Serious Joy:

John Wesley's *Journal*

(Condensed and Gently Paraphrased
for the 21ˢᵗ Century)

Edited by
Robert H. Morris, M.A. Bib. Lit.

Serious Joy: John Wesley's *Journal*

(Condensed and Gently Paraphrased for the 21st Century)

By

Robert H. Morris, Editor

Other published books by the editor:

The Faith of a Seeker: Integrating Science and Scholarship with Christian Experience

Doctor Always on Call

© 2021 Robert H. Morris
March 2021

**Serious Joy: John Wesley's *Journal*
(condensed and gently paraphrased for the 21st Century)**

All rights reserved. No portion of this book may be reproduced, stored in a retrieval system, or transmitted in any form or by any means—electronic, mechanical, photocopy, recording, scanning, or other—except for brief quotations in critical reviews or articles, without the prior written permission of the publisher.

Published in March 2021
by
The Old Paths Publications
www.theoldpathspublications.com
TOP@theoldpathspublications.com

Scripture quotations are mostly from the King James Bible, but the editor has taken the liberty of substituting modern words at some points. Also, John Wesley, who knew Hebrew and Greek very well, often gives his own translation of Scripture. Rather than sort these out, the editor has given the scriptural citation, allowing the reader to check against his or her own translation.

Cover art is by The Old Paths Publications.

Library of Congress Cataloging-in-Publication Data
Library of Congress Control Number: 2021904738

ISBN: 978-1-7365344-7-2

To My Granddaughter,
Star Cheyenne Morris

That the day may come
When you will understand

Robert Morris

Table of Contents

Table of Contents 5
Preface 6
Editor's Introduction 8
VOLUME 1: 1730-1746 13
[Wesley's] Introduction 13
VOLUME 2: 1745 – 1760 191
VOLUME 3: 1760-1773 293
VOLUME 4: 1773-1790 398
Details Of John Wesley's Final Days 497
About The Editor 500

Preface

Why a new work on Wesley after so many books have been written? For two main reasons: First, there have been other condensations of his *Journal*, but none, I believe, like this one. I have attempted to condense without cutting out aspects some may feel uncomfortable with—that is, without trying to remake him in our twenty-first-century image: his totally biblical theology, including belief in the devil and demons, and a real hell; his strong adherence to the Church of England, of which he was an ordained priest; his belief in miracles, of which he gives many instances; his belief in levels of Christian growth, even to perfection, which he considered the peculiar treasure of Methodists; his strong moral stand against abortion, infanticide, and sodomy. Second, my gentle paraphrasing of his language, which is 250 years old, and which I believe will be helpful to modern readers. I've spent many hours, using the *Oxford English Dictionary* (16,000 pages), and the online *Merriam-Webster Dictionary*, finding current words equivalent in meaning to his language, so I believe my renderings are rather precise.

To me John Wesley is a compelling figure, unique, and a great servant of God. One could say he was the Billy Graham of the 18th century, not preaching to as many people as Graham, but actually reaching deeper into people's lives. He formed classes and small circles wherever a Methodist fellowship could be established, questioning them individually and regularly regarding their life and commitment. He went about on foot, sometimes slogging through snow, begging his people to contribute money for the poor who were starving—this not once, but a number of times—then distributing money and goods to the poor families directly. He helped organize workhouses for the unemployed. He went out of his way to visit the sick, praying with them and offering natural remedies that he found to be effective. He treated the mentally ill with compassion. He ministered to prisoners sentenced to be executed and enabled many of them to face death with peace, even with joy. He was sensitive to the issue of chattel slavery—Black people held as absolute, permanent property—and to England's ravishing of India.

Preface

His extraordinarily heavy labor (typically preaching three times a day) spanned over 50 years and only ended with his death. While clinging to the Church of England, he formed a Society of preachers and stewards (= superintendants—ultimately bishops) that would carry on his methods after his death. He also strongly honored his king, and only years after the American Revolution accepted U.S. independence.

By no means was John Wesley perfect. We see his weakness displayed most clearly in his tragic love affair with Sophie Hopkey in Georgia and in the failed marriage which he entered into at age 43 with little forethought, leading to a separation after 17 years that was never reconciled. But this should not blind us to his virtues. He was an extraordinary preacher to whom people flocked by the thousands, and they were moved to repent and to commit themselves to our Lord. By binding them into small groups, he built them up in Christian virtue, urging them on to holiness and to final perfection, of which he gives striking examples, while not claiming it for himself.

We may not follow Wesley's exact discipline today, but we can learn from him, and to that purpose I dedicate this condensation and paraphrasing of his *Journal*.

Editor's Introduction

This introduction to Wesley's *Journal* will be brief and not loaded with scholarly details, but I believe is consistent with good scholarship.

First, my Method. The printed editions of the *Journal* are divided into four volumes of 500-plus pages each. I've worked through all four volumes, abbreviating them by deleting repetitious material and matter less interesting, and so highlighting the more valuable material. The result, I hope, will be readable, enjoyable, and edifying as well.

Second, the Man. Although not fully a Wesley scholar myself, I did read several books by scholars that illuminate his character and figure. These are:

Richard P. Heitzenrater, *Wesley and the People called Methodists* (Abingdon Press: Nashville, 1995).

Franklin Wilder, *The Remarkable World of John Wesley, Pioneer in Mental Health* (Exposition Press: Hicksville, NY, 1978)

Henry D. Rack, *Reasonable Enthusiast: John Wesley and the Rise of Methodism,* 2d ed. (Abingdon Press: Nashville, 1992)

Frederick A. Norwood, *The Story of American Methodism: A History of the United Methodism and Their Relations* (Abingdon Press: Nashville, 1974.)

All these are good books. They clash at points, but taken all together they give a basic understanding of the man, John Wesley.

So who was he? First of all, his life spanned almost the entire 18th century (1703–1791). His father, Samuel Wesley, was the Anglican parish priest at Epworth, on the isle of Axholme in Lincolnshire. Samuel was a faithful priest, considered quite strict by many (or faithful, depending on your viewpoint). He also wrote theological treatises. Perhaps because of his strictness, some in his parish became enemies. By his wife, Susanna, he had 19 children, and this often led to problems due to debts they incurred. Susanna was unusual in the care she gave to raising their children, and I include an extraordinary letter from her to John describing her

Editor's Introduction

manner of child-rearing, which is interesting in its own right—so different from our methods today.

John and his younger brother Charles were Samuel's pride and joy since they became Oxford scholars and Anglican priests. John begins his *Journal* about midway through his Oxford career.

John Wesley was brilliant. Besides being a deep Bible scholar, he was a linguist: He mastered New Testament Greek and Biblical Hebrew, was fluent in Latin and French, and was conversational in German, Spanish, and Italian. He wrote commentaries on some books of the Bible and worked with his brother Charles on a translation of the New Testament.

Something needs to be said about his character. It's my guess that due to an extra-strict upbringing, including some degree of food deprivation, John developed a toughness that carried him to the end of his life: preaching as often as four or five times a day, riding countless hours on horseback, and confronting hostile crowds. His brother Charles, however, was more delicate and often sick. He disagreed strongly with John at time, but always returned to his side as a faithful companion. It is Charles who wrote hundreds of hymns, some still sung today by many denominations.

John Wesley was unfortunate—even unwise—in love and marriage. Perhaps he may have been conflicted sexually following his informal vow of celibacy while at Oxford. (Charles, to the contrary, had a good marriage, with children.) Where the blame for John's failure in marriage lies depends on the scholar one is reading. In Volume I, Wesley hints at his brief love affair with Miss Sophia Hopkey in Savanna. Later volumes of the *Journal* give tidbits of his disastrous marriage to a widow, Mary Vazeille. In fact, we are disappointed in his scant references to his wife and her children, although he is very loving toward children generally throughout his ministry. It seems that Mary was jealous of John's close contact with other women, while he neglected her. They separated after 20 years of marriage and remained so until Mary's death.

Third, the Message. What we will see in this volume is that Wesley goes through several spiritual stages, coming to a mature sense of salvation by faith working through love. As a child, he associated going to heaven with being perfectly good. He carried this with him to Oxford, where with Charles and others he formed the Holy Club. It is the Moravians, en route with him to Savannah, Georgia, who challenged him to an inward faith. Finally back in London, at a fellowship meeting, he listened to the words of Martin Luther that "strangely warmed" his heart and experienced a breakthrough to assurance and joy that he'd never known before. John took a trip of some months to Germany to become better acquainted with the Moravians. It was mostly positive, but later the German "stillness" disturbed him more and more, telling believers not to pray much, not to go to communion, not to read the Bible, not to do good works. Over the next year or so this teaching created disturbances in the Methodist fellowships, and John confronted them sharply.

What John Wesley achieved is a balanced theology that salvation is by faith alone, but that this faith will be accompanied by the "ordinary means of grace" (prayer, Bible reading, the Lord's Supper, corporate worship), and by works done in love.

Besides the "German stillness," Wesley combated the antinomianism[1] originating from some of the same circles. This distortion of the Christian faith, perhaps worst than all, taught that the Christian is under no law at all—not even that of Christ.

Overall, John Wesley took the Anglican theology, the most balanced of the Reformed theologies, and crystallized it into in a compact form.

Fourth, the Method. The title "Methodist" was attached to Wesley's Holy Club early on (although some other dissenters[2] from the Church of England received the jibe as well). This was given in exaggeration and derision, of course; originally it especially meant going regularly to prayers and Holy Communion, but before long Wesley and his followers did develop a method that not only bound

---

[1] Antinomianism = having no law. Wesley references James 2:18, 22 where James writes that he will show his faith by his works. Wesley's view is that salvation is by faith alone, but that true faith will bear fruit

[2] Those formally dissenting from the Church and forming separate congregations. (In this work, Church with a capital "C" will refer to the Church of England, the national church).

them tightly as a fellowship ("Society" is his word), but gave them a powerful program to reach out to all levels of society.

The Methodist "fellowships" (my substitute for Wesley's "Societies," a word foreign to our use of the term today), in a city or area were broken down into classes of no more than 12, which could be of mixed genders, and these were further subdivided into bands or "circles" of single gender. These were accountability groups in the modern sense; at meetings members were expected to confess their sins and their successes in struggling with them. All meetings included hymns and prayers, and normally time for testimonies. To these were added prayer groups in many towns.

At all levels there were strict rules, and Wesley didn't hesitate to expel any who couldn't or wouldn't conform, though hoping for their reformation and restoration. I should add that dismissing a member didn't automatically mean that that member was headed for perdition, although at times Wesley did express such a possibility. Certainly this is not in keeping with our loosely run spiritual groups today.

Fifth, the Mission. John Wesley was an Anglican priest who was never assigned a parish. His father wanted him to take over the rectorship[3] of Epworth, but John wrote a strong letter, which I include, stating why he didn't want to do so. When pressed, Wesley answered someone: "The world is my parish." This freed him to preach on his father's gravestone at Epworth, to preach throughout England, Wales, Scotland, and Ireland. We may question the numbers he gives for his crowds—up to 30,000—but at times he gives the actual basis for these estimates.

This means that, over a period of 50 years, riding some 4000 miles a year, he could preach to hundreds of thousands, even to a total of millions. And he was not alone. Some 100–200 preachers under his leadership swelled the numbers. The movement reached America, survived the struggles of the Revolution, and grew amazingly in frontier America.

---

[3] The rector was a member of the clergy in the Anglican Church in charge of a parish.

Serious Joy (John Wesley's *Journal*)

John Wesley's mission was the reformation of the Church of England and of all denominations, the conversion of nations, the bringing of all souls to God. He reached out to condemned prisoners, the freezing and starving poor, the mentally ill, the rich. His mission knew no bounds.

A note on words: I've preserved Wesley's term "Society" for the Methodist movement as a whole, but substituted "fellowship" for local gatherings, trying to be consistent in this. Also, Wesley uses the word "congregation" for any gathering of people to hear him preach, whereas today we normally reserve the term for a settled body in a particular location (*Webster's Dictionary*). Therefore I've usually substituted "assembly" or "gathering" when the reference is not to a local church.

A note on biblical quotes: The King James Version (1611) was standard in Wesley's lifetime, and most quotes are from it or closely follow it. But John Wesley was a Bible scholar in his own right; in fact he, with his brother Charles, produced their own translation of the New Testament. So his quotations will often vary slightly from the King James. I too, having some knowledge of Greek and Hebrew, have taken the liberty of modernizing the language in some quotes. I have searched and bracketed citations as far as I am able.

The astounding things to me is that, even in this condensed version of his *Journal,* we find Wesley drawing at least a hundred different texts—both from Old and New Testaments—in his sermons. He was truly steeped in the Bible, and didn't just pick out those texts that supported his doctrine.

VOLUME 1: 1730-1746

[Wesley's] Introduction

What then are we to say? [That] Israel, who did strive for the righteousness that is based on the law, did not succeed in fulfilling that law. Why not? Because they did not strive for it on the basis of faith, but as if it were based on works. (Romans 9:30-32)

1. About fifteen years ago, I took the advice Bishop Taylor gave in his *Rules for Holy Living and Dying* and started keeping a better record of how I used my time, writing down how I spent every hour of the day. I kept this up wherever I was till I left England [for Georgia]. After that, my various experiences led me to transcribe [into my journal], from time to time, the more substantial parts of my diary, adding little reflections here and there as they came to mind. What follows is an abridged version of the *Journal*[4] that I composed this way. Here I don't intend to give all the details that I wrote down purely for my own use but which would serve no real purpose for others, however important they were to me.

2. ... I still wouldn't have done this if Captain Williams' sworn statement, published as soon as he left England, hadn't obliged me to do my best to obey God's command: "Do not let what you regard as good be spoken of as evil" [Rom. 14:16]. Keeping this in mind, at last I "make a defense to anyone who asks me a reason for the hope that is in me" [1 Peter 3:15], so that in all these things I "have a clear conscience toward both God and man" [Acts 24:16].

3. I have prefaced my *Journal* with a letter I wrote several years ago, giving a clear account of the rise of that little fellowship at Oxford which others have described in widely different ways. Part of this was published in 1733 without my knowledge or consent. I'll print it as I wrote it, without addition, subtraction, or alteration, as

---

[4] The standard published edition of Wesley's *Journal,* an abridgement of his diary, is about 2000 pages. His dairies have never been published in full. In this book we are further abridging his four-volume *Journal*.

my only concern here is to tell it like it is— the bare truth. [*Only some extracts from this long letter will be printed below.*]

4. Other involvements[5] may not allow me to answer more fully those who say all kinds of evil against me falsely and seem to think that they do God service. It's enough to say that they—and I too—will soon "give an account to him who's ready to judge the living and the dead" [1 Peter 4:5].

---

[5] I.e., preaching, superintending.

Letter To Mr. Morgan, Sen.

Sir, Oxford, Oct. 18, 1730.

I am sorry to trouble you with this letter, but I have an extraordinary reason for doing so. Last Sunday I was informed (as no doubt you will be soon) that my brother [Charles] and I had killed your son—that the severe fasting he had forced on himself at our recommendation made his illness worse and hastened his death ... I am forced to clear myself of this accusation by pointing out to you, as I have to others, that your son gave up fasting about a year and a half ago, and that I began practicing it less than six months ago ...

In November 1729, when I came to live at Oxford, your son, my brother, myself, and one other man, agreed to spend three or four evenings a week together. Our purpose was to read the classics, which until then we had read separately, on weekday nights, and on Sunday some book of theology. The following summer, Mr. M[organ Jr.] told me he had visited the jail to see a man condemned for killing his wife, and that, from the talk he had with one of the debtors, he believed it would help a great deal if we would take time to talk to them now and then. He kept repeating this until, on August 24, 1730, my brother and I walked with him to the castle prison.[6] Our conversation there was so satisfying that we agreed to go back once or twice a week. We hadn't been doing this long when [Mr. Morgan] asked me to go with him to see a poor woman in the town who was sick. When we reflected on this activity, we thought it would be worthwhile to spend an hour or two each week doing this as well, as long as the minister of the parish wasn't against it. But in order not to rely only on our own judgment, I wrote to my father, telling him our whole plan, asking ... him if we should now stop everything or go ahead? Part of his answer, dated September 21, 1730, was this:

"I ... praise God for giving me two sons at Oxford to whom he has given grace and courage to take the offense against the world[7]

---

[6] I.e., Newcastle, a noted prison.
[7] "World" here means fallen creation and its sin.

and the devil, which is the best way to defeat them. You[8] just have one more enemy to conquer: the flesh. If you are careful to subdue it by fasting and prayer, the only thing left for you to do will be to go steadily forward to and expect the crown that doesn't fade away. You have reason to praise God, as I do, that you have so steadfast a friend as Mr. M[organ], who I see is ready to break the ice for you in this most difficult service. ...

"The proper first step is for you to consult with whoever ... has jurisdiction over the prisoners, and the next is to obtain guidance and approval from your bishop ... To God ... I now heartily commit you, as

"Your most affectionate and joyful father."

Following these directions, I immediately went to Mr. Gerard, chaplain to the bishop of Oxford who also was in charge spiritually of the prisoners condemned to die. (At other times the prisoners were left to themselves.) I told him our plan of serving the prisoners to what extent we could and of my own intention to preach there once a month if the bishop approved. The chaplain was all in favor of our plan; he said he could vouch for the bishop's approval and would mention it to him at the first opportunity. Before long he told me he had done this and that his lordship not only gave his permission but was very pleased with our undertaking and wished it success.

Soon after this, a gentleman[9] of Merton College who was one of our little group,[10] now consisting of five persons, told us that the day before he had been laughed to scorn for being a member of "the Holy Club," which had become a common butt of jokes at his college, where they supposedly had found out several of our practices—practices we ourselves knew nothing about! ...

...We kept meeting as usual, supporting each other in our commitments the best we could, taking communion[11] as often as we could (which was once a week), and serving our acquaintances, the

---

[8] Here and in the next sentence, I have changed "they" and "them" to "you."
[9] I.e., someone of position in society by birth, education, or achievement.
[10] Wesley's word is "company."
[11] Wesley's word is "communicating" but the meaning is "to take or receive [holy] communion," which will be my regular substitution.

prisoners, and two or three poor families in the town as we were able ...

Your son already stands before the judgment seat of him who gives righteous judgment, at the brightness of whose presence the clouds part. His eyes are open, and he sees clearly whether it was "blind zeal and a total mistake of true religion, that hurried him on in the error of his way"; or whether he acted like a faithful and wise servant, who, rightly aware that his time was near, hurried to finish his work before his Lord's coming, so that "when weighed in the balance" he might not "be found wanting." ...
Sir, your ever obliged
And most obedient servant.

1735

Tues. OCTOBER 14.—Mr. Benjamin Ingham of Queen's College, Oxford; Mr. Charles Delamotte, son of a merchant in London, who had volunteered a few days earlier; my brother Charles Wesley, and myself, took a boat to Gravesend in order to sail from there for Georgia. We left our native land not because we lacked anything there (God having given us plenty of worldly goods) nor to gain ... riches or honor, but only this: to save our souls and to live wholly to the glory of God ...

Wednesday and Thursday we spent with one or two friends, part of the time on board and the rest on shore, exhorting each other to "lay aside every weight, and sin which clings so closely, and [to] run with endurance the race that is set before us" [Heb. 12:1].

Fri. 17.— I began learning German in order to communicate with the 26 Germans[12] on board. On Sunday, the weather being fair and calm, we held the morning service on the quarterdeck. It was my first time to preach extemporaneously,[13] and after doing so I administered the Lord's Supper to six or seven communicants—a little flock; may God increase it!

Mon. 20.— We thought that denying ourselves even in small ways might, by God's blessing, help us forward spiritually, so we

---

[12] These were Moravians, or Bohemian Brethren.
[13] I.e., without a written text or notes.

stopped eating meat and drinking wine, restricting ourselves to vegetables—mainly rice and biscuits. In the afternoon David Nitschman, bishop of the Germans, and two others, began learning English. Oh, may we not only be of one language but of one mind and one heart!

Tues. 21.— ... Now we began following a regular schedule, usually like this: From 4 to 5 a.m., we each prayed separately. From 5 to 7 a.m., we read the Bible together, carefully comparing it (so as not to lean on our own understanding) with the writings of the earliest ages.[14] At 7 a.m., we ate breakfast. At 8 a.m. there were public prayers. From 9 a.m. to 12 noon I usually studied German, and Mr. Delamotte, Greek; my brother wrote sermons, and Mr. Ingham taught the children. At noon we met to share what we had done since our last meeting and what we planned to do before the next one. About 1 p.m. we ate lunch. After lunch, till 4 p.m., each of us read to those persons he had taken charge of or talked to them individually as needed. Evening prayers were at 4 p.m., and then either the Second Scripture[15] was explained (as it always was in the morning), or the children were catechized and instructed in front of the congregation. From 5 to 6 p.m., again we prayed privately. From 6 to 7 p.m., I read in our cabin to two or three of the passengers (there were about 80 Englishmen on board), and each of my brothers to a few more in their cabins. At 7 p.m. I attended the Germans' public service, while Mr. Ingham was reading between the decks to as many as cared to listen. At 8 p.m. we met again, to exhort and instruct one another. Between 9 and 10 p.m. we went to bed, where neither the roaring of the sea nor the ship's motion could take away the refreshing sleep that God gave us ...

Sat. NOVEMBER 1.—We came to St. Helen's harbor, and the next day into Cowes Road ... We waited for the man of war[16] that

---

[14] Wesley read the Bible in the original languages, Hebrew and Greek. He also used commentaries. The implication here is that he is also using the early church fathers (2st–5rd centuries).

[15] Reference is to the Anglican lectionary, a book giving scriptural passages for each day of the year.

[16] A ship outfitted for war belonging to a particular navy.

was to sail with us. This was a happy opportunity of instructing our fellow travelers ...

Sun. 16.—Thomas Hird and Grace his wife, with their children, Mark, 21, and Phebe, about 17, until then Quakers,[17] were, at their repeated request, and after careful instruction, received for baptism.

Sun.23—At night I was awakened by the ship tossing and the wind roaring, which clearly showed I was unfit [to meet God], because I was not willing to die ...

Thur. DECEMBER 18.—A woman in late pregnancy, who had a high fever and was worn down by violent coughing, asked to receive holy communion before she died. About the time she took it she began to recover, and within a few days was totally out of danger ...

1736

Sat. JANUARY 17.— ... About 9 p.m. the sea washed over us from stem to stern. Three or four of us were in the state cabin. The water broke through the windows and completely covered us, but a bureau protected me from the main force of the wave. About 11 p.m. I lay down in the great cabin and soon fell asleep, not knowing if I would ever wake up and being very ashamed that I wasn't willing to die. Oh, how pure in heart we must be to rejoice that we might appear before God at a moment's notice! Toward morning "He rebuked the winds and the sea, and there was a dead calm" [Matthew 8:26] ...

Fri. 23.—Another storm began that evening. In the morning it got so bad that they had to release the rudder and let the ship be driven by the gale. I could only say to myself, "Why do you have no faith?" still not being willing to die ... About midnight the storm ceased ...

Sun. 25.— ... At 7 p.m. I visited the Germans. For a long time I had noticed their serious[18] conduct. They had given constant proof of

---

[17] The Quakers are a sect that does not practice water baptism or other "outward" ordinances. Today they are divided between those considering themselves Christians and those who do are universalists.

[18] Seriousness and solemnity, as opposed to levity or lightness, were considered by many Protestants (including Puritans and Quakers) of that time as one mark of a true Christian—quite the opposite of most evangelicals today, who feel they're

their humility by humbly serving the other passengers in ways none of the Englishmen would do, for which they didn't ask and wouldn't accept any pay, saying that "it was good for their proud hearts" and "that their loving Savior had done more for them" ... Now there was an opportunity to find out whether they'd been delivered from the spirit of fear, as well as from that of pride, anger, and revenge. Almost as soon as they began their service by singing a psalm, the sea broke over the railing, split the mainsail in two, flowed over the ship, and poured in between the fore and aft decks as if the abyss was swallowing us up. The Englishmen began screaming, but the Germans calmly sang on. I asked one of them later, "Weren't you afraid?" He answered, "No, thank God." I asked, "But weren't your women and children afraid?" He mildly replied, "No; our women and children aren't afraid to die" ...

Thur. FEBRUARY 5.—Between 2 and 3 in the afternoon, God brought us all safe into the Savannah River ...

Fri. 6.—About 8 a.m., we first set foot on American soil. It was a small uninhabited island, over against Tybee. Mr. Oglethorpe[19] led us to a hillock where we all knelt down to give thanks. He then took a boat to Savannah ...

Sat. 7.—Mr. Oglethorpe returned from Savannah with Mr. Spangenberg, one of the German pastors. I soon discerned his [excellent] spirit and asked his advice regarding my own conduct. He said, "My brother, I must first ask you one or two questions. Do you have the witness within you? Does the Spirit of God bear witness with your spirit that you are a child of God?" I was surprised and didn't know how to answer. He noticed this and asked, "Do you know Jesus Christ?" I paused and said, "I know he is the Savior of the world." "That's true," he replied, "but do you know that he's saved *you*?" I answered, "I hope he has died to save me." He simply added, "Do you know this yourself?" I said, "Yes, I do." But I am afraid they were mere words ...

---

supposed to be light-hearted. We'll see later that Wesley made it a rule for himself never to laugh. Fortunately he mellowed some in older age and was considered by his sister to be pleasant company, but he was never accused of frivolity.

[19] James Oglethorpe (1696-1785) founded the colony of Georgia first for the poor who were in debtors' prisons.

VOLUME 1: 1730-1746

Sat. 14.—About 1 p.m., Tomo Chachi, his nephew Thleeanouhee, his wife Sinauky, with two more women and two or three Indian[20] children, came on board. As soon as we came in, they all stood up and shook us by the hand, and Tomo Chachi (with a Mrs. Musgrove interpreting) spoke as follows:

> I am glad you have come. When I was in England I asked that some would speak the great Word to me; and then my nation wanted to hear it; but now we are all in confusion. Yet I am glad you have come. I will go up and speak to the wise men of our nation, and I hope they will hear. But we would not be made Christians like the Spaniards make Christians; we want to be taught before we are baptized.

I answered, "There is but One who sits in heaven who is able to teach man wisdom. Although we have come so far, we don't know if it will please him to teach you through us or not. If he teaches you, you will learn wisdom, but we [by ourselves] can do nothing." We then left ...

Sat. 21.—Mary Welch, aged eleven days, was baptized according to the custom of the early church and the rule of the Church of England, by immersion.[21] The child was sick at that moment, but progressively recovered from that hour.

Sun. 29.— ... We went to public prayers, after which we were refreshed by several letters from England. Reading them, I could only remark how careful our Lord is to repay whatever we give up on his account. When I left England, I had two main fears: one, that I would never again have as many faithful friends as I had there; the other, that the spark of love that began to burn in their hearts would cool and die away. But who knows the mercy and power of God? I am separated from 10 friends for a while, and he has opened a door for me into a whole church. And as for the ones I left behind, his Spirit has gone forth even more, teaching them not to trust in man

---

[20] "Indian," here and elsewhere, refers to Native Americans.

[21] The Church of England allows baptism by immersion, by pouring, and by other means. Wesley, convinced that immersion was the original form of baptism, personally baptized this way when the person's physical condition and circumstances allowed it. But he accepted other forms of baptism and did not quarrel about it.

but "in him who gives life to the dead and calls into existence the things that do not exist" [Rom. 4:17] ...

Sun. MARCH 7.—I began my ministry at Savannah by preaching on the epistle for the day,[22] 1 Corinthians 13. The second lesson,[23] Luke 18, included our Lord's prediction of the treatment that he himself, and later on his followers, would receive from the world: ... "Truly, I say to you, there is no one who has left house or wife or brothers or parents or children, for the sake of the kingdom of God, who will not receive many times more at this time, and in the age to come eternal life" ...

Here I testify against myself that when I saw how many people were crowding into the church, the close attention they paid to the Word, and how serious they all seemed afterwards, it was all I could do not to completely deny what experience, reason, and Scripture all teach. It was hard to believe that by far most of this attentive, serious people, would later trample under foot that Word and say all kinds of evil falsely against me who spoke it ...

Sat. APRIL 17.— ... Not yet finding an open door to pursue our main purpose,[24] we considered how we could be most useful to the little flock at Savannah. And we agreed: 1. to advise the more serious among them to form themselves into a sort of little fellowship and to meet once or twice a week in order to correct, instruct, and encourage each other; then 2. to select from these a smaller group for closer fellowship with each other. We hoped to assist them by talking to each one individually and also by inviting them all to our house. We decided to do this every Sunday afternoon ...

Fri. May 28.— ... Only five attended the first service on Sunday, May 30. At the second service there were 25. The next day, I made Mr. Lassel's will for him. In spite of his great weakness, he roused whenever mention was made either of death or of eternity.

Tues. JUNE 1.—After praying with Mr. Lassel, I was surprised to find one of the most debated questions in theology, love without attachment,[25] settled immediately by this poor old man with no

---

[22] Again, Wesley is using the Church of England lectionary.
[23] See previous note.
[24] I.e., to convert the Indians.
[25] Wesley: "disinterested love."

education or learning, or any teacher except the Spirit of God. I asked him what he thought of Paradise, where he said he was going. He said, "Of course, it is a fine place. But I don't mind that; I don't care what place I am in. Let God put me where he will or do with me what he will, just as long as I can shine for his honor and glory." ...

Thur. 10.—At Frederica we put into practice what we had earlier agreed to do at Savannah. Our plan was this: Sunday afternoons and every evening after public service we would spend some time with the more serious members singing, reading, and discussing. This evening we had only Mark Hird. But on Sunday Mr. Hird and two others asked to join. After a hymn and a little conversation, I read Mr. Law's *Christian Perfection*, then ended with another hymn. ...

Wed. 23.—I had a long conversation with Mr. ____ on the nature of true religion, then asked him why he didn't recommend it to everyone he talked to. He said, "I did that once, and for a little while I thought I was doing a lot of good. But later I found that they never got better and that I myself had gotten worse. So now, though I always try not to offend anyone by my conduct, I don't try to make people religious unless they want to be and so are willing to listen to me. But so far I haven't yet found one such person in America—you and your brother being the only exceptions."

"He who has ears to hear, let him hear!" Notice where this damnable principle leads to! If you just speak to those willing to hear, see how many you will turn from the error of their ways! If you hurt somebody's feelings by trying to do good, so what? So did St. Paul, and so did the Lord of life. Even his word was "the smell of death" as well as "the smell of life" [2 Cor. 2:16]. But should we stop trying for that reason? God forbid! Try to be humbler, calmer, and more careful. Try in a different way than before, but keep trying while God's breath is in you! ...

Sun. 27. About 20 joined us for morning prayer. An hour or two later, a large party of Creek Indians came, which deprived us of our place of worship since they were given the building for their hearing

Thur. JULY 1.—The Indians were given a hearing, and another one on Saturday when Chicali, their head man, dined with Mr. Oglethorpe. After dinner, I asked the gray-headed old man what he thought he was made for. He said, "He that is above knows what he made us for. We know nothing. We are in the dark. But white men know much. And yet white men build great houses, as if they were going to live forever. But white men can't live forever. In a little time, white men will be dust just as I'll be." I told him, "If red men will learn the Good Book, they may know as much as white men. But neither we nor you can understand that book unless we are taught by him who is above, and he won't teach unless you avoid what you already know isn't good." He answered, "I believe that. He won't teach us while our hearts aren't clean. And our men do what they know isn't good; they kill their own children. And our women do what they know isn't good; they kill the baby in the womb. Therefore, he who is above doesn't send us the good book." ...

Mon. SEPTEMBER 13.—Mr. Delamotte and I started reading Bishop Beveridge's *Pandecta Canonum Conciliorum*.[26] Nothing could have convinced us more that both local and general church councils may and have erred, and that the things which they have ruled to be necessary for salvation have no strength or authority unless they are taken out of Holy Scripture ...

Tues. NOVEMBER 23.—Mr. Oglethorpe sailed for England, leaving Mr. Ingham, Mr. Delamotte, and me at Savannah,[27] but with less hope of preaching to the Indians than we had the day we first set foot in America. Whenever I brought this up, I was immediately told, "You can't leave Savannah without a minister!" To this I answered frankly, "I don't feel under any obligation not to leave. I never promised to stay here one month! Before coming, when I arrived, and ever since I have been here, I've publicly stated that I could take charge of the English only until I could go to the Indians." When they said, "Didn't the trustees of Georgia appoint you minister of Savannah?" I replied, "Yes, they did; but I didn't ask for it; it was done without my wish or knowledge. So I believe that this appointment only obliges me to stay until the door opens for me to go to the heathens,[28] and I said this specifically when I agreed to accept that appointment." But although I had no other commitment keeping me from leaving Savannah now, I still couldn't resist the obligation of love. My more serious parishioners kept begging me to watch over their souls a

---

[26] *Encyclopedia of Church Councils*.
[27] Charles Wesley had been assigned to Federica. He had become chronically ill and had returned to England.
[28] "Heathen" refers to those who do not believe in one God, as opposed to Christians, Jews, and Muslims.

little longer, till someone else could come to take my place. I was more willing to do this because the time wasn't right to preach the gospel of peace to the heathens, since all their nations were in tumult. Paustoobee and Mingo Mattaw had told me, in so many words, in my own house, "Now our enemies are all around us; we can do nothing but fight; but if the beloved ones[29] should ever give us to be at peace, then we would hear the great Word." ...

1737

Thur. FEBRUARY 24.— ... Mr. Ingham delivered a letter I wrote to Dr. Bray and his partners, who had sent books to Savannah for a parish library. When ministers receive these libraries, they are expected to tell the donors their method of catechizing the children and further instructing the young people of their parishes. Here is part of what I wrote:

> Our general method is this: A young man who came with me[30] teaches between 30 and 40 children to read, write, and do arithmetic. Before school in the morning and after school in the afternoon, he teaches the catechism to the beginning class and tries to help them to understand, not just to memorize. In the evening he teaches the older children. On Saturday afternoon, I catechize them all, and I do the same on Sunday before the evening service. In church, right after the second passage, I select a few of them to repeat the catechism and I question them on some part, then I try to explain it fully, urging it both on them and the congregation.
>
> After the evening service, those of my parishioners who want to do so meet at my house, as they also do on Wednesday evening, and spend about an hour in prayer, singing, and mutual encouragement. A smaller group (mostly those who intend to take communion the next day) meets here on Saturday evening, and a few of these come to me on other evenings as well, spending half an hour the same way.

Fri. MARCH 4.—I wrote the Georgia trustees an account of our year's expense, from March 1, 1736, to March 1, 1737; which, after deducting extraordinary expenses, such as repairing the parsonage

---

[29] I.e., their ancestors.
[30] I.e., Mr. Delamotte.

and trips to Frederica, amounted, for Mr. Delamotte and me, to 44 pounds, 4 shillings, and 4 pence.[31]

I received guidance from God today on a matter of great importance,[32] and I could only notice, as I have many times before, how totally wrong they are who assert that God won't answer your prayer unless your heart is completely resigned to his will. My heart wasn't completely resigned to his will and so, not daring to depend on my own judgment, I pleaded with him even more earnestly to make up for what I lacked. I knew and was assured that he heard my voice, and he sent forth his light and truth …

Mon. APRIL 4.—I began learning Spanish in order to converse with the Jews in my parish.[33] Some of them seem nearer to the mind of Christ than many who call him Lord …

Sat. 23.— … Finding a young Negro[34] woman at Mr. Thompson's who seemed more intelligent than the rest, I asked her how long she had been in Carolina. She said two or three years, but that she was born in Barbados and had grown up there in a minister's home. I asked if she went to church there. She said, "Yes, every Sunday, to take my mistress's children." I asked what she had learned at church. She said, "Nothing; I heard everything they said but didn't understand a thing." "But what did your master teach you at home?" "Nothing." "Not even your mistress?" "No," she said. I asked … "Do you know who God is?" "No," she replied. I explained, "You can't see him any more than you can see your own soul. It is he that made you and me, and all men and women, and all the four-legged animals and birds, and the whole world … Why do you think he made us, you and me?" "I don't know." "He made you to live with himself above the sky, and you will, in a little time, if you're good. If you're good, when your body dies, your soul will go up there, and lack

---

[31] I.e., about $10,400 in 2020 USD.

[32] Wesley often opened his Bible at random to get guidance. He was in love with Sophia Hopkey (hugs and kisses?), and had suggested marriage, but later drew back because of a former informal vow of celibacy (which he abandoned in his late 30s). Likely here he was seeking guidance about this relationship, and right after this told her he could not marry. She married Mr. Williamson just eight days later.

[33] The Spanish Inquisition had driven most Jews out of Spain in 1492, and many had fled to America.

[34] I will retain Wesley's older word for African-Americans.

nothing, and you will have whatever you want. No one will beat or hurt you there. You will never be sick. You will never be sad or afraid anymore. I can't tell you how happy you will be, because you will be with God."

I can't describe how this humble woman drank in my teaching. The next day she remembered everything, quickly answered every question, and said she would ask him who made her to show her how to be good ...

Wed. 27.— ... Mr. Belinger sent a Negro boy with me to Purrysburg .... He too I found both very eager and able to receive instruction. Perhaps the easiest and most direct way to teach Christianity to the American Negroes would be first to find some of the most serious Christian plantation owners, then, after finding out which of their slaves have good dispositions and understand English, to go from plantation to plantation teaching them, staying as long as necessary in each place. Three or four gentlemen[35] I know in Carolina would be sincerely glad to have such an assistant; he could carry out this work with no more hindrances than preaching the gospel always encounters ...

Sun. MAY 29. Being Whitsunday [Pentecost], four of our students, after being taught daily for several weeks, and as they earnestly and repeatedly requested, were admitted to the Lord's Table. I trust their zeal has stirred many others up to remember their Creator in the days of their youth and to redeem the time, even in the midst of a wicked and adulterous generation.

In fact, it was about this time that we noticed the Spirit of God moving on the minds of many of the children. They started paying better attention to what was said, both at home and at church, and grew remarkably serious in their total behavior and conversation. Who knows but that some of them may grow up "to the measure of the full stature of Christ" [Ephesians 4:13]? ...

Sun. JULY 3.—Right after Holy Communion, I told Mrs. Williamson[36] (Mr. Causton's niece) something in her behavior that I thought needed correction. At this she seemed very angry and said

---

[35] Slaveowners?
[36] Formerly Sophy Hopkey, Wesley's girlfriend (see note above). This sets in motion the controversy that will lead to Wesley fleeing Savannah.

that she didn't expect me to treat her that way and, where the street we were walking on took a turn, she suddenly walked away. The next day Mrs. Causton apologized for her, saying she was sorry for what had happened the day before and asked me to tell her in writing what I disapproved of; so I did that the next day ...

Sat. 23.—Considering the situation I was now in, I stated in a letter to a friend, "I can't see how I'll become crucified with Christ. Here in America, I'm in a situation I neither asked for nor expected, living in comfort, honor, and abundance. This is a strange school for him who has just one business: to train for godliness.[37]

Wed. 27.—I rejoiced to meet that good soldier of Jesus Christ, August Spangenberg,[38] once again; we traveled together to Ebenezer ...

Wed. AUGUST 3.—We returned to Savannah. On Sunday the 7th, I refused Holy Communion to Mrs. Williamson.[39] And Monday the 8th, the Recorder of Savannah issued the following warrant:

> Georgia. Savannah ss.
>
> To all Constables, Petty Constables, and others, whom these may concern:
>
> You all and each of you are hereby required to take the body of John Wesley, Cleric[40]:
>
> And bring him before one of the bailiffs of the said town, to answer the complaint of William Williamson and Sophia his wife, for defaming the said Sophia, and refusing to administer to her the Sacrament of the Lord's Supper, in a public congregation, without cause; by which the said William Williamson is damaged one thousand pound sterling:[41] And for so doing, this is your warrant, certifying what you are to do on the premises.
>
> Given under my hand and seal the 8th day of August, the year of our Lord 1737.
>
> Thomas Christie.

---

[37] "To train for godliness," from 1 Timothy 4:7, Wesley puts here in Greek.
[38] Moravian minister who later became the bishop of the church.
[39] On some technicality.
[40] I.e., clergyman.
[41] $235,000 in 2020 USD.

Tues. 9.—Mr. Jones, the constable, served the warrant, and took me to face Parker, the bailiff, and the recorder. I answered them that giving or refusing the Lord's Supper was a purely ecclesiastical matter, so I did not acknowledge their right to question me about it. Mr. Parker told me, "You still must appear at the next court held in Savannah." Mr. Williamson, standing by, said, "Gentlemen, I want Mr. Wesley to pay bail for his appearance." But Mr. Parker immediately replied, "Sir, Mr. Wesley's word is sufficient." ...

Thur. 11.—Mr. Causton came to my house, and among many other things said, "You'd better settle this matter. To think you treated my niece this way! I've drawn my sword and I'll never put it back in its sheath till I'm satisfied!"

After that he said, "I want you to tell the whole congregation why you refused her." I answered, "Sir, I will do that if you insist, and I hope it will please you to tell her too." He said, "Write her and tell her so yourself." I said, "All right, I will," and after he left, I wrote:

> To Mrs. Sophia Williamson
>
> At the request of Mr. Causton, I am writing once more. The rules I follow are these:
>
> Those intending to partake of Holy Communion shall give their names to the pastor at least some time the day before. You did not do this.
>
> And if any of these have done anything wrong to his neighbors, by word or deed, so as to offend the congregation, the pastor will mention it publicly, so that he will not presume to come to the Lord's Table until he has openly stated that he has truly repented.
>
> If you offer yourself at the Lord's Table on Sunday, I will tell you publicly (as I have done more than once privately) what you have done wrong: And when you have openly declared yourself to have truly repented, I will administer to you the mysteries of God.
>
> Aug.11, 1737.   John Wesley ...

Tues. 16.—Mrs. Williamson swore to and signed an affidavit, insinuating more than it clearly stated, but asserting "that Mr. Wesley had many times proposed marriage to her; all which proposals she had rejected." I requested a copy of this. Mr. Causton replied, "Sir, you may have one from any of the newspapers in America."

Serious Joy (John Wesley's *Journal*)

On Thursday or Friday a list of 26 men was posted who were to meet as a Grand Jury on Monday the 22nd ... To this Grand Jury, Mr. Causton gave a long and earnest charge: "To beware of spiritual tyranny, and to oppose the new, illegal authority wrongfully taken over their consciences." Then Mrs. Williamson's affidavit was read, after which Mr. Causton delivered to the Grand Jury a paper, entitled

> A list of grievances, presented by the Grand Jury for Savannah, this ____ day of August, 1737:
> The majority of the grand jury ... asserted under oath, "That John Wesley, clergyman, had broken the laws of the realm, contrary to the peace of our sovereign lord the king, his crown and dignity:
> 1. by speaking and writing to Mrs. Williamson without her husband's permission;
> 2. by refusing to serve her Holy Communion;
> 3. by not declaring his adherence to the Church of England;
> 4. by dividing the morning service on Sundays ...

Fri. SEPTEMBER 2.—This was my third court appearance since being brought before Mr. P. and the Recorder.

I now moved for an immediate hearing on the first charge ... but was put off till the next court day.

The next court day I appeared again, as well as at the two court sessions following, but couldn't be heard, "because," the Judge said, "Mr. Williamson had left town."

The consensus of the minority of the grand jurors themselves (for they were by no means unanimous concerning these charges), may appear from the following paper, which they transmitted to the Trustees:

> Whereas two sworn statements have been made, one of August 23 and the other of August 31, by the grand jury for the Town and County of Savannah in Georgia, against John Wesley, clergyman:
> We the undersigned members of the grand jury, do humbly ask permission to tell you what we dislike about these charges. Being acquainted with all the circumstances, we are completely persuaded that everything Mr. Wesley is charged with is Mr. Causton's fabrication, intended to destroy Mr. Wesley's reputation rather than to free the colony from religious tyranny, as he called it in his suit ...

As to the first charge, we do not consider that Mr. Wesley acted against any law by writing or speaking to Mrs. Williamson, since it does not seem that he has either spoken in private or written to Mrs. Williamson since March 12 (the day of her marriage) except one letter of July the 5th, which he wrote at the request of her uncle, as a pastor, to exhort and reprove her.

We do not consider the second charge true, because in our humble opinion Mr. Wesley did not assume any unlawful authority. We understand that "every person intending to communicate should signify his name to the curate[42] at least some time the day before" as something Mrs. Williamson did not do, in spite of Mr. Wesley telling the whole congregation they must comply with that directive and previously refusing communion to several for not complying with it.

We do not think the third charge is true, because several of us have heard him state his attachment to the Church of England in a stronger way than by a formal declaration. He has explained and defended the Apostles,' the Nicene, and the Athanasian Creeds, the Thirty-Nine Articles, the whole Book of Common Prayer, and the Homilies of this Church. We understand that a formal declaration is required only of those who have been inducted and ordained to a church office …

On OCTOBER the 7th I consulted with my friends as to whether God was calling me to return to England. The reason I had left there no longer applied, since there still was no possibility of instructing the Indians, nor had I yet found or heard of any Indians on the continent of America who had any desire to be instructed. As for Savannah, I'd never committed myself, either verbally or in writing, to stay there a day longer than I thought suitable … Besides, I probably could serve these unhappy people better in England than I could in Georgia, by reporting to the trustees without fear or favor the actual condition of the colony. My friends, after deeply considering these things, were unanimous that I ought to go, but not yet. So I set these thoughts aside for the moment, being persuaded that when the time came, God would make the way plain, right in my face …

---

[42] A parish priest or member of the clergy assisting the rector in a parish.

Thur. NOVEMBER 3.— ... I again consulted my friends, and we agreed that the time we waited for had come. The next morning I called on Mr. Causton and told him that I intended to set out for England immediately. I posted a notice in the public square to this effect and quietly prepared for my journey.

Fri. DECEMBER 2.— ... That afternoon the magistrates published an order requiring all the officers and guards to keep me from leaving the province and forbidding anyone to assist me in doing so. Now being a prisoner, only just not behind bars ... I saw clearly the time had come for leaving this place; and as soon as evening prayers were over, about 8 p.m., the tide being right, I shook off the dust of my feet and left Georgia after having preached the gospel there—not as I ought, but as I was able—one year and nearly nine months ...

[*Wesley attaches several pages describing Georgia's geography and also the character of the various Native American tribes of what is now the Southeastern U.S., especially listing their virtues and vices.*]

Thur. 22.—I said goodbye to America (may it please God, not forever), going on board the *Samuel,* whose captain was Percy, with a young gentleman who had been in Carolina several months and had been one of my parishioners in Savannah; also with a Frenchman, recently of Purrysburg, who escaped there by the skin of his teeth ...

Wed. 28.—I was irrationally afraid of an unknown danger (the wind being light and the sea smooth). This increased for several days, so I cried earnestly for help, and it pleased God to restore peace to my soul almost instantly ...

1738

Sun. JANUARY 8.—With an overflowing heart, I wrote the following words:

> By that most infallible of proofs—inward feeling—I am convinced:
> 1. of unbelief, having no faith in Christ such as will keep my heart from being troubled, which it could not be, if I truly and rightly believed in God;
> 2. of pride throughout my past life, in that I thought I had what now I find I do not possess;

3. of flagrant forgetfulness, such that in a storm I cry to God constantly, but not in a calm;
4. of a frivolous and excessive spirit, occurring whenever I'm not under pressure; it manifests by my saying things that don't edify others, but mostly by the way I talk about my enemies.
Lord save, or I perish! Save me
1. by a faith that gives peace in life and in death;
2. by a humility that will fill my heart, from now on, with a piercing, unceasing awareness that "so far I have accomplished nothing,"[43] clearly having built without a foundation;
3. by remembering to cry to you every moment, especially when all is calm. Give me faith or I die: give a lowly spirit; otherwise, let my life not be easy[44];
4. by steadiness, seriousness, reverence,[45] sobriety of spirit, avoiding like fire every word that does not tend to edify, and never speaking about any who oppose me or who sin against God without all my own sins laid out before me. ...

Fri.13.—We had a major storm, which forced us to shut all the hatches, the sea breaking over the ship continually. At first I was afraid, but I cried to God and was strengthened. Before 10 p.m. I lay down, bless God, without fear ...

About noon the next day the storm ceased. But first I had determined, God being my helper, not only to preach the word of God to all but to apply it to every single soul in the ship one by one, and if just one or not even one of them will hear, I know my efforts are not wasted.

As soon as I began carrying out this resolution, my spirit revived, so that from that day forward I had no more of the fear and heaviness that until then almost constantly weighed me down ...

Tues. 24.—We spoke with two ships coming from England, who gave us the welcome news that we were only 160 leagues[46] from Land's End. My mind was now full, and I wrote down some of my thoughts as follows:

---

[43] "Nihil est quod hactenus feci" in Latin.
[44] "Mihi non sit suave vivere" in Latin.
[45] Greek Σεμνοτης: "reverence, seriousness."
[46] A league is about 3½ miles; so 560 miles.

I went to America to convert the Indians; but oh, who will convert me! Who will deliver me from this evil heart of unbelief? I have a fine summertime religion; I can talk well, and even believe my own words when no danger is near; but just let death look me in the face, and my spirit is troubled. I cannot truly say, "To die is gain!" [Phil. 1:21] ...

I truly believe that if the gospel is true, I am safe, because I not only have given and do give all my goods to feed the poor. I not only give my body to be burned, drowned, or whatever God decrees for me, but I follow after Christian love (not as I ought to, but as I am able) hoping I can attain it. I now believe the gospel is true. "I show my faith by my works" [James 1:18], by staking my all on it. I would do so again and again a thousand times if I still had to choose. Whoever looks at me can tell that I want to be a Christian ... A wise man advised me some time ago, "Be still, and go forward." Perhaps this is best, to see it as my cross; when it comes, to let it humble me and strengthen all my good resolutions, especially to pray without ceasing, and at other times not to worry about it but to go on quietly in the work of the Lord. ...

But I received mercy for this reason, that in me, as the foremost, Jesus Christ might display his perfect patience as an example to those who were to believe in him for eternal life (1Tim.1:16) ...

Fri. FEBRUARY 3.— ... In the evening I reached London. I had been away almost two years and four months.

I have many reasons to praise God, even though I didn't achieve my purpose for going to that strange land, [America,] in spite of all I had planned to do. I trust that through these experiences he has humbled and tested me, at least to some extent, by showing me what was in my heart. These experiences have taught me to beware of people, and they have given me a certainty that if we acknowledge God in all our ways, when reason fails as a guide, he'll direct our paths, either by lot[47] or by his other means. These experiences have delivered me from the fear of the sea, which I dreaded and held in horror since childhood.

---

[47] For Wesley, opening the Bible at random or literally by casting lots.

Through these experiences God has acquainted me with many of his servants, especially those of the Church of Herrnhut,[48] and they have opened me up to the writings of German, Spanish, and Italian saints. I hope too that some good will come to others through these experiences. All [the Europeans] in Georgia have heard the word of God. Some did believe and started off well [in the Christian race]. Beginning steps were made to publish the good news both to African and American heathens.[49] Many children learned how they should serve God and help their neighbor. And those most concerned[50] were able to learn the true state of their infant colony and so to lay a firmer foundation of peace and happiness for generations to come.

Sat. 4.—I told my friends some of my reasons for returning to England earlier than planned. They all agreed it would be proper to report these to the trustees of Georgia …

In the afternoon I was asked to preach at St. John the Evangelist Church. I spoke on these strong words, "If anyone is in Christ, he is a new creature" [2 Cor. 5:17]. Afterwards I was told that many of the "better people"[51] in the parish were so offended that I was not to preach there anymore.[52]

Tues. 7.—A day long to be remembered! At the house of Mr. Weinantz, a Dutch merchant, I met Peter Boehler, Schulius Richter and Wensel Neiser, who had just then landed from Germany. Finding they didn't know anyone in England, I offered to find them a place to lodge, and did so near my own lodging at Mr. Hutton's. And from that moment on, as long as I stayed in London, I took every opportunity to talk with them.

Wed. 8.—I went to see Mr. Oglethorpe again, but had no opportunity to speak to him as I had planned. Afterwards I waited till the board of trustees permitted me to speak, and gave them a short but plain account of the condition of the colony. My account, I am

---

[48] I.e., the Moravians.
[49] I.e., slaves from Africa and Native Americans.
[50] I.e., the Georgia trustees in England.
[51] I.e., those with money and positions of power.
[52] This is just the first of many instances when Wesley's strong preaching of conversion and holiness closed the doors of many churches to him.

afraid, was very different from many others they had received before, and I believe some of them haven't forgiven me yet.

Sun. 12.—I preached at St. Andrew's Holborn Church on, "If I give away all I have, and if I deliver up my body to be burned, but don't have love, I gain nothing" [1 Cor. 13:3]. These are hard sayings; who can hear them? Apparently here too I won't preach any more …

Fri. 17.—I started out for Oxford with Peter Boehler. There we were received hospitably by Mr. Sarney, the only one remaining here now of many who, before we sailed to America, enjoyed counseling each other and rejoiced when enduring insults for Christ's sake.[53]

Sat. 18.— … I spoke at length with Peter Boehler, but I couldn't understand him, least of all when he said, "My brother, my brother, that wisdom of yours must be pruned away."[54] …

Tues. 28.— … As for my own behavior, I now renewed and wrote down my earlier resolutions:

1. to be absolutely open and honest with everyone I talk to;
2. to try to be earnest and serious, and not to indulge in the least frivolous behavior or in laughter, not even for a moment.
3. to say nothing that doesn't tend to the glory of God, and especially not to talk of worldly things. Others may, and indeed must, do so. But what does that matter to me? And
4. to take no pleasure that doesn't tend to the glory of God, thanking God every moment for all I do enjoy, and therefore rejecting every pleasure in and for which I can't thank him..

Sat. MARCH 4.—I found my brother [Charles] at Oxford recovering from pleurisy. With him was Peter Boehler, by whom, and by the great hand of God, I was, on Sunday the 5th, clearly convicted of unbelief, of lacking that faith by which alone we are saved.[55]

Immediately I thought, "I should stop preaching! How can I, who have no faith, preach to others?" I asked Boehler if he thought I

---

[53] Apparently referring to the Holy Club.
[54] Wesley gives Boehler's sentence in Latin, then translates it for us.
[55] Wesley's added note: "With the full Christian salvation."

should stop. "By no means!" he replied. I asked, "But what can I preach?" He said, "Preach faith till you have it and then, because you have it, you will preach faith."

So on Monday the 6th I began preaching this new doctrine, though my soul shrank from the work. The first person to whom I offered salvation by faith alone was a prisoner sentenced to die; his name was Clifford. Peter Boehler had asked me many times before to speak to him, but I couldn't make myself do so until then, still claiming, as I had for many years, that there was no such thing as [genuine] death-bed repentance.

Fri. 10.—Peter Boehler returned to London. On Tuesday the 15th I set out for Manchester with Mr. Kinchin, graduate of Corpus Christi College, and Mr. Fox, formerly a prisoner in the city jail ...

At the inn in Newcastle, where we arrived about 10 a.m.[?], some we spoke to paid close attention, but a merry young woman who waited on us wasn't affected. We kept on talking, however. When we left, she had a fixed look, not moving or saying a word, and seemed as amazed as if she had seen someone raised from the dead ...

Thur. 23.—I met Peter Boehler again, who amazed me more and more by the testimony he gave of the fruits of living faith—the holiness and happiness that he said accompanied it. The next morning I began reading the Greek New Testament again, resolving to abide by "the law and the testimony"[56] and confident that God would show me by this means if this doctrine was of God.

Sun. 26.—I preached at Whitam on the new creation, and in the evening went to a fellowship meeting in Oxford, where (as I did then at all fellowship meetings), after using a collect[57] or two and the Lord's Prayer, I explained a chapter in the New Testament, then ended with three or four more collects and a hymn.

Mon. 27.—Mr. Kinchin went with me to the castle prison where, after reading prayers and preaching on "It is appointed for men once to die" [Heb. 9:27], we prayed with the man sentenced to be executed. First we used several prayers [from the prayer book], then we prayed as we felt led. The man knelt down, confused and heavy-

---

[56] I.e., the Scriptures, especially the New Testament; cf. Isaiah 8:20.
[57] Short prayer from the prayer book.

hearted, having no rest in his bones because of his sins. After a while he rose up and said eagerly, "I am ready to die now! I know that Christ has taken away my sins and that there's no more condemnation for me!" He remained composed and cheerful when led out to execution, and in his last moments he still displayed a perfect peace, confident that he was "accepted in the beloved" [Eph. 1:6] ...

Sat. APRIL 21.—I met Peter Boehler again. Now I had no objection to how he described faith: that it is (to use the words of our Church) "a sure trust and confidence in God that, through the merits of Christ, our sins are forgiven, and we are restored to favor with God." Nor could I deny the happiness or holiness that he described as fruits of this living faith. The verses, "That very Spirit bears witness with our spirit that we are children of God" [Rom. 8:16], and, "Those who believe in the Son of God have the testimony in their hearts" [1 John 5:10], fully convinced me of [the necessary fruit of happiness], just as "Those who have been born of God do not sin" [1 John 3:9], and "Everyone who believes ... has been born of God" [1 John 5:1], convinced me of [the necessary fruit of holiness]. But I couldn't comprehend what he said about an instantaneous work; I couldn't understand how this faith could be given in a moment—how a man could be instantly changed from darkness to light, from sin and misery to righteousness and joy in the Holy Spirit. I searched the Scriptures again, the book of Acts in particular, and was astonished; almost all the cases I found there were of instant conversion and hardly any occurred as slowly as Paul's, who spent three days laboring in the new birth. My only way out was this: "Granted that God worked this way in the early periods of Christianity, times have changed. Why should I believe that he works the same way now?"

But on Sunday the 2nd I was driven out of this last refuge by the evidence of several actual witnesses, all testifying that God had worked this way in them. They said he had instantly given them such a faith in the blood of his Son that it transported them from darkness into light, and from sin and fear into holiness and happiness. So I stopped arguing; now I could only cry out, "Lord, help my unbelief!"

I asked Peter Boehler again if I should stop teaching others. He said, "No, don't bury the talent God has given you!" Accordingly, on

Tuesday the 25th I spoke clearly and fully at Blendon to Mr. Delamotte's family, of the nature and fruits of faith. Mr. Broughton and my brother [Charles] were there. Mr. Broughton's main objection was that he couldn't believe that I, who had done and suffered so much, had no faith. My brother was very angry and told me I didn't know the trouble I had caused by talking like that. And that is when it pleased God to light a fire [in me] that I trust will never be put out …

Peter Boehler walked with me a few miles, urging me not to stop short of the grace of God. At Gerrard's Cross, I plainly declared to those God placed in my hands the faith as it is in Jesus. The next day I spoke in a similar way to a young man I overtook on the road, and that evening to our friends at Oxford. To them it was a strange doctrine; some, although they didn't argue, didn't know what to make of it, but one or two, wounded by sin, were willing to hear and gladly received it …

Mon. MAY 1.—My brother got sick again and I had to hurry back to London. In the evening I found him at James Hutton's in better health than I expected, but he strongly opposed what he called "the new faith."

This evening we started our little fellowship, which later met in Fetter Lane. Our basic rules were as follows:

> In obedience to the command of God through St. James and by the advice of Peter Boehler, we agree on the following:
> 1. We will meet once a week to "confess our sins to one another and to pray for one another, so we may be healed" [James 5:16].
> 2. Those who meet like this will be divided into several circles or small groups,[58] none with less than five or more than ten members.
> 3. Those present will take turns speaking as openly and honestly, but as briefly as they can, telling what is really in their hearts, including the different ways they have been tempted and delivered since the last meeting.
> 4. All the circles will join together[59] at 8 p.m. every Wednesday evening, beginning and ending with singing and prayer.

---

[58] "Bands or little companies." "Circle" will be my substitution for "band."
[59] "Have a conference."

5. Any who wish to join this fellowship should be asked: "Why do you want to do this? Will you be completely open and honest? Do you object to any of our rules?" (These rules may then be read aloud.)

6. When new members are nominated, all present should state clearly and openly any objections they may have to them.

7. Where there is no reasonable objection, they should be placed into one or more separate circles for a trial period, and a member chosen to help them.

8. After a two-month trial period, if no one objects, they may be accepted into the fellowship.

9. Every fourth Saturday is to be observed as a day of intercessory prayer by the fellowship collectively.

10. On the second Sunday following that Saturday, a general love-feast will be held from 7 to 10 p.m..

11. Members must not disobey the fellowship rules. If they do, they should be warned three times, and if they still do not conform, they should no longer be considered members.

Wed. 3.—My brother had a long and extraordinary conversation with Peter Boehler, and it pleased God then to open Charles' eyes to clearly see the nature of that one true living faith by which "through grace we are saved" [Eph. 2:8].

[*In the following weeks, Wesley preached strongly in different churches in London on justification by faith, and in most of these was told he would not be allowed to preach there again.*]

Wed. 10.—Mr. Stonehouse, vicar of Islington, was convinced of "the truth as it is in Jesus." From this time till Saturday the 13th, I was sorrowful and heavy-hearted, unable to read or meditate, sing or pray or do anything else. Yet I received some refreshment from Peter Boehler's letter ...

Fri. 19.—My brother's pleurisy returned once again.

A few of us spent Saturday night in prayer. The next day being Whitsunday [Pentecost], I heard Dr. Heylyn preach a truly Christian sermon on "They were all filled with the Holy Spirit" [Acts 2:4]. "You can all be filled like that," he said, "unless it's your own fault." I assisted him in serving Holy Communion, since his regular assistant got sick during the service, and then I received the surprising news that my brother had found rest in his soul. From that hour, his body also grew stronger. "Who is so great a god as our God?" ...

Monday, Tuesday, and Wednesday, I was always sorrowful and heavy-hearted. I described something, as well as I was able and haltingly, in the following letter to a friend: ...

> I know that I deserve only wrath, being filled with all that God detests and having nothing good in me to atone for them or to remove the wrath of God. All my works, my good deeds, my prayers, themselves need to be atoned for. So that my mouth is shut; I have nothing to plead. God is holy; I am unholy. God is a consuming fire; I am altogether a sinner, fit to be consumed.
>
> Yet I hear a voice (and is it not the voice of God?) saying, "Believe, and you will be saved. He who believes has passed from death to life. 'For God so loved the world that he gave his only Son, so that everyone who believes in him may not perish but have eternal life'" [John 3:16].
>
> Oh, let no one deceive us by empty words as if we had already attained to this faith![60] We will know it by its fruits. Do we already feel peace with God and joy in the Holy Spirit? Does his Spirit bear witness with our spirit that we are the children of God? Not with mine, nor, I fear, with yours. Oh, Savior of mankind, deliver us from trusting in anything but you! Draw us after you! Let us be emptied of self, and then fill us with all peace and joy in believing, and let nothing separate us from your love, in time or in eternity!

I feel I should give a full account of what happened on Wednesday the 24th after a preface to give its context. Those who can't accept this should ask the Father of lights to give more light to them and to me.

1. I believe that before I was about 10 years old, I hadn't sinned away that "washing of the Holy Spirit" which was given me in [infant] baptism, since I had been strictly trained and carefully taught that I could only be saved by complete obedience, by keeping all the commands of God, and [my parents] made a real effort for me to

---

[60] Wesley's note: "The proper Christian faith." This, for Wesley, was not mere belief in doctrine but new birth—evidenced, as here, by a faith bearing fruit, inwardly and outwardly.

understand them. I gladly accepted those instructions as far as outward duties and sins were concerned, and I often thought about them. But I neither understood nor remembered what was said to me about obedience or holiness of the heart. So in fact I was just as ignorant of the true meaning of the law as I was of the gospel of Christ.

2. For the next six or seven years I was away at school where, no longer being restrained, I more and more neglected even outward duties and almost constantly committed outward sins,[61] knowing them to be wrong, even though to the world they weren't shocking. Still I continued reading the Scriptures and saying my prayers, morning and evening. At this point I hoped to be saved by: 1. not being as bad as other people; 2. still having a religious inclination; and 3. reading the Bible, going to church, and saying my prayers.

3. When I graduated and went to the university, for five years I still said my prayers, publicly and privately, and along with the Scriptures I read other religious books, especially commentaries on the New Testament. But all that time I had no concept of inner holiness; in fact, I kept sinning habitually and consciously. For the most part I was content to do this, except for short periods and brief struggles [of conscience], especially before and after Holy Communion, which I was required to receive three times a year. I can't say how I hoped to be saved at this point, since I was constantly sinning against the little light I had, except for temporary fits of what many clergymen taught me to call "repentance."[62]

4. When I was about 22, my father urged me to enter holy orders. At the same time God's providence directed me to [Thomas à] Kempis' *Christian Pattern,* and I began to see that true religion resided in the heart and that God's law extended to all our thoughts as well as words and actions. I was angry at à Kempis, however, for being too strict, though I read him only in Dean Stanhope's translation. Yet when I read him, I often received comfort that until then I had never known. Also, meeting with a new friend who was pious, I began changing my behavior completely and living a new

---

[61] I.e., actual deeds, not only in the heart.
[62] In other words, he felt contrition at times but continued to sin, and therefore was not truly repentant.

way. I withdrew an hour or two each day as a spiritual exercise. I took communion every week. I guarded myself against all sin of either word or deed. I began aiming at and praying for inward holiness. The upshot was that now, doing so much and living so good a life, I thought surely I was a good Christian.

5. Soon I transferred to another college,[63] and when I did I carried out a plan that I already felt was extremely important: I shook off all superficial friends. I began to value my time more and more. I began to study harder. I guarded more carefully against actual sins. I advised others to be religious,[64] according to the concept of religion by which I modeled my own life. But now I encountered Mr. Law's *Christian Perfection* and his *Serious Call.* Many things in both books offended me, but they convinced me more than ever of the height and breadth and depth of the law of God. The light flowed in mightily upon my soul, and everything took on a new perspective. I cried to God for help and resolved to obey him promptly, as I'd never done before. I made a concerted effort to keep his whole law, inner and outer, to the best of my ability. I was persuaded that he would accept me and that even then I was saved.

6. In 1730, I started visiting the prisons, helping the poor and sick in town, and doing what other good I could by giving either my time or the money I had to the bodies and souls of all [I could help]. To do this, I cut out everything superfluous and even many things usually called necessities of life. This soon made me an object of scorn, and I rejoiced that my name was rejected as evil [cf. Luke 6:22]. The following spring I began keeping the Wednesday and Friday fasts that were commonly observed in the ancient church, eating nothing till 3 p.m. At this point, I didn't know how to go any further. I wrestled with all my might against all sin; I denied myself everything I thought it lawful to do; I was careful to use all the means of grace at all times, both publicly and privately. I neglected no opportunity of doing good, and for that very reason was mistreated ... This was my path for several years, but when I thought I was about to die, none of this gave me any comfort or any assurance of God's acceptance. This

---

[63] Wesley originally was a student of Christ Church, Oxford. He was ordained a deacon in 1725, and the following year elected fellow of Lincoln College, Oxford.
[64] "Religious" in the original sense: "spiritual, pious, godly."

[discovery] surprised me very much, not imagining I had been building on the sand all that time nor considering that "no one can lay a foundation other than that which is laid, which is Jesus Christ" [1 Cor. 3:11].

7. Soon after this a man who practiced meditation convinced me, more than I'd been before, that outer works are nothing by themselves, and in several conversations he taught me how to pursue inner holiness or a union of the soul with God. But now I must say even of his instructions, though at the time I received them as the words of God: 1. that he spoke so recklessly against trusting in outer works that he discouraged me from doing them at all; and 2. that he recommended, as if to make up what was lacking in outer works, silent prayer, and similar exercises as the best way to purify the soul and unite it with God. But in fact these things became my own works just as much as visiting the sick or clothing the naked, and the union with God which I pursued was actually my own righteousness as much as ever before.

8. ... I dragged on heavily this way, finding no comfort or help, till I left England. On shipboard, however, I again became active in good works, and there it pleased God in his mercy to give me 26 Moravians for companions. They tried to show me a more excellent way, but I didn't understand it at first. I was too educated and too wise, and it seemed foolishness to me. So I kept on preaching, while pursuing and trusting in that righteousness "by which no flesh can be justified" [Rom. 3:20].

9. The whole time I was at Savannah I was struggling this way in vain ...

10. In this miserable state of bondage to sin, I was constantly fighting but not overcoming. Up to then I'd served sin willingly; now against my will I still served it. I fell and rose, and fell again. Sometimes I was overcome, and in heaviness; sometimes I overcame and had joy ... I was still under the law, not under grace (along with most so-called Christians), for I was struggling with sin but not set free from it. Nor did the Spirit bear witness with my spirit; it couldn't, for I wasn't seeking it by faith but as if by works of the law.

11. On my return to England in January 1738, being near death and for that reason very anxious, I became convinced that unbelief

was the cause of my anxiety and that the one thing I needed was a true and living faith. Still for me the object of this faith was simply God as such, not faith in or through Christ. I didn't realize that I totally lacked this faith; I just thought I didn't have enough of it. As soon as I arrived in London, God provided for me Peter Boehler. He affirmed that the one true faith in Christ was always accompanied by two fruits: power over sin and constant peace in knowing we're forgiven …

12. … I was forced to retreat to my last stronghold: that experience would never agree with the literal interpretation of those scriptures, and therefore I couldn't admit it to be true until I found living witnesses of it. [Peter Boehler] answered that he could furnish these any time—if I wished, the next day. And so the next day he came with three others, who all testified of their personal experience, that a true, living faith in Christ can't be separated from a sense of pardon for all past, and freedom from all present, sins. … I was now totally convinced, and, by the grace of God, resolved to seek it to the end: 1. by absolutely renouncing all dependence on my own works or righteousness … 2. by adding to the other means of grace continual prayer for this justifying, saving faith, a full reliance on the blood of Christ shed for me, and a trust in him as my Christ, as my sole justification, sanctification, and redemption [1 Cor. 1:30].

13. I continued to seek it this way … till Wednesday, May the 24th. About five that morning, I opened my New Testament on those words: "Thus he has given us, through these things, his precious and very great promises, so that through them you … may become participants of the divine nature" (2 Peter 1:4).[65] Just as I was about to go out, I opened it again on those words: "You are not far from the kingdom of God" [Mark 12:34]. In the afternoon I was invited to go to St. Paul's. The anthem[66] was, "Out of the deep have I called unto thee, O Lord: Lord, hear my voice; etc." [67]

14. That evening, against my will, I went to a fellowship meeting in Aldersgate Street, where someone was reading Luther's preface to the book of Romans. About a quarter of nine,

---

[65] Wesley gives the Greek text before the English translation.
[66] A psalm or hymn sung responsively, with words from Scripture.
[67] A mixture of verses.

while he was describing the change God works in the heart through faith in Christ, **I felt my heart strangely warmed. I felt I did trust in Christ, Christ alone, for salvation, and I received an assurance that he had taken away my sins—even mine—and had saved me from the law of sin and death** [my emphasis] ...

Fri. 26.—I continued to have peace in my soul, but still I was heavy-hearted due to many temptations. I asked Mr. Telchig, the Moravian, what to do. He said, "You must not fight them like you did before but rather flee from them the moment they appear and take refuge in the wounds of Jesus." ...

Sat. 27.—I thought that one reason I lacked joy was that I didn't take enough time for prayer, I resolved to do no work in the morning until I went to church, and instead to keep pouring out my heart before him. And today my spirit was enlarged so that, although I was still attacked by many temptations, I was more than a conqueror. This gave me still more power to trust and to rejoice in God my Savior.

Sun. 28.— I woke up in peace but without joy. I remained in the same calm, quiet state of mind till evening. Then in a large gathering I was attacked harshly as an enthusiast, a seducer, and as one teaching new doctrines. It was the blessing of God that kept me from getting angry. After calmly and briefly answering, I left, but without the tender concern I should have had for those who were seeking to die in the error of their ways ...

Sun. JUNE 4.—This was a true feast-day, because from the time I rose till after 1 p.m. I was praying, reading the Scriptures, singing praise, or calling sinners to repentance. All these days I can hardly remember opening the New Testament[68] on anything except some great and precious promise. I saw more clearly than ever that the Gospel[69] is, in truth, one great promise from beginning to end ...

Wed. 7.—I decided, if God allowed me, to withdraw to Germany for a little while. I had fully intended to do this before leaving Georgia, if it pleased God to bring me back to Europe, and I now clearly saw that the time had come. My mind was too weak to be

---

[68] I.e., at random.
[69] Meaning here, it seems, the New Testament, not one particular Gospel.

torn apart like this, and I hoped that conversation with these holy men,[70] living witnesses of the full power of faith who yet were able to bear with those who were weak, would be God's means of confirming my soul, so that I could go on from faith to faith and from strength to strength.

Thur. 8.—I went to Salisbury to say goodbye to my mother. The next day I left Sarum, and on Saturday came to Stanton Harcourt. Having preached faith in Christ there on Sunday the 11th, I went on to Oxford; and from there on Monday to London, where I found Mr. Ingham just setting out. We boarded a ship the next day, Tuesday the 13th ... We reached the Mease at 8 a.m. on Thursday morning, and an hour and a half later landed at Rotterdam.

There were eight of us in all: five Englishmen and three Germans ...

At Ysselstein, staying with Baron Wattevil was like being at home ... They were living just outside of the town in three or four little houses until a larger house could be built that would hold them all. Saturday the 17th was their intercession day. In the morning, some of our English brethren asked me to administer the Lord's Supper. The rest of the day we spent with all the brothers and sisters, hearing the wonderful work God is beginning to do over all the earth, petitioning him and giving him thanks for the power of his kingdom.

At 6 a.m. we embarked. Beautiful gardens border the river on both sides for much of the way to Amsterdam, which we reached about 5 p.m. ... Here we were entertained until the following Thursday with true Christian hospitality, by Mr. Decknatel, a Mennonite minister, who made sure we lacked nothing while we stayed. Dr. Barkausen, a physician from Russia who had been with Mr. Decknatel for some time, also showed every kindness. Remember them, O Lord, for good!

Mon. 19.—I attended a meeting of one of the fellowships, which lasted an hour and a half. About 60 persons were present. Singing was done in Low German (Mr. Decknatel having translated part of the Herrnhut hymnbook into that language), but the words were so

---

[70] I.e., the Moravians or Bohemian Brethren.

much like German that any who understood the original could understand the translation …

Wed. 28.— … When we embarked at 4 p.m., I couldn't help but notice that the Catholics behaved more decently than we who are called Reformed. As soon as we were seated (and every morning thereafter), they all pulled off their hats and each privately prayed a short prayer for our safe journey. And I credit the boatmen themselves (who on the Rhine are proverbially wicked) that I never heard one of them take God's name in vain, or saw anyone laugh when anything religious was mentioned, so that I believe the glory of joking about sacred things is peculiar to the English!

Sun. JULY 2.— … That evening we came to Mainz, and on Monday the 3rd at 10:30 a.m. to Frankfort.

Faint and weary as we were, they wouldn't let us enter the city since we hadn't brought passes with us, which we never imagined they would have required in a time of general peace. After waiting an hour at the gates, we got a messenger, sending him to Mr. Boehler (Peter Boehler's father). He immediately came, got us entry into the city, and gave us warm hospitality. We set out early in the morning on Tuesday the 4th and about 1 p.m. came to Marienborn …

The family at Marienborn consists of about 90 persons from many different countries. Currently they live in a large house rented by Count [Zinzendorf] which could hold a much larger number; but they are building one about three miles off on the top of a green hill. "Oh, how good and pleasant it is when brothers dwell in unity!" [Psalm 133:1].

Thur. 6.—The Count carried me with him to the Count of Solmes, where I noted with pleasure the German moderation. Three of the young countesses, though full-grown, were dressed in linen, and the count and his son in cloth of simple weave. At dinner the next day, a glass of wine and a glass of water were set beside each one, and if either glass were emptied it was replaced. They all talked freely without putting on airs. At 10 p.m. we took the public carriage again and in the morning we reached Marienborn.

I lodged with one of the brothers at Eckershausen, a mile from Marienborn, where I usually spent the day, mostly in conversation with those who could speak either Latin or English, since I hadn't practiced my German enough to speak it fluently. Here I constantly found what I was looking for, namely, living proof of the power of faith—persons saved from inner as well as outer sin by "the love of God poured into their hearts" [Rom. 5:5], and from all doubt and fear, by the abiding witness of "the Holy Spirit who has been given to them" [cf. John 7:39] ...

Wed. 12.—Today was one of the meetings for nonmembers, where someone from Frankfort asked the question: Can a man be justified and not know it? The count spoke at length and biblically on it to this effect:

1. Justification is the forgiveness of sins.
2. The moment people fly to Christ they are justified,
3. And have peace with God, but not always joy;
4. And they may not know they are justified till a long time afterwards:
5. For the assurance of it is distinct from justification itself.
6. But others may know they are justified by their power over sin, by their seriousness, their love of the brethren, and their "hunger and thirst after righteousness," which things prove the spiritual life has begun.
7. To be justified is the same thing as to be born of God. (*Wesley's comment*—"Not so.")
8. When a man is awakened spiritually, he is born of God, and his fear and sorrow and sense of the wrath of God are the pangs of the new birth ...

Wed. AUGUST 2.— At 4 p.m. there was a love-feast of the married men, eating with "gladness and singleness of heart" [Acts 2:46] and voicing their praise and thanksgiving.

Thur. 3 ... On Friday and Saturday (and every day the following week), I talked at length with the more mature brothers regarding the great work God had done in their souls, purifying them by faith, and with Martin Dober and other teachers and elders of the church, concerning their church discipline ...

Tues. 8.— ... On Wednesday and Thursday I was able to speak with Michael Linner, the oldest member of the church, and also at length with Christian David, who served God as its first founder.

Serious Joy (John Wesley's *Journal*)

I also had the blessing of hearing him preach four times during my few days there, and every time he chose the very subjects I would have chosen if given the chance. Three times he described the condition of those who are weak in faith, who are justified but haven't yet received a new, clean heart, who have received forgiveness through the blood of Christ, but haven't received the constant indwelling of the Holy Spirit ...

[*Omitted are many pages in which Wesley records his conversations with different Moravians. Now Wesley defends his own life and ministry in England as it develops.*]

"If this plan or this undertaking is of human origin, it will fail; but if it is of God, you will not be able to overthrow it—in that case you may even be found fighting against God!"—Acts 5:38–39.

1. WHEN people first started accusing me of things I knew nothing about, I often thought, "If I just had two or three close friends who knew my life and how I acted, they could simply say what they had seen and heard, and all these false accusations would fall away." But I saw my mistake as soon as I had two or three true, not just so-called, friends ... For if anyone dares to speak up for me, they only have to say, "We suppose you are a Methodist, too," and all he has said means nothing to them.

2. Many who knew my lifestyle were afraid to tell the truth, fearing they would be reproached like me, and the few who overcame this fear were rendered ineffective, being immediately lumped with me whom they defended. Shouldn't impartial people say, "You're allowed to answer for yourself"? ... You've heard one side already; hear the other. Weigh both sides; allow for human weakness, and then judge as you want to be judged.

3. In this extract [of my *Journal*], my purpose is to declare to all mankind what the so-called Methodists have done and are doing now—or rather, what God has done and is still doing in our land. For what has appeared recently isn't the work of man. All who consider it calmly must say, "This is the Lord's doing, and it is marvelous in our eyes" [Psalm 118:23].

4. In many ways, this is a work such as neither we nor our parents have known. Quite a number whose sins were most flagrant—that is, drunkards, swearers, thieves, whoremongers, and adulterers—have been brought "from darkness to light and from the power of Satan to God" [Acts 26:18]. Many of these were deeply attached to their sins, having gloried in their shame for a long time, perhaps for many years—yes, even to old age. Many didn't have even an intellectual faith, being Jews, Arians,[71] Deists,[72] or atheists. Nor has God only flexed his muscles in these last days on behalf of the unchurched and sinners, but many of the self-righteous also have believed in him—"the righteous who need no repentance" [Luke 15:7]. Realizing that they were doomed, they then heard the voice that raises the dead and were made partakers of an inward, vital religion, which is "righteousness and peace and joy in the Holy Spirit" [Rom. 14:17].

5. The way God has done this work in many souls is as unusual as the work itself. Generally, if not always, it has been done in a moment. "As the lightning flashing from heaven," so was "the coming of the Son of Man" [Matt. 24:27], either to bring peace or a sword, either to wound or to heal, either to convict of sin or to give remission of sins in his blood. And the other circumstances accompanying it have been equally far removed from what human wisdom would have expected. So the word is true: "My ways are not as your ways, nor my thoughts as your thoughts" [Isa. 55:8].

6. It seems that God intends for these extraordinary events to further manifest his work, to cause his power to be known, and to awaken the attention of a drowsy world. Yet some have used these as the basis for their main objection to the whole work: "We never saw it happen this way," they say, "therefore the work is not of God." As further evidence, they've grossly misrepresented many actual events and have added many fictional ones, without any regard either to truth or probability. A straightforward narration of those things,

---

[71] Arianism, an ancient heresy, held that Christ was a created being and did not exist eternally, and hence was not fully God.
[72] Deists accepted the idea of a Creator, but did not believe that God still intervened in human affairs or that he ever suspended natural law. Therefore they rejected the supernatural.

which were "not done in a corner" [Acts 26:26], is the best answer to these objections. However, I'll sometimes give a more detailed answer to those occurrences that seem the most important.

7. Yet I know that even this won't satisfy the majority of those who are now offended. This is due to the obvious reason that they'll never read it. They want to hear one side and one side only. I know also that many who do read it won't change their minds because they're prejudiced and won't pay attention to anything "this fellow" can say. That's their business. I've done my part and have cleared myself. Yes, I know that many will take great offense at this very account, and this has to be the case from the very nature of the things I'll tell. The best they can do is to call me a fool, a madman, and an enthusiast. But my part is to relate simple truth in as inoffensive a manner as I can. May it have the effect God is pleased to give it and, what's more, may it be for his glory! ...

Sun. SEPTEMBER 17.—I began again to declare in my own country the good news of salvation, preaching three times and afterwards explaining the Holy Scripture to a large gathering in the Minories.[73] On Monday it was my joy to meet with our little fellowship which had grown to 32 persons. The next day I went to the condemned criminals in Newgate Prison and offered them free salvation. In the evening I went to a fellowship meeting in Bearyard and preached repentance and remission of sins. The next evening I spoke the truth in love at a fellowship meeting in Aldersgate Street where some opposed me at first, but not for long, so that nothing but love could be seen when we parted ...

Fri. OCTOBER 6.—I preached at St. Antholin's again. In the afternoon I went to the Rev. Mr. Bedford to tell him privately how he had harmed [the cause of] God and also his brother by preaching and printing that very weak sermon on assurance, which was an *ignoratio elenchi*[74] from beginning to end, seeing the assurance we preach is very different from that which he writes against. We speak of an

---

[73] An area of London.
[74] "ignorance of the clench"?

assurance of our present pardon, not, as he does, of our final perseverance[75] ...

Mon. 9.—I set out for Oxford. While walking, I read the truly surprising narrative of the recent conversions in and around the town of Northampton in New England.[76] Surely "this is the Lord's doing; it is marvelous in our eyes."

I wrote a summary of this to a friend, about the condition of those who are weak in faith. His answer, which I received at Bristol on Saturday the 14th, greatly disturbed me until, after crying out to God, I picked up a Bible, which opened on these words: "Jabez called on the God of Israel, saying, 'Oh that you would bless me and enlarge my border, and that your hand might be with me, and that you would keep me from harm so that it might not bring me pain!' And God granted what he asked" [1 Chron. 4:10].

This, however, along with a sentence in the evening lesson, started me thinking about my own condition more deeply. And here is what happened to me then:

> Examine yourselves, to see whether you are in the faith" [2 Cor. 13:5]. Now the best way to examine ourselves, as to whether we are truly in the faith, is that given by Paul: "If anyone is in Christ, he is a new creation. The old has passed away; behold, the new has come" [2 Cor. 5:17] ...
>
> Such, by the grace of God in Christ, is the thrust of my life; therefore, in this respect, I am a new creature.
>
> But St. Paul tells us elsewhere that "the fruit of the Spirit is love, joy, peace, patience, kindness, goodness, faithfulness, gentleness, self-control" [Gal. 5:22–23]. By God's grace in Christ I find some of these—peace, patience, kindness, gentleness, and self-control—in myself to some degree, but I don't find the others. I can't find in myself the love of God or of Christ.[77] This is why I am numb and my

---

[75] "Final perseverance" is the doctrine that believers will remain faithful to the end, and not sin so as to be finally lost.
[76] Wesley is referring to the first Great Awakening in New England, George Whitefield being the main leader.
[77] This sentence is remarkable, and Wesley will write similarly even in his 60s. It seemed he did not have a felt or passionate love for God and Jesus as he thought he should have, although he often experienced God's love for him and overflowed

mind wanders during public prayer; likewise, even during Holy Communion, I feel cold even when focused on it.

Again, I don't have that "joy in the Holy Spirit," or any solid or lasting joy; nor do I have such a peace that drives out all fear or doubt. When godly men told me that I had no faith, I often doubted if I really had any, and those doubts made me very uneasy until I found relief through prayer and reading the Holy Scriptures.

But overall, even though I don't yet have that "joy in the Holy Spirit" or the full assurance of faith, and much less am I, in the full sense of the words, "a new creature" in Christ, still I trust that I have some measure of faith and am "accepted in the beloved." I trust that "the record that stood against me is erased" [Col. 2:14] and that I am reconciled to God through his Son.

Sun. 15.— ... In the evening, being disturbed by what some said about "the kingdom of God within us," and doubtful of my own condition, I called upon God and received this answer from his Word: "He was also himself looking for the kingdom of God" [Mark 15:43]. But shouldn't I wait in silence and stillness?—this was my immediate thought. I opened my Testament again, on these words: "You see that faith was active along with his works, and faith was completed by his works" [James 2:22].

Fri. NOVEMBER 3.—On Wednesday, at the urgent request of the condemned criminals, my brother and I went to render them the last services. It was the most glorious instance I ever saw of faith triumphing over sin and death. A bystander, seeing one man in particular with tears streaming down his cheeks, while his eyes were gazing upwards, asked him a few moments before he died, "How's your heart now?" He calmly replied, "I feel a peace that I didn't believe possible; and I know it's the peace of God that passes all understanding." ...

Sun. 12.—I preached twice at the Castle Prison. The following week, I began to examine more closely the teaching of the Church of England on the controversial question of justification by faith, and I

---

with gratitude. We might say that W. preached love and acted loved until he had love.

condensed and printed for the use of others[78] the substance of what I found in the Homilies.[79] ...

Tues. DECEMBER 5.—I began reading prayers and preaching in the Gloucester Green workhouse,[80] and on Thursday in the one belonging to St. Thomas' parish. Both days I preached at the castle prison. At St. Thomas's was a young woman, raving mad, screaming and afflicting herself continually. I had a strong urge to speak to her. The moment I started, she became still. Tears ran down her cheeks the whole time I was telling her, "Jesus of Nazareth is able and willing to deliver you." Oh, where is faith on earth? Why are these miserable people allowed to remain completely bound by Satan? Jesus, Master! Give medicine to heal their sickness, and deliver those who right now are tormented by unclean spirits! ...

Mon. 11. Hearing that Mr. Whitefield had arrived from Georgia, I hurried to London, and on Tuesday the 12th God permitted us once more to take sweet counsel together ...

1739

Mon. JANUARY 1.—Mr. Hall, Mr. Kinchin, Mr. Ingham, Mr. Whitefield, Mr. Hutchins, and my brother Charles were present at our love-feast in Fetter Lane, with about 60 brothers and sisters. About 3 a.m., as we continued in urgent prayer, the power of God came so strongly on us that many cried out with overflowing joy, and many fell to the floor. As soon as we had somewhat recovered from our awe and amazement at his Majesty's presence, we broke out with one voice, "We praise you, O God; we acknowledge that You are the Lord!"

Thur. 25.—I baptized John Smith, formerly an Anabaptist, and four other adults at Islington. Of the adults I've known to be baptized recently, only one at the time was born again in the full sense of the phrase; that is, found a thorough, inward change, by the love of God filling her heart. Most of them were only born again in a lower sense, i.e., received the remission of their sins ...

---

[78] Wesley abridged many books and printed them for educational purposes.
[79] I.e., discourses on Bible passages. Reference is to the Book of Homilies used by the Church of England.
[80] I.e., a house or shop providing work for the unemployed poor.

Fri. MARCH 2.—All our brethren recommended me to spend a few days at Oxford, so I went there on Saturday the 3rd. I found a few here ... who hadn't denied the faith or been ashamed of their Lord, even in the midst of a perverse generation. And every day we spent together, we had convincing evidence like we'd never even imagined that "he is able to save completely those who come to God through him" [Heb. 7:25].

One of the most amazing manifestations of his power which I ever remember seeing was the following Tuesday when I visited a woman who was absolutely enraged over "this new way"[81] and who opposed it zealously. I soon learned that disputation just angered her more, so I stopped arguing and asked if we could pray together, and she agreed so far as to kneel down. In a few minutes she began struggling in agony of body and soul, and before long cried out earnestly, "Now I know I'm forgiven for Christ's sake!" She kept speaking along that line, bearing witness to a full hope of immortality. And from that time on, God set her face like flint to declare the faith that she previously persecuted ...

Sat. 10.— ... Thursday the 15th I set out early in the morning, and in the afternoon arrived in London.

During my stay here, I was very busy, between our own fellowship in Fetter Lane and many others, where I was constantly asked to explain Scripture; so when I received another letter from Mr. Whitefield and one from Mr. Seward, earnestly requesting me to come to Bristol without delay, I hadn't been thinking of leaving London. I wasn't eager to leave, and perhaps even less inclined (though I trust I don't hold my life dear, just so I can finish my race with joy) because of the remarkable scriptures[82] we hit on every time we asked what this moving out would lead to, probably allowed to try our faith: "Go up this mountain ... and die on the mountain which you go up, and be gathered to your people" [Deut. 32:49–50]. "And the people of Israel wept for Moses in the plains of Moab thirty days" [Deut. 34:8]. "For I will show him how much he must suffer

---

[81] I.e., the "new way" of zeal and holiness.
[82] Wesley is relying on the method he frequently uses of opening the Bible at random, seeking guidance.

for the sake of my name" [Acts 9:16]. "Devout men buried Stephen and made great lamentation over him" [Acts 8:2].

Wed. 28.—My trip was proposed to our fellowship in Fetter Lane. But my brother Charles could hardly bear to hear it mentioned, till again we appealed to the oracles of God, but he said nothing more after receiving these words as spoken to himself: "Son of man, behold, I am about to take the delight of your eyes away from you at a stroke; yet you shall not mourn or weep, nor shall your tears run down" [Ezek. 24:16]. Our other brothers, however, continued debating the matter with little likelihood of an agreement until finally we all agreed to decide it by lot.[83] This decided that I should go ... [84]

Perhaps it will satisfy some if I explain, before relating this next phase of my life, why for so many years I preferred the university life to any other, especially after my father strongly urged me to accept a pastorate.[85] Here I attach the letter I wrote him several years ago about this:

Oxford, Dec. 10, 1734

Dear Sir,

A parent's authority and the call of God[86] are things so sacred that any question concerning them deserves the most serious consideration ... I'm sure you join me in begging his guidance, who will not allow those who trust him to make fatal errors in their life-choices.

2. I completely agree that the glory of God and the different levels of promoting it are to be our only consideration and guide in choosing any path of life, and therefore that it all revolves around this point: Which ought I to prefer: a college life or that of a parish parson? I do not say that the glory of God is to be my first or main consideration, but my only one ...

5. However, when two different ways of life are offered, I would choose to consider first which one I believe will be best for my own

---

[83] Decision by lot was similar to sacred dice, which we see in Acts 1. The outcome was considered to be from God.

[84] It's not just a matter of leaving London, for John W. will continue to come and go in years ahead. But this is the beginning of a major expansion of his—and the Methodist—ministry throughout the British Isles.

[85] "A cure of souls"; i.e., a parish ministry.

[86] Wesley: "Providence."

soul; which will promote my own holiness. By holiness I do not mean fasting or severe asceticism, as you seem to think, but rather the mind that was in Christ—renewing the soul in the image of God. And I believe the situation I am now in will help advance me in this, because of the special advantages I now enjoy.

6. The first of these is daily conversation with my friends ... who see from afar what that one work is: the recovery of a single eye and a clean heart; who, in order to do so have, according to their ability, absolutely devoted themselves to God, and who follow after their Lord, denying themselves and taking up their cross daily ...

7. Another blessing I enjoy here more than I could expect elsewhere is solitude. Not only do I have as much but as little company as I please. I have no idle visitors ...

9. Another great blessing here is freedom from material concerns. Where else could I enjoy it like I do now? I hear about the cares of the world, but I don't feel them. I receive my income regularly;[87] all I have to do is to take it home. My major expense is food, and this too is provided without any care of mine.[88] ... When I need to buy something, I can do so immediately, without wasting time. Here, therefore, I can be "free from anxieties" [1 Cor. 7:32]. I can "wait upon the Lord without distraction" [1 Cor. 7:35]. And I know what a help this is to being "holy both in body and in spirit" [1 Cor. 7:34].

10. Stirring me up to make the best ... use of these special privileges, I am able to take communion every week and to attend public prayers twice a day. It would be easy to mention ... many disadvantages[89] ... But what others could do, I could not. I'd give way in one month if I overslept, indulged in too much food, or was not regular in studies, or gave in to general lukewarmness in my love for others and slackness in my actions, or to a softness directly opposing the character of a good soldier of Jesus Christ ... I must note, therefore, that the question does not relate to levels of holiness but to holiness itself ... The point is whether or not I will work out my salvation, whether I will serve Christ or Satan ...

14. But, you say that Epworth[90] is a larger sphere of activity than here; there I would have the care of two thousand souls. Two thousand

---

[87] As an Oxford graduate, Wesley could stay in residence and receive a regular stipend as long as he remained unmarried.
[88] Probably in the university dining halls.
[89] E.g., temptations to self-indulgence.
[90] His father's parish, which Samuel Wesley Sr., hoped his son would take over.

souls! I don't see how it's possible for someone like me to take care of 100! The weight on me now is almost more than I can bear; should I increase it tenfold? … Would this be the way to help either myself or others up to heaven? No: the mountains I reared would only crush my soul and make me completely useless to others …

16. If you say, "The love of the people of Epworth towards me may balance these advantages"; I ask, how long will it last? Only till I come to tell them plainly that their deeds are evil, and particularly to apply that general statement, saying to each, "You are the man!"[91] Sir, don't I know what love they had to you at one time and how many of them treated you later? Why, just as everyone will be treated whose business it is to bring light to those who love darkness …

20. My … position is this: Till he is despised [as a Christ-follower], no one is in a saved condition. This flows from the fact that all who are "not of the world" are despised by those who are, so until a man is despised he is "of the world," that is, not in a state of salvation …

22. These are some of my reasons for choosing to stay in the situation I'm now in. As to the flock committed to your care, which you have fed many years with the sincere milk of the Word, I trust in God that your labor will not be in vain. Some of them you have seen gathered into the granary.[92] And for yourself, I have no doubt that when "your warfare is ended," when you are "made perfect through sufferings," you will follow the children God has given you, full of years and victories. And he who cared for those poor sheep before you were born will not forget them when you are dead.

Thur. 29.—I left London and in the evening explained scriptures to a small group at Basingstoke. Saturday the 31st I reached Bristol in the evening and met Mr. Whitefield[93] there. It was hard for me at first to accept this strange way of preaching outdoors, which he did on Sunday. All my life till very recently, I've been such a stickler for "decency and order" that I would almost have thought even the saving of souls to be a sin if not done in a church.

---

[91] 2 Samuel 12:7—what the prophet Nathan said to David about taking Bathsheba and murdering her husband Uriah.
[92] I.e., they are with God.
[93] George Whitefield, a Methodist predestinarian, opened John W. to "field-preaching," which consumed most of John's ministry.

Sun. APRIL 1.—In the evening (Mr. Whitefield having left) I began explaining our Lord's Sermon on the Mount (itself a remarkable precedent for field-preaching, though there were synagogues[94] even then) to a little fellowship that used to meet once or twice a week in Nicholas Street.

Mon. 2.—At 4 p.m., I humbled myself, surrendering all my dignity,[95] and declared in the "highways" the good news of salvation, speaking from the top of a little hill on a parcel of land adjacent to the city to about 3000 people. My text (does not every true minister of Christ fulfill this?) was: "The Spirit of the Lord is on me, because he has anointed me to preach good news to the poor. He has sent me to proclaim freedom for the prisoners and recovery of sight for the blind, to release the oppressed, to proclaim the year of the Lord's favor" [Luke 4:18–19] ...

Wed. 4.— ... In the evening three women agreed to meet together weekly, with the same purpose as those at London: to confess their faults to one another and pray one for one another, that they might be healed [James 5:16]. At eight, four young men agreed to meet for the same purpose. How dare anyone deny this to be—at least in substance—a means of grace, ordained by God, unless he is going to affirm with Luther, in the fury of his "faith-only" doctrine, that James is "an epistle of straw"? ...

Sun. 8.—At 7 a.m. I preached to about 1000 people at Bristol, and afterwards to about 1500, on the top of Hannam Mount in Kingswood. I called to them in the words of the prophet who proclaimed the good news: "Ho, everyone who thirsts, come to the waters; and you that have no money, come, buy and eat! Come, buy wine and milk without money and without price" [Isa. 55:1]. About 5000 were present in the afternoon at Rosegreen (on the other side of Kingswood). I stood among them and cried, in the name of the Lord, "If anyone thirsts, let him come to me and drink. Whoever believes in me, as the Scripture has said, 'Out of his heart will flow rivers of living water'" [John 7:38] ...

---

[94] Wesley: "churches"; i.e., buildings for worship. The Gospels often mention synagogues. Actually, both the words for "church" and "synagogue" mean "assembly" in Greek, as in James 2:2, when "synagogue" refers to a church.

[95] A reference to 2 Samuel 6:22, when David danced before the ark.

Sat. 14.—I preached at the poor-house, 300 or 400 inside and more than twice that many outside, to whom I explained those comforting words, "When they could not pay, he cancelled the debt of both" [Luke 7:42] ...

Wed. 18.—In the evening, L.S. (formerly a Quaker, but baptized the day before), R.M., and a few others, were received into the fellowship, but R.M. could hardly speak or look up ... We poured out our grief before God and told him of her trouble. He soon showed that he's a God who hears prayer: She felt in herself that being justified freely, she had peace with God through Jesus Christ. She rejoiced "in hope of the glory of God" [Rom. 5:2], and "the love of God was poured into her heart" [Rom. 5:5] ...

Thurs. 25.—While I was preaching at Newgate Prison on these words, "Whoever believes has everlasting life" [John 5:24], I was led, without any forethought, to proclaim strongly and explicitly that God wills all people to be saved this way and to pray that, if this were not the truth of God, he would not allow the blind to stray from the path, but if it were, he would bear witness to his Word." Immediately one, two, three, then more sank to the ground; they dropped on all sides as if hit by lightning. A woman cried aloud. We sought God on her behalf, and he turned her heaviness into joy. Another woman was in the same agony, so we called on God for her too, and he spoke peace to her soul ...

Fri. 26.—All Newgate Prison rang with the cries of those whom the word of God cut to the heart; two of whom were filled with joy in a moment, to the astonishment of those who saw them.

Sun. 28.—I declared [at Newgate Prison] the free grace of God to about 4000 people from these words: "He who did not spare his own Son but gave him up for us all, how will he not also with him graciously give us all things?" [Rom. 8:32]. In that very hour, one who had remained in sin a long time, despairing of finding mercy, received a full, clear sense of his pardoning love and power to sin no more. I then went to Clifton ... From Clifton we went to Rosegreen, where we estimated there were nearly 7000, and from there to the Gloucester Lane fellowship, after which we held our first love-feast in Baldwin Street. Oh, how has God renewed my strength, who 10 years ago used to get so faint and weary from preaching just twice in one day!

Mon. 29.—We understood that many had been offended by those who cried out under the power of God. Among these was a physician who was afraid there might be fraud or deceit taking place. But today while I was preaching in Newgate, a woman he'd known many years was the first to break out into loud cries and tears. The doctor could hardly believe his eyes and ears. He stood right next to her and observed every symptom, till great drops of sweat ran down her face and all her bones shook. And now he didn't know what to think, being clearly convinced it was neither deception nor any natural cause. When both her soul and body were healed in a moment, he acknowledged the finger of God.

Tues. MAY 1.—Many were offended again, and even more than before, because at Baldwin Street my voice could hardly be heard in the midst of the groanings of some and the cries of others, calling aloud "to him who is mighty to save" [Isa. 63:1]. I asked all who were sincere to join me in earnestly requesting the Prince exalted for us, that he would "proclaim deliverance to the captives" [Luke 4:18] …

A Quaker standing by was greatly displeased at the way these people were "pretending," and was biting his lips and frowning, when he himself dropped down as if hit by lightning. It was painful to see the agony he was in. We begged God not to charge him with folly, and he soon lifted up his heart and cried aloud, "Now 1 know you are a prophet of the Lord!"

Wed. 2.—At Newgate, another mourner was comforted. I was asked to step over to a nearby house to look at a letter written against me as "a deceiver of the people," by teaching that God "wills all men to be saved." One who long had asserted the contrary was there, when a young woman came in (who could already say, "I know that my Redeemer lives") all in tears and in deep anguish of spirit. She said she had been reasoning with herself how these things could be, till she was perplexed more and more, and she now found the Spirit of God had departed from her. We began to pray, and she cried out, "He's come to me; he's here! I rejoice in God my Savior again!" Just as we rose from giving thanks, another woman staggered four or five steps and then dropped down. We prayed with her, then left her strongly convicted of sin and earnestly groaning for deliverance ...

Wed. 9.—We took ownership of a parcel of land near St. James's churchyard, in the Horse Fair area, where our plan was to build a preaching-room[96] large enough to contain both fellowship groups of Nicholas and Baldwin Street and any of their acquaintances who might want to attend with them whenever scripture was explained. On Saturday the 12th the first stone was laid to the sound of praise and thanksgiving.

At first I had no intention of being personally involved, either in the cost of this work or in supervising it, having appointed 11 trustees whom I thought would naturally carry these burdens. But I quickly learned my mistake; first, with regard to the expense, for the whole enterprise would have stood still if I hadn't immediately taken it on myself to pay all the workmen. The result was that, before I realized it, I had contracted a debt of more than 150 pounds.[97] And I had to do this any way I could, the financial pledges of both fellowships not amounting to one quarter of the sum. As to the supervision of the work, I soon received letters from my friends in London, Mr. Whitefield in particular, backed with a message by one who had just come from there, stating that neither he nor they would have anything to do with the building, nor would they contribute anything towards it, unless I would instantly discharge all the trustees and do everything in my own name. They gave many reasons for this, but just one was enough: that such trustees would always have the power to control me, and if I didn't preach the way they liked, they could evict me from the building I had erected. And so I yielded to their advice and, calling all the trustees together, with no one opposing, cancelled the papers drawn up earlier and

---

[96] Wesley's preaching-rooms, often just called "rooms," could be nice buildings, convenient for preaching, but were deliberately not called "churches," so as not to compete with the Church of England. It was only in his last years that the sacraments were administered in them and they came to be called churches. In each "room" he reserved an upstairs apartment where he and his brother Charles could stay when in the area preaching.

[97] About $35,000 in 2020 USD. Wesley's income was mainly from his publications, which only at the end of his life proved considerable. Throughout his career his lived on 30 pounds a year, about $7000 in 2020 USD.

personally took over the management. It is true that I had no money, nor any clear way or likely means of getting it; but I knew that "the earth is the Lord's and the fullness thereof" [Psalm 24:1], and set out in his name, doubting nothing ...

Sun. 13.— ... Now my usual public activity was this: Every morning I read prayers and preached at Newgate Prison. Every evening I explained a passage of Scripture at one or more of the fellowships. On Monday afternoon I preached in the open air near Bristol; on Tuesday, at Bath and Two-Mile Hill alternately; on Wednesday at Baptist Mills; every other Thursday, near Pensford; every other Friday, in another part of Kingswood; on Saturday afternoon and Sunday morning, in the Bowling Green (near downtown in the city); on Sunday at 11 a.m., near Hannam Mount; at 2 p.m., at Clifton; and at 5 p.m., on Rosegreen. And so far, my strength is sufficient for the day ...

Wed. 16.—While I was proclaiming at Baptist Mills, "He was wounded for our transgressions" [Isa. 53:5], a middle-aged man began violently beating his chest and crying to him "by whose stripes we are healed." During our prayer, God put a new song in his mouth. Some mocked him, while others acknowledged the hand of God—in particular, a woman of Baptist Mills, who was now convicted of her own need of an advocate with God, went home full of anguish, but in a few hours she was filled with joy, knowing he had "blotted out all her transgressions." ...

Sun. 20.—... Seeing many rich people at Clifton Church, my heart ached for them, and I earnestly wished that even some of them might "enter the kingdom of heaven." But full as my heart was, I didn't know where to begin in warning them to flee from the wrath to come, till my New Testament opened on these words: "I came not to call the righteous, but sinners to repentance" [Luke 5:32]. As I appealed to them, my soul was enlarged so that I felt I could have cried out, like poor vain Archimedes,[98] "Give me a place to stand, and I will shake the earth!"—although in a different sense than his. God sent forth lightning along with rain, but this didn't hinder about

---

[98] The Greek philosopher Archimedes theorized that given a fulcrum and a long-enough lever, he could move the world.

1500 from staying at Rosegreen. Our scripture was, "It is the glorious God that makes the thunder. The voice of the Lord is mighty in its work; the voice of the Lord is a glorious voice" [Isa. 30:30]. In the evening, he spoke to three whose souls were all storm and tempest, and immediately there was a great calm.

During this entire time, I was almost constantly asked, either by those who purposely came to Bristol to find out about this strange work, or by those corresponding by mail, how such things could be? I was constantly being warned (usually based on gross misrepresentations) not to pay attention to visions or dreams, or to imagine that people had remission of sins because of their cries or tears or merely outward professions. This is the substance of what I wrote to one who had written me many times on this subject:

> The difference between us revolves mainly, if not completely, around matters of fact. You deny that God works these effects now, at least not this way. I affirm both, because I have heard these things with my own ears, and have seen them with my eyes. I have seen (as far as something of this kind can be seen) many persons changed in a moment from the spirit of fear, horror, and despair to the spirit of love, joy, and peace, and from sinful desire, till then reigning over them, to a pure desire to do the will of God. These are matters of fact, which I have seen and heard, and almost daily still do. What I can say regarding visions or dreams is this: I know several people in whom this great change was accomplished through a dream or during a strong visualization of Christ either on the cross or in glory. This is the fact; people can judge it as they please. And that such a change was accomplished appears, not just from their shedding tears or falling into fits or crying out (these are not the fruits, as you seem to suppose, by which I judge), but from the whole import of their life—till then, wicked in many ways, but from that time on, holy, just, and good.
>
> I'll show you one who was a lion till then and is now a lamb; one who was a drunkard and is now the model of sobriety; the man who resorted to prostitutes who now hates "even the garment stained by the flesh" [Jude 1:23]. These are living examples for what I assert, namely, that God does now, as long ago, gives remission of sins and the gift of the Holy Spirit, even to us and to our children; yes, and that always suddenly, as far as I have known, and often in dreams or in the

visions of God. If this is not so, I stand a false witness before God. For these things I do, and by his grace will, testify ...

Mon. 21. –Today our Lord answered for himself; for while I was driving home these words, "Be still, and know that I am God" [Psalm 46:10], he began to flex his muscles, not in a closed room, or in private, but in the open air and before more than 2000 witnesses. One, and another and another were struck to the ground, trembling greatly at the presence of his power. Others cried with a loud and bitter cry, "What must we do to be saved?" And in less than an hour seven persons, wholly unknown to me till then, were rejoicing and singing, and with all their might giving thanks to the God of their salvation ...

Sat. 26.—One came to us in deep despair, but after we spent an hour in prayer went away in peace. The next day, having observed in many a zeal not suiting the sweetness and gentleness of love, I preached at Rosegreen (to the largest gathering I ever had there, I believe over 10,000 people) on these words:

"You don't know what kind of spirit you have, for the Son of Man didn't come to destroy men's lives, but to save them" [Luke 9:56]. At the evening fellowship, eleven were deeply convicted of sin and soon were comforted ...

Tues. 29.—Without realizing it, I had a conversation with a famous nonbeliever, one who strengthened the non-religious in this area. He seemed a little surprised and said that he would pray to God to show him the true way of worshiping him ...

Mon. JUNE 4.—Many came to me and pleaded with me not to preach outdoors in the afternoon, because several persons had conspired to do terrible things. This report being spread abroad brought many of the so-called "better" people,[99] and added, I believe, 1000 more to the regular gathering. The scripture to which God providentially directed me, not by my own choice, was, "Fear not, for I am with you; be not dismayed, for I am your God; I will strengthen you, I will help you, I will uphold you with my righteous right hand" [Isa. 41:10].

---

[99] I.e., the social elite.

Tues. 5.—The people of Bath were excited about what a prominent man was supposedly going to do to me there, and they begged me not to preach, because no one knew what might happen. This only served to gain me a much larger audience, among whom were many of the rich and great in society. I told them plainly, "The Scripture had concluded them all under sin" [Gal. 3:22]—high and low, rich and poor, all together. Many of them seemed to be a little shocked and were becoming serious when their "champion" appeared and, walking up to me, asked me by what authority I did these things? I replied, "By the authority of Jesus Christ, transmitted to me by the [bishop who is] now the archbishop of Canterbury, when he laid his hands upon me and said, 'Take authority to preach the gospel.'" ... Here he paused a while, and having regained his composure, said, "I'd like to know why these people come here?" Hearing this, a woman said, "Sir, leave him to me. Let an old woman answer him." "You, Mr. Nash, take care of your body. We take care of our souls, and we come here for the food of our souls." He didn't answer a word, but simply walked away ...

Mon. 11.—I received a letter from London (after several others) urging me to get there as soon as possible: "Our brethren in Fetter Lane are in great confusion due to the lack of your presence and advice." I therefore preached in the afternoon on these words, "Therefore I testify to you this day that I am innocent of the blood of you all, for I did not shrink from declaring to you the whole counsel of God" [Acts 20:27]. After the sermon, I commended them to the grace of God in whom they had believed. Surely God still has a work to do in this place. I haven't found such love in England, nor so childlike, open, and teachable a spirit as he's given to this people.

Yet during this whole time I had many thoughts about the unusual way I ministered among them. But after frequently laying it before the Lord and calmly weighing whatever objections I heard against it, I could only adhere to what I had some time previously written to a friend who had freely expressed his feelings about it. Here I attach part of that letter to place the matter in a clear light.

DEAR SIR,

The best reply I can make for the kind freedom you use is to return the same to you. Oh, may the God whom we serve sanctify it to us both and teach us the whole truth as it is in Jesus!

You say that you cannot reconcile some parts of my behavior with the character you have known me to have through the years. Nor will you ever; therefore I have renounced that character on every possible occasion. I told everyone on our ship, everyone at Savannah, everyone at Frederica, and that over and over in explicit terms, "I'm not a Christian; I'm only pursuing and hoping I may attain it." …

Now please let me tell my principles in this matter: **I see the whole world as my parish** [my emphasis], meaning that in whatever part of it I am in, I consider it fitting, right, and my solemn obligation to proclaim to all who will hear, the glad tidings of salvation. This is the work which I know God has called me to, and I am sure that his blessing attends it. So I am greatly encouraged to be faithful in fulfilling the work he has given me to do. I am his servant, and as such, I act according to the plain direction of his word, "As I have opportunity, I do good to everyone" [Gal. 6:10]. And his providence clearly agrees with his Word; it has cut me loose from everything else, so I can attend do this one thing singlemindedly "and go about doing good" [cf. Acts 10:38] …

I am, &c. [100]

Wed. 13.—In the morning I reached London, and after taking Holy Communion at Islington, I once again had an opportunity to visit my mother, whom I had not seen since my return from Germany …

Thur. 14.—I went with Mr. Whitefield to Blackheath, where I believe there were, 12- or 14,000 people. I was a little surprised when he asked me to preach in his place. I did this, though inwardly I recoiled, on my favorite subject, "Jesus Christ, whom God made our wisdom and our righteousness and sanctification and redemption" [1 Cor. 1:30].

I felt great compassion for the rich people there, to whom I made a special appeal. Some of them seemed to listen, while others drove their carriages away from such an uncultured preacher …

---

[100] "I am your obedient servant, etc." —the usual flourish concluding a letter.

Sat. 16.—We met at Fetter Lane to humble ourselves before God and confess that he was just to withdraw his Spirit from us, since we were unfaithful in many ways. We acknowledged that we had grieved him by our divisions: "Each one of you says, 'I follow Paul,' or 'I follow Apollos'" [1 Cor. 1:12]; by our leaning again on our own works and trusting in them, instead of on Christ; by stopping with the little beginnings of sanctification which he has been pleased to work in our souls; and above all by blaspheming his work among us, ascribing it either to nature, to the force of imagination and natural disposition, or even to the delusion of the devil. That same hour, we found God to be with us again as in the beginning. Some lay prostrate on the ground; others burst out, as in one accord, into loud praise and thanksgiving, and many openly testified that there had been no day such as this since this past January the 1st.

Sun. 17.—I preached at seven in Upper Moorfields, I believe to 6- or 7000 people on, "Ho, everyone who thirsts, come to the waters" [John 7:37]. In the afternoon I saw poor R.T., who had left our fellowship and the Church.[101] We didn't argue but prayed, and in a little while the scales fell off of his eyes. He gladly returned to the Church and that evening was readmitted into our fellowship ...

Fri. 22.— ... In the afternoon I preached at the Fish Ponds, but with no life or spirit in me, dreading that God might set me aside and send other workers into his harvest. This was the thought filling me as I came to the fellowship, and I began in much weakness to explain, "Beloved, do not believe every spirit, but test the spirits to see whether they are from God" [1 John 4:1]. I told them that they must not judge the spirit by which anyone spoke, either by how they looked or by what others said, or even by their own inner feelings—nor by any dreams, visions, or revelations that they claim to have received, no more than by their tears, or any involuntary effects on their bodies. I warned them that all these were, in themselves, of a doubtful, disputable nature; they might be from God or they might not, and were therefore not simply to be relied on, anymore than simply to be condemned, but to be tried by a further rule: to be

---

[101]I.e., the Church of England.

brought to the only certain test: the law and the testimony"[102] [Isaiah 8:20] ...

Fri. JULY 6.— ... I spent the afternoon with Mr. Whitefield, who had just arrived from London, and went with him to Baptist Mills, where he preached on the "Holy Spirit, which all who believe are to receive," adding a severe but just rebuke to those who preach as if there were no Holy Spirit.

Sat. 7.—I had an opportunity to talk with [Mr. Whitefield] of those outward signs which had so often accompanied the inward work of God. I found his objections were chiefly grounded on gross misrepresentations of fact; but the next day he had an opportunity to become better informed. For, no sooner had he begun applying his sermon, inviting all sinners to believe in Christ, than four persons sank down close to him, almost at the same time. One of them lay unconscious and immobile; a second trembled violently; the third person's body convulsed, but he made no noise except for groaning; the fourth, shaking violently, called on God with strong cries and tears. From now on, I trust we will all let God carry on his own work however it pleases him ...

Mon. 30.—Two persons were in great pain, both their souls and bodies being almost torn in two. We cried to God but received no answer; he didn't yet give any degree of deliverance.

One of these had been very zealous against those who cried out and made a noise, being sure that they could keep from doing it if they wanted to. She still held that opinion until the moment she was pierced as if by a sword and fell trembling to the ground. She then cried aloud, though not distinctly, because she swallowed her words. She continued in such pain for 12 or 14 hours, and then her soul was set free. But her master (for until then she was a servant at a gentleman's house in town) wouldn't let her return to him, saying he wouldn't have anyone in his house who had received the Holy Spirit.

Tues. 31.—... About this time, someone put *A Caution against Religious Delusion* into my hands. I thought it my duty to write to its author, which I therefore did in these words:

---

[102] I.e., the Scriptures.

Reverend Sir, ...

3. ... Our coming to Christ, as well as theirs, requires a great and powerful change. It requires not just an outward change, from stealing, lying, and all evil conduct, but a thorough change of heart, an inward renewal in the spirit of our mind. Accordingly, "the old man" implies infinitely more than outward evil conduct; it is "an evil heart of unbelief," corrupted by pride and a thousand deceitful lusts. Consequently, the "new man" must imply infinitely more than outward good conduct; it requires a good heart, "which after God is created in righteousness and true holiness" [Eph. 4:24], a heart full of the faith that works by love and produces all holiness of conduct.

4. What I call the "new birth" is the change from the first to the latter of these conditions. But you say I am not content with this plain and easy concept of it, but fill myself and others with fantastic notions about it. Oh, sir, can you prove this? And if you cannot prove it, what can you do to make it right, either with God or with me, or to the world, for publicly asserting what is grossly false? ...

6. Now it is certain a man may lack ["a true trust and confidence of the mercy of God through our Lord Jesus Christ."], although he can truly say, "I am sexually pure, I am sober, I treat others justly, I help my neighbor, and I observe God's ordinances."[103] And however such a man may have behaved in these respects, he is not to think well of his own condition till he experiences something within himself that he has not yet experienced, but which he may be sure he will, if God's promises are true: that something is a living faith, a sure trust and confidence in God, that by the merits of Christ his sins are forgiven and he is reconciled to the favor of God.[104] And from this will spring many other things, which till then he has not experienced, such as the love of God shed abroad in his heart, the peace of God that passes all understanding, and joy in the Holy Spirit—joy that can be felt but that is "unspeakable and full glory" [1 Peter 1:8].

7. These are some of those inward fruits of the Spirit which must be felt, wherever they are; and without these I cannot find in sacred Scripture that any man is "born of the Spirit." I beg you, sir, by the mercies of God, that if so far you know nothing of such inward feelings, if you do not "feel in yourself these mighty workings of the Spirit of Christ," at least you would not contradict and revile. When the Holy Spirit has truly kindled your love towards God, you will

---

[103] I.e., church attendance, communion.

[104] Much of Wesley's language here is from the Articles of the Church of England.

know these to be very evident results. You hear the wind and feel it striking your body. The same way, you will know you are under the guidance of God's Spirit, by feeling it in your soul, by the actual peace and joy and love you feel within, as well as by its outward and more distant effects.

I am, &c. ...

Fri. AUGUST 10.—I had the satisfaction of speaking with a Quaker and then with an Anabaptist[105] who, I trust, have had a good measure of the love of God shed abroad in their hearts. Oh, may those of every persuasion who have this spirit increase a thousand-fold, however many they may be! ...

Fri. 17.—Many of our fellowship met at our appointed time, 1 p.m., and agreed that all the members of our fellowship should obey the Church [of England], to which we belong, by observing all Fridays in the year as days of fasting or abstinence. We also agreed that as many as able should then meet to spend an hour together in prayer ...

Mon. SEPTEMBER 3.—I talked at length with my mother, who told me that until recently she'd hardly ever heard of immediate forgiveness of sins or of God's Spirit bearing witness with our spirit even being mentioned. Much less did she imagine that this was the common privilege of all true believers. "Therefore," she said, "I never dared ask it for myself. But two or three weeks ago, while my son Hall was uttering those words, when offering the communion cup to me, 'The blood of our Lord Jesus Christ, given for you,' the words struck through my heart, and I knew that God, for Christ's sake, had forgiven me all my sins." ...

Thur. 6.—A woman who began to feel herself a sinner sent for me, but when a refined lady unexpectedly came in, I hardly had a chance to speak. The fourth person in the group was a poor, uneducated girl who began telling us what God had done for her soul. The rest looked at each other in amazement but didn't say a word. I then exhorted them not to stop crying out to God till they could say, as she did, "My beloved is mine, and I am his. I'm as sure

---

[105] Anabaptists were radical 16th century reformed Christians from whom the Amish and Mennonite are descended.

of it as that I'm alive, for his Spirit bears witness with my spirit that I'm a child of God." ...

Thur. 13.—A serious clergyman wanted to know on what points we differed from the Church of England. I answered, "To the best of my knowledge, on none; the doctrines we preach are the doctrines of the Church of England—indeed, the fundamental doctrines of the Church, clearly laid down in her prayers, articles, and homilies."

He asked, then, in what points then did I differ from the other clergy of the Church of England? I answered, "In no points from those clergy who adhere to the doctrines of the Church; but I do differ from the clergy who dissent from the Church (without admitting it) on these points:

> First, they speak of justification either as the same thing as sanctification or as something that follows it. I believe justification to be wholly distinct from sanctification, and that it necessarily precedes it.
>
> Second, they speak of our own holiness or good works as the cause of our justification or for the sake and on account of which we are justified before God. I believe that neither our own holiness nor good works are any part of the cause of our justification, but that the death and righteousness of Christ are the sole, complete cause of it, or for the sake and on account of which we are justified before God.
>
> Third, they speak of good works as a condition of justification, necessarily preceding it. I believe there is no good work prior to justification; therefore these are not a condition of it; rather we are justified by faith alone, since until that time we are ungodly and therefore unable to do any good work.[106] It is faith without works; faith, though it produces all, includes no good work.
>
> Fourth, they speak of sanctification or holiness as if it were an external thing, as if it consisted chiefly, if not wholly, in these two points: 1. in doing no harm; 2. in doing good (so-called), i.e., using the means of grace and helping our neighbor. I believe that it is an inner thing, namely, the life of God in the soul of man and man's partaking of the divine nature; the mind that was in Christ; or, the renewal of our heart after the image of him who created us.

---

[106] Wesley is speaking here of "good works" prior to faith as not proceeding from the changed heart—the true good works that faith will effect; he follows Luther in his "Preface to the Book of Romans" here.

Finally, they speak of the new birth as an external thing, as if it were no more than baptism, or at most a change from outer wickedness to outer goodness, from an immoral to what is called a virtuous life. I believe it to be an inward thing: a change from inner wickedness to inner goodness, an entire change of our inmost nature from the image of the devil (in which we are born)[107] to the image of God. It is a change from the love of the creature to the love of the Creator, from earthly appetites to heavenly and holy emotions—simply put, a change from the nature of the spirits of darkness to those of the angels of God in heaven.

There is, therefore, a wide, intrinsic, fundamental, irreconcilable difference between us, so that if they speak the truth as it is in Jesus, I am exposed as a false witness before God. But if I teach the way of God in truth, they are blind leaders of the blind.

Sun. 16.—I preached at Moorfields to about 10,000, and at Kennington Common, I believe, to almost 20,000, on those words of the calmer Jews to Paul, "We would like to hear what your views are, for with regard to this sect we know that everywhere it is spoken against" [Acts 28:22]. At both places I described the real difference between what is generally called Christianity and the true old Christianity,[108] which under the new name of Methodism is also now everywhere maligned ...

Fri. 28.—[*At Turner's Hall*] I received fresh proof that "whatever you ask in prayer, you will receive, if you have faith" [Matt. 21:22]. A middle-aged woman asked me to offer thanks to God for her. As many witnesses then present testified, a day or two before, she had really been out of her mind and was tied down to her bed. But after others prayed for her, she had instant relief and was restored to a sound mind.

Mon. OCTOBER 1.—I rode to Oxford, and found a few [members of our fellowship] who had not yet neglected meeting together; to whom I explained that "holiness without which no one will see the Lord" [Heb. 12:14] ...

---

[107] Wesley believed in Augustine's doctrine of original sin; even an unbaptized infant is damned or in a state less than blessed.

[108] Wesley felt he was leading a movement to restore primitive Christianity.

Wed. 3.—I had some free time to take a good look at the shattered condition of things here. The poor prisoners, both in the castle and the city prisons, now had no one to care for their souls—none to instruct, advise, comfort, and build them up in the knowledge and love of the Lord Jesus. Now no one visited the workhouses,[109] where we used to find people arousing the utmost compassion. Our little school, where about 20 poor children at a time had been taught for many years, was on the point of breaking up, since no one now supported or visited it. And most of those in the town who were knitted together in love and who strengthened each other's hands in God, were torn apart and scattered abroad. "It's time for you, Lord, to put forth your hand!"

At 11 a.m., a little group of us met to earnestly seek God for the remnant that was left. He immediately gave us a good sign: A woman who had long been bitter, full of wrath, strife and envy, especially against one whom she had once tenderly loved, rose up and showed the change God had worked in her soul by hugging and kissing her [Christian] sister with many tears. We found the same spirit reviving in others as well, so that we left them hoping that the seed that had been sown even here "will take root downward and bear fruit upward." [2 Kings 9:30] ...

Sun. 7.—A few, I trust, out of 2- or 3000, were awakened when I explained these words, "You did not receive the spirit of slavery to fall back into fear, but you have received the Spirit of adoption as sons by whom we cry, 'Abba! Father!'" [Rom. 8:15] ...

Between 5 and 6 a.m. I called on all who were present (about 3000) at Stanley, on a grassy spot near the town, to accept Christ as their only "wisdom, righteousness, sanctification, and redemption" [1 Cor. 1:30]. I was strengthened to preach as I'd never been before, and continued almost two hours.[110] The darkness of the night and a little lightning, instead of decreasing the number, increased the seriousness of the audience. I finished the day by explaining part of our Lord's Sermon on the Mount to a small, serious company at Ebly ...

---

[109] I.e., providing lodging for the poor and work for the able-bodied.
[110] Wesley usually kept his sermons to about an hour.

Thur. 11.—It was a comfort to us when a man who was a notorious drunkard and who constantly took the Lord's name in vain came in. Now he's been washed and old things have passed away; such is our God's power. In the evening our Lord rose up on many who were under conviction "with healing in his wings" [Mal. 4:2], and others, who till then were indifferent and unconcerned, felt the two-edged sword that came out of his mouth [cf. Rev. 1:16].

One of these, in the agony of her soul, cried aloud to God for help, and this upset many others, who strongly rebuked her, telling her to keep quiet. She kept on in great torment all night, finding no rest either of soul or body. But while a few were praying for her in the morning, God delivered her out of her distress ...

Mon. 15.—*[In Abergavenny]* ... I felt in myself a strong inner resistance to preaching here. However, I went to Mr. W. (whose land Mr. Whitefield had preached on) to ask for its use. He said he would gladly do so if the minister wasn't willing to let me use the church. I immediately wrote a note to the minister, and after he refused, Mr. W. invited me to his house. About 1000 people stood patiently even though, being after sunset, it was bitter cold, while, from Acts 28:22, I simply described the plain, old religion of the Church of England, which people now almost everywhere speak against, calling it by the new name of Methodism. An hour later, I explained it a little more fully in a nearby house, showing how "God exalted [Jesus] at his right hand as Leader and Savior, to give repentance ... and forgiveness of sins" [Acts 5:31] ...

Thur. 18.—I tried to cut them off from all false supports and vain dependencies by explaining and applying that fundamental truth: "And to the one who does not work but trusts him who justifies the ungodly, his faith is counted as righteousness" [Rom. 4:5] ...

Sat. 20.—I returned to Bristol. I haven't seen any other part of England as pleasant for 60 or 70 miles at a stretch as the parts of Wales I've been in. And truly most of the inhabitants are ripe for the gospel. I mean (as strange as this may sound) that they earnestly want it to be taught to them, while being as totally ignorant of it as any Creek or Cherokee Indians. This is not to say they don't know the name of Christ. Many of them can say both the Lord's Prayer and the creed, and some even the whole catechism. But beyond what they have memorized, nine out of ten of them whom I talked to know nothing of gospel salvation or of the faith by which alone we can be saved, than Chicali or Tomo Chachi.[111] Now, who would rather let these poor creatures perish for lack of knowledge than that they should be saved, even by the exhortations of Howell Harris, or an itinerant preacher? ...

Tues. 23.—In riding to Bradford, I read over Mr. Law's book on the new birth. It is philosophical, speculative, dangerous, Boehmenistic,[112] void, and vain! ...

When I returned in the evening, I was implored to go back to see a young woman in Kingswood (and here I just tell the facts, letting the reader judge). So I went. She was 19 or 20 years old, but apparently couldn't read or write. I found her in bed, with two or three people holding her down. It was a terrible sight: Indescribable anguish, horror, and despair appeared on her pale face. The thousand distortions of her whole body showed how the dogs of hell were gnawing at her heart ... She then began praying to the devil. We began singing,

> Arm of the Lord, awake, awake!

She immediately sank down as into sleep; but, as soon as we stopped singing, she broke out again with unspeaking intensity, "Stony hearts, break! I am a warning to you. Break, break, poor stony hearts! Won't you break? What more can be done for stony hearts? I am damned so you can be saved. Now break, now break, poor stony hearts! You don't have to be damned, but I do!" She then fastened her gaze on the corner of the ceiling and said, "There he is, yes, there he is; come, good devil, come take me away. You said you would dash my brains out; come do it quickly. I'm yours; I'll be yours. Come right now and take me away." We interrupted her by calling again upon God, at which she sank down as before. Then another young woman began to roar as loudly as this one had done. At this point my brother came in, it being about 9 p.m. We kept

---

[111] Native Americans with whom Wesley had conversed in Georgia; see above.
[112] I.e., following the teaching of Jakob Boehme (1575—1624), a German mystic and theologian.

praying till past 11, when God instantly spoke peace to their souls—first to the tormented young woman, and then to the other one, and they both joined in singing praise to him who had subdued the enemy and the avenger ...

Sat. 28.—A message came for me to go to Kingswood again, to one of those who had been very sick before. A heavy rain began just as I set out, so I was completely soaked in a few minutes. Just then the woman, who was three miles away, cried out, "There comes Wesley, galloping as fast as he can!" When I got there, I was numb from cold, more fit for sleep than for prayer. She burst out in a horrid laughter and said, "No power, no power; no faith, no faith. She is mine; her soul is mine. I have her and won't let her go."

We begged God to increase our faith. Meanwhile her spasms grew worse and worse, so that you would have guessed, by the violence of the convulsions, that her body would be torn to pieces ... We threw ourselves into prayer again and didn't stop until, about 6 p.m., she began singing with a clear voice, while looking calm and cheerful, "Praise God from whom all blessings flow!" ...

Wed. 31.—I drove home vigorously, to those who imagine they believe but don't, "As the body apart from the spirit is dead, so also faith apart from works is dead" [James 2:26]. The power of God was present in an unusual way at the meeting of the circles in the evening. Six or seven were deeply convinced of their unfaithfulness to God, and two were filled again with his love. But poor Mary W. remained like someone without hope; her soul refused comfort. She could neither pray nor bear to hear us praying. At last she cried out, "Give me the book and I'll sing." She began giving out line by line, but with an expression such as training could never reach:

> Why do these cares my soul divide,
> If thou indeed hast set me free?
> Why am I thus, if God hath died,
> If God hath died to purchase me?
> Around me clouds of darkness roll;
> In deepest night I still walk on:
> Heavily moves my damned soul ...

At this point, we were forced to interrupt her. We again resorted to prayer, and her heart was comforted, though she was not fully set free ...

1741

[The following section largely deals with Wesley's painful break with the Moravians, who had led him to realize that salvation is by faith alone. When he writes the opening letter, which serves as his preface, the Moravians have begun preaching quietism: One seeking salvation is to stop all outward "works": church attendance, taking communion, reading the Bible, good deeds, and even much prayer. The effective result is antinomianism, the position that Christians are free from all law, even the moral law and the commands of Christ. To Wesley, this strikes at the very heart of true Christianity. It becomes a problem in his movement for some years and ensnares a few of his best preachers. I will skip over much of this material, as it becomes repetitive. Still I'll let Wesley state his case on these practical and biblical issues. Strangely, the letter is dated from 1744, perhaps when final corrections were made.]

To The Moravian Church,[113]

More Especially That Part Of It Now Or Recently Residing In England

1. At last I am forced to write my current thoughts and feelings about you, using the truth as I see it. This is not just for my own sake that, if I judge wrongly, I may become better informed. It is also for the sake of all who either love or sincerely seek the Lord Jesus. Many of these have been totally at a loss what to think, all the more so because they couldn't help but notice, as I often have with a sad heart, that few have written about you (aside from those who approve of you excessively) who weren't clearly prejudiced against you ... My own understanding is that no one can judge you or help others to judge you rightly unless he can speak of you as the friend whom he loves as his own soul.

---

[113] Wesley's note: "So-called by themselves, though improperly." He did not consider them a true church.

2. But now I write not just for their sake but also for yours. Perhaps the Father of lights, the giver of every good gift, will use even me as his humble instrument to speak to your hearts. My constant petition and prayer to God is that you may clearly see what is that good and perfect will of the Lord, and fully discern how to separate the wheat from the chaff among you …

4. What unites my heart to you is the excellence, in many respects, of the doctrine you teach: your laying the true foundation that "God was in Christ, reconciling the world to himself" [2 Cor. 5:19]; your declaring the free grace of God to be the cause, and faith the condition, of justification; your bearing witness to the great fruits of faith: "righteousness, and peace, and joy in the Holy Ghost" [Rom. 14:17]; and the Spirit's sure mark: "No one born of God makes a practice of sinning" [1 John 3:9].

5. I extol the grace of God that is in many of you, enabling you to love him who first loved us, teaching you to be content whatever the situation you are in, causing you to trample underfoot the lust of the flesh, the lust of the eye, and the pride of life, and, above all, enabling you to love each another in a way unknown to the world.

6. I praise God that he has delivered you and still delivers you from those outward sins that are widespread on earth: No cursing, no vain or false swearing, no profaning God's name is heard among you. No robbing or stealing, no gluttony or drunkenness, no fornication or adultery, no bickering or open hostility (those scandals of the Christian name[114]) are found within your gates; no pastimes but such as become saints, which may be enjoyed in the name of the Lord Jesus. You give no weight to outward adornment, but rather seek the ornament of a serious, meek, and quiet spirit. You aren't lazy in business, but work to earn the bread you eat, and you manage the "means of unrighteous wealth"[115] wisely so you may have to give to others also, to feed the hungry and to clothe the naked.

7. I love you and regard you for your excellent discipline, hardly inferior to that of the apostolic age. Those holding offices are in proper subordination, each knowing and keeping in his place. You carefully divide the people you care for, so that all may receive their appropriate food. You make provision for all who serve the church to frequently and freely confer; therefore you have exact and up-to-date knowledge of every

---

[114] I.e., these are notorious in so-called Christian nations and among nominal Christians.

[115] Cf. Luke 16:9: "mammon of unrighteousness" (KJV).

member's condition, and you readily distribute either spiritual or material relief, as each one needs it.[116]

8. Now some of you may say, "If you grant all this, what more do you want?" The following extract [of my *Journal*] will answer you fully. In it I first relate in a straightforward way, among other things, many facts and conversations between us in the order in which they occurred, and then I'll sum up what I can't yet commend so that it may be tested by the Word of God.

9. I've tried to do this with a gentle hand, stating no more than I believe absolutely necessary, carefully avoiding all sharp and unkind expressions that I foresee would annoy or offend you beyond the actual thing implied, trying everywhere to speak consistently with what's settled in my heart, that you are (though I can't call you rabbi or infallible) still far, far better and wiser than I.

10. And if any of you will strike me in a friendly way and rebuke me, if you'll show me how I may be in error, either in the substance or style of the following account or in any part of it, I will, by the grace of God, confess it before angels and men in whatever way you shall require.

     Meanwhile do not cease to pray for
       Your weak
       but still affectionate brother,
       JOHN WESLEY.
        London, June 24, 1744.

On Thur., NOVEMBER 1, 1739, I left Bristol, and on Saturday reached London. The first person I met there was a woman whom I had left strong in faith and zealous for good works, but now she told me that Mr. Molther[117] had convinced her that she never had had any faith at all. His counsel was that until she received faith she should be still and stop doing all outward works. She had therefore done so and didn't doubt that soon she would receive the benefits.

In the evening Mr. Bray also highly recommended "being still before the Lord." He went on speaking at length of the danger that attended outward works and the foolishness of people who "keep running about to church and sacrament," as he said he'd done until recently.

---

[116] Wesley uses some of the same means in administering his movement.
[117] A Moravian minister.

Sun. 4.—Our fellowship met at 7 a.m. and stayed silent until 8. Then one spoke of looking to Jesus and encouraged us all "to lie still in his hand."

In the evening I met the women of our fellowship at Fetter Lane, where some of our brethren strongly implied that none of them had true faith and then asserted plainly: 1. that until they had true faith they ought to be still; that is, as they explained, to abstain from the so-called "means of grace," the Lord's Supper in particular; 2. that the ordinances are not means of grace, Christ being the only means.

Wed. 7.—Wanting very much to understand the basis for this, I had a long discussion with Mr. Spangenberg. I agreed with everything he said about the power of faith. I agreed that whoever by faith is born of God doesn't practice sin, but I could *not* agree that no one has any faith at all who is subject to any doubt or fear, or that until we have true faith, we ought to abstain from the Lord's Supper and the other ordinances of God.

At 8 p.m., our fellowship met at Fetter Lane. We sat an hour without anyone speaking. The rest of the time was spent in discussion after someone raised a question about the Lord's Supper, many insisting that people shouldn't receive it till they had the full assurance of faith.

I noticed more and more every day how Satan was taking advantage of us. Many who once knew in whom they had believed were thrown into fruitless speculation and filled with doubts and fears from which they couldn't escape. Many were led to deny the gift of God and to affirm they'd never had any faith at all, especially those who'd fallen back into sin and thus into darkness. Almost all these had stopped using the means of grace, saying that they must now cease from their own works; they must now trust in Christ alone; they were poor sinners and could do nothing except lie down at his feet.

Until Saturday the 10th, I don't believe I met one woman of the fellowship who wasn't about to throw away her confidence in God. Finally I did find one who, when many tried to persuade her that she had no faith, replied with a spirit they couldn't resist: "'I know that the life that I now live, I live by faith in the Son of God, who loved me, and gave himself for me' [cf. Gal. 2:20]; and he has never left me one moment since the hour he was made known to me in the breaking of bread."

What can we learn from the undeniable fact that she who lacked faith received it in the Lord's Supper? Just this: 1. that there are means of grace, i.e., outward ordinances that ordinarily convey the inward grace of God to people, communicating saving faith to those who until then don't have it; 2. that one of these means is the Lord's Supper; and 3. that one who doesn't have this faith ought to wait for it, using this as well as the other means that God has ordained.

Fri. 9.—I showed how we are to examine ourselves as to whether we are in the faith [cf. 2 Cor. 13:5], and after that I recommended to all, but especially to those who believed, *true stillness*—that is, waiting on God patiently, in lowliness, meekness, and complete submission, in all the ways of his holy law and the works he has commanded ...

Thur. 15.—My brother [Charles] and I set out for Tiverton. About 11 a.m. I preached at Burford. On Saturday evening I explained at Bristol the nature and extent of Christian perfection, and at 9 a.m. the next morning I preached at Bath on "I know that nothing good dwells in me" [Rom. 7:18] ...

Mon. 19.—[*In Bristol*] I pleaded with those who had believed "to beware of two opposite extremes: one, while they were in light and joy, thinking that the work was complete, when it had actually just begun; and the other, thinking when they felt oppressed that the work hadn't begun, after learning that it hadn't been completed." ...

Tues. 20.—We set out, and on the afternoon of Wednesday the 21st came to Tiverton. My poor sister was grieving almost as someone without hope. Yet we could only rejoice at hearing, from someone who had cared for my brother[118] throughout his weakness, that several days before he passed away God had given him a calm and full assurance of his claim on Christ. Oh, may everyone now opposing it be so convinced that this doctrine is of God! ...

---

[118] Samuel Wesley, Jr. (1690–1739), an ordained Anglican minister and school headmaster.

Serious Joy (John Wesley's *Journal*)

Tues. 27.—At his request, I wrote Mr. D. a short report on what had been done in Kingswood and of our ongoing work there. My account was as follows:

There are few who have lived a long time in the west of England who haven't heard of the coalminers of Kingswood. They've always had a reputation of having no fear either of God or man. They were so ignorant of the things of God that they seemed just one degree above the beasts that perish, and had no desire for instruction or the means to get it if they wanted it.

Last winter many people spoke mockingly of Mr. Whitefield: "If he wants to convert heathens, why doesn't he go to the Kingswood coalminers?" This past spring he did just that, and since thousands of them had never set foot in a place of public worship, he pursued them into their own wilderness, to seek and save the lost. When he was called away to another place, others went into the highways and hedges to compel them to come in. By the grace of God, their labor was not in vain. Now the whole scene has changed. Kingswood is no longer filled, like it was a year ago, with the sound of cursing and blasphemy. It's no longer filled with drunkenness and uncleanness and the idle pastimes that naturally lead to these things. It's no longer full of feuds and fighting, clamor and bitterness and wrath and envying; instead, there's peace and love. A great many of the people are mild, gentle, and easy to deal with. They don't cry out or strive, and their voice is rarely heard in the streets [cf. Matt. 12:19]—not even in their own neighborhoods, except when they're at their usual evening pastime, singing praise to God their Savior.

So that their children, too, might know the things that make for their peace, it was proposed some time ago to erect a building in Kingswood, and after many difficulties, foreseen and unforeseen, last June the foundation was laid. The site chosen was in the middle of the woods between London and Bath roads, not far from what's called Two-Mile Hill, almost exactly three miles from Bristol.

Here a large building was constructed for the school, having four small rooms at each end to house the schoolteachers—and perhaps, if it pleases God, some poor children as well. Two persons are prepared to teach as soon as the building is ready for them; the framing is nearly completed, and we hope that it will all be finished this coming spring or early next summer.

It's true that the teachers will receive no salary; still this undertaking is at great expense. But he who feeds the young ravens will take care of that; he has the hearts of all men in his hand. If he puts it in your heart or in the hearts of any of your friends to help in bringing this work of his to completion in this world, don't look for an earthly reward, but it will be remembered on that day when our Lord will say, "As you did it to one of the least of these my brothers, you did it to me" [Matt. 25:40].

Wed. 28.—We left Tiverton and the next day reached Bristol. On Friday, many of us prayed together for a woman who was tormented. She got wilder and wilder for about two hours, and then our Lord gave her rest.

That evening, five people were in the same kind of agony. I ordered them to be taken outside so their screams wouldn't drown out my voice or distract the assembly. But after the sermon I had them brought into the room again, where a few of us continued in prayer to God, determined not to leave until we had a peaceful answer from him; this lasted till 9 a.m. the next morning. Before then, three of them sang praise to God, and the others got some relief, though they were not completely set free ...

Thur. DECEMBER 13.— ... I ... must maintain (at least until I have a clearer light), that 1. The justification Paul speaks about to the Romans and which is in our Church Articles is not twofold; it is one and just one. It is the present remission of our sins, or our initial acceptance by God. 2. It is true that the merits of Christ are the sole basis for our justification. But it is not true that this is all that Paul and our Church mean by being justified by faith only; nor is it true that either Paul or the Church mean, by faith, the merits of Christ. 3. Rather, by saying we are justified by faith only, both Paul and the Church mean that the condition of our justification is faith alone and not good works, insofar as "all works done before justification have in them the nature of sin."[119] And lastly, that the faith which is the sole condition of justification is the faith that is in us by the grace of

---

[119] Quoting from the Articles of the Church of England.

God. It is "a sure trust that a man has that Christ has loved him and died for him."[120] ...

Wed. 19.—I ... came to London but with a heavy heart. Here every day I found the terrible effects of our brethren's reasoning and their debates with each other. Barely one in 10 still kept their first love, and most of the rest were in great confusion, biting and devouring each another. I pray God "that you are not consumed by one another" [Gal. 5:15].

Mon. 24.—After staying late into the evening at Fetter Lane, I went to a smaller group, where we continued exhorting one another with hymns and spiritual songs, and poured out our hearts to God in prayer. Towards morning, one of us was overwhelmed with joy and love, and couldn't help showing this by crying out loudly and weeping. This very much upset another woman; she said that it was just due to natural disposition, imagination, and nerves. Oh jealous God, do not lay this sin to her charge, and let's not be wise beyond what is written [in Scripture]! ...

Mon. 31.—I had a long, involved conversation with Mr. Molther himself. I weighed all his words carefully, requested that he explain what I didn't understand, and asked him again and again if I wasn't mistaken in what he said. I'd ask, "Is this what you mean, or not?" So I think, if God has given me any understanding at all, I can't be much mistaken in what he meant.

As soon as I came home, I begged God to help me and not to allow "the blind to miss the road" [cf. Deut. 27:18]. Then I wrote down what I believed to be the difference between us, as follows:

> As to faith, you believe that:
> 1. There are no degrees of faith, and that no man has it to any degree until all things have become new for him, until he has the full assurance of faith, the abiding witness of the Spirit, and the clear sense that Christ dwells in him ...
>
> Whereas I believe:
> 1. There are degrees of faith and that a man may have some degree of it even before all things become new for him, before he has

---

[120] Ibid.

the full assurance of faith, the abiding witness of the Spirit, or the clear sense that Christ dwells in him.

2. Therefore, I believe that there is a degree of justifying faith (and consequently a condition of being justified) short of and usually preceding this ...

4. And, in general, that the gift of God, which many received since Peter Boehler came into England, namely, "a sure confidence of God's love for them," was justifying faith,

5. And that the joy and love attending it were not from natural disposition, temperament, or imagination, but a measure of joy in the Holy Spirit, and of the love of God shed abroad in their hearts ...

I believe:

The way to attain faith is to wait for Christ and be still
> While using "all the means of grace."

Therefore I believe it right for those who know they have no faith (i.e., that is, overcoming faith)
> To go to church,
> To take communion,
> To fast,
> To pray as much privately as they can, and
> To read the Scripture

(Because I believe that these are "means of grace," i.e., they ordinarily convey God's grace to unbelievers; and,
That it is possible for a man to use them without trusting in them),
> To do all the earthly good one can,
> And to strive to do spiritual good—

Because I know, many fruits of the Spirit are borne by those who do not have them themselves;[121] and that those who do not have faith, or only in the least degree, may have more light from God, more wisdom for the guiding of other souls, than many that are strong in faith ...

1740

Tues. JANUARY 1.—I tried to explain to our brethren the true Christian scriptural "stillness" by defining fully these solemn

---

[121] It is not clear what Wesley means by this statement. Does he mean, by those without faith? Here he seems to differ from Luther and from his own statements elsewhere.

phrases, "Be still, and know that I am God" [Psalm 46:10]. On Wednesday the 2nd I strongly urged them all to "stand in the old paths" [cf. Jer. 6:16] and to stop disturbing each other's souls by needless disputes and arguments over words. They all seemed convicted. We then lifted our voices in prayer for God to heal all our falling away, and he sent us such a spirit of peace and love as we hadn't known for many months ...

Mon. 21.—I preached at Hannam, four miles from Bristol. In the evening I collected money from our assembly for the relief of the poor who lived outside of Lawford's Gate. They had no work because of the bitter cold and received no help from their local parish, and so were reduced to utmost necessity. I took another collection on Thursday and a third on Sunday, which enabled us to feed 100 and sometimes 150 a day of those we found to need it most ...

Thur. 31.— ... I had now resolved, if God allowed me, to spend some time in Bristol, but contrary to my expectations, I was irresistibly called away. A young man who had no interest in religion had come to Bristol a few months earlier. One of his acquaintances brought him to hear me. He liked what he heard and for a while behaved well, but his seriousness soon wore off. He returned to London and fell in with his old buddies. Some of these led him to commit a robbery on the highway for which he was arrested, tried, and convicted. Now he very much wanted to talk to me, and in a letter to his friend he wrote this: "I want him to swear, by the living God, that he will come and see me before I leave this world." ...

Wed. FEBRUARY 6.—I visited this poor young man who lay in prison sentenced to die. Truly God has begun a good work in his soul. Oh, may it be brought to perfection! ...

Tues. 12.—The young man to be executed the next day handed me a note, reading in part:

> Since I must give account to the God of justice and truth before whom I will appear naked tomorrow:
> I came to Bristol planning to go abroad, either as a doctor or serving in any other suitable capacity. Unfortunately, I met Mr. Ramsey there. He told me, after one or two conversations, that he was serving Mr. John Wesley, and that he would introduce me to him,

which he did. I must say I was always fond of the teaching I heard from [Mr. Wesley]. However, I regret to say that I agreed with Mr. Ramsey that between us, as I recall, we would steal more than 30 pounds[122] out of the money collected to build the school in Kingswood.[123]

I acknowledge that God is just in catching me stealing that which was consecrated, in taking money that was dedicated to God, but I trust now that he has forgiven me for this and all my other sins, washing them away in the blood of the Lamb.

Feb. 12, 1739-40[124]   GWILLAM SNOWDE

The next morning, when I was told that his execution had been delayed for six weeks, and later, that he had been ordered to be deported, I didn't know whether to be glad or sad.[125] But God knows all his works! ...

Tues. 26.—I heard a complaint (as I had several times before) that many of our brethren were not only abstaining from God's ordinances but were also constantly disturbing those who used them and arguing with them whether they wanted to or not. The same complaint was made again the next night at the fellowship meeting. Then I openly confronted them with what they had done, pleaded the case with them, and earnestly begged them not to trouble or confuse the minds of their brethren any more, and that at least they should not hinder those who still waited for God in the ways he has appointed ...

Wed. MARCH 12.—After getting urgent requests to visit the soldier in Bridewell[126] who had received the death penalty, I took time for this. I continued to do so once a day, which gave me opportunity to declare the gospel of peace to several desolate souls who also were confined there.

Tues. 25.—The morning teaching of the Bible began at 5 a.m., as I hope it always will in the future. Thursday the 27th I met with

---

[122] About $7000 in 2020 USD.
[123] Apparently Snowde was guilty of both crimes mentioned.
[124] There was an adjustment of the calendar which is not important to us here.
[125] Wesley's concern is that at the present the young man is in right relationship with God but that he might stray from God as time goes on.
[126] Originally a palace for Henry VIII, Bridewell became a poorhour and prison.

Joseph Chandler, a young Quaker who had sometimes spoken in their meeting. We had never spoken to each other before, and in fact, I didn't know his name or what he looked like. But some had gone to the trouble of taking to him as if from me a formal challenge to debate, and later they told him I'd stated openly to the fellowship that I had "challenged Joseph Chandler to debate, and that he promised to come but had broken his word." Joseph immediately sent to find out from me personally if these things were true. If only those who consider themselves better Christians[127] had done like this honest Quaker, how many false rumors like this one that they now believe to be true would have vanished into thin air? ...

Sat. 29.— ... I think it was about this time that the soldier was executed. For some time I'd visited him every day, but when the love of God was poured into his heart [cf. Rom. 5:5], I told him, "Don't expect to see me anymore. He who has now begun a good work in your soul, will, I trust, preserve you to the end, but I believe Satan will separate us for a time." And just the next day I was informed that the warden[128] [of the prison] had given a strict order: "Neither Mr. Wesley nor any of his people are to be allowed in, for they are all atheists." But did that condemned man die like an atheist? Let my death be like his!

Tues. APRIL 1.—While I was explaining the first half of Acts 23 (which fit the occasion beautifully, although I didn't plan it that way), the flood's roar began. Some children of the devil had tried to disturb us several nights earlier, but now it seemed like the whole host of the enemy came together with one purpose. Not only the court and the alleys, but the street all up and down was filled with people shouting, cursing, swearing, and ready to swallow the earth with violence and rage. The mayor sent an order for them to disperse, but they paid no attention to it. Next, the chief constable came personally. Until then, he had been rather prejudiced against us, but they insulted him in so gross a manner that I believe it completely opened his eyes. Finally the mayor sent several of his officers, who

---

[127] I.e., better than the Quakers, who did not practice the outward ordinances (e.g., baptism, communion).
[128] Wesley: "commanding officer."

arrested the ringleaders and didn't leave till all the rest dispersed. Surely he has been to us "God's servant for good" [Rom. 13:4].

Wed. 2.— ... I called at Newgate Prison in the afternoon and was informed that the unfortunate people sentenced to die very much wanted to speak to me, but that this wouldn't happen since Alderman Beecher had just then sent a special order that they could not. I call on Alderman Beecher to answer for these souls at the judgment seat of Christ ...

Sat. 12.—Preaching at Lanvachas on the way, in the afternoon I reached Bristol and heard the sad news that ____, a leader of those who had caused us trouble, had hung himself on April 1st. It seems he was still alive when cut down, but that he died in less than an hour. Another one who caused disturbance had been in great pain for some days and many times had sent requests for our prayers. A third came to me personally and confessed that he was hired that night and deliberately gotten drunk, but when he came to the door he couldn't move or open his mouth—he didn't know why ...

Sat. 19.—I received a letter from Mr. Simpson and another one from Mr. William Oxlee, telling me that our poor brethren in Fetter Lane[129] were again in great confusion, and earnestly requesting for me to go to London immediately if possible.

Mon. 21.—I started out, and the next evening reached London. On Wednesday the 23rd, I went to see Mr. Simpson. He told me that all the confusion was caused by my brother [Charles], who was preaching in favor of the ordinances; whereas believers, he said, are not subject to ordinances, and unbelievers have nothing to do with them. "They ought to be still; otherwise they will be unbelievers all the days of their life." ...

Now I was at a total loss as to what course of action to take, finding no solid ground on which to set my feet. These useless disputes followed me wherever I went and constantly filled my ears. On Wednesday the 30th I went to my friend—friend, that is, up to this point!—Mr. S., at Islington. But he also immediately raised the subject, telling me that now he was fully convinced that no one has

---

[129] Wesley had started the Fetter Lane fellowship ("society") early on in London with the Moravians. Now a split is in process.

faith to any degree until he is as perfect as God is. I asked, "Then don't you have any degree of faith at all?" He said, "No, because I don't have a clean heart." I turned and asked his servant, "Esther, do you have a clean heart? "She said, "No, my heart's desperately wicked, but I don't have any doubt or fear. I know my Savior loves me and that I love him; I feel it all the time." I then told her master, "This overthrows all your reasoning; this is the condition that you deny exists." ...

In the evening, at the Fetter Lane fellowship, one of the first things that sprang up was the question of the ordinances. But I begged us not to be constantly debating but rather to give ourselves to prayer ...

Fri. MAY 9.—I was a little surprised at some who were shaken by Satan in an unusual way: They had such a strong spirit of laughter that they couldn't resist it, although it was painful and distressing to them. If I hadn't experienced the same thing 10 or 11 years ago, I could hardly have believed what they told me. My brother and I used to spend part of Sunday walking in the meadows and singing hymns. But one day, just as we were starting to sing, he burst into loud laughter. I asked him if he was out of his mind and started to get angry, but right away I began laughing as loudly as he did. There was no way we could stop, even though we were almost torn to pieces, and we had to go home without singing another line ...

Mon. JUNE 9.—A woman came to me from Deptford, saying she was sent by God. I listened to her, and she spoke words that were impressive and true.[130] But I remembered not to judge anything before the time [cf. 1 Cor. 4:5].

Wed. 11.—I went with Mr. Ingham to Islington, my purpose being to talk with Mr. Molther.[131] But they said he was so sick that no one could talk to him. In the evening I went to Fetter Lane, and confronted our poor, confused, shattered fellowship on how they had strayed from the faith. Just as I feared, they couldn't receive what I said. Now, however, I'm innocent of their blood ...

---

[130] Perhaps prophecy about Wesley's future ministry.
[131] I.e., the Moravian minister who was spreading the doctrine of stillness. See above.

Fri. 20.—I mentioned this to our fellowship and, without discussing the different views, begged all those who were weak in the faith to welcome each other, not to quarrel over opinions [cf. Rom. 14:1], but simply to pursue holiness and the things that make for peace.

Sun. 22.—Seeing that God's work would be totally destroyed if I delayed, I began executing a plan I had long considered, to strike at the root of the great delusion. Therefore, led by these words of Jeremiah [6:16], "Stand by the roads, and look, and ask for the ancient paths," I took time to write down a straightforward account of the work God had begun among us, and of the way the enemy had sown his weeds among the good seed, as follows:

> After we had wandered for years in the "new" path of salvation by faith plus works, about two years ago it pleased God to show us the "old" way of salvation by faith only. Many soon tasted this salvation, being justified freely, having peace with God, rejoicing in hope of the glory of God [Rom. 5:2], and having his love poured into their hearts [Rom. 5:5]. These now followed the path of his commandments; they performed their whole duty to God and man. They walked in all the ordinances of the Lord, and through his appointed means received daily grace to help in time of need, and went on from faith to faith.
>
> But eight or nine months ago, certain men rose up, speaking contrary to the teachings we had received. They asserted ...
>
> I plan to consider all these assertions. The first is that weak faith is no faith.

By weak faith, I understand: 1. a faith that is mixed with fear, particularly fear of not enduring to the end; 2. a faith that is mixed with doubt as to whether we have not been deceived and whether our sins are in fact forgiven; 3. a faith that has not yet fully cleansed the heart from all its idols. In these senses, I find the faith of almost all believers to become weak soon after they first have peace with God.

Yet, that weak faith is real faith appears: 1. from Paul: "As for the one who is weak in faith, welcome him" [Rom. 14:1]; 2. from John, speaking of believers who were little children, as well as of young men and fathers [1 John 2:12–13]; and 3. from our Lord's own words: "Why are you afraid, O you of little faith?" [Matt. 8:26]; "O you of little faith, why did you doubt?" [Matt. 14:31]; "I have prayed for you (Peter) that your faith may not fail" [Luke 22:32].

So Peter did have faith then; yet his faith was so weak that not only doubt and fear, but gross sin overcame him that same night.

Nevertheless he was clean because of the word Christ had spoken to him [cf. John 15:3]—that is, he was justified, even though it is clear he did not have a clean heart.

Therefore, there are different degrees of faith; and weak faith may still be true faith.

Tues. 24.— ... In the evening I preached on, "Do not throw away your confidence, which has a great reward" [Heb. 10:35]. [*Part of his sermon follows:*]

"You who have known and felt your sins forgiven, do not throw away your confidence, 1. even if your joy dies down, your love grows cold, and even if your peace itself is strongly attacked; 2. even if you meet with doubt or fear or strong and constant temptation; yes, 3. even if you find sin still alive in you and thrusting its sword at you fiercely so as to make you fall ...

"Finding that sin still remains in you doesn't prove that you are not a believer. Sin does remain in those who are justified, but it doesn't rule over them, for at first they do not have a clean heart, and all things have not yet become new. But don't fear even if you have a sinful heart; in a little while you'll be clothed with power from on high, by which you can purify yourselves [so as to be pure] even as he is pure, and be holy, as he who has called you is holy." ...

Fri. JULY 18.—A few of us joined with my mother in the great sacrifice of thanksgiving,[132] and then considered how to proceed with our poor brethren of Fetter Lane. We all saw that things were coming to a head and therefore agreed unanimously what we would do.

Sun. 20.— ... In the evening I went with Mr. Seward to the love-feast[133] in Fetter Lane. I said nothing until it was over, then read a paper, substantially as follows:

---

[132] I.e., Holy Communion or the Eucharist, a word meaning "thanksgiving."
[133] At the love-feast, reminiscent of the early church, simple food (often just bread and water) was shared, along with brief testimonies. The love-feast began and ended with singing and prayer.

About nine months ago, certain of you began to speak contrary to the doctrine we had received up till then. Essentially, what you asserted is this:

1. There is no such thing as weak faith. Whenever there is any doubt or fear, or whenever there is not, in the full sense, a new, clean heart, there is no justifying faith.

2. Persons ought not to use the ordinances of God, which our Church calls "means of grace," before they have a faith that excludes all doubt and fear and involves a new, clean heart.

You have often affirmed that "to search the Scriptures, to pray, or to take communion before we have this faith, is to seek salvation by works and that, until these works are abandoned, no one can receive faith."

I believe these assertions flatly contradict the Word of God. I have warned you of this again and again, and have begged you to turn back to "the law and the testimony" [Isa. 8:20]. I have borne with you a long time, hoping you would turn back, but now, since I find you more confirmed in the error of your ways, the only thing I can do is to release you to God. You who are of the same mind as I am, follow me!

Then, without saying anything more, I left, along with 18 or 19 members of the fellowship ...

Wed. 23.—Our little group met at the Foundry[134] instead of Fetter Lane. God has already given us about 25 brothers, all of who think and speak the same thing. In addition, 47 or 48 of the 50 women who belonged to circles[135] asked to share our lot ...

Mon. AUGUST 4.—I ate dinner with one who told me very simply, "Sir, I thought last week that there could be no such thing as the rest you described—none in this world wherein we could be so free as to not even want to be released from pain. But God has taught me better, because on Friday and Saturday, when I was in greatest pain, not for a single moment did I want relief; I just wanted God's will to be done."

---

[134] The Foundry was the first Methodist building in London, originally a metalworks factory. (Originally spelled "Foundery")

[135] Wesley's word is "bands." Those familiar with Wesley may be comfortable with this word, but "circles" catches the idea: smaller groups for accountability and support.

In the evening, many people gathered at Long Lane, planning to make a disturbance. They had found a woman to get things started, well known in that area as someone with no fear of either God or man. The moment she burst out, I turned to face her directly and told her of our Lord's love for her soul. We then prayed that he would confirm his word of grace. She was struck to the heart and her shame was obvious. From her I turned back to the others, who melted like ice as if they had lost their strength; but surely some of them will find him who is their rock and their strong salvation …

Sun. 10.—Taking Galatians 6:3 as my text, I earnestly warned all who had tasted the grace of God: 1. not to think they were justified before they had a clear assurance that God had forgiven their sins and with it a calm peace, the love of God, and dominion over all sin; and 2. even after they had this, not to think they were anything special but rather to press forward for the prize of their high calling—a clean heart, thoroughly renewed "after the likeness of God in true righteousness and holiness" [Eph. 4:14][136] …

Fri. 22.—I was asked to pray with a hardened old sinner, believed to be at the point of death. He didn't know me and never had heard me preach. I spoke a long time before he opened his mouth. But no sooner did I say "the Savior of sinners," than he burst out, "Yes indeed, the Savior of sinners! I know it, because he's saved me! He told me so on Sunday morning, and he said I wasn't going to die yet—not until I've heard his children preach his gospel and have told my old partners in sin that he's ready to save them, too." …

Thur. 28.— … Now the disputes were over, and everything was quiet and calm. So on Monday, September 1st, I left London, and the next evening found my brother at Bristol, quickly recovering from his fever. At 7 p.m., God saw fit [for me] to apply those words to the hearts of many backsliders, "How can I give you up, O Ephraim? How can I hand you over, O Israel? How can I make you like Admah? How can I treat you like Zeboiim? My heart recoils within me; my compassion grows warm and tender" (Hosea 11:8) …

---

[136] Note the main points: Wesley expects believers to persist seeking until they receive the assurance of salvation, and he expects them to put away outward sin immediately, while seeking inward holiness.

Fri. SEPTEMBER 5.—Our Lord brought back many who had been driven away. In the evening we cried out to him with all our might, praying for brotherly love to continue and grow, and so it did, according to our faith.

Sat. 6.—I met the circles in Kingswood and warned them, with all authority, to beware of going beyond what is written [cf. 1 Cor. 4:6][137] and to seek to know nothing but Christ crucified [cf. 1 Cor. 2:2].

Mon. 8.—We started out early in the morning and reached London the evening of the next day. On Wednesday the 10th I visited a woman in wrenching pain, wasting away with sickness, yet in everything giving thanks and rejoicing in hope of the glory of God. When we left her, we went to visit someone whose life was threatened by smallpox, yet who wasn't asking to live or even for relief—just for the holy will of God to be done. If these are unbelievers, as some of the "still" brethren recently told them, I will gladly be an unbeliever all my days …

Sun. 14.—As I returned home in the evening, no sooner had I stepped out of the stagecoach than the mob that had gathered around my door completely surrounded me. I rejoiced and praised God, knowing this was the moment I had long been waiting for. Immediately I spoke to those nearest me of "righteousness and the judgment to come" [Acts 24:25]. At first not many could hear me because of the uproar, but the silence kept spreading until I had a quiet, attentive audience, and when I left them they all were very loving and gave me many blessings …

Mon. 22.—Needing a little time to withdraw, which was almost impossible for me to do in London, I went to Mr. Piers' at Bexley, where mornings and evenings I taught the Sermon on the Mount but was free the rest of the day to do other things. On Saturday the 27th I returned [to London] …

Sun. OCTOBER 19.—I found a man who was a fresh example of that astonishing truth that the servants of God are never distressed. His body was almost torn apart with pain, but God had made his bed

---

[137] I.e., not to promote opinions that went beyond plain teachings of Scripture.

easy in his sickness, so that he was constantly thanking God and glorifying his goodness ...

Thur. 23.—I was told of an awful judgment of God. A wretched man who was here last week, swearing and blaspheming and striving with all his might to hinder the Word of God, afterwards bragged to a lot of people that he would come back on Sunday, and that then no one would shut him up. But on Friday God laid his hand on him, and on Sunday he was buried ...

Mon. 27. The surprising news of poor Mr. S.'s death was confirmed. Surely God will uphold his own cause. You are righteous, O Lord! ...

Mon. NOVEMBER 3.—We distributed to many poor members of our fellowship, as each had need, articles of clothing which those who could spare them had brought for that purpose ...

Sun. 16.—After receiving communion at St. James, our parish church, with a large congregation, I visited several sick people. Most of them had the spotted fever, which I was told had taken many lives and from which few recovered. But God said, "You can come so far [and no farther]" [cf. Job 38:11]. I believe that everyone we visited recovered ...

Tues. 25.—After several methods were proposed for employing those out of work, we decided to try one that several of our brethren recommended. Our aim was to meet their need while providing for them as inexpensively as possible. In order to do this, we set up 12 of the poorest, along with a trainer, in the fellowship preaching-room. There they worked for four months, until spring came, carding and spinning cotton. And the plan succeeded; they stayed busy and were sustained, costing us little more than the value of their labor ...

Mon. DECEMBER 1.—Finding that many of our brothers and sisters had been offended by others, I set times for the accusers to come and speak face to face with the accused. Nearly every day this week, some of them came, and most of the offenses vanished. Where doubt remained, I could only advise them to look into their own hearts and to suspend judgments until God brings to light the things now hidden in darkness [cf. 1 Cor. 4:5].

Fri. 12.—Having received many unsettling reports regarding our little fellowship in Kingswood, I left London and on Saturday evening, after some difficulty and danger due to a great deal of ice on the road, came to my brother at Bristol, and he confirmed what I didn't want to hear.

Sun. 14.—I went to Kingswood intending, if it pleased God, to spend some time there, hoping I might be his instrument to heal the divisions that had arisen, so that we might again, with one heart and one mouth, glorify the Father of our Lord Jesus Christ.

Mon. 15.—I began explaining, both morning and evening, our Lord's Sermon on the Mount. During the day I tried to heal the jealousies and misunderstandings that had arisen, warning and exhorting everyone, "See that you don't fall by the wayside" …

Sun. 21.— … In the evening, at our love-feast at Bristol, 70 or 80 of our brothers and sisters from Kingswood attended in spite of the heavy snowfall. We all walked back together through the most violent sleet- and snow-storm I ever remember. The snow was over knee-deep in many places, but our hearts had been so warmed that [as we waded through it] we rejoiced and praised God for the consolation we had received …

Thur. 30.— … At 6 p.m., when the body of Alice Philips was brought in the building, I explained: "Today you will be with me in Paradise" [Luke 23:43]. This was the woman whose master fired her last year "for receiving the Holy Spirit." Then she hardly had a place to lay her head, but now she has a home with God, eternal in the heavens.

Wed. 31.—Many from Bristol came over to meet with us, and our love for each other was greatly strengthened. At 8:30 p.m., the building was filled from one end to the other, and we ended the year by wrestling with God in prayer and praising him for the wonderful work he had already done on earth.

1741

Thur. JANUARY 1.—I explained, "Anyone who is in Christ is a new creation" [2 Cor. 5:17]. But I discovered that many of our brethren had no ears to hear, having argued so much that they lost both their faith and their love. In the evening, overflowing with the words God gave me, I explained those words of Paul—which indeed is true of every true believer—"For me to live is Christ, and to die is gain" [Phil. 1:21] ...

Mon. 12.—In the evening we were so filled with the spirit of prayer and thanksgiving that I hardly knew how to teach until I found where it is written, "My song will be always of the lovingkindness of the Lord. With my mouth I will always show thy truth from one generation to another" [cf. Psalm 42:8].

All today until evening, Mrs. J. was in great agony, then sitting up suddenly she said, "They've just finished; they've just finished! C. prayed and Humphreys preached (which in fact we later learned they had), and they are coming here as fast as they can!" Right after that, they came in. She immediately cried out, "Why did you come here? You can't pray; you know you can't!" And they couldn't open their mouths; so after a while they had to leave her like she was.

Many came to see her on Tuesday, and to each one she said something about either his or her actual[138] sins or the sins in their hearts, and things so personal that several of them left more quickly than they entered. In the afternoon Mr. J. sent to Kingswood for me. She told him, "Mr. Wesley won't come tonight; he'll come in the morning. But God has begun and he'll end the work by himself. Before six in the morning I'll be well." And about 5:45 the next morning, after resting quietly a while, she burst out, "Peace to you (her husband)! Peace to this house! The peace of God has filled my soul! I know that my Redeemer lives!" And for several days her mouth was filled with his praise, and all she talked about was his wonderful works ...

Mon. 19.—From several reports, I found it absolutely necessary for me to be in London. I therefore asked the fellowship to meet in the evening and, having settled things the best I could, on Tuesday I set out, and on Wednesday evening met our brethren at the Foundry ...

Sun. FEBRUARY 1.—A personal letter written to me by Mr. Whitefield had been printed without either of us giving permission, and a large number of copies were handed out to our people, both at the door and inside the Foundry itself. I got a copy and, after

---

[138] I.e., outward, bodily.

preaching, related the actual facts to the congregation. I told them, "I'll do just what I believe Mr. Whitefield would do if he himself were here"—then I tore it to pieces in front of them all. Everyone who had received a copy did the same, so that in two minutes there was not a whole copy left. Ah poor Ahithophel![139] *Ibi omnis effusus labor!*[140] ...

Thur. 12.—My brother returned from Oxford and preached on "the true way of waiting for God." This immediately dispelled the fears of some and the vain hopes of others, who had confidently asserted that Mr. Charles Wesley was already practicing stillness and would not come back to London.

Mon. 16.—As I preached in Long Lane, the enemy host gathered together. One big rock (and they threw many) went just over my shoulder, but no one got hurt, for "his kingdom rules over all" [Psalm 103:19].

Having settled affairs to my liking, on Tuesday, February 17th, I left London. In the afternoon I reached Oxford, and leaving my horse there, set out on foot for Stanton-Harcourt. Nightfall, along with heavy rain, overtook me in about an hour. Being wet and weary and not sure of my way, although ashamed that I wasn't fully resigned to God's will, I couldn't help praying silently, "Oh, that you would 'hold the waterskins of the heavens!' [Job 38:37]. Or at least give me light, or a reliable guide, or some help however you know best!" Soon the rain stopped, the moon broke out, and a friendly man caught up with me, who sat me on his own horse and walked by my side until we came to Mr. Gambold's door.

Wed. 18.—Wednesday I walked to Burford, on Thursday to Malmsbury, and the next day to Bristol. On Saturday the 21st I investigated as thoroughly as I could the divisions and offenses which, in spite of the earnest warnings I had given, had broken out afresh in Kingswood. That afternoon I met a few of the circles there, but the atmosphere was cold and uneasy. On Sunday the 22nd I tried to show them the basis of many of their mistakes from these words,

---

[139] Ahithophel was David's counselor who went over to Absalom and gave wise counsel on how to defeat David. God used Hushai the Archite to overturn Ahithophel's counsel (2 Samuel 17).

[140] Meaning roughly: "All the wasted labor!"

"You have no need that anyone should teach you" [1 John 2:27], a text frequently used to support the worst enthusiasm.[141] Mr. Cennick and 15 or 20 others approached me after the sermon. I told them they'd been wrong to speak against me behind my back. Mr. C., Ann A., and Thomas Bissicks, as spokesmen for the rest, replied that they'd said nothing behind my back that they wouldn't say to my face, which was that my preaching praised man's faithfulness and not the faithfulness of God.

That evening we held our love-feast in Bristol. Mention was made that many of our brethren at Kingswood had formed a separate fellowship. Therefore when our love-feast ended, I related to them fully the result of the separations that had been made from time to time in London, and also the cause of this, namely, Mr. C[ennick]'s preaching a doctrine different than they had first received. The natural result was that when my brother and I preached just what we had from the beginning, many criticized and spoke against us both, causing endless strife and confusion.

T.B. replied, "Why, you do preach false doctrine! You preach that there is righteousness in man." I said, "And there is, after the righteousness of Christ is imputed to him through faith. But who told you that what we preach is false doctrine? Who but Mr. C[ennick] would have made you believe this?" Mr. C[ennick] answered, "You do preach righteousness in man! I did say this, and I'll say it again. We're still willing to have joint meetings with you, but we'll also meet separately, because we want to confirm each another in the truths that you speak against."

I replied, "You should have told me this before and not have replaced me in my own house, stealing the hearts of the people and separating friends by private accusations." He said, "I've never accused you privately." I said, "My brethren, you be the judge," and read as follows:

> To the Reverend Mr. George Whitefield.
> My DEAR BROTHER,   Jan. 17, 1741.
> So that you may come quickly, I have written a second time.

---

[141] Originally meaning "inspired by God (or a god)"; in this period, religious extravagance and imagination.

I sit solitary, like Eli, waiting to find out what will happen to the ark [cf. 1 Sam. 4:13]. And while I wait, fearing that it will be carried away from among my people, my trouble increases daily. How gloriously did the gospel once seem to flourish in Kingswood! I spoke of the everlasting love of Christ with sweet power. But now Brother Charles is allowed to open his mouth against this truth, while the frightened sheep stare and flee as if there were no shepherd among them. It is just as if Satan were now warring against the saints in an unusual way. Oh, pray for the troubled lambs who are left in this place that they may not faint. They surely would if preaching would do it, because those who listen to the sermons have nothing to rest on but their own faithfulness.

With universal redemption,[142] Brother Charles pleases the world, and Brother John follows him in everything. I believe no atheist can preach against predestination more than they do, while all who believe in election are counted as enemies to God, and are called that.

Fly, dear brother. It's as if I am alone. I'm in the midst of the plague. If God permits you to come, hurry!

Mr. C[ennick] stood up and said, "Yes, that's my letter. I sent it to Mr. Whitefield, and I don't take back anything in it or believe I was wrong to send it!"

Noticing that some of our brethren began to speak in anger, I asked him to meet me at Kingswood on Saturday when each of us could speak more freely, and to let everything rest until then.

Tues. 24.—The circles met at Bristol, and I read over the names of the United Society,[143] being determined that no one who behaved disorderly would remain in it. Therefore I took note of every person, 1. to whom any reasonable objection was made, and 2. who was not known to and recommended by some who could be depended on to

---

[142] I.e., the doctrine that redemption is offered to all, not just to the elect.

[143] Wesley defined his "United Society" as "a company of men having the form and seeking the power of godliness, united in order to pray together, to receive the word of exhortation, and to watch over one another in love, that they may help each other to work out their salvation." Each "society" (fellowship) was subdivided into classes of about 12 each. It would be wrong to see it as a denomination at this point. Wesley considered it a renewal movement within the Church of England.

be truthful ... This way about 40 separated from us, I trust only for a season.

Sat. 28.—I met the Kingswood circles again, and took time to listen to all who wanted to speak, after which I read the following paper:

> Many witnesses testify that a few members of the fellowship of circles[144] in Kingswood have made it a common practice to scoff at the preaching of Mr. John and Charles Wesley. They have criticized and bad-mouthed them behind their backs, while claiming to their faces to love and esteem them; they have actively tried to prejudice other members of that fellowship against them; and in order to do this, have falsely represented and slandered them at various times.
>
> Therefore, not for any of their opinions, whether right or wrong, but for the reasons just given, namely, for scoffing at the Word and the ministers of God; for malicious reports, for going behind our backs and speaking evil; for their deception, lying, and slandering,
>
> I, John Wesley, by the consent and with the approval of the Kingswood fellowship, declare the persons above-mentioned no longer to be members. They will not be considered such until they openly confess their fault and do whatever they can to remove the scandal they have created.

They seemed a little shocked at first when they heard this, but Mr. C[ennick], T.B., and A.A. soon recovered and said that they had heard both my brother and me preach Catholicism many times. However, they would join with us if we were willing, but that they wouldn't admit they had done anything wrong.

I asked them to consider it one more time and to give us their answer the following evening.

The next evening, MARCH the 1st, they answered the same as before. Still not knowing how to break fellowship, I urged them to wait a little longer and to wrestle with God to know his will about them.

Fri. 6.— ... On Saturday the 7th all members of the fellowship who could do so met together. I told them that plain dealing was

---

[144] Wesley: "the Band Society."

best, and so, setting all our opinions aside, I would tell them plainly how I thought many of them were at fault; namely:

1. belittling God's servants and making light of his ordinances; 2. not speaking or praying when they met until they were strongly moved to do so; and 3. separating from their brethren and forming a different fellowship ...

T.B. replied, "Our belief in election is the real reason you're separating from us." I answered, "In your heart you know that's not true. There are several predestinarians in our fellowships, both in London and Bristol, and never yet have I expelled any from either one for holding that opinion."

He said, "We'll disband our fellowship on condition you receive Mr. C[ennick] and let him preach as you did before." I replied, "My brother has wronged me, but he hasn't said, 'I repent.'" Mr. C[ennick] said, "Except for not speaking up to defend you, I don't see that I've wronged you at all." I answered, "It seems, then, that all that's left is for each of you to choose which fellowship you prefer." Then, after a short time of prayer, Mr. C[ennick] left, and about half of those present went with him ...

Mon. 23.—I visited the sick in Kingswood. One woman really surprised me. Her husband had died of the fever[145] some days earlier. Immediately after he died she got sick, next her oldest daughter, then another and still another of her children. Six of them were now sick all round her, lacking medicine, money, and food, and without seeing any way to get it. At such times, who but a Christian can say from the heart, "Blessed be the name of the Lord!"?

Now everything at both Kingswood and Bristol was settled, even beyond my expectation, so I granted my brother's request and, setting out on Wednesday the 25th, the next day came to London ...

Wed. APRIL 15.—At Greyhound Lane, I explained the last part of Ephesians 4. Physically, I was so weak I could hardly stand up, but my spirit was greatly strengthened.

All day Thursday I felt myself growing weaker, and on Friday the 17th I could hardly get out of bed. When I did get up, I had to lie down again almost immediately. Nevertheless, in the evening I

---

[145] Probably the spotted fever (see above).

dragged myself out to Short's Gardens. I had difficulty climbing the stairs, and my voice was almost gone. I could hardly make myself heard as I read these words: "Those whom he foreknew he also predestined" [Rom. 8:29]. But in a moment both my voice and strength came back, and from then on, for some weeks, I found physical strength such as I haven't had since I landed in America [six years ago].

Mon. 20.—I was deeply concerned for those who were tossed to and fro by every wind of doctrine [cf. Eph. 4:14], and for many of these once more entangled in sin and under Satan's control, so I begged God to show me what this would lead to and opened my Bible on these words: "Nothing was missing, whether small or great, sons or daughters, spoil or anything that had been taken. David brought back all" [1 Sam. 30:19] …

Wed. MAY 6.—We had agreed to meet on this day to pray and humble ourselves before God; perhaps he would show us his will about reuniting with our brethren of Fetter Lane. At 1 p.m. all the circles, both men and women, met for this purpose. And our Lord didn't reject our prayer or leave himself without a witness among us. It was clear to everyone, even to those who previously were the most eager for it, that the time hadn't come [for reunification], 1. because the others had not given up their most essentially wrong doctrines; and 2. because many of us had found so much deception in their words that we could hardly tell what they really believed and what they didn't.

Thur. 7.—I reminded the United Society that many of our brothers and sisters were short even of essential food. Many had no suitable clothes; many were out of work due to no fault of their own; and many were sick and in danger of dying. I said I'd done what I could to feed the hungry, to clothe the naked, to provide work for the poor, and to visit the sick, but that by myself I couldn't accomplish these things, and therefore requested all whose hearts agreed with mine: 1. to bring whatever clothes they could spare to be distributed among those who needed them most; and 2. to each to give a penny[146] a week, or whatever they could afford, for the relief of the poor and sick.

I told them that my plan was to employ all the women who were out of work and who wanted to do so in knitting for the time being. I said, "To these we will first give the usual wage for what work they do and then add more as they need it. Twelve persons are appointed to inspect them and to visit and provide things needed for the sick. These are to visit all the sick in their districts every other day, and to meet on Tuesday evening to give account of what they've done and discuss what can be done further." ...

Thur. 21.—In the evening I published the great decree of God, eternal and unchangeable (but so sadly misunderstood and misrepresented by fools who think they are wise): "Whoever believes ... will be saved, but whoever does not believe will be condemned" [Mark 16:16].[147]

Sat. 23.—At a meeting of the fellowship stewards[148] (who receive and pay out what's contributed each week), we realized that we needed to cut back on expenses, which were exceeding the contributions. We agreed to let two of the teachers at Bristol go, because the current funds are barely enough to pay three teachers, two male and one female, at Bristol, and two teachers, one male and one female, at Kingswood[149] ...

Sun. JUNE 7.—I preached in Charles Square on "An hour is coming, and is now here, when the dead will hear the voice of the Son of God, and those who hear will live" [John 5:25]. A furious storm burst on us halfway through the sermon, but such things don't affect those who seek the Lord. His power was all the more present to heal—so much so that the hearts of many of us were dancing for joy, praising our glorious God who makes thunder ...

Sat. 13.— ... From [Markfield] I went to Hemmington. Here too, the building couldn't contain the people, so some stood outside

---

[146] About $1.00 in 2020 USD.
[147] Wesley's probable reference is to "bare belief," as opposed to faith that bears fruit.
[148] Or superintendents; particularly responsible for finances.
[149] Elsewhere W. states that the teachers at Kingswood receive no pay; so this must have changed over time.

around the door and at both windows while I showed them what we must do to be saved.

After I finished preaching, someone in our assembly took offense at a man they considered despicable, notorious in that whole area for cursing, swearing, and drunkenness, even though he was now gray-headed and almost 80 years old. He came to me, grabbed my hands, and said, "I don't know if you are a good man or a bad man, but I know that the words you speak are good. I never heard anything like this in all my life. Oh, that God would drive them home to my poor soul!" He then burst into tears and could say no more ...

Mon. 15.—I set out for London, and on the way read that famous book, Martin Luther's *Commentary on the Epistle to the Galatians*. I was ashamed of myself! I used to value this book just because I heard others praise it and because, from time to time, I'd read some excellent sentences quoted from it. But what can I say, judging it now for myself after seeing it with my own eyes? ... How blasphemously does he speak of good works and of the law of God; constantly coupling the law with sin, death, hell, or the devil, and teaching that Christ delivers us from all of these! Why, it can no more be proved by Scripture that Christ delivers us from the law of God, than that he delivers us from holiness or from heaven. Here, I sense, is the real source of the great error of the Moravians: They follow Luther for better or for worse, hence their "no works, no law, no commandments." But who are you to "speak evil against the law and judge the law"? [cf. James 4:11] ...

Thur. 18.—I asked about the requirements to complete the Bachelor of Divinity degree, and told Mr. Gambold the topic of my sermon before the university, but he seemed to think it didn't matter. "Because," he said, "everyone here is so prejudiced that they won't pay attention to anything you say." I don't know if that's true; however, I must deliver my own soul, whether they listen or not ...

Thur. 2.—I met Mr. Gambold again, who told me plainly that he was ashamed to be seen with me and therefore must be excused from attending our fellowship meeting with me. At least this is plain dealing! ...

Thur. 9.—Being in the Bodleian Library, I landed on Mr. Calvin's account of the Michael Servetus[150] case. Calvin inserts several of Servetus' letters in which he states explicitly: "I believe the Father is God, the Son is God, and the Holy Spirit is God." Mr. Calvin, however, portrays him as an out-and-out monster—an Arian, a blasphemer, and what-not—besides calling him "dog," "devil," "pig," and so on---the usual names Calvin gives his opponents. At the same time, he utterly denies having caused Servetus' death. "No," he says, "I merely advised our magistrates, since they have the right to use the sword to restrain heretics, to arrest and try him as one of the worst heretics, but after he was judged guilty, I said not one word about executing him"! ...

Mon. 13.—I returned to Oxford, then on Wednesday rode to Bristol. I learned that my brother [Charles] had already gone to Wales, and so I came [to Bristol] just in time. My timing was right for another reason, too; a spirit of enthusiasm was breaking out on many. They claimed that whatever entered their imagination was the will of God—not what was written, but whatever was impressed on their hearts. If these impressions are received as the rule of action instead of the written Word, I believe there's no error so wicked or absurd that we can't fall into, and that without remedy ...

Wed. 22.—At the repeated urging of some who were [at Oxford], I went over to Abingdon. There I preached on "What must I do to be saved?" Both the yard and the building were full, but scarcely have I ever seen so stupid and senseless a people, both in the spiritual and the natural sense. Yet God is able even from "these stones to raise up children for Abraham" [Matt. 3:9] ...

Sat. 25.—It became my turn (which happens once every three years) to preach at St. Mary's to the whole university. The harvest truly is plentiful. For whatever reason, they came. I have seldom seen such a large congregation at Oxford. My text was the confession of poor Agrippa: "You almost persuade me to be a Christian" [Acts

---

[150] Michael Servetus (1511–1553), a Spanish theologian, wrote against the classical understanding of the Trinity and against infant baptism. When visiting Geneva, he was arrested and, with Calvin's consent, if not at his direction, was burned as a heretic. Wesley seems to have some sympathy for him.

26:28]. I have "cast my bread upon the waters"; let me "find it again after many days" [Eccl. 11:1] ...

Fri. 31.—Hearing that Jane Muncy, one of our sisters, was sick, I went to see her. She was in one of the first women circles at Fetter Lane, and when the debate about the means of grace began, she stood in the gap and contended earnestly for the ordinances once delivered to the saints. Not long after that, when leaders ordered the unmarried men and women not to speak to to each other, she again withstood to the face those who were "teaching as doctrines the commandments of men" [Matt. 15:9] ... Many times, after she had performed loving service until 8 or 9 p.m., she then sat down and worked with her hands until 12 or 1 a.m.—not that she lacked anything herself, but that she might have to give to others for their necessities ...

Now after she had worked harder than all the rest, God singled her out to suffer. At first a high fever seized her. When this happened, they moved her to another house, where she accomplished something she was unaware of: The homeowner, who had no concern for spiritual things, observed her and was convicted. It was then that he began to understand and take to heart the things that bring one peace in the end.

In a few days her fever dropped, or rather seemed to settle into an internal infection, so that she couldn't breathe without great pain, and this grew worse day and night. When I came in, she stretched out her hand and said, "Have you come, you blessed of the Lord? Praised be the name of my Lord for this!" I asked, "Are you growing weak [in faith], now that you are disciplined by him?" [cf. Heb. 12:5ff.]. She said, "O no, no, no; I'm not getting weak; I don't complain; I rejoice continually!" I said, "But can you give thanks in everything?" She replied, "Yes, I do, I do!" I said, "God will give you comfort in your sickness." She cried out, "He does, he does! I don't lack anything. He's always with me, and I have nothing to do but praise him." ...

Wed. AUGUST 12.—I visited a man whom God is purifying by fire as an answer to the prayers of his wife. He was just starting to beat her (which he often did), when God immediately struck him. His hand dropped and he fell on the ground, having no more strength than a newborn baby. He has had to stay in bed ever since, but rejoices in hope of the glory of God …

Thur. 20.—A clergyman had sent a message that if I would preach in the evening on the text he chose, he would come to hear me, so I preached on that text, Matthew 7:26, and strongly applied our Lord's warning to "beware of false prophets"—that is, all preachers who do not speak as the oracles of God.

Mon. 31.—I began my preaching series on the Book of Common Prayer. On Tuesday, September 1st, I read Mr. Whitefield's account of God's dealings with his soul. I know much of this to be true. "Oh, let not steadfast love and faithfulness forsake you; bind them around your neck; write them on the tablet of your heart" [Prov. 3:3].

Thur. SEPTEMBER 3.—James Hutton had sent me word that Count Zinzendorf wanted to meet me at 3 p.m., so I went then to Gray's Inn Walks. The substantial part of our conversation [in Latin], which I dare not conceal, was as follows. To spare the dead,[151] I do not translate. (*I am omitting this letter, found on pp. 323-326 of Vol. 2 of Wesley's* Journal) …

> Thus have I declared, and in the most straightforward way I can, the real issue between us and the Moravian brethren. It is an unpleasant task that I have delayed undertaking, at least as long as I could with a clear conscience; but now at last I am forced to speak the bare facts as they are, so as not to hinder the work of God.
>
> I am very aware of the objection that has so often been made, namely, "You are inconsistent. You tenderly loved, highly esteemed, and zealously commended these very men, and now you don't love or esteem them at all. You not only don't commend them but are bitter against them and even speak abusively of them before the whole world."
>
> This is partly true, and partly false. So that the whole case may be better understood, I must give a short history of what has occurred between us from the beginning.

---

[151] It is not clear if Wesley means Zinzendorf, who died in 1760.

Serious Joy (John Wesley's *Journal*)

[After reviewing his history with the Moravians and how they benefited him, Wesley says he has read all their books published in English. Then he refutes, point by point, what he finds objectionable in their writings. He concludes:]

O my brethren, let me earnestly entreat you once again, in his name who is my Lord and yours, "if there is any comfort from love ... any affection and sympathy" [Phil. 2:1], pick the fly out of the ointment, separate the precious from the worthless! I beg you to reconsider your whole work and see if Satan has gained an advantage over you. "Excellent things have been spoken of you, O city of God." But may not "he who has the sharp two-edged sword" say "yet I have a few things against you"? [Rev. 2:12–14]. Oh, that you would repent of these, that you might be "a glorious church, without spot or wrinkle or any such thing!" [Eph. 5:27].

Permit me, above all, to press on you three things, with all the earnestness of love. First, regarding your doctrine, to purge out from among you the leaven of antinomianism that affects you so deeply and to no longer "make void the law through faith" [Rom. 3:31]. Second, regarding your discipline, to call no one on earth the rabbi, master, or lord of your faith [Matt. 23:8–9]. I know that subordination is needed. I can show you a kind of subordination that in fact satisfies all Christian purposes, yet is as far removed from your kind as the heavens are from the earth. Third, regarding your practice, to renounce all craft, cunning, subtlety, dissimulation, and wisdom that is falsely so called; to put away all false appearance and all guile out of your mouth; "to behave in this world with all simplicity and godly sincerity" [cf. 2 Cor. 1:12]; to speak plainly to all, whatever it costs you, seeking only, "by open statement of the truth, to commend yourselves to everyone's conscience in the sight of God" [2 Cor. 4:2].

Sun. SEPTEMBER 6.—Observing that some had begun to use their liberty as a cloak for license to sin, I drove home, in the morning, those words of St. Paul that are worthy to be written in the heart of every believer: "'Everything is permissible'—but not everything is beneficial" [1 Cor. 6:12, 10:23 NIV], and, in the evening, our Lord's essential admonition "that they ought always to pray and not lose heart" [Lk. 18:1].

Mon. 7.—I visited a young man in St. Thomas Hospital, who was constantly praising God while in great pain. At the request of many of the patients, I spent a short time with them, encouraging them and praying for them. Oh, what a harvest there might there be if any who love souls and who have the time would regularly visit these places of distress, and in the tenderness and meekness of wisdom would teach and encourage those on whom God has laid his hand[152] so they will know and take advantage of their day of visitation![153] ...

Thur. OCTOBER 1.—We set out for Wales but missed the ferry crossing the River Severn in the morning, and it was sunset before we got to Newport. We asked if there was a guide we could hire to lead us to Cardiff, but none was available. Right after that, a young man came in who said he was going to Lanissan, a little village two miles to the right of Cardiff, so we decided to go there. At 7 p.m. we set out. It rained quite heavily, and as there was no moonlight or starlight we couldn't see the road or each another or even the heads of our horses. But God's promise didn't fail; he gave his angels charge over us, and soon after 10 p.m. we arrived safely at Mr. Williams' house at Lanissan.

Fri. 2.—We rode to Fonmon Castle. We found Mr. Jones' daughter sick with the smallpox, but he was able cheerfully to put her and everything else into the hands of the One in whom he now believed. In the evening I preached at Cardiff in the Shire Hall, a large and comfortable place, on "God gave us eternal life, and this life is in his Son" [1 John 5:11]. Since there had been a feast in the town that day, I felt it necessary to add a few words on excessive drinking. While I was saying, "As for you drunkards, you have no part in this life; you are still in death; you are choosing death and hell," a man cried out loudly, "I'm one, and that's where I'm going." But I trust that God that very hour began to show him and others a more excellent way.

Sat. 3.—About noon we came to Pontypool. A clergyman stopped me on the first street, and a few more after him soon

---

[152] I.e., in sickness.
[153] "Day of visitation" can be negative (their sickness) or positive (God visiting to help); Wesley believes that sickness can help people turn to God.

recognized who I was. I found that their love had not been cooled at all by the bitter enemies who had been among them. True pains had been taken to set them against my brother and me by men who "know not what manner of spirit they are of" [Luke 9:55], but instead of arguing we sought God in prayer, and all our hearts were knit together as in the beginning.

In the afternoon we came to Abergavenny. Those who are bitter in spirit have been here too, yet Mrs. James (now Mrs. Whitefield) received us gladly, as she had done previously. But we could only find two or three to join with us in the evening besides those of her own household …

Sat. 17.— … I preached at Cardiff at 3 p.m., and about 5 p.m. left there to go to Fonmon Castle. In spite of the pitch-black night and our not knowing the road, before 8 p.m. we safely reached the assembly that had been waiting for us for some time …

Tues. 20.— At 11 a.m. I preached at the prison [at Cardiff] on "I came not to call the righteous but sinners to repentance" [Lk. 5:32]. In the afternoon, I was asked to meet one of the "honorable"[154] women, whom I found to be simply a sinner groaning under the mighty hand of God. About 6 p.m., at Mr. W.'s request, I preached once more on those words, "He whom you ignorantly worship I declare unto you" [Acts 17:23] …

Fri. 23.—I visited several others who were sick of the same disorder [as at the previous house]. Surely our Lord will work greatly by this sickness. I don't find that it comes to any house without leaving a blessing behind it. In the evening I went to Kingswood and found Ann Steed also praising God, even in the fire of pain, and testifying that all her weakness and pain worked together for good.

Sun. 25.—After communion at All-Saints, I started on horseback for Kingswood, but before reaching Lawrence Hill, my horse fell down and, while trying to get up again, fell on top of me. Two women ran out of a nearby house, and when I got up they helped me inside. I adore the wisdom of God: In this house were three persons who had started to run well, but Satan had hindered them. Now, however, they determined to start out again, and not one of them has

---

[154] I.e., upper-class.

looked back since. In spite of this delay, I got to Kingswood by 2 p.m.

The words God enabled me to speak there and later at Bristol (and I must express myself this way, because I dare not ascribe it to my own wisdom) were like a hammer and a flame. And we received the same blessing at the fellowship meeting but even in greater measure at the love-feast following it. I don't remember anything like it for many months [before this]: Loud voices were heard from one end of the assembly to the other, not of grief but of overflowing joy and love. "Oh, continue to give your lovingkindness to those who know you, and your mercy to those who have true hearts!" …

Fri. NOVEMBER 20. I began reading Mr. Laval's *History of the Reformed Churches in France,* full of the most amazing examples of men's wickedness and of God's goodness and power. About noon the next day, I took a stagecoach as far as Kingswood School, where one of the teachers lay near death (or so we thought) having received no benefit from all the medicines she'd taken. We decided to try one more remedy: We poured out our souls in prayer to God. From that hour she began to regain strength and in a few days was out of danger.

Sun. 22.— Not being allowed to go to church yet,[155] I took communion at home. I was advised to stay home for a while longer, but didn't feel it was necessary, and so on Monday the 23rd I went to the New Room, where we praised God for all his mercies. I explained the text systematically for about an hour, without feeling at all faint or weary, on "What shall I render to the LORD for all his benefits to me? I will lift up the cup of salvation and call on the name of the LORD" [Psalm 116:12].

I preached once every day this week, and it didn't give me any problems.

Sun. 29.—I thought I might be up to doing more, so I preached both at Kingswood and at Bristol. Afterwards I spent nearly an hour with the fellowship, and about two hours at the love-feast, but my body couldn't keep pace with my mind yet. I had another bout of

---

[155] Wesley was sick and under doctor's orders to rest.

fever the next day, which didn't last long, and I slowly continued to regain my strength ...

Wed. DECEMBER 9.—God humbled us on the evening [of the 8th] by our losing more than 30 of our little company. I was obligated to exclude them as no longer honoring the gospel of Christ. I thought it best to openly state their names along with the reasons they were excluded. Then we all cried out to God that this might be for their edification and not their destruction.[156]

Fri. 11.—I went to Bath ... I returned to Bristol the next day, and that evening a man asked to talk to me. I could tell he was totally confused, and for a while he couldn't speak. Finally he said, "It was I who interrupted you at the New Room on Monday. I haven't had any rest since, day or night, and couldn't have any till I'd spoken to you. I hope you'll forgive me, and that it will be a warning to me all the days of my life." ...

Sun. 20.—I preached once more at Bristol on "Little children, keep yourselves from idols" [1 John 5:21]. Immediately after that, I forced myself to part from those with whom my heart was now more united than ever, and I believe their hearts were the same as mine. Oh, what poor words are those: "You diminish the reverence and respect which people owe to their pastors."[157] Love is all in all, and all who are alive to God must pay this to every true pastor. Whenever a flock is duly fed with the pure milk of the Word, they will be ready (if it were possible) to pluck out their eyes and give them to those that are over them in the Lord.

Mon. 21.—I took the stagecoach and on Wednesday came to London.

Thur. 24.—I found that it was good for me to be here, especially while I preached in the evening. The fellowship met afterwards, and we could hardly separate, our hearts overflowing in love to each other ...

Thur. 31.—The unusual overflowing of peace and love that I felt to all led me to believe that some trial was at hand. At 3 p.m. my

---

[156] When Wesley expelled someone from his "society," it was almost always his hope that they would return after changing either their ways or their attitudes. He also didn't assume that someone leaving his fellowship was going to be damned.

[157] Apparently by physical expressions of affection.

fever came back, but since it wasn't so high, I was unwilling to break my word, and therefore at 4 p.m. I committed to the earth the body of one who had died in the Lord a few days before. Nor could I keep from exhorting the huge crowd that had gathered round her grave, to cry to God that they might die the death of the righteous and their end might be like hers. I then intended to lie down, but Sir John G. came [to my lodging] and sent word that he wanted to speak to me, so I went to him, and from him into the pulpit, knowing God could renew my strength. I preached as this woman, who was now with God, had requested, on the words that had refreshed her soul a little before she departed, after a long night of doubts and fears: "Your sun shall no more go down, nor your moon withdraw itself; for the LORD will be your everlasting light, and your days of mourning shall be ended" [Isa. 60:20] ...

1742

Fri. JANUARY 1.—After a night of quiet sleep, I woke up in a high fever but without any sickness, thirst, or pain. I agreed, however, to stay in bed on one condition: that everyone who wanted to do so would be allowed to speak with me. I believe 50 or 60 people did so today, and I felt no worse for this. In the evening I sent for all of the circles who were in the building that we might magnify our Lord together. As a close relative was with me when they came, I asked her later if she was offended. "Offended?" she said, "I wish I could always be here among you. I thought I was in heaven."

That night as well, by God's blessing, I slept well, to the amazement of those around me—the pharmacist in particular, who said he had never seen such a fever in his life. My temperature was clearly lower in the morning, but about 2 p.m. I had a higher fever than ever. Otherwise, I would have met with the circles. But the Lord's will is good ...

Mon. 4.—I woke up in perfect health ... and preached morning and evening every day for the rest of the week. On Saturday, while I was preaching at Long Lane, an ignorant mob lifted up their voices. I lit into them without delay.[158] Some pulled off their hats and shut

---

[158] Rebuking them for their ungodly behavior and language.

their mouths; the rest crept away, one after another. All who remained were quiet and attentive ...

Mon. 11.—Twice I went to Newgate Prison at the request of poor R.R., who lay there awaiting execution, but they refused to let me in. Receiving a short note from him the day he was to die, I asked Mr. Richards to try to get in, but he came back with another refusal.

It was over two years prior to this, lacking necessities and in distress, that [R.R.] appealed to me at Bristol for help. I took him in and used him temporarily writing for me and keeping my accounts. A little later, I gave him a position in the little school operated by our United Society. Many suspected him during that time, including his friend Gwillim Snowde,[159] but there was no clear proof of wrongdoing, so after three or four months they both quietly returned to London. But God wasn't deceived and they didn't escape from his hand. Gwillim Snowde was soon arrested for robbery and, when condemned, sent for me and confessed that what lay heaviest on his conscience was his having repaid us evil for good. I believe it was the desire of poor R., too, to tell me all he had done. But it was too late now; I wasn't allowed to see or speak with him. So he who earlier wouldn't receive the Word of God from my mouth now wanted what he couldn't get, and on Wednesday he was sacrificed to the justice of a long-offended God. Oh, consider this, you who now forget God and don't know the day of your visitation! ...

Thur. 21.—Once again I visited many who were sick, but found no fear either of pain or death among them. One of these, Mary Whittle, said, "I'll go to my Lord tomorrow; but before I go, he'll finish his work." The next day she lay quiet for about two hours, and then, opening her eyes, she cried out, "It's done! It's done! Christ lives in me! He lives in me!"—and died a moment later ...

Mon. 25.—While I was explaining at Long Lane, "The one who practices sin is of the devil" [1 John 3:8 NASB], his servants were outraged. They not only made all the noise they could, but violently shoved many people to and fro, hitting others and breaking down part of the building—even though, as I asked [our people] earlier, no one moved or answered them a word ... I then told them, "You'd

---

[159] See note above.

better stop acting like this. I've been ordered by the justice of the peace, who is God's servant in this matter, to inform him of those who break the laws of God and the king. And I'll have to do it if you keep this up; otherwise, I'd be taking part in your sin." After I said this, they behaved more outrageously than before. When this happened, I said, "Let three or four calm men take hold of the one in front, and turn him over to a constable so the law can take its course." They did so, and brought him into the building, cursing and blaspheming horribly. I asked five or six to go with him to Judge Copeland, to whom they told the bare facts. The judge immediately bound him over to the next sessions at Guildford.

I noticed that when this man was brought into the house, many of his buddies were shouting, "Richard Smith, Richard Smith!" who, as it seemed later, was one of their fiercest leaders. But Richard Smith didn't reply; he'd fallen into the hands of One higher than they; God had struck him to the heart. God did the same to a woman who was saying things not fit to be repeated and throwing whatever she could get her hands on; he caught her in the very act. She came into the house with Richard Smith, fell upon her knees before us all, and strongly exhorted him never to turn back, never to forget the mercy God had shown to his soul. Since that time, we never had any serious interruption or disturbance at Long Lane, even though we stopped prosecuting the case when the offender showed submission and promised better behavior ...

Mon. FEBRUARY 1.—I found, after excluding some who didn't walk according to the gospel, that about 1100 remained in our fellowship who are, I trust, of a more excellent spirit ...

Fri. 5.—I set out, and with some difficulty reached Chippenham on Saturday evening. The weather was so rough and the wind so boisterous that I had a hard time staying on my horse. On Sunday about noon I came to Kingswood, where there were many of our friends from Bath, Bristol, and Wales. Oh that we may always love one another with a pure heart fervently like this! ...

Mon. 15.—Many of us met to consider a suitable way to pay off our fellowship's debt, and finally we agreed: 1. that every member of the fellowship who could should contribute a penny[160] a week; 2. that the whole fellowship should be divided into little groups or classes, about twelve in each class, and; 3. that one person in each class should receive what the rest contributed and bring it in to the stewards each week ...

Sun. 28.—In the evening I set out for Wales ... [On Tuesday evening,] although weak and in pain, I explained at Fonmon how Jesus saves us from our sins. The next morning, at 8 a.m., I preached at Bolston, a little town four miles from Fonmon. From there I rode to Lantrissent and sent a message to the minister asking for the use of his church. His answer was that he would gladly do so, but the bishop had forbidden him. By what law? I haven't been convicted of heresy or any other crime. By what authority then am I now not allowed to preach? By sheer arbitrary power ...

Fri. MARCH 5.—I talked with a woman who often used to say, "I pray to God I never have this new faith. I hope I don't know my sins are forgiven until I'm about to die." But some weeks ago, as she was reading the Bible at home, the light broke in on her soul. She knew all her sins were blotted out and cried aloud, "My Lord and my God!" [John 20:28] ...

Wed. 10.—I was with a gentlewoman[161] whose illness has puzzled the most prominent physicians for many years. They couldn't explain it rationally or find any remedy for it. The simple fact is, she's been tormented by an evil spirit that pursues her day and night. Yes, you can try all your drugs again and again, but in the end it will plainly be seen that "this kind cannot be driven out by anything but prayer and fasting" [Mark 9:29].

Fri. 12.— ... Our Lord was gloriously present with us at the watch-night, so that my voice was lost in the cries of the people. After midnight, about 100 of us walked home together, singing and rejoicing and praising God ...

Sun. 21.—In the evening I rode to Marshfield, and on Tuesday afternoon came to London ...

---

[160] About $1.00 in 2020 USD.
[161] I.e., a woman of the upper class.

Thur. 25.—I picked out several earnest and sensible men to meet with me. I explained to them the great difficulty I'd had for a long time of knowing the people who wanted to be under my care. After lengthy discussion, they **all agreed there could be no better way to come to a certain and thorough knowledge of each person than to divide them into classes, like those at Bristol, under the supervision of those I could most trust. This is how our classes in London originated, for which I can never praise God enough** [my emphasis]. The extraordinary usefulness of this system has been more and more obvious ever since ...

Fri. APRIL 9.—We had our first watch-night in London. We usually choose for this solemn service the Friday night nearest the full moon, either before or after it, so those of the congregation who live at a distance can see their way home. The service begins at 8:30 p.m. and continues till a little after midnight. We've often found a special blessing at these times. Usually the congregation is deeply in awe, perhaps partly due to the silence of the night, but especially when we sing this concluding hymn:

> Hearken to the solemn voice!
> The awful midnight cry!
> Waiting souls, rejoice, rejoice,
> And feel the Bridegroom nigh.

Fri. 16.—Since it was Good Friday, I was asked to visit someone at Islington who was sick. There I found several old acquaintances who once loved me as the apple of their eye. After being with them just a little while, I was convinced that if I stayed just a week among them (unless the providence of God plainly called me to stay longer), I would be as still[162] as poor Mr. S. I felt their words thrilling through my veins, so soft, so pleasing to my flesh! It made it seem that our [Methodist] religion was heavy and coarse, not as delicate and refined as theirs. I wonder how any person of discernment (who doesn't have faith) can withstand them!

Fri. 23.—I spent a pleasant hour with Mr. Wh[itehead]. I believe he's sincere in all he says concerning his desire to join hands with all

---

[162] I.e., only meditating, as opposed to prayer, church attendance, and good deeds.

who love the Lord Jesus Christ. But if (as some want to persuade me) he's not, the loss is all on his side. I'm just as I was; I go on my way, whether he goes with me or stays behind ...

Mon. 26.—I visited a woman who was grieving as one without hope for her son who had turned back to wickedness. I advised her to wrestle with God for his soul. Two days later God brought the wandering sheep home, fully convinced of the error of his ways and determined to choose the better path ...

Sun. MAY 9.—I preached in Charles Square to the largest assembly I've ever seen there. Many of the lower-class people tried to interrupt me, but they found, after a while, that they wasted their efforts. A more serious woman was very angry at the listeners, as she later confessed, but she was quickly rebuked by a rock that hit her forehead and knocked her to the ground. Instantly her anger was gone and pure love filled her heart.

Wed. 12.—I waited with Mr. Whitefield to see the Archbishop of Canterbury, and again on Friday, and also to see the Bishop of London. I trust that if we're called to appear before princes we won't be ashamed.

Mon. 17.— ... On Thursday the 20th I set out. The next afternoon I stopped for a short while at Newport-Pagnell, and then rode on till I overtook a serious man, with whom I immediately fell into conversation. He soon let me know what his opinions were; therefore I said nothing to oppose them. But that didn't satisfy him. He was anxious to know if I held to the doctrine of the decrees[163] as he did," but I told him over and over," we'd better stick to practical things, lest we get angry at each another." And so we did for two miles, till he caught me unawares, and dragged me into the dispute before I realized it. He then grew hotter and hotter, and told me my heart was rotten, and he supposed I was one of John Wesley's followers." I told him, "No; I'm John Wesley himself." Upon which

Improvisum aspris veluti qui sentibus anguem pressit—[164]

---

[163] I.e., Calvin's doctrine of double predestination—of the elected and the damned.
[164] He stepped on the unforeseen just as (one would) a snake in rough thorn-bushes. (Translation by Anne Taylor)

he would gladly have simply run away. But since I had a better horse, I kept close to his side and tried to show him his heart till we came into the streets of Northampton ...

Tues. 25.—I set out early in the morning with John Taylor, who since then has moved to London, and on the evening of Wednesday the 26th I reached Birstal, six miles beyond Wakefield.

John Nelson had written to me some time earlier, but at that time I thought little of seeing him. Hearing he was at home, I sent for him to come to our inn. He did, then immediately carried me to his house and gave me an account of the strange way he had been led since we parted in London.

He had a good business there and a large income. But from the time he found peace with God, it was constantly on his mind, though he didn't know why, that he had to return to his hometown. He did so about Christmas of 1740. His relatives and friends soon began to ask what he thought of this new faith and whether he believed that anyone could really know that his sins were forgiven. John told them pointblank that this "new faith," as they called it, was the "old faith" of the gospel, and that he himself was as sure his sins were forgiven as he was that the sun shone. The word soon got around, and more people came to ask about these strange things. Some demanded that he prove the great truths which these questions naturally led him to mention. And so, without realizing it, he was led to quote, explain, compare, and apply several passages of Scripture. He did this, at first sitting in his house, till those gathered there increased so much that the house couldn't hold them. Then he stood at the door, which he had to do in the evening as soon as he came from work. God immediately set his seal to what was spoken, and several believed and therefore declared that God was merciful to them in their unrighteousness and had forgiven all their sins ...

Thur. 27.— ... We came to Newcastle about 6 p.m., and after a little refreshment walked into the town. I was surprised; I don't remember ever seeing so much drunkenness, cursing and swearing—even from the mouths of little children—in such a short time. Surely this place is ripe for him who did "not come to call the righteous but sinners to repentance" [Luke 5:32] ...

Sun. 30. At 7 a.m., I walked down to Sandgate, the poorest and most looked-down-upon part of the town. Standing at the end of the street with John Taylor, I began singing the 100th Psalm. Three or four people came out to see what was going on, and soon they increased to 400 or 500. I suppose there might have been 12- or 1500 before I finished preaching; to them I applied those solemn words, "He was wounded for our transgressions; he was crushed for our iniquities; upon him was the chastisement that brought us peace, and with his stripes we are healed" [Isaiah 53:5].

When I finished, I noticed that the people stood staring at me with open mouths and great astonishment. I told them, "If you want to know who I am, my name is John Wesley. At 5 p.m., with God's help, I plan to preach here again."

At 5 p.m., the hill I planned to preach on was covered from top to bottom. I never saw so many people together, even in Moorfields or at Kennington Common. I knew it was impossible for even half of them to hear, although my voice back then was strong and clear, and I stood where I could keep them all in my sight, since they were ranged on the side of the hill. The word of God which I set before them was, "I will heal their backsliding; I will love them freely" [Hosea 14:4]. After preaching, the people almost trampled me underfoot out of pure love and kindness. It took me a while to get out of the crowd. I then went back by a different way than by the one I came. But several reached our inn before me, and they urgently begged me to stay with them a few days, or at least one day more. But I couldn't agree to this, having given my word to be at Birstal, God willing, on Tuesday night ...

Sat. JUNE 5.—I rode horse,[165] heading for Epworth ... Since I hadn't been in Epworth for many years,[166] I went to an inn in the middle of the town, not knowing whether there would still be any there unashamed to acknowledge me as an acquaintance. But one of my father's old servants, with two or three poor women, soon recognized me. I asked her, "Do you know any in Epworth who earnestly want to be saved?" She answered, "I do, by the grace of

---

[165] Wesley's means of transportation unless stated otherwise.
[166] Epworth was Wesley's place of birth. His father Samuel had been rector there, and it remained the home of his mother and unmarried sisters.

God, and I know I am saved through faith." I asked, "Then do you have the peace of God? Do you know that he's forgiven your sins?" She replied, "Thank God, I do know it, and many here can say the same thing."

Sun. 6.—A little before the service began, I went to Mr. Romley, the curate, and offered to assist him either by preaching or reading prayers. But he didn't want my help. The church was completely full in the afternoon, since a rumor had spread that I was going to preach. But the sermon on "quench not the Spirit" didn't meet the expectations of many hearers. Mr. Romley told them that one of the most dangerous ways of quenching the Spirit was by enthusiasm, and he described the character of an enthusiast in a very flowery and oratorical manner. After the sermon John Taylor stood in the churchyard as the people were coming out and gave notice: "Since Mr. Wesley was not permitted to preach in the church, he intends to preach here at 6 p.m."

Therefore I came at 6 p.m. and found such an assembly as I believe Epworth never saw before. I stood near the east end of the church on my father's tombstone, and loudly proclaimed, "The kingdom of heaven is not a matter of eating and drinking but of righteousness and peace and joy in the Holy Spirit" [Rom. 14:17] ...

Wed. 9.—I rode over to a nearby town where I waited to see a justice of the peace, a man of integrity and understanding, before whom, I was informed, their angry neighbors had carried a whole wagonload of these "new heretics." But when the justice asked what they had done, there was complete silence, for those who had brought them had forgotten [to consider] this point. Finally one said, "Why they pretended to be better than other people, and besides, they prayed from morning to night." Mr. S. asked, "But have they done anything else?" "Yes, sir," said an old man; "An't please your worship, they have convarted my wife. Till she went among them she had such a tongue! And now she's as quiet as a lamb." "Carry them back, carry them back," replied the justice, "and let them convert all the foul-mouthed women in the town!" ...

Sat. 12.—I preached on the righteousness of the law and the righteousness of faith. While I was speaking, several dropped down as if dead, and among the rest such a sound was heard of sinners groaning for the righteousness of faith that it almost drowned out my voice. But many of them soon lifted up their heads with joy and gave thanks aloud, now sure that they had received their soul's desire, the forgiveness of their sins ...

Sun. 13.—At 7 a.m. I preached at Haxey on "What must I do to be saved?" [Acts 16:30]. From there I went to Wroote, where my father had served as rector for several years as well as at Epworth. Mr. Whitelamb offered me use of the church, and I preached the next morning on "Ask and it will be given to you" [Matt. 7:7] and in the afternoon on the difference between the righteousness of the law and the righteousness of faith. But the church couldn't hold all the people, many of whom came from far away—I trust not in vain.

At 6 p.m., planning to leave town the next morning, I preached for the last time in the Epworth churchyard, to a huge crowd that had gathered from all around, on the opening of our Lord's Sermon on the Mount.[167] I stayed with them for almost three hours, and even then we hardly knew how to part. Oh, let none think his labor of love is lost because he doesn't immediately see the fruit! My father toiled here almost forty years but saw little fruit of all his labor. I, too, took some pains among his people, and my strength, like his, seemed spent in vain. But now the fruit appeared: There were hardly any in the town to whom either my father or I had formerly ministered, where the seed sown so long ago didn't spring up now, bringing forth repentance and remission of sins ...

Thur. 17.—I began preaching about 5 a.m. on "the righteousness of faith" [Rom. 4:13], but halfway through my sermon I had to stop speaking because our hearts were so filled with God's love and our mouths with prayer and thanksgiving. Once we were satisfied with this, I went on to call sinners to the salvation ready to be revealed ...

One of the listeners sometime previously had been deeply convinced of her ungodliness, so much that she cried out day and night, "Lord save me, or I perish." The neighbors all agreed that she was stark raving mad, so her husband put her in the care of a physician who bled her a lot, gave her a strong emetic to make her vomit, and applied some chemicals that raised blisters. But when all

---

[167] I.e., the Beatitudes (Matthew 5:1–12).

this proved of no use, she was soon pronounced incurable. [Her husband] though, thought that he would speak to one more person, a woman who had done a lot of good in the neighborhood. When Mrs. Johnson came, she soon saw the true nature of the disease, having gone through the same thing herself. She ordered all the medicines to be thrown out and urged the patient to look to Jesus. The woman was able to do so by faith this evening, and he healed the brokenhearted ...

Sat. 26.—I was asked to visit Mr. Walker, "the pillar of the church" in this area. As soon as I came in, he attacked me with all he had for saying that people could know their sins were forgiven, and he brought a large book to prove me wrong. I asked if it was the Bible, and when he said no, I asked no more questions but quietly laid it down. This made him even angrier, upon which I considered it best to shake his hand and take my leave ...

Sun. 27.—I preached in Painswick at 7 a.m. on the spirit of fear and the spirit of adoption. I went to church at 10 a.m. and heard a remarkable sermon, asserting that we are justified by faith alone; but that this faith, which is the condition for justification, is the complex of all Christian virtues, including all holiness and good works in the very concept of faith ...

When the afternoon service was ended at Runwick, I stood and cried to a huge crowd of people, "To the one who does not work but trusts him who justifies the ungodly, his faith is counted as righteousness" [Rom. 4:5]. I ended the day on Hampton Common by explaining to a large congregation the essential difference between the righteousness of the law and the righteousness of faith ...

I left Bristol on the evening of Sunday, July the 18th, and on Tuesday came to London. I found my mother on the brink of eternity, but she had no doubt or fear or any wish except "to depart and to be with Christ" as soon as God called her.

Fri. JULY 13 [16]. About 3 p.m., I went to see my mother and found that her change was near. I sat down on the bed. She was in her final struggle, unable to speak, but I believe fully conscious. Her face was calm and serene and her eyes fixed upward while we commended her soul to God. From 3 to 4 p.m., the silver cord was loosening and the wheel breaking at the cistern [cf. Eccl. 12:6]. And then, without any struggle or sigh or groan, her soul was set free. We stood round the bed and fulfilled her last request, made shortly before losing her speech: "Children, as soon as I am released, sing a song of praise to God."

Sun. AUGUST 1.— ... For the benefit of those who are entrusted, as she was, with the care of a large family, I must add one more letter which she sent me many years ago:

> Dear Son,   July 24, 1732
>
> According to your wish, I have collected the main rules I kept in educating my family, which I now send you as they came back to mind, and if you think they may be useful to anyone, you may arrange them as you please.
>
> The children's lives were always regulated from birth, according to their capacity, as in dressing and undressing themselves, making their beds, etc. The first quarter of the day commonly passed in sleep.[168] After that, they were, if possible, laid in their cradles while still awake and rocked to sleep; and they were kept rocking until it was time for them to wake up. This was done to bring them to a regular procedure of sleeping; which at first was three hours in the morning, and three in the afternoon; afterwards two hours [each, morning and evening, and so on], till they needed none at all.
>
> When they became a year old, and some even earlier, they were taught to fear the rod and to cry softly, which spared them much of the correction they might otherwise have had, and that most disgusting noise of children crying was rarely heard in the house. Instead, the family usually lived in as much quietness as if there hadn't been a child among them.
>
> As soon as they had grown strong enough, they were limited to three meals a day. At dinner their little table and chairs were set next to ours where they could be supervised; and they were allowed to eat and drink as much small-beer[169] as they wanted, but not to ask for anything aloud. If they did want something, they would whisper to the maid waiting on them, who then came and spoke to me. As soon as they could handle a knife and fork, they were seated at our table. They were never allowed to choose their food but always made to eat whatever the family provided.

---

[168] Six to nine a.m.?
[169] I.e., diluted beer.

Mornings they ... always had soft or liquid food, and sometimes at nights. But whatever they had, at those meals they were never allowed to eat more than one dish, and of that a small-enough portion. Drinking or eating between meals was never allowed except in case of sickness, which seldom occurred. Nor were they permitted to go to the kitchen to ask any thing of the servants when they were at meals. If we knew that they did, they were certainly whipped and the servants severely reprimanded.

At six, as soon as family prayer was over, they had their supper; at seven, the maid washed them and, beginning with the youngest, she undressed and got them all to bed by eight. At that time she left them in their separate rooms awake; for in our house I didn't allow anyone to sit with a child until it fell asleep.

They were used to eating and drinking what was given to them, so that when any of them was sick it wasn't difficult to make them take the most unpleasant medicine, for they dared not refuse it, though some of them would immediately throw it up. I mention this to show that a person may be taught to take anything, even if their stomach rejects it ...

I insist on conquering the will of children early in life, because this is the only strong and rational foundation of a religious education, without which both precept and example will be ineffective. But when this is thoroughly done, children are capable of being governed by the reason and faith of their parents until their own understanding comes to maturity and the principles of religion have taken root in their minds ...

The children of this family were taught the Lord's Prayer as soon as they could speak, which they were made to say on rising and at bedtime regularly; to which, as they grew bigger, they added a short prayer for their parents and some church prayers, a short creed and some portion of Scripture as their memories could bear.

They were very early made to distinguish the Sabbath from other days, before they could well speak or walk. As soon as this was done, they were taught to be still during family prayers and to ask a blessing immediately afterwards, which they used to do by signs before they could kneel or speak.

They were quickly made to understand that they would get nothing they cried for, and taught to speak properly for what they wanted. They weren't allowed to ask even the lowest servant for anything without saying, "Please give me such and such," and the servant was scolded if she ever let them omit that word "please."

Taking God's name in vain, cursing and swearing, profanity, obscenity, rude and ugly names, were never heard among them. Nor were they ever permitted to call each other by their proper names, without adding "brother" or "sister." ...

During the six hours of school, loud talking and playing weren't allowed; all the children were kept at their work. It is almost incredible what a child can be taught in three months by real diligence, if they have reasonable ability and good health. Every one of them except Kezzy could read better in that time than most women ever do.

Getting up from their seats or leaving the room wasn't permitted unless for a good reason, and running into the yard, garden, or street, without permission was treated as a capital offense ...

We had some other bylaws which slipped my memory earlier, or else I would have inserted them in their proper place. I mention them here because I think they are useful:

1. We noticed that cowardice and fear of punishment often lead children to lie; then it becomes a habit they can't break. To prevent this, we made it a law that those accused of something of which they were guilty, if they would honestly confess it and promise to change, they wouldn't be whipped. This rule prevented a great deal of lying ...

2. No sinful action, such as lying, playing at church or on the Lord's day, disobedience, quarrelling, etc., would ever pass unpunished.

3. No child should ever be scolded or whipped twice for the same fault; and if they reformed, they should never be blamed for it afterwards.

4. Every notable act of obedience, especially when it went against their own inclinations, should always be praised and frequently rewarded, according to the situation ...

Wed. 11.—[Samuel Prig] sent me a note demanding payment of 100 pounds,[170] which he had loaned me about a year before to pay the workmen at the Foundry. On Friday morning at 8 a.m. he came and said that he wanted his money, and couldn't wait any longer. I told him that I would try to borrow it and asked him to come in the evening, but he said he couldn't stay that long and must have it at 12 noon. I didn't know where to get it, but between 9 and 10 a.m., a man came and offered me the use of 100 pounds for a year—after

---

[170] About $23,500 in 2020 USD.

two others had already come making the same offer! I accepted the bank note which one of them brought and saw that God is over all! ...

Sat. SEPTEMBER 3 [4].—I was urgently asked to visit a poor murderer in Newgate who was very troubled both in body and soul ... I did go and found, surprisingly, that all the doors were now open to me. I exhorted the sick criminal to cry to God with all his might for grace to repent and believe the gospel. It wasn't long before the rest of the felons flocked round, to whom I spoke strong words concerning the Friend of sinners, which they received with as much amazement as if it had been a voice from heaven. When I went down into the common hall (as I think they called it), one of the prisoners there asked me a question, which gave me the opportunity to speak with them also. More and more kept running together as I declared that God wasn't willing for any to perish, but that all should come to repentance [cf. 2 Pet. 3:9] ...

Sun. 12.—I was asked to preach in an open place, commonly called the Great Gardens, lying between Whitechapel and Coverlet's Fields, where I found a huge crowd had gathered. Aware that most of them were poorly acquainted with the things of God, I called upon them in the words of our Lord, "Repent, and believe the gospel!" [Mark 1:15]. Many savages among the people tried hard to disturb those who were of a better mind. They tried to drive a herd of cows in among them, but the dumb beasts were wiser than their masters. They then showered us with stones, one of which struck me right between the eyes, but I felt no pain at all, and when I had wiped away the blood, I went on testifying with a loud voice that God has given, to those who believe, "not the spirit of fear, but of power and love and of a sound mind" [2 Tim. 1:7]. And by the spirit that now was evident in the whole assembly, I clearly saw what a blessing it is when it is given to us to suffer for his name's sake, even in the least degree ...

Tues. 28.— ... A little before noon I came to Windsor. I was soon told that many rowdy people had formed a conspiracy, declaring again and again that there would be no preaching there that day. In order to make sure of this, they'd provided enough gunpowder and other things several days earlier. But since they passed by Burnham Fair on the way, they agreed to go there first and have some fun. So they went there and threw some of their firecrackers upon their brother mob at Burnham, but these, not being Methodists, didn't take it kindly, turned against them, and chased them. They took refuge in a house. But that wasn't good enough, for those outside soon forced their way in and grabbed as many as they could find, and these, when formal complaint was made, were sent to jail. The rest ran away, so that when I came no one hindered or interrupted us. In the evening I came to London. I planned to spend two weeks there and then return to Bristol …

Mon. OCTOBER 11.—Since Mr. Richards got sick, I delayed my journey. He was much better on Tuesday, so I set out the next morning, and before 7 p.m. reached the midway house, four miles this side of Hungerford.

I now learned that it was good that I didn't start out on Monday to be at Bristol on Tuesday night, as I usually did, for all the travelers who went that way on Tuesday were robbed. But on Thursday the road was clear, so I came safe to Kingswood in the afternoon and in the evening preached at Bristol …

Wed. NOVEMBER 3.—Two so-called prophets asked to speak with me. They told me they had a message for me from God, which was that very soon I would be born again. One of them added that they would stay in the building till it was done unless I made them leave. I answered solemnly, "I won't make you leave," and led them down into the fellowship room. It was rather cold, and they had nothing to eat or drink. However they sat from morning till evening. They then slipped quietly away, and I haven't heard anything from them since …

Thur. 18.—I couldn't help but notice the different ways it pleases God to work in different places. The grace of God flows here in a wider stream than it did at first either at Bristol or Kingswood. But it doesn't sink as deeply here as it did there. Few are thoroughly convicted of sin, and hardly any can witness that the Lamb of God has taken away their sins …

Thur. 25.— … I never saw a work of God in any other place [as the Hospital in London], so evenly and gradually advancing; it keeps rising step by step. Not as much seems to be accomplished at any one time as has often occurred at Bristol or London, but something happens every time. It's the same with individual souls. I saw none with that triumphant faith which has been so common in other places. But the believers go forward, calm and steady. Let God do what seems good to him …

Wed. DECEMBER 1.—We had several sites offered on which to build a preaching-room[171] for the fellowship, but none suited us, and perhaps there was providence in our not finding any as yet, for this kept me at Newcastle, whether I wanted to stay or not.

Sat. 4.— … Today a gentleman called and offered me a piece of ground. On Monday a contract was drawn up by which he agreed to put me into possession on Thursday, upon payment of 30 pounds.[172]

Tues. 7.—I was so sick in the morning that I had to send for Mr. Williams to come to the preaching-room. He afterwards went to Mr. Stephenson, a merchant in the town, who had an easement through the ground we intended to buy. I was willing to purchase it. Mr. Stephenson told him, "Sir, I don't want cash. But if Mr. Wesley wants ground, he can have a piece of my garden adjoining the lot you mention. I give my word. For 40 pounds[173] he can have a piece 16 yards wide and 30 long."

Wed. 8.—Mr. Stephenson and I signed a contract, and I took possession of the ground. But I couldn't rightly go back on my agreement with Mr. Riddle. So I agreed to buy his ground at the same time. Altogether our parcel is 40 yards long. We planned to build the preaching-house in the middle, leaving room for a small courtyard in front and a little garden behind the building …

Mon. 13.—I moved into a lodging adjacent to the ground where we were preparing to build. But the hard freeze forced us to delay the work. I never felt such intense cold before. In a room where a constant fire was kept burning, even though my desk was within a yard of the chimney, I couldn't write continuously for a quarter-hour without my hands becoming numb …

---

[171] Wesley did not call his preaching-rooms "churches," because the sacraments weren't administered in them, and he didn't intend them to be rivals to the Church of England. This changed at the end of his career.
[172] About $7000 in 2020 USD.
[173] $9400 in 2020 USD.

Mon. 20.—We laid the first stone of the house. Many came from all around to see it, but no one scoffed or interrupted while we praised God and prayed that he would prosper the work of our hands. Three or four times in the evening I was forced to interrupt my preaching so we could pray and give thanks to God …

Thur. 23.—It being estimated that such a building as we planned couldn't be finished for less than 700 pounds,[174] many were confident it would never be finished at all, and others that I wouldn't live to see it roofed. I thought differently, not doubting that, since it had been started for God's sake, he would provide what was needed to finish it.

Sat. 25.—[Christmas.] [*A member is gravely ill.*]The physician told me that he'd done all he could and that Mr. Meyrick couldn't live through the night. I went upstairs and found the people around him, all crying. His legs were cold and, it seemed, dead already. We all knelt down and called on God with strong cries and tears. [Mr. Meyrick] opened his eyes and called for me, and from that hour continued to regain strength until he was restored to perfect health. I'm still waiting for someone to either disprove this fact or account for it rationally.

Sun. 26.—From these words, " Sing we merrily unto God our strength: make a cheerful noise unto the God of Jacob" [Psalm 81:1, Wesley], I used the occasion to point out the usual way of keeping these days "holy" in honor of the birth of our Lord; namely, by gluttony and drunkenness, by pagan—and worse than pagan—amusements (with what always goes with them: passion and strife, cursing, swearing, and blasphemy), and by dancing and card-playing, equally conducive to the glory of God. I then described the right way of keeping a day holy to the Lord: by special prayer, public and private; by thanksgiving; by hearing, reading, and meditating on his Word, and by talking of all his wondrous works …

Wed. 29.—After preaching as usual in the square, I went on horseback to Tanfield. More than once the wind nearly blew me off my horse. However at 3 p.m. I reached the Leigh, and explained to a crowd of people the salvation that is through faith. Afterwards I met

---

[174] $165,000 in 2020 USD.

the fellowship in a large upper room, which rocked back and forth with the violence of the storm. But indoors all was calm, and we rejoiced together in hope of a kingdom which can't be moved. ...

1743

Sat. JANUARY 1. ... In the evening I reached Epworth.

Sun. 2.—At 5 a.m. I preached on "So it is with everyone who is born of the Spirit" [John 3:8]. About 8 a.m. I stood on my father's tomb and preached on Hebrews 8:11. Many from the nearby towns asked if it wouldn't be good, since it was communion Sunday, for them to receive it? I told them, "By all means; but it would be more respectful first to ask permission of Mr. Romley, the curate." One man did so, speaking for the rest, to whom the curate replied, "Please tell Mr. Wesley that I won't serve him communion, because he's unfit."

How wise is our God! There couldn't have been any place under heaven more suitable for this first to happen to me than at my father's home, my birthplace, and the very place where, "according to the strictest party of our religion," I had so long "lived as a Pharisee"! [Acts 26:5]. It was also most fitting that he who thrust me away from the very table where I myself had so often distributed the bread of life should be one who owed all he was in this world to the tender love which my father had shown to his family, as well as to him personally ...

Mon. 24.—I preached at Bath ... Several of the upper class asked to stay for the fellowship meeting, where I explained the nature of inward religion, the words flowing through me faster than I could speak. One of them, a notorious unbeliever, hung over the seat in front of him in an indescribable posture, and when he went out, left a half-guinea[175] with Mary Naylor for the use of the poor.

The following days I spoke with each member of our fellowship in Kingswood. **I can't understand how any minister can hope ever to render his account with joy**[176] **unless, as Ignatius**[177]

---

[175] Worth about $120 in 2020 USD.
[176] Cf. Hebrews 13:17.
[177] Ignatius of Antioch was an apostolic father; i.e., he personally knew one of the twelve apostles: John.

advises, he "knows all his flock by name [my emphasis]; not overlooking the men servants and maid servants" …

Tues. MARCH 1. I preached at two in Pelton, five miles south of Newcastle. A crowd of people had gathered from all the nearby towns, and (which gave me even more joy) from all the nearby coalmines. Riding home, I noticed a little village called Chowden, which they told me consisted solely of coalminers. I decided to preach there as soon as possible; for they are sinners and need repentance.

Sun. 6.—In the fellowship meeting, I read aloud the rules that all our members are to follow, and asked all to seriously consider whether or not they were willing to abide by them. I knew very well that this would unsettle many of them and, therefore, on Monday the 7th I began visiting the classes again, lest "those who are lame should not altogether miss the way" [cf. Heb. 12:13] …

Sun. 13.—I went in the morning to speak individually with the members of our fellowship at Tanfield. From the terrible examples I found here, and indeed in all parts of England, I am more and more convinced that the devil himself wants nothing more than this: that the people of any location should be half awakened and then left to themselves to fall asleep again. Therefore, I resolve, by the grace of God, not to strike a single blow anywhere if I can't follow through on that blow …

Thur. 17.—As I was preaching at Pelton, one of the old coalminers, not much accustomed to things of this kind, in the middle of the sermon began shouting with all his might for pure satisfaction and with a joyful heart. But their usual show of approval, which somewhat surprised me at first, was slapping me on the back …

Mon. 28.—I was amazed to find it to be plain fact, which before I couldn't believe, that three of the dissenting ministers … had agreed to exclude all those from Holy Communion who would't stop listening to us. Mr. A. publicly declared that we were all Catholics and that our doctrine was pure Catholicism. And Mr. B., at the conclusion of a series of sermons which he preached expressly against us, went even one step further; for after he confessed that "many texts in the Bible are for them," he added: "But you should pay no mind to those texts, for the Catholics have put them in!" ...

Fri. APRIL 1.—Being Good Friday, I very much wanted to visit a little village called Placey, about 10 marked miles north of Newcastle. It's inhabited solely by coalminers, who've always been foremost in ignorance and wickedness in every way. Their grand assembly used to be on the Lord's Day, on which men, women, and children met together to dance, fight, curse, and swear, and play at chuck, ball, span-farthing, or whatever came to hand. I felt great compassion for these poor creatures from the time I first heard of them, and even more so because everyone seemed to despair of them. Between 7 and 8 a.m. I set out with John Heally, my guide. The north wind, unusually strong, drove the sleet in our face, which froze as it fell and soon crusted over our faces. When we came to Placey, we could hardly stand up. As soon as we had partially recovered, I went into the town square and declared him who "was wounded for our transgressions; he was crushed for our iniquities" [Isa. 53:5].

The poor sinners quickly gathered together and gave close attention to the things I said. In the afternoon, in spite of the wind and snow, they did the same, as I begged them to receive him for their King; to "repent and believe in the gospel" [Mark 1:15] ...

Fri. 22.—I rode to Painswick, and on Saturday the 23rd, through heavy rain, to Bristol.

I now had a week of rest and peace, which refreshed both my soul and body. Sunday, May the 1st, I had opportunity to receive the Lord's Supper at St. James, our parish church. We had another refreshing hour in the afternoon as I explained: "This is the covenant that I will make with the house of Israel after those days, declares the LORD: I will put my law within them, and I will write it on their hearts. And I will be their God, and they shall be my people" [Jer. 31:33].

Tues. MAY 3.—I set out for Wales, accompanied by one of my Oxford students. That night we could go no farther than the Bull, five Welsh miles beyond Abergavenny. The next morning we came to Builth just as the church prayers began. Mr. Phillips, the rector of Maesmennys, who had invited me to come, soon recognized me, and we began a friendship which I trust will never end. I preached standing on a tomb at the east end of the church at 4 p.m., and again at 7 p.m. Mr. Gwynne and Mr. Prothero (justices of the peace) stood on either side of me, and all the people in front of us, catching every word with serious and eager attention.

Tues. 17.—My brother set out for Cornwall where, according to the accounts we had received, many who previously neither feared God nor regarded persons began to inquire what they must do to be saved. But the same lack of prudence which had given rise to all the disturbances in Staffordshire had broken out here too and turned many of our friends into bitter and implacable enemies. Violent persecution was a natural consequence of this, but the power of God prevailed over all …

Sun. 29.—Being Trinity Sunday, I began officiating at the chapel in West Street near the Seven Dials, on which, by a strange series of providences, we have a lease for several years. I preached on the Gospel for the day, part of the third chapter of St. John, and afterwards administered the Lord's Supper to several hundred communicants. I was a little afraid at first that my strength wouldn't be sufficient for the business of the day when a service of five hours (from 10 a.m. to 3 p.m.) was added to my usual activities. But I truly believe God tended to that, and those who want to call it "enthusiasm" may do so. I preached at the Great Gardens at 5 p.m. to an enormous gathering on "You must be born again" [John 3:7]. Then the leaders met (who filled in for me whenever I wasn't speaking in public), and after them the circles. At 10 p.m. I wasn't as tired as I was at 6 a.m.

The following week I spent visiting members of our fellowship. On Sunday June the 5th, the service at the chapel lasted till nearly 4 p.m., so I found it necessary, for the time being, to divide the communicants into three groups so we won't have over 600 at once.

Wed. JUNE 8.—I ended my round of visiting, throughout which I found great cause to bless God, as so few out of 1950 souls had drawn back to perdition.[178]

---

[178] I.e., final damnation—not because they left Wesley's fellowship, but because he felt these were returning to lives of sin and unbelief.

VOLUME 1: 1730-1746

Sat. 18.—I received a full account of the terrible riots which had occurred in Staffordshire. I wasn't surprised at all, nor would I have wondered if, after the advices they had so often heard from the pulpit as well as from the bishop's chair, the zealous high churchmen had risen up and cut all who were called Methodists to pieces.

Mon. 20.—Determined to help them as much as I could, I set out early in the morning, and after preaching at Wycombe about noon, in the evening came to Oxford. Tuesday the 21st we rode to Birmingham, and on the morning of Wednesday the 22nd to Francis Ward's at Wednesbury.

Although I knew that everything done here was contrary both to law and to justice and mercy, still I didn't know how to advise those who were suffering or how to obtain redress for them. At that time, I wasn't well-acquainted with the process of English law, having had reservations about it for a long time.[179] But since many of these reservations had now been taken away, I thought it best to find out if the laws of the land could be of any help. I therefore rode over to the lawyer, Littleton, at Tamworth, who assured us, "You might have an easy remedy, if you resolutely prosecute, in the manner the law directs, those rebels against God and the king" ...

Mon. JULY 18.—I set out from Newcastle with John Downes of Horseley. We rode four hours to Ferry Hill, about 20 marked miles. After resting there an hour, we rode on at a gentle pace, and at 2 p.m. came to Darlington. It seemed to me that my horse wasn't well, and John thought the same of his, though they were both young and had been well the day before. We ordered the stableman to find a horse doctor,[180] which he did right away, but before the men could find out what was wrong, both horses lay down and died.

I rented a horse to go to Sandhutton and rode on, asking John Downes to follow me. From there I rode to Boroughbridge on Tuesday morning, and then walked on to Leeds ...

Sat. AUGUST 6.—A suitable chapel was offered to me in Snow's Fields, on the other side of the water. It seems to have been

---

[179] Perhaps this was a "separation of church and state issue with Wesley"; he felt he shouldn't call on the legal authorities to intervene in persecutions.
[180] Wesley "farrier," one who shoes horses, but in that period also a horse veterinarian.

built on purpose by a poor erring Arian[181] to defend and spread her wrong belief. But the wisdom of God brought that plan to nothing and ordered, by his overruling providence, that it should not be used to crucify the Son of God afresh, but to call all to believe on his name.

Mon. 22.— ... Before reaching Kensington, I found my mare had lost a shoe. This gave me the opportunity of talking personally, for nearly half an hour, both to the blacksmith and his servant. I mention these little circumstances to show how easy it is to redeem every bit of time, if I may put it this way, when we feel any love to those souls for whom Christ died.

Tues. 23.—I came to Kingswood in the afternoon, and in the evening preached at Bristol.

Wed. 24.— ... For some time I had had a strong desire to join forces with Mr. Whitefield as far as possible and to put an end to needless disputation, so I wrote down my views as clearly, as I could express them, in the following words:

> There are three points in dispute: 1. Unconditional Election. 2. Irresistible Grace. 3. Final Perseverance.[182]
>
> With regard to the first, Unconditional Election, I believe that God, before the foundation of the world, unconditionally chose certain persons to do certain works, such as Paul to preach the gospel; that he has unconditionally chosen some nations to receive special privileges, the Jewish people in particular; that he has unconditionally chosen some nations to hear the gospel, such as England and Scotland now, and many others in past ages; that he has unconditionally chosen some persons to many special advantages, both with regard to worldly and spiritual things.
>
> And I do not deny, though I cannot prove it to be so, that he has unconditionally elected some persons to eternal glory.
>
> But I cannot believe that all those who are not thus elected to glory must perish everlastingly or that there is one soul on earth who will never have a possibility of escaping eternal damnation.

---

[181] I.e., a follower of Arius, an ancient heretic who taught that the Son was not of the same substance as the Father, therefore not fully God.

[182] These are the three key points in which Wesley differed with predestinarians, just as earlier he listed his differences with the Moravians (antinomians).

VOLUME 1: 1730-1746

With regard to the second, Irresistible Grace, I believe that the grace which brings faith, and thereby salvation, into the soul, is irresistible at that moment; that most believers may remember some time when God did irresistibly convict them of sin; that most believers do at some other times find God irresistibly acting upon their souls.

Yet I believe, that the grace of God, both before and after those moments, may be and has been resisted, and that in general it does not act irresistibly; rather we may comply with it or not. And I do not deny that in some souls the grace of God is irresistible to the point that they cannot but believe and finally be saved.

But I cannot believe that all those must be damned in whom it does not irresistibly work like this, or that there is one soul on earth who has not and never had any other grace than such as does in fact increase his damnation, and was designed of God so to do.

With regard to the third, Final Perseverance, I am inclined to believe that there is a state attainable in this life, from which a man cannot finally fall. And when he has attained this, he can say, "Old things are passed away: all things in me are become new." ...

Sun. 28.—... From the church I went to the Castle [Prison], where some thought half the adults in the city had gathered. It was an awesome sight, so huge a gathering in that solemn amphitheater! They were all silent and still while I fully explained and drove home that glorious truth, "Happy are they whose lawless deeds are forgiven, and whose sins are covered" [Rom. 4:7].

From there I went to visit poor Mr. V., the clergyman, lying under a death sentence. For some time he had pretended to be crazy, but I soon stopped his play-acting, and he seemed to have plenty of sense when angry. I planned to pin him into a corner right then, but two meddlesome and insolent gentlemen forced their way into the room so that I could say no more and had to leave him in their hands.

The young man who was to die the next day was of quite another spirit. He appeared deeply touched as we spoke and even more so during our prayer. And no sooner were we gone than he broke out into a bitter cry. Who knows but he might be heard by the One who made him? ...

Sat. SEPTEMBER 3.—I rode to a place called Three-Cornered Down, nine or ten miles east of St. Ives, where we found 200 or 300 tin-miners, who had been waiting for us for some time ... A man who lived close by invited us to lodge at his house and escorted us back to the village green in the morning. We arrived there just as the day dawned. I made strong application of those gracious words, "I will heal their backsliding, I will love them freely" [Hosea 14:4], to 500 or 600 serious people ...

Fri. 9.—I rode 10 or 12 miles southeast of St. Ives, aiming for St. Hilary Downs. I found the downs but no gathering—neither man, woman, or child. But by the time I had put on my gown and cassock, about 100 assembled, to whom I earnestly called "to repent and believe the gospel." And if just one heard, it was worth all the effort ...

Sat. 10.— ... There were prayers at St. Just in the afternoon, which didn't end till 4 p.m. I then preached at the Cross[183] to, I believe, 1000 people, all who behaved in a quiet and serious manner. At 6 p.m. I preached at Sennan, near Land's End, and set a time for the little assembly, mostly old, gray-headed men, to meet me again at 5 a.m. But on Sunday the 11th many of them gathered between 3 and 4 a.m. So between 4 and 5 a.m. we began praising God, and I fully explained and applied "I will heal their backslidings; I will love them freely" [Hosea 14:4] ...

Between 8 and 9 a.m. I preached at St. Just, on the level green near the town, to the largest gathering (so they told me) that had ever been seen in these parts. I called out, with all the authority of love, "Why will you die, O house of Israel?" [Ezek. 18:31]. The people trembled and were still. I hadn't known such an hour before in Cornwall.

Soon after 1 p.m. we had a similar gathering on the north side of Morva Church. The Spirit of the great King was in our midst, and I was filled both with substance and words, even more so than at St. Just. To you, Lord, I credit my strength ...

Mon. 12.—I preached at 1 p.m. on Trezuthan Downs, and in the evening at St. Ives. Such fear of God fell on us while I was speaking that I could hardly utter a word, but most of all this was during

---

[183] A monumental cross in the town marketplace, common in English towns at that time.

prayer, when I was carried along in the Spirit as hardly ever before in my life.

For some time I'd had a great longing to go and proclaim the love of God our Savior, if just for one day, in the Isles of Scilly, and occasionally I'd mentioned this to a few people. This evening three of our brethren came and offered to take me there if I could get the mayor's boat, which they said was the best sailing vessel of any in the town. I sent him a note, and he immediately let me borrow it. So the next morning, Tuesday the 13th, John Nelson, Mr. Shepherd, and I, with three other men and a pilot, sailed from St. Ives. It surprised me that we were trying to go fifteen leagues[184] in a fishing boat on the high sea, especially when the waves began to swell and mount up higher than our heads. But I called to my companions, and we all joined together in singing heartily and with a good courage,

> When passing through the wat'ry deep,
> I ask in faith His promis'd aid,
> The waves an awful distance keep,
> And shrink from my devoted head.
> Fearless their violence I dare:
> They cannot harm; for God is here.

About 1:30 p.m. we landed on St. Mary's, the main inhabited island …

We immediately called on the governor with the usual gift, a newspaper. I offered him a copy of my *Earnest Appeal* as well. The rector not being willing for me to use the church, I preached at 6 p.m. on the street to almost the whole town, plus many soldiers, sailors, and workmen, on "Why will you die, O house of Israel?" [Ezek. 18:31]. It was such a blessed time that I could hardly come to a conclusion. After the sermon I gave them some little books and hymnals, which they were so eager to receive that they nearly tore both them and me to pieces …

Fri. 16.— … In the evening, as I preached at St. Ives, Satan began fighting for his kingdom. The rabble of the town burst into the hall and made a great disturbance, yelling and hitting whoever stood

---

[184] A nautical mile is about 3½ land miles; so here a little over 50 miles.

in their way, as though possessed by Legion himself.[185] I tried to persuade our people to stand still, but some were so zealous and others so afraid that they didn't listen. Finding the uproar to be increasing, I went into the middle and brought the leader of the mob up with me to the desk.[186] I took just one blow to the side of the head, after which we reasoned with him until he grew more and more gentle, and finally tried to quiet his comrades ...

Tues. 20.— ... We reached Gwenap a little before six, and found the plain covered from end to end. Some estimated there were 10,000 people, to whom I preached Christ our "wisdom, righteousness, sanctification, and redemption" [1 Cor. 1:30]. I couldn't finish until it was so dark that we could hardly see each other, and those on all sides paid the closest attention, none speaking, stirring, or even looking at those beside them. Surely here, though in a temple not made with hands, God was "worshiped in the beauty of holiness!" [cf. Psalm 29:2].

One of those present was Mr. P., once our violent opponent. Before the sermon began, he whispered to one of his friends, "Captain, stand beside me; don't leave me." He soon burst into a flood of tears, and right after that began sinking down. His friend caught him and kept him from falling to the ground. Oh, may the Friend of sinners lift him up!

Wed. 21.—I was awakened between 3 and 4 a.m. by a large group of tin-miners. Afraid of being be too late, they had gathered around the house and were singing and praising God. At 5 a.m. I preached once more on "Believe on the Lord Jesus Christ and you will be saved" [Acts 16:31]. All of them eagerly devoured the Word. Oh, may it be health to their soul and marrow to their bones!

We rode to Launceston that day. On Thursday the 22nd, as we were riding through a village called Sticklepath, someone stopped me in the street and suddenly asked, "Isn't your name John Wesley?" Immediately two or three others came up and told me I had to stop there. So I did, and before we had spoken many words, we found we

---

[185] I.e., Satan; cf. Mark 5:9.
[186] Apparently, the desk on which Wesley stood to preach.

had kindred spirits. I learned they were called Quakers, but that didn't bother me, seeing that the love of God was in their hearts ...

Mon. 26.—I longed to speak plainly to a young man who went with us over the New Passage. For that purpose I rode with him three miles out of my way; but I couldn't get anything I said to stick. As soon as we parted, walking over Caerleon Bridge, he stumbled and almost fell. I caught him, and began to speak of God's care over us. Immediately I could see tears in his eyes, and he seemed to feel every word I said, so I spoke without sparing him. I did the same to a poor woman who led my horse over the bridge, to our landlord and his wife, and to one who came in from time to time, and they all seemed very appreciative ...

Sun. OCTOBER 2.—Afraid I wouldn't have enough strength to preach more than four times that day, I only spent half an hour in prayer with our fellowship in the morning. At 7 a.m. and in the evening I preached in the prison, at 11 a.m. in Wenvo Church, and in the afternoon in Porth Kerry Church, on "Repent, and believe the gospel" [Mark 1:15].

Mon. 3.—I returned to Bristol and spent several days examining and purging our fellowship, which still consisted (after many were dropped from membership) of more than 700 persons. The next week I examined the fellowship in Kingswood, in which I only found fault with a few things ...

Thur. 20.— ... At Francis Ward's in the afternoon, I was writing when a shout went up that "the mob" was "around the house." We prayed that God would scatter them, and it was so: One went this way and another that, so that, within half an hour, not a man was left. I told our brethren, "Now is the time for us to go," but they urged me strongly to stay. In order not to offend them, I sat down, though I could see what was about to happen. Before 5 p.m. the mob surrounded the house again in even greater numbers. They all shouted, "Bring out the preacher; we demand the preacher!" I asked a certain man to take their captain by the hand and bring him into the house. After exchanging a few sentences, the lion became a lamb. I asked him to go and bring one or two more of his angriest comrades. He brought in two who were ready to eat the very ground with rage, but in two minutes they were as calm as he. I then told them to make way so I could go out among the people. As soon as I was in their midst, I called for a chair to be brought and, standing up, I asked, "What do you want with me?" Some said, "We want you to go with us to the judge." I said, "I'll be glad to go." I then spoke a few words, which God applied to them, so that they shouted with all their might, "He's an honest gentleman, and we'll defend him with our lives!" I asked, "Should we go to the judge tonight or in the morning?" Most of them cried, "Tonight, tonight"; whereupon I led and 200 or 300 followed, the rest returning wherever they came from ...

In the meantime I got my strength and voice back, and broke out aloud into prayer. And now the man who had just been heading the mob turned around and said, "Sir, I will give my life for you. Follow me, and not one soul here will touch a hair of your head." Two or three of his comrades echoed his words and quickly closed in around me. At the same time the gentleman in the shop cried out, "It's a shame, it's a shame; let him go." ...

The people then, as if by common consent, fell back to the right and left; while these three or four men took me between them and carried me through them all. But on the bridge the mob rallied again; therefore we took a side path over the mill dam and then through the meadows, till a little before 10 p.m. God brought me safe to Wednesbury, having lost only one flap of my waistcoat and a little skin from one of my hands.

I never saw such a chain of providences before, so many convincing proofs that the hand of God is on every person and thing, overruling all as it seems good to him ...

Tues. 25.—A man in the town promised us the use of a large hall, but he was pressured to renege on this promise before preaching time. I then intended going to the market-cross, but the rain prevented this, so we were somewhat at a loss till we were offered a very suitable place by "a woman who was a sinner." There, at about 1 p.m., I declared him whom God has exalted to give repentance and remission of sins, and God so confirmed the word of his grace that I marveled that anyone could withstand him.

However, the prodigal held out till the evening, when I described the sins and faith of the woman who washed our Lord's feet with tears and wiped them with the hairs of her head [Luke

7:44]. She then was broken all to pieces—as, indeed, was almost the whole assembly—and afterwards she came to my lodging, crying out, "Oh, sir, what must I do to be saved?" By now I had learned her situation and said, "Flee for your life. Return immediately to your husband." She said, "But how can I do it? How can I go there? He is over a hundred miles away. I just received a letter from him, and he is at Newcastle-upon-Tyne." I told her, "I am heading to Newcastle in the morning; you can go with me. William Blow will let you ride behind him." And so he did. Glory be to the friend of sinners! He has plucked one more brand out of the fire. You poor sinner; you received a prophet in the name of a prophet, and he who sent him has found you ...

Fri. 28.—We rode with William Holmes, an Israelite indeed,[187] from Epworth to Syke-House. I preached there at 10 a.m. and hurried on to Leeds. From there I hoped, by setting out early in the morning, to reach Wensley-Dale before it was dark, but this simply was not going to happen. So at dusk, understanding we had five or six more miles to ride, I thought it best to find a guide. In less than an hour, it being very dark, I realized we were had missed the road: We were in a large meadow near a river and (it seemed to me) almost surrounded with water. I asked our guide, "Do you know where you are?" and he honestly answered, "No, I don't." So we rode on the best we could, till about 8 p.m. we came to a little house, where we were directed into a lane which led to Wensley.

Sun. 30.—Mr. Clayton read prayers, and I preached on "What must I do to be saved?" [Acts 16:30]. I showed in the plainest words that merely acting religiously would not bring us to heaven; that none could go there without inward holiness, which was only attained by faith. As I went back through the churchyard, many people of the parish were vigorously debating. But at length, one who was more learned than the rest brought them all firmly over to his opinion: "That [Mr. Wesley] was a Presbyterian Catholic"!

Mon. 31.—We set out early in the morning and in the evening came to Newcastle.

---

[187] Meaning one of true faith, without hypocrisy; cf. John 1:47.

Wed. NOVEMBER 2.—The following notice was posted around the town:

> For the benefit of Mr. Este.
> By the Edinburgh Company of Comedians, on Friday, Nov. 4, will be acted a comedy, called, "The Conscious Lovers": to which will be added, a Farce, called "Trick upon Trick; or, Methodism Displayed."

On Friday a huge crowd of spectators were assembled in the Moot Hall[188] to see this. They believed there were at least 1500 people present. Several hundred sat on rows of seats erected upon the stage. Soon after the comedians had begun the first act of the play, suddenly all those seats fell down, their supports breaking like rotten sticks. The people were thrown on top of each other, pitched about five feet forward, but not one of them hurt. After the rest of the spectators quieted down, the actors went on. In the middle of the second act, all the shilling[189] seats made a cracking sound, and sank down several inches. Loud noise and shrieking followed, and as many as could make it to the door left and didn't return. In spite of this, when the noise died down, the actors went on with the play. At the beginning of the third act, the entire stage suddenly sank about six inches. The actors fled from the stage, but after a little while they began again. At the end of the third act, all the sixpenny[190] seats fell to the ground without any warning. A cry arose on every side, the people supposing that many were crushed to pieces; but upon inquiry, not a single person (such was the mercy of God!) was either killed or dangerously hurt, 200 or 300 still remaining in the hall. Mr. Este (who was to act the Methodist) came upon the stage and told them, "In spite of this, he was determined to enact the farce." While he was speaking, the stage sank six inches more, on which he ran offstage in the utmost confusion, and the people ran out the door as fast as they could, no one bothering to look behind them.

Which is most surprising: that those players acted this farce the next week, or that some hundreds of people came again to see it?[191]

---

[188] An old term for a town meeting-hall.
[189] About $12 in 2020 USD.
[190] About $6 in 2020 USD.
[191] Wesley is always looking for the hand of God in events. Here he notes that no one was seriously hurt. He likely saw the farce against the Methodists as deserving some measure of divine judgment.

Sun. 6.—We had a sound, practical sermon at St. Nicholas Church in the morning, and another one at St. Andrew's in the afternoon. At 5 p.m. I preached to an open-hearted gathering on the Prodigal Son [Luke 15]. How many of these that were lost now have been found?

During the next week I tried to speak personally to all members of the fellowship. I found that their number had neither increased nor decreased, but that many had increased in the knowledge and love of God …

Thur. 17.—I preached at the Spen on "Christ Jesus our wisdom, righteousness, sanctification, and redemption" [1 Cor. 1:30]. I've seldom seen an audience so strongly moved since I first preached at Bristol: Men, women, and children wept and groaned and trembled violently; many were unable to stay within these bounds, crying with a loud and bitter cry. It was the same at the meeting of the fellowship, and likewise in the morning while I was showing the happiness of those "whose lawless deeds are forgiven, and whose sins are covered" [Rom. 4:7], following which I spoke with 12 or 14 of them individually and found good reason to believe that God had given them to "taste of the good word and of the powers of the age to come" [Heb. 6:5].

Sun. 20.—After preaching at Newcastle morning and evening, I earnestly exhorted the fellowship members to beware of bad-mouthing each other and of judging those who didn't follow us …

Sat. 26.—I went on to Nottingham. On the morning of Sunday the 27th I spoke in our preaching-house at 5 a.m., and about 8 a.m. at the High Cross on, "Why will you die, house of Israel?" [Ezek. 33:11]. I went there again from St. Mary's in the afternoon and proclaimed to a huge crowd: "Jesus Christ, the same yesterday, today, and forever" [Heb. 13:8]. I didn't see a single scoffer or anyone making light of what I said; rather each and all appeared serious and attentive.

Mon. 28.— … In the afternoon I rode to Markfield. After preaching there twice on Thursday the 29th, I went on to Hinckley and preached to a large, quiet assembly. We rode to Market-Harborough that day, the next to Hockley, and on Thursday, December 1st, to London.

Here all my time for some weeks was occupied in speaking one by one to the members of the fellowship. I was obligated to remove many of these. There remained about 2020 persons.

1744

Sun. JANUARY 8.—In the evening I rode to Brentford, on Monday to Marlborough, and the next day to Bristol.

Wed. 11.—I began examining the fellowship, and none too soon, for the plague had broken out. I found many crying out, "Faith, faith! Believe, believe!" but making little account of the fruits of faith, either of holiness or good works. In a few days they came to themselves, and had a more thorough understanding of the truth as it is in Jesus ...

Wed. FEBRUARY 1.—Just before the time I had planned to start preaching at the chapel, I was seized with such pain as I don't remember ever having before in my life. But I forgot it as soon as I had read my text, Psalm 18:1 and following: "I will love thee, O Lord, my strength." And from then on I didn't feel it.

About this time the soldiers abroad began to meet together, as we learned from the following letter:

Ghent, Feb. 2, 1744.

SIR,

I make bold to send you these lines. February 18, 1743, we began our march for Germany. I was then very downcast and my heart was ready to break. But the day we marched to Maestricht, I found the love of God shed abroad in my heart, so that I thought my very soul was dissolved in tears. But this didn't last more than three weeks, and then I was in heaviness again, till on April 24th, as I was walking in the fields, God broke my hard heart in pieces. And yet I wasn't delivered from the fear of death. I went to my quarters very sick and weak, in great physical and mental pain. By morning I was so weak I could hardly go on. But this proved a sweet night to my soul, for now I knew there was no condemnation for me, believing in Christ Jesus.

June 16. This day we engaged the French at Dettingen. As the battle began, I said, "Lord, in you have I trusted, let me never be confounded." Joy overflowed my soul, and I told my fellows in arms, "If I fall this day, I shall rest in the everlasting arms of Christ." Now I felt I could be content to be cast into the sea, for the sake of my dear brethren, so their eyes might be opened, and they might see, before it was too late, the things that belong to their peace.

When we came to winter-quarters, there were but three of us joined together [in Christian fellowship], but now, by the blessing of God, our number has increased to 12, and we have reason to believe that the hand of the Lord is with us. I request, for the sake of him whom we follow after, that you would send us some instructions how to proceed in our little fellowship. My mouth has become God's mouth, and he has blessed even my word to some of their souls. All praise and glory and honor be to him and to the Lamb forever and ever!

From your affectionate brother, J. H.

Wed. 15.—We were informed of the intended French invasion; they were expected to land at any time. I therefore exhorted the assembly, in the words of our Lord: "Stay awake at all times, praying that you may have strength to escape all these things that are going to take place and to stand before the Son of Man" [Luke 21:36].

Thur. 16.—In the evening, after explaining and commenting on the third chapter of Jonah, I urged everyone to "turn from his evil way, and cry mightily to God," and enlarged on these words: "Who knows? God may turn and relent and turn from his fierce anger, so that we may not perish" [Jonah 3:9].

We observed Friday the 17th as a day of solemn fasting and prayer. In the afternoon, when many came together, I exhorted them now, while they had opportunity, to make to themselves friends of the mammon of unrighteousness: to deal their bread to the hungry, to clothe the naked, and not to hide themselves from their own flesh [cf. Isa. 58:7]. And God opened their hearts, so that they contributed nearly 50 pounds,[192] which I began laying out the very next hour, in linen, wool cloth, and shoes, for those whom I knew to be diligent and yet in need. In the evening I explained Daniel 3; and those words in particular: "If this be so, our God whom we serve is able to deliver us from the burning fiery furnace, and he will deliver us out of your hand, O king. But if not, be it known to you, O king, that we will not serve your gods or worship the golden image that you have set up" [vv.17-18].

---

[192] About $12,000 in 2020 American dollars.

Sat. 18.—I received an account from James Jones, of another kind of invasion in Staffordshire: the substance of which as follows:

On Monday, January 23rd, a mob gathered together at Darlaston, a mile from Wednesbury. They attacked a few people who were going to Wednesbury, and among the rest, Joshua Constable's wife, of Darlaston. Some of them threw her down, and five or six held her down, so another could rape her; but she continued to fight back till they changed their plan, beat her severely, and went away.

Mon. 30.—The rabble gathered again, broke into Joshua Constable's house, tore part of it down, broke some of his belongings to pieces, and carried the rest away, in particular all his shop goods, worth a considerable amount. But not satisfied with this, they searched for him and his wife, swearing they would knock their brains out. Their little children, meantime, as well as they themselves, wandered up and down, no one daring to help or take them in, afraid of risking their own lives.

Mon. February 6.—I accompanied [Charles Wesley] part of his way, and in the afternoon came back to Wednesbury. I found that the fellowship was meeting, and commending themselves to God in prayer, having been informed that many, both at Darlaston and other places, had bound themselves by an oath, to come on Shrove-Tuesday[193] (the next day) and plunder all the Methodists in Wednesbury.

We continued in prayer till the evening. I asked as many as could to meet me again at 8 a.m.; but I had just started to speak when one came running at full speed and told us that a hostile crowd was coming into the town and had broken into a few houses already. I immediately withdrew to my father's house; but he didn't dare to receive me, nor did anyone else, until finally Henry Parks took me in, and early in the morning I left for Birmingham.

The mob had been gathering all Monday night, and on Tuesday morning they began their work. One after another, they assaulted all the houses of those called Methodists: they first broke all their windows, leaving no glass, lead, nor frames unbroken, then they made their way inside the houses, and all the tables, chairs, chests of drawers; with whatever was not easily movable, they dashed in pieces, especially shop goods and furniture of every kind. What they couldn't

---

[193] Or Mardi Gras.

break up, such as feather beds, they cut in pieces and strewed about the room. William Sitch's wife was lying sick, but that was all the same to them; they pulled away her bed and cut it in pieces. (Had the French come in that place, would they have done more?) All this time none offered to resist them; in fact for the most part, both men and women fled for their lives; only the children stayed, not knowing where to go.

Clothes and things which were of value or easily salable, they carried away, each loading himself with as much as he could carry, of whatever he liked best.

Some of the gentlemen who had set the mob to work, or threatened to turn away coalminers or other miners out of their service who didn't come and do his share, now drew up a paper for those of the fellowship to sign, to the effect that they'd never invite or again receive any Methodist preacher. On this condition, they told them they'd stop the mob at once; otherwise they must take the consequences.

They offered this to several [Methodists], but they all declared, "We've already lost our goods, and nothing more can follow but the loss of our lives, which we will lose too, rather than wrong our consciences."

On Wednesday the mob divided into two or three groups, one of which went to Aldridge, four miles from Wednesbury, and plundered many houses there as they had already done in several other villages. Here too they loaded themselves with clothes and goods of all sorts, as much as they could carry. They came back through Walsal with their spoils, but the gentlemen of Walsal, being forewarned of their coming, raised a body of men who met them, took away what they had, and laid it up in the town hall. Notice was then sent to Aldridge that everyone who had been plundered might come and take their own goods.

Mr. Wood of Wednesbury likewise told several they should have what could be found of their goods, on condition they would promise not to receive or hear these preachers any more.

On Friday, in the afternoon, I went from Birmingham, planning to go to Tipton-Green, but finding the mob was still raging up and down, I returned to Birmingham, and soon after (having so far no more purpose in these parts) set out for London ...

Mon. 27.—This was the day I had set to leave the city, but understanding that a proclamation had just been made requiring all

Catholics to leave London by the following Friday, I decided to stay another week in order to cut off all occasion of reproach.[194] What made me more willing to stay was to obtain more clothes for the poor before I left London.

For this purpose I made a second collection which amounted to about 30 pounds,[195] but realizing that all the money collected wouldn't meet one-third of the need, I decided to go around to the classes and beg for the rest till I'd gone through the whole fellowship.

Fri. MARCH 2.—I began to carry out this plan. While I was at a house in Spitalfields, a justice of the peace came with the parish officers searching for Catholics. I was glad to have the opportunity to talk with them at length, both of our principles and practices. When I went out, a rather large crowd accompanied me to the door of the house to which I was going, but they didn't hurt us at all; they just stared with open mouths and yelled as loud as they could.

Wed. 14.—I tried to clear up the misunderstandings which had arisen [in Bristol] by hearing the parties face to face. It was, as I suspected, a mere difference of words, of which they then were all so fully aware that I believe they won't as easily fall into this snare of the devil again.

Thur. 15.—I talked at length with the stewards of Kingswood School regarding the state of their schools and of the fellowship there, and then with the headmaster, the headmistress, and the children, and found great cause to bless God on their behalf. In the evening I preached at Bristol, on, "I will love thee, O Lord, my strength" [Psalm 18:1], and after committing myself to their prayers, rode to Marchfield ...

Thur. 22.—I gave the fellowship an account of what had been done with regard to the poor. By the contributions and collections, I'd received about 170 pounds,[196] with which over 330 poor people had been provided with needed clothing. Thirty or forty still remained in need, and since some debts had been incurred for the

---

[194] Wesley had often been accused of being Catholic ("Papist"), so he avoids the implication that his leaving the city by that date might have.
[195] About $7000 in 2020 USD.
[196] About $40,000 in 2020 USD.

clothes already distributed, the next day being Good Friday, I made one more collection of about 26 pounds.[197] This treasure, at least, neither rust nor moth shall corrupt, nor thieves break through and steal [cf. Matt.6:19].

Sat. 24.—My brother and I agreed it was enough for one of us to stay in the city, while the other tried to strengthen our brethren in other parts. So on Monday the 26th I set out, and came in the evening to Newbury …

We stopped at a house in the afternoon in which the first person we met was so drunk that she couldn't speak plainly, and with an effort could only curse and swear. In the next room we found three or four more merry people keeping Easter in much the same way, but we soon spoiled their merry-making. They earnestly regarded the things they little regarded before, and didn't know how to express their thanks for our advice and for a few little books that we left with them …

Sat. 31.—Stopping at Chard, I came unexpectedly on a poor woman who was earnestly groaning for redemption. At noon we spent an hour with a little gathering in Axminster, and hastened on toward Crockern Wells, but with the sleet and snow falling so fast, we couldn't reach it till after 9 p.m.

Sun. APRIL 1.—I rode to Sticklepath. At 1 p.m. I preached in an open place on "This is the testimony, that God has given us eternal life, and this life is in his Son" [1 Jn. 5:11]. A storm of rain and sleet began while I was preaching, but those who had gathered didn't move. At 5 p.m. I preached again. Many of the poor people followed me to the house where I lodged and wouldn't agree to part till I had spent another hour in exhortation, prayer, and thanksgiving.

I read today the strange account of John Endicot, governor of New England, and his associates there, who beat and imprisoned so many of the poor Quakers and murdered William Robinson, Marmaduke Stephenson, and others. Oh, who would have looked for Father Inquisitors at Boston! Surely these men didn't cry out against Catholic cruelty!

---

[197] About $6100 in 2020 USD.

Mon. 2.—I preached at 5 a.m., then rode on for Launceston. The hills were covered with snow as in the depth of winter. About 2 p.m. we came to Trewint, very wet and weary, having been beaten by the rain and sleet for some hours. I preached in the evening to many more than the house would hold on the happiness of him whose sins are forgiven. In the morning, Degory Isbel took pains to guide us over the great wasteland, all the paths being covered with snow, which in many places was piled too deep for horse or man to pass through. The sleet was at our back for the first seven miles; we then had a sunny but bitterly cold day. I preached at Gwenap in the evening to a plain, simple-hearted people, and God gave us comfort in each other.

Wed. 3.—About 11 a.m. we reached St. Ives. I was a little surprised, upon entering John Nance's house, to be received by many who were waiting for me there with a loud though not bitter cry, but they soon recovered and we poured out our souls together in praises and thanksgiving.

As soon as we went out we were greeted, as usual, with a great shout and a few stones or pieces of dirt. But in the evening no one opened their mouth while I proclaimed, "I will love thee, O Lord, my strength ... I call upon the LORD, who is worthy to be praised, and I am saved from my enemies" [Psalm 18:1,3].

Thur. 5.—I viewed the ruins of the house that the mob had pulled down a little while before, for joy that Admiral Matthews had beaten the Spaniards. Such is the Cornish method of thanksgiving! I suppose if Admiral Lestock had fought too, they would have knocked all the Methodists on the head ...

Fri. 6.—I spoke with the members of the fellowship individually, and noticed with great satisfaction that persecution had driven away only three or four, while greatly strengthening the rest. The persecution here was due in great measure to the unwearying labors of Mr. Hoblin and Mr. Simmons, gentlemen worthy to be had in everlasting remembrance for their unwearying efforts to destroy heresy. *Fortunati ambo! Si quid mea pagina possit, Nulla dies unquam memori vos eximet aevo.* [If my page (writing) could have done anything, no day would ever have taken you from eternal memory!—rough translation].

Sat. 7.—I have recorded a partial account of the late riot, which (to show the deep regard of the actors in it for his Majesty) was on the very same day that his Majesty's proclamation against rioters was read. Yet I see that a great deal of good has come from it already, especially the great peace we now enjoy.

About 11 a.m., John Nance and I set out for Morva. With both the wind and rain hitting straight in our faces, we were wet through and through before we came to Rosemargay, where some of our brethren met us. I found there had been a shaking among them, caused by the confident assertions of some that they had seen Mr. Wesley a week or two ago with the Pretender[198] in France, and others, and that he was in prison at London. Yet the main body still stood firm together, and were not removed from the hope of the gospel ...

Tues. 10.—I asked others how Dr. B., a person noted for good sense and learning, could speak evil of this way, after he had seen such a change in the most forsaken of his parishioners? But I was satisfied when Jonathan Reeves informed me that when the doctor asked him who had been made better by this preaching, and he replied, "The man right here in front of you (John Daniel) for one, who never before knew any work of God upon his soul." The doctor answered, "Get out of here! You are a bunch of lunatics!" and taking him by the shoulder, actually shoved him to the door. See here! What it is that the world calls madness? Knowing that God has done a work on our souls!

In the afternoon I walked over to Zunnor and, after preaching, put the new fellowship in order.

Wed. 11.—This being the public fast day, the church at St. Ives was well filled. After reading those strong words, "If they have called the master of the house Beelzebub, how much more those of his household?" [Matt.10:25]. Mr. H. fulfilled them, by vehemently declaiming against the new sect as enemies of the Church, Jacobites,[199] Catholics, and what not! After church we met and spent

---

[198] "Bonnie Prince Charles," pretender to the British throne.
[199] Jacobites (17th and 18th centuries, wanted to restore Stuarts to the British monarchy.

an hour in prayer, not forgetting the poor sinner [i.e., Mr. H.], sinning against his own soul.

In the evening I preached at Gwenap, standing on the wall in the calm, still evening, with the sun setting behind me and almost an innumerable multitude[200] in front, behind, and on both sides. Many likewise sat on the little hills, at some distance from the bulk of the gathering. But they could all hear distinctly while I read, "The disciple is not above his Master" [Matt. 10:24], and the rest of those comforting words which day by day are fulfilled in our ears.

Thur. 12.— ... About 6 p.m. I reached Morva, wet through and through, the rain having continued with hardly any letup. However, a little group had gathered together, to whom I preached on "Ask, and it will be given to you" [Matthew 7:7]. The next day I had time to dry my clothes at Mr. John's near Penzance. At noon I preached on the Downs, not far from his house, about 3 p.m. at Gulval, and at St. Ives in the evening.

Sat. 14.—I took my leave of St. Ives, then preached at 2 p.m. in Cambourn, and at Gwenap in the evening.

Sun. 15.—I preached here again at 5 a.m., and at 8 a.m. in Stithian parish. The place was a green, triangular plot of ground, capable of holding 8- or 10,000 adults. I stood on one of the walls that enclosed it. Many sat on the other two walls. Some thousands stood between and received the word readily.

At 5 a.m. I preached at Gwenap on a little hill near the usual place. It rained from the time I began till I finished. I felt no pain while I spoke, but the moment I finished, and all the time I was with the fellowship afterwards, my teeth and head ached so badly that I was almost out of my senses. I lay down as soon as I could and fell asleep. In the morning (blessed be God) I felt nothing wrong.

Mon. 16.—In the afternoon we came again to Trewint.

Here I learned that notice had been given that I would preach that evening in Laneast Church, which was very crowded. Mr. Bennet (the minister of Laneast) carried me afterwards to his house,

---

[200] W. gives numbers up to 30,000 at various places, and in some instances computes by measurement (e.g., so many per six feet squared). While these can't be corroborated today, there's no reason to dismiss them as pure guesses.

and (though over 70 years old) came with me in the morning to Trewint, where I had promised to preach at 5 a.m.

Before we parted, Degory Isbel informed me of an accusation against me, current in those parts. It was one which I really didn't expect, no more than that other one, vehemently asserted at St. Ives, of my bringing the Pretender with me last fall, under the name of John Downes. It was, that "I called myself John Wesley, whereas everybody knew Mr. Wesley was dead." ...

Thur. 19.—Having a sloop ready, which came on purpose, we crossed the Channel in about four hours. Some of our friends were waiting for us on the shore. About 1 p.m. we came to Fonmon Castle. I found a natural wish: "Oh, for ease and a resting-place!" [But the answer I received is,] not yet, but eternity is at hand! I preached at 6 p.m. and at 5 a.m. ...

Sat. 21.—I rode to Garth in Brecknockshire and on Sunday the 22nd preached in the church there, both morning and afternoon. On Monday the 23rd I preached in Maesmennys Church, and afterwards in the churchyard at Builth. I noticed only one man with his hat on, probably through inattention, for he likewise knelt down on the grass with the rest as soon as I began to pray ...

Wed. 25.—We rode over the still snowy mountains. At noon I preached at Killigaer, in the evening at Cardiff, and the next evening at Fonmon. On Saturday the 28th I returned to Bristol ...

We had a remarkable blessing ... at 5 a.m. on Wednesday, May the 9th ...

Fri. MAY 11.—I preached at Sheffield and on Saturday the 12th, about 10 a.m., at Barley Hall. In the afternoon I rode to Epworth, and immediately went to Mr. Maw's to thank him for his good services to Mr. Downes and for his honest and open testimony for the truth, before the court at Kirton. It wasn't his fault that those "honorable" men didn't regard the laws either of God or the king. But they were determined that he would be a soldier, right or wrong, "because he was a preacher." So, to make it sure, they sent him away as a prisoner to Lincoln Jail!

My first plan was, to have gone the shortest way from Sheffield to Newcastle. But it was best I didn't, considering the panic that had spread everywhere. I came just in time to remind all the poor frightened sheep "that even the hairs of our head are all numbered" [cf. Matthew 10:30] ...

At 2 p.m. many of our brethren at Epworth met, whom I cheerfully commended to the grace of God. We were riding gently towards Fishlake when two or three people met us and begged us not to go that way, for they said the town was all up in arms and many were waiting for us on the road, most of whom had made themselves very drunk, and so were ripe for any kind of mischief; so we rode to Sykehouse another way. Some came there in a great hurry to tell us that all the men in the congregation would be pressed [into military service]. Others stated that the mob was on its way right then and that they would surely set the house on fire or pull it down to the ground. I told them, "Then our only way is to make the best use of it while it's still standing." So I began to explain the 10th chapter of Matthew, and no one opened his lips against us.

Tues. 15.—After comforting the little flock at Norton, I rode the shortest way to Birstal. Here I found our brethren partly mourning and partly rejoicing on account of John Nelson. On Friday the 4th of this month, they told me, the constables took him, just as he had ended his sermon at Atherton, and the next day carried him before the commissioners at Halifax, the most active of whom was Mr. Coleby, vicar[201] of Birstal, Many were ready to testify that he was not in any respect a person such as the Act of Parliament specified. But they got no hearing; he was a preacher; that was enough, so he was sent as a soldier at once! ...

Mon. 21.—I rode to Newcastle, and passed a quiet week.

Mon. 28.—I began visiting the classes in the town, and on Sunday, June the 3rd, those in the country, which I'd never found so much in earnest before. I trust that not only are there none whose conduct is disorderly, but hardly a slacker left among them.

Fri. JUNE 8.—I preached at night on John 17:3. The house was too small for the gathering, and most of them stayed either indoors or outdoors till the end of the midnight hymn.

Sun. 10.—I preached at Biddick about 8 a.m., at Tanfield as soon as morning prayer was over, at Spen about 3 p.m., and in

---

[201] Church of England clergyman receiving a salary but not tithes in a parish.

Newcastle at 6 p.m. I ended the day by praising God with the fellowship.

Mon. 11.—I left Newcastle, and in the afternoon met John Nelson at Durham, with Thomas Beard, another quiet and peaceable man, who had recently been torn from his trade and his family and sent away as a soldier—that is, banished from all that was near and dear to him, and forced to dwell among lions for no other crime, either committed or pretended, than that of calling sinners to repentance. His soul wasn't at all terrified by his adversaries, yet his body, after a while, sank under its burden. He was then lodged in the hospital at Newcastle, where he still praised God continually. His fever increasing, his blood was let,[202] his arm became infected, then he developed gangrene and it was cut off. After two or three days God signed his discharge and called him up to his eternal home …

Tues. 12.—In the evening I came to Knaresborough. About 9 p.m., I was told that the house we were in was surrounded by men, women, and children [intending on mischief]. I asked those inside to prop open the doors and let all who wanted to to come in. When the house was full, I came downstairs. The noise died down and I proclaimed "Christ our wisdom, righteousness, sanctification, and redemption" [1 Cor. 1:30]. Only one drunk man gave a little interruption, but his friends soon shoved him outdoors. So let all Satan's devices fall on his own head! I trust this mob didn't come together in vain …

Sat. 16.—In the evening I preached at Sykehouse and, by setting out early in the morning, on Sunday the 17th preached at 8 a.m. in Epworth. I came here just at the right time, for two such sermons as Mr. Romley preached this day, so very bitter and totally false, I can't say I ever heard before.

After the evening service I preached on Romans 3:22 to a much larger audience than in the morning, and I believe that all who had honest hearts were greatly comforted.

Mon. 18.—I left Epworth, and on Wednesday the 20th in the afternoon met my brother [Charles] in London.

---

[202] Blood-letting was a standard medical practice of the day for fevers and other conditions.

Mon. 25.—and the following days, we spent in conference with many of our [preaching] brethren, arriving from several places, who desire nothing but to save their own souls[203] and the souls of those who hear them, and surely, as long as they continue to be of such a mind, their labor will not be in vain in the Lord.

The next week we worked to purge the fellowship of all who didn't walk according to the gospel. By this means we reduced the number of members to less than 1900, but number is an inconsiderable circumstance. May God increase them in faith and love!

Mon. JULY 9.—My brother set out for Cornwall. For the next two weeks, I had a great deal of trouble trying to keep an unwary man from destroying his own and many other souls. On Monday the 23rd when I set out for Bristol, I flattered myself that the work was done, but on my return, I found I had accomplished absolutely nothing, so on Thursday, August the 2nd, I was forced to declare, in the gathered Society, that Thomas Williams was no longer in fellowship with us.

Fri. AUGUST 10.—I preached to the debtors in Newgate, and asked two or three of my friends to visit them weekly. I had a serious, well-behaved audience; perhaps God may give us some fruit here as well.

Wed. 15.—I went to Bedlam[204] at the repeated request of Mr. S., who had been confined there more than two years. This was the man who, while he was speaking against my brother and me to the fellowship at Kingswood, was in a moment struck raving mad. It seems that finally God has heard our prayers on his behalf and has restored him to a sound mind.

Tues. 21.—I set out with a few friends for Oxford. On Wednesday my brother met us coming from Bristol. On Friday the 24th, St. Bartholomew's Day, I preached, I suppose, the last time at St. Mary's. Let it be so; I am now clear of the blood of these men; I have fully delivered my own soul.

---

[203] "Desiring nothing but to save their own souls" is a code-phrase of Wesley's for those earnest in seeking and serving God.

[204] "Bedlam," originally "Bethlehem," was the first hospital founded for the mentally ill (then called "lunatics," "insane"), in 1247.

The beadle[205] came to me afterwards and told me that the vice-chancellor had sent him for my [sermon] notes. I sent them without delay, admiring the wise providence of God. Perhaps few men of note would have given a sermon of mine a reading if I had put it into their hands, but by this means it came to be read, probably more than once, by every prominent man in the University.

I left Oxford about noon, preached at Wycombe in the evening, and on Saturday the 25th returned to London.

Sat. SEPTEMBER 1.—I talked at some length with George Newans, the supposed Shropshire Prophet. I am inclined to think he believes himself, but I can't believe God has sent him.

Wed. 5.—A man sent me word that he had now found the right way of worshiping God, and therefore, he must give up prayer and the rest of our will-worship and join himself with the Quakers. However, in the evening, he ventured among us once more and God smote him to the heart, so that he knew and felt and declared aloud that he had no need of going elsewhere to find the power of God for salvation.

Thur. 6.—I committed to the dust the remains of Elizabeth Marsh, a young woman who had received a sense of the pardoning love of God about four years before her death, and had never left her first love. She had scarcely known health or ease from that hour but never murmured or complained about anything. I saw her many times after she was confined to her bed and found her always quiet and calm, always cheerful, praising God in the fire, though longing to depart and to be with Christ. I couldn't tell that her mind was ever clouded, even for a moment, from the beginning of her illness, but a few days before she died, she told me, "I am concerned because I said something in haste today. One told me, 'You'll recover within ten days'; and I said, 'I don't want to recover.'" ... She'd lost her voice when I prayed with her the last time, and commended her soul to God ...

I could only speak a few words at her grave, but when I returned to the Foundry, God made his Word as a flame of fire. I spoke from that passage in Revelation: "Then one of the elders addressed me,

---

[205] One who delivers messages or executes mandates.

saying, 'Who are these, clothed in white robes, and where have they come from?' I said to him, 'Sir, you know.' And he said to me, 'These are the ones coming out of the great tribulation. They have washed their robes and made them white in the blood of the Lamb'" [7:13–14] ...

A young servant of Mrs. Clark of Newington went home deeply stirred. The next day he was taken ill, and every day grew worse, so when I came to the house on Monday the 10th (though I knew nothing of him or of his illness before that), he was gasping for breath. It was a sad sight: both his words and his eyes "witnessed huge affliction and dismay"; death stared him in the face, and he didn't know God. All he could say was, "For God's sake, pray for me."

When John Nelson arrived, we interceded for the life for our brother, in full confidence of the promise.[206] All through the day, as his illness increased, so did his terror, but the next day God gave him life from the dead. He told me, "Now I am not afraid to die, for I know God loves me. I used not to love you or your people, but now I love you as my own soul. I love you all; I know you're the people of God, and that I'm just going to him." He continued praising God as long as he could speak, and when he could no longer do so, his eyes were fixed upwards. Between 1 and 2 a.m. on Wednesday morning he cried out, "I've lost my God! Where is he? I can't see him!" But he soon recovered and said, "Now I've found him, and I won't lose him anymore." About 7 p.m. I prayed with him, and praised God on his behalf, and not long after that he died.

Fri. OCTOBER 14.—I performed the last rites (by his request) over his body, which was interred in the presence of a huge crowd of people, at a small distance from that of Elizabeth Marsh.

Sun. 16.—All this summer, our brethren in the west [of England] had trials as hard and fiery as those in the north of England; the war against the Methodists, so called, being everywhere carried on with far more vigor than that against the Spaniards. I had accounts of this from all parts; one of which was as follows:

---

[206] The promise that God responds to the fervent prayers of his people.

VOLUME 1: 1730-1746

REV. SIR,

The word of God has free course here; it runs and is glorified, but the devil rages horribly. Even at St. Ives, we can't shut the doors of John Nance's house to meet with the fellowship without the mob immediately threatening to break them open. They now triumph over us more and more, saying, "It's obvious that nothing can be done against them." And in other places it's worse. I was going to Crowan on Tuesday a week ago. On the road two of our brothers met me. When we came within a mile of the house we saw a great mob from a distance, but they were going another way. We then left our horses at the house of a friend and went ahead on foot. Within a quarter mile of the place where I was going to preach, two people met us who used to be persecutors, but they now begged me, for God's sake, "not to go up; for if I did, they said, there would surely be murder; if there wasn't already, for many had been knocked down before they left."

Taking their advice and listening to the pleas of those who were with me, I turned back to the house where we left our horses. We had been there just a short time when many of the people came, very bloody, having been beaten badly. But the main cry of the mob was after the preacher, whom they sought in every corner of the house, swearing bitterly, "They only wanted to knock him on the head, and then they would be satisfied."

Not finding me there they said, however, that they would catch me on Sunday at Cambourn. But it was Mr. Westell's turn to preach that Sunday. While he was preaching there at Mr. Harris's house, a tall man came in and pulled him down. Mr. Harris demanded his warrant. But he swore that, warrant or no warrant, he must go with them; so he carried him out to the mob, who took him away to Church Town. They kept him there till Tuesday morning and then carried him to Penzance where, in the afternoon, he was brought before three justices and asked many questions, to which they required him to answer upon oath. Then Dr. Borlase wrote his mittimus,[207] by virtue of which he was to be committed to the House of Correction at Bodmin as a vagrant. So they took him as far as Cambourn that night, and the next day on to Bodmin.

    I request your continual prayers for me,
        Your weak servant in Christ,
            HENRY MILLARD ...

---

[207] The warrant written by an officer committing a prisoner to confinement.

The judges who met at the next quarter-session at Bodmin, knowing a little more of the laws of God and man, declared Mr. Westell's commitment to be contrary to all law, and set him at liberty without delay ...

Sun. NOVEMBER 4.—Poor Richard Jeffs who, in spite of his former conviction, was now determined to renounce us and join the Quakers, took the risk, however, of going once more to the Lord's Table. He had no sooner received the elements than he dropped down and cried with a loud voice, "I've sinned; I have sinned against God!" At that instant many were pierced to the heart. I could hardly speak for some time. Several mourners were filled with strong consolation, and all said, "Surely God is in this place!" ...

Sun. 11.—In the evening I rode to Brentford. A group of very drunk men were in the inn where I lodged the next night. My human nature suggested, "Why should you speak to them at all? At best it will be wasted effort; for you can be sure that none of them will mind one word you say." However, we spoke a few words to them. One of them immediately rose up and said, "It's all true," followed us as well as he could into our room, and appeared deeply convicted, with a strong desire to serve a better Master.

Tues. 13.—In the evening we reached Bath, and the next morning rode to Bristol. After spending a few days there and at Kingswood, on Saturday the 24th I came again to London ...

Sun. DECEMBER 2.—I was with two people who believe they are saved from all sin. Whether this is so or not, why shouldn't we rejoice in the work of God, as far as it is unquestionably wrought in them? For instance, I ask John C., "Do you always pray? Do you rejoice in God every moment? Do you give thanks in everything—in loss, in pain, in sickness, weariness, disappointments? Do you ask for nothing? Do you fear nothing? Do you feel the love of God continually in your heart? Do you have a witness in whatever you speak or do, that it's pleasing to God?" If he can solemnly and deliberately answer in the affirmative, why don't I rejoice and praise God on his behalf? **Perhaps, because I have too complex an idea of sanctification, or of a sanctified man; and so, for fear he shouldn't have attained all I include in the idea of sanctification, I can't rejoice in what he has attained** [my emphasis].

VOLUME 1: 1730-1746

After having often declared the same thing before many witnesses, this day Mr. Williams wrote a solemn retraction of the gross slanders he had been propagating for several months concerning my brother and me. This he concluded in these words:

> Though I don't doubt that you can forgive me, yet I can hardly forgive myself. I have been so ungrateful and disobedient to the most tender of friends, who through the power of God were my help in all my temptations.—
>
> I request your prayers on my behalf, that God may restore, strengthen, establish, and settle me in the grace to which I've been called. That God may bless you and your dear brother, and that we may be all united again in one fellowship, is the prayer of him who, for the future, hopes to be
> "Your obedient Son and Servant,
> For Christ's sake,
> THOMAS WILLIAMS ...

Mon. 3.—I answered [a] letter I had received from Flanders, and a portion of which is attached here.

> Ghent, Nov. 12, O. S. 1744.
>
> REV. SIR, ...
>
> Dear Sir, we've never met face to face. I don't think I've seen you more than once, when I saw you preaching on Kennington Common, and then I hated you as much as now, by the grace of God, I love you. The Lord pursued me with convictions from early childhood, and I often made many good resolutions, but finding just as often that 1 couldn't keep them (since they were made wholly in my own strength), at length I left off all striving and gave myself over to all manner of lewdness and profanity. I continued that way for some years, till the battle of Dettingen. The balls then flew very thick about me, and my comrades fell all around me, yet I was preserved unhurt. A few days after this, the Lord was pleased to visit me again. The pains of hell got hold of me; the snares of death encompassed me. I dared no longer commit any outward sin, and I prayed God to be merciful to my soul. Now I was at a loss for books, but God took care of this too. One day, while I was working, I found an old Bible in one of the train wagons. To read this, I soon forsook my old

companions—all but one, who was still a thorn in my flesh, but not long after that he got sick and died ...

When the Lord finally opened my eyes, and showed me that "by grace we are saved, through faith," I began immediately to declare it to others, though I hadn't as yet experienced it myself. But on October 23rd, as William Clements was at prayer, I suddenly felt a great change in my soul. My eyes overflowed with tears of love. I knew I was, through Christ, reconciled to God, which inflamed my soul with fervent love to him, whom I now saw to be my complete Redeemer.

Oh, the tender care of Almighty God in bringing up his children! How are we bound to love so indulgent a Father, and to fall down in wonder and adoration of his great and glorious name for his tender mercies!—Dear Sir, I beg you will pray for him who is not worthy to be a doorkeeper to the least of my Master's servants.

JOHN EVANS

He continued both to preach and to live the gospel till the battle of Fontenoy. One of his companions saw him there, lying across a cannon, both his legs having been taken off by a chain shot, praising God, and exhorting all who were around him; which he did till his spirit returned to God.

Mon. 17.—In the evening I rode to Brentford. Many miserable people tried to create a disturbance just as I began to preach, and used one of their number, utterly void of shame, to lead the way, but he acted his part with such a degree of impudence and stupidity that when I turned around and asked to whom he belonged,[208] his comrades were ashamed to acknowledge him as one of their own. So some went away and the rest stood still, and we had a quiet and pleasant hour.

Sun. 23.—I was unusually lifeless and heavy till the love-feast in the evening when, just as I was straining to speak, I had to stop whether I wanted to or not, because the blood gushed out of both my nostrils so 1 couldn't add another word. But in a few minutes it stopped, and all our hearts and mouths were opened to praise God.

The next day, however, once again I was like as a dead man, but in the evening, while I was reading prayers at Snow's Fields, I found such light and strength as I never remember having had before. I saw

---

[208] I.e., whether to God or to Satan.

every thought—as well as every word and action—just as it was rising in my heart, and whether it was right before God, or tainted with pride or selfishness. I never knew before (I mean not as at this time) what it was "to be still before God."

Tues. 25.—I woke up by the grace of God in the same spirit, and about 8 a.m., being with two or three that believed in Jesus, I felt an awe and a tender sense of the presence of God that greatly confirmed me in it, so that God was right before me all day long. I sought and found him everywhere, and could truly say, when I lay down at night, "Now I have lived a day."

Thur. 27.—I went to see the lawyer whom I had hired to defend me in the suit recently begun against me in chancery court, and here I first saw that foul monster, a chancery bill! It was a scroll of forty-two large pages, to tell a story that needed just forty lines, and stuffed with such stupid, senseless, improbable lies—many of them, too, totally beside the point—such as, I believe, would have cost the head of whoever drafted it in any heathen court either of Greece or Rome. And this is equity in a Christian country! This is the English method of righting wrongs! ...

1745

Sat. JANUARY 5.— ... I had often wondered at myself, and sometimes mentioned it to others, that 10,000 cares of various kinds were no more weight or burden to my mind, than 10,000 hairs were to my head. Perhaps I began to credit something of this to my own strength; and this could be the reason why, on Sunday the 13th, strength was withheld and I felt what it was to be troubled about many things. One thing and another harassing me continually, they seized on my spirit more and more till I found it absolutely necessary to fly for my life, and that without delay. So the next day, Monday the 14th, I mounted my horse and rode toward Bristol.

Between Bath and Bristol, I was urgently requested to stop at the home of a poor man, William Shalwood. I found him and his wife sick in one bed and with little hope of either of them recovering. Yet after prayer I believed they would "not die, but live, and declare the lovingkindness of the Lord." The next time I dropped by, he was sitting downstairs and his wife was able to leave the house.

As soon as we came into the [preaching-]house at Bristol, the burden of my soul was lifted of that terrible weight that had lain on my mind, more or less, for several days ...

Wed. 30.—Our whole family gathered at St. James,' our parish church. At twelve we met together to pour out our souls before God and to provoke one another to love and good works. I set apart the afternoon for visiting the sick. Blessed be God, this was a day of peace in my spirit ...

Thur. 31.—I rode to Coleford, about 20 actual miles southeast of Bristol. The coalminers here weren't quite as famous as those at Kingswood used to be [for rowdiness]. I preached near the roadside, for the preaching-house couldn't contain even a tenth of the gathering. No one opposed me, or mocked, or smiled. Surely some of the seed has fallen on good ground ...

Mon. FEBRUARY 18.—I set out with Richard Moss for Newcastle on Wednesday the 20th. Soon after we passed through Leicester, a gentleman of that town overtook us and accompanied us to Loughborough, ate dinner with us there, then rode back to Leicester. His main business, I found, was to talk with me. He said he had been in low spirits for a long time, had had the very best advice, and taken many purges[209] and yet was as bad off or worse than ever. I explained his case to him at large, and advised him to apply to that Physician who alone heals the broken in heart[210] ...

Fri. 22.—There was so much snow around Boroughbridge that our progress was very slow; so much so that night fell on us when we were still six or seven miles short of the place where we planned to lodge. But taking the risk, we pushed on across the wasteland and about 8 p.m. came safe to Sandhutton.

Sat. 23.—We found the roads much worse than they'd been the day before, not only because the snows were deeper, which made even the raised roadways in many places impassable (and turnpikes weren't known in these parts of England till some years later), but also because the hard freeze following the thaw had made all the ground like glass. We were often obliged to walk, it being impossible

---

[209] Enemas and other drugs to cleanse the digestive tract.
[210] Wesley tried to exercise discernment in deal with mental-emotional issues. Here he felt it was a spiritual condition that prayer could help.

to ride, and our horses fell down several times while we were leading them, but not once while we were riding them, during the whole journey. It was past eight before we got to Gateshead Fell, which appeared to be a pathless waste of white. The snow filling up and covering all the roads, we were at a loss how to proceed, until an honest man of Newcastle caught up with us and guided us safely into the town.

I've had many difficult journeys before, but none like this, between wind and hail, rain and ice and snow, and driving sleet and piercing cold. But that's all behind me now; those days will return no more, and are therefore as if they'd never been …

On Monday and Tuesday, I carefully inquired as to who were offended at each other—this being the sin which of all others most easily besets the people of Newcastle. And as many of them as were able to meet, I heard them face to face. It was now an easy thing to remove their offenses, for God was in the work, and they were all as willing to be reconciled to each other as I was to have them be.

February 27th, being Ash Wednesday, after the public prayers, the little church[211] in our house met together. Misunderstandings were cleared up, and we all agreed to set out anew, hand in hand and, by the grace of God, to help one another forward in running the race that is set before us.

Sun. MARCH 3.—As I was walking up Pilgrim Street, hearing a man calling for me, I stood still. He came up, using rough language mixed with many oaths and curses. Several people came out to see what the matter was, upon which he shoved me two or three times and went away.

Upon inquiry, I found this man had long been notorious for abusing and throwing stones at any of our family who went that way. So I didn't let the opportunity pass by, but on Monday the 4th, sent him the following note:—

ROBERT YOUNG,

---

[211] Wesley rarely uses the word "church" for his fellowships ("Societies"), but does so here. "Church" in his journal normally refers to a congregation of the Church of England, and "congregation" seems to be his meaning here.

I EXPECT to see you between today and Friday and to hear from you that you are aware of your fault; otherwise, in pity to your soul, I shall be obliged to inform the Magistrates of your assaulting me yesterday in the street.
I am
Your real Friend,
JOHN WESLEY.

Within two or three hours, Robert Young came and promised to behave differently. So this gentle reproof, even if it didn't save a soul from death, at least prevented a multitude of sins.

Sun. 10.—We had a helpful sermon at All-Saints in the morning, and another at our own church in the afternoon. I was very refreshed by both, and united in love both to the two preachers and to the clergy in general.

The next day I wrote to a friend as follows:

Newcastle-upon-Tyne, March 11, 1745.

This morning I have been drawing up a short account of the case between the clergy and us. I leave you to make any use of it as you believe will be to the glory of God.

1. About seven years ago, we began preaching inward, actual salvation, attained by faith alone.

2. For preaching this doctrine, we were forbidden to preach in the churches.

3. We then preached in private houses, as occasion offered; and when the houses could not contain the people, we preached in the open air.

4. For this, many of the clergy preached or printed against us as both heretics and schismatics.

5. Persons who were convicted of sin begged us to advise them more particularly how to flee from the wrath to come. We replied that if they would all come at one time (for they were numerous) we would try to do that.

6. For this we were represented, both from the pulpit and the press (we have heard it with our ears and seen it with our eyes), as introducing Catholicism, raising sedition, practicing both against Church and state, and all manner of evil was publicly said both of us and those who were accustomed to meet with us ...

9. But now several of the bishops began to speak against us, either in private conversation or in public.

10. With this encouragement, several of the clergy stirred up the people to treat us as outlaws or mad dogs ...

12. And they do so still, wherever they are not restrained by their fear of the secular Magistrate.

Thus the case stands at present. Now, what can we do, or what can you our brethren do toward healing this breach, which is highly desirable, that we may withstand with joint force the still increasing flood of Catholicism, Deism, and immorality?

Ask anything of us what we can do with a safe conscience, and we will do it immediately: Will you meet us here? Will you do what we ask of you, so far as you can with a safe conscience? ...

Sat. 16.—I visited some of the sick; for I couldn't see them all in one day. I found many very burdened, through various temptations, added to that of bodily pain, but none sorrowing as those without hope, though some deeply mourning after God.

The following week I visited the fellowships in the country. On Thursday the 28th, a gentleman called at our house who told me his name was Adams, that he lived about 40 miles from Newcastle, at Osmotherley in Yorkshire, and had heard so many strange accounts of the Methodists that he couldn't rest till he came to find out for himself. I told him he was welcome to stay as long as he pleased, if he could live on our lenten fare.[212] This caused no difficulty for him, and he was happy to stay till the following Monday, when he returned home fully satisfied with his trip.

Sat. APRIL 6. Mr. Stephenson, of whom I bought the ground on which our preaching-house is built, finally came, after more than a two-year delay, and executed the documents. So I'm freed from one more care. May I, in everything, make my request known to God!

We met at 4 a.m. on Easter morning and had great joy in the Lord. I preached on "The Lord is risen indeed" [Luke 24:34], and at Southbiddick at 7 a.m. In the evening many of our brethren from all around were present and we again praised God with joyful lips ...

---

[212] I.e., reduced, coarser diet for Lent.

Tues. 16.— I preached at 5 a.m. on Romans 3:22 to a large gathering, part of whom had sat up all night, afraid they wouldn't wake up in the morning. Many of them, I found, either were, or had been, Catholics. Oh, how wise the ways of God are! How am I brought, without any care or thought of mine, into the centre of the Catholics in Yorkshire? Oh, that God would arise and maintain his own cause and utterly abolish all the idols!

Following the sermon, an elderly woman asked me bluntly, "Do you think water baptism is an ordinance of Christ?" I said, "What did Peter say? 'Can anyone withhold water for baptizing these people, who have received the Holy Spirit just as we have?'" [Acts 10:47]. After I had spoken just a few more words, she cried out, "That's right! That's right! I *will* be baptized," and so she was the same hour. About 8 p.m. I reached Sykehouse, and preached to a little gathering there.

Wed. 17.—I rode past Epworth to Grimsby. The northeast wind was full in our face and bitterly cold. I began preaching before 8 a.m., but to such an assembly as I hadn't seen lately: so stupidly rude and noisy, egged on by their main speaker, a drunken alehouse-keeper. I singled him out, and stuck to him till he chose to withdraw. The rest soon calmed down and behaved very quietly till the service ended ...

Fri. 19.—William Fenwick rode with me to L____d: the minister there had told him again and again, "Be sure to bring Mr. Wesley with you when he comes. It's for my soul—for the good of my poor soul." When we were alone, he told me, "Sir, I have read your writings; but I couldn't believe them till very recently. Now I know your doctrine is true: God himself has shown it to me. A few days ago my soul was in great agony, praying to God to forgive my sins; and there was such a light about me as I can't express, and I knew God had heard my prayer, and my heart was filled with the love of God; and ever since then I pray and praise him all day long."

I asked if he he'd told this to anyone else? He said, "I began to tell it to one I thought a very good Christian, but he seemed to think I was crazy, so I spoke no more, and indeed I don't know any that would listen to me."

I told him, "You'll meet with many such trials as this, and others which you aren't yet aware of." He answered, "I know that I can't bear them by myself. I have no strength, unless I always watch and pray. But I do pray always. And what are trials to me? I'm not in the world; I live in eternity. I can't turn any way without seeing God. He's with me continually, and on every side." ...

Sun. 28.—I preached at 5 a.m. ... about a mile from Altringham, on "Watch and pray, that ye enter not into temptation" [Matt. 26:41]. A plain man came to me afterwards and said, "Sir, I find Mr. Hutchings and you don't preach the same way. You tell us to read the Bible and pray and go to church, but he tells us to let all this alone, and says, 'If we go to church and communion, we'll never come to Christ.'"

... At five I preached at Mill-Town near Chapel-in-the-Frith. The poor miller near whose pond we stood tried to drown out my voice by letting out the water, which fell with a great noise. But it was labor lost, for the strength of my voice was so increased that I was heard to the very edges of the assembly.

Mon. 29.—I preached at Taddington in the Peak and rode from there to Sheffield, where I preached on the floor of the former preaching house (which the good Protestant mob had just pulled down), to the largest and one of the quietest assemblies I ever remember to have seen there ...

Thur. MAY 2.—I rode to Markfield. The church was full, even though the notice was so short. But I was sorry to hear that some of the nearby churches are likely to be rather empty, for I found that the "still" brethren had spread themselves into several of the adjacent parishes. And the very first "sins" their hearers leave off are reading the Bible and "running to the church and communion." ...

Sun. 5.—The number of people even at 5 a.m. forced me to preach outdoors. About 1 p.m. I preached at Tipton-Green and about 4 p.m. at Wednesbury. A few people at first threw some clods of dirt, but they were quickly glad to retreat, so that there was no interruption at all while I applied these gracious words of our Lord, "Come unto me, all ye that labor and are heavy laden, and I will give you rest" [Matt. 11:28].

I hurried from there to Goston's Green, near Birmingham, where I had arranged to preach at 6 p.m. But it was dangerous for anyone standing to listen, for the stones and dirt were flying from every side, almost without stop, for nearly an hour. Still very few people went away. I afterwards met the fellowship and exhorted them, in spite of men and devils, to continue in the grace of God ...

Sat. 11.—I came to London. The one who sowed tares, I found, hadn't been idle, but rather had shaken many, and moved some from their steadfastness who once seemed to be pillars. The next week, finding no other way to convince some who were very much in love with that solemn trifle, my brother and I were at the pains of reading over Robert Barclay's *Apology*[213] with them. Being willing to receive the light, their eyes were opened. They saw his nakedness and were ashamed.

Thur. 23.—We had one more conversation with one who had often strengthened our hands, but now earnestly exhorted us (What is man?) "to return to the Church; to get rid of our lay-assistants; to dissolve our fellowships, to stop preaching outdoors, and to accept honorable stipends."

Wed. 29.—... I wish everyone would take note that the points in question between us and either the German or English Antinomians are not points of opinion, but of practice. **We break fellowship with no man for his opinion.**[214] **We think and let think** [my emphasis] ...

Sunday, JUNE 9.—In the evening I rode to Colebrook; on Monday to Marlborough; and on Tuesday to Bristol. The Antinomians had taken true pains here also to seduce those who were showing their faith by their works, but they had reaped little fruit of their bad labor, for upon the most diligent inquiry, I couldn't find

---

[213] Robert Barclay's *Apology for the True Christian Divinity* was, and remains, the outstanding defense of the Quaker theology, in which the inner light within each person carries equal weight with the Bible.

[214] Note that while Wesley had strong views on predestination and antinomianism, he accepted in fellowship those with these views who practiced godly living and did not quarrel about opinions.

seven persons out of 700 who been turned out of the old Bible-way.[215]

We left Bristol early on Friday the 14th, and on Sunday morning reached St. Ginnys. The church was moderately filled with serious listeners, but few seemed to feel what they heard. I preached both morning and afternoon, and also on Monday evening, when many assented to and approved of the truth.

Tues. 18.—Being invited by the rector of St. Mary Week (about seven miles from St. Ginnys), to preach in his church, we went there in the afternoon. I hadn't seen in these parts of Cornwall either so large a church, or so large a congregation. From there we rode to Laneast, where Mr. Bennet read prayers and I preached on, "The redemption that is in Jesus Christ" [Rom. 3:24].

Wed. 19.— ... Being told here of what had happened to Mr. Maxfield, we turned aside toward Crowan Church-town; but on the way we were informed that he had been taken away from there the night before. It seems that the valiant constables who guarded him, having received timely notice that a body of 500 Methodists were coming to take him away by force[216], had hurriedly carried him two miles farther to the house of a Henry Tomkins.

Here we found him, not at all terrified by his adversaries. I asked Henry Tomkins to show me the warrant. It was ordered by Dr. Borlase and his father, and Mr. Eustick, to the constables and overseers of several parishes, requiring them to apprehend all such able-bodied men as had no lawful calling or sufficient maintenance, and to bring them before the previously-mentioned gentlemen at Marazion on Friday the 21st to be examined whether they were proper persons to serve his Majesty in the army.

It was endorsed (by the steward of Sir John St. Aubin) with the names of seven or eight persons, most of whom were well known to have lawful callings, and a sufficient maintenance thereby. But that made no difference; they were called Methodists, therefore soldiers

---

[215] I.e., the way of faith bearing fruit, as in note above.
[216] Apparently only a few Methodist rode to see what they could do to help Mr. Maxfield, and Wesley is enjoying the humor of the constable imagining it to be a terrifying number.

they must be. Underneath was added, "A person, his name unknown, who disturbs the peace of the parish."

A word to the wise! The good men easily understood that this could be none but the Methodist preacher, for who "disturbs the peace of the parish" like one who tells all drunkards, whoremongers, and those who swear and use profane language, "You are in the high road to hell?" ...

About 2 p.m., Mr. Thompson and I went into the room where the justices and commissioners were. After a few minutes, Dr. Borlase stood up and asked if we had any business. I told him, "We do: We wish to be heard concerning one who was lately apprehended at Crowan." ... They delayed the affair of Mr. Maxfield (as we expected they would) to the very last. About 9 p.m. he was called. I would have gone in then, but Mr. Thompson advised me to wait a little longer. The next information we received was that they had sentenced him to go for a soldier. Hearing this, we went straight to the commission-chamber, but the honorable gentlemen[217] were gone.

They had ordered Mr. Maxfield to be put on board a boat immediately and carried to Penzance.[218] We were told they had first offered him to be the captain of a man of war that had just come into the harbor, but he answered, "I have no authority to take such men as these, unless you would give them to me for at least a week to preach and to pray to my people."

Sat. 22.— ... We heard today that as soon as Mr. Maxwell came to Penzance, they put him down in the dungeon, and that the mayor being inclined to let him go, Dr. Borlase had gone there on purpose to read the Articles of War in the court and delivered him to one who was to serve as the officer ...

Tues. 25.—We rode horseback to St. Just. I preached at 7 a.m. to the largest gathering I've seen since my arrival. At the meeting of the earnest, loving fellowship, all our hearts were on fire, and again at 5 a.m. while I explained, "There is no condemnation to them that are in Christ Jesus" [Rom. 8:1].

---

[217] Wesley is sarcastic here. They hold positions of honor but are not acting honorably.
[218] Penzance is a port in southwest England.

When the preaching was ended, the constable, by warrant from Dr. Borlase, arrested Edward Greenfield, a tin-miner 45 years old with a wife and seven children. Three years ago he was outstanding for cursing, swearing, drunkenness, and all manner of wickedness, but for a while he had put those old things away, and now was remarkable for a quite the opposite behavior.

I asked a little gentleman at St. Just what objection there was to Edward Greenfield. He said, "Why, the man is well enough in other things, but the gentlemen can't bear his impudence. Why, Sir, he says, he knows his sins are forgiven!"—and for this reason he's sentenced to exile or even death!

Tues. JULY 2.—I preached in the evening at St. Just. Not only did I notice several gentlemen there whom I suppose never came before, but a large group of tin-miners who stood at a distance from the rest, and a large crowd of men, women, and children besides, who didn't seem to know why they were there. Almost as soon as we had finished singing, a sort of gentlewoman began her show. I've seldom seen a poor creature take so much pains. She scolded, screamed, spit, stomped, and wrung her hands, made faces, and distorted her body in all sorts of ways. I paid no attention to her at all, good or bad, nor did almost anyone else. Afterwards I heard she had been raised a Catholic, and when [at first] she was told that we were [Catholics], she rejoiced greatly. No wonder she should be angry to the same extent when she found out otherwise.

Mr. Eustick, a neighboring gentleman, came just as I was finishing my sermon. The people parted to the right and left, and he came up to me and said, "Sir, I have a warrant from Dr. Borlase, and you must go with me." Then turning round, he said, "Sir, are you Mr. Shepherd? If so, you are mentioned in the warrant, too. Be pleased, sir, to come with me." We walked with him to a public house,[219] near the end of the town. Here he asked me if I was willing to go with him to the doctor. I told him, Yes, right then, if he wished. "Sir," he said, "I must conduct you to your inn, and in the morning, if you'll be so good as to go with me, I'll show you the way." So he escorted me back to my inn and left.

---

[219] Either a tavern or a building for public use.

Wed. 3.—I waited till nine, but no Mr. Eustick came. I then asked Mr. Shepherd to go ask for him at the house where he had been lodging; *si forte edormisset hoc villi* ["if perhaps he has slept off this bit of wine"]. He met him coming, or so he thought, to our inn. But after waiting some time, we asked again, and learned he had turned aside to another house in the town. I went there and asked, "Is Mr. Eustick here?" After some delay, one said, "Yes," and showed me into the parlor. When he came down, he said, "Oh, Sir, will you be so good as to go with me to the doctor?" I answered, "Sir, I came for that purpose." ... But he was in no hurry; so we were an hour and a quarter riding three or four miles. As soon as we came into the yard, he asked a servant, "Is the doctor at home?" upon his answering, "No, sir; he is gone to church," he soon said, "Well, sir, I've executed my commission. I've done, sir; I've no more to say." ...

Thur. 4.—I rode to Falmouth. About 3 p.m. I went to see a gentlewoman who had been doing poorly for a long time. Almost as soon as I sat down, the house was surrounded by a large crowd of people. A louder or more confused noise could hardly be heard in the taking of a city by storm. At first Mrs. B. and her daughter tried to quiet them. But they wasted their time; they might as well have tried to still the raging of the sea. They were soon glad to shift for themselves, and leave K.E. and me to do as well as we could. The rabble roared with all their throats, "Bring out the Canorum! Where is the Canorum?" (a meaningless word, which the Cornish generally use instead of "Methodist"). No answer being given, they quickly forced open the outer door and filled the hallway. Only a wainscot partition was between us, which was not likely to hold up long. I immediately took down a large mirror which hung against it, supposing the whole side would fall in at once. When they began their work, with many bitter curses, poor Kitty was utterly astonished, and cried out, "Oh, Sir, what must we do?" I said, "We must pray" ... All the hinges gave way at once, and the door fell back into the room. I immediately stepped forward into the midst of them and said, "Here I am. Which of you has anything to say to me? To which of you have I done any wrong? To you? Or you? Or you?" I kept speaking till I came, bareheaded (for I purposely had taken my hat off so all could see my face), into the middle of the street; and then raising my voice, said, "Neighbors, countrymen! Will you let me speak?" They cried vehemently, "Yes, yes. He shall speak. He shall. Nobody shall hinder him." But having nothing to stand on, and no advantage of height,[220] I could only be heard by a few. However, I spoke without stopping and, as far as my voice reached, the people were still, till one or two of their captains turned around and swore that not a man would touch me ...

I never saw before, no, not at Walsal itself, the hand of God so plainly shown as here ... Here, although the hands of perhaps some hundreds of people were lifted up to strike or throw, yet they were one and all stopped in midair, so that not a man touched me with one of his fingers, nor was anything thrown from beginning to end, so that I didn't even have a speck of dirt on my clothes. Who can deny that God hears prayer, or that he has all power in heaven and earth?

I took a boat at about a half-hour past five.[221] Many of the mob waited at the end of the town, but seeing that I had escaped from their hands, they could only revenge themselves with their tongues, but a few of the fiercest ran along the shore to intercept me at my landing. I walked up the steep narrow passage from the sea, at the top of which the man in front stood. I looked him in the face, and said, "I bid you goodnight." He didn't speak, nor moved hand or foot till I was on horseback. Then he said, "I wish you were in hell," and turned back to his companions.

As soon as I came within sight of Tolcarn (in Wendron Parish) where I was to preach in the evening, many people met me, running for their lives, and begged me to go no farther. I asked, "Why not?" They said, "The churchwardens and constables, and all the heads of the parish, are waiting for you at the top of the hill, and are determined to get you. They have a special warrant from the justices in session at Helston who will stay there till you are brought." I rode directly up the hill, and observing four or five horsemen, well dressed, went straight to them and said, "Gentlemen, do any of you have anything to say to me? I am John Wesley." ... And I don't

---

[220] Wesley was rathr short.
[221] Probably a.m., but uncertain.

know what would have happened to me for making so bold an assertion, except that Mr. Collins, the Minister of Redruth (accidentally, as he said) came by. As he approached me, he said that he knew me at Oxford, and my first antagonist fell silent, then another kind of dispute began: whether this preaching had done any good. I appealed to facts [of people changed for the better]. He allowed, after many words, that people were better for the present, but he added, "To be sure, by and by they will be as bad, if not worse, than ever." ...

I rode from there to a friend's house, a few miles away, and found the sleep of a laboring man is sweet. I was informed there were many here also who had an earnest desire to hear "this preaching." But they didn't dare, Sir V. having solemnly declared, and that in the face of the whole congregation, as they were coming out of church, "If anybody of this parish dares listen to these fellows, they won't come to my Christmas feast!" ...

Sat. 6.—I rode with Mr. Shepherd to Gwenap. Here too we found the people in the greatest turmoil. Word was brought that a large group of tin-miners, deliberately made drunk, were coming to do terrible things. I tried hard to settle the minds of the people, but fear had no ears, so many went away. I preached to the rest on, "Love your enemies" [Matt. 5:44]. The event showed this also was a false alarm, a trick of the devil to hinder people from hearing the Word of God.

Sun. 7.—I preached at 5 a.m. to a quiet assembly, and about 8 a.m. at Stithians. Between 6 and 7 a.m. in the evening we came to Tolcarn. Hearing the mob was rising again, I began preaching immediately. I'd been speaking less than a quarter-hour before they came in sight. One Mr. Trounce rode up first, and began talking to me, at which point he was roughly interrupted by his comrades. Yet as I stood on a high wall and kept my eyes on them, many were softened, and grew calmer and calmer. When some of their heroes noticed this, they went around and suddenly pushed me down. I landed on my feet, not being hurt at all, and finding myself close to the angriest of the horsemen, I took hold of his hand and held it fast while I made my case. Although he was beyond being convinced, both he and his partners grew much calmer, and we parted very civilly ...

Wed. 10.—In the evening at Trevouan, in Morva, I began to explain in detail "Come, everyone who thirsts, come to the waters" [Is. 55:1]. In less than a quarter hour, the constable and his companions came and read the proclamation against riots. When he finished, I told him, "We'll do as you demand; we'll disperse within an hour,[222] and went on with my sermon. After preaching, I had planned to meet just with our fellowship, but many others also followed with such earnestness that I couldn't turn them away, so I exhorted them all "to love their enemies, as Christ hath loved us." They felt what was spoken; cries and tears were on every side, and all could bear witness ...

Mon. 15.—Mr. Bennet met us at Trewint, and told us that Francis Walker had been driven away from there[223] but had since been an instrument of great good wherever he had gone. Indeed I never remember so great an awakening in Cornwall working in so short a time, among young and old, rich and poor, from Trewint all the way to the seashore.

I preached between 4 and 5 a.m., and then went on to Laneast church, where I read prayers and preached on "There is no condemnation to them that are in Christ Jesus" [Rom. 8:1]. Oh, how pleasant a thing is even outward peace! What wouldn't a man give for it but a good conscience? ...

Wed. 17.—I rode to Mr. Thompson's near Barnstaple, and the next evening to Minehead. Early on Friday the 19th we embarked and in about four hours crossed the channel and reached Fonmon.

Here we were as if in a new world, in peace and honor and abundance. How soon should I melt away in this sunshine! But the goodness of God would not allow it. In the morning I rode to Cardiff, where also there had been much disturbance, but now all was calm. I preached there in the evening. God gave a blessing with his Word, and we rejoiced greatly before him ...

Tues. 23.—I preached about noon at Maesmennys, to a larger congregation than the church could contain. About 3 p.m. I preached at Builth. Five of us clergy were present, two justices of the peace,

---

[222] The riot act required dispersal within an hour.
[223] Apparently driven from Trewint, but continuing his work elsewhere in Cornwall.

and almost all the adults in the town. I hadn't known so solemn a season before since we came into Wales ...

Thur. AUGUST 1.—and the following days, we had our second [annual] conference,[224] with as many of our brethren that labor in the Word as could be present. During my stay here, I took the opportunity of visiting the little fellowships round Bristol, in Wiltshire and Somersetshire ...

Sun. SEPTEMBER 8.—In the evening I asked the fellowship to stay so that we might commend each other to God,[225] since we didn't know how he might see fit to use us before we saw each other's face again.

Mon. 9.—I left London, and the next morning called on Dr. Doddridge at Northampton. It was about the time when he usually explained a portion of Scripture to the young gentlemen under his care. He asked me to take his place, and perhaps the seed wasn't sown altogether in vain.

In the evening, the church at Markfield was full while I explained, "The Scripture imprisoned everything under sin" [Gal. 3:22].

Wed. 11.—I preached at Sheffield. I had intended to go around by Epworth, but hearing of more and more disturbances in the north, I judged it best to go straight on to Newcastle.

Thur. 12.— I came to Leeds, preached at 5 p.m., and at 8 p.m. met the fellowship, after which the mob pelted us with dirt and stones much of the way home. The next evening the gathering was much larger, and so was the mob meeting us on our return. They were also in higher spirits, being ready to knock out all our brains for joy that the Duke of Tuscany was Emperor. What a sad consideration is this—that the bulk of the English nation will not suffer God to give them the blessings he would, because they would turn them into curses. He can't, for instance, give them success against their enemies, for they would tear their own countrymen in pieces. He

---

[224] The annual conferences became important vehicles for the strengthening and spread of Methodism. Through them, John and Charles Wesley gradually began to share their power so that, when the Wesley brothers died, a fairly smooth transition was possible.

[225] Essentially, praying for one another.

can't trust them with victory, lest they should thank him by murdering those that are quiet in the land.

On Saturday and Sunday I preached at Armley, Birstal, and Leeds, and on Monday the 16th I rode to Osmotherley.

Tues. 17.—I saw the poor remains of the old chapel on the brow of the hill, as well as those of the Carthusian monastery, called Mount Grace, which lay at the foot of it. The walls of the church, of the cloister, and some of the cells, are fairly intact, and one may still discern the partitions between the little gardens, one of which belonged to every cell. Who knows but some of the poor superstitious monks, who once served God here according to the light they had, may meet us by-and-bye in that house of God, not made with hands, eternal in the heavens?

Wed. 18.—About 5 p.m. we came to Newcastle at a suitable time. We found that the inhabitants generally were in great dismay, news having just arrived that at 2 a.m. the morning before, the Pretender had entered Edinburgh. A flood of people were with us in the evening, to whom I explained the third chapter of Jonah, insisting particularly on that verse, "Who can tell if God will return and relent and turn away from his fierce anger, that we perish not?" [Jonah 3:9].

Thur. 19.—The Mayor, Mr. Ridley, summoned all the householders of the town to meet him at the Town Hall, and requested as many of them as were willing to sign a paper to the effect that they would risk their goods and lives to defend the town against the common enemy. Fear and darkness were now on every side, but not on those who had seen the light of God's face. We rejoiced together in the evening with solemn joy, while God applied those words to many hearts: "Do not be afraid, for I know that you seek Jesus who was crucified" [Matt. 28:5].

Fri. 20.—The Mayor ordered the townsmen to carry arms and to take turns standing guard, above and beyond the guard of soldiers, of whom several companies had been brought into the town on the first alarm. Now, too, Pilgrim Street Gate was ordered to be walled up. Many began to be very concerned for us in the house where we were staying, because it stood outside the walls. But no! The Lord is a wall of fire unto all who trust in him!

I had asked all our brethren to join with us this day in seeking God by fasting and prayer. About 1 p.m. we met and poured out our souls before him, and we believed he would send a peaceable answer.

Sat. 21.—The same day these actions were taken, the news of General Cope's defeat came.[226] Orders were now given for the doubling of the guard and for walling up Pandon and Sally-Port Gates. In the afternoon I wrote the following letter:

To the Worshipful Mayor of Newcastle.

SIR,

My not visiting you at the Town Hall was not owing to any lack of respect. I revere you for your office's sake, and much more for your zeal in executing it. I would to God every magistrate in the land would follow such an example! Much less was it owing to any disaffection to His Majesty King George, but I didn't know how far it might be either necessary or proper for me to appear on such an occasion. I have no fortune at Newcastle; I have only the bread I eat and the use of a little room for a few weeks in the year.[227]

All I can do for His Majesty, whom I honor and love, I think, not less than I did my own father, is this: I cry to God day by day, in public and in private, to put all his enemies to confusion, and I urge all who hear me to do the same, and in their various social degrees to exert themselves as loyal subjects, who so long as they fear God, can only honor the King.

Permit me, Sir, to add a few more words, out of the fullness of my heart. I'm persuaded that you fear God and have a deep sense that his kingdom rules over all. To whom, then, I ask you, should we flee for help but to him who, by our sins, we have justly displeased? Oh Sir, isn't it possible to stop these overflowings of ungodliness—the open, flagrant wickedness, the drunkenness and profaneness, which so abound even in our streets? I just feel free to suggest this. May the God whom you serve direct you in this and all things! This is the daily prayer of,

---

[226] Cope was a general and a member of parliament. He had some military successes but is noted for his defeat at the Battle of Prestopans in 1745.

[227] Newcastle upon Tyne is not far inland and is near the Scottish border, therefore vulnerable to attack. John and Charles Wesley retained rights to preach and to stay in a room in the preaching-room the Methodists had built.

VOLUME 1: 1730-1746

> SIR,
> Your obedient Servant, for Christ's sake,
> J. W.

Sun. 22.—Cannons were mounted on the walls, and every preparation was made for thwarting an assault. Meantime our poor neighbors on both sides were busy taking away their goods; and most of the best houses in our street were left without either furniture or inhabitants. Those inside the walls were almost equally busy carrying away their money and goods, and more and more of the gentry[228] every hour rode south as fast as they could. At eight I preached at Gateshead in a broad part of the street near the Catholic chapel, on the wisdom of God in governing the world. How all things do tend to further the gospel!

Never before have I seen such a well-behaved congregation in any church in Newcastle as that at St. Andrew's this morning. The place indeed seemed to be the house of God, and the sermon Mr. Ellison preached was strong and weighty, which he almost couldn't finish for his tears.

All this week the alarms from the north continued, and the storm seemed nearer every day. Many wondered why we would stay outside the walls. Others told us we must get away quickly, for if the cannon began to fire from the top of the gates, they would throw all the houses over on us. This made me look closely at how the cannons on the gates were fixed, and I could only admire the providence of God, for it was obvious that: 1. They were all fixed in such a manner that no shot could touch our house; 2. The cannon on Newgate protected us on one side, and those upon Pilgrim Street Gate on the other, so that none could come near our house either way without being torn to pieces.

On Friday and Saturday, many messengers of lies terrified the poor people of the town, as if the rebels were coming to swallow them up. Upon this the guards were increased, and a large number of country gentlemen came in with their servants, horses, and arms. Among those who came from the north was one whom the mayor ordered to be arrested on suspicion of his being a spy. As soon as he

---

[228] Those of "gentle" birth, below the nobility and above the working-class.

was left alone, he cut his own throat, but a physician coming quickly sewed up the wound, so that he lived to reveal the plans of the rebels which were thereby effectively prevented.

Sun. 29.— ... Mr. Nixon, the gentleman who had a few days previously, upon being arrested, cut his own throat, being still unable to speak, wrote as well as he could, that "the plan of the Prince (as they called him) was to seize on Tinmouth Castle, which he knew was well provided both with cannon and ammunition, and from there to march to the hill on the east side of Newcastle, which entirely commands the town." And if this had been done, he would have won the day and gained the town without a blow. The mayor immediately sent to Tinmouth Castle and lodged the cannon and ammunition in a safer place ...

Wed. OCTOBER 9.—Supposing the danger was over for the present, I preached at 4 p.m. in Gateshead at John Lyddel's on 1 Corinthians 16:13: "Be watchful, stand firm in the faith, act like men, be strong." And then I took to horse with Mr. Shepherd and in the evening reached Sandhutton.

Thur. 10.— We dined at Ferry-Bridge where we were conducted to General Wentworth, who did us the honor of reading all the letters we had with us. We spent the night at Doncaster, not at all pleased with the drunken, cursing, swearing soldiers who surrounded us on every side. Can these wretches succeed in anything they undertake? I fear not, if there be a God that judges the earth.

Fri. 11.—I rode to Epworth and preached in the evening on the third chapter of Jonah. Today I read part of the *Meditations of Marcus Antonius*. What a strange emperor, and what a strange heathen, giving thanks to God for all the good things he enjoyed!—in particular for his good inspiration, and for twice revealing to him in dreams things whereby he was cured of (otherwise) incurable ailments. I have no doubt but this is one of those many who shall come from the east and the west, and sit down with Abraham, Isaac, and Jacob, while the children of the kingdom, nominal Christians, are shut out ...

Tues. 22.—I came to Newcastle in the evening, just as Mr. Trembath was starting the first verse of a hymn, and, as soon as it ended, I began preaching without feeling any lack of strength.

Wed. 23.—I found all things calm and quiet; the consternation of the people was over; but the seriousness which it had occasioned in many continued and increased.

Sat. 26.— I sent Alderman Ridley the following letter:

SIR,
THE fear of God, the love of my country, and the regard I have for His Majesty King George, constrain me to write a few plain words to one who is no stranger to these principles of action.

My soul has been pained day by day, even in walking the streets of Newcastle, at the senseless, shameless wickedness, the ignorant profanity, of the poor men to whom our lives are entrusted. The continual cursing and swearing, the wanton blasphemy of the soldiers in general, must needs be a torture to the sober ear, whether of a Christian or an honest unbeliever. Can any that either fear God or love their neighbor, hear this without concern, especially if they consider the interest of our country, as well as of these unhappy men themselves? For can it be expected that God should be on their side who are daily offending him to his face? And if God is not on their side, how little will either their number or courage or strength avail!

Is there no one who cares for these souls? Surely there are some who ought to do so; but many of these, if I am rightly informed, receive large pay and just do nothing.

I would to God it were in my power, to any degree, to supply their lack of service. I am ready to do what lies within me to call these poor sinners to repentance, once or twice a day, while I remain in these parts, at any hour, or at any place; and I desire no pay at all for doing this, except what my Lord shall give at his appearing ...

If it be objected that I would only fill their heads with peculiar whims and notions, that might easily be known. Only let the officers hear with their own ears, and they may judge whether I do not preach the plain principles of manly, rational religion.

Having myself no knowledge of the general, I took the liberty to make this offer to you. I have no interest herein, but I should rejoice to serve, as I am able, my king and country. If it be judged, that this will be of no real service, let the proposal die and be forgotten. But I beg you, sir, to believe, that I have the same glorious cause, for which you have shown so becoming a zeal, earnestly at heart, and that therefore I am, with warm respect,
SIR,

Serious Joy (John Wesley's *Journal*)

Your most obedient Servant ...

Fri. NOVEMBER 1.—A little after 9 a.m., just as I began preaching on a little mound in front of the camp, the rain (which had continued all morning) stopped and didn't begin again till I finished, A lieutenant attempted to make some disturbance. However, when I finished, he tried to make amends by getting up where I stood and telling the soldiers that all I said was very good ...

Sun. 10.—I preached at 5 a.m., and at 8 a.m. in Wednesbury, about 1 p.m. at Tipton-Green, and at 4 p.m. to almost the whole town, rich and poor, as in the beginning.

Mon. 11.—I preached at Birmingham. The next morning I set out and on Wednesday the 13th reached London.

Thur. 28.—I wrote "A Word to a Drunkard." On Friday the 29th I spent an hour with Mr. Lampe, who had been a Deist for many years, till it pleased God by my Earnest Appeal to give him a better understanding.

VOLUME 2: 1745 – 1760

Mon. DECEMBER 2.—The alarm still increased in London on account of the rebels approaching. But how easy are all these things to those who can commit both soul and body to a merciful and faithful Creator!

About this time I received some further accounts from the army, the substance of which was as follows:

October 10, 1745

REVEREND SIR,

I WILL acquaint you with the Lord's dealings with us since last April. We marched from Ghent to Allost on the 14th, where I met with two or three of our brethren in the fields. We sang and prayed together and were comforted. On the 15th I met a small company about three miles from the town, and the Lord filled our hearts with love and peace. On the 17th we marched to the camp near Brussels. On the 18th I met a small gathering on the side of a hill and spoke from those words, "Therefore let us go to him outside the camp and bear the reproach he endured" [Heb. 13:13]. On the 28th I spoke from those words of Isaiah: "Thus says the LORD who redeemed Abraham, concerning the house of Jacob: 'Jacob shall no more be ashamed; no more shall his face grow pale'" [Isa. 29:22]. On the 29th we marched close to the enemy, and when I saw them in their camp, my heart was moved toward them in love and pity for their souls. We slept with our weapons all night. On the morning of April 30th, the cannon began to fire at 4:30, and the Lord took away all my fear, so I went to battle with joy. The balls flew on either hand, and the men fell in abundance; but nothing touched me till about 2 p.m. Then I received a ball through my left arm, and rejoiced so much more. Soon after that I received another in my right arm, which forced me to leave the field. But I scarce knew whether I was on earth or in heaven. It was one of the sweetest days I ever enjoyed.

WM. CLE—TS.

1746

Wed. JANUARY 1.—I preached at 4 a.m. on, "I am God Almighty; walk before me, and be blameless" [Genesis 17:1].

We dined with poor John Webb, now thoroughly poisoned by by Robert Barclay's *Apology,* which he was sure would do him no hurt, till all his love to his brethren was swallowed up in feeble-mindedness[229] about questions and strife of words.

Wed. 8.—I waited on Mr. B., rector of _____, who had sent to me as soon as he had read my *Further Appeal.*[230] He said, "Sir, all this is sad truth. But what can we do to help it?" I went afterwards to another clergyman, who had likewise sent and asked to speak with me. How is this? I thought the publication of this tract would have enraged the world beyond measure, but to the contrary, it seems nothing ever was published which softened them so much!

Mon. 13.—I had a visit from Mr. S., an honest, zealous Anabaptist teacher. Finding he wanted to argue, I let him argue and answered him point by point till between 11 and 12 o'clock. By that time he was willing to take a breather. Perhaps he may be less fond of dispute for the time to come.

Mon. 20.—I set out for Bristol. On the road I read over Lord King's account of the primitive church. In spite of the strong prejudice of my education, I was ready to believe that this was a fair and impartial essay, but if so, it would follow that bishops and presbyters are essentially of one order; and that originally every Christian congregation was a church independent of all others![231] ...

Tues. FEBRUARY 18.—We pushed on through thick and thin, and with great difficulty reached Stanley. From there, after an hour's stop, we hurried on. The streams were so swollen by the late rains that the regular roads were impassable, but our guide, knowing the country, carried us round through the fields so we escaped the dangerous waters and soon after sunset reached Evesham, wet and dirty enough.

Wed. 19.—We rode to Birmingham, where many of our brethren from surrounding areas met us in the evening.

---

[229] Wesley: "dotage."
[230] Wesley: "Farther Appeal."
[231] If the church was founded on the pattern of the synagogue, this would be true. Cf. Acts 20, where "pastor," "overseer [= "bishop" (ἐπίσκοπος)]," and "elder" seem to be used synonymously in Paul's farewell speech.

Thur. 20.—We set out at daylight. Before reaching Aldridge-Heath, the rain changed into snow, which the northerly winds drove right in our faces and crusted us over from head to foot in less than an hour's time. We asked a man who lived at the entrance of the wasteland which was our best way to Stafford. "Sir," he said, "'tis 1000 pounds to a penny that you don't get there today. Why, 'tis four long miles to the far side of this common, and on a clear day I'm not sure to go right across it; and now all the roads are covered with snow, and it snows so that you can't see in front of you." However, we went on, and I believe we didn't get 10 yards out of the way till we got to Stafford.

In the evening we reached Roger Moss's house. I preached on Romans 3:22 and organized a few into a fellowship.

Fri. 21.—We ate breakfast at Bradbury-Green and from there rode on to Marsden. The next day, Saturday the 22nd, we reached Leeds. I preached at 5 p.m. As we went to our house, a mob followed us, throwing whatever was at hand. I was struck several times—once or twice in the face—but not hurt at all. I walked straight to the city magistrate and told him what had happened. He promised to prevent similar occurrences in the future …

Mon. 24.—I preached at Skircoat Green near Halifax to a large group of Quakers. The good man of the house, about 80 years old, had formerly been a speaker among them, but due to fear of man he desisted, and so quenched the Spirit that he was in darkness for nearly 40 years until, hearing John Nelson declare the love of God in Christ, light sprang up in his soul again …

Sat. MARCH 1.—I visited the sick; their number increased daily in every part of the town. It seems that 2000 of the soldiers alone have died since their encampment, the fever or dysentery sweeping them away by whole companies in spite of all the physicians could do.

Wed. 5.—I preached at Wickham at noon, in the evening at Spen, the next day at Burnupfield, and on Saturday the 8th in the Square at Placey. A violent storm, which was driven straight at us by the northeast wind, began in the middle of the sermon, but the congregation disregarded it.

Sun. 9.—This was a day of solemn joy, yet in the afternoon I felt very downcast, due to my failure to speak plainly to some who were deceiving their own souls. I don't wonder at the last words of St. Augustine and of Archbishop Usher, "Lord, forgive my sins of omission."

I preached on Monday at Horseley, on Tuesday at Biddick, and on Wednesday the 12th at Sunderland, where I tried to bring the little fellowship into some kind of order. In the afternoon, being at Mrs. Fenwick's and seeing a child there 10 or 12 years old, I asked, "Does your daughter know Christ or know she needs him?" She replied with much concern, "I'm afraid not; nothing has ever affected her at all." Immediately that word came into my mind, "Before they call, I will answer." I was going to say, "Come, let's call on God to show her she needs a Savior," but before I could speak the words, the child turned away her face and began crying as if her heart would break. The only words I could get from her were, "My sins, my sins!" We then sought God to carry on his own work.

Mon. 17.—I took my leave of Newcastle, and set out with Mr. Downes and Mr. Shepherd, but when we came to Smeton, Mr. Downes was so sick that he couldn't go any farther. When Mr. Shepherd and I left Smeton, my horse was so lame that I was afraid I'd have to stay there too. We couldn't tell what was wrong, yet he would hardly put his foot to the ground. By riding that way seven miles, I was worn out and my head ached more than it had for some months. (What I assert here is the bare fact; let each account for it as he or she sees fit.) I then thought, "Can't God heal either man or beast by any means, or without any?" Immediately my weariness and headache were gone, and my horse's lameness at the same moment. Nor did he limp any more either that day or the next. This too is a very odd occurrence!

Tues. 18.—I rode to Pontefract; on Wednesday to Epworth; and on Thursday, by Barley-Hall, to Sheffield. I was glad to have the opportunity here to talk with a child I'd heard about. She'd been convicted of sin some weeks earlier by the words of her older brother (about eight years old), dying as [with the spirit of someone] 100 years old, in the full victory of faith. I asked her bluntly, "Do you love God?" She said, "Yes, I do love him with all my heart." I said,

"Why do you love him?" She answered, "Because he has saved me." I asked, "How has he saved you?" She replied, "He has taken away my sins." I said, "How do you know that?" She answered. "He told me himself on Saturday, 'Your sins are forgiven,' and I believe him, and I pray to him without a book. I was afraid to die, but now I am not afraid to die, for if I die, I'll go to him."

Fri. 21.—I came to Nottingham. For a long time I had long wondered what hindered the work of God here; but upon inquiry the case was clear: So many of the fellowship were either triflers or behaving lawlessly that the blessing of God couldn't rest on them; so I made short work, cutting off all like them at a stroke, and leaving only that little handful who (as far as could be judged) were really in earnest to save their souls.

Sat. 22.—I came to Wednesbury. The antinomian teachers had labored hard to destroy this poor people.

Sun. 23.—I talked an hour with their chief, Stephen Timmins. I wondered if pride hadn't made him mad. An unusual wildness and fierceness in his manner, his words, and the whole way of his behavior, almost caused me to think God had given him up into the hands of Satan for a season …

Thur. APRIL 3.—I spent an agreeable hour with our old fellow-laborer, Mr. Humphreys. I found him open and friendly, but rigorously tenacious of the unconditional decrees.[232] Oh, that opinions should separate best friends! This is bigotry all over …

Tues. 22.—I rode with Mr. Piers to see a man who called himself a prophet. We spent about an hour with him, but I couldn't think at all that he was sent by God: 1. because he seemed full of himself, vain, willful, and opinionated; 2. because he spoke with extreme bitterness both of the king, of all the bishops and all the clergy; 3. because he tried to talk Latin, but couldn't, plainly showing that he didn't understood his own calling.

Wed. 23.—At the earnest request of a friend, I visited Matthew Henderson, condemned for murdering his mistress. A real, deep work of God seemed already to have begun in his soul. Perhaps, by

---

[232] Referring to Calvin's doctrine of God's unconditionally electing some to salvation and the rest to damnation.

driving him too fast, Satan has driven him to God, to that repentance which shall never be repented of.

About this time I received a letter from John Nelson, whom I'd left at Birmingham; part of which was as follows:

Birstal, April 22, 1746

AFTER I left Wednesbury I stayed two nights at Nottingham, and had large gatherings, but while I was meeting the fellowship the second night, there came a mob, raging as if they would pull the house to the ground. As soon as we finished meeting, the constable came and arrested me, saying I must go before the mayor for making a riot, so he took me by the arm and led me through the streets, the mob accompanying us with curses and shouts. God gave me the power as we went to speak very plainly to the constable and to all who were near me till one cried out, "Don't carry him to the mayor, for he is a friend of the Methodists, but to Alderman _____." Upon this he turned, and led me to the alderman's. When we were brought in he said, "Sir, I have brought you another Methodist preacher." He asked my name, and then said, "I don't know why you can't stay home. You can see that the mob won't let you preach in this town." I said, "I didn't know this town was governed by the mob. Most towns are governed by the magistrates." He said, "What? Do you expect us to take your side, when you take the people from their work?" I said, "Sir, you are uninformed. We preach at 5 a.m. and 7 p.m., and these are the hours when most people are in their beds in the morning, and at night either at play or at the alehouse." Then he said, "I believe you are the cause of all the trouble that has come upon this nation." I said, "What reason do you have to believe that? Can you prove that one Methodist in England assisted the rebels with either men, money, or arms?" He answered, "No, but it has been observed that there's always been such a people before any great evil fell upon the land." I said, " ... We've been sent to persuade them to forsake their sins in repentance, that the heavy judgments of God may not consume such a people, and unless there's a general reformation, God will be avenged of such a nation as this." Then he said, "Don't preach here," but God opened my mouth, and I didn't stop setting life and death before him. The constable began to be uneasy, and said, "What must we do with him?" "Well," he said, "I understand he's leaving town tomorrow; I think you must take him to your house." But he asked to be excused. Then the justice said, "You may go where you came from." When I had gone a little way through the mob, he came to the door, and called, "Mr. Nelson, wait a minute!" Then he ordered the constable to conduct me to the house he had brought me from and take care that the mob didn't hurt me. This seemed to cause him great humiliation; but he was obligated to do it. So he brought me to our brethren again, and left us to give thanks to God for all his mercies.

Fri. MAY 23.—I signed over the preaching houses in Bristol and Kingswood and, the next week, that at Newcastle, to seven trustees, reserving only to my brother and myself the liberty of preaching and lodging there …

Sat. JUNE 28.—I asked more details of Mrs. Nowens concerning her little son. She said, "He appeared to have a continual fear of God and an awful sense of his presence; that he frequently went to prayers by himself, and prayed for his father, and many others by name; that he had a very tender conscience, being aware of the smallest sin, and crying and refusing to be comforted when he thought he had displeased God in anything; that a few days ago he broke out into prayer aloud and then said, 'Mama, I will go to heaven soon, and be with the little angels; and you will be there too, and my papa; but you won't go so soon'; that the day before, he went to a little girl in the house, and said, 'Polly, you and I must go to prayers. Don't mind your doll; kneel down now; I must go to prayers: God tells me to.'" When the Holy Spirit teaches, is there any delay in learning? This child was then just three years old! A year or two after this he died in peace …

Sun. JULY 6.—After talking at length with both the men and women leaders,[233] we agreed it would prevent great expense, of health as well of time and of money, if the poorer people of our fellowship could be persuaded to stop drinking tea. We resolved to begin with ourselves and set the example. I expected some difficulty in breaking off a 26-year-old custom; and, sure enough, the three first days my head ached more or less all day long, and I was half asleep from morning to night. The third day, on Wednesday afternoon, my memory failed almost entirely. In the evening I sought help in prayer. On Thursday morning my headache was gone; my

---

[233] Leaders of circles and classes.

memory was as strong as ever; and I've found no inconvenience but rather a conscious benefit in several respects from that very day to this.

Thur. 17.—I finished the little collection which I'd made among my friends for a lending-stock.[234] It didn't quite reach 30 pounds, but a few persons later made it up to 50[235]; and by this modest sum above 250 poor people were relieved in one year ...

Wed. AUGUST 13.—I preached at Lanzufried. As soon as we came out of the church, a poor woman met us whom Satan had bound in an unusual manner for several years. She followed us to the house where our horses were, weeping and rejoicing and praising God. Two clergymen were there besides me and the house was full of people. But she couldn't keep from declaring to them all what God had done for her soul. And the words that came from her heart entered our hearts. I hardly ever heard such a preacher before. Everyone around her was in tears, regardless of their place in society, for there was no resisting the Spirit by which she spoke ...

At 6 p.m. I began preaching [at Leominster] on a tombstone near the south side of the church. The crowd roared all around, but my voice soon prevailed, and more and more of the people were melted down, till they began ringing the church bells. But still they didn't win the day, because my voice prevailed. Then the organs began playing with all their might. Mr. C., the curate,[236] went into the church and tried to stop them, unsuccessfully. So I thought it best to move to the grain market. The whole assembly followed, joined by many others who wouldn't have come to the churchyard. Here we had a quiet time, and I showed them what that "sect" is which everyone is speaking against. A long line followed us to our inn, but I heard no one say anything against us. A Quaker following me told me, "I was much displeased with thee, because of thy last *Appeal,* but my displeasure is gone. I heard thee speak, and my heart clung to thee."

Fri. 15.—I preached at five to a large gathering of willing hearers. We ate breakfast with a lovely old woman, worn out with

---

[234] The purpose being to give small loans to the working poor.
[235] Almost $12,000 in 2020 USD.
[236] I.e., the parish priest.

sickness and pain, but full of faith and love, and breathing nothing but prayer and thanksgiving.

About 10 a.m. we came to Kington, three hours' ride (which they call eight miles[237]) from Leominster. I preached at one end of the town. The assembly divided itself into two parts. Half stood near, the other half remained a little ways off and muttered defiance. But the bridle from above was in their mouth, so they made no disturbance at all.

At four, we had another kind of congregation at Maesmennys, many who had drunk deeply of the grace of God. I examined them: "Do you now believe?" And the Word was like a two-edged sword. After taking a sweet leave of this loving people, we rode with honest John Price of Mertha, to his house. We had four hours' rain in the morning, but a fair, mild afternoon, at the close of which we came to Cardiff.

Sun. 17.—I preached at Wenvo Church morning and afternoon, and at 5 p.m. in the Castleyard at Cardiff, to the far greatest gathering which I'd ever seen in Wales. All stood uncovered and attentive and, I trust, few went away empty.

Mon. 18.—I rode with Mr. Hodges to Neath … The multitude of people obliged me to preach in the street on "Repent, and believe the gospel" [Mark 1:15]. One man would have caused an interruption and had hired a drunken fiddler to back him up. But finding none to join them, they were ashamed, so the gentleman stole away on one side and the fiddler on the other.

Tues. 19.—I preached again at 5 p.m. Whatever prejudice remained now vanished away as a dream, and our souls were knit together with each other as having all drunk into one spirit.

About 10 a.m. I preached on my return at Margum on "By grace ye are saved, through faith" [Eph. 2:8]. Since many were present who didn't understand English very well, one repeated to them in Welsh the substance of what I'd said. At 1 p.m. we came to Bridge-End, where I preached on a small grassy spot not far from the church on "Jesus Christ, made of God unto us wisdom, righteousness, sanctification, and

---

[237] The Welsh mile was about 3 ½ English miles, so here about 28 miles.

redemption" [1 Cor. 1:30]. It being the time of the yearly revel,[238] we had many strangers from all parts. But none misbehaved and none opened their mouth, for the fear of God was upon them. In the evening I preached at Fonmon Castle on the fruits of the Spirit. I concluded the day with the little fellowship there, rejoicing and praising God ...

Fri. SEPTEMBER 5.—I inquired concerning John Trembath's late illness. It was a second relapse into the spotted fever, at the height of which they gave him white wine, cold milk and apples, and as many plums as he could swallow. I can see no way to account for his recovery, but that he hadn't finished his work then. In the evening I preached at St. Ives.

Sat. 6.—I rode to Trewillard, in the parish of St. Just. I found no fellowship in Cornwall as spiritually alive as this. Yet I had to rebuke a few of them for neglecting meetings, which is always the forerunner of greater evils ...

Tues. 9.— ... W.T. of. Sithney rode with me to Gwenap. He was a constant companion of Mr. N.'s, as long as he would join with him in riot and drunkenness. But when his drunkenness ended, so did Mr. N.'s friendship.

When he heard that one John O., a tin-miner, was preaching, he went on purpose to make fun of him. But the word of God struck him to the earth. Yet he struggled in the net, sometimes wanting to go again, sometimes resolving never to go anymore. But one day, visiting at his sister's, he picked up a little girl about four years old and said, "They tell me you can sing hymns. Come on, sing me a hymn." She began immediately:

> My soul, don't delay,
> Christ calls thee away:
> Rise! Follow thy Saviour, and bless the glad day!
> No mortal doth know
> What he can bestow;
> What peace, love, and comfort—go after him, go!

He jumped up at once and went to the preaching, and that same night he found peace to his soul.

---

[238] Merry-making, including much drinking and bawdyness.

Thur. 11.—E.T. (W.T.'s sister) rode with me to Cambourn. When she heard her brother had gone over to false doctrine, she went over to Sithney on purpose to win him back. But finding that neither gentle words, nor name-calling, nor oaths, nor curses, nor blows would work, she went away, renouncing him and all that belonged to him, fully determined not to see him anymore.

Six weeks later she met him at Redruth, and asked him to enter a house. After they sat down, she burst into tears and said, "Brother, follow those men in God's name, and send me word when any of them preaches in your house, and I'll come and hear him."

He asked, "How is it that you came to be so changed?" She replied, "Two weeks ago, I dreamed a man stood near me and said, 'Don't say anything bad about these men, for they are the servants of God.' I said, 'What, are you one of them? I defy you all. I will keep to my church.' He said, 'And when you're at church, what are you thinking about, even at the Lord's Table?' And he went on telling me all that was in my heart, and every word went through me, and I looked up, and saw him very bright and glorious; and I knew it was our Savior, and I fell down at his feet; and then I woke up."

A week later she went to Sithney, where Mr. M. was preaching, saying, "Is there any of you that has shut your doors against the messengers of God? Suppose our Lord shut the door of mercy against you?" She cried out, "It is I!" and dropped down. And she didn't have any rest till God made her a witness of the faith that she once persecuted.

Sat. 13.— ... At six I preached at Sithney. Before I finished night fell, but the moon shone bright on us. I intended after preaching to meet the fellowship, but that wasn't practical, the poor people so eagerly crowding in on us. So I met them all together and encouraged them not to leave their first love.

Sun. 14.—For the sake of those who came from far away, I delayed preaching till 8 a.m. Many from Helstone were there, and most of those who previously had distinguished themselves by making riots, but the fear of God was on them; they all stood with their heads uncovered and calmly listened from beginning to end.

About 1 p.m. I began preaching near Portkellis to a much larger audience, and about 4:30 p.m. at Gwenap to a huge crowd of people on "To me to live is Christ, and to die is gain" [Phil. 1:21]. At first I was afraid my voice wouldn't reach them all, but my fear was without cause, for my voice was so strengthened that I believe thousands more might have heard every word. At the close of my sermon I read them the account of Thomas Hitchins's death; and the hearts of many burned within them so that they couldn't conceal their desire to go to him and be with Christ. At 6 p.m. we took to horse, and about 9 p.m. (having bright moonshine) reached St. Columb.

Mon. 15.—A guide met us at Camelford and conducted us to St. Mary Week. Mr. Bennet caught up with us on the road, and Mr. Thompson joined us soon after, having lost his way. We also picked up Mr. Meyrick and Butts, who were wandering around lost. It was the time of the yearly revel, which obliged me to speak very plainly. Thence we rode to Laneast, where there was a much larger assembly, and of quite another spirit …

Thur. 18.— … Before I preached, I was completely exhausted and had a high fever simply through fatigue; but on riding to Middlesey I revived, and on the morning of Friday the 19th, I rose up quite well. "My strength will I ascribe unto Thee." …

Tues. 23.—I went to Rood, where the mob made loud threats. I decided, however, to look them in the face, and at noon I cried to the largest assembly by far which I'd ever seen in these parts: "Seek the Lord while he may be found; call upon him while he is near" [Isa. 55:6]. The mockers stood still as if astonished and didn't speak or stir till I'd finished my sermon.

Between 5 and 6 a.m., I preached at Bearfield, and the next evening at Blewberry. While I was meeting the fellowship afterwards, one serious backslider who'd been for some time as if in the belly of hell, was struck to the earth and roared aloud. He didn't stop till God restored the pearl he'd lost. Doesn't our God abundantly pardon? …

Sat. OCTOBER 4.—My brother and I took up our cross, and talked at length with Mr. G.; but he still insisted: 1. that there was no repentance at all prior to saving faith; 2. that naked faith alone was the only condition of everlasting salvation; and, 3. that no works need be preached at all, and neither were necessary both before and after faith. [239] ...

Wed. NOVEMBER 12.—In the evening, at the chapel, my teeth hurt me badly. When I returned to the house where I was staying, Mr. Spear gave me an account of the rupture he had had for some years, which, after the most eminent physicians had declared it incurable, was perfectly cured in a moment. I prayed, submitting to the will of God; my pain ceased and returned no more ...

I received ... from several of our brethren abroad, an account of the deliverance God had recently accomplished for them.

REV. SIR, Bush at Brabant, Oct. 17.

For a long time I've wanted to write, but had no opportunity till we came to our winter quarters. When we came over, we thought we would have had B. Haime with us as before, but we were disappointed. We were about three weeks into our march, and endured a great deal through the heat of the weather and from lack of water. At Villear camp, we lay so near the enemy and were forced to mount so many guards that we had hardly any time to ourselves, nor had J. Haime any time to meet with us ... So when the French had gotten past us, our regiment retreated, or we would have been surrounded. In our retreat, we turned around twice and fired on the enemy, and so came off with little loss, though they fired after us with large cannon shot—I believe 24-pounders.

We lost one brother of Graham's regiment, and two of ours, Andrew Paxton, shot dead in our retreat, and Mark Bend, who was wounded and left on the field. The Lord gave us all an extraordinary courage on that day and a word to speak to our comrades, as we advanced toward the enemy, to tell them how happy they were that had made their peace with God. We likewise spoke to one another, while the cannon were firing, and we could all rely on God and resign to his will.

A few of us meet here twice a day and, thanks be to God, his grace is still sufficient for us. We desire all our brethren to praise God on our behalf, and we desire all your prayers, that the Lord may grant

---

[239] As Wesley made clear in other places, he believed that salvation is by faith alone. What he objected to was "naked faith" or "bare belief" in the gospel, without fruit. In fact, he expected fruit in a person seeking God for salvation, as preliminary evidence of faith, and certainly after salvation.

us to be steadfast, unmoveable, always abounding in the work of the Lord.
I remain
Your loving brother,
S. S.

Sun. MARCH 23.—In the evening I preached at Birmingham. Here another pillar of the Antinomians came to me, looking over his shoulder, and said, "Don't think I want to be in your fellowship, but if you are free to talk with me, you may." I'll record the conversation, as dreadful as it was, in the very way it happened, so that every serious person may see full-blown antinomianism for what it is, and may know what these men mean by their favorite expression, "perfect in Christ, not in themselves."

"Do you believe you have nothing to do with the law of God?" "No; I'm not under the law. I live by faith." "Living by faith, do you have a right to everything in the world?" "Yes I do. Since Christ is mine, all is mine." "Then can you take anything you want anywhere—let's say, out of a shop, without the knowledge of the owner?" "I can, if I want it, for it is mine; but I won't give offense." "Do you also have a right to all the women in the world?" "Yes, if they agree." "But is that not a sin?" "Yes, to the one who thinks it's a sin, but not to those whose hearts are free." That wretched man, Roger Ball, affirmed the same thing in Dublin. Surely these are the firstborn children of Satan! ...

Wed. APRIL 9.—In the afternoon I buried Ann Clowney, a poor woman whom many thought could never be a believer because she was simple-minded. (She was very weak in understanding, but not actually mentally retarded.) But in her time of sickness and pain, none could deny the work of God in her. Nor did she die as a simple-minded person ...

Mon. MAY 12.—I ate dinner with a gentleman who is fully convinced that there's no such thing as either virtue or happiness on earth. He said he'd "found, by repeated experiments, that despite outward appearances, everyone living was, in the end, completely selfish and truly miserable." I wouldn't be surprised if every rational Deist thought the same. In fact they must, if they are consistent. For surely all humans are both miserable and selfish, however they appear, who lack faith, even that "evidence of things not seen" [Hebrews 11:1], evidence of the Being whose existence they question ...

Fri. 23.—I signed the preaching-houses in Bristol and Kingswood this day, and the week following that at Newcastle, to seven trustees, only reserving to my brother Charles and myself the liberty of preaching and lodging there ...

Sat. JUNE 7.—In the afternoon, an old friend (now with the Moravians) tried hard to convince me that I couldn't continue in the Church of England because I couldn't essentially agree with her decrees—"for this," he said, "was necessary to continuing in any church." What he meant was, not continuing in any church but that of the Brethren. But if that were the case, I couldn't be a member of any church under heaven! **For I must still insist on the right of private judgment; I dare call no man rabbi** [or teacher--my emphasis]. I can't yield either essential faith or obedience to any man or body of men under heaven ...

Wed. AUGUST 6.—I preached at Oak Hill. How can it be so? I haven't known as many people earnestly mourning after God in any fellowship of this size in England and so unreproachable in their behavior, and yet not one person has found a sense of the pardoning love of God from the first preaching here to this day!

When I mentioned this to the fellowship, one might have thought the sounds of mourning to have reached the very sky. My voice was quickly drowned out. We kept crying to God loudly and bitterly, until I was forced to leave them between 4 and 5 a.m. and mount horse for Shepton ...

Mon. 18.—I rode with Mr. Hodges to Neath. Here I found 12 young men whom I could almost envy. They lived together in one house and constantly gave away whatever they earned beyond the necessities of life. They told me that most of them were predestinarians, but they were so far from being bigoted in their opinion that they wouldn't allow a predestinarian to preach among them unless he would lay aside all dispute. And on these terms they gladly received those of the opposite opinion ...

Sat. SEPTEMBER 13.—I said farewell to our brothers and sisters of St. Ives, and between 1 and 2 p.m. began preaching in front of Mr. Probis's house at Bray on the promise given to them who believe. Many there till then had been strongly opposed to me, but from that time on they no longer were.

Tues. 23.—I went on to Rood, where the mob made loud threats. I decided, however, to look them straight in the face, and at noon I cried, to the largest gathering by far that I'd ever seen in these parts: "Seek the Lord while he may be found; call upon him while he is near" [Isa. 55:6]. Those who showed contempt stood like men in shock; they neither spoke nor stirred till I finished my sermon ...

Thur. DECEMBER 4.—I told the fellowship about my plan of giving medicines[240] to the poor. About 30 persons came for help the next day, and in three weeks about 300. We continued doing this for several years, till the number of patients increased beyond what we could afford. But during this time, through the blessing of God, many who had been sick for months or years were restored to perfect health ...

Mon. 15.—I spent most of this week at Lewisham writing *Lessons for Children,* consisting of the most useful passages of Scripture with just a few brief explanatory notes ...

Mon. 29.—I resumed my vegetarian diet which I had discontinued for several years, and found it helpful to both my soul and body. But after two years a severe diarrhea hit me in Ireland and forced me to eat meat again ...

1747

Tues. FEBRUARY 15.— I was very weak and faint, but on Monday the 16th I rose shortly after 3 a.m., lively and strong, and discovered that all my complaints had vanished like a dream.

The day before I was surprised at how mild the weather was, such as I seldom find in my travels. But now I stopped wondering; the wind came straight from the north and blew so hard and sharp that by the time we reached Hatfield, neither my companions nor I had much use of our hands or feet ... However, before 2 p.m. we

---

[240] By this time Wesley had developed a whole system of remedies apart from standard pharmaceuticals that he found effective.

reached Baldock, where someone met us and guided us safely to Potten.

About 6 p.m. I preached to a serious gathering. On Tuesday the 17th we started out as soon as we had good light, but it was hard work going forward because the ice wouldn't bear or break well under the horses' hooves. The untracked snow covered all the roads, so we had difficulty keeping our horses on their feet. Meanwhile the wind grew stronger and stronger, till it was ready to throw us and our horses down. But after a short rest at Bugden we pushed on, and in the middle of an open field ran into heavy rain and sleet such as we'd never met before. It drove through our greatcoats and our light coats, our boots, and everything, freezing as it fell, even on our eyebrows, so we hardly had any strength and could barely move by the time we reached our inn at Stilton …

Wed. 18.—The servant at the inn came and said, "Sir, no one can travel today. So much snow has fallen during the night that the roads are totally covered." I told him, "At least we can walk 20 miles a day, leading our horses." So in the name of God we set out. The northeast wind pierced us like a sword and had driven the snow into uneven heaps, so the main road was impassable. Still we kept on, by foot or on horseback, till we came to the White Lion at Grantham …

On the road we caught up with a clergyman and his servant, but my toothache kept my mouth shut. We reached Newark about 5 p.m. Soon after we sat down to eat, another clergyman came and asked for our fellow traveler. It wasn't long before we got involved in serious discussion. He told me that some of our men had often preached in his parish, and his judgment was: 1. that their preaching at Hunslet had done some good, but more harm; because 2. those who attended it only turned from one wickedness to another—they had only traded Sabbath-breaking, swearing, or drunkenness, for slandering, backbiting, and bad-mouthing; and 3. those who didn't attend it were provoked by it to return evil for evil. So the first group was, in effect, no better, and the second group was worse than before …

[*Part of Wesley's answer:*] "'Those who have left their outward sins,' you affirm, 'have only changed drunkenness or Sabbath-breaking for backbiting and bad-mouthing.' I answer: If you affirm this of them all, it is blatantly false. We can name many who left cursing, swearing, and backbiting, drunkenness and bad-mouthing altogether, and who to this day are just as fearful of slandering as they are of cursing or swearing. And if some are not yet fully aware of this snare of the devil, we hope they soon will be. Meantime, see that you bless God for what he has done, and pray that he would deliver them from this death also.

"You further assert that 'their neighbors are provoked by the preaching to return evil for evil, and so, while the first group is no better, the second group is worse than before.'

"I answer: 1. These are worse than they were before, but why? Because they 'despise the Spirit of grace' anew; they despise the long-suffering love of God that would lead them (as is does their neighbors) to repentance. And by laying the blame for this on those who will no longer run amuck with them into sin, they only fulfill the Scriptures and fill up the measure of their own iniquity.

"I answer: 2. There is still no proportion at all between the good, on the one hand, and the harm on the other, because those who reject the goodness of God used to serve the devil and they are still his servants. But those who accept God's goodness are brought from the power of Satan to serve the living and true God." ...

Tues. 24.—At noon I examined the little fellowship at Tetney. I haven't seen any other like it in England. In the class report, which includes an account of contributions for the poor, I noticed that one gave eight-pence, often ten-pence a week; another 13, 15, or 18 pence; another, sometimes one, sometimes two shillings.[241] I asked Micah Elmoor, the leader (an Israelite indeed, who now rests from his labors), "How is this? Are you the richest fellowship in all England?" He replied, "I guess not, but all of us who are single have agreed to give ourselves and all we have to God, and we do it gladly. This way we are able to provide hospitality to all the strangers who come to Tetney from time to time, who often have no food to eat nor any friend to lodge them." ...

Sun. MARCH 1.—I arrived in Osmotherly about 10 a.m., just as the minister (who lives some miles away) came into town. I sent him an offer of my services and told him that, if it pleased him, I would

---

[241] One pence = about $1 in 2020 USD; one shilling = $12 USD.

assist him either by reading prayers or by preaching. When he got my message, he immediately came and said he would be very glad for my assistance. As we walked to the church together, he said, "Would it be too much for you to read prayers and preach too?" I told him I would be glad to do that, and so I did. When the service ended, Mr. D. said, "Sir, I'm sorry I don't have a house to offer you hospitality. Please let me know whenever you come this way." Several persons asked where I would preach in the afternoon, and one asked Mr. D. if he would allow me to preach in the church. He said, "Yes, whenever Mr. Wesley wants to." We had a large assembly at 3 p.m. Those who previously had been the most bitter in opposition now seemed to be melted into love. Everyone realized that we weren't Catholics. How wisely does God order everything in its time!

Mon. 2.—I rode to Newcastle. The next day I met the stewards, men who have shown themselves to be above reproach in every way. They are of one heart and mind. I found all in the preaching-house to be of the same spirit, pouring out their souls to God many times a day together, and breathing nothing but love and brotherly kindness ...

On Monday the 9th, and on Tuesday and Thursday, I examined the classes. Often I'd been told that it was impossible to distinguish the true from the false without the supernatural gift of discernment of spirits. But now I saw more clearly than ever that this could be done without much difficulty. It requires only two things: courage and steadiness in the examiner, and common sense and honesty in the leader of each class. Say, for instance, I visit the class in the Close, of which Robert Peacock is the leader. I ask, "Does this or this person in your class live in drunkenness or any other outward sin? Does he attend church services and use the other means of grace? Does he meet you as often as he can?" Now if John Doe has common sense, he can give a true answer to these questions, and if he is honest, he will. And if not, someone else in the class has both and will answer for him ... My gist is this: I don't say the truth can't be known, but that it can't be hidden without a miracle ...

The fellowship which the first year had 800 members has now fallen to 400. But as an old proverb says, the half is more than the whole. We won't be ashamed of any of these when we confront our enemies in the gate ...

Fri., 13.—In some of the following days I took a few hours to read *The History of the Puritans*. I am amazed! First, at the despicable spirit of persecution that drove these venerable men out of the church, and with which Queen Elizabeth's clergy were as deeply stained as Queen Mary's ever were; secondly, at the weakness of these holy confessors, many of whom spent as much time and energy arguing about surplices and hoods as they did kneeling at the Lord's Supper.

Thur. 19.—I pondered: "What would I do now if I knew that I had only two days to live?" All outward things are settled according to my wishes; the preaching-houses at Bristol, Kingswood, and Newcastle are safe ... My will is made. What more do I need to do except to commend my soul to my merciful and faithful Creator?

I spent a few days each week examining the fellowships around Newcastle, and found great cause to rejoice over them ...

Sun. APRIL 5.—We set out early, and about 8 a.m. went out into the market-place at Hexham. A crowd soon ran together, most of them as wild as untamed colts. Many had promised to do mighty things, but the bridle was in their teeth. I cried aloud: "Let the wicked forsake his way, and the unrighteous man his thoughts" [Isa. 55:7]. They felt the sharpness of the two-edged sword and sank into seriousness all around, so much so that I didn't hear one unkind or ill-mannered word till we left them, standing and staring at each other ...

Mon. 6.—Being told that there were many large coal mines a few miles north or northwest of Durham, I rode to a village in their midst called Renton and proclaimed, "The Lord God, gracious and merciful" [Exod. 34:6]. A great number of people listened eagerly to every word spoken. They knelt down when I prayed, sang in their own way when I sang, and crowded into the house I entered. They were all crying out, "Ah, they were only too long a-coming! Why didn't they come sooner?" ...

Fri. 10.—Having settled all the fellowships in the country, I started examining Newcastle's again. It was my special concern to remove, if possible, every hindrance to brotherly love. And I found one odd hindrance creeping in that had already caused much trouble: the notion that we must not justify ourselves. (This is an offspring of the mystic theology.) It's contrary to the scriptural injunction: "Be ready to give an answer for the hope that is in you" [1 Pet. 3:15]. Because we failed to do this in time, some offenses had become incurable. I therefore found it necessary to tear this up by the roots, explaining the duty of examining ourselves, and requiring all who wished to remain with us to justify themselves, whenever they were blamed unjustly, and not to swallow up both peace and love in their voluntary humility …

Sun. 19.—(Easter) About 9 a.m. I preached to a large gathering at Renton and reached Osmotherley before 6 p.m. Finding that Mr. D. the rector had, as I expected, been savagely attacked by neighboring clergy and aristocrats, in order to spare him any further difficulty on my account, I didn't take him up on his promise to use his church, but rather stood on a tombstone nearby. My text was, "The Lord is risen indeed!" [Luke 24:34]. How wisely does God order everything! Some won't hear the word of God outside of a church, and for their sakes we're often permitted to preach in churches. Others won't hear it inside of a church, and for their sakes we are often compelled to preach in the highways …

Tues. 28.—I preached at 8 a.m. at Pudsey, and from there rode to Dewsbury where I was to preach at noon. But first I paid a visit to the minister, Mr. Robson, and it proved to be an appropriate time. Many little offenses had risen up, magnified by those who sought just such occasions. But we spoke our minds freely, and the snare was soon broken.

After the sermon, Mr. Robson, having sent me a note to call on him again, I went and spent such a precious hour as I haven't had since leaving London. We left each other in tears. Who knows how great a work God can do in even a short time? …

Thur. MAY 14.—I rode to Barley-hall. As soon as I finished my sermon, William Shent told me he'd just come from Leeds, where he'd left Mr. Perronet in a high fever. I had no time to spare; however at 3 a.m. on Friday the 15th I set out, and between 7 and 8 a.m. came to Leeds. By the blessing of God, he recovered from that hour …

Sun. 31.—At 7 a.m. I preached in Moorfields to a large, well-behaved congregation. Mr. Bateman asked me to preach a sermon for charity at St. Bartholomew the Great, his church, in the afternoon. I had a hard time getting into the church, because not only the church itself but all the entrances were crowded with people on top of each other. They made so much noise that at first I was afraid my labor would be in vain, but as soon as the service began, all was still and my fear vanished. I hope God gave us this day as a token for good. If he will work, who will stop his hand? ...

Sat. JUNE 6.—I arranged to talk to those who had applied to us for bodily needs. I found there had been about 600 in about six months. More than 300 of these came two or three times, then we saw them no more. About 20 of those who came constantly didn't seem to be either better or worse. Over 200 were clearly better, and 51 completely cured. The entire expense, from beginning until now, was about 30 pounds[242] ...

Mon. 15.—Our conference began, ending on Saturday the 20th. The minutes of everything that transpired were later transcribed and published ...

Tues. 23.—We mounted horses at 3 a.m., stopped for breakfast at Chippenham, and had dinner at Kingswood. From there I walked to Bristol. About 7 p.m. I went to the Old Orchard, where there was a large crowd of both rich and poor. We had a solemn and joyful hour. Surely these fields are white unto harvest! ...

Sat. 27.—At Plymouth-Dock, about 6 p.m., I went to the place where I had preached last year. A little before we finished the opening hymn, the famous lieutenant came with his retinue of soldiers, drummers, and a mob. When the drums ceased, a gentleman barber began to speak, but the crowd quickly drowned out his voice with their shouts as their numbers and their fierceness increased. After waiting about 15 minutes, seeing the violence of the rabble increasing, I walked down into the thickest of them and took the captain of the mob by the hand. He immediately said, "Sir, I'll see you safe to your lodging. No one will touch you. Gentlemen, back off. I'll knock down the first man that touches him." We walked on

---

[242] About $7000 in 2020 USD.

in great peace ... till we came to Mr. Hide's door. We then parted in much love. I stayed in the street nearly a half-hour after he left, talking with the people, who now had forgotten their anger, and went away in good humor and high spirits ...

Sun. JULY 5.—I began preaching at Gwennap about 5:30 a.m. I was afraid my voice wouldn't be strong enough for such a huge crowd. But my fear was groundless since the evening was calm and the people all paid attention.

It was harder for me to be heard when I met with the fellowship. On the one hand, there were the cries of those who were pierced as if by a sword and, on the other hand, those who were filled with joy unspeakable ...

Thur. 9.—The stewards of all the fellowships [in the county] met. I now tried diligently to find out what exhorters there were in each fellowship; whether they had gifts suitable for the work; whether their lives were especially holy, and whether there appeared to be any fruit of their labor. I found, overall: 1. that there were no fewer than 18 exhorters in the county; 2. that three of these had no gifts at all for the work, either natural or supernatural; 3. that a fourth had neither gifts nor grace, but was a dull, empty, self-conceited man; 4. that a fifth had considerable gifts, but had evidently made shipwreck of the grace of God. These five I therefore decided to set aside immediately and advise our fellowships not to hear them; 5. that J.B., A.L., and J.W. had gifts and grace and had been much blessed in the work; and finally, that the rest might be helpful when there was no preacher in their own or the neighboring fellowships, provided they did nothing without the advice of those more experienced than themselves ...

Tues. AUGUST 4.—I set out for Ireland. We rode hard that day to Builth, where I preached in the evening on the Prodigal Son ...

Sat. 8.—Before 10 a.m. we came to St. George's-quay. Soon after we landed, I heard the church bells ringing, so I went there at once. About 3 p.m. I wrote a note to the curate of St. Mary's, who replied that he'd welcome my help. So I preached there, another gentleman reading prayers, to as rowdy and senseless a congregation as I ever saw. After the sermon, Mr. R. thanked me affectionately and asked me to be his guest in the morning.

Mon. 10.—I met the fellowship at 5 a.m., and preached at 6 on "Repent, and believe the gospel" [Mark 1:15]. The room, large as it was, couldn't hold the people, who all seemed to taste the good word.

Between 8 and 9 a.m. I went to Mr. R., the curate of St. Mary's. He showed plenty of good will, praised my sermon highly, and begged to see me the next morning. But at the same time he expressed deep-rooted prejudice against laymen preaching outside of church, and said that the archbishop of Dublin was determined not to allow any such irregularities in his diocese.

I went to our brothers and sisters so we could pour out our souls before God. Then I went to wait on the archbishop myself, only to find that he had left town …

Between 6 and 7 p.m. I went to Marlborough Street. Our preaching-house at the time was originally designed as a Lutheran church and holds about 400 people, but four or five times that number can stand in the yard. Many rich people were there, along with ministers of every denomination. My text was, "Scripture hath concluded all under sin" [Gal. 3:22]. I spoke clearly and strongly, but no one seemed to be offended. If my brother Charles or I could have stayed here for a few months, I think there might have been a larger fellowship here than even the one in London …

Sat. 15.—I stayed in my lodging and spoke to all who came, but found hardly a single Irishman among them. At least 99 percent of the native Irish remain in the religion of their forefathers. The Protestants in Dublin and elsewhere all came here recently from England. And it's no wonder that the Catholics live and die as such, when the Protestants find no better ways to convert them than penal laws and acts of Parliament …

Mon. 17.—I started examining the fellowship [in Dublin] this day and finished the next. It had 240 members, many who seemed strong in faith. The people here are of a more teachable spirit than in most parts of England. But for that very reason, they need to be watched more carefully, being equally capable of making good and bad impressions …

Tues. SEPTEMBER 1.—I reached Cardiff between 7 and 8 p.m., and immediately went to the preaching-room. My strength just lasted till I finished preaching, then I was very glad to lie down and rest ...

Sat. 19.—Mrs. Baddily asked me to go upstairs to her son, who had been in poor condition for several days. For a year or two he had been an example to the whole family, till he began spending more and more time talking with "a good sort" of men. Then he grew cooler and cooler to the ways of God, and after a few months left our fellowship. He had decided, he said, to stick to his church and live a sober life, and that was enough. Soon even that was too much. He grew tired of his church and dropped it and sobriety altogether. Now, his mother told me, he was as dead as a stone to all the things of God. I spoke a few words to him, then went to prayer. And God broke his heart. He continued weeping and praying all that day and night, and at 6 a.m. he died ...

Mon. 28.—I spoke with a woman who, not long before, was so overwhelmed with troubles that one night she was going to end it all by throwing herself into the New River. As she passed by the Foundry, it being a watch-night, she heard some people singing. She stopped and went in, listened a while, and God spoke to her heart, after which she no longer wanted to put an end to her life but instead to die to sin and to live to God ...

Fri. OCTOBER 9.—We had a watch-night at the chapel. Feeling weak, I was afraid I couldn't go through with it. But the longer I spoke, the more strength I had—so much so that at midnight all my weariness and weakness were gone, and I was like someone refreshed with wine ...

Mon. NOVEMBER 2.—In the afternoon I rode to Reading. Mr. J.R. had just sent word to his brother that he had hired a mob to tear down his preaching-house that night. This evening Mr. S. Richards caught up with a large group of bargemen walking towards it, and he immediately hailed them. He asked if they would go with him to hear a good sermon, saying, "I'll make room for you, and would if you were twice as many." They said they would go, with all their hearts. "But friends," he said, "wouldn't it be better to leave your clubs behind? They might scare some of the women." They threw them all away, and walked quietly with him to the preaching-house, where he set them in a pew.

When I finished my sermon, one of them, till then their captain, and a head taller than his fellows, stood up, looked around the congregation, and said, "Everything the gentleman says is good. I say so, and not a man here dares to say otherwise." ...

Sun. 22.—I spent an hour with Mary Cheesebrook, a unique example of the mercy of God. About six years ago she was without God in the world, being kept as a mistress. An acquaintance brought her one evening to the chapel in West Street, where God gave her a new heart. She wept profusely; she "plucked out the right eye and cast it from her,"[243] and from that time on earned what she needed for life and godliness by hard labor. She never missed an opportunity to come to the preaching. Often, after a hard day's work at Mayfair, she came to the Foundry, running most of the way. Every Saturday, after paying her small debts, she gave away whatever money was left, trusting that tomorrow would take care of itself ...

[*As she was dying*] I found something still lay on her mind. I urged her to speak freely, and she told me that she had an eight-year-old daughter who, after she was gone, would have no one to take care of her soul or body. I answered, "Be at peace about this as well; I'll take care of the child." From that time she lay two or three weeks in bed, quietly waiting for the salvation of God ...

Fri. DECEMBER 25.—We met at 4 a.m., and solemnly rejoiced in God our Savior. I found my own soul greatly revived this day, and so did many others. On this and the following days, I strongly urged wholly giving ourselves up to God and renewing our covenant in every respect that the Lord might truly be our God ...

1748

Fri. JANUARY 1.—We began the year at 4 a.m. with joy and thanksgiving. The same spirit was in our midst at noon and in the evening. Surely we will finally present ourselves "a living sacrifice, holy, acceptable to God" [Rom. 12:1].

Wed. 6.—I had an hour's conversation with Counselor G., notorious for many years for having contempt for all religion. Recently he had formed an acquaintance with Mr. R., as a result of

---

[243] I.e., cut off her immoral relationship.

which he soon turned on his wife. She told him, "Sir, here is a better answer to your objections than I'm able to give," and asked him to seriously read the *Earnest Appeal.* He did so, and was thoroughly convinced that there is reality in religion.

I believe he told me his whole heart. He stayed till the watch-night service ended and seemed very moved. Let just a little seed be sown and God can make it increase …

Sun. 17.—I made a public collection toward a lending-fund for the poor. Our rule is to lend only 20 shillings[244] at once, which is to be repaid weekly within three months. I began this about a year and a half ago. At that time 30 pounds, 16 shillings[245] were collected, and out of this no fewer than 255 persons have been relieved in 18 months. Dr. W., hearing of this plan, sent a guinea[246] toward it, and so did a prominent Deist the next morning …

Tues. FEBRUARY 9.—I met about 60 of the fellowship in Bristol for consultation about enlarging the preaching-room and, in fact, to make it safe, because there was real danger of it falling on our heads. In two or three days 230 pounds[247] were subscribed. We immediately got experienced builders to give us estimates for the work, and I appointed five stewards outside our fellowship to supervise it …

Sun. MARCH 6.— … In the evening I preached at Llanygorse. When I finished, Mr. Jones repeated in Welsh the substance of what I had said, and did the same that afternoon. The next morning we returned to Holyhead and found the passenger boats there that we had left.

I was determined not to stay another day at an inn, so in the afternoon found lodging in a private house, not a bow-shot from the town, and moved there immediately.

My audience that evening was larger than ever, and several of the upper-class agreed to come the next evening, but they were too late, because at midnight the wind became fair, and before 1 a.m. we sailed out of the harbor.

---

[244] About $240 in 2020 USD..
[245] About $7250 in 2020 USD.
[246] About $126 dollars.
[247] About $54,000 in 2020 USD.

Tues. 8.—The gentle breeze soon lulled me fast asleep, but I was awakened before 5 a.m. by a fierce storm that continued for two or three more hours and brought us within sight of Howth, and then, with a light breeze, brought to Black Rock about 4 p.m.

Here we rented horses and so rode to Dublin: Mr. Meriton, Swindells, and I. We reached our preaching-house in Cork Street, while my brother Charles was meeting with the fellowship. It took some time for my voice to be heard, due to the noise of the people shouting and praising God. I spent the rest of the week disposing of all the business I could, and settled with my brother everything related to our work ...

Mon. 14.—I began at 5 a.m., an unheard-of thing in Ireland. I explained part of the first chapter of Acts and purpose, God willing, to go through the book in order.

Wed. 16.—I investigated the condition of the fellowship. Inflated accounts had been sent me from time to time of large numbers added to it, so I was confident I would find 600 or 700 members. But what is the actual fact? I had left 394 members, and I now doubt if there are 396.

Let this be a warning to us all, not to give in to that hateful habit of painting things larger than life. Let our conscience not allow us to magnify or exaggerate anything. Let us speak under, rather than above, the truth. **We, of all people, should be exact in what we say, so that none of our words should fall to the ground** [my emphasis] ...

Fri. 25.—I preached at Marlborough Street at 5 a.m., to the largest gathering I have yet seen in a morning. At 2 p.m. I began in Ship Street with many rich people and aristocrats present. I was very tired, having examined classes all day, but my fatigue disappeared after I spoke two sentences; I was strengthened in body and soul ...

Fri. APRIL 1.—At 6 p.m. I preached from the window of an unfinished house facing the market-house, which wouldn't have held half those who gathered. My text was: "You know the grace of our Lord Jesus Christ" [2 Cor. 8:9]. I've hardly ever seen a better-behaved or more attentive gathering. Indeed, I've never seen so mannerly a people as the Irish in general, either in Europe or in America ...

VOLUME 2: 1745 – 1760

Mon. 11.—At 5 a.m., in Athlone, I preached the terrors of the Lord as strongly as I could. Still those who are ready to devour every word don't appear to digest any of it.

In the evening there seemed to be more emotion in the assembly than I'd ever seen before, and it was in a way I'd never seen before. It didn't work just in one here and one there, but in all. Perhaps God is working here in a way we haven't known before, moving with a slow and even motion through the whole body of people so that they all might be aware of themselves and turn to the Lord.

Tues. 12.—I rode my horse to Clara, where I soon learned that in an hour there was to be a famous cockfight that almost the whole countryside was coming to watch. Hoping to get some of them to use their time in a better way, I began preaching in the street as soon as possible. One or two hundred stopped, listened a while, pulled off their hats, and forgot their planned amusement …

Sun. 24.—I preached at Skinner's Alley at 5 a.m. and on Oxmantown Green at 8 a.m. My body was weak, but I was refreshed by the seriousness and earnestness of the gathering. Taking advantage of the occasion, I told them I would preach there again in the afternoon, which I did to a much larger and equally attentive audience. When I got to my lodging I was glad to lie down, having a sore throat and also a fever. But when the fellowship met, I made the effort to creep in among them, and immediately my voice was restored. I spoke without pain for nearly an hour altogether. And we rejoiced greatly over each other, knowing that God would order all things well.

Mon. 25.—Finding my fever higher than before, I thought it best to stay in bed and to fast a few days on apples and apple-tea. On Tuesday I was pretty well and would have preached, except that Dr. Rutty, who had visited me twice, insisted on my resting for a while …

Wed. 27.—In the evening, at a fellowship meeting, I read letters, my voice being weak but I think audible. While I was reading a young woman dropped down and cried out very loudly, but in a few minutes her sorrow turned to joy and her mourning into praise …

Thur. 28.—This was the day set for my going out into the country … So about 6 a.m. I mounted up. About 9 a.m. I paid a call at Killcock. The old landlord was down with the gout and his wife had a variety of disorders. But when I told her, "The Lord chastens those whom he loves, and all these are tokens of his love," she burst out, "O Lord, I offer you all my sufferings, my pain, my sickness! If you love me, that's enough. Here I am; take me and do with me as you will." …

Thur. MAY 5.—Though my diarrhea kept getting worse (which was caused by eating a rotten egg at Birr), I didn't want to break my promise and so made the effort to ride that afternoon to Mountmelick …

Fri. 6.—More people came at 5 a.m. than I'd ever seen at that time anywhere in Ireland, and my heart was so moved toward them that, in spite of weakness and pain, I energetically applied for more than an hour these solemn words, "The kingdom of God is at hand; repent, and believe the gospel" [Mark 1:15] …

Mon. 9.—Not having had even one hour of sound sleep from the time I lay down till the time I rose, I doubted whether I could preach. However, I went to the market-place as usual, and found no lack of strength till I had fully declared "the redemption that is in Jesus Christ" [Rom. 3:24]. Afterwards I'd planned to thoroughly settle the fellowship, but was unable to sit up so long.

Many warned me not to go out at night, the wind being extremely cold and gusty. But there was no way I could spare myself at such a time as this. I preached on "Come unto me, all you who labor and are heavy laden" [Matt. 11:28]. And when I finished, I felt at least as well as before I began …

Tues. 10.—Instead of going straight to Tullamore, I couldn't feel easy without going around by Coolylough—I didn't know why. For then I didn't know that Mr. Handy's wife, who had been put to bed a few days earlier, had a strong desire to see me once more before I left the kingdom. She couldn't help praying for this, even though her sister stopped her again and again, telling her it just couldn't happen. Before their debate ended, I entered the room, so they wondered and praised God …

Wed. JUNE 15.—I preached once more at St. Bartholomew's. How strangely has the scene changed! When we preached in a London church 10 years ago, there was a lot of laughter and ruckus among the upper-class people of the parish. And now all are calm and quietly attentive, from the least to the greatest ...

Fri. 24.—This was the day we had appointed for opening the school at Kingswood. I preached there on "Train up a child in the way he should go, and when he is old, he will not depart from it" [Prov. 22:6]. My brother Charles and I served the Lord's Supper to many who came from far away. We then agreed on the general rules of the school, which we had printed up shortly afterwards ...

Sun. JULY 3.—Mr. Hay, the rector, reading prayers, I once again had the comfort of receiving the Lord's Supper at [my home parish of] Epworth. After the evening service, I preached at the Cross again, to almost the whole town. I can see clearly that we've often misjudged when we've measured the work of God here and in other places by the numerical increase of our fellowship. The fellowship here isn't large, but God has worked in this whole area: Sabbath-breaking and drunkenness are no longer seen in the streets; cursing and swearing are rarely heard. Wickedness now hides its head. Who but God knows that, sooner or later, he may completely take it away? ...

Tues. 5.—We rode to Coningsby on the edge of the fens.[248] Mr. B., a Baptist minister, had written to me at London, begging me to lodge with him whenever I came to Coningsby, yet he had left town that very morning. But a man rode after him and brought him back in the afternoon. Scarcely had I sat down in his house before he started arguing about baptism. I tried to brush the matter aside for a while, but finding that of no use, I engaged him in earnest, and we kept at it for about an hour and a half. After that we let the matter rest and confirmed our love for one another ...

Sun. 10.—I began urging all who loved their own souls to solemnly renew their covenant with God, the nature of which I explained at length on the mornings of the following week ...

On Wednesday, Thursday, and Friday, I examined the classes and found not only an increase in number but also more of the life and power of religion among them than I'd ever found before.

---

[248] I.e., swamps, marshlands.

I observed the same thing in all the rural fellowships, among whom I spent one or more nights every week ...

Wed. 20.—We mounted up between 8 and 9 a.m. ... I sent a message to the commander of the fort requesting the use of a grassy spot near his house, which he readily granted. At 7 p.m. I preached to an estimated 2000 people. In general, I found them to be just as I expected: serious and decent, but not easily convinced of anything. For who can tell them what they didn't already know?

Thur. 21.—After preaching, we walked around the walls which they were repairing and rebuilding. I couldn't help but notice how different things appeared today than they did yesterday, especially after I'd preached at noon. Yesterday people yelled at us all along the street, but today no one opened his mouth as we walked along, and even the children were silent. The grown-ups pulled off their hats on all sides, so we might have thought we were at Newcastle. It's a good thing that honor is balanced with dishonor, and praise with blame.

At 7 p.m. I preached to a far larger assembly than before. And now the word of God was as a fire and a hammer. I began over and over, after I thought I had finished, and the last words were even stronger than the first ...

Sun. 31.—At 8 a.m. I preached in the street at Sunderland, and again at 1 p.m. From there I rode straight to Castle-garth, and found a crowd gathered. Many all around me were in tears while I opened and applied those comforting words: "He heals those who are broken in heart, and gives medicine to heal their sickness" [cf. Psalm 147:3].

Wed. AUGUST 3.—I found it absolutely necessary to publish the following advertisement:

> WHEREAS one Thomas Moor, alias Smith, has lately appeared in Cumberland and other parts of England, preaching (as he calls it) in a clergyman's habit, and then collecting money of his hearers: This is to certify, to whom it may concern, that the said Moor is no clergyman, but a cheat and an imposter, and that no preacher in connection with me, either directly or indirectly asks money of anyone.
> John Wesley

Thurs. 4.—I preached in the evening at Spen and on Friday the 5th about noon at Horsley. As I rode to my lodging, my headache grew much worse. But since many people were coming from all around, it being the monthly watch-night, it didn't feel right to send them away. While I was speaking I almost forgot my pain, but had to go to bed as soon as I finished.

Sat. 6.—My pain was much worse than before, so I applied cloths dipped in cold water. Immediately my head was well but I felt very sick otherwise. When I lay down, the headache returned and the sickness ceased; when I sat up, my headache ceased and my sickness returned. In the evening I took ten grains of ipecacuanha,[249] which took effect in about 10 minutes. After that was done I was in perfect health, with neither headache nor sickness ...

Tues. 16.—We left Newcastle ... Some gentlemen of Yarm strongly asked me to preach there in the afternoon. I refused for a while, being weak and tired, thinking that preaching three times in the day and riding 50 miles on horseback would be enough work. But they wouldn't accept my refusal, so I went with them about 2 p.m. and preached at 3 in the market-place to a large crowd of people, who gathered with just a few minutes' notice. About 7 p.m. I preached in the street at Osmotherly, it raining all the time, but no one went away. At 5 a.m. we mounted up and in the afternoon of Wednesday the 17th came to Leeds ...

Sun. 28.—Mr. U., the minister of Goodshaw, invited me to preach in his church. I began reading prayers at 7 a.m., but realizing that the church would barely hold half those coming, after prayers I went outside and, standing on the churchyard wall in a shaded spot, explained and drove home these words in the second lesson: "Almost you persuade me to be a Christian" [Acts 26:28].

I wonder about those who still speak of field-preaching as something indecent. What's more indecent than at St. Paul's Church, when many of the congregation are asleep, or talking, or looking around, and not paying attention to a word the preacher says. On the other hand, there is great decency in a churchyard or field when the

---

[249] an emetic

whole assembly behaves and looks as if they were seeing the Judge of all and hearing him speak from heaven.

At 1 p.m. I went to the market-cross in Bolton. There was a huge crowd of people, many of them completely wild. As soon as I started speaking, they began shoving this way and that, trying to throw me down from the steps I was standing on. They succeeded once or twice, but I climbed up again and continued my speech. Then they began throwing rocks, and at the same time one got up on the Cross itself to push me down, which caused me to notice how God rules even small circumstances: One man was screaming right in my ear when a rock hit him on the cheek, then he was still. Another was forcing his way down to me when a rock hit him on the forehead, bounced off, making blood run down, and he came no farther. A third, who was close to me, stretched out his hand, and that very instant a sharp rock hit the joints of his fingers. He shook his hand and was very quiet till I finished my message and went away ...

Fri. SEPTEMBER 2.—I preached at Wednesbury in the afternoon, and from there rode to Meriden. Riding with few stops, the next day we reached St. Alban's, and the Foundry on Sunday morning.

The following week I examined the classes and settled all the business for which I'd come to London. Monday the 12th I preached at Reading, then rode on to Hungerford. Tuesday the 13th I preached in the newly built preaching-room at Bristol ...

Mon. 19.—I rode to Camelford and preached about noon, with no one trying to interrupt me this time. From there I went to Port Isaac and preached in the street at 5 p.m. to almost the whole town, no one saying an unkind word. It rained most of the time, but I think that no more than five people left.

Tues. 20.—The preaching-room was full at 4 a.m. I ate breakfast around 7 a.m. at Wadebridge with Dr. W., who for many years was a steady, rational infidel. But when he read my *Appeal,* it pleased God to touch his heart, and now he is striving to be altogether a Christian

Sun. 25.—Believing my strength would not be sufficient to preach five times a day, I asked John Whitford to preach at 5 a.m. ...

I found tonight that God can wound by the gospel as well as by the Law, although the cases of this are very rare and we have no ground in Scripture to expect them. While I was driving home "We pray you in Christ's stead, be reconciled to God" [2 Cor. 5:20], a young woman, spiritually asleep until then, was cut to the heart and sank to the ground. Afterwards, however, she couldn't give a clear, rational account of how she came under conviction ...

Sat. OCTOBER 1.—I preached at Waywick about 1 p.m., then rode quietly on to Bristol.

The following week I examined the fellowship, removing every careless person and anyone who willfully and obstinately refused to meet his brothers and sisters weekly. By this means their number was reduced from 900 to about 730 ...

Tues. NOVEMBER 1.—being All-Saints' Day, we had a solemn assembly in our London chapel, and I must point out that we had done so on this day for several years. Surely, "Very dear in the sight of the Lord is the death of his saints" [Psalm 116:15].

Sun. 13.—Sarah Peters, a lover of souls, a mother in Israel [Judg. 5:7], went to rest ... It was her special gift and her constant concern to seek and save the lost, to support the weak, to comfort the feeble-minded, to bring back those who had gone astray. And in her doing this, God endowed her, above fellow-believers, with the love that "believes, hopes, and endures all things" [1 Cor. 13:7].

"She used to say," one closely acquainted with her says, "'I think I'm all spirit. I always have to keep moving. I can't rest, day or night as long as I can gather in souls to God.' Yet she'd often complain of her weakness and imperfections and cry out, 'I'm an unprofitable servant!' Sometimes I was envious that she carried her charity too far, not keeping what she needed for herself. But she'd reply, 'I can live on one meal a day, so I can give to those who have no food at all.'"

On Sunday, October the 9th, she went with another person to see the criminals facing execution at Newgate Prison. They asked especially about John Lancaster, who had requested them to come. [*Ministry continued to him and other prisoners until the day of their execution.*] ...

The prisoners begged that those whom God had sent to minister to them be allowed to spend the last night with them. But when she came at 10 p.m., she was absolutely forbidden to enter. Yet the six prisoners in the cell spent the night wrestling with God in prayer. When she was allowed in at 6 a.m., some of them were saying ecstatically, "Oh, what a happy night we've had! What a blessed morning this is! We long for the hour when our souls will be set free!" The jailer said, "I never saw people like this before." When the bellman came at noon to tell them, "Remember you are going to die today," they cried out, "Good news! Good news!" ...

All the people who saw them along the way seemed to be amazed, but even more so when they came to the place of execution. An awe overwhelmed the crowd. As soon as the executioner had finished preparing John Lancaster[250] and the two others with him, John called for a hymnbook and sang a hymn with a clear, strong voice. And after the chaplain had prayed, he announced then sang the 51st Psalm. He then took leave of his fellow sufferers with the most tender affection, blessed the persons who attended him, and commended his own soul to God.

It seems worth noting even a little incident that followed this. Lancaster's body was carried away by a group hired by the physicians, but a sailors' crew went after them, took the body from them by force, and carried it to his mother, so that it was decently buried in the presence of many who praised God on his behalf.

One thing that amazed those who were there was that, even after death, there were no marks of violence on his body. His face was not bloated or disfigured, or even changed from its natural color. He lay there with a calm, smiling countenance, as in a sweet sleep ...

Wed. 16.—In the afternoon I preached to a small group at Wandsworth who had just begun to seek God, but starting out for them was rough: The rabble gathered from every side whenever they met, throwing dirt and rocks and abusing both men and women in the worst way. The abused registered a complaint with a nearby judge, and he promised to render justice, but Mr. C. walked over to his house and argued in favor of the rioters to the effect that they were all dismissed ... A few days later Mr. C., walking over the same field, dropped down and never said another word! Surely the mercy

---

[250] John Lancaster had responded to Wesley's preaching, but later had helped steal money from the Kingswood School treasury. He repented of his act as we see evidence here.

of God wouldn't allow a man who meant well to continue being the tool of persecutors …

1749

Mon. JANUARY 2.—I'd planned to leave with a friend for Rotterdam, but felt it very urgent to reply to Dr. Middleton's book against the Church Fathers. I postponed my voyage and spent nearly 20 days at that unpleasant task …

Tues. MARCH 14.—Having scheduled one hour a week for the purpose, I met the children of our four schools together: namely, the boys boarded in the new preaching-house, the girls boarded in the old one; the boys taught by James Harding and the girls taught by Sarah Dimmock. Soon we could see the effects on the children, some deep and lasting …

Fri. APRIL 7.—We reached Garth. On Saturday the 8th I married my brother Charles and Sarah Gwynne. It was a solemn day, as suited the dignity of a Christian marriage …

Mon. 24.—I had a cold, which kept getting worse for several days, plus a swelling in my cheek which also kept getting worse, causing a lot of pain, so I sent for Dr. Rutty. While waiting for him, I applied boiled nettles, which took away the pain right away. After that I used warm molasses, which reduced the swelling, so when the doctor arrived I was almost well. However, he advised me not to go out that day. But I had made an appointment to read the letters[251] that evening. I returned to my lodging as early as I could with no inconvenience …

Tues. MAY 16.—How is it that the frequency and greatness of God's works make us less, rather than more, aware of them? A few years ago, if we heard of one notorious sinner truly converted to God, it was a matter of solemn joy to all who loved or feared him, but now, when many people of all kinds and positions in society daily turn from the power of darkness to God, we pass over it lightly as a common thing! O God, give us thankful hearts! …

Fri. JUNE 2.—In the evening an upper-class woman told me that Dr. B. had claimed to her and many others: 1. that both John and

---

[251] Likely encouraging letters from distant brothers and sisters.

Charles Wesley had been expelled from the University of Oxford long ago; 2. that there was not a Methodist left in Dublin, or anywhere in Ireland, except Cork and Bandon, the government having rooted out all the rest; 3. that there were no Methodists left in England, either; and, 4. that fundamentally it was all Jesuitism.[252] Alas for poor Dr. B! God be merciful to you, a sinner!

Sat. 3.—At the request of many in the town, after finishing my evening sermon, I answered Dr. B's claims for myself and have reason to believe it blessed many of the congregation ...

Sat. 17.—As the wind was fierce in the evening, I preached in our newly built preaching-house. Toward the end of the sermon I asked, "Who among you will give yourselves, soul and body, to God?" A woman cried out, almost shaking the building, "Oh, I will, I will!" And as soon as she could stand up, she came forward to witness before the whole congregation. It was Mrs. Glass. Her words pierced like lightning. Soon another person gave witness to the same resolution. And before long, Mrs. Meecham, who had been sorrowing as without hope, lifted up her head with joy and continued singing and praising God until dawn the next day ...

Tues. 27.—I had a two-hour conversation with J.S., a Quaker. He spoke in the very spirit and language that poor Mr. Hall used before he made shipwreck of the grace of God. I found it good to be with this man; it enlivened and strengthened my soul ...

Sun. JULY 2.—I preached at 8 a.m. in Portarlington and again at 2 p.m. I hardly knew how to end, all the people seemed so deeply affected. The fellowship now counts 100 members, full of zeal and good desires, and in just one week the whole appearance of the town has changed. Open sinfulness is not seen; the fear of God is on all sides, and rich and poor ask, "What must I do to be saved?" I thought to myself: How long will this continue? In most, only until the birds of the air come and devour the seeds. Many of the rest, when persecution or disrespect begins, will immediately take offense, and in the few remaining, some will fall away either through other desires, the cares of the world, or the deceitfulness of riches.[253] ...

---

[252] I.e., of the Roman Catholic Society of Jesus, or Jesuits.
[253] Wesley is referring to Jesus' Parable of the Sower in Matthew 13 and Mark 4.

Wed. 19.—I finished translating *Martin Luther's Life*. No doubt he was a man highly favored by God and a blessed instrument in his hand. But oh, what a pity that he had no faithful friend!—none that would risk everything to rebuke him plainly and sharply for his rough, incorrigible spirit and his bitter zeal for opinions that so greatly obstructed the work of God ...

Tues. 25.—I rode over to Kingswood and looked closely into the condition of our school there. It concerned me to find that some of our rules had been habitually neglected. I therefore considered it necessary to reduce the family, allowing none to stay there who were not clearly satisfied with the rules and committed to following them all ...

Wed. SEPTEMBER 6.—I reached Newcastle, rested one day, preached two evenings and two mornings with an uncommon blessing, and on Friday set out to visit the northern fellowships. I began at Morpeth, where I preached at noon on one side of the market-place. We were afraid the market would draw people away from the sermon, but just the contrary: Vendors left their stalls and there was no buying or selling till I finished my sermon ...

Wed. 20.—I set out for the western fellowships. In the evening, at Hinely Hill, our hearts were all melted down as we considered our great high priest who, though he has gone into the heavens, is still "touched with the feelings of our infirmities" [Heb. 4:15]. A deep sense of his love led many to call on him with "strong cries and tears," and many others with groaning that couldn't be uttered ...

Sun. 24.—After preaching at 8 a.m. at the Gins, between 1 and 2 p.m. I preached again at Hensingham to as many as my voice could command on "Repent, and believe the gospel" [Mark 1:15]. Then I hurried to the church, and in the middle of the service suddenly felt stricken. I shook all over, and in a few minutes had a fever. I thought of taking an emetic right away in order to vomit and of going to bed. But as I left church I heard there was a great gathering in the market-place, and I couldn't send them away empty. And while I was speaking to them, God remembered and strengthened me both in soul and body ...

Fri. 29.—I set out again for Whitehaven. The windstorm was strong and hit me straight in the face so that I could barely stay on my horse, especially while I rode over the broad, bare backs of the high hills that lay in my way. But I kept going the best I could till I came to the brow of Hatside. Then a fog fell so thick that I soon lost the road and didn't know which way to turn. But I knew where to find help—namely in God—in either small or great difficulties. The fog vanished in a moment and I saw Gamblesby at a distance, the town I was going to ...

[Here Wesley inserts a letter he received about this time:]

Rev. and dear Sir,

    The sincere love to your worthy person and faithful performance of your holy office which the Lord kindled in my heart during your time in Savannah, Georgia, has not lessened, but rather increased, since God's providence called you away from us and showed you another field for your ministry ....

    The Lord has graciously joined us in mutual love and harmony in our congregations, and has not permitted the Hernhutters, falsely called Moravians, nor other false teachers, to creep in among us. We are hated by wicked people, which keeps them from settling among us, though we love them sincerely and would have as many settle among us as would keep such orders as Christianity and the laws of England require them to do. This is all I thought needful to tell you about for the present. I continue with due regard and cordial wishes for your prosperity in soul and body, reverent and dear Sir,

                                  Yours most affectionately,
                                        John Martin Bolzius

What a truly Christian piety and simplicity breathe in these lines! And yet I refused to admit this very man to the Lord's Table when I was at Savannah because he wasn't baptized—that is, not baptized by a minister who had been episcopally ordained.

Can anyone carry high church zeal higher than this? How well, since then, have I been beaten with my own staff! ...

Thur. OCTOBER 5.—At Leeds Mr. Whitefield preached at 5 a.m., and about 5 p.m. he preached at Birstol. God gave him strong and persuasive words which, I trust, sank deep into many hearts.

Fri. 6.—I preached at 5 a.m., then rode back to my brother Charles, whom I had left at Leeds. At noon we spent an hour with several of our preachers, encouraging and praying. About 1 p.m. I preached to a crowd of upper- and lower-class, rich and poor, but even this number was much larger at 5 p.m. just as my strength was increased, both of soul and body. I cried aloud to them all to look to Jesus, and hardly knew when to quit ...

Fri. 13.—At the meeting of the select society,[254] such a flame broke out as was never there before. We felt such a love for each other that we couldn't express; also such a spirit of supplication and such joy to know all the providences of God and confidence that he wouldn't withhold from us any good thing ...

Wed. 18.—At the request of John Bennet, I rode to Rochdale in Lancashire. Just as we entered the town, we found the streets lined on both sides with crowds of people yelling, cursing, blaspheming, and gnashing their teeth at us. Seeing it wasn't practical to preach outdoors, I went into a large room, open to the street, and called aloud: "Let the wicked forsake his way, and the unrighteous man his thoughts" [Isa. 55:7]. God's Word prevailed over the fierceness of man. No one opposed me or interrupted, and there was a remarkable change in the behavior of the people as we later went through the town.

We came to Bolton about 5 p.m. No sooner had we started down Main Street than we realized that the lions at Rochdale were lambs compared to those of Bolton. They followed us, yelling loudly, to the house we went to, and as soon as we entered, sealed all the entrances and filled the street from one end to the other ... When the first stone came in among us, I expected a shower to follow ... But their plan was not to attack from a distance; now they had gotten a bell to call all their forces together. Soon someone ran up and told us that the mob had burst into the house ... Believing the time had now come, I walked down into the thickest of them. Now they had filled all the rooms downstairs. I asked for a chair. The wind died down, and all was calm and still. My heart was filled with love, my eyes with tears, and my mouth with reasons. They were amazed; they were ashamed; they were melted down; they devoured every word. What a turn this

---

[254] The select society in each locality was composed of persons (male and female) selected by Wesley or his assistants for training in Methodist principles and for furthering their spiritual growth.

was! Oh, how God changed the counsel of the old Ahithophel into foolishness[255] and brought all the drunkards, swearers, Sabbath-breakers, and plain sinners in that place to hear of his bountiful redemption! ...

Sat. 21.—Speaking with several people here, I realized that now we weren't among publicans and sinners but among those who, a while ago, supposed they needed no repentance. Many of them had long been "exercising themselves unto godliness," in much the same way as we had done at Oxford, but now they were thoroughly willing to renounce their own, and accept "the righteousness which is of God by faith" [Phil. 3:9] ...

Tues. 24.—I preached in Wednesbury at 4 p.m. to a nobler people and was greatly comforted by them, and the same on the morning of Wednesday the 25th. How much does a praying congregation strengthen the preacher! ...

Mon. 30.—I withdrew to my quarters in Kingswood in order to write part of the volume of sermons that I had promised to publish this winter ...

Sun. DECEMBER 3.—At Snowsfields, as usual, I preached at 5 and 10 a.m. and again at 5 p.m., besides meeting the class leaders, the circles, the preachers, and our own family. But I felt no weariness either of body or mind. Blessed be my strong Helper! ...

Wed. 27.—I saw the two Germans whom God has so wonderfully blessed in their labor of love among his ancient people, the Jews. Many Jews in Poland, Russia, Prussia, and some parts of Germany, have come, by the unceasing efforts of these two, to search the Scriptures "whether these things were so" [Acts 17:11]. And over 600 of them have given proof that they have a saving knowledge of God and of "Jesus Christ whom he has sent" [cf. John 17:3] ...

1750

Sun. FEBRUARY 4.—I preached at Hayes. How it has changed here in a year or two! Instead of the parishioners leaving the Church, people now come from many miles around. The church was also filled in the afternoon, and everyone behaved well except the choir

---

[255] 2 Samuel 15-17.

members, whom I rebuked in front of the congregation, and some of them were ashamed ...

Thur. 8.—About 12:15, an earthquake began at the edges of the town. It started in the southeast, ran through Southwark, under the river, then from one end of London to the other. It was observed at Westminster and Grosvenor Square at 12:45 ... There were three distinct shakings, or waves to and fro, along with a hoarse, rumbling noise like thunder. How gently does God deal with this nation! Oh that our repentance might prevent heavier signs of his displeasure! ...

Sun. 18.—At Snowsfields today, wherever we assembled, God let his power be known, but especially at the love-feast. The honest simplicity with which several spoke, declaring the way God had been dealing with them, set the hearts of others on fire. And the flame kept spreading till, having stayed nearly an hour longer than usual, we really had to leave ...

Thur. 22.— Several times after being sent for, I went to see a young woman in Bedlam. But I hadn't talked with her long before someone came to tell me that none of "these preachers" were to come there. So we're forbidden to go to Newgate Prison for fear of making them wicked, and to Bedlam Hospital for fear of driving them mad!

Tues. 27.—I finally forced myself to leave London. We had dinner a little beyond Colnbrook, spoke plainly to everyone in the house, and left them very thankful and with good resolutions.

I preached at Reading in the evening, and on Wednesday the 28th we rode our horses with the north wind straight in our faces. It was so cold I could hardly feel my hands or feet by the time we reached Blewbury. After speaking one by one with members of the fellowship, I preached to a large gathering. In the evening I met my brother Charles at Oxford and preached to a small, serious group ...

Fri. MARCH 2.—In the afternoon we came to Bristol. Soon many miserable comforters were with me, complaining of the lack of lively preachers, of the hurt the Germans had done to some, and R.W. to others, and the almost universal coldness, heaviness, and deadness among the people.

I knew only One who could help, so we called upon God to arise and maintain his own cause. And this evening we had a token for good, because his Word was like a two-edged sword.

Sun. 4.—I asked John W. to preach at 5 a.m., and I was no longer surprised at the deadness of his hearers. I preached at Kingswood at 8 a.m., and God spoke to many hearts, yes, and even to a few at Connam. But the greatest blessing was in the evening at Bristol, when we were all convinced that God had not "forgotten to be gracious" [cf. Psalm 77:9].

Tues. 6.—I began writing a short French grammar. We observed Wednesday the 7th as a day of fasting and prayer. I preached at 5 a.m. on "Repent, and do the first works" [Rev. 2:5] ...

Thur. 8.—I asked all the preachers in Bristol to meet me at 4 p.m. and again every day I was in town. In the evening God split the rocks again. I was amazed at the words he gave me to speak. But he does whatever pleases him ...

Sat. 10.—With the teachers of Kingswood School I discussed at length the children and their management. They all agreed that one of the boys made it his business to corrupt the rest. I wouldn't allow him to remain under the roof any longer, but sent him home that very hour ...

Sun. 11.—I would gladly have spent more time in Bristol, since I found increasing evidence that God was reviving his work there, but the reports I received from Ireland made me feel it my duty to get there as soon as possible. So on Monday the 19th I started out with Christopher Hopper for the New-passage. When we got there, there was a strong wind, coming almost straight at us; still we managed to cross in less than two hours and got to Cardiff before dark. There I preached at 7 p.m. and felt very refreshed ...

Wed. 21.—We rode to Builth, where I preached at noon. Between 4 and 5 p.m., Mr. Philips set out with us for Royader. I wasn't well at all in the morning; still I went on to Llanidloes and then lay down. After an hour's nap I felt much better and rode on to Machynlleth ...

Fri. 23.—After overnight in the inn at Dolgelly, we heard the rain beating down when we woke up. We mounted up at 5 a.m. and it rained without stop all the while we rode. When we came to the mountain, four miles from the town—by which time I was wet from my neck to my waist—I had a hard time not slipping over the head of my mare, since the wind was almost ready to carry us away. Nevertheless about 10 a.m. we arrived safely in Dannabull, praising him who saves both man and beast.

Since our horses were very tired and we ourselves were completely wet, we rested the rest of the day, especially since several members of the family understood English—a rare thing in these parts. We spoke directly to them about spiritual things, and they seemed very affected, especially when we all joined in prayer ...

Sun. APRIL 8.—I preached morning, afternoon, and evening, and then urged the fellowship to stand fast in the good old Bible-way and not to move from it to the right or the left.

I found Mr. Lunell in a high fever with little hope that he would live. But he revived the moment he saw me and fell into a breathing sweat. He began to recover from that time. Perhaps I was sent for this purpose also ...

Thur. 12.—We dined at Mr. P.'s. A young married woman was there, until recently a zealous Catholic who had converted several Protestant heretics to the Roman faith. But when she set upon some of the Methodists, they converted her—or, at least, convinced her of the great truths of the gospel. Immediately her relatives—her husband especially—renounced her. But none of these things moved her; she desires nothing on earth but to experience the faith she once persecuted.

In the evening a man who had reasoned himself out of all his Christianity sent for me, now doubting whether the soul would survive the body. Surely even theoretical faith is the gift of God; without him, we can't even hold this securely ...

Sat. 14.—Several of the Methodists that were charged as vagrants in the fall appeared at the Lenten sessions before the grand jury. But as no one appeared against them, they were acquitted, with honor to themselves and shame to their persecutors. These, by bringing the matter to court, plainly showed that "there is law even for Methodists." It also gave his Majesty's judge an occasion to declare the total illegality of all riots and there being no excuse for tolerating—much less causing—them on any pretence whatsoever ...

Wed. 18.—A woman who, when she turned to God, had been expelled from her home and shunned by all her relatives (all good Protestants), was now received into the "house of God, not made with hands." We rejoiced over her in the evening with great joy. Happy are those who lose all but gain Christ!

Wed. 25.—At Closeland I dined at Mr. K.'s, who had lived utterly without God for about 70 years, but now God had made him and most of his household "partakers of like precious faith" [2 Peter 1:1]. When I first entered his home, he was in agony due to a pain he had endured for about 45 years. I advised to apply hot nettles. The pain soon ceased, and he rose up and praised God.

Thur. 26.—I examined the class of children, many of whom are rejoicing in God. Then I searched for the lost sheep, and left all whom I spoke with determined to return to him. About noon I read the letters, and in the afternoon rode cheerfully to Mount-melick. I found the fellowship greatly increased in grace but fewer in number—something I hardly remember having met with before in all England and Ireland.

Sun. 29.—I preached at 8 a.m., at 2 p.m., and finally at 5 p.m. when our worst opponents were there, but by their seriousness and close attention, they gave us reason to hope they will oppose us no more.

Mon. 30.—I baptized a man and a woman, former Quakers, as I did one other the night before. Afterwards I visited the sick …

Tues. MAY 1.—In Tullamore, I found that many of the first had become the last, having returned "as a dog to his vomit" [Prov. 26:11] … In meeting the fellowship, I rebuked them sharply for their lukewarmness and covetousness. In that hour the spirit of contrition came down, and all of them seemed broken in pieces. At the same time my voice, which had been very hoarse, was restored in a moment, so I could once more sing praise to God …

Sun. 13—About 5 p.m. I preached at Ahaskra to an audience that came from all around. Oh, what a harvest there might be in Ireland if only the poor Protestants didn't hate true Christianity worse than either Catholicism or heathenism! …

Sun. 20.---Understanding that my usual preaching site would not contain those wanting to hear, about 8 a.m. I went to Hammond's-marsh. The gathering was large and very attentive. Some of the riffraff collected a ways off, but little by little they came nearer and mixed in with the assembly ...

That afternoon, a rumor spread that the mayor planned to keep me from preaching on the Marsh that evening, so I asked Mr. Skelton and Mr. Jones to go see him and ask about it. Mr. Skelton asked if he disapproved of my preaching there, adding, "Sir, if so, Mr. Wesley won't do it." He replied in anger, "Sir, I'll not allow any mobbing." Mr. Skelton: "Sir, there was none this morning." The mayor: "There was. Aren't there enough churches and meeting-houses? I won't allow any more mobs and riots." Mr. Skelton: "Sir, neither Mr. Wesley nor those who heard him made either mobs or riots." The mayor then said plainly, "I'll have no more preaching, and if Mr. Wesley tries to preach, I'm prepared for him." ...

Mon. 21.—I rode on to Bandon. From 3 p.m. till after 7, the mob of Cork marched in grand procession and then burned me in effigy near Dant's-bridge.

While they were doing this, Mr. Haughton took the opportunity to go down to Hammond's-marsh. He called at a friend's house there, where the man's wife took care to lock him in. But seeing that many people had gathered outside, he opened the window and preached to them through it. Many seemed deeply affected, even of those who previously were persecutors, and they all quietly withdrew to their own homes before the mob got to them ...

Sun. 27.—At 8 a.m. we had a glorious shower of rain such as usually follows a calm. After church I began preaching again on "the Scripture has concluded all under sin" [Gal. 3:22]. In the evening a huge crowd flocked together such, I believe, as had never before been seen in Bandon, and the fear of God was in their midst. The whole multitude seemed to be deeply in awe while I expanded on "God forbid that I should glory except in the cross of our Lord Jesus Christ" [Gal. 6:14] ...

Tues. JUNE 5.—I returned to Limerick. As I examined the classes there, I couldn't help but notice 60 of the Highland Regiment of soldiers—men fit to appear before princes. Their zeal "according to knowledge" [cf. 1 Peter 3:7] has stirred up many, and they continue speaking for God and are not ashamed ...

Serious Joy (John Wesley's *Journal*)

Fri. 15.—We set out at 4 a.m. and reached Kilkenny, about 25 old Irish miles, about noon. This is by far the most pleasant and most fruitful country I've seen in all of Ireland. After lunch our way passed by Dunmore, the residence of the late Duke of Ormond. We rode through the park for about two miles, the river running beside us. I never saw in England, Holland, or Germany a place so delightful. The walks, each consisting of four rows of ashes, the tufts of trees sprinkled up and down, interspersed with the smoothest and greenest lawns, are beautiful beyond description. But what does its owner, the Earl of Arran, have? He can't even behold it with his eyes ... I finally lay down to sleep about midnight. I think this was the longest day's journey I ever rode, being 50 old Irish, that is, about 90 English miles ...

Sat. 23.—I listened as two women in our group expressed their prejudices against each other. This went on for three hours and they grew more and more angry to the point of being deranged. I saw that prayer was the only remedy, so a few of us wrestled in prayer for over two hours. When we stood up, one woman ran and fell on the other's neck. Anger and revenge vanished and melted away into love. Only one person continued in agony of soul. We sought God on her behalf and didn't let him go till she too was set free ...

Tues. JULY 3.—I preached in the evening on the Connaught side of the river. Then I met with the fellowship, but when I was ready to dismiss them, no one seemed willing to leave. We were standing there just looking at each other when a cavalryman walked out into the middle of the room and said, "I have to say something. I was like Saul; I persecuted the children of God ... I hated you especially, Mr. Wesley, and said all kinds of evil things about you. I was going to see a woman last night when one of my buddies met me and asked me if I'd go to the watch-night service. I came out of curiosity, but paid no attention to what was said the first half of the sermon. Then God struck me to the heart and I couldn't keep standing; instead I dropped to the ground. Last night I didn't sleep a wink and came to you in the morning, but couldn't speak. From you I went to a few of our brothers, who prayed with me till my burden fell off. And now, by God's grace, I'll part from you no more. I'm ready to go with you all over the world."

His words were like fire, kindling a flame that spread throughout the assembly. We praised God with one heart and voice. Then I spoke a benediction the second time, but the people stood motionless as before until another cavalryman stepped out from among his fellows and said, "I was a Pharisee from my youth, having a strict form of godliness, yet I always lacked something—I didn't know what—until something inside led me—I couldn't say why—to hear you preach. And since you came here, I've done that. I saw right away that what I lacked was faith and the love of God, and he gave me both here last night. Now I can rejoice in God my Savior." ...

Thur. 19.—When the fellowship met, some sinners whom I didn't know were so convicted in their consciences that they couldn't keep from confessing their faults in front of all their brothers and sisters. I had just admitted one of these to membership, and another I had just excluded, but he pleaded so earnestly to be on trial a little longer that I couldn't refuse him. We wrestled with God on his behalf that sin might no more rule over him ...

Mon. AUGUST 6.—I rode to St. Mewan and found a large assembly, despite the rain, waiting for me. As I came out, a huge man ran right into me. I thought it was an accident, till he did it a second time and began cursing and swearing. At this I stepped aside out of the path, but he pursued me fiercely through the crowd and planted himself right by my side. Toward the end of the sermon his expression changed and after a while he took off his hat. When I finished, he squeezed my hand and went away as quiet as a lamb ...

Thur. 9.—At 1 p.m. I preached in the street to three times as many as the preaching-room would have held. After that I visited a poor old woman a mile or two outside of town. Her trials had been unusual: inexpressible agonies of mind joined with all sorts of bodily pain—not, it seemed, from any natural cause, but from Satan's direct operation. But now her joys were just as unusual: She needed little sleep having, for the past several months, seen, as it were, the unclouded face of God, and she praised him day and night ...

Wed. 15.—Reflecting on an odd book, *The General Delusion of Christians with Regard to Prophecy,* which I read during this trip, I was fully convinced of something I had long suspected: 1. that the Montanists, in the 2nd and 3rd centuries, were real, scriptural

Christians; and 2. that the main reason the miraculous gifts were so soon withdrawn was not only that faith and holiness were well-nigh lost, but that dry, orthodox men began even then to ridicule whatever gifts they themselves didn't have and to dismiss them all as either madness or fakery ...

Fri. 17.—Through all Cornwall I find the fellowships have suffered great loss due to lack of discipline. The ancients wisely said, "The soul and body make a man; the Spirit and discipline make a Christian." ...

Tues. 28.—In the evening I preached in Laneast church to a large and attentive congregation. What can destroy the work of God in these parts but zeal for and quarreling about opinions? ...

Mon. SEPTEMBER 17—My brother set out for the north but returned the next day in very poor condition. How little do we know the counsels of God! But we know they are all wise and gracious.

Wed. 19.—When I came to our apartment in the evening I found him much worse. He hadn't slept for several nights and expected to have no rest unless it was from opioids. I went downstairs to our brothers and sisters and we made our request known to God. When I went up again he was in a sound sleep which continued till morning ...

Tues. OCTOBER 23.—Riding through Holt, I paid a visit to the minister, Mr. L., one of the most zealous adversaries we've in England. I found a calm, sensible, impressive old man, and we spent over an hour in friendly debate ...

Fri. NOVEMBER 30.—I rode through a fierce storm to Windsor and preached to a serious gathering. About 1 p.m. I preached at Brentford, and gathered up the poor remains of the shattered fellowship. How firmly did they stand in the midst of storms! But once the sun shone, they melted away ...

1751

Sat. FEBRUARY 2.—Having received a full answer from Mr. P., I was clearly convinced that I ought to marry. For many years I stayed single because I believed I'd be more useful to God in a single state than in a married one. And I praise God who enabled me to do so. Now I was as fully convinced that, in my present circumstances, I might be more useful in the married state. Acting on this clear conviction, and upon the advice of my friends, I entered the state of matrimony a few days later.[256]

Wed. 6.—I met with the single men and gave them many reasons why it was good for those who had that gift from God to remain "single for the kingdom of heaven's sake" [cf. Matt. 19:12], there being exceptions to the general rule.

Sun. 10.—After preaching at 5 p.m., I was in a hurry to take leave of the congregation at Snowsfields, planning to set out in the morning for the north when, in the middle of London Bridge, both my feet slipped on the ice and I fell down heavily, my ankle-bone hitting the top of a stone. I got up with help and made it to the chapel, determined not to disappoint the people. After preaching, I had my leg wrapped by a doctor, then with difficulty walked to Seven-dials. I had a lot of trouble getting up into the pulpit, but then God comforted many of our hearts.

I took a coach back to Mr. B.'s, and from there was carried in a chair to the Foundry, but was unable to preach since my sprain grew worse. So I moved to Threadneedle Street, where I spent the rest of the week partly in prayer, reading, and conversation, and partly in writing a Hebrew grammar and lessons for children ...

Sat. MARCH 30.—I rode to Birmingham and found God in the midst of the congregation.

Sun. 31.—I earnestly warned the fellowship against idle disputes and vain quarrels, then preached on "If you are led by the Spirit, you are not under the Law" [Gal. 5:18]. The hearts of many were melted, so neither they nor I could hold back our tears. But they were mainly tears of joy, from a real awareness of the liberty by which Christ has set us free ...

Tues. APRIL 2.—I preached in the evening at Wednesbury where, in spite of the rain, every man, woman, and child stayed to the end. I warned them earnestly not to lean on broken reeds—that is, on opinions of any kind—and even the predestinarians received it in love and told me it was very suitable for the occasion.

---

[256] This leaves a negative impression, since Wesley tells us nothing about the woman he is marrying, about their courtship and engagement. It seems an impulsive act on his part. Did he truly love her?

Wed. 3.—I finished visiting the classes, which had been shattered by the sowers of strange doctrines. At 1 p.m. I preached at Tipton-green, where the Baptists also have been ravaging the flock. This forced me, in speaking of these words, "Arise, and be baptized, and wash away thy sins" [Acts 22:16], to spend almost 10 minutes in controversy, which is more than I've done in public for many months—perhaps years—previously ...

Wed. 24.—We reached Musselburgh, Scotland, between 4 and 5 p.m. I had no intention of preaching in Scotland and didn't imagine that anyone there wanted me to do so. But I was wrong. If nothing else, curiosity brought out a large number of people together in the evening. And whereas in the kirk[257] (Mrs. G. informed me) there used to be laughing and talking and the utmost inattention, it was quite the contrary here: they were as still as statues from the beginning of the sermon to the end ...

Sat. MAY 11.—We returned to Epworth to a poor, dead, weak-minded people. This didn't surprise me when I learned: 1. that some of our preachers had collected and spread all the evil they heard about me; 2. that some had stopped using our hymns as well as the doctrine they once preached; and 3. that one frequently spoke against our rules, and the others simply neglected them. Nothing but God's mighty power could have kept the people as well as they were ...

[A letter Wesley wrote to an unnamed Anglican minister.]

Rev. Sir,　　　　　　　　　　　　London, August 15, 1751

1. I take the liberty to inform you that a poor man, recently of your parish, was with me some time ago, along with two others who live in or near Wrangle. If what they affirmed was true, you were much involved in some recent affairs there. In short: A riotous mob, several times, in particular on July 7 and August 4, assaulted a group of quiet people, striking many of them, beating others to the ground, and dragging others away. After abusing them in various ways, they threw them into drains or other deep waters, putting their lives in danger. But that wasn't enough for them; they broke into a house, dragged a poor man out of bed and drove him out of the house naked

---

[257] Scottish word for "church."

while also damaging his goods. At the same time they threatened to treat all of them the same or worse if they didn't stop worshiping God in the way they believed to be true and right.

2. The victims, I am told, went to a nearby justice of the peace to apply for legal remedy, but got none—far from it. The justice himself told them they got what they deserved and that if they kept on (worshiping God according to their conscience) the mob would treat them the same way again.

3. I grant that some of those people might act in passion or with ill manners. But even if they did, was there any proportion between the fault and the punishment? Or if punishment is due, does the law say that a riotous mob should carry it out?

4. I grant further, that this gentleman supposed the doctrines of the so-called Methodists to be atrocious. But is he sure about this? Has he read their writings? If not, why does he pass judgment before he hears the evidence? If he has, and thinks them wrong, yet is this a method of refuting error to be used in a Christian—a Protestant—country? And especially in England, where everyone may think for himself, since he must give an account to God?

The sum of our doctrine, with regard to inward religion (insofar as I understand it), is contained in two points: loving God with all our hearts, and loving our neighbor as ourselves. And as for outward religion, two more points: doing all to the glory of God, and treating everyone as we would like them to treat us. I believe no one will easily refute this by Scripture and sound reason, or prove that we preach or hold any other doctrine as necessary to salvation.

Sir, I thought it my duty, though a stranger to you, to say this much, and to ask of you two things: That the damage these poor people have sustained may be repaid, and next, that in the future they may be allowed to enjoy the privilege of Englishmen: to serve God according to the dictates of their own conscience. On these conditions they are very willing to forget all that is past.

Wishing you all happiness, spiritual and temporal, I remain, Reverend Sir,
Your affectionate brother and servant ...

Sat. 17.—I called on a gentleman in the city whom I hadn't seen in a good while. I found him thin and pale, appearing to be developing tuberculosis. I asked him if he didn't think a journey would be better for him than a lot of medicine and if he'd set out with me and my wife for Cornwall on Monday—to which he willingly agreed ...

Wed. OCTOBER 30.—After preaching at West Street Chapel in the evening, I walked to Lambeth to see Miss S., who for several days had expressed a strong desire to see either my brother Charles or me. When I arrived, her sister told me she was unconscious and hadn't spoken for several hours. But as soon as I took her by the hand she spoke, declaring full hope of immortality. I prayed with her and praised God on her behalf. An hour or two later, her spirit returned to God ...

Tues. NOVEMBER 19.—I began writing a letter to one who compared the Catholics to the Methodists. This was heavy work which I wouldn't choose except sometimes it has to be done. One of the ancient writers well put it: "God made practical theology necessary, and the devil made it controversial." But it is necessary: We must "resist the devil," or he won't "flee from us" [James 4:7].

1752

Sun. MARCH 15.—While I was preaching at West Street in the afternoon, there occurred one of the most furious storms I ever remember. Right in the middle of my sermon, a large part of a house opposite our chapel was blown down. We heard the noise but didn't know the cause. For this reason God spoke even more strongly to our hearts, and we rejoiced greatly, confident in his protection. Between 4 and 5 a.m. my wife, daughter,[258] and I mounted horses, with tiles still rattling down from the houses on both sides, but they didn't hurt us ...

Thur. 26.—We rode on, through wind and snow, and reached Manchester. That night I was grieved to hear everywhere, from my entering Cheshire till now, that John Bennet was still speaking all kinds of evil against me, saying that Mr. W. preached nothing but

---

[258] Wesley married Molly Vazeille, a widow with four children, in 1751, when he was 48. Their marriage was never a good one, largely due to his constant travels and her jealousy of the women he saw and who wrote him letters (which she opened). She left him in 1771 and they remained separated thereafter. I did not find this in my copies of his *Journal*, but Wikipedia reports that he wrote: "I did not forsake her, I did not dismiss her, I will not recall her."

Catholicism, denying justification by faith, and making nothing of Christ. Lord, lay not this sin to his charge! ...

Sun. APRIL 5.—About 1 p.m. I preached at Birstal. Noticing that several sat on the side of the opposite hill, I later asked a man to measure the ground, and we found it was 140 yards from the place where I stood. Yet the people there heard perfectly well. I didn't think any human voice could have reached that far ...

Sat. 11.—I preached at R____, once a place of furious riot and persecution, but now quiet and calm since the bitter rector has gone to give an account of himself to God.

Sun. 12.—I preached at Wakefield; as the bells were ringing people in I went straight to Mr. W. in the vestry. The congregation's behavior surprised me; I saw no one careless or unaffected while I expounded, "What does it profit a man if he gains the whole world but loses his own soul?" [Matt. 16:26]. Doesn't God have the hearts of all people in his hand? Who would have thought I'd be preaching in Wakefield Church to such an attentive congregation a few years ago, when all the people were like roaring lions, and the honest man didn't dare let me preach in his churchyard lest the mob pull down his buildings?

Mon. 13.—In the evening I preached at Sheffield in the shell of the new preaching-house. All is at peace here now since the trial at York, at which the officials were sentenced to rebuild the preaching-house that the mob had pulled down. Surely the magistrate giving the order has been the minister of God to us for good! ...

Thur. 16.—I walked over to Burnham. I hadn't thought of preaching there, doubting that my strength would be sufficient to continue preaching three times a day as I'd done most days since I came from Evesham. But finding a house full of people, I couldn't hold back. The more I use my strength, the more I have. I'm often very tired the first time I preach in a day, a little less the second time, but after the third or fourth time, I rarely feel weakness or weariness ...

Mon. 20.—I rode by way of Hainton to Coningsby. The next day I preached at Wrangle, where we expected some disturbance but didn't find any. The sentence imposed on the recent rioters (though it wasn't heavy, since they plea-bargained) has secured peace ever since. It's a real mercy to impose the weight of the law on those who flaunt it! It prevents many inconveniences to the innocent and much sin to the guilty ...

Fri. 24.—At Mighton-car, a huge crowd gathered, thousands of them serious, but others acting as if possessed by Moloch. Rocks and clods of dirt flew all around, but they neither hurt nor disturbed me. After finishing my speech, I looked for my coach, but the coachman had driven away. We were at a loss what to do till a gentlewoman invited my wife and me to ride in her coach. This caused her some trouble: Not only were there nine of us in the coach—three on each side and three in the middle—but the mob was right on us, throwing whatever was in their hands in the windows, which we didn't think it prudent to shut. But a large gentlewoman who sat in my lap shielded me so I wasn't touched ...

Sat. 25.—I went to see the room provided for preaching but found it wasn't more than 15′ x 15′ square. I then looked at a yard that was offered, but it was filled with rocks, which I didn't like—ammunition for the devil's drunken companions. Just then it began to rain, upon which a gentleman offered me a large, spacious barn. I began preaching to a few, but the number kept increasing as I went on. I haven't known such a time since leaving London; tears fell like rain, and no one opposed or mocked ...

The man and his wife at whose house we dined had been bitterly persecuted by both their mothers. They were some of the first whose hearts were touched. Immediately after preaching, they came up into our chambers and confessed, with many tears, how eagerly they had opposed the truth of God and troubled their children for clinging to it. How wise are all the ways of God! If it hadn't been a fair-day, they wouldn't have been there ...

Mon. 27.—We reached Osmothersly. After preaching in the evening, I was asked to visit a woman who had been a notorious scoffer at all religion; but now, they said, "was in a strange way." I found her in a strange way indeed: either raving mad or possessed of the devil. She herself said the devil had appeared to her the day before, and after some talk, had jumped on her and had grievously tormented her ever since. We prayed with her, and her agonies ceased. She fell asleep and awoke the next morning calm and easy ...

VOLUME 2: 1745 – 1760

Thur. MAY 14.—At 5 a.m. the soldiers were a good part of the gathering. At noon they came again in companies. One of them, T.W., came from the Highlands last year and went through Westmoreland to drum up recruits. He had been strictly warned, before leaving Scotland, not to go near the Methodists on any account. But in Kendal he met two or three of them, after which they were never a day apart. Before long, God clearly assured him of his pardoning love. Two weeks later he was ordered to follow his regiment to Berwick, where he's constantly encouraging his comrades to be "good soldiers of Christ Jesus," and many have already enlisted under that banner ...

Wed. 20.—I preached at Biddick to a crowd of coalminers, though it rained constantly. All of them, even some who had long drawn back, seemed to be melted down like wax before a flame. I don't remember seeing so strong and general an influence on an assembly in some years ...

Tues. 26.—In the evening we came to Allandale and found the poor fellowship almost completely shattered. Negligence and offenses had eaten them up. When I entered the room, I was just like one of them, having no life or strength and hardly able to speak or stand. But immediately we had a token for good. My voice and strength were completely restored and I cried aloud, "How shall I give you up, Ephraim?" [Hos. 11:8]. The mountains flowed down again at his presence, and the rocks once again were broken in pieces ...

Sat. JUNE 6.—We reached Chipping and immediately were informed that several there were conferring as to how to keep me from preaching. Mr. Milner, hearing they were meeting in the house next door, went there and brought them all to us; they were the churchwardens and three or four other men. I spend about a quarter-hour in calm and friendly debate with them, and they left much cooler than they came ...

Tues. 9.—I preached at 6 a.m. to many people near Ewood and with an unusual blessing. From there we rode to Todmorden. The minister was slowly recovering from a severe paralysis, with which he was struck immediately after preaching a harsh sermon against the Methodists ...

Sat. 13.—The preaching-house was more filled this evening than the evening before, while I applied that gracious invitation, "Come to me, all who are weary and heavy-laden" [Matt. 11:28] ...

Mon. JULY 6.—Finding no ship ready to sail, I decided to return to Whitehaven, so my wife and I mounted horses between 9 and 10 a.m., and in the evening I preached at Manchester ...

Fri. 17.—We boarded a ship on Monday the 13th but, due to contrary winds, it was Friday evening before we reached Dublin. The preaching-house here is about the same size and shape as the one in Newcastle, but since it has deep balconies on three sides, it will hold more people ...

Mon. 27.—I preached in Edinberry at 1 p.m. and at Closeland in the evening. Tuesday the 28th I preached at Portarlington, though I was very sick and it was painful for me to speak, but it was a comfortable pain. I was able to praise God from my heart for his fatherly visitation.

Wed. 29.—I rode to Mount-mellick, but was so hoarse I could only preach in the preaching-house. Friday the 31st: Not well enough to ride horseback, I borrowed Mr. P.'s chair[259] to Tullamore, and on Saturday reached Cooly-lough and met many of my friends from all around. Now I found my strength increasing daily—sufficient for each day.

Sun. AUGUST 2.—I baptized Joseph English, formerly a Quaker, and two of his children ...

Tues. 4.—I preached about noon at Street to a civil but unconcerned audience, and about 6 p.m. at Abidarrig, a mile from Kenagh. Many Catholics were present, and I felt a great concern for them. I couldn't refrain from addressing them in particular, exhorting them to rely wholly on the one Mediator between God and man ...

Sat. 23.—We reached Cork. On Sunday the 24th, in the evening, I proposed to the fellowship our building a preaching-house. The next day ten people pledged 100 pounds.[260] Another 100 was pledged in three or four days, and a parcel of ground bought. Now I saw God's providence doubled in our not sailing last week: If we

---

[259] Probably a light vehicle drawn by one horse (a buggy?), per Oxford English Dictionary.
[260] About $23,500 in 2020 USD.

had, this building probably wouldn't have been built, and most likely we ourselves would have been shipwrecked, since over 30 ships, we learned, were lost on these coasts in the recent storm ...

Mon. OCTOBER 2.—Against the wind, I rode once more to Bandon. Although my coming was unexpected, the building was too small to contain half the people who gathered, so I preached in the street, both that evening and at 5 a.m. on Tuesday morning, the moon giving us sufficient light until the sun took its place ...

Thur. 26.—The body of Elizabeth Man being brought into the preaching-room, I spoke on "Blessed are the dead who die in the Lord" [Rev. 14:13]. She is a clear example of grace so changing the heart as to leave no trace of her natural disposition! I recall her being fretful, peevish, grumbling, discontented about everything. But for more than a year before she died, God laid the axe to the root of the tree: All her peevishness and fretfulness was gone; instead, she was always content, always thankful ... Often her soul was so filled with love and praise that her body was overwhelmed. On Sunday morning she said, "I'm going to die." She had intense pains all day, but they didn't stop her prayer and praise; she kept exhorting those around her till about 3 a.m., having finished her work, she was set free.

Sun. 29.—This was a day beneficial to my soul. More than once I felt trouble and heaviness, but I called on the name of the Lord and he gave me a clear, full approval of his way and a calm, thankful acceptance of his will.

I stand amazed at the goodness of God. Others are attacked on the weak side of their soul, but with me it is the opposite: If I have any strength at all (and I only have what has been given to me) it is in forgiving injuries; and on this side I am attacked more often than on any other. But Lord, don't leave me here one hour to myself, or I will betray myself and you! ...

Mon. NOVEMBER 6.—During the rest of this and the following month, I prepared the remainder of the books for the Christian Library for publication; a work that has set me back over 200 pounds.[261] I hope the generation after me will realize its value ...

---

[261] About $47,000 in 2020 USD.

1753

Sun. JANUARY 7.—I had breakfast with M.Y., an unusual example of mercy. For a long time he was like "a dog turned back to his vomit" [Prov. 26:11], and wallowed in sin of all kinds. But his wife never gave up on him, and he couldn't escape from the hell inside him, till one day she told him, "Go upstairs and seek God; you don't know—maybe he will still bless you." He went, but with a dull, heavy heart, and stayed about two hours. When he came down, she stared at him and asked, "What's the matter? What's happened to you? You look different." He said, "Yes, because I've found the Lord." And from that hour he has tried to walk worthy of God, who has once again called him "to his kingdom and glory." ...

Thur. FEBRUARY 8.—A proposal was made for transferring all my temporal business, books and all, entirely to the stewards so that, in London at least, I might have no care except that of the souls committed to my charge. Oh, when will it really happen? From this very day?

In the afternoon I visited many sick people. Who couldn't be moved by such sights? Nothing like these is to be found in any pagan country. If any of the Indians in Georgia were sick—which rarely happened until they learned gluttony and drunkenness from the Christians—his neighbors gave him whatever he needed. Oh, who will convert the English into honest heathens!

On Friday and Saturday I visited as many more as I could. I found some in their cells underground; others in attics, half-starved with cold and hunger, added to weakness and pain. But every single one of them who was able to crawl about was working. It is wicked and devilishly false to object that "They are poor because they are lazy." If you took the time to see these things with your own eyes, would you spend your money on baubles and luxuries? ...

Wed. 28.—We rode horses to Bristol, where I read Mr. Prince's *Christian History*. It's amazing how differently God has carried on his work in England and in America! In America, over 100 of the established clergy, men of age and experience, and noted for sense and learning in those parts, are zealously involved in the work. Here, almost all the aged, experienced, learned clergy are zealously fighting against it, and only a handful of raw young men are involved in it, without reputation, university learning, or superior intelligence. And yet in America, the work has seldom flourished more than six months at a time, then there's been a general decay until the next revival, whereas in England what God has accomplished by these detested instruments has continued to steadily increase for 15 years, and whenever it has declined in one place, it has gloriously increased in others …

Fri. MARCH 16.—I returned to Bristol, and on Monday the 19th set out with my wife for the north. I preached in the evening at Walbridge, near Stroud. Many people stood outside since the house was too small, but neither before nor after—much less during—my preaching, did I hear any voice or any footstep, so great was the silence with which they came, listened, and left …

Thur. APRIL 5.—I rode to Bolton and found the fellowship exactly twice as large as it was when I was here last, and they are growing in grace no less than in number, walking closely with God, lovingly and prudently with each other and wisely toward outsiders …

Mon. 9.—Mr. Milner rode with us to Kendal, where I preached in a large, comfortable room (the weather not allowing me to preach outdoors) where Mr. Ingham's fellowship used to meet. I was disturbed at how the people came in and sat down, making no pretence of prayer or interjection to God, and their sitting during the hymn, which not a single one (though they knew the tune) sang with me. But it was totally different after the sermon, for God spoke through his Word. At the second hymn every person stood up and most of them sang audibly, and most of the fellowship followed us to our inn, not leaving us until we went to bed …

Sun. 15.—We ate lunch at Dumfries, a clean, well-built town, having two of the most elegant churches that I've seen, one at each end of the town. We reached Thorny-hill in the evening. What sorry reports currently circulate in England about the inns in Scotland! Here, as well as everywhere we stayed in our whole journey, we not only had everything we needed, but everything right at hand, in good order, and as clean as I could want it …

Fri. 20.—[After preaching outdoors the day before in Glasgow, I planned to preach there again, but the rain made it impractible.] So

Mr. G., the rector of the college church, asked me to preach in his church, where I began between 7 and 8 a.m. Surely with God nothing is impossible! Who would have believed, 25 years ago, either that the minister would have asked it or that I would have agreed to preach in a Scottish kirk? ...

Thur. 26.—I spoke one by one with the fellowship members and found they'd been outrageously harassed by a few extreme predestinarians who finally had left us. It was a good thing that they saved me the trouble, because I can have no connection with those who will be contentious. I reject them not for their opinion but for their sin—their unchristian temperament and practice, for refusing reproof, for hating peace and their own brethren—and therefore, God himself ...

Fri. MAY 4.—We held our first general quarterly meeting of all the stewards around Newcastle, in order to thoroughly understand both the spiritual and temporal condition of every fellowship ...

Sun. 13.—I began preaching in York at 7 a.m., and God applied it to the hearts of the hearers. There were tears and groans all around me, among high-class and low. It seemed as though God were bending the heavens and coming down. The flame of love went before him; rocky hearts were broken in pieces, and the mountains of mercy flowed down at his presence.

I had planned to leave for Lincolnshire that morning, but finding that a day of God's power had come, I sent a brother to preach there in my place, and after preaching as scheduled at Stamford-bridge and at Pocklington, I returned to York in the evening. Let us work together with God when, where, and as he pleases!

Every night while I stayed, many of the rich and respectable crowded in among us. Isn't "God able to raise up children to Abraham even of these stones?" [Matt. 3:9] ...

Tues. 22.—Most of our preachers met and had open discussion, and we did so, morning and afternoon till the end of the week. Our conference ended with the same blessing as it began, God allowing us not only to be one in heart but one in judgment ...

Tues. 29.—I preached at Keighley, where the loving spirit and exemplary behavior of one young man has been a means of convincing almost the whole town—except for his own household ...

Tues. JULY 3.—I rode over to Mr. K.'s at Taddington, "an Israelite indeed." After lunch Dr. Halles invited us to his home and showed us several experiments. How well do science and religion agree in a man of good understanding!

Sun. 8.—After preaching at the chapel, morning and afternoon, I took horse with Mr. P. We had planned to ride only two or three hours in order to shorten the next day's ride. But a young man caught up with us near Kingston and persuaded us to change our plan. So we only rested half an hour at Cobham and, leaving between 9 and 10 p.m., rode on easily in a calm, moonlit night, and about midnight reached Godalming. We mounted up again at 4:30 a.m. and got to Portsmouth about 1 p.m.

I was surprised to find so little fruit here after so much preaching. That damnable affliction of disputation had almost destroyed all the seed that had been sown. And this useless quarreling they called "contending for the faith." I believe that the whole faith of these poor wretches is mere opinion ...

At 6:30 p.m. I preached in the market-place to a large assembly, but they weren't as serious as those at Portsmouth. The children made a lot of noise, and many grownups were talking aloud almost the whole time I was preaching. But it was very different at 5 a.m.; again there was a large assembly, but this time every person seemed to realize that this was the word by which God would judge them in the last day ...

Tues. 17.—At their earnest request, I preached to the poor coalminers confined in Newgate Prison because of the recent riot. They wouldn't hear the gospel while they were free; God grant that they may benefit from it now! ...

Mon. 23.—I rode to Launceston and held the first general meeting of the stewards for the eastern part of Cornwall. In the evening I preached in perfect peace—a great blessing, if the price we pay isn't too high; that is, **if the world doesn't begin to love us because we love the world** [my emphasis] ...

Sat. 28.—After preaching to the little flock at Zennor, we rode on to St. Just, and found an assembly at 6 p.m. such as we used to have 10 years ago. I didn't find another fellowship in the county as

alive to God as this one. Lately 50 or 60 have been added to it, including many children filled with peace and joy in believing.
...

Sun. 29.—In the morning I woke up between 2 and 3 a.m. My bowels had been loose for several days. On Sunday it got worse by the hour, but I was determined, with God's help, to preach where I was expected to. Now, along with diarrhea, I had a constant headache, forceful vomiting, and cramps in my feet or legs several times an hour. But God enabled me to be completely content and resigned to him. I requested someone to preach in my place in Ludgvan at noon, at Helstone in the evening, and another on Tuesday noon at Porkellis while promising, if able, to meet them in the evening ...

Tues. AUGUST 14.—I willingly accepted the offer of using the preaching-house recently built for Mr. Whitefield at Plymouth-dock. It behooves us to thus trample on bigotry and party-zeal. Shouldn't all who love God love one another? ...

Fri. 24.—I attempted once more to bring Kingswood school into order. Surely the importance of this work is clear, even with the difficulties that attend it. I have spent more money and time and care on this than almost any other work I have ever undertaken; still it tries my patience to the limit. But it's worth all the effort ...

Fri. OCTOBER 5.—I crossed over to Portsmouth. Here I found people who had disputed themselves out of the power and nearly out of the very form of religion. Still I labored—and not altogether in vain—to soften and compose their jarring spirits, both that evening and the next day. On Sunday at 5 p.m. I began at Portsmouth-common. I admired not so much the great number of people as their unusually decent behavior, which ran through the whole assembly. After the sermon I explained to them at length the nature and purpose of our fellowships and asked any who were willing to join to see me either that evening or in the morning ...

Mon. 22.—I was extremely weak when I rose but determined, if possible, to keep my word, and so set out soon after 4 a.m. for Canterbury. I was forced to stop at Welling, but after resting an hour was much better. However my sickness returned soon after I began riding my horse, and it stayed with me to Brompton, near Chatham.

In the evening I preached to a serious gathering; also at 5 a.m. We reached Canterbury about 1 p.m., when almost immediately I was seized with the cold fit of an ague.[262] About midnight I fell asleep, and woke up well at 7 a.m.

Wed. 24.—I preached in the evening with no inconvenience, and also at 5 a.m. But about 9 a.m. I began shivering again. After the hot fit, I lay in a heavy sweat till 8 p.m. Then I gradually cooled till I fell asleep, and rested sweetly till the morning.

Fri. 25.—Determined to use the interval of health, I hired horse and buggy and reached Brompton in the evening, and spoke, as well as I was able, God bearing witness to the word of his grace.

Sat. 26.—I arrived in London, having received no harm but rather having benefited from my journey.

Thur. NOVEMBER 1.—I began visiting the classes, although I found, by the loss of my voice, that my physical strength hadn't recovered as much as I'd thought …

Sun. 4.—I rode to Hayes since I'd promised I would, though I felt very sick. It was with great difficulty that I read prayers, preached, and administered the sacrament. I had an easier time with the evening service, but at night my strength completely failed. I would have taken some rhubarb the next day but didn't have time, as I had classes to meet from morning to night.

Thur. 8.—During the night my disorder came back worse than ever since I left Cornwall. I would have taken some ipecacuanha in the morning, but had no time to spare, since every hour of my day was scheduled until 4 p.m., and by that time all my symptoms were gone so that I just needed a little food and rest …

Wed. 14.—As we rode home, the wind was strong and piercingly cold. It blew straight in our faces, so the open buggy was no protection and my feet were almost frozen. When I got home, pain had settled in my left chest and I had a heavy cough and a slow fever. But in a day or two, by following the directions of Dr. Fothergill, I got much better, and on Sunday the 18th I preached at Spitalfields and administered the sacrament to a large congregation …

---

[262] Alternating chills and fever.

Serious Joy (John Wesley's *Journal*)

Mon. 26.—Dr. Fothergill told me plainly that I mustn't stay in town a day longer. He added: "If anything will help you, it must be the country air, rest, donkey's milk, and daily horse riding." So, as I wasn't able to sit on a horse, about noon I took a coach for Lewisham.

In the evening, not knowing what God's will for me might be, and to prevent silly eulogies, I wrote as follows:

> Here lies the Body
> Of
> John Wesley
> A BRAND PLUCKED OUT OF THE BURNING:
> WHO DIED OF A CONSUMPTION IN THE FIFTY-FIRST YEAR
> OF HIS AGE,
> NOT LEAVING, AFTER HIS DEBTS ARE PAID,
> TEN POUNDS BEHIND HIM:
> PRAYING,
> GOD BE MERCIFUL TO ME, AN UNPROFITABLE SERVANT !

He ordered that this, if any, inscription, should be placed on his tombstone.

Wed. 28.—I found no change for the better, the medicines that helped me before now having no effect. About noon, the time that some brothers and sisters in London had set apart for joining in prayer, an idea came to my mind to try an experiment. I ordered some powdered sulfur to be mixed with the white of an egg and spread on brown paper, which I then applied to my side. The pain was gone in five minutes and the fever in half an hour, and from that point on I began to regain strength. The next day I was able to ride horse and continued doing so throughout the month of December.

Fri. DECEMBER 14.—Having finished all the books that I intended for the *Christian Library*, I went against the doctor's order not to write and began recording a *Journal* for the press. In the evening I went to prayers with the family without any bodily trouble ...

1754

Sun. JANUARY 6.—I began writing notes on the New Testament, a work I probably never would have attempted if I hadn't been too sick to travel or preach, yet well enough to read or write ...

Mon. 14.—In the evening one or two of our neighbors asked to join in our family prayers. Soon a few more made the same request, so I had a little gathering every night. After a few nights, I began to add a short exhortation, thus preparing myself for a larger gathering ...

Thur. 31.—My wife, wanting to render her last services to her poor dying son, left for London and arrived a few days before he went home [to be with the Lord], rejoicing and praising God ...

Wed. FEBRUARY 27.—My brother Charles came down from London, and we spent several days together, comparing the translation of the Evangelists[263] with the original ...

Tues. MARCH 19.—Having finished the rough draft, I began writing for publication the *Notes on the Gospels.*

Tues. 26.—I preached for the first time after a space of four months. What reason do I have to praise God, that he has not completely taken the word of truth out of my mouth! ...

Sun. MAY 12.—I tried to convince Mr. Green, the rector, that it wasn't good that he had tried to refute the sermon I had preached the previous Sunday morning that same afternoon, but he was absolutely set in his position. I then asked, "Will you meet me halfway? I'll never preach publicly against you; will you do the same for me?" But he rejected any such agreement and walked away as if that was the end of it. He told everyone he met that I had put him away, but indeed it wasn't I. I adore the providence of God. He has put himself away, and I won't ask him to come again until he has sounder judgment and a more teachable spirit ...

Wed. 22.—Our conference began, and the spirit of peace and love was in our midst. Before we dismissed, we all signed an agreement not to act independently of each another. So the recent breach has only united us more closely than ever ...

JUNE 2.—(Being Whitsunday [Pentecost]) I preached at the Foundry, which I hadn't done before in the evening. I still haven't

---

[263] I.e., the Gospels: Matthew, Mark, Luke, and John.

fully recovered my voice or my strength. Perhaps I never will, but I'll use what I have ...

Mon. AUGUST 5.—I set out for Canterbury, and on the way read Mr. Baxter's *History of the [Church] Councils*. It's amazing, and would be totally incredible except that his evidence is irrefutable. What wretches they were who, in almost every age since St. Cyprian, governed the church! One council was constantly cursing another and handing them over to Satan—all who didn't receive their edicts, though often frivolous, sometimes false, unintelligible, even self-contradictory! Surely Islam was let loose to reform the Christians! ...

Tues. SEPTEMBER 3.—We rode at an easy pace to Taunton. After resting a while, a man asked me to step inside to see his father who was dying of tuberculosis. He had always been a very honest, moral man, but now found this was not the one thing he needed, and he seemed to want to know Christ and the power of his resurrection ...

Mon. 9.—I preached at Charlton, a village six miles from Taunton, to a large gathering assembled from the towns and countryside for many miles around. Sometime earlier all the farmers had agreed to dismiss from their employment and to hire no one who went to hear a Methodist preacher. One of their leaders, Mr. G., soon after that, was convinced of the truth and asked those very men to preach at his house. Many of the other accomplices came to hear, with their servants and employees gladly following. So Satan's whole plan fell to the ground, and God's Word grew and prevailed ...

Tues. 17.—I rode to Trowbridge, where a man who found peace with God while he was a soldier in Flanders, and since his discharge has prospered greatly in business and has built a preaching-house at his own expense. He very much wanted me to be the first to preach there, but before I finished the opening hymn, the room was so crowded and therefore so hot, that I had to go and stand outside at the door. There was a crowd of listeners, rich and poor. Oh, that they may not all hear in vain! ...

Fri. OCTOBER 4.—I came to London. On Monday the 7th I withdrew to a little place near Hackney, once a seat of Bishop

Bonner and still bearing his name. Here it was as if I were in a college.

Twice a day we joined in prayer. The rest of the day, aside from about an hour for meals and another for walking before lunch and dinner, I spent quietly in my study ...

1755

Mon. APRIL 7.—I was advised to take the Derbyshire Road to Manchester. We stopped for refreshments six miles beyond Lichfield. Noticing a woman sitting in the kitchen, I asked, "Are you not well?" and found she had just been taken ill on her journey with the symptoms of pleurisy. She was glad to hear of an easy, cheap, and almost infallible remedy: a handful of nettles, boiled a few minutes, and applied warm to the side ...

Soon after we remounted, we came upon a poor man creeping along on two crutches. I asked where he was going. He said it was to Nottingham, where his wife lived, but both his legs had been broken while his was on ship and he had spent all his money. He appeared very thankful [for our help] and ready to acknowledge the hand of God ...

Thur. 24.—In less than four hours we rode the eight (so-called) miles to Newell-hay. Just as I began to preach the sun broke out and shone very hot on the side of my head. I knew if that continued I wouldn't be able to speak long, so I lifted my heart up to God. In a minute or two the sun was covered with clouds, which continued until the service ended. Anyone who wants to do so may call this chance, but I call it an answer to prayer ...

Sat. 26.—At 7 a.m. I preached to a large, serious assembly, and again at 4 p.m. When I began in a meadow near the preaching-house, the wind was so strong I could hardly speak. But the winds, too, are in God's hand. In a few minutes that trouble ceased; we found the Spirit of God breathing in the midst of us, and great was our rejoicing in the Lord ...

Wed. 30.—[My brother Charles and I] began reading together *A Gentleman's Reasons for his Dissent from the Church of England.* It's an elaborate and brilliant tract, and forcefully presents its case, but it doesn't yield one proof that it's lawful—much less our duty—for us to separate from the Church ...

Tues. MAY 6.—Our conference began at Leeds. The point on which we asked all the preachers to speak their minds fully was "whether we ought to separate from the Church?" Whatever was put forward on one side or the other was seriously and calmly considered, and on the third day we all reached the general conclusion that whether it was lawful or not to separate, it was by no means advisable.

Mon. 12.—My wife and I rode to Northallerton ...

MAY 18.—(Being Whit-Sunday [Pentecost].) I preached about 8 a.m. at Gateshead-fell and returned to Newcastle before the service at St. Andrew's began. At the Lord's Supper many received an unusual blessing and felt God had not left the Church of England.

The following week I spoke to the members of our fellowship individually and found much fewer than I expected to be prejudiced against the Church—a total of no more than 40, I think. And I trust the plague is now stopped ...

Sat. JUNE 7.—One of the cathedral clergymen sent for Mr. Williamson, who had invited me to preach in his church, and told him, "Sir, I hate persecution, but if you let Mr. Wesley preach, it will be the worse for you." In spite of this he requested my services, but I declined. Perhaps there is providence in this as well. God won't allow my little remaining strength to be spent on those who won't hear me except in an honorable way ...

Mon. 9.—I said farewell at York to the richest fellowship, as individuals, that we have in England. I hope this place will not prove, as Cork has for some time, the Capua[264] of our preachers. When I reached Epworth, the congregation was waiting, so I immediately went to the town Cross and we gloried greatly in our Lord.

Tues. 10.—I met the stewards of the Lincolnshire fellowships, who gave us an acceptable account of the work of God in every place ...

Mon. 16.—I preached in the evening at Nottingham, and on Thursday afternoon reached London. From a deep sense of the

---

[264] From the history of Capua, Italy, Wesley may mean a false ally.

amazing work that God has done in England in recent years, I preached in the evening on Psalm 147:20: "He has not dealt this way with any nation"—no, not even with Scotland or New England. In both these nations God has bared his arm, but not in as astonishing a manner as among us here in England ...

Tues. 24.—Observing in that valuable book, Mr. Gillies' *Historical Collections,* the custom of Christian congregations in all ages to set aside times of solemn thanksgiving, I was amazed and ashamed that we had never done so after all the blessings we had received. And many to whom I mentioned it gladly agreed to set apart a day for that purpose.

Mon. 30.—I started out for Norwich and reached it the next day in the evening. Since a large assembly was waiting, I had to preach even though I was quite weary. The following two days I spoke to each member of the fellowship and on Friday, July the 4th, mounted horse again, though I didn't feel like I could ride five miles. But God strengthened both man and beast, and I reached Bury the same night and London the next night, much less weary than when I left Norwich.

Mon. JULY 7.—This was our first day of solemn thanksgiving for the innumerable spiritual blessings we have received. And I believe it was a day that won't soon be forgotten.

Sun. 27.—I buried the body of Ephraim B., once a pattern to all who believed. But when he stopped fasting and denying himself in general, he sank lower and lower till he lost both the power and the form of religion. When he got sick, at first he was in deep despair, but a great deal of prayer was made for him. Toward the end, it pleased God to shine his face on him once again. So I trust his backsliding only cost him his life, and that he may still live with God forever.

About this time I was very moved by a letter sent from a gentleman in Virginia. Here it is in part:

> The poor Negro slaves here never heard of Jesus or his religion till they arrived here in America. And their masters generally neglect them as though they don't have immortal souls like their own. These poor Africans are the main object of my compassion and, I believe, the proper object of your love as well.

The population of Virginia is estimated to be about 300,000, and about half of these are believed to be Negroes. The number of those who attend my ministry isn't clear, but I think about 300 attend regularly. I've never been so struck with the appearance of an assembly as when I glanced at one part of the house, beautified (so it seemed to me) with many black faces, attentive to every word they heard, and some of them covered with tears. About 100 of them have been baptized after being instructed in the great truths of religion and have shown their understanding by lives of strict virtue ...

Wed. AUGUST 6.—I mentioned to the congregation another means of increasing serious religion, frequently practiced by our ancestors, and accompanied by great blessing, namely: joining in a covenant to serve God with all our heart and all our soul. For the following several mornings I explained this, and on Friday many of us kept a fast to the Lord, imploring him to give us wisdom and strength to commit ourselves to the Lord our God and to be faithful to our commitments.

Mon. 11.—Again I explained the nature of such a commitment and of doing so in a way pleasing to God. At 6 p.m. we met for that purpose at the French Church in Spitalfields. After I had gone over the nature of the proposed covenant, in the words of that blessed man, Richard Alleine, all the people stood up to testify of their consent, about 1800 people. I hardly ever saw such a night before. Surely its fruit will remain forever ...

Sat. 30.—About 5 p.m. I found the assembly waiting in a wide, adequate part of the street in Redruth. I was very tired, and my friends were so glad to see me that they didn't think of offering me something to eat or drink. But my weariness disappeared when I started speaking. Surely God is in this place too ...

Wed. SEPTEMBER 3.—At 4 a.m. Mrs. M. came into my room in tears and told me she'd apparently seen our Lord standing by her, calling her by name, and that ever since she'd been filled with joy unspeakable. Soon after that her sister came in in a similar condition, and later her niece, who like them melted into tears and refused to be comforted. But which of these will endure to the end? At least for now God is among them ...

The example of W.T. has done a lot of good here. He was utterly without God when his father died and left him a small estate along with many debts. Seven or eight years ago he found peace with God. He sold his estate, paid off his debts, and with what he had left opened a small shop. God blessed him in that in an unusual way. Meanwhile, his behavior is such that more and more of his neighbors say, "Well, this is a work of God!" ...

Sat. 13.—Once again I preached at St. Just, on the cornerstone of their new fellowship hall. That evening, as we rode to Claiborne, John Pearce of Redruth told of a remarkable occurrence: While he was living at Helstone, when their class was meeting one evening, one of them cried out in a peculiar tone of voice: "We can't stay here; we must go to [a certain house in a different part of town]!" Immediately they all got up and went there, though neither she nor they knew why. Shortly after they left, a spark fell into a barrel of gunpowder in the next room and blew up the house. So God preserved those who trusted in him and prevented the slander of others.

At 1 p.m. I preached on faith, hope, and love. I was surprised at the behavior of the whole assembly; it seems at last that God is moving on all their hearts. About 5 p.m. I preached at St. Agnes, where all but two or three received the truth in love, and these few soon walked away. From there I rode to Cubert. At noon I was very tired, but at the end of the day was as fresh as in the morning ...

Fri. OCTOBER 3.—I rode over to Pill, a place, like Kingswood, famous for many generations for stupid, brutal, wild wickedness. But what is all the power in the world and the devil when the day of God's power comes? It seems that many of the inhabitants now want to turn from the power of Satan to God ...

Mon. 13.—About noon I preached at Shepton-mallet and in the evening at Coleford, where the congregation has grown so much that they need to enlarge their building ...

Wed. NOVEMBER 5.—Mr. Whitefield came to see me. We have no more disputes; we love each other and join hands to promote the cause of our common Master ...

Fri. DECEMBER 12.—As I was returning from Zoar, I felt as well as usual entering Moorfields, but there my strength entirely gave out, and I was taken with such a faintness and weariness that I had difficulty getting to my lodging. I couldn't help but think how good it would be (supposing we are ready for the Bridegroom) to sink down and steal away at once, without any of the hurry and ceremony of dying! Yet it's still better to glorify God by our death as well as by our life ...

Tues. 23.—I was in the robe-chamber, adjoining the House of Lords, when the king put on his robes. His brow was deeply furrowed with age and clouded with care. And is this all the world can give even to a king? All the grandeur it can afford? A blanket of ermine around his shoulders, so heavy he can hardly move under it! A huge heap of borrowed hair, with a few plates of gold and glittering stones upon his head! Alas what a mere trinket is human greatness! And even this will not endure ...

1756

Thur. JANUARY 1.—We had a large gathering at 4 a.m. How divided people are in their expectations regarding the coming year! Will it bring a flood of temporal calamities, or otherwise, of spiritual blessings? Perhaps both: temporal calamities leading to spiritual blessings ...

Fri. FEBRUARY 6.—The national fast-day was glorious, a day such as London has hardly seen since the Restoration.[265] Every church in the city was filled, and on every face was a solemn seriousness. Surely God hears prayer, and our tranquility will be prolonged.

Even the Jews observed this day with special solemnity. The form of prayer in their synagogue began, "Come, and let us return unto the Lord, for he has torn, and he will heal us"; and concluded with these remarkable words: "Incline the heart of our Sovereign Lord King George, as well as the hearts of his lords and counselors, to use us kindly, and all our brethren, the children of Israel; that in his days and in our days we may see the restoration of Judah, and

---

[265] The restoration of the monarchy in England in 1660 following Oliver Cromwell.

that Israel may dwell in safety, and the Redeemer may come to Zion. May it be thy will! And we all say Amen." ...

Wed. 25.—I dined with Colonel _____ who said, "No men fight like those who fear God. I had rather command 500 like them than any regiment in his Majesty's army." ...

Mon. MARCH 1.—I set out for Bristol. Later I received the copy of a letter dated March 2nd from Rev. Davies in Virginia; what follows are some extracts:

> When the books [you sent] arrived, I announced after sermon, asking any Negroes who could read, and white people who could not afford them but would use them well, to come to my house. For some time after that, the slaves, whenever they had an hour's leisure, hurried to me and received them with all the marks of true gratitude. All the books were useful, but none more so than the Psalms and hymns, which satisfied their special taste for hymns. Some of them spent all night in my kitchen; a few times, when I woke up at 2 or 3 a.m., a flood of sacred hymns poured into my bedroom. Some of them spent the whole night in this practice.
>
> The benefits of this charity are already evident. It convinces the heathen that, however careless about religion most white people are, there are some who consider it important. Some of their masters have been stimulated to imitate us and are ashamed that strangers on the other side of the Atlantic take pains to teach their servants while they neglect to do so. The Negroes who can already read are progressing in learning. This has stirred up others to learn to read, because I'll only give books to those who can read as a reward for their efforts. I'm told that in almost every home in my congregation, and in many other places, they spend every free hour trying to learn ...
>
> Thousands of Negroes in this colony still remain grossly ignorant and are as pagan as they were in the wilds of Africa. More than a few of these are within the bounds of my ministry. But they are not all like this; my ministry has had an effect on some. Two Sundays ago, I was pleased to see 40 of their black faces at the Lord's Table, several of whom gave unusual evidence of their sincerity in religion. Last Sunday I baptized seven or eight who had been catechized for some time. Indeed, many of them seem determined to press into the kingdom ...
>
> I have distributed some of the books among the poor white people, telling them to circulate them among those of their neighbors

who would seriously read them, so as to make them as useful as possible, and some of them have shared with me what deep impressions they received by reading them …

Tues. APRIL 6.—A sister told me of an outstanding example of the power of faith. "Many years ago," she said, "I fell and sprained my ankle, so that I thought it would never completely recover. But seven years ago this past September, I was coming home from preaching on a very dark night when I stumbled over a piece of wood and fell with the whole weight of my body on my lame foot. I thought, 'O Lord, I won't be able to attend preaching again for many weeks!' Immediately a voice in my heart said, 'Name the name of Christ and you will stand.' I jumped up, stretched out my foot, and said, 'Lord Jesus Christ, I name your name. Let me stand!' And my pain stopped; I stood up; and my foot was as strong as ever." …

Sun. 11.—I met with about 100 children who are catechized all together twice a week. Thomas Welsh began this some months ago, and its fruit can already be seen. What a pity that all our preachers everywhere don't have the zeal and wisdom to follow his example!

Tues. 13.—I had breakfast with one of the loveliest old men I ever saw: John Garret, a Dutchman by birth, and a speaker among the Quakers …

Mon. 26.—I started out for Cork, intending to visit as many fellowships as I could on the way. In the afternoon I came to Edinderry, where the little fellowship has built a spacious preaching-house. I had planned on preaching outdoors, but the sharp wind drove us into the house. Although they had no prior notice, the gathering filled it from one end to the other, except that a few found it too hot and quickly left while I proclaimed, "You must be born again" [John 3:7] …

Tues. MAY 4.—We rode to Portarlington where, on Wednesday the 5th, at the request of several who couldn't attend the early preaching, I preached in the assembly room at 10 a.m. on "You must be born again." Many of the so-called "best" people in the town were there and seemed amazed. Even more came in the evening, among whom I found an unusual liberty of spirit. For the moment they seem very affected, but how soon will the thorns grow up?

VOLUME 2: 1745 – 1760

Thur. 6.—I rode to Kilkenny. One of the cavalrymen soon discovered we were there. A few of them, along with some from the town, are united and constantly meet together. I preached in the barracks, in one of the officers' rooms. Still, in Ireland, military has the priority ...

Wed. 12.—In the evening I preached in the new preaching-house at Cork, nearly as large as the one in Dublin, and with an interior more elegant in every way, though costing 400 pounds[266] less ...

Wed. JUNE 16.—I rode over to Newmarket and preached to an earnest assembly of poor people. In the morning, at the request of the nearby upper class, I delayed preaching till 10 a.m. Many of them were present then and seemed quite astonished. Perhaps they will remember it—for a week.

In the afternoon I rode to Ballygarrane, a town of Palantines[267] who came over in Queen Anne's time. They maintain much of the temperament and manners of their own country and have no resemblance to those among whom they live. I found real life among this plain, natural, serious people. The whole town came together in the evening and praised God for the consolation. Many who aren't connected with us [Methodists] walk in the light of God's countenance. In fact, they've imitated us by dividing themselves into classes, and lived in perfect harmony with our brethren ...

Thur. 24.—I went on to Ennis, a town consisting almost wholly of Catholics except for a few Protestant gentlemen. One of these, the chief person in the town, had invited me to his house. He walked with me to the courthouse where I preached to a huge, wild, spiritually dead multitude, both Protestants and Catholics, many of whom would have been disruptive if they dared.

Fri. 25.—Mr. Walsh preached at 6 a.m., first in Irish, then in English. The Catholic priest arranged his service to be at the same hour, and his man came again and again with his bell, but not one-tenth of his people would stir. At 8 a.m. I preached to a far more serious assembly, and the word seemed to sink into their hearts ...

---

[266] About $94,000 in 2020 USD.
[267] Originally, members of the German court.

Tues. JULY 13.—A large gathering at Longford was present at 5 a.m. and didn't move despite some heavy showers. At noon I preached at Cleg Hill, and again at 5 p.m. in the barrack-yard, where there was a greater gathering of people than before. Mr. P., the minister of a neighboring parish, and another clergyman who came with him, received the truth in love, and Mrs. P., his wife, found rest to her soul.

But how is it that almost everywhere, even when there's no lasting fruit, so great an impression is made at first on a considerable number of people? The fact is this: Everywhere the work of God rises higher and higher till it reaches a peak, and it seems to stay there for a while, then it gradually sinks again …

Sun. 18.—A little before noon (the usual time in Ireland) the morning service began at Rosemead Church, where Mr. Booker preached a useful sermon. I preached at 5 p.m. to many plain country people and two coaches full of the upper class. Oh, how hard it is for these [upper class] to enter into the kingdom of heaven!

Mon. 19.—As soon as we entered Ulster, we noticed a difference. The earth was tilled just as in England, and the cottages were not only neat but had doors, chimneys, and windows. The first town we came to, Newry, allowing for the difference in size, is laid out much like Liverpool. I preached soon after 7 p.m. to a large assembly and to a good part of them again at 5 a.m. Afterwards, I spoke to the members of the fellowship, consisting of Anglicans, dissenters, and Catholics. But there is no striving among them unless it's to "enter in at the narrow gate" [Matt. 7:13] …

Fri. 23.—The rector, with his curate, called on me; they openly voiced their objections [to my preaching], and we spent about two hours in free, serious, friendly conversation. How much evil might be avoided or removed if other clergymen would follow their example! …

Fri. AUGUST 6.—On this and the next day I finished my business in Ireland so as to be ready to sail at an hour's notice.

Sun. 8.—The wind was fair and we were about to set sail, but as we were boarding ship the wind turned full east. I find it very useful to be in suspense; it is an excellent way of breaking our will. May we be ready either to stay longer on this shore or to launch into eternity! …

Wed. 25.—[Back in England once again,] we rode on to Bristol.

Thur. 26.—About 50 of us [Methodist preachers] meeting, the Rules of the Society were read and carefully considered item by item, but we didn't find a single one that could be omitted. So we agreed to abide by them all and to recommend them [to our fellowships] with all our might …

Mon. SEPTEMBER 6.—I took passage in a carriage and on Tuesday evening came to London.

Wednesday and Thursday, I settled my temporal affairs. For about 18 years now, I've been writing and printing books. And how much in that time have I gained by printing? Going over my accounts, I found that as of March 1, 1756 (the day I last left London), by printing and preaching together I had gained a debt of 1236 pounds[268] …

Sun. OCTOBER 3.—My diarrhea returned as severe as ever, but I disregarded it while performing the service at Snowsfields in the morning and afterwards at Spitalfields, till I went to the Lord's Table to administer the supper. Then a thought came to my mind: "Why shouldn't I seek God in the beginning rather than at the end of an illness?" I did so and found immediate relief, so I no longer needed any kind of medicine …

Mon. 11.—I went to Leigh. Where we ate dinner, a poor woman came to the door with two little children. They and their mother seemed half-starved, and the woman was shivering with the ague. She was extremely thankful for a little food, and even more so for a few pills that almost always cure this disorder …

Sat. 16.—I baptized Hannah C., formerly a Quaker. As usual, God bore witness to his ordinance. A solemn awe spread over the assembly, and many couldn't hold back their tears …

Mon. NOVEMBER 1.—This was a day of triumphant joy, as All-Saints' Day generally is. How superstitious are those who refrain from giving God solemn thanks for the lives and deaths of his saints!

---

[268] About $291,000 in 2020 USD.

Tues. 9.—Having purchased a device on purpose, I had several persons electrified who were sick with various disorders. Some of them found an immediate, and some a gradual, cure. From then on I set aside some hours every week, and later on an hour every day, so that any who wanted to could try the benefit of this surprising medicine ... We've used this method ever since, and to this day, hundreds, perhaps thousands, have received unspeakable good, and I haven't known any man, woman, or child who's been hurt by it ...

Sun. DECEMBER 26.—I buried the remains of Joseph Yarner, an Israelite indeed. The peace that filled his heart during his last hours gave such a glow to his countenance that it remained after his death, to the surprise of all who remembered the cloud that used to hang over him ...

1757

Mon. JANUARY 3.—I visited a poor dying backslider, full of good resolutions. But who can tell when these indicate a real change of heart? And when they don't---when they spring only from fear—what will they profit a person before God?

Mon. 10.—I walked to Bishop Bonner's with Mr. D., who recently entered Cambridge full of good intentions. May God keep him humble and simple of heart! Then his keen mind and learning will do him good; but how great are the odds against him!

Wed. FEBRUARY 16.—Calling on a friend, I found that he had just be taken with all the symptoms of a pleurisy. I advised him to apply a plaster of sulfur, and in a few hours he was perfectly well. Now why should this patient have taken a lot of drugs and lost 20 ounces of blood? For what purpose? Why, to please the doctor and pharmacist. Enough! Good reason! ...

Sun. 27.—After the services at Snowsfields, I found myself much weaker than usual, and afraid I wouldn't be able to complete the day's work, equal to preaching eight times. So I prayed that God would send me help, and as soon as I finished preaching at West Street, a clergyman who had come to the town for a few days offered me his services. So when I asked for strength, God gave me strength, and when I asked for help, he gave me that too.

VOLUME 2: 1745 – 1760

For a long time I'd wanted to see the little flock in Norwich, but I couldn't rightly do this before rebuilding part of the Foundry there as my lease obligated me to. Now a sum of money sufficient for that purpose was given to me unexpectedly by someone I didn't know personally. So on Monday the 28th I set out, and preached in Norwich on Tuesday evening, March 1st. Mr. Walsh had been there preaching for 12 or 14 days, and God had blessed. After I preached, I signed a contract with a builder and gave him part of the money, which I had in hand. On Wednesday and Thursday I settled all our spiritual and temporal affairs and on Friday and Saturday returned with Mr. Walsh to London …

Mon. APRIL 11.—At 5 p.m., about 1200 members of our society met me at Spitalfields. I expected two to help me, but no one came. I kept preaching till between 7 and 8 p.m.; by then I was barely able to walk or speak. But I looked up [to heaven] and received strength. At 9:30 p.m., God broke in mightily upon the congregation. Great indeed was our glorying in him; we were filled with consolation. And when I went to my apartment between 10 and 11 p.m., I was no more tired than at 10 in the morning …

Thur. 28.—I talked with a man who, on the advice of his pastor, had calmly and deliberately beaten his wife with a big stick till she was black and blue almost from head to foot. And he insisted that it was his duty to do so because she was ornery and bad-tempered, and that he was full of faith all the time he was doing it, and had been so ever since.[269] …

Thur. MAY 5.—I asked John Johnson about Miss Judith Berresford. Here is part of his account:

> She was always an innocent, sober young woman, outwardly godly until convicted of sin and soon after that justified. She was a model of both devotion and diligence. In spite of having wealth and being sickly, she always kept busy. When she had no work to do [at home], she worked for the poor. And the whole character of her behavior was such that it's still a common saying, "If Miss Berresford hasn't gone to heaven, nobody ever will." …

---

[269] Wesley implies his strong disapproval of this behavior and this spirit.

When her weakness kept her in her room, she rejoiced with joy unspeakable, especially when she was freed from all her doubts about Christian perfection. No one ever thirsted for this more, and she exhorted all her brothers and sisters to press after it ...

As soon as I came to Ashbourn, she sent for me, and broke out: "I'm at my journey's end. What a mercy that I, who have done so little for God, should so soon be taken up to him! Oh, I'm full of the love of God!" ... I asked, "Have you felt any sin remaining in you lately?" She said, "I felt pride a few weeks ago." And it seems this was the last time. She added, "I have no will of my own now; God's will is mine. I can bring my dearest friends before the Lord, and while I'm praying for them, the glory of the Lord overpowers me so that I'm lost and adore the God of heaven in silence." She cried out, "Tell everyone for me that perfection is attainable, and exhort all to press after it." ...

On Saturday morning at 6 a.m. she said, "My Savior will come today and take his bride." Yet about 8 a.m. she said, "If you had felt what I have this morning, it would have killed you. I had lost sight of God." (Perhaps in the last conflict with 'principalities and powers.') From this point on she was filled with joy but said very little. Her eyes were still lifted up to heaven till her soul was released, with so much ease that I didn't know when she drew her last breath.

So died Judith Berresford, as if 100 years old, but at the age of 24 ...

Sun. 15.—I rode to Birstal. The congregation here was three times as large as at Bradford. They stood, one above another, on the circular slope of the hill, my voice commanding them all. Though I spoke longer than usual, I felt no weariness or weakness. Shall not "they that wait upon the Lord renew their strength"? [Isa. 40:31]. Yes, as long as the sun and moon endure ...

Wed. JUNE 1.—We rode on to Glasgow. A mile before we got there, we met Mr. Gillies, who had ridden out to meet us.

In the evening they set up a "tent" (so they called a covered pulpit) in the Poorhouse yard, a very large and spacious place. The pulpit faced the infirmary, with most of the patients at or near the windows. Next to this was the hospital for the insane; several of whom gave serious attention. And isn't God also able to give them the spirit of a sound mind? [2 Tim. 1:7]. After my sermon, they brought four children to be baptized. I was at the kirk while the minister baptized several immediately after the sermon, so it wasn't up to me as to their manner of baptism. I believe this removed a great deal of prejudice ...

Sat. 4.—I was pleased with the seriousness of the people in the evening, but still prefer the behavior of the English congregations. I can't get used to men sitting [rather than kneeling] during prayer, or wearing their hats while they are singing praises to God ...

Sun. 5.—At 7 a.m., the assembly was as large as my voice could reach, and I didn't spare them at all, so if anyone wants to be deceived, I'm clear of his blood. In the afternoon we estimated that at least 2000 left because they couldn't hear, but several thousand heard distinctly, the evening being calm and still. After preaching I met as many members of the praying fellowship as cared to come. I earnestly advised them to meet Mr. Gillies every week, and at their other meetings, not to talk loosely, and in general (as their custom had been) on some topic of religion, but rather to examine each other's hearts and lives ... Later, speaking to members of the fellowship, I was pleasantly surprised to find that more than two-thirds knew in whom they had believed. And the tree was known by its fruit. The national shyness and stubbornness were gone, and they were as open and teachable as little children. At 7 p.m., 45 or 46 of the 50 cavalrymen and crowds of the townspeople attended preaching. Has the time come when even these wise Scots will become fools for Christ's sake? ...

Mon. 13.—From Morpeth we road to Placey. The fellowship of coalminers here may be an example to all the fellowships in England. No person ever misses his circle or class; they have no disagreements of any kind among them, but with one heart and one mind "provoke one another to love and good works" [Heb. 10:24] ...

Sun. 19.—Not long after the rain began, which forced me to preach indoors at Newcastle, I took up a collection for the poor, many of whom can barely stay alive due to the current scarcity ...

Mon. 27.—We rode across the Tyne to Prudhoe, a little town on the top of a high hill. I preached at the side of Mr. H.'s house, and suppose that all the people of the town who could get out were present [in the evening], and most of them at 5 a.m. At both times, it pleased God to make bare his arm, not just to wound, but also to heal.

Tues. 28.—I returned to Newcastle hoarse and weak. But who can be spent in a better cause? ...

Sun. JULY 10.—In the evening, talking with the fellowship, I saw more than ever the care of God over those who fear him. What stopped their growing in grace? Why, they had a well-meaning preacher in their midst who was inflaming them more and more against the clergy. He couldn't advise them to attend public ordinances, for he himself never went to church or partook of the sacrament. I actually didn't know all this, but God did, and he, by his providence, wisely prepared for the consequences that would naturally have followed. William Manuel was conscripted into military service, so now the people go to church and receive the sacrament as they did before ...

Tues. 19.—I preached on a ground next to the [preaching-]house. Toward the end of my sermon, the woman I was lodging with became offended by another woman who sank down and cried for mercy. But she herself was the next to drop down, and cried as loudly as the first one, and so did several others right after her. When we prayed for them, one was soon filled with peace and joy in believing. In the morning I left the rest refusing to be comforted until Christ should be revealed in their hearts ...

Mon. 25.—We rode to Rotherham. When I arrived, I had no strength and no voice left. However, an hour later I was able to preach to the largest gathering, I believe, that was ever seen there.

Tues. 26.—I was unable to sit up for more than two or three hours at a time. Still, I preached in the morning and evening and spoke personally with each member of the fellowship ...

Thur. 28.—About noon I preached at Woodseats and in the evening at Sheffield. Indeed I do live by preaching!

Tues. SEPTEMBER 6.—I went on to Cambourne, and rejoiced to hear that the gentleman who conscripted Mr. Maxfield no longer persecutes the Methodists, and won't allow anyone else to do so. Also, in the recent famine, he helped many of the poor and saved many families from starvation. I preached at 6 p.m. on "I will heal their backsliding" [Hos. 14:4], and God put his Word into effect.

Several who had left the fellowship for some years came after the sermon and asked to be re-admitted. Oh, how should our hearts yearn for all who once ran well! This is the very thing we need. How many souls might we still pluck out of the jaws of the lion! …

Wed. 21—A large assembly attended St. Ewe in the evening, many of them from Mr. Walker's fellowships. Some had come from St. Columb, 12 miles away. And they didn't come in vain; the flame of love ran from heart to heart, and hardly any remained unmoved …

Sun. 25.—At St Austle, the whole church service was performed by Stephen Hugo, a clergyman over 90 years old. He has been vicar there between 60 and 70 years. Oh what might a man full of faith and zeal have done for God in such a length of time! …

About 2 p.m. I preached at St. Stephen's near a solitary house on the side of a barren mountain. Since neither the house nor the courtyard could contain the people, we went into a meadow where everyone could kneel, as they generally do in Cornwall, as well as stand and hear. And they did hear and sing and pray as if their lives depended on it. I didn't see anyone careless or inattentive among them.

About 5 p.m. I preached at St. Austle to a very well-behaved people. But when will they be wounded in order to be healed? …

Tues. 27.—We rode to Liskeard, to me one of the largest and most pleasant towns in Cornwall. I preached in a broad, convenient place located in the middle of the town. Not a single person made any noise at all. At 6 a.m. the next morning I had almost the same gathering. After that I examined the fellowship and was agreeably surprised to hear that every one of them had found peace with God. And what was even more remarkable, none of them had left their first love. Today, not one of them is in darkness! …

Mon. OCTOBER 10.—I rose at my usual time,[270] but the soreness and swelling of my face, due to my catching cold on Saturday, made it impractical for me to preach. In the evening I applied boiled nettles, which took away the pain in a moment and caused the swelling to go down in a few hours.

---

[270] I.e. 4 a.m.

Sun. 16.—I began visiting the classes at Kingswood. They are steady, but not zealous. It's impossible for them to stay on the fence long; they must go forward or go backward ...

Mon. 24.—I preached about noon at Bath and in the evening at Escot near Lavington.

Tues. 25.—As I was returning to Bath, a man met me near Hannam and told me that the schoolhouse at Kingswood had burned down. I didn't feel a moment's grief, knowing that God does all things well ... [I learned that] a partition took fire immediately; from there it spread to the roof of the building. Plenty of water was brought, but they couldn't get near where it was needed, since it was so filled with flame and smoke that no one could go inside ... John How, a young man who lived next door, ran up a long ladder with an axe in his hand, chopped a hole in the roof, which provided a vent for the flames and smoke ... Men were then able to get to the door of the leads[271] and pour water down through the tiling, so the fire was quickly put out. It had consumed only part of the partition with a box of clothes, some damage to the roof, and some to the floor below.

It's amazing that so little damage was done, because the fire, which began in the middle of the long room ... was raged so that it broke every pane of glass except two in the windows on both east and west ends ... What can we say to these things but that God set the boundaries beyond which it couldn't pass? ...

Wed. NOVEMBER 23.—I was shown Dr. Taylor's new meeting-house, perhaps the most elegant one in Europe. It's an octagon, constructed of the finest brick, with 16 sash-windows below, the same above, and eight skylights in the dome (which are purely ornamental). The inside is furnished in the most elegant taste and is as clean as any nobleman's reception hall. The communion table is made of fine mahogany; even the latches of the pew-doors are polished brass. How can it be that the old, coarse gospel should find its way here? ...

Sat. 26.—I returned to London. There was much confusion while I was gone, due to some indiscreet words spoken by one who seemed to be strong in the faith.

---

[271] Meaning uncertain.

Mon. 28.—I heard everyone involved face to face, but was totally unable to judge whether there was willful sin, lying on either side, or merely human weakness. For the present I leave it to the Searcher of hearts who will bring everything to light in due season.

Wed. 30.—I had another long hearing of the same complicated case, but with no more success. One side flatly affirmed what the other side flatly denied. This is strange, but it's stranger that those who seem so strong in faith should have no union of spirit with each other ...

1758

Christmas week I rode down to Bristol where Sunday, JANUARY 1, we began the New Year with the great assembly at 4 a.m., rejoicing and praising God.

Tues. 3.—At the request of several of my friends, I wrote *A Letter to a Gentleman of Bristol,* in order to protect them from seeking salvation by works, on the one hand, and from antinomianism, on the other. From those who lean to either extreme, I'll receive no thanks, but "wisdom is justified by her children" [Mt. 11:19].

Wed. 4.—I rode to Kingswood and rejoiced over the school, which finally is what I've wished it to be for so long: a blessing to all in it and an honor to the whole body of Methodists ...

Fri. 13.—My business at Bristol being finished, I rode to Newbury and the next day to London. Now, if it be God's will, I'd be glad to have a little rest. If not, let me rejoice to be without it.

Tues. 17.—I preached at Wandsworth. A gentleman who has come from America has once again opened a door in that desolate place. In the morning I preached in Mr. Gilbert's house. Two Negro servants of his and a Mulatto seem to be quite awakened. Shall not God's saving health be made known to all nations? ...

Fri. MARCH 10.—Both our horses were lame, so I set out in the morning in a stagecoach between 4 and 5 a.m., but the ice made such bad driving that my companion reached Stamford with the lame horses as soon as I did ... I knew no coach could go the rest of the way, so all we could do was to hire horses and a guide ... I'd heard that a man called Richard Wright lived around there who knew the road over the moor perfectly. Hearing someone speaking that we couldn't see, I called out, "Who's there?" He answered, "Richard Wright." We agreed on his fee and he quickly mounted his horse and rode forward boldly. The northeast wind blew right in our faces and I heard them saying, "It's very cold!" But neither my face, my hands, nor my feet were cold, and between 9 and 10 p.m. we reached Epworth. After traveling more than 90 miles, I was only slightly more tired than when I got up in the morning …

Thur. 30.—Considering how short the notice given was, we had a large gathering in the evening but a very small one in the morning, April the 1st. This didn't surprise me when I was told that the 5 a.m. preaching had been discontinued for about a year and a half. Also at 8 a.m. on Sunday the 2nd, the congregation was small. I realized that the people of Dublin had neither seen nor heard much of self-denial since T. Walsh left the kingdom …

Tues. APRIL 18.—Among the letters I read in public last week was one from Mr. Gillies, telling about a society recently formed at Glasgow, Scotland, for promoting Christian knowledge among the poor, mainly by distributing Bibles and other religious books to them. I could only express my amazement that nothing of this sort had been tried in Ireland and asked whether it wasn't time for such a society to be formed in Dublin. This morning Dr. Tisdale showed me a paper that the archbishop had just sent to each of his clergy, urging them to found a society for the distribution of books among the poor. Thanks be to God for this! It's all the same whether it's we or they who do it, just so long as God is known, loved, and obeyed …

Sat. 29.—I think most of the Protestants in the town attended the evening service. Many Catholics also stood around the edges of the gathering, though liable to heavy penance for doing so. It seemed appropriate for me to preach much longer than I am used to. As Thomas à Kempis[272] said, "He rides easily whom the grace of God carries."

Mon. MAY 1.—I tried to end the bitter contentions that had nearly torn the fellowship to pieces. I heard the opposing parties face

---

[272] Catholic priest in the 14th-15th centuries, famous for his book, *Imitation of Christ*.

to face and asked them to speak fully. God blessed this; the snare was broken, and they were warmly reconciled. Just one person had no patience and renounced us all. But within an hour God broke her heart too, and she begged pardon with many tears. So there is reason to hope that they will, for the time to come, "bear one another's burdens." ...

Sun. 7.—I preached at 8 a.m. and at 5 p.m. Afterwards, I was asked to make a collection for a distressed family. Mr. Booker, the minister of the parish, was willing to stand at the door to receive it, and encouraged all who passed by to be merciful according to their ability ...

Wed. 10.—I suppose all the inhabitants of the village, along with many others, were present at 5 a.m. Among them was a poor woman, sick in bed 10 days before, who had walked four Irish (seven English) miles with her child in her arms for me to baptize it. Another woman, who lives at Terryhugan, had earnestly requested the same thing if she gave birth before I left the country. She did so two or three hours before the preaching, so God gave her what she asked of him ...

Sat. 27.—We entered the county of Sligo, the most populated that I've seen in the kingdom. We counted eight villages within seven miles, and the town itself is not much smaller than Limerick. The countryside around it is fertile and well-improved—even the mountains to the very top. It sits two miles from the sea and has a large harbor flanked by mountains on both sides.

The mob had been in action all day, but they were only dealing with market racketeers who had bought up all the grain around there to starve the poor while loading a Dutch ship that lay at the quay. But the mob brought it all out into the market and sold it for the original owners at the common price. And they did this with all the calmness and composure imaginable, without hitting or hurting anyone ...

Fri. JUNE 2.—I rode to Hollymount and preached in the churchyard. Then I visited my antagonist, Mr. Clark, who was in bed very sick ...

Sun. 4.—Since they celebrate the Lord's Supper here only four times a year, I administered it in the evening to about 60 people.

Hardly one of them went away empty. Many were filled with consolation …

Fri. 9.—About 8 a.m. I preached at Ahaskra to a congregation of whom four-fifths were Catholics. Would to God the government would grant to all the Catholics in the land the same liberty of conscience, that none might hinder them from hearing the true Word of God! Then hearing, they can judge for themselves …

Wed. 21.—We began our small conference with 14 preachers present. We settled everything here that we judged useful to the preachers or to the fellowships, and considered how to do away with anything that might be a hindrance to the work of God …

Thur. 29.—How unspeakable is the advantage, from the viewpoint of common sense, that middle-class people have over the rich! There is so much paint and affectation, so many senseless words and customs, among people of high rank! It fully justifies the remark made 1700 years ago: "In such an elevated condition of life, common sense is generally very rare."[273]

Sun. JULY 2.—I preached on the island near Limerick morning and evening, standing on the side of a large hollow next to the old military camp. The ground sloped upward, so the people sat on the grass, row above row. I'd never seen such an amphitheater before in which thousands of listeners could be so well accommodated, and they seemed earnest to hear our Lord's invitation: "Come, for all things are now ready!" [Luke 14:17].

At that time I didn't realized that I had strained my voice, but in the morning I was very hoarse. This got worse through the day, together with pressure and an obstruction in my chest. On Tuesday I began spitting blood and found I had pain in my left side and noticeable loss of strength and a deep wheezing cough—the same symptoms I had a few years ago. Immediately I applied a plaster of sulfur to my side and used a mixture of roasted lemon and honey which I licked. On Wednesday the 5th, my side was no longer hurting, my hoarseness was mostly gone, so in the evening I made the effort to preach again, though not without difficulty. I had planned to preach the next day at Shronill, about 24 English miles

---

[273] The original of this quote is in Latin; Wesley's editors have translated it.

from Limerick, and at Clonmell, about the same distance from Shronill, but seeing that my strength was not sufficient, and yielding to the advice of friends, I rested another day ...

Sat. 8.—The assembly was large, but my voice was so weak that many couldn't hear. Sunday the 9th, after burying James Massiot, I preached to a large crowd on "Blessed are the dead who die in the Lord" [Rev. 14:13]; and the longer I spoke, the more my voice was strengthened ...

Tues. 11.—In the evening I preached on the main street at Bandon. Now needing all my voice, it was given to me again, only I had a little pain in my side which ended while I was preaching ...

Sun. 30.—I began meeting the children in Cork in the afternoon, although with little hope of benefiting them. But I hadn't spoken long on our natural state without God until many of them were in tears, and five or six so affected that they couldn't help but cry aloud to God. When I began to pray their cries increased, soon drowning out my voice. I haven't seen such a work among children for 18 or 19 years ...

Mon. AUGUST 7.—Not having heard from the captain of the boat on which we were to sail from Ireland back to England, I went to the center of Cove. Many people came running together, but they were far too wild and noisy for me begin with a hymn or a scriptural text as I usually do, so I immediately lit into as many as could hear in an ad lib and casual way. In a few minutes the whole assembly was quiet and fairly attentive. They continued growing more serious till I finished with a hymn and a short prayer ...

Thur. 17.—I went to the Bristol cathedral to hear Handel's *Messiah*. I doubt if the congregation was ever as serious at a sermon as they were during this performance. In many parts, especially several of the choruses, it exceeded my expectation ...

Tues. OCTOBER 3.—A man of Warminster who was at Bristol last week has asked me to visit him at home. I did so this morning and preached in his yard to a large gathering of saints and sinners, rich and poor, Anglicans, Quakers, and Presbyterians (both of the old and new way). We expected some disturbance, but there wasn't any. Everyone behaved well, and instead of curses or stones we had many blessings as we rode through the town for Salisbury ...

Mon. 16.—I rode to Canterbury. As we entered the city, a stone flew out of the pavement, striking my mare on the leg with such force that she suddenly dropped down. I kept my seat till, struggling to rise, she fell again and rolled over on me. When she rose I tried to rise too, but found I couldn't use either my right leg or thigh. But a good barber came out, picked me up, and helped me into his shop. Feeling very sick, I asked for a glass of cold water, which gave me immediate relief.

Tues. 17.—I had reason to rejoice over the little flock here, now free from all divisions and offenses. And on Saturday I cheerfully returned to London after being away nearly eight months ...

Sun. NOVEMBER 5.—We went to St. Peter's Church, since the Lord's Supper was being administered here. I can hardly remember ever seeing a more beautiful parish church—the more so because its beauty doesn't spring from extra adornments but from its very form and structure. It's quite large and unusually high, and the sides are almost all windows, giving it an awesome and venerable look, but at the same time surprisingly cheerful ...

Thur. 9.—We rode to Mr. Berridge's at Everton. For many years he was seeking to be justified by his works, but a few months ago he was thoroughly convinced that "by grace [we] are saved through faith" [Eph. 2:8]. Immediately he began to proclaim aloud the redemption that is in Jesus, and God confirmed his own Word exactly as he did at Bristol, beginning by working repentance and faith in the hearers, and with the same strong outward evidence ...

Wed. 29.—I rode to Wandsworth and baptized two Negroes belonging to Mr. Gilbert, a gentleman recently arrived from Antigua. One of these is deeply convicted of sin; the other rejoices in God her Savior and is the first African Christian I've personally known. But won't our Lord, in due time, also have these heathens "for his inheritance?" [Psalm 33:12] ...

Wed. DECEMBER 27.—I felt so sick that I didn't know how I'd get to church. Between 9 and 10 a.m. I was told that some hot-tempered men in the parish wouldn't agree to my preaching there. I saw God's hand in this and was thankful, since it gave me a little more time to rest. In the afternoon, the sun came out, clearing away the fog, and we had a pleasant ride to Bury. Yet shortly after arriving, I was so sick that I didn't know how I could preach. But an hour's nap refreshed me so that I found no lack of strength as I preached. Still my disorder got worse during the night, but while preaching in the morning I felt well, and no more sickness or complaint at all …

Fri. 29.—I found the fellowship in Colchester had decreased since L.C. went away, yet the other preachers were just as good as he. But that's not enough; **experiential evidence has shown us that even if a man preaches like an angel, he'll neither gather nor preserve a fellowship that's been started unless he visits them from house to house** [my emphasis]…

Sat. 30.—I returned to London and received an urgent letter from Bristol, because of which I took horse on Monday morning,

1759

JANUARY 1, arriving there the next evening. After resting two days (only preaching morning and evening), I examined the members of the fellowship one by one. This is one great purpose in my coming. Another was to provide for the poor. Accordingly, on Sunday the 7th I preached a sermon for them, to which it pleased God to give his blessing, so the collection was far more than twice what it used to be …

Tues. FEBRUARY 27.—I walked with my brother Charles and Mr. Maxfield to L.H.'s. After breakfast, in came Mr. Whitefield, Madan, Romaine, Jones, Downing, and Venn, with some "persons of quality" and a few others. Mr. Whitefield, I found, was to have administered the sacrament, but he insisted on my doing it, after which, at the request of L.H., I preached on 1 Corinthians 13. Oh, what are the greatest men to the great God? Like the finest dust on a balance scale …

Mon. MARCH 5.—Examining the fellowship, I found that out of the 126 members I had left in October, we'd lost only 12, and in their place we've gained 40. Many of these whom we left in sorrow and heaviness are now rejoicing in God their Savior.

Tues. 6.— …In the evening I asked those who wanted to join in a fellowship to speak to me the next evening. About 20 did so, but most of these seemed like frightened sheep. And this is no wonder, when they've been accustomed so long to hearing all kinds of evil about me.

Fri. 9.—I preached morning and evening at the Foundry. How pleasing it would be to my flesh to stay in this quiet, little place, where finally we've weathered the storm! But no! I'm not to take thought for my own ease but for advancing the kingdom of God ...

Sun. 18.—I served the Lord's Supper to almost 200 communicants. I never remember such a solemn time in the city of Norwich before. Since a good part of them were dissenters, I asked everyone to use the posture he chose. If I had directed them to kneel, probably half would have sat up, but as it were, all but one knelt down.

Feeling I needed to see our people once more at Colchester, I took to horse between 4 and 5 a.m. The freezing air was very sharp for several hours, but then it was a fair, mild day. About 2 p.m. it began to rain, but we reached Colchester before we got soaked through.

The preaching room was crowded in the evening, forcing many to leave. Wednesday the 21st I baptized seven adults, two by immersion, and in the evening (as their own ministers had cast them out for going to hear Methodists) I served the Lord's Supper to them and many others whom their teachers had rejected for the same reason ...

Sun. MAY 6.—I received a great deal of comfort at the old church in Liverpool in the morning and at St Thomas's in the afternoon. It was as if both sermons had been made for me. I pity those who can find no good at church. But how can they, if prejudice bars them from the grace of God? ...

Sat. 12.—Reflecting today on the case of a poor woman who had constant pain in her stomach, I noted the inexcusable negligence of most physicians in cases of this sort. They prescribe drug after drug without knowing the root cause of the disorder ... Where did this woman's pain originate? ... From fretting about the death of her son ... Why don't all physicians consider how far bodily disorders are caused or influenced by the mind and, in these cases, which are out of their realm, call in a minister, just as ministers call in physicians? But why are these cases out of their realm? Because they don't know God. It follows, then, that no one can be a complete physician without being an experienced Christian …

Sun. 20.—I preached at 8 a.m. in an open place at the Gins, a village on one side of Lorton. Many were there who never had and never would come to the preaching-room. Oh, what a victory would Satan gain if he could put an end to field-preaching! But I trust that he never will—at least not till my head is laid to rest …

Mon. JUNE 4.—After preaching at Alnwick, I rode on to Newcastle. Certainly, if I didn't believe there was another world, I'd spend all my summers here, since I don't know any place in Great Britain as pleasant as this. But I seek another country, and therefore am content to be a wanderer on the earth …

Wed. 13.—I never saw as large an assembly at Sheephill as we had at 6 p.m. What's lacking in this whole region? Only more laborers …

Sun. 24.—I preached in the street at 8 a.m. in Sunderland, about 1 p.m. at South-shields, and about 5 p.m. in North-shields. Most of the audience seemed to hear as if their lives depended on it. So these lions have become lambs. Oh, for zealous, active, faithful workers! How white the fields are unto harvest!

On Monday and Tuesday evening I preached outdoors near the Keelmen's Hospital, to twice the number we would have had in the preaching-room. It's no wonder the devil hates field-preaching; so do I. I love a comfortable room, a soft cushion, a handsome pulpit. But where is my zeal if I don't trample all these underfoot in order to save one more soul? …

Fri. 29.—About 11 a.m. I started out for Swalwell on a fair, mild morning. But in half an hour the rain poured down so heavily that in a few minutes I was soaked from head to foot. And when I got there, I didn't know where to position myself to preach, because the house wouldn't contain a third of the people. Just then the dissenting minister sent a message offering me the use of his meeting-house. I immediately went there and found a large assembly, and a blessing in their midst …

Sun. JULY 1.—While the fellowship was gathering, I visited a young woman who some days previously had been suddenly struck with what they called madness. And it was madness, but a devilish madness, as many symptoms made clear. However after we had a time of prayer, she fell asleep, and never raged or cursed any more.

Mon. 2.—I rode to Durham and right away went to the meadow by the riverside where I preached two years ago. The assembly was now half again as large as before, but the sun scorched my head so that I was barely able to speak. I paused for a little while and asked God to provide us a covering if it would be to his glory. And in a moment it happened: A cloud covered the sun, which bothered us no more. Should willful humility conceal these tangible proofs that God still hears prayer? ...

Tues. 10.—In the afternoon I rode to York, where I thought I would rest a few days, being almost worn out, but it was judged quite necessary that I should go to Hull, lest the little flock be discouraged; so on Friday the 13th I set out early ... I had a far finer gathering at Hull, so for once the rich have the gospel preached to them! ...

Sun. 15.—I began reading an account of the recent work of God at Everton to the fellowship, but couldn't finish. At first there were only silent tears all around, but before long several couldn't keep from weeping aloud. A sturdy young man suddenly dropped down, roaring as if in the agonies of death. I didn't try to read any more and instead began wrestling with God in prayer. We continued that way until almost 9 p.m. What a day of jubilee it was! ...

Sun. 22.—In Haworth at 10 a.m. Mr. Milner read prayers, but the church wouldn't nearly contain the assembly, so after prayers I stood on a scaffold close to the church while the people stood in the churchyard. Those receiving communion alone filled the church. The gathering was nearly doubled in size in the afternoon, yet even so, most weren't merely curious listeners but people fearing God ...

Thur. 26.—I preached in Gildersome at noon and at Morley in the evening. A fire has suddenly broken out here where it was least expected, and it spreads wider and wider. When God works, who can hold back his hand? ...

Mon. AUGUST 6.—Mr. B. came and told me that Alice Miller (15 years old) had fallen into a trance. I immediately went downstairs and found her sitting on a stool and leaning against the wall with her eyes open and fixed upward. I moved my hand [suddenly] like I was going to hit her, but they didn't move. Her face showed an inexpressible mixture of reverence and love, while silent tears rolled down her cheeks ... I don't know if I've ever seen a human face so beautiful—somehow covered with a smile, as from joy, mixed with love and reverence ... Her pulse was regular. After about half an hour I noticed her countenance change into the form of fear, pity, and distress. Then she burst into a flood of tears and cried out, "Dear Lord, they'll be damned! They'll all be damned!" But in about five minutes her smiles returned, and only love and joy appeared on her face. About 6:30 I observed distress take place again; she wept bitterly and cried out, "Dear Lord, they'll go to hell! The world will go to hell!" Soon after that she said, "Cry aloud! Spare not!" And in a few moments her features were composed again and revealed a mixture of reverence, joy, and love. Then she said, "Give God the glory."

About 7 p.m. she came back to her senses and I asked, "Where have you been?" "I've been with my Savior." "In heaven or on earth?" "I can't tell, but I was in glory." "Then why did you cry?" "Not for myself but for the world, because I saw that they were on the brink of hell." "Who did you want to give the glory to God?" "Ministers who cry aloud to the world; otherwise they will be proud, then God will leave them and they'll lose their own souls."

I preached at 8 p.m. on "The wicked shall be turned into hell, and all the people who forget God" [Psalm 9:17]. The whole assembly was very attentive, but only one or two cried out, and I didn't notice any fainting away either then or in the morning. I've observed these outward symptoms accompanying the beginning of a general work of God. Thus it was in New England, Scotland, Holland, Ireland, and many parts of England. But after a while the manifestations gradually decrease while the work goes on more quietly. Those whom it pleases God to use in his work ought to be passive in this regard, choosing nothing but leaving all the circumstances of his own work entirely to him.

Tues. 7.—After preaching at 4 a.m. because of the harvest, I mounted up and rode at an easy pace to London. I truly wanted a little rest, having ridden in seven months over 2400 miles.

Wed. 8.—Our conference began. Our time was almost entirely used in examining whether the spirit and lives of our preachers were suitable to their profession. On Saturday, in the afternoon, we concluded. The unanimity and love reigning among us were great, and if any feared or hoped the contrary, they were happily disappointed.

Sun. 12.—I dreaded looking forward to the day's work, feeling my strength wasn't sufficient for it. But God took care of that, for although I was very weak at Snowsfields in the morning, I was stronger at noon, and after preaching in the fields and meeting the fellowship, I felt no weakness at all …

Thur. 30.—I preached at the Tabernacle in Norwich to a large, rude, noisy assembly. I took note of the kind of teachers they had been used to and determined to correct them or leave them. Therefore the next evening, after sermon, I reminded them of two things: 1. that it was not decent to begin talking out loud as soon as the service ended and scurrying to and fro as at a wrestling-match; and 2. that it was a bad habit to gather into cliques just after sermon and turn the house of worship into a coffee-house. So I requested that none would talk under that roof but leave quietly and silently. And on Sunday, September the 2nd, I was pleased to observe that everyone left as quietly as if they had been accustomed to doing so for many years …

Sun. SEPTEMBER 9.—[*At Kemnal*] I met the fellowship at 7 a.m., and told them plainly that they were the most ignorant, self-conceited, self-willed, fickle, stubborn, disorderly, disjointed fellowship that I knew in the three kingdoms. And God applied it to their hearts, so that many were benefited, and I didn't find one that was offended ….

Mon. 10.—After riding in the hot sun all day, I had a fever from the moment I entered the house where we were staying. But that didn't keep me from preaching on the lawn, and afterwards meeting the fellowship. Then I lay down as soon as I could, but couldn't sleep more than a quarter-hour at a time till between 2 and 3 a.m. I don't remember losing a night's sleep before, sick or well, since I was six years old. But it's all the same: God can give strength either with or without sleep. I rose at my usual time and preached at 5 a.m. without feeling faint or drowsy …

Fri. 14.—I returned to London. Saturday the 15th, having previously left orders for immediately repairing West Street Chapel, I went to see what had been done, and found cause to praise God for this also. The main timbers were so rotten that you could poke your finger into them in many places. Probably if we had waited till spring the whole building would have fallen to the ground …

Sun. 23.—By far most of the huge assembly in Moorfields were deeply serious. Just one such hour might convince an impartial person of the effectiveness of field-preaching.[274] What building, except St. Paul's cathedral, would contain such a congregation? And if it would, what human voice could have reached them there? By long experience I find I can command three times the number in the open air than I can under a roof. And who can say that the time for field-preaching is over while: 1. greater numbers than ever attend, and 2. the converting, as well as the convicting, power of God is notably present with them? …

Mon. OCTOBER 1.—During my stay at Bristol, I spent all my leisure time finishing the fourth volume of *Discourses,* probably the last that I'll publish.

Mon. 15.—I walked up to Knowle, a mile from Bristol, to see the French prisoners. Over 1100 of them, we were told, were confined in that small place, with nothing to lie on but a little dirty straw, and nothing to cover them but a few stinking thin rags both by day and night, so that they were dying like rotting sheep. I was moved with compassion and preached that evening on Exodus 23:9: "You shall not oppress an alien, for you know the heart of an alien, seeing you were aliens in the land of Egypt." Eighteen pounds were contributed immediately, which were made up to 24[275] the next day. With this we bought linen and woolen cloth, which were sewn into shirts, vests, and pants. Several dozen pairs of socks were added, all of which were carefully distributed where the need was greatest. Shortly after this, the Corporation of Bristol sent a large quantity of mattresses and blankets. And before long contributions came in from

---

[274] "Field-preaching" can refer to all preaching outside of church buildings.
[275] 18 pounds = about $4,200; 24 pounds = about $5,600 in 2020 USD.

London and various parts of the kingdom, so I think that from this time on they were pretty well provided with the necessities of life ...

Sat. NOVEMBER 17.—I spent an agreeable and profitable hour with Lady G.H. and Sir C. H. It's a good thing that a few of the rich and noble are called. Oh, that God would increase their numbers! But I would be glad (if it were God's will) that it should be done by the ministry of others. If I could choose, I would still (as I have done until now) preach the gospel to the poor ...

Fri. 23.—The roads were so slippery that it was with great difficulty that we reached Bedford. We had a fairly large gathering, but with the stench from the pigs under the room we could hardly stand it. Was ever a preaching-place over a hog-sty before? Surely people who come to hear it in such a place love the gospel ...

Sun. 25.—In the afternoon God was present with us in a remarkable way, though rather to comfort than to convict. I noticed a remarkable difference since I was here before in the manner of the work. Now none were in trances, cried out, fell down, or were convulsed; only some trembled mightily, a low murmur was heard, and many were refreshed with the flood of peace.

The danger was to regard extraordinary circumstances such as outcries, convulsions, visions, and trances too much, as if these were essential to the inward work, so that it couldn't go on without them. But perhaps the [greater] danger is to regard them too little, to condemn them altogether, to imagine God was not in them at all and that they were a hindrance to his work. Whereas the truth is: 1. God suddenly and strongly convicted many that they were lost sinners, resulting in sudden outcries and strong bodily convulsions; and 2.that to strengthen and encourage those who believed and to make his work more evident, he favored several with divine dreams and others with trances and visions; 3. that in some of these, after a while, human nature became mixed with divine grace; and finally 4. that Satan also imitated this work of God in order to discredit the whole work. Yet it isn't wise to give up these manifestations any more than it is to give up the whole work of God, which doubtless it was at the first. It's still partly so today, and he'll enable us to discern how far, in every case, the work is pure, and where it mixes or degenerates ...

Wed. 28.—I returned to London, and on Thursday the 29th, the national day set aside for general thanksgiving, I preached again in the chapel near the Seven Dials, morning and afternoon. I believe the oldest person in England hasn't seen a thanksgiving day observed like this before. It had the solemnity of the general fast. All shops were closed; the people in the streets all appeared serious; the prayers, lessons, and the whole public worship service were completely appropriate for the occasion. The prayer for our enemies, in particular, was very striking; perhaps it's the first of its kind in Europe. There was no noise, hurry, bonfires, or fireworks in the evening, and no public amusements. This is indeed a Christian holiday, a "rejoicing unto the Lord." The next day we received news that Sir Edward Hawke had scattered the French fleet.

Sun. DECEMBER 9.—For the first time, I held a love-feast for the whole Society [in London]. Wednesday the 12th I began reading over the Greek New Testament and the notes with my brother Charles and several others, carefully comparing the translation with the original and correcting or enlarging the notes as we saw fit …

1760

Sun. JANUARY 13.—I preached again in West Street Chapel, now enlarged and completely repaired. When I took this building 18 years ago, I didn't seriously think that the world would bear with us until now. But the right hand of the Lord reigns over all; therefore we endure to this day …

Mon. 28.—I began examining the classes in London, doing so more carefully than ever before. After going through them individually, I found the society here now contained about 2350 members, few of whom we could discern to be just casually committed and none, we hope, living in willful sin.

Tues. FEBRUARY 5.—I baptized an upper-class woman at the Foundry, and the peace she immediately found was fresh proof that the outward sign, received properly, is always accompanied by inward grace …

Tues. MARCH 4.—In the evening I preached at the new house at Wednesbury. Few congregations exceed this in either number or in seriousness. At 5 a.m. the assembly was far larger than the morning assembly at the Foundry. Indeed, hunger after the Word has from the beginning been the distinguishing mark of this people ...

Sat. 8.—We went on to Burslem, near Newcastle-under-Line, a scattered town on the top of a hill whose inhabitants were mostly potters. A crowd of them assembled at 5 p.m. Every face showed deep attention, although so far with deep ignorance. But if the heart is turned toward God, in due time he will enlighten the understanding ...

Wed. 12.—[*Now in Leeds*] I'd asked all who could of the towns around who believed they were saved from sin to meet me, and I spent most of this day examining them one by one. I couldn't accept the testimony of some, but regarding the far greater part it's plain (unless they are deliberately lying): 1. that they feel no inward sin and, to the best of their knowledge, commit no outward sin; 2. that they see and love God constantly and pray and rejoice and always give thanks; and 3. that they always have as clear a witness from God of sanctification as they have of justification. Now I rejoice in this, call it what you please, and I would to God that thousands had arrived at this point—after that, let them experience as much more as it pleases God ...

Fri. APRIL 18.—I went with Miss F. to see the French prisoners sent from Carrickfergus. They were surprised at hearing as good French spoken in Dublin as they could have heard in Paris,[276] and still more at being exhorted to heart-religion, to the "faith that works by love" [Gal. 5:6] ...

Mon. 28.—I rode to Rathfriland, seven Irish miles from Newry, a small town built on the top of a mountain ... The Presbyterian minister had written to the Catholic priest to keep his people from hearing me. But they wouldn't be kept back: Protestants and Catholics flocked together to the meadow where I preached and sat on the grass, still as night, while I exhorted them to "repent, and believe the gospel" [Mark 1:15].

---

[276] Wesley implies that he himself, and perhaps Miss F., spoke excellent French.

VOLUME 3: 1760-1773

[WESLEY] TO THE READER:
I am aware that there are many details in the journal below that some serious people won't believe and that others will ridicule. But I can't help this, lest I cover up things that I feel it my solemn duty to declare. I can't do otherwise, so long as I'm persuaded that this was a real work of God and that he's done this and all "his marvelous works, that they ought to be kept in remembrance." I only ask that those who think differently from me will bear with me as I do with them, and that those who think like me that this was the most glorious work of God which has ever been done in our memory may be encouraged to expect themselves to be partakers of all the great and precious promises, and that without delay, seeing that "Now is the accepted time! Now is the day of salvation!" [2 Peter 1:4].

London, January 31, 1767 …

Tues. MAY 6, 1760.—I had a long conversation at Carrickfergus with Monsieur Cavenac, the French general, not on the circumstances but the essence of religion. Nothing seemed to surprise him; instead he said more than once and with emotion, "Why this is my religion! There is no true religion besides it." …

Sat. 10.—I preached, morning and evening, in Mr. B.'s house, to a well-behaved assembly of various denominations: Anglicans, Catholics, Presbyterians, and Cameronians. One seceder also ventured in, but the moment he heard "Our Father, who art in heaven," he quickly ran away[277] …

Mon. 19.—We rode to Castlebar, where I preached in the evening. I was especially concerned for the poor backsliders. It seemed like most of us said in our hearts, "If they want to go to hell, let them go." Not so! Rather let us pluck the "brands," willing or unwilling, "out of the burning."

Mon. JUNE 23.—As it was the quarterly meeting, the stewards from all the country fellowships were present: a group of solid, sensible men. Nothing is lacking in this kingdom except zealous, active preachers, adhering to order and strict discipline …

---

[277] Some "non-credal" denominations avoid using the Lord's Prayer in public worship.

Thur. 26.—I preached at 5 a.m. in a large, spacious [preaching-]room obtained since I was here last. I had breakfast with Mr. A. and dinner with Mr. K., but have seldom seen two such families. They had feared God for many years and served him in the best way they knew how. Nothing was lacking except for them to hear "the more excellent way" [1 Cor. 12:31], which they embraced whole-heartedly ...

Sat. 28.—At 5 a.m. the assembly was larger than it had ever been at that time. After breakfast I rode out with Mr. K. and with Mr. D., who, hearing I had a sorry horse, offered me the use of one of his horses during my stay in Ireland.

That evening, it being market-day, so that the market-house was filled with people, I sent a note to the colonel, who readily gave me freedom to preach in the barracks-yard. He himself came to hear as did several of the officers. It was a solemn conclusion of the happiest birthday which I had known for many years ...

Tuesday, JULY 1.—We mounted up about 4 a.m., and it was good that we did, because our 37 Irish miles, so-called, were little less than 70 English miles. I preached at a friend's house soon after 3 p.m., then, getting a fresh horse about the size of a donkey, rode on with more comfort than dignity to Aghrim.

Wed. 2.—In the evening I preached at Birr, with more satisfaction than for several years, finding many more alive to God than ever and provoking each other to love and good works. I had planned to set out in the morning, but their love compelled me to stay a day longer, which gave me leisure to complete the account of the fellowship. Presently the fellowships in Connaught contain just over 200 members; those in Ulster, about 250; and those in Leinster, 1000 ...

Wed. 9.—I rode over to Killiheen, a German settlement about 20 miles south of Limerick. It rained all the way, but the earnestness of the poor people made us forget it. In the evening I preached to another colony of Germans at Ballygarane; the third is at Court Mattrass, a mile from Killiheen. I don't suppose three such towns can hardly be found again in England or Ireland. There is no cursing or swearing, no Sabbath-breaking, no drunkenness, no ale-house in any of them. Surely these poor foreigners will rise up in the judgment against those that are round about them! ...

Mon. 21.—At 6 p.m. I preached at the camp near Caire, to a large and serious congregation of soldiers. From there we rode on to Clonmell where I preached near the barracks at 8 a.m. to a wild, staring people, but of necessity quiet because they were in awe of the soldiers. We rode in the afternoon to Waterford where our friends had obtained a spacious enclosed place. I preached there three evenings, with great hope of doing good. Our large room was full every morning. Oh, why should we despair of any souls that God has made? ...

Sun. AUGUST 24.—At 7 a.m. I took leave of my friends, and about noon embarked on the *Nonpareil* for Chester. We had 40 or 50 passengers on board, half of whom were cabin passengers. I was afraid it wouldn't be an easy time with so many upper-class people. We started out with a fair wind, but at 4 p.m. the wind died down, leaving us in a dead calm. At this point I made the gentlemen the offer of preaching, which they gratefully accepted. While I was preaching the wind sprang up fair, but the next day we were becalmed again. That afternoon they asked me to give them another sermon, and again the wind sprang up while I was speaking and continued till about noon on Tuesday we landed at Parkgate ...

Thur. 28.—I spent ... two days with the preachers, who had been waiting for me all week,, and their love and unanimity was such that it soon made me forget all my labor [of the previous week].

Monday, SEPTEMBER 1. I set out for Cornwall, preaching at Shepton, Middlesey, and Tiverton, on the way.

Wed. 3.—I reached Launceston and found what was left of a dead, scattered fellowship. But it's no wonder, since they hardly have any discipline and only one sermon every two weeks.

On Friday the 5th I found another fellowship in the same condition at Gamelford, but their deadness here was due to bitterness against each other. In the morning I heard the opposing parties face to face, and they resolved and promised on all sides to let the past be forgotten. Oh, how few have learned to forgive "one another, as God for Christ's sake has forgiven us"? [Eph. 4:32].

Sat. 6.—We had an exceptionally lively gathering in the evening at Trewalder. In fact, the whole fellowship stands firm and "adorns the doctrine of God our Savior" [Titus 2:10] …

Sun. 7.— … In examining the fellowship of Port Isaac, I found much reason to bless God on their behalf. They diligently observe all the rules of the Society, with or without a preacher. They constantly attend church and take communion and meet at the appointed times. As a result, 30 out of 35, their total number, continue to walk in the light of God's countenance.

Mon. 8.—A gentleman followed me to my inn at St. Columb's and carried me to his house where there were three or four others as friendly as himself. One of them rode with me seven or eight miles and gave me a welcome account of two young clergymen, Mr. C. and Mr. Phelps, who had the care of three adjoining parishes. Surely God has a favor for the people of these parts; he gives them such serious, lively ministers! By these and the Methodists together, the line is now drawn, with only small breaks, all along the North Sea from the eastern point of Cornwall to Land's End …

The congregation at St. Agnes in the evening was, I suppose, double that at Port Isaac. We had almost as many on Tuesday the 9th at 5 a.m. as the preaching-house could hold. Afterwards I examined the fellowship and was surprised and grieved to find that, out of 98 persons, all but three or four had forsaken the Lord's Table. I told them my thoughts very plainly. They seemed convicted and promised to no longer give place to the devil …

Fri. 19.—I rode to Illuggan. We had heavy rain before I began but hardly any while I was preaching …

Sat. 20.—In the evening I stood in my old place on the main street at Redruth. A crowd, rich and poor, calmly listened. So the roughest town has become one of the quietest ones in England.

Sun. 21.—I preached in the same place at 8 a.m. Mr. C. of St. Cuthbert preached at the church, morning and afternoon, and strongly confirmed what I had spoken. At 1 p.m., the day being mild and calm, we had the largest assembly of all, but it rained all the time while I preached at Gwenap. We ended the day with a love-feast at which James Roberts, a tinsmith of St. Ives, told how God had dealt with his soul …

VOLUME 3: 1760-1773

Mon. 22.—I preached at Penrhyn ... On Wednesday evening, having met with the fellowships and preached 30 times in 11 days, I felt somewhat exhausted, but a day's rest took care of that, so on Friday the 26th I preached again at noon near Liskeard. In the afternoon there was strong wind and rain, and when we reached Saltash, no boat would venture out, so we had to lodge there.

Sat. 27.—The wind being as strong as ever, we had no hope of crossing here, so we decided to ride around by the new bridge. The rain continued falling to our left and right, but for almost 20 miles we didn't have a single drop, and not a heavy shower all day. We arrived safely at Plymouth Dock soon after 4 p.m.

I saw a dismal scene here, finding most of the people dead as stones, and when I took an account of the fellowship, only 34 out of 70 were left. At 7 p.m. and again at 5 a.m., I strongly exhorted them to return to God. The next day at 8 a.m. and also at 5 p.m. I did the same, and God made his Word like a hammer. At the meeting of the fellowship as well, strong and effective words were given to me. Many were convicted anew; many backsliders were cut to the heart, and I left once more between 60 and 70 members ...

Sun. OCTOBER 12.—In the afternoon I had appointed the children [of the Kingswood School] whose parents were of the Society to meet me at Bristol. Thirty of the children came today and more than 50 others on the following Sunday and Thursday. About half of these I divided into four classes: two of boys and two of girls, and I appointed proper leaders to meet them separately. I met them all together twice a week, and it wasn't long before God began to touch some of their hearts.

On [Thursday, Friday, and Saturday] I spoke individually with members of the fellowship. As many of them increase in worldly goods, the great danger I now see is their relapsing into the spirit of the world, and then their religion is just a dream ...

Fri. 24.—I visited the French prisoners at Knowle, and found many of them almost naked again. Hoping to provoke others to jealousy, I made another collection for them, and ordered the money to be spent for linen and waistcoats, which were given to those most in need.

Sat. 25.—King George was gathered to his fathers. When will England have a better prince?

Many of us agreed to observe Friday the 31st as a day of fasting and prayer for the blessing of God on our nation and especially on our current Majesty. We met at 5 a.m., at 9 a.m., at 1 p.m., and at 8:30 p.m. I expected to be a bit tired, but was more alert after midnight than I was at 6 a.m. ...

Mon. NOVEMBER 24.—I visited as many of the sick as I could. How much better is it, when possible, to take help to the poor rather than just sending it? And this both for our sake as well as for theirs. For theirs, since it provides so much more comfort to them, since we may then help them spiritually as well as materially, and for our own sake, since it is more apt to soften our hearts and make us naturally care for each other ...

1761

JANUARY 2nd, I wrote the following letter:--

To the Editor of the London Chronicle.

Sir, Of all the centers of woe this side of hell, I suppose few exceed or even equal Newgate [Prison in London]. If any place of horror could exceed it a few years ago, Newgate in Bristol did, so great was the filth, the stench, the misery and wickedness, that shocked all who had a spark of humanity. How surprised I was when I visited there a few weeks ago! 1. Every part of it, upstairs and down, even the pit where the felons are confined at night, is as clean and neat as a gentleman's house, it now being a rule that every prisoner must wash and clean his cell thoroughly twice a week. 2. There is no fighting or brawling. If anyone thinks he's mistreated, the matter is immediately referred to the warden, who listens to both sides face to face and decides the matter at once. 3. The usual grounds for quarreling are removed, for very rarely does anyone cheat or wrong another, being sure that if he does and it's found out, he'll be committed to stricter confinement.

4. There is no drunkenness ...

5. Nor any whoredom ...

6. ... Those willing to work at their callings are provided with tools and materials, partly by the warden, who gives them credit at a moderate profit, partly by alms given occasionally, which are divided

with the most prudence and impartiality. And so at present, among others, there is a shoemaker, a tailor, a brazier, and a coach-maker working at their trades.

7. Only on the Lord's Day they don't work or play, but dress as clean as they can and attend the public service in the chapel, every person there attending. No one is excused unless sick, in which case he's provided with both advice and medicine.

8. And to further assist them in matters of greatest importance, besides a sermon every Sunday and Thursday, they have a large Bible chained on one side of the chapel which any prisoner may read. By the blessing of God on these regulations, the prison now has a new face. Nothing offends the eye or ear, and overall it's like a quiet, serious family. And doesn't the warden of Newgate deserve to be remembered … ? May the Lord remember him on that day! Meantime, will no one follow his example?

Your humble servant,
John Wesley

Mon. 12.—I rode to Colchester, and after spending two or three pleasant days, on Friday the 16th went on to Bury. I would gladly have stayed a day or two here longer, if only on account of the severe weather, but I had work to do elsewhere, so I mounted up soon after preaching the morning of Saturday the 17th, though as bitter cold a day as most I've known. A piercing wind hit us just as we rode out of the gate at daybreak. It was no use looking up; I felt I might lose one of my eyes, and the wind hit one eye as if I'd received a blow, so that I couldn't use it for a while. To make matters worse, not having good directions, we soon lost our way. However we hobbled on through miserable roads till about 3 p.m. we got to Norwich …

Tues. 20.—I asked about Yarmouth, a large and well-populated town, as famous for wickedness and ignorance as any seaport in England. Some have tried to call them to repentance but at the risk of their lives. What more could be done? Last summer God sent the regiment in which Howell Harris was an officer. He preached every night, with no one daring to oppose him, and by this means good seed was sown. Many were stirred up to seek God, and some of them now earnestly invited me to come over. I went this afternoon and preached in the evening. Soon the preaching-house was overflowing, and instead of the expected ruckus, all were as quiet as at London.

Indeed, the Word of God was quick and powerful among them, and it was the same at 6 a.m. the next morning. At 11 a.m. I delivered my farewell sermon. I didn't see anyone who wasn't deeply affected. Oh, fair blossoms! But how many of these will "bring forth fruit to perfection"?

That afternoon I rode back to Norwich and took account of the fellowship there. I found about 330 who made professions to meet in classes, but many of them were like bullocks unaccustomed to the yoke. Where or what will they be a year from now?

Thur. 22.—We had our first watch-night at the tabernacle, and I couldn't help but notice that although I preached the law from beginning to the end of my sermon, yet many were very comforted. So it is plain that God can send either terror or comfort to the heart by whatever means it pleases him.

Sunday the 25th was a day of solemn rejoicing. At 8 a.m., 11 a.m., 2 p.m., and at 5 p.m., God was notably present in the assemblies, filling their hearts with love and their mouths with praise.

In some of the following days, I visited the rural fellowships.

Fri. 30.—[*Back in London.*] After preaching at the Foundry in the evening, I met the small groups as usual. While a poor woman was speaking a few simple words out of the fullness of her heart, a fire was kindled and ran like a flame among the stubble, through the hearts of almost all who heard. So when it pleases God to work, it doesn't matter how weak or how lowly the instrument! ...

Sun. FEBRUARY 1.—Many were comforted and strengthened both at the Lord's Supper and at the evening service. I think all jealousies and misunderstandings have disappeared, and the whole fellowship is well-knitted together. But how long they'll continue this way, considering the unparalleled fickleness of the people in these parts, only God knows. Still, he's working now, and we rejoice in this ...

Tues. 3.—About noon I preached at Harston, five miles beyond Cambridge. Mr. Berridge's labor here hasn't been in vain. Several have found peace with God, and a more natural, loving people I've seldom seen. They had gathered from all around. It pleased God to give a manifestation of his love to one woman in the middle of my sermon. She praised God aloud and inflamed many hearts with love and gratitude ...

Fri. 13.—Being the general fast-day, the chapel in West Street, as well as other churches, was completely filled with serious listeners. Surely God is pleased even with these outward humiliations, as an acknowledgment that he rules over all events. And they give some restraint, even if for a season, to the floods of ungodliness. Besides, we shouldn't doubt that there are some good people in most of the congregations that assemble, and we know that "the effective fervent prayer of even one righteous man avails much" [James 5:16] ...

Tues. 24.—I withdrew to Lewisham and copied the list of our Society. I deleted about 160 to whom, at present, I can do no good. The number of those who remain at present is 2375.

Fri. 27.—At noon I met about 30 people who had experienced a deep work of God and set a time to meet them every week. Whether they are saved from sin or not, they are certainly full of faith and love and especially helpful to my soul ...

Wed. MARCH 4.—At the chapel in Lewisham, I'd barely entered the room where a few believers had met together when one began to tremble violently and soon sank to the floor. After a great struggle she burst out into prayer, which quickly changed into praise. She then declared, "The Lamb of God has taken away all my sins." She added many strong words to the same effect, rejoicing with joy unspeakable.

Fri. 6.—I met again with those who believe God has delivered them from the root of bitterness. Their number increases daily. I believe 15 or 16 have received the same blessing this week ...

Sun. 15.—I struggled to preach indoors at 8 a.m., but in the afternoon didn't know what to do, having pain in my side and a sore throat. But I was determined to speak as long as I could. I stood at one end of the house, and the people (estimated at 8- or 10,000) in the adjoining field. My text was: "I count all things loss for the excellency of the knowledge of Jesus Christ my Lord" [Phil. 3:8]. By the time I finished preaching, my complaints were gone. At the love-feast in the evening, many men and women told their experience in a way that affected all who heard. For example one said, "For 17 or 18 years I thought God had forgotten me. Neither I nor anyone in our house could believe, but now, blessed be his name, he has saved me and all in my house and has let me, my wife, and our seven children, rejoice together in God our Savior."

Wed. 18.—Talking with several at Wednesbury, I found that God is working here as in London. We have reason to hope that one prisoner was fully set free through the sermon Saturday morning and another through that on Saturday evening. One or more received remission of sins on Sunday, another on Monday morning, and on Wednesday still another believed the blood of Jesus Christ had cleansed him from all sin. In the evening I could hardly believe it, but more than one heard him say, "I will, be thou clean!" [Matt. 8:3]. In fact, he was so wonderfully present till midnight that it seemed he would have healed the whole congregation ...

Mon. 23.—After preaching at 5 a.m., I hurried and reached Leeds about 5 p.m., where I had asked all the preachers in that region to meet me, and we had a happy meeting both that evening and the next morning. Afterwards I asked about the condition of the fellowships in Yorkshire and Lincolnshire. I found that the work of God increases all around, but especially in Lincolnshire, where there has been no work like this since that time I preached at Epworth on my father's tomb ...

Fri. 27.—I rode to Bridgefield, in the middle of the Derbyshire Mountains, and cried out to a large assembly, "If anyone thirsts, let him come to me and drink" [John 7:37]. And indeed they did drink in the Word as the thirsty ground does the rain. About 6 p.m. I preached at Stockport. Here I asked about a young man who a while back was earnestly seeking salvation, but it wasn't long before he grew cold and left the fellowship. A few months later he left the world—and that by his own hand! ...

Sun. 29.—We had an unusual blessing, both morning and afternoon. In the evening I met with the believers and strongly urged them to go on to perfection. To many of them it seemed like a new doctrine. However, they all received it in love, and a flame was kindled which I trust neither men nor devils will ever be able to quench ...

VOLUME 3: 1760-1773

Mon. APRIL 13.—I left the fellowship at Liverpool, only slightly increased numerically but considerably strengthened, now being entirely united in judgment and in love.

About noon, I preached to a serious assembly at Downam-Green, near Wigan, but to a far more serious one in the evening at Bolton. I've found few places like this: All disputes have been forgotten and the Christians truly love each other. When I visited the classes on Wednesday the 15th, I didn't find a single one walking disorderly, nor one lazybody. They seemed, one and all, to be seriously seeking salvation ...

Mon. 27.—I preached at 8 a.m. in the market-place at Wigton. When I began, the gathering consisted of one woman, two boys, and three or four little girls, but in 15 minutes we had most of the town. I was quite struck by the peculiar self-sufficiency of many of them, visible in their faces and conduct. This forced me to use extraordinary plainness of speech. They took it well. Who knows but that some may benefit? ....

Tues. 28.—We rode partly over the mountains, partly with mountains on both sides, between which was a clear winding river, and about 4 p.m. we reached Edinburgh.

Here I met Mr. Hopper, who had promised to preach in the evening in a large room, formerly an Anglican meeting-house.

Wed. 29.—It being extremely cold, I preached in the same room at 7 a.m. Some of the reputable listeners cried out in amazement, "Why, this is sound doctrine! Is this the man of whom Mr. Wh[itehead] used to talk against so much?" Talk as he will, I won't retaliate ...

Sat. MAY 2.—At Aberdeen. In the afternoon, I sent a message to the principal and regent asking permission to preach in the college commons. This was readily granted, but it began to rain, so I was asked to go into the hall. I suppose this is at least 100 feet long, with seating all around. The assembly was large despite the rain and fully as big at 5 a.m. the next morning.

Sun. 3.—I heard two useful sermons in the kirk, one preached by the principal of the college, the other by the divinity professor. A huge crowd afterwards gathered in the college commons, and all who could hear seemed to receive the truth in love. I then added about 20 to the little fellowship. Fair blossoms! But how many of these will bring forth fruit? ...

Mon. 4— ... In the afternoon, I was walking in the library of Marischal College when the principal and the divinity professor approached me, and the latter invited me to his lodgings, where I spend a very pleasant hour. In the evening, the people coming were so eager they almost ran over each other. It took a while before they were still enough to hear, but then they devoured every word. After preaching, Sir Archibald Grant, whom business had called out of town, sent and asked to speak with me. I couldn't do so then, but promised to visit him on my return to Edinburgh, God willing.

Tues. 5.—I accepted the principal's invitation and spent an hour with him at his home. I didn't notice any stiffness at all, rather the good breeding of a man of sense and learning. I suppose that both he and all the professors, along with some of the magistrates, attended my preaching in the evening. I opened up all the windows; still the hall was as hot as a hot bath. But this didn't hinder either the attention of the people or the blessing of God ...

Thur. 7.—Leaving nearly 90 members in the fellowship, I rode over to Sir A. Grant's, near Monymusk, about 20 miles northwest of Aberdeen ...

About 6 p.m., we went to the church. It was pretty well filled with such people as we didn't expect so near the Highlands. As surprised as we were at their appearance, we were even more so at their singing. Thirty or forty sang an anthem after the sermon, with such voices and execution that I doubt any cathedral in England could have surpassed them ...

Sat. 16.— ... About noon I preached at Warksworth to an assembly as quiet and attentive as that at Alnwick. How long will we forget that God can raise the dead? Weren't we all dead until he quickened us? ...

Sun. 17.—In the evening, a crowd of people and a small regiment of soldiers gathered in the market-place at Alnwick. In the morning the soldiers were to march for Germany. I hope some of them "have put on their armor" [cf. Eph. 6:11-17] ...

Thur. 21.—Among the believers at Gatesbead-Fell who met in the evening, God had kindled a burning desire for his full salvation.

Asking how it was that in all these parts we scarcely have one living witness of this, I received from every person the same answer: "We see now that we sought salvation by our works. We thought it would come gradually; we never expected to receive it in a moment, by faith, as we did justification." No wonder, then that you have been fighting all these years as one beating the air! ...

Mon. 25.—I rode to Shields and preached in an open place to a hearing crowd. Many of them followed me to South-Shields, where I preached in the evening to almost double the number. How ripe for the gospel are these also. What is needed except more laborers?

More! Why, isn't there here, as in every parish in England, an appointed minister who takes care of all their souls? There is one here who has responsibility for all their souls, but what care he takes of them is another question. He may neither know nor care whether they are going to heaven or hell. Does he ask man, woman, or child, any question about it, from one Christmas to the next? Oh, what account will such a pastor give to the Great Shepherd in that day!

Tues. JUNE 9.—I preached at 9 a.m. but had to stand outdoors because of the crowd of people. The sun shone right in my face, but after a brief prayer I paid no attention to it. Later I met the fellowship, and arrived just in time to stop them from all turning dissenters, which they were on the point of doing, being disgusted at the curate, whose life was no better than his doctrine ...

We had a long stagecoach ride from there to Swaldale, where I found an earnest, loving, simple people, whom I also urged not to leave the church, though they didn't have the best ministers. I baptized a man and two women who had been raised among the Anabaptists, and I believe all of them received such a blessing as they couldn't express ...

Sun. 14.—In Sunderland, after Mr. G. finished reading prayers, I spoke very plainly to as many as could crowd into the church. Out of so "many that are called," won't some "be chosen"? [Matt. 22:14] ...

Mon. 15.—In the afternoon I rode to Hartlepool, but had difficulty preaching. Both my strength and my voice were gone—and usually they go away together. I can preach three times a day three days in a week, but now I had far exceeded this, besides meeting classes and exhorting the fellowships. I had to lie down a good part of Tuesday, but that afternoon I preached at Cherington and in the evening at Hartlepool again, but with difficulty.

Wed. 17.—I rode to Stockton where shortly before preaching time my voice and strength were restored at once ...

Sat. 20.—At Yarm, at noon, I applied these words: "Now abide faith, hope, and love, but the greatest of these is love" [1 Cor. 13:13].

This evening it rained at Hutton-Rugby till 7 p.m., the hour of preaching, but God heard our prayer, and from the time I began we had only some scattered drops. After sermon, the fellowship alone filled the new preaching-house, so mightily has the Word of God prevailed since Alexander Mather labored here ...

Sun. 21.—At 5 a.m. I preached at Potto, a mile from Hutton. When I began, I was very weak, but God renewed my strength and so applied his word that it seemed everyone had to believe it. But Scripture cannot be broken; some seed will still "fall by the wayside" and some "on stony ground" [cf. Mark ch. 4].

Mon. 22.—I spoke one by one to members of the fellowship at Hutton-Rugby. They totaled 80 in all, of whom nearly 70 were believers, and probably 16 renewed in love. Here are two small groups of children, one of boys, one of girls, most of them walking in the light. Four of those who seem to be saved from sin are of one family, and they all walk holy and unblameable, adorning the doctrine of God their Savior ...

At Guisborough a gentleman of the town asked me to preach in the market-place, and a table was set up for me to stand on. But it was in a bad neighborhood, because the smell of stinking fish almost suffocated me, and the people roared like the waves of the sea. But the voice of the Lord was mightier, and in a few minutes the whole crowd was still and listened attentively while I proclaimed "Jesus Christ, made by God for us wisdom, righteousness, sanctification, and redemption" [1 Cor. 1:30] ...

Fri. JULY 3.—We returned to York, where I was asked to visit a poor convict in the castle prison ... The plain fact was this: Some time back, a man who lived near Yarm helped others to run some illegal brandy. His share was four pounds. After he completely left that bad work and was following his own business as a weaver, he was arrested and sent to York jail, and soon after a declaration comes down "that Jac. Wh. had landed a vessel ladened with brandy and geneva at the port of London and sold them there, whereby he was indebted to his Majesty 577 pounds[278] and upwards"; and to tell this worthy story the lawyer takes up 13 or 14 sheets of paper, stamped three times.

Oh England, England! Will this reproach never be rolled away from you? Is there anything like this to be found among Catholics, Turks, or heathens? In the name of truth, justice, mercy, and common sense, I ask: 1.Why do men lie, for lying sake? Is it only to keep their hands in the money? Why say it was the port of London when everyone knows that brandy was landed 300 miles from there? What contempt, what hatred of truth! 2. Where is the justice of swelling four pounds to 577? 3. Where is the common sense of taking up 14 sheets to tell a story that can be told in 10 lines? 4. Where is the mercy in thus grinding the face of the poor, thus sucking the blood of a poor prisoner, reduced to begging? Wouldn't this be the worst iniquity, if the paper and writing together were only sixpence a sheet, when they have stripped him of what little he has and not left him 14 pennies in the world? ...

Wed. 8.—I rode to Knaresborough, where we didn't expect to receive a friendly reception, but the Lord is King. Our preaching-house being too small, I preached in the town assembly room. Most of the people looked wild enough when they came in, but they were tame before they went out, and behaved as decently and seriously as the assembly at Otley.

Indeed, the mob never was as furious here as they formerly were at Otley where the good magistrate directed the mob: "Do what you want to them, just so you don't break any bones." But can't a man cut his neighbor's throat without breaking his bones? ...

Sun. 12.—I had an appointment to be at Haworth, but the church wouldn't nearly hold the people who came from all around. However, Mr. Grimshaw had provided for this by erecting a scaffold outside of one of the windows, where I went after prayers, while the people all went out into the churchyard. The afternoon assembly was

---

[278] Four pounds = about $940 in 2020 USD; 577 pounds = about $136,000.

even larger. What has God accomplished in the midst of these rough mountains! ...

Mon. 13.— ... About noon [on the 14th] I preached at Bacup, a village in Rosendale. The new preaching-house is large but wasn't big enough to contain the gathering. Soon after 5 p.m. I preached at Heptonstall. The fellowship here has been severely hurt by two leaders getting into new opinions. One of them attacked me directly for "denying the righteousness of Christ." We discussed this for an hour. The outcome was that one was quite convinced of my view and the other, to my relief, asked me to find someone to replace him as leader ...

Sun. 19.—From Leeds I hurried back to the love-feast at Birstal. It was the first that had been held there. Many were surprised when I told them, **"The very purpose of a love-feast is a free and open sharing, in which every man and woman has the freedom to speak whatever may be to the glory of God"** [my emphasis]. Several then did speak, and not in vain. The flame ran from heart to heart, especially while one woman was declaring very simply how God had set her soul at full liberty during the morning sermon through the words, "I will, be thou clean" [Mark 1:41]. Two men spoke to the same effect, and two others said they had found peace with God. We then joyfully poured out our souls before God and praised him for his mighty works ...

Fri. 24.—My sermon was based on the words, "In many things we offend all" [James 3:2]. I observed: 1. As long as we live, our soul is connected to the body; 2. Since it's connected this way, it can't think without the help of bodily organs; 3. Since these organs aren't perfect, we're liable to mistakes, both theoretical and practical; 4. Yes, and a mistake may cause me to love a good man less than I ought, which is a faulty or wrong temper; 5. For all these we need the atoning blood, as we do for every defect or omission; therefore 6. We all must say daily, "Forgive us our trespasses." ...

Sun. 26.—About 1 p.m. I preached to the usual assembly at Birstal. What a work God is doing here too! Six people in one class this week have found peace with God and two this morning in the class meeting. While I was praying Sunday evening that God would give us a token for good, James Eastwood was set at liberty, as were

VOLUME 3: 1760-1773

William Wilson and (before him) Elizabeth, his wife, and Martha, his daughter, with Agnes Gooddel the next Wednesday. Joseph Newsam and Richard Hellewell, both 16 years old, have been added; so the oldest of our believers now cry out, "We never saw it like this before!" ...

Thur. AUGUST 6.—I preached about 9 a.m. at Hatfield-Wood House and about 1 p.m. at Syke House to by far the largest assembly that's been seen at these places for many years. Whoever will may boast that "Methodism (the revival of true religion) is coming to nothing." But we know better and are thankful to God for its continual increase.

Sat. 8.—I preached at Winterton to such an assembly as I suppose never met there before. From there we rode to Barrow, where the mob was ready to receive us, but their courage failed them. They yelled two or three times and let us pass by unmolested.

As soon as I came out to preach, they gave another yell, but as more and more of the angry ones came within hearing range, they lost all their fierceness and sank into calm attention. So I ended my speech with quietness and satisfaction ...

Fri. 14.—We rode to Bellingford and on Saturday to Norwich. After spending a few days there, and a few more at Yarmouth and Colchester, I returned to London on Saturday the 22nd.

I found the work of God swiftly increasing here. The assemblies in every place were larger than they'd been for several years. From day to day, many were convicted of sin. Many found peace with God. Many backsliders were healed—in fact, filled with joy unspeakable—and many believers entered into a rest such that they never imagined they could receive. Meantime, the enemy was not lacking in his efforts to sow tares among the good seed. I saw this clearly but dared not use force lest I root up the wheat with the tares [cf. Matt. 13:25ff.].

Tues. SEPTEMBER 1. Our conference began, ending on Saturday. After spending two more weeks in London, warning both the preachers and the people against running into extremes on either hand, on Sunday the 20th at night I took the stagecoach, and on Monday the 21st came to Bristol ...

Wed. OCTOBER 21.—The condemned prisoners asked me to give them one more sermon, and on Thursday, Patrick Ward, who was to be executed that day, sent a message asking me to administer the sacrament to him. He was 21 years old and had hardly ever had a serious thought till he shot the man who was about to take away his gun. From that instant he felt a change inside and never swore anymore. His whole behavior in prison was serious and composed; he read, prayed, and wept a lot, especially after one of his fellow prisoners found peace with God. Gradually his hope increased up till now and was greatly strengthened at the Lord's Supper. But he still complained, "I'm not afraid, but I don't want to die. I don't feel that warmth in my heart; I'm not sure my sins are forgiven." He went into the cart [taking him to the gallows] about noon in calmness, but mixed with sadness. But 15 minutes later, as he wrestled with God in prayer, seeming unaware of anyone near him, he said, "The Holy Spirit came on me, and I knew that Christ was mine." From that moment his whole conduct breathed a peace and joy beyond expression till, after spending about 10 minutes in private prayer, he gave the sign [to the executioner [that he was ready] ...

Sunday, NOVEMBER 1.—Back in London, I found the same spirit that I had left here, both in the morning and evening services.

Mon. 2.—At 5 p.m. I began a series of sermons on Christian perfection. At 7 p.m. I began meeting the classes ...

Mon. 16.—I withdrew to Lewisham, having many things to write.

Fri. 20.—I spent an hour at St. George's Hospital. The behavior of two or three patients there has done unspeakable good. Deep prejudices have been torn up by the roots, and much goodwill to the truth has followed. Oh, what may not just one believer do who seeks nothing but the glory of God! ...

Sun. 29.—We had a peaceable love-feast in London, at which several declared the blessings they had recently received. We don't need to worry about what names to call them, while they themselves are beyond dispute. Many have and many do experience an unspeakable change. After being deeply convicted of inbred sin, especially of pride, anger, self-will, and unbelief, in a moment, they feel all faith and love—no pride, no self-will, or anger. And from that moment they have continual fellowship with God, always rejoicing, praying, and giving thanks. Some may ascribe such a change to the devil, but I ascribe it to the Spirit of God. And I say, let whoever feels this at work in them, cry to God that it may continue, which it will if they walk closely with God—otherwise it won't ...

Mon. DECEMBER 21.—I withdrew again to Lewisham and wrote *Farther Thoughts on Christian Perfection.* If the cautions given in this work had been taken, how much scandal might have been prevented! And why weren't they taken? Because my own familiar friend was even then forming a party against me ...

Sat. 26.—I made special inquiry into the case of Mary Special, a young woman then living in Tottenham Court Road. She said, "Four years ago, I had a lot of pain in my breasts, then hard lumps. Four months ago, my left breast broke open and kept running continually. On recommendation I went to St. George's Hospital. They bled me several times and gave me hemlock three times a day, but I didn't get better; the pain and the lumps were the same, and both my breasts were hard and as black as soot. A week ago yesterday I went to Mr. Owen's where there was a prayer meeting. Mr. Bell saw me and asked, "Do you have faith to be healed?" I said, "Yes." He prayed for me, and in a moment all my pain was gone, but the next day I felt a little pain again. I cupped my hands on my breasts and cried out, "Lord, if you will, you can make me whole." It was gone! And from that hour I have no pain, no soreness, no lumps, no swelling; both my breasts were perfectly well and have been ever since."

Now here are plain facts: 1. She was sick. 2. She is well. 3. She was healed in a moment. Which of these can be denied?

Tues. 29.—In order to remove some misunderstandings, I requested all parties concerned to meet with me. They all did but T.M., who flatly refused to come. Is this just the first step toward a separation? Alas for that man! Alas for the people!

Thur. 31.—We ended the year, as usual, with a solemn watch-night. Oh, may we end our lives in the same way, blessing and praising God!

1762

Fri. JANUARY 1.—I think we had nearly 2000 of our Society at Spitalfields in the evening, where Mr. Berridge, Mr. Maxfield, and Mr. Colley assisted me, and we found God in our midst while we devoted ourselves to him in the most solemn and explicit way ...

Sun. 3.—In Everton, I read prayers and preached, morning and evening, to a large and lively assembly. In general, the people were more settled than when I was here before, but they were in danger of running from one extreme to another. Instead of thinking, as many did, that none can possibly have true faith except those who have trances or visions, they were now ready to think that whoever had anything like this had no faith at all ...

Sun. 10.—At Potton I preached at 6 a.m., then at Everton I read prayers and preached both morning and afternoon and administered the sacrament to a large number of communicants. At 4 p.m. we mounted up, reaching Grandchester shortly before 7 p.m. Finding a group gathered there, I spent a very pleasant half-hour with them, and by the blessing of God was no more tired when I went to bed than when I had risen in the morning ...

Wed. 13.—We rested from our labor. How can those who never work taste the sweetness of rest? ...

Fri. MARCH 5.—I had a long conversation with Joseph Rule, nicknamed the White Quaker. He seemed to be a calm, loving, sensible man, very devoted to God ...

Fri. 12.—The national fast was observed all over London, with great solemnity. Surely God is well pleased with this acknowledgment that he governs the world, and even the outward humiliation of a nation may be rewarded with outward blessings ...

Fri. APRIL 1[2].— ... It was at this time that Mr. Grimshaw died. He was born September 3, 1708 ... One day in 1742, being in the utmost agony of mind, he clearly saw, as it were, Jesus Christ pleading for him with God the Father and gaining a free pardon for him. At that moment all his fear vanished and he was filled with joy unspeakable. "Now," he said, "I was willing to deny myself and to embrace Christ for my all in all. Oh, what light and comfort my soul enjoyed, and what a taste of the pardoning love of God!"

All this time he was entirely ignorant of the people called Methodists, although later he thought it his duty to favor them and to

VOLUME 3: 1760-1773

work with them in his community. He was also a stranger to their writings till he came to Haworth on May the 26th of this year. And the good effects of his preaching soon became visible. Many of his flock became deeply concerned for their salvation, and were shortly afterwards filled with peace and joy through believing. As in ancient times, the whole congregation has often been seen in tears on account of their rebellion against God and of his goodness in still sparing them.

His animated way of representing the truths of God caused much talk, and many hundreds came to Haworth Church out of curiosity. Long after the novelty passed, they received so much benefit that the church continued to be full of people, many who came from far away, and this for a period of 20 years ...

Mr. Grimshaw used all his strength and abilities even to his last illness, and his labors were not in vain in the Lord. He saw a real change take place in many of his flock, and a reduction of the commission of sins in the parish in general. He saw the name of Jesus exalted and many souls happy in knowing him and walking as becomes the gospel. He was happy in himself, being kept by the power of God, unblameable in his conduct. He was happy in being beloved in the last years of his life by everyone in his parish who, whether he could persuade them to forsake their sinful ways or not, had no doubt that Mr. Grimshaw was their true friend. And so, at his departure from this life, a general concern was visible throughout his parish. His body was interred in a manner more ennobling than all the pomp of a royal funeral, as he was followed to the grave by a huge crowd, with affectionate sighs and many tears, by those who cannot still hear his well-beloved name without weeping for the guide of their souls, to whom each of them was dear as children to their father ...

Mon. 19.—I left Dublin, and could look back with satisfaction on my days there. I had reason to believe that God had been at work in a very unusual way. Many who once argued and bad-mouthed were now convicted of the truth as it is in Jesus. Many who had long rebelled against God had returned to him wholeheartedly. Several mourners had found peace with God, and some believe he has saved them from all sin. Many more are on fire for this salvation, and a spirit of love runs through all the people.

That evening I came to Newry, where I found a very different set of circumstances. Offenses had broken the fellowship into pieces, leaving only 32 out of nearly 100. But God still has a few names left here; if they stand firm, God will maintain his own cause ...

Thur. MAY 13.—I hoped that the Catholics at Athlone finally had a shepherd who cared for their souls. He was stricter than his predecessors and considered a man of piety as well as of learning; accordingly, he had given them strict orders not to work on the Lord's Day. But I found he allowed them to play as much as they pleased, especially at cards; in fact, he said it was their duty to do so, to "refresh both their bodies and minds." Alas, for the blind leader of the blind! Doesn't he have the greater sin?[279]

Sun. 16.—I had told the fellowship last week that I'd never seen a congregation behave so badly in Ireland at church as in Athlone: laughing, talking, and looking around during the whole service. I had added: "This is your fault, for if you attended the church, as you ought to have done, your presence and example certainly would have influenced the whole congregation"—and so it appeared. Today I saw not one laughing, talking, or looking around; instead, a remarkable seriousness spread from one end of the church to the other.

Mon. 17.—I preached at Ahaskra to all the Protestants in or near the town, but the priests wouldn't allow the Catholics to come. What would a magistrate do in this case? Most likely he would tell the priest, "Sir, as you enjoy freedom of conscience, you will allow it to others. You yourself are not persecuted, and you will not persecute them."

Wed. 26.—In the afternoon we reached Galway. There was a small fellowship here and (what is unusual) all of them were young women. Between 7 and 8 p.m. I began preaching in the courthouse to a mixed multitude of Catholics and Protestants, rich and poor, who seemed completely amazed. At 5 a.m. I preached again and spoke as

---

[279] Many of us today would agree with the Catholic priest in this rather than with Wesley, seeing Sunday as a day of recreation as well as of worship.

plainly as possible, but to most of them it just seemed to be "the sound of many waters." ...

Sun. 30.—At Limerick I preached in the old military camp. The place being so pleasant, the evening so calm, and the short distance from the town, conspired to draw the people together from all around. Many officers and soldiers were among them and behaved very decently. The following evenings I preached at the same place, in large part for the sake of the soldiers, it being within a musket-shot of the place they were conducting maneuvers. Two evenings, in fact, an officer ordered a large company to conduct maneuvers on the very spot we were using, but the moment I began, they laid down their arms and joined the rest of the assembly ...

Fri. JUNE 11.—and Saturday, I had long conversations with a person of renown, but I found no one in town who expected that any good could be done to such a sinner as him. Such a sinner! Why weren't we all such sinners? We were "dead in sin" [cf. Rom. 8:10], and is he more than dead?

Sun. 13.—Having been told that I was preaching over the heads of the soldiers, who only understood hell and damnation, I left them this evening after strongly applying the story of Dives and Lazarus [Luke 16:19ff.]. They seemed to understand this, and all but two or three young officers behaved as men fearing God ...

Sat. 26.—I visited the classes and urged them to "be zealous and repent" [Rev. 3:19]. This work penetrated their hearts, so when we met in the evening, they didn't seem to be the same. They seemed to breathe quite another spirit, each stirring up his neighbor. I don't know when I've seen so deep and general an impression made in such a short time ...

Sun. 27.—Thomas Jones died, an honest man whom God raised from nothing by his constant diligence to a sizable fortune; yet when riches increased, he didn't set his heart on them. Some years ago he retired from business, but was still employed full-time building and doing good. He was rough by nature and so was his speech, which caused him some trouble; nevertheless he was generous and compassionate, never weary of well-doing. When he got sick, he was constantly in prayer, for a while with fear and distress, but when I came from Bandon I saw no sign of these things. I believe his fear had vanished, and he waited calmly, though with earnest desire, for the salvation of God.

Wed. 30.—I rode to Limerick. I had promised to come again if our brethren found a suitable place to build a preaching-house. Now a place was offered, proper in every respect.

Sat. JULY 3.—I met the fellowship and asked what each was willing to pledge toward the preaching-house. A considerable sum was pledged immediately …

Tues. 6.—I rode to Carrick-on-Sure. Having been told that there was a family here too in which both the man and his wife feared God, I immediately sent a message to the house. The woman came shortly, who told me that her husband had died the previous Saturday, leaving her with nothing but four little children and an unshakable confidence in God. Her words, her appearance, her conduct, were all coherent and showed the dignity of Christian sorrow. I could only admire that God had sent me just at this time! And her tears were turned into tears of joy.[280] …

Sun. 11.—At 6 p.m. I began preaching in the old bowling-green near the castle. Masses of people, Protestants and Catholics, gathered from all around. They were very still during the first part of the sermon. Then the Catholics ran together, began shouting, and would have gone further, but they were held back—they didn't know how. I turned to them and said, "Be quiet or leave!" Their noise died down, and we didn't hear from them anymore, so I picked up where I'd left off and went on with my sermon, ending without interruption …

Tues. 13.—I rode to Birr. About 40 people attended the evening preaching and about half that many the next morning. The only way I saw to do any good was to preach outdoors in the evening. Then I had hundreds of listeners, and God himself spoke to many cold hearts. The next morning at 5 a.m. the room was full and light sprang out of darkness, so that many poor, withered souls began to revive and to rejoice again in God their Savior …

Tues. 20.—We had our quarterly meeting at Cooly-Lough. On Wednesday I preached at Clara, on Thursday the 22nd at Tyrrell's Pass, and on Friday I went on to Edinderry. Here I found some who

---

[280] Wesley implies that he helped the widow financially.

for a long time had been laboring in the fire, trying to work themselves into holiness. To show them a more excellent way, I preached on Romans 10:6-8. They found that this was the very thing they lacked, and at the meeting of the fellowship, God confirmed the word of his grace in such a powerful way that many wondered how they could help but believe.

Sat. 24.—I rode to Dublin and found the flame not only still burning but increasing. The gathering used to be small on Saturday night but now was as large as formerly on Sunday ...

Tues. 27.—I received a comforting letter from Edinderry: "When you came here, Satan had gained such an advantage over us that few even of the fellowship would read your sermons, saying they were nothing but the law, but now God has taught us better. His power fell on us first in your preaching, but much more so when the fellowship met. At that time many who were in heaviness were filled with consolation, and two of the first believers were compelled to declare that they believed God had cleansed them from all sin."

Thur. 29.—I was told of a remarkable instance of divine mercy. A harmless, spiritually dead young woman came to one of the prayer meetings in Dublin. While they were praying, she felt herself to be a sinner and began crying aloud for mercy. And when the group rose to disperse, she cried out bitterly, "What, must I leave without Christ?" They began praying again, and in a little while she was praising God loudly for his pardoning mercy.

The case of Alexander Tate was just as remarkable. He and his wife were present when a few met for prayer. Her sorrow quickly turned to joy. Her husband, who before that was only a little awakened spiritually, was just then cut to the heart and felt the wrath of God abiding on him. He didn't stop crying to God till his prayers and tears were swallowed up in thanksgiving. So here are two cases of persons both convicted and converted in the same hour ...

Fri. AUGUST 6.—Asking how the revival began at Macclesfield, I was told the following: Last March, after a long period of dryness and barrenness, one Monday night John Oldham preached. When he finished and was leaving, a man fell down and cried out for mercy. In a short time so did several others. John came back and wrestled with God in prayer for them. About midnight he left, leaving some of the brethren who were determined to continue wrestling until they had a peaceful answer from God. They continued in prayer till 6 a.m., and nine prisoners [of Satan] were set free.

They met again the following night, and six or seven were filled with peace and joy in believing. So were one or two others each night till the following Monday, when there was another general rain of grace, and many believed that the blood of Christ had cleansed them from all sin.

I spoke to these (40 in all) one by one. Some said they had received that blessing 10 days, some seven, some four, some three days, after they found peace with God, and two of them the next day. But no wonder, since one day with God is as 1000 years? [2 Peter 3:8] ...

Mon. 9.—I preached at Eland and Birstal on my way to Leeds, where our conference began on Tuesday morning. And we had plenty of reason to praise God for his gracious presence from beginning to end.

Sun. 15.—I preached about 1 p.m. at Birstal, and the next morning and evening at Leeds. Then I rode about 18 miles. Monday morning I preached at Sheffield, and in the evening reached Derby. I had sent word that I didn't plan to preach, but after resting a while in my room, I came down and found the house full of people. I spoke to them half an hour in a familiar way and then spent some time in prayer. I believe God touched some of their hearts; in fact, it appeared that everyone was moved ...

Sat. 21.—My brother Charles and I had a long conversation with Mr. Maxfield and openly told him what we didn't like [in his ministry]. We found that in some things he had been blamed without cause; others he promised to change. So we were complexly satisfied with our dialogue, believing all misunderstandings had been removed ...

Sun. 29.—I preached at 8 a.m. on Southney Green to a very quiet assembly. Then we attended services at the cathedral, where the sermon was useful and the whole service performed with great solemnity and decency. I'd never heard such an organ before, so large, beautiful, and finely pitched. And the music of *Glory Be to God in the Highest,* to me exceeded even *The Messiah* itself. I was very pleased to partake of the Lord's Supper with my old opponent, Bishop Lavington. Oh, may we sit down together in the kingdom of our Father! ...

Sun. SEPTEMBER 6.—At 1 p.m. I preached in the main street at Redruth, where rich and poor alike were attentive. The wind was so fierce at 5 p.m. that I couldn't stand in the usual place at Gwenap. But nearby was a hollow able to hold many thousands of people. I stood on one side of this natural amphitheater toward the top, with the people below and on all aides, and expanded on the words in the Gospel for the day, Luke 10:23: "Blessed are the eyes which see the things that you see and the ears that hear the things that you hear." ...

Mon. 7.—In Mullion, a flame was kindled almost as soon as I began to speak, and it grew brighter and brighter all the time I was preaching as well as during the meeting of the fellowship. How tender are the hearts of this people! Such is the benefit of true Christian simplicity! ...

Wed. 15[16?].—We held our quarterly meeting. The next day I arranged for the children to meet. I expected 20, but it looked like we had 80, all of them needing and many wanting to be taught.

The more I talk with the believers in Cornwall, the more I'm convinced that they've suffered great loss due to not hearing the doctrine of Christian perfection clearly and strongly enforced. And this can only be helped by keeping in them an expectation every hour of being perfected in love. I say to expect it every hour, because to expect it at death or some time in the future is just about the same as not expecting it at all ...

Tues. 21.—I rode to Port Isaac. Here the stewards of the eastern circuit met. What a change has been accomplished in one year's time! The abominable practice of cheating the king is no more found in our fellowships, and since this accursed thing has been put away, the work of God increases everywhere. Our Society, in particular, has more than doubled, and they are all alive to God ...

Fri. OCTOBER 1.—I preached at Taunton and Shepton Mallet, and on Saturday the 2nd rode on to Bristol. The following two weeks I visited as many as I could of the fellowships in the country, and set those of Bristol and Kingswood in order.

Sat. 19[?].—Being told that James Oddie, who was coming to Bristol, had to stop at Newport with a pleuritic fever, I went to him immediately. He recovered from that hour,[281] and in two or three days followed me to Bristol ...

The next week I went to many of the fellowships in Somersetshire ...

Thur. 28.—A woman who had adorned the gospel in life and death had asked me to preach her funeral. I went with a few friends to her house and sang in front of her body in the room where her body lay. I did this to show my approval of that solemn custom[282] and to encourage others to follow it. As we walked, our group swiftly grew larger, so we had a large group in the room. Who knows but that some of these may bless God for it to all eternity?

Many years ago my brother Charles often said, "Your day of Pentecost hasn't fully come, but I don't doubt that it will, and you'll hear of people sanctified as often as you do now of people justified." Any unprejudiced reader will see that now it *had* fully come. Just so we did hear of people sanctified in London and most parts of England, and in Dublin and many other parts of Ireland, as often as of those justified, even though instances of justification were far more frequent than they'd been for 20 years previously. That many of them didn't keep the gift of God is no proof that it wasn't given to them. That many do keep it today is a matter of praise and thanksgiving. And many have gone to him whom they loved, praising him with their last breath; just as in the spirit of Ann Steed, the first witness in Bristol of the great salvation who, being worn out with sickness and racking pain, after she had commended to God all who were around her, lifted up her eyes, cried aloud, "Glory, hallelujah!" and died ...

Wed. NOVEMBER 24.—Deciding to hear for myself, I stood where I could hear and see without being seen. George Bell prayed for nearly an hour. I couldn't help but admire his fervor of spirit. Later I told him what I didn't admire: 1. his screaming now and then in such a strange way that one could hardly tell what he was saying;

---

[281] Like by a combination of Wesley's prayers and his treatment methods, which were often effective.

[282] I.e., of singing before a dead body.

2. his thinking he had the miraculous discernment of spirits; and 3. his sharply condemning those opposing him …

Mon. DECEMBER 6.—and the following days, I corrected my *Notes on the Book of Revelation.* Oh, how little do we know of this deep book—at least, how little do I know! I can barely guess, and can't affirm a single point, regarding that part of it which is still unfulfilled …

Sun. 19.—From Matthew 18:3, I tried to show those who use the Word without understanding it what Christian simplicity actually is and what it isn't. It's not ignorance or folly; it's not emotionalism or credulity; it's faith, humility, willingness to be taught, and freedom from evil thinking …

Wed. 22.—I heard George Bell one more time and was convinced he mustn't continue to pray at the Foundry. I'm willing to bear the reproach of Christ, but not the reproach of emotionalism, if I can help it.

Sat. 25.—We met in the Spitalfields Chapel to renew our covenant with God, and he did indeed move in the midst of the congregation, answering as if by fire.

Sun. 26.—In order not to do anything hastily, I permitted George Bell to come once more this evening in the West Street Chapel and again Wednesday evening at the Foundry. But it was worse and worse. Now he spoke as if from God something I knew God had not spoken. And so I asked him not to come there anymore …

Fri. 31.—Now I stepped back and looked on the past year—a year of unusual trials and unusual blessings. Many had been convicted of sin; many had found peace with God; and in London alone, I believe, at least 200 have been brought into glorious liberty. Yet I've had more concern and trouble in six months than in several previous years. What the end will be I don't know; but it's enough that God knows.

1763

Sat. JANUARY 1.—A woman told me, "Sir, I have several men in my employment. Now if one of my employees won't obey me; am I not right to fire him at once? Please tell me, will you apply this to

Mr. Bell?" I answered, "It's right to fire an employee, but what would you do if he were your son?" ...

Fri. 7.—I asked George Bell, along with two or three of his friends, to meet me with one or two others. We took great pains to convince him of his mistakes, especially the one he had recently taken up, "that the end of the world was to come on February 28th," which at first he was strongly against, but we could make no impression on him. He was as unmoved as a rock ....

Mon. MARCH 7—I took the stagecoach for Norwich and, after spending a few quiet, pleasant days in Norwich, Yarmouth, and Colchester, without any problem or contention, on Sunday the 19th returned to London.

Mon. 28.—I withdrew to Lewisham and wrote the sermon on "Sin in Believers," in order to remove the error that some were trying to promote, that there's no sin in any who are justified.

Mon. APRIL 11.—Leaving things, so it seemed, pretty well settled in London, I took the stagecoach for Bristol. Here, on Tuesday the 19th, I paid the last office of love to Nicholas Gilbert, who was a good man and an excellent preacher. He likely would have been of great use, but God saw it best to take him away by a fever in the dawn of his usefulness.

Sat. 23.—I returned to London. On Thursday the 28th I was at Westminster where I was scheduled to preach, when word was brought to me about 5 p.m. "that Mr. M. would not preach at the Foundry."

So the break is made, but I'm clear that I've done all I possibly could to avoid it. I immediately walked away and preached on "If I am bereaved of my children, I am bereaved" [cf. Gen. 43:14] ...

Monday, MAY 2.—and the following days, I was employed full-time visiting the fellowship and settling the minds of those who had been confused and distressed by 1000 misrepresentations. Indeed, a flood of slander and evil-speaking (which was easy to foresee) was poured out on every side. My purpose was still to go straightforward in the work to which I was called ...

Sun. 29.—I preached at 7 a.m. in the high-school yard at Edinburgh. It being the time of the national general assembly, which brought not only the ministers but many of the nobility and upper class and many more in the afternoon at 5 p.m., I spoke as plainly as ever in my life, but I never knew any in Scotland offended by plain dealing. In this respect, the North Britons are an example to all humankind ...

Tues. 31.—I rode to Alnwick and was refreshed among a people who don't have just the form but the spirit of true religion: fellowship with God and the living power of faith divine ...

Mon. JUNE 5[6].—I rode to Barnard Castle and preached in the evening to such an assembly as I never saw there before, not just with respect to number but also to seriousness and tranquility. I planned after preaching to meet with the fellowship, but most of the people were so eager to hear more that I just had to let in as many as the room would hold, and it was a time of God's power. They all seemed to take the kingdom by force as they stormed heaven with fervent prayer.

Tues. 6[7].— ... There is something remarkable in the way God revived his work in this area. A few months ago the people in this circuit generally were spiritually lifeless. Samuel Meggot realized this and advised the fellowship at Barnard Castle to devote every Friday with fasting and prayer. The very first Friday they met together God broke in on them in a wonderful way, and his work has been increasing among them ever since. The nearby fellowships, hearing of this, agreed to follow the same rule, and soon received the same blessing. **Isn't the neglect of this plain duty—I mean fasting—ranked by our Lord with charitable giving and prayer, one general occasion of deadness among Christians? Can anyone willingly neglect it and be guiltless?** [my emphasis] ...

Sun. 12.—I used the preaching-room in the morning, preached in the afternoon at the market-place, and about 1 p.m. to those who gathered from all around, in Haxley Parish, near Westwood-side. At each place I tried to settle the minds of the poor people who had been harassed by a new doctrine, which honest John C. and his converts had been diligently spreading among them, that there is no sin in believers; instead, the moment we believe, sin is destroyed, root and branch. I trust that this plague too is stayed. But ought not those unstable ones to be ashamed, who are so easily tossed about by every wind of doctrine?

Serious Joy (John Wesley's *Journal*)

I had asked Samuel Meggot to give me a fuller account of the recent work of God at Barnard Castle. Part of his answer follows:

June 7, 1763

Within 10 weeks, at least 20 people in this town have found peace with God, and 28 the pure love of God. Before you left us this morning, one found peace and another the second blessing, and after you left two more received it. One of these had belonged to the fellowship before, but after he turned away had bitterly persecuted his wife, especially after she claimed to be saved from sin.

He furiously came to drag her out of the fellowship meeting. Someone cried out, "Let's pray for him." Soon he ran away, and his wife went home. It wasn't long before he rushed in like a madman and swore he would kill her. Someone said, "Aren't you afraid that God might smite you?" He replied, "No, let God do his worst. I'll get rid of her and the brats and myself, too, and we'll all go to hell together." His wife and children fell down and burst into prayer. His expression changed and he became quiet as a lamb. Before long he was overwhelmed with dread and very distressed. The hand of God was on him and gave him no rest, day or night. On Tuesday afternoon, he went to the woman who prayed for him when he went to drag his wife out, begging her with many tears to pray for his deliverance. On Thursday he wrestled with God till he was sopping wet with sweat, just as if he'd been dipped in water. But that evening God wiped away his tears and filled him with joy unspeakable.

This morning, while Brother Story was praying, God bore witness in his heart that he had purified him. When he rose from his knees, he couldn't help but declare it. He ran to his wife, not to kill her but to gather her in his arms, that they might praise God and weep over one another with tears of joy and love ...

Thur. 16.—At 5 p.m. I preached at Dewsbury, and on Friday the 17th reached Manchester. Here I received a detailed account of a remarkable incident. A noted drunkard of Congleton used to amuse himself, whenever there was preaching there, by standing beside the preaching-house, cursing and swearing at the preacher. One evening he had a fancy to step in and "hear what the man had to say." He did this, but it made him so uneasy that he couldn't sleep at all that night. In the morning he was so uneasy that he walked in the fields, but nothing helped till it came to his mind to go to one of his drinking buddies who was always ready to mock the Methodists. He told him how he was and asked what he should do. "Do?" said Samuel, "Go and join the fellowship!" "I will, because I was never so uneasy in my life." They both did so without delay. But soon David cried out, "I'm sorry I joined, because I'll get drunk again and they'll throw me out." He stood firm for four days, but on the fifth his old friends persuaded him to "take one pint," then another and another, till one of them said, "See, here is a drunk Methodist!" David jumped up, knocked him over in his chair, then drove the rest out of the house, broke the door open, picked up the landlady, carried her out and threw her into the kennel, then ran into the fields, tore his hair, and rolled up and down on the ground. A day or two later there was a love-feast and he crept in, staying at the rear so none could see him. While Mr. Furz was praying, David was seized with a dreadful agony of both body and mind. This caused many to wrestle with God for him. After a while he jumped to his feet, stretched out his hands, and cried aloud, "All my sins are forgiven!" This was Samuel H. David burst through the people, caught him in his arms, and said, "Come, let's sing the Virgin Mary's song; I never could sing it before: "My soul doth magnify the Lord, and my spirit doth rejoice in God my Savior." And their behavior showed the reality of their words …

Fri. 24.—Finding it imprudent to leave London during the agitation that continued following Mr. M.'s separation from us, I decided not to leave before the conference. This began on Tuesday, July the 19th, and ended on Saturday the 23rd, and it was a great blessing that we had peace among ourselves while so many were arming themselves for battle.

Mon. AUGUST 1.—I began visiting the classes again, and found less loss than one might have expected, considering that most of those who had left us spoke all kinds of evil with no fear or shame. Poor creatures! But he who led them into this has the greater sin …

Sat. 27.—[*At Swansea*] At 7 a.m. I preached to 100 or 200 people, many of whom seemed full of good desires. But as there is no fellowship, I expect no deep or lasting work …

Thur. SEPTEMBER 1.—I began explaining a second time, after a 20-year interval, the epistle of 1 John. How plain, how full, and how deep a summary of genuine Christianity!

Sat. 3.—I described the one undivided "fruit of the Spirit," part of which people are always trying to separate one from the other. But this can't be so; no one can retain peace or joy without meekness and long-suffering, or without fidelity and temperance. Unless we have the whole fruit, we can't keep any part of it for long ...

Wed. 14.—I preached at Bath on "Now is the day of salvation." Afterwards I was very refreshed by the conversation of a woman who had recently come from London, in spite of her unusual way of thinking, peculiar to herself. How much preferable is her irregular warmth to the cold wisdom of those who despise her! I would gladly be as she is, taking her wildness and fervor together! ...

Fri. 23.—I preached again at Bath. Riding home, we saw a coffin being carried into St. George's Church with many children following it. When we got closer, we found they were our own children, attending the body of one of their schoolmates who had died of the smallpox. And by this means God touched many of their hearts in a way they never knew before.

Mon. 26.—I preached to the prisoners in Newgate Prison, and in the afternoon rode over to Kingswood School, where I held a solemn watch-night and took the opportunity to speak intimately with the children. One is dead, two have recovered, seven are still sick, and the hearts of all are like melting wax.

Tues. 27.—I left the congregation at Bristol after opening and applying these words by which no living person shall be justified: "Thou shalt love thy neighbor as thyself" [Lev. 19:18; Matt. 22:39]. I believe a noted Deist who was present will not easily forget that hour. At least then he was deeply affected and felt he needed "an advocate with the Father" [cf. 1 John 2:1]...

Sat. OCTOBER 1.—I returned to London and found our preaching-house in ruins, large parts torn down to make a major repair, but enough remaining for my personal lodging. Six feet square is sufficient for me by day or night ...

Sun. 2.—All this week I tried to firm up those who had been shaken with regard to the important Christian doctrine of perfection, either by its wild defenders or by wise opponents who took advantage of that wildness. It must be that such offenses will come, but "woe be to him by whom the offense comes" [Luke 17:1].

Mon. 10.—I set out for Norwich, stopping at Hertford on my way, where I began preaching between 10 and 11 a.m. Those expecting disturbance were gladly disappointed, because the whole assembly was quiet and attentive. I have no doubt that a lot of good may be done even here if our brothers and sisters live what we preach. In the evening I preached in the New Room at Bedford, where we finally see some fruit for our labor.

Tues. 11.—I rode through miserable roads to Cambridge and from there to Lakenheath. The next day I reached Norwich, and found a strong presence of God in the assembly, both that evening and the next day. Friday evening I read to them all the rules of the Society, adding: "Those who resolve to abide by these rules may stay with us, and only those." I then related what I'd done since I first came to Norwich and what I would continue to do; in particular, that I would immediately put an end to preaching during the church services. I added, "For many years I've had more trouble with this fellowship than with half the fellowships in England put together. With God's help I'll try you one year longer, and I hope you'll bring forth better fruit." …

Tues. 25.—I rode to Colchester and found a strange unrest in the fellowship caused by the indiscretion of ____, who had lit a fire that he couldn't put out and had set every man's sword against his brother. I heard them all face to face, but it was no use; they had no regard either to Scripture or reason. But on Thursday evening, at the meeting of the fellowship, God was moved on their behalf. The stony hearts were broken; anger, revenge, and suspicions fled away. The hearts of all were again united together and his banner over us was love [cf. Sg. of Sol. 2:4] …

Sun. NOVEMBER 13.—I felt the power of God in preaching, but far more at the Lord's Table. At the same time, a man who had been wandering away from God for many years and who wanted to attend the service but couldn't, found that the Spirit of God wasn't hindered or confined to one place. God found the poor backslider in his own home and revealed Christ anew in his heart …

Fri. 18.—I finished visited the classes in London and noticed that since last February, 175 persons have left us. One hundred and six left on account of Mr. M.; few of them will return till they are truly humbled.

I stood here, looking back on recent developments. Before Thomas Walsh left England, God began the great work which has continued ever since without much letup. During this whole time, many have been convicted of sin, many justified, and many backsliders healed. But the special work of this season has been what St. Paul calls "the perfecting of the saints" [Eph. 4:12]. Many in London, in Bristol, in York, and other parts of England and Ireland have experienced such a deep and total change as they never imagined possible. After a deep conviction of inherent sin, of their total fall from God, they've been so filled with faith and love—usually in a moment—that sin vanished, and they found from then on no pride, anger, wrong desire, or unbelief. They could "rejoice evermore, pray without ceasing, and in everything give thanks" [1 Thes. 5:15-18]. Whether we call this the actual destruction or merely the suspension of sin, it is the glorious work of God. This is such a work, considering its depth and extent, that we never saw in these kingdoms before ...

1764

Thur. FEBRUARY 2.— Again I preached in the Foundry, on which repair work had been going on for several weeks. Now it's not only solid and safe, whereas before the main timbers were rotting, but it's also clean and decent and able to contain several hundred more people ...

Mon. MARCH 12.—I set out for Bristol.

Fri. 16.—I met several serious clergymen. For a long time I have wished for an open, acknowledged union between all who teach these fundamental truths: original sin and justification by faith, producing inward and outward holiness. But all my efforts have so far been unproductive; God's time hasn't yet fully come ...

Fri. 30.—I met with those who believe God has redeemed them from all their sins, about 60 in all. I couldn't find that any among them walked unworthily of their profession. Many are watching them to find evil, but they are overcoming evil with good. I found nothing of self-conceit, stubbornness, impatient arguing, or London emotionalism among them. They have learned better of him who was meek and lowly of heart, to adorn the doctrine of God their Savior ...

Sat. 31.— ... At noon I preached in a yard near the bridge in Doncaster, the preaching-room being too small to contain the people. The wind was strong and biting cold, and the whole time blew on the side of my head. That afternoon I got a sore throat almost as soon as I reached Epworth. I did preach, however with difficulty, but afterwards could hardly speak. Being better the next day, April 1st, I preached about 1 p.m. at Westwood-side, and shortly after 4 p.m. in the market-place at Epworth to a large assembly. At first few could hear, but the more I spoke, the more my voice was strengthened, till near the end all my pain and weakness were gone and all could hear clearly.

Mon. APRIL 2.—I had a day of rest.

Tues. 3.—I preached about 9 a.m. at Scotter, a town six or seven miles east of Epworth, where a fire has suddenly broken out, many being convicted of sin almost at once, and many justified. But there were many enemies stirred up by a bad man who told them, "There is no law for Methodists." Therefore constant disorder followed till, after a while, an upright magistrate took charge of the matter and so handled the rioters and the man who got them going that they've been quiet as lambs ever since.

From there we rode to Grimsby, once the deadest, now the liveliest place in the county. Here there's been a rapid increase both of the fellowship and of those who attend preaching, so that the preaching-house, even though galleries have been added, is still too small. On the morning of Wednesday the 4th, I explained at length the nature of Christian perfection. Many who'd doubted about it before were now fully convinced. What's left now is only to experience what we believe.

In the evening the mayor and all the upper-class people of the town were present, and so was our Lord in an unusual way. Some dropped down as if dead, but after a while rejoiced with joy unspeakable. One woman was carried out in violent fits. I went to her after the service; she was convulsing strongly from head to foot, and shrieking in a dreadful way. The unclean spirit did indeed tear her, but his reign was short. In the morning both her soul and body were healed, and she testified to both the justice and mercy of God.

Wed. 11.—When I came to York at 5 p.m., I felt fresher than at 7 a.m. During the sermon, many received real comfort, and one old Christ-follower, over 70 years old, was now first able to call him Lord by the Holy Spirit ...

Sun. 29.—Since the ground was wet due to heavy rain, I used the preaching-house both morning and evening. I soon discerned the spirit of the people. There's no discord or contention here; rather all are peaceably and lovingly striving together for the hope of the gospel. What can hurt the Methodists (as we are called) but the Methodists themselves? If only they don't fight each other, brother taking up a sword against his brother, "no weapon formed against them shall prosper" [Isa. 54:17] ...

Sat. MAY 19.—I preached to the poor coalminers at Placey, who are still an example of righteousness to the whole county. As we rode to our lodging, we stopped at a large house I'd often heard about. The front is truly noble. In the house I didn't see anything remarkable except what was remarkably bad: pictures such that an honest heathen would be ashamed to allow in his home unless he wanted his wife and daughters to be prostitutes. And this is quite the fashion! What proof of the taste of our present age!

Sun. 20.—Between 8 and 9 a.m. I preached in Gateshead to an attentive crowd. I believe we had twice that number at the Fell around 2 p.m. About 5 p.m. I preached to another assembly outside Pandon Gate. I don't know if I've ever preached before to three such gatherings in one day that required me to speak in my loudest voice from beginning to end. But it made no difference; I was no more tired in the evening than if I had sat still all day ...

Sat. JUNE 2.—At 7 p.m. I preached in the college commons at New Aberdeen, but the assembly was so large that many weren't able to hear. However, many did hear and I think felt, my application of "You are not far from the kingdom of God" [Mark 12:34].

All we lack here is a larger preaching-house, and the foundation for one has already been laid. It's true that we don't have much money, and our Society is poor, but we know the One in whom we have believed ...

Mon. 11.—We mounted up about 11 a.m. after preaching in Inverness. While we were dining at Nairn, the innkeeper said, "Sir, the gentlemen of the town have read the little book you gave me on Saturday and would pleased to hear a sermon from you." I agreed; the bell was immediately rung; and the people quickly gathered in the kirk. Oh, what a difference is there between South and North Britons! Everyone here at least loves to hear the Word of God, and none says anything unkind to another, because they are seeking to save their souls ...

Tues. 12.—The whole family at our inn, 11 or 12 in all, gladly joined us in prayer at night; in fact such was the case at every inn where we lodged, for among all the sins they have imported from the English, the Scots—at least the ordinary people—haven't learned to scoff at sacred things ...

Sun. JULY 1.—At Bradford I preached at 7 a.m. to a larger gathering, I believe, than ever assembled there before, and all were as serious as death. About 1 p.m. I preached at Birstal on "Now is the day of salvation" [2 Cor. 6:2]. The people stood by thousands, covering both the plain and the sides of the adjacent hill. It was a glorious opportunity. At 5 p.m. the assembly in Leeds was almost as large but not as deeply affected ...

Thur. 5.— ... On the morning of Saturday the 7th, I rode to Huddersfield and preached between 11 and 12 a.m. The church was pretty well filled, considered the short notice. At 1:30 we rode for Manchester. The sun was burning hot and the wind was at our back, but soon the sky became overcast and the wind blew in our faces all the way there. I had difficulty preaching that evening, my voice being very weak, since I had preached three times a day for 10 days, and mostly outdoors.

Mon. 9.—The stewards from different places gave a good report of the work of God among them, steadily increasing everywhere. In the evening, many curious unbelievers (people who don't believe the Christian revelation) came to the preaching-house. I preached on "You shall love your neighbor as yourself" [Lev. 19:18; Matt. 22:39], and proved them to be sinners on their own principles. Some of the braver ones trembled, I hope leading to a better outcome than that of poor Felix.[283]

Wed. 11.—I gave our brothers and sisters a solemn warning not to "love the world or the things of the world." This is one way Satan will surely attempt to overthrow the present work of God. Many Methodists (so-called) are rapidly growing rich. What but the mighty power of God can keep them from setting their hearts on their riches. And if so, the life of God vanishes away ...

Thur. 19.—After preaching at Little Leigh, I rode on to Macclesfield. Here I heard a pleasing account of Mrs. K. who was in the fellowship in London from childhood, but after she married a rich man, dared not acknowledge a poor despised people. Last year she broke through and came to see me. I spoke a few words to her which never left her, not even in the mortal sickness that overtook her a few months later. All her talk then was of heaven till, feeling her strength quite gone, she said with a smile, "Death, you are welcome," and gave up her spirit ...

Fri. 20.—At noon we made the same arrangement at Congleton as when I was here last. I stood in the window, having all the women inside the preaching-house that it would hold, with the men standing below in the meadow, along with many of the town's people, who behaved unruly enough. Scarcely have I felt such enlargement of heart since I came from Newcastle. The savages resisted for a long time but were finally overcome, except for five or six of them. Surely man will not long have the upper hand; God will win the victory for himself ...

Sun. 29.—At Pembroke, the minister of St. Mary's sent me word that he would be very glad for me to preach in his church, but before the service began, the mayor send a message to forbid it. So the minister preached a very useful sermon himself. The mayor's behavior disgusted many of the upper class, who determined to hear [preaching] where they could. Accordingly, they all flocked together in the evening from all parts of town, and perhaps their taking up this cross may profit them more than my sermon in the church would have done ...

---

[283] Cf. Acts 24. King Felix trembled at Paul's preaching but didn't convert.

VOLUME 3: 1760-1773

Mon. AUGUST 6.—Our conference began. The main point I aimed at was a good understanding with all our brethren of the [Anglican] clergy who are whole-heartedly engaged in extending living religion ...

Mon. 13.—Again I was as busy as at the conference, visiting classes from morning till night.

Sat. 18.—I preached for the first time in our new chapel at Snowsfields on "Oh how pleasant are your tabernacles, O Lord of hosts!" [Psalm 84:1] ...

Mon. 20.—I went to Canterbury and dedicated our new chapel by preaching on "One thing is needful" [Luke 10:42]. How is it that many Protestants, even in England, don't know that no other consecration of church or chapel is allowed, much less required, in England, than the performance of public worship in it? ... It's true that Archbishop Laud composed a consecration liturgy, but it was never proposed, much less established in England. Let this be remembered by all who talk so idly of preaching in unconsecrated places ...

Mon. SEPTEMBER 17.—Two people from London who were at Bath for their health had walked over to the preaching. Afterwards we all spent an hour singing and in serious conversation. The flame blazed higher and higher till the woman asked if I would allow her to pray. I never heard such a prayer before. It was completely original, odd and disconnected ... and yet like a flame of fire. Every sentence pierced my heart and, I believe, the hearts of everyone present. For many months I haven't met with anything like it. It was good for me to be here ...

Sat. 22.—I was refreshed at hearing the testimony of Mary G., once a determined foe to the doctrine of perfection, opposing it eagerly and with many reasons, but now a happy witness to it. During her time of most heated opposition, she could never rest easy in any known sin, and finally this made both pride and anger so bitter to her that she could have no peace till she was fully delivered from them.

Sun. 23.— ... On Monday, Tuesday, and Wednesday I visited the fellowships in Somersetshire. The following days I met the classes in Bristol and carefully inquired into the character and behavior of each person. I did this especially because I had been told as fact that there were many in the fellowship who behaved disorderly. I found one woman and one man whom, I fear, fit that description. Let anyone more clear-sighted than I find two more, and I will thank him.

Sun. 30.—The whole fellowship met in the evening and in union renewed their covenant with God in the form recommended by Mr. Richard Allein, and many felt that God was there. It was a day of his power not to be forgotten, a day both of godly sorrow and strong consolation ...

Tues. OCTOBER 16.—In the evening, the whole congregation at Norwich seemed very moved while I expanded on those solemn words, "He died for all, that they who live might no longer live for themselves, but for him who died for them and rose again" [2 Cor. 5:15]. The move of God was noticeable in a higher and higher degree the two following evenings. If I could stay here a month, I think there would be a fellowship little inferior to that in Bristol. But that can't be; if they will bear sound doctrine only from me, they will still believe a lie ...

Sun. NOVEMBER 4.—I proposed to the leaders that we assist the Society for the Reformation of Manners, considering their heavy debt. One leader asked, "Shouldn't we pay our own debt first?" After some discussion, we agreed to try to do this. The general debt of the Society in London, due mainly to repairing the Foundry and chapels and by building at Wapping and Snowsfields, was about 900 pounds.[284] I set this before the Society in the evening, and asked them all to put their shoulders to the plow, either by an immediate contribution or by pledging what they could pay either on the first of January, February, or March ...

Thur. 8.—At 10 a.m., and also every morning, I met the preachers that were in town and read with them *The Survey of the Wisdom of God in the Creation*. [Back at Oxford,] I had many students at the university and took pains teaching them, but to what effect? What has become of them now? How many of them think about either their tutor or their God? I've had some pupils since then

---

[284] About $212,000 in 2020 USD.

who reward me well for my labor. Now I live; for "you stand fast in the Lord" [Phil. 4:1] ...

Mon. 19.—and the other afternoons of this week, I took up my cross and went personally to the outstanding people in our Society in every part of town. By this means, within six days, almost 600 pounds[285] were pledged toward our common debt, and this was done with the utmost cheerfulness. I just remember one exception: A gentleman who squeezed out ten shillings[286] as if it were so many drops of blood ...

Sat. DECEMBER 8.—I saw a man who, many years ago, was a servant of God to us for good by repressing the madness of the people: Sir John Gonson. He was a magistrate for almost 50 years and has lived to be more than 90 years old. Even in his decline he is majestic in appearance, having few wrinkles and not stooping at all, though dropping into the grave, having no strength and little memory or understanding. Bishop Stratford rightly prayed, "Lord, let me not live to be useless!" And Sir John had his wish: He had a stroke in the evening, praised God all night, and died in the morning ...

Thur. 27.—I preached and administered Holy Communion at the New Chapel in Snowsfields.[287] How well does God order all things! By losing the first chapel we have gained both a better house and a larger congregation.

Fri. 28.—Between 2 and 3 a.m. John Matthews sent for me. For some months he had often said, "I have no more doubts of being in heaven than if I were already there." A little before we came someone asked, "How are you now?" He replied, "The Lord protects; he's always near."

When I entered his room, he was fully conscious but too weak to speak. Exactly at 3 a.m. I began to pray, and I had hardly prayed two minutes when, without any struggle or even a sigh or groan, he fell asleep [in death].

---

[285] About 141,000 in 2020 USD.
[286] About $120 in 2020 USD.
[287] This is departure for Wesley, who prior to this only used his chapels or preaching-rooms for preaching. The Methodist buildings are now proper churches.

I've hardly ever been acquainted with a man of such flawless behavior. For 20 years, I don't recall his doing or saying anything that I would disapprove of ...

1765

Sun. JANUARY 6.—The whole [London] fellowship met in the evening. The service lasted from 5 p.m. till nearly 9, and I don't remember as solemn a season since the first time we joined in renewing our covenant with God.

Wed. 9.—In the evening I preached at High Wycombe and Thursday the 8th at Witney. The congregation here, though formed so recently, could be a pattern for all England. When the services ended, no one spoke, evenings or mornings. All left the house and yard silently. In fact, when I followed many of them, I didn't hear anyone utter a sound until they entered their own homes ...

Sun. 20.— ... I used all my free time this week revising my letters and papers; many of them I threw in the fire. Perhaps some of the rest may see the light when I'm gone ...

Mon. FEBRUARY 25.—I preached at 7 p.m. in a preaching-house built for the General Anabaptists. [288] It is one of the most elegant buildings I've ever seen, and was quite filled both this and the following evening with serious and attentive listeners. Now there seems to be a general call of God to the town; surely some will hear the voice that raises the dead. We returned to Norwich on Wednesday and left there on Thursday morning on a wonderful day of ice and snow, sleet, and wind. However, we reached Lakenheath in the afternoon. Considering the weather, there was a large gathering. Mr. I. read prayers, and I preached with great liberty of spirit on "What does it profit a man if he gain the whole world and lose his own soul?" [Mark 8:36].

Sun. MARCH 10.—I made a collection in our congregation for the poor weavers who have lost their jobs. It amounted to 40 pounds. In the evening our own fellowship met and contributed 14 pounds[289] more to relieve a few of their own distressed members ....

---

[288] Anabaptists reject infant baptism; they include Mennonites, Amish, Hutterites, but are to be distinguished from Baptist denominations.

[289] 40 pounds = $9400; 14 pounds = $3500 in 2020 USD.

VOLUME 3: 1760-1773

Fri. APRIL 26.—About noon I preached at Musselborough, where there are still a few living souls. In the evening we had another blessed time at Edinburgh, and I bid a solemn farewell to the people. Yet I didn't know how I'd be able to ride. At Newcastle I'd found a small rising, less than a pea, but in six days it was as large as a small egg, and hard. On Thursday it broke open. I was afraid that riding wouldn't agree with this, especially on a hard-trotting horse. Still, trusting God, I set out early on Saturday morning. Before I reached Glasgow, the rising was much smaller, and in two or three days it was all gone. If it was a boil, it wasn't like any I've ever heard about, because it was never sore or gave me any pain ...

Sun. MAY 12.—At 8 a.m. I preached again at Linen Hall to as large a gathering as the night before—the largest I've seen in the north of Ireland. About 11 a.m., Mr. Knox went with me to church and led me to a pew where I sat next to the mayor. What? What have I to do with honor? Lord, let me always fear, not desire it.

The afternoon service wasn't over till about 6:30. At 7 p.m., I preached to all the people of the city. I think that almost everyone felt the presence of God there. Scarcely have I ever seen such a general impression on a gathering ...

Wed. 22.—I encouraged the little fellowship to avoid laziness, wastefulness, and uncleanliness; on the contrary, to be patterns of diligence, thrift, and cleanliness ...

Sat. 25.—Ever since I came to Derry, I've been amazed at the honesty throughout this city. No one is afraid to leave his house open all day, and the door is latched only at night. Theft is hardly ever heard of here, and no one fears it. For this reason, the inhabitants never think of themselves as sinners. Oh, what a pity that honesty should be a hindrance to salvation! Yet that's so if a person puts it in the place of Christ ...

Tues. 28.—In the evening I stood at my usual place in the market-house at Sligo, but how changed was the scenery! I haven't seen anything like this since entering the kingdom of Ireland. Such a total lack of good sense and good manners, indeed even of common decency, was shown by quite a few of the audience! It's good that I visited Sligo after Londonderry; honor and dishonor balance each other. Haven't we done anything here yet? If not, then it's high time to begin and try to see if something can be done now. The next two days I spoke as strongly as I could, and my labor wasn't in vain. The audience increased considerably and appeared to have a different spirit. They behaved better the second night than the first and much better the third night. I believe many of them had a fresh call from God, and at the meeting of the fellowship he was powerfully present, so that despite their loss of numbers I could only hope that there would be "a blessing in the remnant."

Thur. JUNE 6.—I was led on my way by Lt. Cook, who took part in all the military actions at Fort William Henry, at Louisborough, Quebec, Martinico, and Havana. He gave me a clearer account of those notable scenes of Providence than I'd ever heard before. Though he was often at the battlefront against Indians, French, and Spaniards, and in the most intense fire, both while charging and retreating, he never received a wound. The odd saying of King William is true: "Every bullet has its billet[290]." ...

Sat. 8.—I rode to Limerick and found the preaching-house just completed. I liked it best of any in the kingdom: neat, even elegant, but not gaudy.

Sun. 9.—In the evening I preached at Mardyke. The heat was stifling even at 6 p.m.; still there was a large gathering both of Protestants and Catholics. Some of the latter behaved with remarkable indecency, talking and laughing as if at a play. I turned toward them and rebuked them. They took it well, and didn't laugh or talk anymore.

During the following week I spoke to each member of the fellowship, and they gave me great satisfaction. Several of them show by reasonable proofs that they have given God their whole heart. Many others are groaning after full salvation, and all the rest are free from outward sin and blame. Why can't every Christian community reach this point?

Fri. 14.—About noon I preached at Ballygarane to the remnant of the poor Palatines. Since they were unable to get food and clothing here, in spite of their diligence and thrift, some are scattered

---

[290] "Billet" is private housing commandeered by the military. The sense: Every bullet has its own lodging place.

up and down Ireland and some have gone to America. I'm astonished! Don't landlords have common sense, or even common humanity, to allow such tenants as these to be starved? ...

Sun. 16.—At 7 a.m. I preached in the market-place in Killfinnan. Nearly the whole town—Irish, English, and Germans, Protestants and Catholics—soon gathered. At first most of the Catholics stood back, as did some of the upper-class people, but little by little they drew in and mixed with the assembly, and I believe all of them felt that God was there.

When I went to my lodging, they crowded after me and quickly filled the house. I made urgent appeals and prayed again until I realized it was truly time for them and for me to go to rest ...

Sun. 23.—... Monday and Tuesday I spoke individually to members of the Cork fellowship. They now number 295—50 or 60 more than for some years. This is partly due to preaching outdoors and partly to the prayer meetings in several parts of the city. These have caused the awakening of many gross sinners, the recovering of many backsliders, the strengthening of many who were weak and wavering, and the bringing of many people of all sorts to public preaching. At 7 p.m. I went once again to Blackpool, where the congregation was far larger than before. Many Catholics crept in among them, while a few stood apart. Oh, what a day of God's power this is! May he fulfill in us all his good pleasure!

Fri. 28.—After giving our brothers and sisters a solemn warning not to "love the world nor the things of the world" [1 John 2:15], I left them with more satisfaction than ever, having reason to hope that they will no longer be tossed to and fro but steadily adorn the doctrine of God our Savior ...

Mon. JULY 1.—I rode to Waterford and preached in a little courtyard on our "great High Priest, who has passed into heaven for us" [Heb. 4:14]. But I soon realized I was shooting over the heads of my listeners. I should have spoken of death or judgment. On Tuesday evening I suited my discourse to my audience, which had increased considerably, but still much more so the following evening. Almost every face showed deep attention. The preaching-room was full on Thursday morning and the poor people were so affectionate that it was hard to part from them, which we did with many prayers and blessings ...

Wed. 17.—I preached in the Grove at Edinderry. Many Quakers were there, it being the time of their General Meeting, as well as people of all sorts. Here I came upon the journal of William Edmundson, one of the Quaker preachers in the last century. If the original person equaled the picture (which I have no reason to doubt), what a congenial man he was! Apart from his opinions, what a spirit he had! What faith, love, gentleness, long-suffering! Could mistakes send such a man as this to hell? No! I am so far from believing this that I dare say, "Let my soul be with the soul of William Edmundson!" ...

Wed. 24.— ... Thursday and Friday mornings I spent in a conference with our preachers. In the afternoons I spoke to members of the fellowship. I had left 450 and now find over 500—more than they ever were since I landed in Ireland. And not only have they increased in number, but many are rejoicing in the pure love of God, and many more refuse to be comforted till they can bear witness to the same confession ...

Wed. 31.—At the earnest request of a friend, I allowed Mr. Hunter to paint my portrait. I sat only once, from about 10 a.m. to 1:30 p.m., and in that time he began and ended the face with a striking likeness ...

Sun. AUGUST 11.—I preached about 7 a.m. at the Fell to our honest, lively coalminers, and about 2 p.m. in the square at Hartley, about 11 miles from Newcastle. From there I hurried back to Garthheads, where I found the largest gathering there for many years. Afterwards, several hundred of us met in the preaching-room and solemnly renewed our covenant with God. About 8 p.m. I was so tired I could hardly stand up, but after speaking another hour all my weariness was gone, and I was as lively and strong as at 8 a.m. ...

Fri. 16.—I rode over to Chester and preached to as many as the new preaching-house would hold. We also had large gatherings on Saturday, morning and evening. How the grace of God fits with his providence! A new preaching-house not only brings a new congregation, but likewise (something we have seen again and again) a new blessing from God, and no wonder, if every labor of love finds an immediate reward.

Sun. 18.—The house contained the morning assembly, but in the evening crowds were forced to go away. Just so truth wins its way against all its foes, if it is steadily declared with meekness of wisdom ...

Wed. SEPTEMBER 11.—Sensing that my voice was beginning to fail, I decided to preach for a while only twice a day. In the evening I preached on a small parcel of land at Newlin to a large assembly. No one misbehaved except a young gentleman who seemed to understand nothing about the matter.

Thur. 12.—Coming to St. Just, I learned that John Bennets had died a few hours earlier. He was a wise and good man who for over 20 years had been like a father in our Society. Shortly before his death he questioned each of his children concerning their abiding in the faith. Being satisfied, he told them, "Now I have no doubt that we'll meet again at the right hand of our Lord." He then cheerfully committed his soul to God and fell asleep.

To the large gathering in the evening, I drove home these solemn words: "There is no work, nor device, nor knowledge, nor wisdom in the grave where you go" [Eccl. 9:10] ...

Sun. 15.— ... At 1 p.m. I preached at Lelant, three miles from St. Ives, and at 5 p.m. on the same meadow to a larger gathering than before. Indeed the whole town seems moved, the truths we preach being confirmed by the lives of the people ...

Sat. OCTOBER 5.—I spent some time with the children at Kingswood. They are all healthy; they behave well; they learn well. But alas! Except for two or three, there is no spiritual life in them ...

Fri. 11.—We observed a day of fasting and prayer ...

Mon. 28.—I had breakfast with Mr. George Whitefield, who seemed to be a very old man, worn out in his Master's service, although he's hardly more than 50 years old. Yet it pleases God that I, now in my 63rd year, find no disorder, no weakness, no decay, no difference from what I was at 25, except that I have fewer teeth and more gray hair! ...

Mon. DECEMBER 2.—I went to Canterbury, of which I had received reports that the fellowship there had "all fallen from grace," if they ever had any. I determined to get to the bottom of this, and so I questioned them one by one and was pleasantly surprised to find them all, without exception, upright and blameless in their behavior ...

Thur. 5.—I rode back to Feversham. I was told right away that the mob and the magistrate had agreed to drive Methodism, so-called, out of town. After preaching, I told them what we had been constrained to do[291] by the magistrate at Rolvenden, who might have been richer by several hundred pounds if he never had meddled with the Methodists. I concluded: "Since we have both God and the law on our side, if we can have peace by fair means, we'd rather have it that way and we'll be very glad, but if not, we *will* have peace [by legal means]." ...

Wed. 18.—Riding through the borough, my mare's feet flew up and she fell with my leg under her ... However, I went on to Shoreham ... and recovered some strength so as to be able to walk a little on level ground ...

Thur. 26.—I would have been glad for a few days' rest, but that wasn't possible in this busy season. However, having electricity applied morning and evening, my lameness was cured, though slowly ...

1766

Wed. JANUARY 1.—A large gathering met in the Foundry at 4 p.m. and ushered in the new year with praise and thanksgiving. In the evening we met, as usual, in the church as Spitalfields to renew our covenant with God. This is always a refreshing season at which some prisoners are set at liberty.

Fri. 3.—Mr. B. came to see me, now calm and in his right mind. God has repressed his furious, bitter zeal by means of Mr. Whitefield. Mr. Whitefield made the first breach among the Methodists; oh, may God empower him to heal it! ...

Tues. 14.—The frozen road being very rough, our carriage broke down before daylight. However, it was patched up well enough to get us to Budsdale, and in the evening I preached at Yarmouth. The

---

[291] I.e., take the matter to a higher court.

work of God was increasing here when poor B.W. was converted to Calvinism. Immediately he declared open war, tore the Society in pieces, took all he could to himself, completely quit the Church, and caused a scandal such as won't soon be removed. But doubtless he who turned that young man's head thinks he has done God's service …

Fri. 24.—I returned to London.

Tues. 28.—The brethren met to consider our temporal affairs. One proposed we should first pay off the debt of the Society, which was 500 pounds. Towards this 270 was immediately pledged. At a second meeting, this was increased to 320 pounds.[292] Surely God will supply the rest.

Fri. 31.—Mr. Whitefield came to see me. He breathes nothing but peace and love. Dogmatism can't stand before him; rather it hides its head wherever he goes …

Wed. FEBRUARY 5.—A man came to see me who'd been cheated out of a large fortune and who was now starving for lack of food. I wanted to clothe him and send him back to his own country, but being short of money, I asked him to come back in an hour. Before he returned, a man from whom I expected nothing put 20 guineas[293] in my hand, so I ordered the poor man to be clothed from head to foot, and sent him immediately to Dublin …

Thur. MARCH 6.—The brethren met once again to deal with our Society's debt, and they didn't dismiss till the whole amount of 610 pounds[294] was met and exceeded …

Wed. 12.—I rode over to Kingswood, and having told my whole mind to the teachers and assistants, spoke to the children in a far stronger way than I ever had before. I'll kill or cure; I'll have one or the other—a Christian school, or none at all …

Wed. 19.—We stopped at a little inn about 16 miles from Evesham. But as Duncan Wright and I had our hoods on, the good woman was frightened and unwilling to take us in. So we rode a mile or two farther to another house, where we came in good season.

---

[292] 500 pounds = $118,000; 270 pounds = $63,500; 320 pounds = $75,000 in 2020 USD.
[293] About $47,000 in 2020 USD.
[294] About $143,000 in 2020 USD.

After a short conversation, the woman of the house said, "I'm afraid things aren't as well with me as they once were. Before I married, I used to kneel down in the cow-house to pray to God for whatever I needed. But now I'm loaded down with worldly care, yet God hasn't forgotten me. Last winter, when my husband lost the use of all his limbs, I prayed to God for him, and he got well." This woman knew nothing about the Methodists, but God is near to all who call on him[295] ...

Wed. APRIL 23.—I preached at Horncastle at 5 a.m., in Torrington at 9 a.m., and about 2 p.m. at Scotter, where the poor people now enjoy great quietness because of Sir. N.H. About 6 p.m. I preached at Ferry. I'd rather not preach more than two or three times a day, but when I'm called to do more, it's all the same to me. I find strength according to my need ...

Sun. 27.—I rode over to Miserton and visited a young woman who a year or two ago was first struck with deep depression, then with mental confusion. We were quickly convinced of the source of her disorder. Let physicians do all they can; in the end it will be found out that "this kind goes out only by prayer and fasting" [Matt. 17:21] ...

Tues. 29.—I preached at Yarm in the evening and the next evening at Newcastle. I don't know why, but I've felt more weariness this spring than I have for many years, unless it is due to my falling at Christmas. Perhaps that weakened the springs of my whole body more than I was aware of.

Thur. MAY 1.—I enjoyed a little rest. I haven't changed at all in this regard. I love quietness and silence as well as ever, but if I'm called into noise and tumult, all is well ...

Sat. 10.—I spent an agreeable hour in the home of a Quaker, a man of wealth. His spirit put me in mind of Thomas Keene. May your last end be like his! ...

Mon. 26.—I spent some hours at our National Assembly. My point of view is very far from that of Mr. Whitefield's; he greatly commends the solemnity of this meeting. I've seen few less solemn; I was shocked at the behavior of many of the members. If a preacher

---

[295] Wesley implies that he helped the woman significantly.

had behaved like that at our conference, he would have lost his place among us ...

Thur. JUNE 5.—The weather being fair, we had a larger gathering than ever to which, after preaching, I used the opportunity to repeat most of the more reasonable objections that had been made against us in Scotland. I then gave our reasons in response to these objections, and everyone seemed completely satisfied.

To sum up what I said: I love plain dealing, don't you? I'll do so now; please bear with me.

I have no pretenses; rather I show you all I really am, all I intend to do, and all I actually do. **I'm a member of the Church of England, but I love good people of every church.**

My foundation is the Bible. Yes, you can call me a Bible-bigot. I follow it in all things great and small [my emphasis].

Therefore: 1. I always pray a short, private prayer when I attend a public worship service. Don't you do the same? If not, why not? Isn't this according to the Bible?

2. I stand whenever I sing the praise of God in public worship. Doesn't the Bible give you clear examples of this?

3. I always kneel before the Lord my Maker when I pray in public worship.

4. In public I generally use the Lord's Prayer, because Christ has taught me, when I pray, to say ... And I advise every preacher connected with me, whether in England or Scotland, to follow me in this ...

Sun. JULY 27.—At Bradford there was such a large crowd, and the rain so dampened my voice, that many on the outskirts of the assembly couldn't hear well. They've just built a preaching-house 54-feet side to side, the largest octagon we have in England, and it's the first to have a roof built with common sense, rising only a third of its width, yet it's as firm as any in England without stressing the walls. Why should any roof rise higher? Only by lack of skill or lack of honesty in the builder ...

Thur. 31.—At Heptonstall I preached with great enlargement of heart on "Now is the day of salvation" [2 Cor. 6:2]. The renegade Methodists who had turned Calvinists, then Anabaptists, made much confusion here for a while. But now that they've moved away, the poor people are at peace again ...

Sun. AUGUST 3.—When the prayers at Haworth Church ended, I preached from a little scaffold on the south side of the church on these words in the Gospel: "Oh, if you had only known the things that belong to your peace!" [Luke 19:42]. Those receiving communion alone filled the church—a sight not seen since Mr. Grimshaw's death. In the afternoon, the audience was believed to be the largest that had ever been there; but strength was given to me in proportion to the assembly, so I believe all could hear ...

Sun. 10.—At Birstal, after Mr. Eastwood read prayers, I came out in the churchyard and preached to four times as many as the church could hold on "Are not Abana and Pharphar better than all the waters of Israel?" [2 Kings 5:12]. About 1 p.m. I preached at Daws-Green. I estimated the gathering, closely wedged together, to extend 40 yards one way and about 100 the other. Supposing five people to stand in a square yard, that would amount to 20,000 people. I began preaching at Leeds between 5 and 6 p.m. to a similar gathering. This was the hardest day's work I've had since leaving London, being obliged to speak at each place from beginning to end as loudly as I could. But my strength was sufficient for the day.

Tues. 12.—Our conference began and ended on Friday evening. We've never had one that was happier or more profitable. It began and ended in love, and with a solemn sense of the presence of God ...

Sun. 17.—[*Back in London,*] it was at the earnest request of one whose heart God has turned again that I unexpectedly found myself here, if for no other purpose than to confirm my union with Mr. Whitefield, which amply rewards my labor. My brother [Charles] and I conferred with him every day. Let other honorable men do what they may; we resolved, by the grace of God, to go hand in hand, through honor and dishonor ...

Wed. 20.—I rode to Bristol, and the next day turned over the management of Kingswood House to stewards whom I could depend on. This has taken a heavy load off my shoulders. Blessed be God for able and faithful men who will do his work without any temporal reward ...

Tues. SEPTEMBER 9.—Riding to St. Ives, I stopped by to visit Alice Daniel at Rosemargay, a woman with whom I lodged 22 or 23 years ago. Her sons have all gone away from her and she just has one daughter left, who is always sick. Her husband is dead, and she can't read her Bible any longer because she's completely blind. But she has no complaints; rather she cheerfully waits till her appointed time comes to leave this world. How many of these jewels may lie hidden here and there, forgotten of men but precious in the sight of God! ...

Sun. 14.—I preached at St. Agnes at 8 a.m. The assembly in Redruth at 1 p.m. was the largest I'd ever seen there, but small compared to the one at 5 p.m. in the natural amphitheater at Gwenap, by far the finest site I know in the kingdom. It is a round, green hollow, gently shelving down about 50 feet deep, but I suppose it's 200 feet across one way and nearly 300 feet the other. I believe there were fully 20,000 people and, the evening being calm, all could hear ...

Sun. OCTOBER 5.— ... Several evenings this week I preached at Bristol on the education of children. Some gave that lame excuse: "Oh, he has no children of his own."[296] But many of a nobler spirit acknowledged the truth and pleaded guilty before God ...

Sun. NOVEMBER 16.—I strongly impressed on my hearers the importance of religion in the home, the essential desire of Methodists. Many were ashamed before God, and at length adopted Joshua's resolution: "As for me and my house, we will serve the Lord" [Josh. 24:15] ...

Sun. 30.—I preached on the education of children, something in which we are shamefully lacking. Many are now deeply convicted of this, and I hope they won't stifle that conviction ...

1767

Sat. JANUARY 31.—From the words of our blessed Lord, "Whoever follows me will not walk in darkness" [John 8:12], I showed at length that God never abandons anyone unless they first abandon God and that, aside from bodily disorders on the one hand

---

[296] Wesley's wife had four children by her deceased first husband. Wesley rarely mentions them in his journal.

and strong temptation on the other, every believer may be happy as well as holy and may "walk in the light all the days of their life." ...

Tues. FEBRUARY 10.—I baptized a young woman raised among the Anabaptists. God bore witness to his ordinance and gave her such a blessing that she couldn't express it in words ....

Wed. 25.—I drew up a list of the current fellowship in Norwich, numbering 160 members. But I'm far more comfortable with it now than when it numbered 600. These know what they are about, and most are not ignorant of Satan's devices.

Thur. 26.—I set out for London. A good part of the day we had strong wind and rain right in our faces. However, we pushed on to Lakenheath. Despite the severe weather, the church was pretty well full in the evening. The next morning we reached Hockerill, and London on Saturday afternoon.

Ash-Wednesday, MARCH 4.—I had dinner at a friend's home along with Mr. Whitefield, still breathing nothing but love ...

Thur. 12.—On this and the two following days I examined the fellowship in Bristol. I still find most to be in peace and love, and none blamable as to their outward behavior, but life, power, and "wrestling with God" are lacking; few are agonizing to be altogether Christians ...

Thur. APRIL 9.—I wasn't glad to hear that some of those who have seceded from the Church of England had settled in these parts also. Those whom I've come across are less charitable than the Catholics themselves. I've never met a Catholic who held it as a principle to murder heretics, but a seceding minister who was asked, "Wouldn't you, if you could, cut the throats of all the Methodists?" replied, "Why, didn't Samuel chop Agag in pieces before the Lord?" [1 Sam. 15:33]. I haven't yet met a Catholic in this kingdom who would tell me to my face that all but themselves must be damned. But I've seen seceders who will readily say that none but themselves could be saved. And this is the natural consequence of their doctrine, since they believe: 1. that we are saved by faith alone; 2. that faith is holding such and such opinions; so it follows that those who don't hold those opinions have no faith and therefore can't be saved ...

Wed. 15.—I rode to Armagh. Half an hour before preaching time, an officer came and said, "Sir, the sovereign (i.e. the mayor) orders me to tell you that you shall not preach in his town." In order to test this, I walked to the market-house at 6 a.m. I had just started preaching when the "sovereign" came. His name was Harcourt, I was told. He was talking loudly and rapidly when a gentleman came and said, "Sir, if you aren't allowed to preach here, you are welcome to preach in Mr. McGough's avenue." Mr. McGough, one of the chief merchants in the town, personally showed us the way. I believe three times as many people flocked together as would have heard me in the market-house. So the wise providence of God brought good out of evil! And his Word had free rein ...

Sat. MAY 9.—I rode to Ennis but found there was no longer any preaching and that the fellowship had vanished. So, having no business there, I left Ennis in the morning, preached at Clare about 8 a.m., and in the evening at Limerick. The constant rain kept me from preaching outdoors this week, and I was offended by the small gatherings in the preaching-house. I'm afraid my glorying with regard to many of these fellowships has ended ...

Mon. 18.—In the Old Camp, I spoke to members of the fellowship individually. Most of them seemed to be honest and upright, but a general faintness seems to have spread among them; there was no zeal, no liveliness of grace ...

Sun. 24.—Today the Old Camp could barely contain the assembly, all crowded together. Afterwards we had a solemn meeting of the fellowship, in which God caused many of the broken bones to rejoice. Now they are back on their feet again; may they run with patience the race set before them! ...

Sun. 31.— ... I wanted to preach outdoors at Cork in the evening, but the wind and rain didn't allow it. Two years ago I left over 300 in the fellowship; now I find 187. What has caused such a decline? I believe the real cause is this:

Some two or three years ago, when the fellowship was about as small as it is now, Thomas Taylor and William Penington came to Cork. They were zealous men and sound preachers, very active and strict disciplinarians, not respecting persons. They appointed prayer meetings in several places and preached outdoors at both ends of the city. The number of listeners quickly increased; the fellowship increased, and so did the number both of the convicted and the converted. I came when the fire was burning brightest ... More and more people were stirred, and there was a greater awakening here than in any part of the kingdom.

But misunderstandings crept in between the class leaders and between some of them and the preachers, and these were multiplied when one of the leaders was expelled from the fellowship. Some believed him to be at fault, some not, neither side having patience with the other. And so a flame of anger swallowed the flame of love, and many were destroyed by it. At the same time, some of our brothers and sisters accepted a new opinion and zealously spread it. This zeal was almost as destructive as the previous one, and the effect of both was that the Spirit of God was grieved, his blessing was withheld, and the flock was scattered. When they are convicted of their sin and humbled before him, then, and not till then, he will return ...

Wed. JUNE 17.— ... [At Athlone.] At 7 a.m. I preached in the new house, which Mr. S. has built entirely at his own expense. As usual, the assembly was both large and serious. I rested the four following days, only preaching mornings and evenings.

Sun. 21.— ... In the evening I preached in the barracks. I don't know that I ever saw such an assembly in Athlone before: rich and poor, Protestants and Catholics, coming from all around, and everyone paying close attention while I explained the solemn declaration (part of the Gospel for the day): "If they won't listen to Moses and the prophets, neither will they be persuaded even if one rose from the dead" [Luke 16:31] ...

Fri. 26.—Finding that some of the most earnest people in the Mountmelick fellowship were deeply prejudiced against each other, I asked them to come before me, face to face, and I tried hard to remove their prejudices. I used both argument and persuasion, but all in vain. Seeing that reason was of no benefit, we took to prayer. Suddenly the power of God broke in on them; the angry ones on both sides burst into tears and hugged each others' necks. All anger and prejudice melted away, and they were united as cordially as ever ...

Sat. JULY 4.—Now having finished my circuit, I went cheerfully on to Dublin ...

VOLUME 3: 1760-1773

Tues. 14.—A poor backslider whom 10 days ago I found to be dying in deep despair told me, "Now I'm not afraid to die. I see Jesus right in front of me, his face full of glory." Examples like this certainly don't prove that a saint can't fall, even forever, but only that God is "compassionate and full of mercy, not willing that any should perish" [2 Peter 3:9] …

Tues. 21.— … On Wednesday and Thursday we held our little conference in Dublin. We observed Friday as a day of fasting and prayer, ending it with the most solemn watch-night I ever remember in Ireland. Between 7 and 8 p.m. I felt very tired, but less and less as the service went on; and at the conclusion, a little after midnight, I felt fresher than at 6 in the morning.

Sun. 26.—This was an especially pleasant day. But it tried my strength at the end, since I was speaking with hardly a pause from a little after 5 p.m. till between 9 and 10 p.m.

Mon. 27.—Having a severe cold, I hoped that riding would take it away. So I mounted up a little after 4 a.m. and reached Newry in the evening. But my voice was still so weak that I don't think many of those assembled in the market-house could hear me. And my coughing was so forceful at night that I hardly slept more than a quarter-hour at a time. Nevertheless, I preached at 5 a.m. without much difficulty …

Sat. AUGUST 1.—Since both my horse and I were a bit tired, I took the stagecoach to Edinburgh.

Before leaving Glasgow, I heard such an unusual story that I asked to hear it from the man himself. He was a sexton,[297] yet for many years had shown little concern about religion. I have written down his very words and leave everyone to use their own judgment regarding them: "Sixteen weeks ago, I was walking an hour before sunset behind the high kirk, and looking to one side, saw a man close to me, who looked me in the face and asked me how I was doing. I said, 'Pretty well.' He said, 'You've had many troubles, but what good have you made of them?' He then told me everything I've ever done, even the thoughts of my heart, adding, 'Be ready for the

---

[297] A church officer or employee who cares for the church property, rings the bells, digs graves, etc.

second coming!' Then suddenly he was gone, I couldn't tell how. I trembled all over and had no strength left in me; I sank to the ground. From that time I groaned continually under the load of sin, till at the Lord's Supper it was all taken away!"

Sun. 2.—[*At Edinburgh*] I was sorry to find both the fellowship and the assemblies smaller than when I was here last. I attribute this mainly to the kind of preaching that has been generally done. The people have been told so often and so strongly of their coldness, deadness, heaviness, and lack of faith, but rarely of anything that would generate gratitude. This has driven many away, and those remaining have been kept cold and dead.

At 8 a.m. I strongly encouraged them, and about noon preached at Castle Hill on "There is joy in heaven over one sinner that repents" [Luke 15:7]. The sun shone very hot on my head, but all was well, for God was in our midst. In the evening I preached on Luke 20:34ff., and many were comforted, especially while I was expanding on those deep words, "Nor can they die anymore, but are equal to the angels and are the children of God, being the children of the resurrection." ...

Sat. 8.—At the request of Mr. Whitaker of New England I preached, then made a collection for the Indian schools of America. A large sum of money has now been collected, but will money convert heathens? Find preachers of David Brainerd's spirit, and nothing can stand before them. But without this, what will gold or silver do? No more than lead or iron. Gold and silver have indeed sent thousands to hell but have never yet brought a soul to heaven ...

Tues. 18.—I met in conference with our assistants and a select number of preachers plus, on Thursday and Friday, Mr. Whitefield, Howell Harris, and many stewards and local preachers.[298] Love and harmony reigned from beginning to end. But we all need more love and holiness, and to that end, to cry continually, "Lord, increase our faith!" [Luke 17:6] ...

Mon. 31.—I rode to Carmarthen, and a little before 6 p.m. went down to the Green. The gathering was nearly as large as at Brecknock, but not as flippant, being almost all poor or middle-class

---

[298] Local preachers stayed in a particular community; others were circuit riders.

people. I therefore preached the gospel directly to them They took it in hungrily. And though I was faint and weary when I began, I was soon like "a giant refreshed with wine." ...

Wed. SEPTEMBER 2.—Asking, I found that the work of God in Pembrokeshire had been greatly hindered, mainly by Mr. Davis's preachers, who had been constantly complaining about ours, and thereby frightening many people from hearing or coming near them. This had sometimes provoked our preachers to retort, which always made bad matters worse. Therefore the advice I gave them was: 1. Let all the people abstain from talking behind others' backs, from gossiping and bad-mouthing; 2. Let all our preachers abstain from repaying bad-mouthing with bad-mouthing, either publicly or privately, as well as from disputes; 3. Let them never preach controversy but plain, practical, and experiential religion ...

Mon. 7.—At Neath, I'd planned to preach outdoors, but rain didn't allow me to. The preaching-house was very crowded, and the power of God was in the midst of the assembly. Prejudice gave way before it, and the many lies which most had heard about me vanished into the air. The same power rested on them early in the morning. The bigots on all sides were ashamed and felt that in Jesus Christ nothing avails but the "faith that works by love" [Gal. 5:6] ...

Wed. 23.—About noon I preached at Buckland and in the evening at Frome, but here the house was too small and many were forced to go away. So the next evening I preached in a meadow where a crowd of all denominations attended. It seems that God finally is giving a more general call to this town as well. Previously, the people seemed in every sense to be "rich and increased in goods and lacking nothing" [Rev. 3:17].

Fri. 25.—I was asked to preach at Freshford, but the people dared not come to the
preaching-house because of the smallpox, of which Joseph Allen, an Israelite indeed, had died the day before. So they placed a table near the churchyard. No sooner had I begun to speak than the bells began to ring, arranged by a nearby gentleman. But it was labor lost, because my voice prevailed and the people heard me distinctly. In fact, a man who was quite deaf and who hadn't been able to hear a

sermon for several years, told his neighbors with great joy that he'd heard and understood all from beginning to end! ...

Sun. OCTOBER 11.—I preached at 8 a.m. in Prince's Street, Bristol, and a little before 5 p.m. near the New Square where, despite the sharp wind, the audience was very large. I permitted all of Mr. Whitefield's society who wished todo so to join us for the love-feast that followed. I hope we will "not know war anymore, unless it's with the world, the flesh, and the devil" ...

Tues. 27.—I rode to Weedon where, being refused the use of the church, I accepted the offer of the Presbyterian meeting-house and preached to a crowded audience ...

Fri. NOVEMBER 20.—I preached to the criminals awaiting execution in Newgate on "Today you will be with me in paradise" [Luke 23:43]. All of them were struck and melted into tears. Who knows but that some of them may reap in joy? ...

Mon. DECEMBER 7.—I went on to Yarmouth and found "confusion twice confounded." Not only had B.W.'s fellowship fallen apart, but ours seemed to be rapidly doing the same. They had almost all left the Church again, being full of prejudice against the clergy and against each other. But since two or three retained their humble, simple love, I had no doubt that there would be a blessing in the remnant. My first business was to reconcile them to each other, which was accomplished by hearing the contending parties, first separately, then face to face. What remained was to reconcile them to the Church, and this was done partly by reasoning and partly by persuasion ...

1768

Mon. JANUARY 4.—During my leisure hours this week, I read Dr. Priestley's ingenious book on electricity. He seems to have accurately collected and digested all that is known of this curious subject. But how little that is! We do indeed know its use—at least to some degree. We know it's a thousand medicines in one; especially that it's the most effective medicine in nervous disorders of every kind that's ever yet been discovered. But theoretically, we know nothing; we are soon "lost and bewildered in the fruitless search" ...

VOLUME 3: 1760-1773

Fri. FEBRUARY 26.—I translated from French one of the most useful pamphlets I ever saw for those who want to be "fervent in spirit" [Rom. 12:11]. How little does God regard human opinions! How many false opinions are held by all the members of the Church of Rome, yet how highly favored of God many of them have been!

Sun. MARCH 6.—In the evening I went to Brentford, and on Tuesday the 8th reached Bristol. There I found no decay in the work of God, although it didn't go on as vigorously as at Kingswood. Here the prayer meetings have been greatly blessed; some have been convicted or converted almost every day; and almost 70 members have been added to the fellowship in about three months' time. The school is also flourishing. Several of the children remain serious, and all of them are in better order than they've been for some years.

Mon. 14.—I started out on my northern circuit and preached at Stroud in the evening.

Tues. 15.—About noon I preached at Painswick and in the evening at Gloucester. For quite a while here the mob was both noisy and mischievous, but an honest magistrate took control of the matter and quickly tamed the beasts among the people. And any magistrate might do so if he's willing; so wherever a mob continues any length of time, this is to be imputed not so much to the rabble as to the justices …

Fri. 25.—I went a little out of my way to Burslem and preached in the new preaching-house there. The one at Congleton is about the same size, but better designed and better finished. We had an assembly of elegant people at Congleton, but they paid earnest attention. It seems the behavior of the fellowship in this town has convinced all of its people except the curate, who still refuses to serve communion to any who won't promise to listen to "these preachers" anymore …

Wed. 30.—I rode to a little town called New Mills in the High Peak of Derbyshire. I preached at noon in their large new chapel which (since preaching-houses need air) has a casement in every window three inches square! That's the custom of this country …

Tues. APRIL 5.—About noon I preached at Warrington, not, I'm afraid, to the taste of some of my hearers, since my topic led me to speak strongly and explicitly on the Godhead of Christ. But I can't help that; I must insist on it as the foundation of all our hope …

Tues. 19.—I rode through heavy rain to Glasgow. On Thursday and Friday, I spoke to most of the members of the fellowship. I doubt we have few fellowships in Scotland like this. Most of those I spoke with not only have found peace with God but continue to walk in the light of his countenance. That wise and good man, Mr. G., has been of great service to them, encouraging them by all possible means to continue in the grace of God.

Sat. 23.—I rode over the mountains to Perth. I had received wonderful reports of the work of God in this place, so I expected to find a large and lively fellowship. But instead, I didn't find more than two believers and barely five spiritually awakened people in it. Finding I had to begin all over, I spoke very plainly in the evening to about 100 people in the preaching-room, but seeing that this accomplished nothing, on Sunday the 24th I preached about 8 a.m. at the end of Watergate. A crowd soon assembled to whom I cried, "Seek the Lord while he may be found; call on him while he is near" [Isa. 55:6]. Everyone paid close attention, and I had a little hope that some were benefited.

At the Old Kirk we had useful sermons, both in the morning and at 5 p.m. Immediately after the 5 p.m. service I preached on "God forbid that I should glory except in the cross of our Lord Jesus Christ" [Gal. 6:14]. The assembly was so large that I feared many couldn't hear. After preaching, I explained the nature of a Methodist fellowship, adding that I wouldn't consider anyone in Perth a member unless they spoke to me before I left the city. Four men and four women did speak to me, two of whom I think were believers, and one or two more seem to be just waking up spiritually and groping after God. In truth, the kingdom of God among these people is just like a grain of mustard seed …

Mon. MAY 2.—I set out early from Aberdeen and about noon preached in Brechin. After my sermon, the provost[299] asked to see me and said, "Sir, my son has had epileptic fits from infancy. Dr. Ogylvie prescribed for him many times and finally told me he could

---

[299] The chief magistrate of a Scottish burgh.

do nothing more. I asked Mr. Blair last Monday to speak to you. On Tuesday morning my son told his mother that he'd just been dreaming that his fits were gone and that he was completely well. Soon after that I gave him the drops you advised, and now he is completely well; he hasn't had one fit since."

In the evening I preached to a large audience at Dundee. They paid attention but seemed to feel nothing. The next evening I spoke more strongly—to their hearts rather than to their minds—and I believe a few felt the Word of God as sharp as a two-edged sword ...

Thur. 5.— ... About this time a remarkable work of God broke out among the children at Kingswood School. One of the teachers sent me a short report as follows:

Rev. and Dear Sir,   April 27, 1768

On Wednesday the 20th God broke in on our boys in a surprising way. We have noticed a seriousness in some of them for a while back. But that night, while they were in their own rooms, the power of God came upon them, even like a mighty rushing wind, which made them cry out for mercy. Last night, I hope, will never be forgotten, when about 20 of them were in great distress. But God soon spoke peace to two of them, J.G. and T.M. I've never seen a greater display of his love; they indeed rejoice with joy unspeakable. As for myself, I've seldom felt such power. We don't need to admonish them to pray, for that spirit runs through the whole school, so this building may well be called a house of prayer. Even as I write this, the cries of the boys from their rooms are sounding in my ears. There are many still lying beside the pool,[300] who wait every moment to be put in. They have reached this point: "Lord, I won't, I can't rest without your love." Since I began to write, eight more have been set free and now rejoice in God their Savior ... Their age is from eight to fourteen. There are just a few who resist this work, but it's not likely that they'll do so for long, for the prayer of those who believe in Christ seem to carry everyone before them. Among the coalminers likewise the work of God increases greatly; two of their sons were justified this week. The number added to the fellowship since the conference is 130 ...

                                                                                                       James Hindmarsh

---

[300] A reference to the pool of Siloam in Jerusalem, where, according to the Gospel, when the waters were stirred, the person who entered the water first was cured (John 5:1-4).

Thur. JUNE 2.—At noon I preached at a farmer's house near Brough in Westmoreland. The sun was quite hot, but some shade trees covered both me and most of the assembly. A little bird perched on one of the trees and sang without ceasing from the beginning of the service to the end. Many of the people came from a distance, and I don't believe any of them regretted their efforts …

Fri. 3.— … In running down one of the mountains yesterday, I sprained my thigh. It was worse today, but as I rode to Barnard Castle, the sun shone on it so hot that before I reached town, it was nearly well. In the evening the commanding officer ordered there to be no military training and that all the Durham Militia (what a contrast!) might be free to attend the preaching. So we had a little army of officers as well as soldiers who all behaved well. Many of them were also present at 5 a.m. I haven't found so deep and lively a work in any other part of the kingdom as runs through this whole circuit, especially in the valleys that wind between these horrible mountains. I returned to Newcastle in the evening …

Sun. AUGUST 14.—Hearing that my wife was dangerously ill, I took the stagecoach immediately and reached the Foundry before 1 a.m. I found that her fever had abated and the danger was gone, so about 2 a.m. I set out again, and in the afternoon came to Bristol, not tired at all.

Our conference began on Tuesday the 16th and ended on Friday the 19th. Oh, what can we do for more workers? We can only cry to "the Lord of the harvest." …

Mon. 29.—I rode to St. Columb, intending to preach there, but finding no place that was even nearly suitable, I was going to mount my horse again when a man offered me the use of his meadow near the town. A large assembly quickly gathered to whom I explained the nature and pleasantness of religion. Seldom have I seen a people behave so well the first time I preached to them …

Thur. SEPTEMBER 1.—The grass was too wet for us to stand in the meadow, but we found an open place where I called a listening crowd to return to him who has not "forgotten to be gracious" [Psalm 77:9].

VOLUME 3: 1760-1773

Fri. 2.—I preached at noon to an earnest group at Zennor and in the evening to a far larger gathering at St. Just. Being told that one of our sisters in the next parish, Morva, who in the past had provided hospitality to our preachers, was now worn out and hadn't heard a sermon for many years, on Saturday the 3rd at noon I went to Alice Daniel's and preached near the house on, "They who are counted worthy to obtain that world and the resurrection from the dead, are equal to the angels, and are the children of God, being the children of the resurrection" [Luke 20:36]. I have always thought there is something venerable in persons worn out with age, especially when they retain their understanding and walk in the ways of God.

Sun. 4.—I went to St. Creet's Church, where I heard an excellent sermon. Between 1 and 2 p.m. I confirmed it by explaining that happy religion which our Lord describes in the eight Beatitudes ...

Wed. 7.—[*At Penzance*] After the early preaching, the select society met, such a group of lively believers, full of faith and love as I've never found in this county before. On this and the three following days I preached at as many places as I could, though at first I doubted whether I could preach eight days in a row, mostly in the open air, three or four times a day. But my strength was equal to my task; I hardly felt any weariness from first to last ...

Thur. 15.—We held our quarterly meeting at Medros, but it wasn't like before when the whole Society was afire. Now the love of many has grown cold ...

Fri. 23.—I rode cross-country to Charlton and found the assembly waiting. In the evening we went on to Lympsham, but not without difficulty. The water had risen, so it wasn't easy either to ride or walk. My horse got in a ditch over his back with water. Nor was I able to get to my lodging by the foot path till a good man hoisted me up on his shoulders, and so we waded through ...

Thur. 29.—I rode to Frome. The people here seem more alive to God than most I have seen in the circuit. And this is strange, because in this town alone is there such a mixture of all opinions: Anabaptists, Quakers, Presbyterians, Arians, Antinomians, Moravians, and so forth. If any hold to the truth in the midst of all these, surely the power must be of God.

Fri. 30.—We observed a day of fasting and prayer, and it was a good day for many, who no sooner called than God answered them by the joy in their heart.

Sun. OCTOBER 2.—I preached at Kingswood on "Quench not the Spirit" [1 Thes. 5:19]. Perhaps this people now have ears to hear and will no longer despise prophesying, which by doing so they have often quenched the Spirit and have destroyed his work in their hearts ...

Fri. 7.—I spent a very satisfying hour with the children at Kingswood School. It gave me reason to hope that the grace of God is still working among them. Some are still alive to God, and all behave so well that I can say I've never seen schoolboys like them.

Sun. 9.—I began examining the fellowship in Kingswood, which has increased both in grace and in number. This is due mainly to prayer meetings, which God still blesses greatly. On Monday and Thursday I examined the fellowship at Bristol, and had reason to rejoice over these too, although there is still a heavy spirit on many, in fact on all who are "not going on to perfection."

Fri. 14.—I had dinner with Dr. Wrangel, one of the King of Sweden's chaplains who has spent several years in Pennsylvania. His heart seemed truly united with the American Christians and he strongly pleaded for us to send some of our preachers to help them, for multitudes there are as sheep without a shepherd ...

Thur. DECEMBER 1.—The storm was strong enough to carry away both man and beast, but it slackened about noon so that, after preaching at Margate, I had a pleasant ride to Canterbury.

I observed something curious here, which I pass on to all our preachers. The people of Canterbury have been so often reproved (and often without cause) for being dead and cold, that it has completely discouraged them and made them cold as stones. **How delicate a thing it is to reprove! To do it well requires more than human wisdom** [my emphasis] ...

Wed. 14.—I watched the Westminster scholars act the "Adelphi of Terence," an entertainment not unworthy of a Christian! Oh, how do these heathens shame us! Their very comedies contain both excellent sense, the liveliest portraits of men and manners, and such fine strokes of genuine morality as are seldom found in Christian writings ...

1769

Sun. JANUARY 1.—We met as usual at Spitalfields Chapel to renew our covenant with God. And we never do this without a blessing. Many were comforted and many strengthened.

Mon. 9.—I spent a pleasant and profitable hour with Mr. Whitefield, recalling former times and the way God prepared us for a work which it hadn't even entered our hearts to imagine ...

Fri. 27.—I returned to London. That same day, Elizabeth Vandome went to her rest ... About three weeks ago, she had a remarkable dream: She thought she saw Mr. W[esley] laboring with all his might to keep the people from falling into a deep pit which very few of them were aware of. She awoke with a strong concern about this and was very emotional. Last Tuesday evening she asked us to sit her up in bed to meet her class. Her voice was faltering. She earnestly exhorted them all to live near to God and to stay close to one another, and she added: "I'll soon join the church above." Those were her last words. All was silent rapture till, on Friday morning, without sigh or groan she released her spirit to God.

Such a living and dying witness of the perfect love of God, which she enjoyed for 28 years, ought to silence the doubts and objections of reasonable and honest people.

...

Sat. FEBRUARY 18.—We rode to Norwich.

Sun. 19.—At 7 a.m. I administered the Lord's Supper to about 170 serious communicants. One person then found peace with God and many were comforted. In the evening, finding that the preaching-house wouldn't contain a third of the assembly, I had to stand in the open air, a sight not seen in Norwich for many years. Yet all the people stood still and paid close attention, except for two or three wild Antinomians. I preached on the Gospel for the day, the woman of Canaan. I believe God spoke to many hearts, but who will obey his voice?

Mon. 27.—I had one more agreeable conversation with my old friend and fellow-worker, George Whitefield. His soul seems to still be vigorous, but his body is rapidly sinking. Unless God intervenes with his mighty hand, he must soon finish his work ...

Mon. MARCH 13.—I set out for the north. We had fine weather for a while, then the wind rose and the rain came down heavily. We were soaking wet before we reached Stroud, but didn't take cold at all. At 6 p.m. the preaching-house was quite filled as usual, though the wind and rain kept many strangers to our faith away. The people seemed to be alive in the Spirit and ready to drink in the Word. After preaching we had a love-feast at which many men and women spoke with simplicity what God had done for their souls ...

Tues. 21.—I went to Park Gate and about 11 a.m. boarded the *King George*. We had mild weather and smooth water all day. The next day the west wind blew fresh, yet about 5 p.m. we sailed into Dublin Bay, where we hired a fishing boat that took us to Dunlary. Here we took a carriage and got to Dublin about 8 p.m.

On Thursday, Friday, and Saturday, I tried to soothe the ferment which still continued in the Society. I heard the preachers face to face once and twice, and tried to remove their little misunderstandings. And they did come a little closer to each other, but jealousy remained, and without removing that entirely, there can be no heartfelt agreement. ...

Wed. APRIL 5.—I rode to Terryhugan, where the poor people had raised what they called a tent to screen me from the north wind. My heart was enlarged as I urged them "not to receive the grace of God in vain" [2 Cor. 6:1]. Then we rode to Lisburn. The wind was still piercing cold, yet it didn't prevent a crowd of people from coming to the Linen-hall, an open square called by this name, as are all the Linen-halls in Ireland ...

Tues. 11.— ... Thursday and Friday I preached at Dawson's Grove and Kilmararty, and on Sunday the 15th rode to Derry Anvil, a little village where the roads run out, surrounded by bogs, just like my old parish of Wroote in Lincolnshire. But the assembly here was very large and very alive. I talked with several of them who believed they have been saved from sin and found no reason not to believe them. And I met with many more in these parts who witness to the same confession ...

VOLUME 3: 1760-1773

Mon. 17.—In the evening, and twice on Tuesday, I preached to a genteel yet serious audience in Mr. McGough's Avenue at Armagh. But only God can reach the heart …

Wed. 19.— … We mounted up about 10 a.m., having been asked to visit Kinnard, 10 or 11 miles out of our way, where a little fellowship had been formed recently that was very alive to God. At the end of the town, I met a messenger from Archdeacon C., who asked me to stay overnight with him, and soon after I met another messenger who told me, "The Archdeacon requested me to dismount at his door." I did so, and found an old friend whom I hadn't seen for 34 or 35 years. He received me with the warmest affection and after a while said, "We've been building a new church, which my neighbors expected me to open, but if it pleases you to do it, it will be just as well." Hearing the bell, the people flocked together from all parts of the town, and received the Word with ready minds. I saw the hand of God in this, for the strengthening of this loving people, several of whom believe that the blood of Christ has "cleansed them from all sin." …

Thur. 20.— … Both this and the following evenings I spoke very plainly to the members of the fellowship. Nowhere else in Ireland have our most able preachers taken more pains, but to how little effect? They have no small groups and only 24 persons in the fellowship! Most of these are coldhearted, and the audience in general is dead as stones. However, it's up to us to deliver our message and up to the Lord to do what seems fit to him.

Tues. 25.—Again I set times to meet with the singers and the children, both of which had been discontinued. In fact, a general laxness had prevailed since the morning preaching was abandoned. And it's no wonder; whenever this is abandoned, the glory departs from us …

Mon. MAY 1.—I rode to Augher. Since the day was very hot, I arrived faint and weary, and before I finished my sermon, my head was swimming and I could barely keep standing. But I had a good night's rest and rose as fit as when I left Dublin.

Tues. 2.—I began preaching at Sydare about 5:30 a.m., and it was a day of God's power. The sermon made a general, if not a universal, impression; no one appeared unmoved. This forced me to prolong my prayer as I hadn't done in several years, so I didn't dismiss the audience until almost 8 a.m. ...

Thur. 4.—Near Swadling Bar I found a people as innocent, as earnest, and as loving as even at Tonny-Lommon. About 6 a.m. I preached at the end of the town, even the Catholics seeming as attentive as the Protestants, and I believed thousands of these would soon become zealous Christians, except for their deplorable priests, who won't enter the kingdom of God themselves and do all they can to hinder those who would ...

Sat. 6.—In the evening I preached near the Market-house in Sligo to a large, fairly quiet audience, but soon realized I was shooting over their heads in talking of "salvation by faith." So at 8 a.m., Sunday the 7th, I adjusted my message to their capacity and preached on "Where the worm doesn't die and the fire isn't quenched" [Mark 9:46]. The effect was that the evening gathering was such as I hadn't seen here for many years ...

Sat. 13.—We rode to Limerick. This evening I used the preaching-room, and again at 8 a.m. the next morning, Pentecost Sunday, but was shocked at how few attended. That evening I preached in the Old Camp, where the gathering was larger than it had been for several years; likewise on Monday and Tuesday evening. Still I didn't find any wounded among them—nothing more than a calm, dull attention.

Wed. 17.—I preached at Ballygarane at noon and in the evening at Newmarket. One gentlewoman, strongly prejudiced against this way, at first stood at a distance, then she came a little nearer, afterwards she sat down, and after a brief period hid her face. She attended again in the morning, being strongly convicted of sin, especially of belittling the real Word of God.

We observed Friday the 19th as a day of fasting and prayer for a revival of God's work. Many attended, both at 5 and 9 a.m. and at 1 p.m., but many more so at the watch-night. It was then that God touched the hearts of the people, even of those twice dead.

Sun. 21.—I was hoping to preach in a field in the afternoon, but rain didn't allow this. Yet I didn't regret my disappointment, so great was God's power in our midst. I believe few were untouched, many deeply wounded [as to their need of salvation], and many rejoiced with joy unspeakable. The same power was present the next morning and evening, both to wound and to heal. God swung his two-edged sword all around in a way I hadn't seen here for many years. Oh, how ready he is to answer every "prayer that doesn't go out of false lips." ...

Thur. 24[25].—I had a cool, pleasant ride to Cork, where I soon heard how cold and careless the people were. I asked, "But isn't the fellowship alive, at least?" "No, they are the coldest of all." "What then? Are we to be careless too? No! Let's stir up the gift of God that's in us all the more." In the evening I began to speak very plainly and I soon saw some fruit: The assembly at 5 a.m. wasn't much less than it was in the evening. Many saw their loss. Again God gave me very sharp though loving words. I trust this also is a token for good, and Satan won't triumph over us for long ...

Tues. JUNE 6.— ... On Thursday the 8th I once more took my leave of the loving people of Limerick and set out for Waterford. We intended to dine at Tipperary but were given wrong directions. Finally we stumbled on a little town called Golding, and here I found poor Michael Weston, who wandered here from Westminster a few months ago in search of an estate. I clearly saw the providence of God directing me here before he actually starved ...

Wed. 14.—I preached in the Market-house at Passage to as dull an assembly as I've ever seen. They would've been rude as well, but they were in awe of Mr. Freestone, who gave anyone who disregarded his warning signs a blow on the head with his stick. By this means the whole multitude was fairly quiet and many seemed very affected ...

Thur. 15.—I started preaching a little before 5 a.m. on "the kingdom of God within us" [Luke 17:21]. The hearts of the hearers, without exception, seemed to be like melting wax. Surely it wasn't for nothing that Satan fought so hard to keep the gospel from this place.

In fact, in recent years there hasn't been more severe persecution anywhere in the kingdom of Ireland than here. The mob, encouraged by their superiors, beat and abused whomever they pleased, broke open their houses, and did whatever they wanted to do. A wretched clergyman supported them in this and applied to the Methodist preachers 2 Timothy 3:6-7 (the very text of that unhappy gentleman at Bristol which he read, then dropped down in the pulpit). After he'd painted them black as devils, he added, "I don't have time to finish now; next Sunday I'll give you the rest." But the next morning he was struck in a strange way: He couldn't bear to be alone for a moment. He cried out, "Those hobgoblins, don't you see them? There, there! The room is full of them!" After staying that way for several days, he screamed, "See that hobgoblin at the foot of my bed! Oh that scroll, that scroll that he holds up to me! All my sins are written on it!" Not long after that, without showing the least sign of hope, he went to his reward ...

Sun. JULY 2.—I read Mrs. Rowe's *Devout Exercises of the Heart*. It is far superior to anything of hers which I've ever read, in style as well as in reason. Her experience is plain, sound, and scriptural, not whimsical or mystical at all, and her language is clear, strong, and simple, without the affected flourishes that offend those with a keen ear or who can judge good writing.

At 9 a.m. we had a serious assembly to whom I could speak of the deep things of God. And the new preaching-house contained them fairly well, but in the evening it was far too small. So I stood in the little yard beside the house. Many soft people sat inside, but most of the assembly stood in the meadow and the gardens on either side. In all the world I haven't seen a people so easy to be convicted or persuaded as the Irish. What pity that these tendencies don't always lead to the best results!

Mon. 3.—I rode to Coolylough, where we held our quarterly meeting, and preached at 11 a.m. and in the evening. While we were singing, I was surprised to see the horses who were there gathering around us. Is it true, then, that horses, as well as lions and tigers, have an ear for music? ...

Sat. 15.— ... After returning to Dublin, all the following week we had a remarkable blessing, both at the morning and evening services. On Wednesday and Thursday we held our little conference at which most of the preachers in Ireland were present. We agreed to set apart Friday the 21st for a day of fasting and prayer. At every meeting, especially the last one, the Lord refreshed us in an unusual way. About 10 p.m. I was a bit tired, but before the clock struck 12 my weariness was all gone. It seemed to be the same with the whole congregation, and prayer was swallowed up in praise ...

Tues. AUGUST 1.—Our conference in England began, and we never had a more loving one. On Thursday I mentioned the situation of our brethren in New York who had built the first Methodist preaching-house in America and were badly needing money, but needing preachers even more. Two of our preachers, Richard Boardman and Joseph Pillmoor, volunteered for this service, by whom we decided to send 50 pounds[301] as a token of our brotherly love ...

Wed. 16.—At Haverfordwest, I examined the members of the fellowship, now the liveliest fellowship in Wales. Many of them are rejoicing in the love of God, while many are groaning for full redemption ...

Sat. 19.—About 8 a.m. I preached at Neath; about 3 p.m. in the church at Bridge End (where the rain doubled the assembly by stopping work on the harvest), and at 7 p.m. in the assembly room at Cowbridge on, "Lord, are there few that will be saved?" [Luke 13:23]. I was able to drive it home, I believe with some effect.

Wed. 23.—I went on to Trevecka. Here we found a crowd of people from all around who had come to celebrate the Countess of Huntingdon's birthday and the anniversary of her school, which opened August the 24th last year. I preached in the evening to as many as her chapel could hold; it is very neat, or rather elegant, as is the dining room, the school, and the whole house. About 9 p.m., Howel Harris asked me to give a brief exhortation to his family, and I did so, then went back to my lady's and lay down in peace ...

Tues. SEPTEMBER 5.—Last week, as I rode to Plymouth Dock, I read most of Homer's *Odyssey*. I always imagined it was like Milton's *Paradise Regained,* "the last faint effort of an expiring muse." But how mistaken I was! Homer's latter poem is far superior to the former! Certainly it has its blemishes, such as making Ulysses swim nine days and nights without nourishment; his incredible escape from Polyphemus (unless the goat was as strong as an ox), and his introducing Minerva at every turn, without any *dignus*

---

[301] About $12,000 in 2020 USD.

vindice nodus [*worthily betrayed?*]. But his many beauties as a whole make up for these flaws. Was anyone ever so happy in their descriptions, so exact and consistent in their characters, and so natural in telling a story? In addition, he continually inserts the finest strokes of morality, which I can't find in Virgil, on all occasions recommending the fear of God, with justice, mercy, and truth. He is inconsistent with himself only in one thing: He makes his hero say, "Wisdom never lies." And, "Him, who on whatever pretext, can tell lies, my soul abhors him as the gates of hell." Meantime he himself, on the slightest pretext, deliberately tells lies over and over—yes, and is highly commended for doing so, even by the goddess of Wisdom …

Tues. 12.—I investigated the condition of the Kingswood school. The problem now is the number of children. Instead of 30, as I wanted, we now have almost 50, which is a burden to our teachers. And it's almost impossible to keep them in exact an order as we might do with a smaller number. However, this still comes closer to being a Christian school than any other I know in England …

Tues. 19.—Between 12 and 1 p.m., I preached at Fresh-ford and on White's Hill near Bradford in the evening. This gave many the opportunity of hearing who wouldn't have come to the preaching-room. I had planned to preach there again the next evening, but a gentleman in the town asked me to preach at his doorway. The beasts of the town were fairly quiet till I had nearly finished my sermon. Then they raised their voices, especially one, called a gentleman, who had filled his pockets with rotten eggs. But a young man snuck up behind him, slapped his pockets on both sides, and smashed them all at once. So the gentleman reeked of perfume all over, though not as sweet as balsam! …

Sun. OCTOBER 8.—I let all of Mr. Whitefield's society who wanted to do so to attend our love-feast. I suppose there were 1000 of us in all, and we didn't go away empty …

Tues. 10.—I preached at Shaftesbury at noon and in the evening at Salisbury. Here it was like I was in a new world; the assembly was alive and the fellowship much more so. How pleasant it would be to always be with such people! But that is not our calling …

Tues. 17.— ...Having made an appointment to preach at Oxford at 10 a.m., I had a problem. I didn't want to preach in the dissenting meeting-house, yet I couldn't see how to avoid it. But the owners cut the knot for me by locking up the doors, so I preached in James Mears's garden, and to such an assembly as I hadn't had in Oxford since I preached in St. Mary's Church ...

Fri. NOVEMBER 3.—[*In Norwich*] I tried to gather up the fragments of the poor fellowship, shattered to pieces by Presbyterians, Anabaptists, and disputers of all kinds, but especially by one unhappy man who had risen from among ourselves. In the evening I strongly exhorted them to "repent, and do the first works" [Rev. 2:5] ...

Mon. 6.—and the following days in Yarmouth, I visited as many of the people, sick and well, as I possibly could, and on Friday the 9th left them more united than they had been for many years. I took the stagecoach again and the next afternoon came to London ...

Mon. DECEMBER 4.—I went to Chatham. Those who called themselves Mr. Whitefield's people refused me the use of their preaching-room, so I preached in the barracks to an attentive crowd, and our hearts were sweetly enlarged and knit together. One of Mr. Whitefield's society, grieved at the bigotry of his brethren, invited me to preach in his house the next morning, since the barracks weren't open, which I did to as many as his house could hold ...

Tues. 26.—I read the letters from our preachers in America, telling us that God had begun a glorious work there, and that both in New York and Philadelphia crowds flock to hear, and behave with great seriousness, and that the Society in each place already contains over 100 members ...

1770

Mon. JANUARY 1.—About 1800 of us met together. It was a solemn season as we openly "declared the Lord to be our God, and so he declared us to be his people" ...

Tues. 30.—Someone told me that Mrs. Kitely at Lambuth wasn't expected to live many more hours and that she had a strong desire to see me before she died. I went as quickly as possible, but when I got there, she seemed unconscious as well as speechless. I disregarded these facts but spoke to her immediately, and right away her understanding and speech returned, testifying to a hope full of immortality. Having had her desire fulfilled, she died just two days before her husband, "a perfect pattern of true womanhood."

She was a good wife, a good mistress of her house, and "her works shall praise her in the gates" [Prov. 31:31]. How well did her death suit her life! After many years of doing good, she redeemed a poor, friendless young man from prison, caught the jail-virus, and died ...

Fri. FEBRUARY 23.—I was invited to hear Mr. Leloni sing at the Jewish synagogue. Never before have I seen a Jewish congregation behave so decently. Indeed, the place itself is so solemn that it might put in awe those who have any thought of God ...

Thur. MARCH 15.—I met the select society in Worcester, and am impressed with how swiftly God has deepened his work in them! I've seen very few in Bristol or London who are clearer in their experience. The account all those I had time to question gave of themselves was scriptural and reasonable. Assuming they spoke the truth, they are witnesses of the perfection which I preach. Of course I know that they *may* fall from this, but that they *must* fall, I totally deny ...

Sat. 17.— ... On the evening of Sunday the 18th I preached a funeral sermon for Elizabeth Longmore in the house at Wednesbury. I think she was the first witness to Christian perfection that God raised up in this area. I gave some account of her experience many years ago. From that point on, her whole life conformed to her profession of faith, holy and unblamable in every way. Often she didn't have food to eat, but that didn't keep her from "rejoicing evermore." She had a lot of trouble due to her poor apostate husband, along with sharp pain and failing sickness. But she was above it all, still seeing her Father's hand, and "in everything giving thanks." Her death was like her life: "No cloud could arise to darken the skies, or hide for a moment her Lord from her eyes."

All was noon-day; she praised God with every breath till he took her to himself ...

Wed. 21.—On the following days, I went on slowly through Staffordshire and Cheshire to Manchester. On this journey, as well as on many others, I noticed a mistake that almost everyone makes, and I ask all travelers to take note of it, which may save them from trouble and danger. Almost 30 years ago I was thinking, "How is it that no horse ever stumbles while I'm reading?" (I commonly read history, poetry, and philosophy on horseback, being occupied otherwise at other times.) The only account I can give for this is that then I throw the reins on his neck. Then I began watching, and I solemnly state that in riding over 100,000 miles, I can only recall two horses (and they would fall head over heels anyway) falling or stumbling while I rode with a slack rein. To imagine, therefore, that a tight rein prevents stumbling is a major error. I have repeated this test more often than most men in the kingdom can do. A slack rein will prevent stumbling, if anything will, but in some horses, nothing can do so ...

Good Friday APRIL 13.—Notice having been mistakenly given that I would be preaching at Carlisle, I was obliged to leave Whitehaven immediately after the morning preaching. I preached at Cockermouth at 1 p.m. and then rode on to Carlisle. Here it was the day of small beginnings, the fellowship consisting of only 15 members. I preached at 6 p.m., and as many as could hear behaved with utmost seriousness. Afterwards I walked to Houghton, a village two miles from Carlisle, and slept peacefully on a hard, clean bed ...

Tues. MAY 8.—In Old Aberdeen, I viewed the small remains of the Abbey. I don't know of anything like it in all of North Britain. Pacing it, I found it to be 100 yards long, and the width proportional. Part of the west end, still standing, shows it was fully as tall as Westminster Abbey. The south end of the cross-aisle is also still standing, near the top of which is a large circular window. The zealous Reformers, they told us, burned this down. God save us from reforming mobs! ...

Mon. 28.—In Newcastle I again began meeting with the children—something neglected for several months. And we had a sign for good: Two or three were cut to the heart, and many seemed very moved ...

Mon. JUNE 11.—I took cheerful leave of the loving people of Newcastle, about noon preached at Durham, and in the evening in front of Mr. Watson's door to a large assembly at Stockton.

Tues. 12.—At 5 a.m. I preached in the new preaching-house, built curiously when the situation seemed desperate, by God touching the heart of a wealthy man, who bought the ground and built it without delay. I preached at Norton at noon, and afterwards met with those who can "rejoice evermore, and pray without ceasing" [1Thes. 5:17]. We had another happy opportunity in the evening at Yarm, where I found a greater number of those who believe God has enabled them to love him with all their heart and soul ...

Fri. 15.—I was pleasantly surprised to find that the whole road from Thirsk to Stokeksley, which used to be very bad, was now better than most turnpikes. The gentlemen had raised enough money to repair it effectively; they have done so for several hundred miles in Scotland and throughout all Connaught in Ireland; and they undoubtedly might do so throughout all England without saddling the poor people with the despicable turnpike fees forever ...

Sat. 16.—I found that our preacher [in Whitby], James Brownfield, had set up his own ministry. The reasons he gave for leaving the Methodists were 1. that they went to [the Anglican] Church, and 2. that they held to perfection. I earnestly begged our Society to leave him to God, and say nothing about him, good or bad ...

Sun. 17.— ... We had a poor sermon at church. However, I went again in the afternoon, remembering the words of Philip Henry: "If the preacher doesn't know his duty, I bless God that I know mine."

Between 1 and 2 p.m. I met the small groups, being nearly two-thirds of the fellowship. Their openness and the spirit in which they spoke were quite surprising. One plain woman cried and spoke and cried again, so there were tears all around. I suppose that if I could have stayed long enough, one or another would have spoken till nightfall ...

Sun. 24.—I met the select society at 6 a.m. and was pleased to find that some who had lost the great blessing for months or years had recovered it and even more. At 8 a.m. I preached to a people prepared for the Lord; at 9 a.m. I met the children; at 5 p.m., by taking out the benches, we made room for the greater part of the gathering. Afterwards I spent an hour with the fellowship, and so ended a busy, happy day ...

Thur. 28.— ... I can hardly believe that today I have entered my 68th year of life! How marvelous are the ways of God! How he has kept me, even from childhood! From 10 to 13 or 14, I had little but bread to eat and not much of that. I believe that instead of hurting me, it laid the foundation of lasting health. When I grew up, after reading Dr. Cheyne, I chose to eat sparingly and drink water. This was another major factor in benefiting my health till I was about 27. Then I started spitting blood, which continued for several years. A warm climate cured this. After this I nearly died from a fever, but it left me healthier than before. Eleven years later, I was in the third stage of tuberculosis, but in three months it pleased God to remove this also. Since that time I've had neither pain nor sickness,[302] and now am healthier than I was 40 years ago! This is God's doing! ...

Sun. JULY 1.—Being very concerned about the poor parishioners of Haworth who hear and hear, but are no more affected than stones, I spoke to them in the most cutting way I could. May God apply it to their hearts!

On Monday and Tuesday I preached at Bingley and Bradford, and on Wednesday I rode to Halifax. Here I was able to probe deeply into an extraordinary case: On January 26, 1760, a young woman 22 years old felt very cold in her feet that evening. Soon after that, she was seized with convulsions. This disorder continued almost daily in spite of all the medicines given by the best physicians. One of her fits began just before we entered her room. At first she fell back in her chair, seemed to be unconscious, and struggled like someone strangling in her throat and chest. After two or three minutes she jumped up, turned around many times, then dropped down and began beating her head against the stone floor. She quickly got up, jumped up many times, ran to and fro, with many odd gestures. She hit her head, tore her hair, and tried to run into the fire. Being forced into a chair, she said many things we couldn't understand. She was violently agitated again from head to foot, then said wildly, "Where

---

[302] Wesley seems to forget or disregard some of his minor illnesses.

am I? Who are these people? I want my father. I'll go to my father." In about an hour she came to her senses ...

When old Dr. A. was asked what her disorder was, he replied, "It's what they used to call being bewitched." And why wouldn't they call it that now? Because the infidels have hooted witchcraft out of the world, and the Christians, largely complying, have joined them in the cry. I'm not much surprised that many of them talk like infidels regarding this, but sometimes I wonder at the flippant, cocky, indecent way that some of them trample on men much wiser than themselves—speaking so dogmatically against what the whole world, heathen and Christian, believed in past ages, and that thousands, learned and unlearned, firmly believe even today. I refer you to Dr. Smollett and Mr. Guthrie, who speak concerning witchcraft in a way that must be offensive to any sensible persons who can't give up their Bible ...

Fri. 13.—At Horncastle, our brethren asking me to preach in the market-place, I cried to an unbroken multitude, "What does it profit a man if he gains the whole world and loses his own soul?" [Matt. 16:26]. The power of God was on them, and they all listened calmly until I commended them to God.

This was the first day I've felt weary (the extreme heat drinking up my spirits) since I set out from London ...

Wed. 18.—About noon I preached at Crowle. This is the place where the former rector, my father's contemporary, ordered these words inscribed on his tomb:

> Here lies the body of Solomon Ashburn,
> Forty years Rector of this Parish.
> All day long I have stretched out my hands
> To a disobedient and opposing people.
> So I gave them up to their own hearts' lusts,
> And let them follow their own imaginations.

They did follow them for many years, but finally God has visited them ...

Mon. 23.—I preached at Doncaster and Rotherham, then on Tuesday and Wednesday at Sheffield. On Wednesday evening my heart was so enlarged that I didn't know how to end. Do some say that I preach longer when I'm unproductive? On the contrary: I never go longer except when I'm full of preaching matter. Still I consider that my audience may not go along with me. So it's unusual if I exceed my hour more than fifteen minutes ...

Sat. AUGUST 18.—I gave a solemn warning to a large gathering on Redclliff Hill from these awesome words, "The time is coming when judgment must begin with the house of God." Surely it will, unless a general repentance prevents a general judgment.

Mon. 20.—I rode on to Tiverton, and from there through Launceston, Camelford, Port Isaac, St. Cuthbert, St. Agnes, and Redruth, to St. Ives. Here God has made all our enemies to be at peace with us, so I could have preached in any part of the town. But instead I chose a meadow where those who chose could sit down, either on the grass or on the "hedges" (for that's the Cornish term for their broad stone walls, which are usually covered with grass.) Here I drove home "Fear God and keep his commandments, for this is the whole duty of man" [Eccl. 12:13].

Sun. 26.—Being asked to preach in the town for the sake of some who couldn't climb the hill, I began near the market-place at 8 a.m. on "Without holiness, no man shall see the Lord" [Heb. 12:14]. We had useful sermons at church both morning and afternoon, delivered in a strong and earnest manner. At 5 p.m. I preached again, with almost all the town present, and thousands from the countryside all around, to whom I explained, "The Son of God was manifested to destroy the works of the devil" [1 John 3:8].

Mon. 27.—I was surprised to find that the select society [in Tiverton] had been totally neglected. I got a few of them together, but didn't find any who hadn't given up their confidence. At 9 a.m. I renewed the children's meetings, which had also been given up for a long time. But I've seldom seen such a dead group. I hardly found a single spark even of the fear of God among them.

In the evening I preached in front of our preaching-house at St. Just on "I saw the dead, both great and small, standing before God" [Rev. 20:12]. It was a glorious hour. The same spirit breathed on us at the meeting of the fellowship. At such times, who doesn't feel that nothing is too hard for God? ...

Thur. 30.—I rode to Falmouth and preached at 2 p.m. near the church to a greater number of people than I've ever seen there before, except the mob 25 years ago. I preached at Penryn in the evening, Friday noon in Crowan, and that evening at Trevorga, near Redruth ...

Sat. SEPTEMBER 1.—I walked to the top of that famous hill, Carn-Brae. Here are many monuments of antiquity, hardly to be found in other parts of Europe: enormous Druid altars, simply being huge rocks supported one upon another, and basins, hollowed on the surface of the rock, supposed to contain holy water. Probably these are contemporary with Pompey's Theater, if not with the pyramids of Egypt. And are they any better for this? What difference does it make to the living or the dead if they've withstood the wear of time for 3000 or 300 years? ...

Mon. 3.— ... After visiting Medros, Plymouth, and Collumpton, I came on Friday the 7th to Taunton. Shortly after preaching I mounted up. The rain forced us to hurry, but after a while the saddle slipped up to my horse's neck, then slid under his belly. I had to throw myself off or I would have fallen under him. I was slightly bruised, but soon mounted again and rode to Lympsham, and the next day to Bristol ...

Tues. 18.—Most of the children [of Kingswood School] went to see the body of Francis Evans, one of our neighbors who died two or three days earlier. About 7 p.m., Mr. Hindmarsh met them all at the school and gave an exhortation suitable for the occasion. He then led out with the hymn,

> Am I born to die,
> To lay this body down?
> And must my trembling spirit fly
> Into a world unknown?

This increased their concern, so it was with difficulty that they contained themselves till he began to pray. Then A.M. and R.N. cried out for mercy, and very soon another and another, till all but two or three were compelled to do the same thing, and as long as he continued to pray, they kept up their loud and bitter cry ... After prayer, Mr. H. said, "Those of you who are determined to serve God may go and pray together." Fifteen of them did so and kept wrestling with God with strong cries and tears till about 9 p.m.

Wed. 19.—At morning prayer, many of them cried out again, though not as strongly. From that moment, their whole spirit and conduct were changed; they were all serious and loving to each other. This seriousness and mildness continued on Thursday, and they walked together, talking only of the things of God. On Friday evening their concern increased even more, causing them to burst out again into strong cries. On Saturday the 22nd they seemed to lose none of their concern and spent all their spare time in prayer.

Sun. 23.—Fifteen of them gave me their names, "being resolved," they said, "to serve God." In the afternoon I gave them a strong exhortation, and Mr. Rankin did the same after me. Their very appearances were changed and they drank in every word.

Tues. 25.—During the time of prayer in the evening they were affected just as last Tuesday. The two other maids were present then, and both were cut to the heart ...

All the while it was noticeable that there was an unusual revival of the work of God in all the fellowships in the area. In Kingswood, within a few months, it increased from 118 to over 300 members, and every day more and more were convicted of sin, and more and more were enabled to rejoice in God their Savior ...

Mon. NOVEMBER 5.—I met with the leaders in Norwich and inquired about the condition of the fellowship. In all England I don't find any people like those in Norwich. They are as unstable as water. Out of 200 whom I left here last year, 69 are gone already! What a blessing is knowledge when it is sanctified! What stability can be expected when it isn't? For no matter how strong their affections are now, what hold can you have on a people who don't know either books or people—neither themselves nor the Bible, neither natural nor spiritual things? ...

Sat. 10.—I returned to London and received the sad news of Mr. Whitefield's death, confirmed by his executors, who asked me to preach his funeral sermon on Sunday the 18th. In order to write this, I withdrew to Lewisham on Monday, and the following Sunday went to the chapel in Tottenham-court Road. A huge crowd had gathered from all parts of the town. At first I was afraid that many in the congregation wouldn't be able to hear, but it pleased God to strengthen my voice so that even those at the chapel doors did hear clearly. It was an awesome occasion. Everyone was still as night.

Most appeared to be deeply moved, and many received an impression which I hope will not soon be erased ...

Fri. 23.—Since the trustees of the Tabernacle at Greenwich had asked me to preach Mr. Whitefield's funeral sermon there too, I went over there today to do so. But this building also was too small for the congregation. Those who couldn't get in made some noise at first, but after a little while all were quiet. Here likewise I trust God has given a blow to that bigotry[303] which has prevailed for many years ...

1771

Tues. JANUARY 1.—A large assembly met at Spitalfields in the evening in order to renew, with one heart and voice, their covenant with God. And this was not in vain; the Spirit of glory and of God, as usual, rested on us ...

Fri. MARCH 8.—I went over to Kingswood School and found several of the boys still alive to God ...

Sat. 23.—Having arrived in Dublin early on Sunday morning, I immediately began asking about the condition of the fellowship there. Plainly, there had been a constant disturbance for at least the past two years which had caused the people to stumble, had weakened the hands of the preachers, and had greatly hindered the work of God. I wanted to know the root cause of this, and in order not to act rashly, decided to hear the different parties separately at first, then face to face. After talking with the preachers, I talked with the class leaders in the evening at length. And from the spirit I felt in them all, I had real hope that all hindrances would be removed. Wednesday evening I met with the leaders again and allowed them to explain themselves further. On Friday I arranged a special meeting at which some spoke with great passion. But I restrained both sides so that they parted in peace.

Sat. 30.—I used the new preaching-house near the Barracks about 6 p.m. Many attended here who can't, and many who won't, come to the other end of the town. So I'm persuaded that preaching here two or three times a week will do much for God's glory.

---

[303] Prejudice and conflict between Arminians and predestinarians (Wesley was Arminian; Whitefield a predestinarian).

Sun. 31.—The class leaders, stewards, and preachers spoke their minds freely to each other. Now I saw that the evil might be entirely removed since all parties wanted peace.

On Monday, Tuesday, and Wednesday I visited the classes and found that a general spiritual faintness had run through the fellowship. Yet for several days God has given a general blessing and strengthened many of the weak-minded. On Tuesday I preached again at the new house, and many were comforted.

On Wednesday evening I read to the leaders the following paper: 1. **To more easily discern whether the members of our fellowships are trying to work out their own salvation, they are divided into little groups, called classes. One person in each of these is termed a leader, and it's his or her business: 1. to see everyone in the class once a week; to ask how their souls fare; to advise, reprove, comfort, or encourage them; 2. to receive what money they are willing to give toward the expenses of the fellowship; and 3. to meet the assistant and the stewards once a week.**

2. This is the sole business of a leader or of any number of leaders. But the assistant, where several leaders meet together, may ask their advice on anything regarding the temporal or spiritual welfare of the fellowship. He may or may not do this as he sees best. I often do it in the larger fellowships; on many occasions I've found that in many counselors there is safety ...

In the Methodist discipline, the ranks are these [*below the two Wesleys*]: the Assistant, the Preachers, the Stewards, the Leaders, the people.

But here the leaders, who are next to the lowest rank, had gotten out of their place. They were at the top, above the stewards, the preachers, and even the assistant himself ...

Wed. APRIL 10.—I preached in the courthouse at Molingar to a serious and decent assembly, but they seemed quite unconcerned. Those who met at the courthouse at Longford in the evening were of quite another spirit. They drank in every word while I explained, "Lord, are there few who will be saved?" [Luke 13:23]. Who can despair of doing good in any place? None in this kingdom seemed as barren as at Longford, and that for many years. For nearly 20 years we labored only to find no fruit, but all of a sudden the seed so long hidden has sprung up and promises a plentiful harvest ...

Tues. 30.—I rode to Cork, and on Wednesday, May the 1st, to Bandon, but the northeast wind kept me from preaching in the street. This didn't concern me so much because my business was mainly with the fellowship. I labored to gather up those who had been scattered, to awaken those who were drowsy, to bring to life those who were dead, and to unite all together in following after peace and holiness ...

Sat. MAY 18.—I dined at Mr. ____'s. I haven't seen another family like this in the kingdom of Ireland. He and Mrs. ____ are in person, in understanding, and in temperament, made for each other, and their 10 children are in such good order as I haven't seen in many years—indeed, never since I left my father's house. May they never depart from the good way! ...

Fri. 24.—I spoke individually to members of the fellowship in Limerick. I haven't found any fellowship in Ireland, compared numerically, so rooted and grounded in love. We observed this as a day of fasting and prayer, and were comforted together ...

Mon 27.—We pushed through strong wind and rain and reached Galway in the afternoon. About 6 p.m. I preached in the courthouse, the neatest one I've seen in Ireland. Many soldiers who were to march to Dublin the next day willingly attended, and not a few of the townspeople, but (what is rarely seen in Ireland) there were five or six men to one woman. I was able to drive my points home, and many were stunned if not wounded. The following evening the number of townspeople was doubled, among them the mayor and some other people of fashion. Again I spoke with the utmost plainness and could only hope that there will be a work of God even in Galway.

Wed. 29.—We had heavy rain and strong wind all day long. Still I reached Ballinrobe between noon and 1 p.m. and preached in the courthouse to 40 or 50 listeners. Five miles short of Castlebar, we took shelter for a while in a little cabin. The poor man brought us the best thing he had: a glass of rum. We talked a little with him and his wife, sang a hymn, had a time of prayer, then, since the rain let up, rode cheerfully on to Castlebar.

VOLUME 3: 1760-1773

Thur. 30.—I preached about noon at Cappavica, four miles from Castlebar. I spoke with such closeness and sharpness as I can only do at certain times. In fact it's a gift of God and can't be attained even by nature and art combined ...

Thur. JUNE 6.—We came to Swadlingbar, and seemed to be in another world. The people were all alive, full of faith and love, and panting after the whole likeness of God. The assembly in the evening greatly refreshed me both by their spirit and by their number; they made

> the hills and the dales
> resound with praises;

singing with the Spirit and with the understanding too. I haven't heard such voices since we left Cork, nor seen such an earnest people since we left Limerick.

Fri. 7.—About noon I preached at Tonnylammon, four miles short of Inniskillen, to a similar gathering, deeply thirsting for the full salvation of God. In the afternoon we rode to Mr. A.'s at Sidare ... Here a tent was set up on a green, grassy place, in the middle of a large crowd of people, ripe for the gospel. So I cried out in the Lord's words, "If any are thirsty, let them come to me and drink" [John 7:37], and it's not easy to describe the thirst, the passionate desire that could be seen in much of the audience ...

Fri. 14.—About noon I preached at the New-buildings, two miles from Londonderry. Some time back, the people were very much like the coalminers of Kingswood, equally without God in the world and famous for all kinds of wickedness. But old things have passed away, and now they are prominent for the fear of God and the love of their neighbor. I preached there again on Sunday the 16th and administered the Lord's Supper to the fellowship. I think they were all in tears, but for most they were tears of joy and love.

Mon. 17.—I met with the singers for the last time. I organized them two years ago, but since the preachers following me took no care or thought about them, of course they fell apart, and no wonder, for **nothing will work in the Methodist plan unless the preacher has his heart and hand in it. Therefore every preacher should**

consider that it's not just his business to mind this or that thing, but everything [my emphasis] ....

Sun. 23.—At Caladon, in the evening, such a crowd assembled and stood so close together that, although we were in the open air, the heat was suffocating. Surely God will have a people in this place! At least the poor will receive the gospel ...

Fri. 28.— ... Today I entered the 69th year of my life. I'm still a wonder to myself. My voice and strength are the same as at age 29. This too is God's doing ...

Fri. JULY 12.—I returned to Dublin ... On Monday and Tuesday, I reviewed the classes. The fellowship has dwindled from over 500 members to under 400 in two years, but I trust they will now increase since the offenses are removed and brotherly love is restored.

On Thursday and Friday we had our small conference, a solemn and useful meeting.

Sun. 21.—At the meeting of the fellowship, many were comforted, and all seemed determined to start afresh and take the kingdom of heaven by force [cf. Matt. 11:12] ...

Mon. 29.—I went on to Worcester. Our brethren had chosen a place for me in a broad street not far from the cathedral, where there was room for thousands of people. And we soon had plenty of company—part serious, part like a wild donkey's colt—but after a while the serious part won out and silenced or drove away the rabble, till we had a tolerable degree of silence and finished in peace ...

Tues. AUGUST 6.—We had more preachers than usual at the conference as a result of Mr. Shirley's circular letter. At 10 a.m. on Thursday morning he came with nine or ten of his friends. We discussed freely for about two hours, and I believe they were satisfied that we weren't such "dreadful heretics" as they had imagined, but were tolerably sound in the faith ...

Thur. 22.—I rode to Dala, a little village at the mouth of Milford Haven. It seemed to me that our preachers had spent a lot of effort here to little effect. All the people, without exception, seemed as dead as stones, completely quiet and unconcerned. I told them just what I thought, and it pierced their hearts like a sword. They felt the truth and wept bitterly. I don't know where we've found more of the presence of God. Will we at last have fruit here too? ...

Fri. SEPTEMBER 6.—I spent an hour with our children at Kingswood. It's strange! How long will we have to keep weaving Penelope's web?[304] What's happened to the wonderful work of grace that God accomplished in them last September? It's gone; it's lost, vanished! There's hardly a trace of it remaining! Then we must start all over, and in due season we'll reap if we don't faint.

Mon. 9.—I read Dr. Cadogan's ingenious *Treatise on Chronic Distempers.* It's certainly true that "very few of them are actually hereditary"; that most of them derive from laziness or intemperance or irregular passions. But why should he condemn wine completely, which is one of the noblest cordials[305] in nature? Stranger still, why should he condemn bread? Great whims belong to great people ...

Thur. 26.—I preached once more at Bath to an elegant audience on "Knowledge puffs up." But I trust that many of them can witness that "Love builds up" [1 Cor. 8:1]—builds up both in holiness and happiness ...

Wed. OCTOBER 16.—I preached at South Lye. It was here that I preached my first sermon 46 years ago. One man who heard it was in my audience today; most of the rest have gone to their long home ...

Tues. 22.—I went down to Sheerness and preached in the New Room, but it wouldn't hold the gathering. I believe that all who could hear found that God was there. Both morning and evening I warned them against getting sick from opinions and quarreling about words, which have been the main obstacles to the work of God here from the beginning.

Thur. 24.—I returned to Chatham and on Friday to London.

Sat. 26.—Mr. N. gave me a sad account of his being dismissed from the Tabernacle. Surely that won't be the state of affairs at the Foundry, when my head is laid to rest! If I thought they would [treat

---

[304]In Homer's *Odyssey,* Odysseus' faithful wife Penelope wove a web by day and undid it by night to ward off suitors while hoping her husband will return.
[305] I.e., stimulating medicines or drinks.

me that way], I would do just as I'm doing now, all the good I can while I'm alive ...

Thur. NOVEMBER 7.—At Lynn, the prisoners asked me to give them a word of encouragement and received it with great eagerness. Who knows but that one or two may retain it? In the evening, those who couldn't get in were noisy at first, but after a while they went away quietly ...

Sat. DECEMBER 21.—I met an old friend, James Hutton, whom I hadn't seen for 25 years. The years seemed to make no difference; both our hearts were wide open, and we shared just as we did in 1738 when we met in Fetter Lane.

Mon. 23.—and all the following days, when not tied up otherwise, I spent an hour in the morning with our preachers as I used to do with my pupils at Oxford ...

Mon. 30.—At my brother Charles' request, I sat again for my portrait ...

1772

Wed. JANUARY 1.—As usual, we met in the evening in order to solemnly and explicitly renew our covenant with God ...

Thur. 16.—I started out for Luton. The snow was so deep on the road that it was only with difficulty and some danger that we finally reached the town. I was offered the use of the church. The freezing air was very biting, and the glass had been taken out of the windows. However, for the sake of the people, I accepted the offer, though I could just as well have preached in the open air. I suppose four times as many people were present as would have been in our preaching room, and about 100 came in the morning. So I didn't regret my journey through the snow.

Fri. 17.—The usual road was blocked by snow, so we had to take a detour to Hertford. I found that the poor children whom Mr. A. kept in his school had increased to about 30 boys and 30 girls. I immediately went to the girls. As soon as I began speaking, some of them burst into tears, and they became more and more emotional. But that stayed within bounds till I began to pray. Then a cry went up which spread from one to another till almost all cried for mercy and wouldn't be comforted.

But what a different scene it was with the boys! They seemed as dead as stones and hardly seemed to mind anything I said—in fact, some of them could hardly keep from laughing. But I pressed on and set before them the terrors of the Lord. Soon one was cut to the heart, then another and another, and in 10 minutes most of them were only a little less affected than the girls. Except at Kingswood, I haven't seen such a work of God upon children for over 30 years. I spoke very plainly in the evening on "the narrow way that leads to life" [Matt. 7:14]. But the men were very different than the children; they were affected just as much as so many horses ...

Wed. FEBRUARY 12.—On my way back, I read a very different book, published by an honest Quaker on that detestable chief of all iniquities called the slave trade.[306] I've read nothing like it in the heathen world, ancient or modern. And it infinitely exceeds, in every respect of barbarity, whatever Christian slaves suffer in Muslim countries.

Fri. 14.—I began to carry out a plan, long in my thoughts, to print as accurate an edition of my works as a book publisher would do. Surely I ought to be as exact for God's sake as he would be for money! ...

Fri. 21.—I met several of my friends who had begun raising money so I wouldn't have to ride on horseback any longer. I can't ride so well since I got hurt a few months ago. If they keep this up, fine. If not, I'll have strength according to my need ...

Fri. MARCH 20.—I rode to Markfield through heavy rain. Despite the severe weather, the church was pretty well filled, not merely with curious listeners but with earnest people seeking to save their souls. We also found some like these in Leicester in the evening, along with many who gave it little thought—to whom, therefore, I spoke in a quite different manner, urging them to wake up from sleep. I believe God applied his Word, because the building, large as it was, was nearly filled at 5 a.m. the next morning, and all seemed willing to receive that important truth, "Without holiness no one shall see the Lord" [Heb. 12:14] ...

---

[306] Likely John Woolman's *Some Considerations on the Keeping of Negroes* (*Part One*, 1753, and/or *Part Two*, 1762), printed by Benjamin Franklin.

Sun. 22.— ... In the evening I preached at Derby. Both the preaching room and the yard beside it were crowded, yet many went away. After preaching, the people hung around the doors and couldn't be persuaded to leave, so finally I allowed them to come in along with our fellowship and strongly urged them to worship God in spirit and in truth ...

Wed. 25.—We went on to Congleton, where all is now peace and love. Now there's no one left who speaks against the Methodists except the curate, Mr. Sambach. He does his best to drive them from the Church, but they won't leave it yet; they love both her liturgy and her doctrine, and don't know where to find any better ...

Mon. 30.—At 1 p.m. I preached in Warrington. I believe all the young gentlemen of the academy were there, to whom I declared and proved the use of reason from the words of St. Paul: "In sinfulness be children, but in understanding be adults" [1 Cor. 14:20] ...

Sun. APRIL 5.— ... I preached at Manchester in the evening, but the preaching house was way too small; crowds had to go away. The intellectual knowledge of the truth has risen here, from the least to the greatest, but how far short is this from experiential knowledge! Still, it's a step toward it, not to be despised.

Mon. 6.—I drank tea at A.O.'s in the afternoon. But I was shocked. The children who used to cling to me and to drink in every word had been at a boarding school! They had unlearned all religion and even seriousness; instead they had learned pride, vanity, putting on airs, and whatever would guard them against the knowledge and love of God. Methodist parents who would send your girls straight to hell, send them to a fashionable boarding school! ...

Sun. 12.—At 8 a.m. we had our usual assembly of plain, earnest people. But at 5 p.m. (who would imagine it?) we had almost all the upper-class people of the town, and "the power of the Lord was present to heal them" [Luke 5:17], so that few, I believe, were unaffected. The same power was present at the meeting of the children. Never in all my life was I so affected with any part of the Song of Solomon as while one of the girls was reciting it!

Mon. 13.—At 5 p.m. we had all the upper-class again, along with several clergymen. And again the Spirit applied the Word; for the moment even the rich seemed to be moved ...

Sat. 18.—I set out for Glasgow. You might have thought it was the middle of January rather than April. Snow covered the mountains on both sides and the air was bitter cold, so I preached indoors, both this evening and Sunday morning. But Sunday evening the crowd forced me to stand in the street. My text was, "What God has cleansed, don't call it common" [Acts 10:15]. That gave me the opportunity to attack their miserable bigotry regarding opinions and modes of worship. Many seemed to be convinced, but how long will the impression last? ...

Tues. MAY 5.—In the evening I preached in the new house at Arbroath (properly Aberbrotheck). There's truly a change in this town. It was proverbial for wickedness, Sabbath-breaking, cursing, swearing, drunkenness, and general contempt for religion. But now, no open wickedness, no oaths heard, no drunkenness seen in the streets, and many haven't just ceased from evil and learned to do good but are witnesses of the inward kingdom of God: "righteousness, peace, and joy in the Holy Spirit!" [Rom. 14:17] ...

Sat. 23.—I went on to Alnwick and preached in the town hall. What a difference between an English and a Scotch congregation! The Scotch judge themselves rather than the preacher, and their aim is not only to know but to love and obey ...

Tues. JUNE 2.—We rode to New Orygan in Teesdale. The people were very attentive, but I don't think they were deeply affected. From the top of the next big mountain, we could see Wardale. It's a lovely sight. The green, gently-rising meadows and fields on both sides of the little river, clear as crystal, were sprinkled with countless little houses, three out of four of which (if not nine out of ten) have sprung up since the Methodists came here. Since that time, the beasts have turned into humans and the wilderness into a fruitful field.

Since it was very cold, I considered it best to preach in the preaching-house, though many of the people couldn't get in. Just as I began praying, a man started screaming so loudly that my voice was almost completely drowned out. I asked him to hold himself in the best he could, and he did so fairly well. I then applied the Gospel account of the woman of Canaan [Matt 15:22ff.], and the people devoured every word.

Serious Joy (John Wesley's *Journal*)

Wed. 3.—I asked to speak with those who believed God had saved them from inward sin. I questioned them thoroughly, 20 in all: 10 men, eight women, and two children. I stood in doubt about one man and one or two women. The experience of the rest was clear, especially that of the children: Margaret Spencer, 14 years old, and Sally Blackburn, one year younger. But what a contrast there was between them! Sally Blackburn was completely calm; her appearance, her speech, her whole bearing was like she was 60 years old. Peggy was just the opposite: all fire; her eyes sparkled; all her features spoke; her face was all alive, and she looked like she was ready to fly to heaven! Lord, let neither of these live to dishonor you! Instead, take them unspotted to yourself! ...

Thur. 5[4].—At 5 p.m. I said farewell to this blessed people. I was a little surprised, looking on them carefully, to observe more beautiful faces than I'd ever seen before in a congregation, many of the children especially, 12 or 14 of whom, mainly boys, were fully in my view. But I grant that much more might be due to grace than nature—to the heaven within—than shone outwardly ...

In this part of Wardale, the people in general are employed in the lead mines ... At Christmas, two of the lay preachers in Allandale decided to visit Wardale. Before entering the town, they knelt down on the snow and earnestly sought the Lord that he would open the heart of some worthy person to receive them in their home. The first house they knocked at they were welcomed, and stayed there four days. Their word was with power, so that many were convicted and some converted to God. One of these exhorters was Jacob Rowell. They continued visiting at intervals all winter. By the beginning of summer some 20 spiritually alive, steady people had joined together. After that these gradually increased to 35 and maintained about that number for 10 years. Then there was a remarkable revival among them by means of Samuel Meggot, so that they increased to 80, but four years later they had dwindled to 63. From then on they increased again, and in August were 120 ...

Tues. 23.—About 11 a.m. I preached at Driffield. The sun was scorching hot, but I was screened well enough by a shade tree. In the evening I preached at Beverley, and on Wednesday the 24th in the new house at Hull—extremely well finished and, on the whole, one of the prettiest preaching-houses in England. The next evening we were quite crowded. Being told that many Antinomians were present, I preached on "God sent his own Son, that the righteousness of the law might be fulfilled in us who walk not after the flesh but after the Spirit" [Rom. 8:1] ...

Tues. AUGUST 4.—Our conference began. Generally, during our conferences, since I was talking from morning till night, I asked one of our brethren to preach in the morning. But now, having many things to say, I decided with God's help to preach mornings as well as evenings, and I found it made no difference at all: I was no more tired than with my usual work—that is, no more than if I had been sitting still in my study from morning to night ...

Fri. 14.—About noon, at the request of my old friend, Howel Harris, I preached at Travecka on "the narrow gate" [Matt. 7:14], and we found our hearts knit together as at the beginning. He said, "I have borne with these cocky and ignorant young men, so-called students, till I can't in good conscience bear it any longer. They preach barefaced reprobation[307] and overall antinomianism, so I've been forced to oppose them to the face, even in public assemblies." It's really no surprise that they preach that way. What better can we expect from novices with little understanding, little learning, and no experience?

After spending a very pleasant day or two at Brecknock, on Monday the 17th I preached in the castle at Carmarthen, and on Tuesday the 18th in the new preaching house at Haverfordwest, by far the neatest in Wales. The fellowship here has grown considerably, and not just numerically. After I preached on Wednesday evening, we had a meeting such as I've seldom known. Almost everyone spoke through tears, as well as they could, and with utter simplicity, and many appeared to know "the great salvation" [Heb. 2:3]: to love God with all their hearts ...

Fri. SEPTEMBER 4.—I went over to Westwood and spoke at length to the children, as I did on Saturday and Sunday. I found that there had been a fresh revival of God's work among them some months ago, but it soon ended, which I attribute mainly to their total

---

[307] Foreordination to damnation.

neglect of private prayer. Without this, no other means they enjoyed could benefit them.

Sun. 6.—I preached on the quay at Kingswood and near King's Square. To this day, field preaching is a cross I bear, but I know my mission and see no other way to "preach the gospel to every creature" ...

Wed. 30.—I began visiting members of the fellowship in Kingswood from house to house, going from west to east. For sure this will be a heavy cross, unpleasant to flesh and blood, but I've already seen how unspeakably useful it will be to many souls ...

Wed. OCTOBER 21.—At Witney I had free conversation with some of the most agreeable Christians I know. In the morning I met the select society, 21 total. All but one seemed to be rejoicing in the pure love of God. It wouldn't be surprising if their influence spreads to the whole fellowship or even the whole town ...

Thur. 29.—[*Back in London*] I made an accurate record of the Society, which had increased considerably over the year, and there's reason to believe that many of the members are now somewhat established and will no longer be driven to and fro like reeds shaken by the wind ...

Sun. NOVEMBER 1.—I served the Lord's Supper, as usual, to the fellowship and had at least 50 more partakers than at this time last year. In the evening, many hundreds had to leave since they couldn't squeeze into the preaching room. For those inside, it was a blessed season; God watered them with the dew of heaven. And so it was at 5 a.m. Even to part in this manner is sweet; but how much sweeter it will be to meet before the throne! ...

Tues. 3.—I went on to Colchester. The gathering in the evening was a little smaller than at Norwich. The next evening I made an accurate record of the fellowship; it had increased a little since last November, but most of them were ground down by poverty. They've been this way ever since I've known them, but now they are in greater need than ever through loss of business. Few of our fellowships are rich, but I don't know any in the kingdom as deplorably poor as this one.

Sat. 7.—I returned to London in the stagecoach with very intelligent and agreeable company.

Sun. 8.—In teaching on Psalm 15, I was led to speak more strongly and explicitly than I had for a long time on the universal love of God. Perhaps in the past, out of our desire to live peaceably with all people, we haven't declared in this respect the full counsel of God. But since Mr. Hill and his allies have cut us off from this hope and proclaimed implacable war, we see it is our calling to go straight ahead, declaring to all mankind that Christ tasted death for all "to cleanse them from all sin" [1 John 1:7].

Mon. 9.—I began to explain, mostly in the mornings as I did a few years ago, that summation of all the Holy Scriptures, 1 John ...

Wed. DECEMBER 2.—I preached in the new preaching-house in the parish of Bromley. In speaking individually to members of the fellowship, I was surprised at the openness and simplicity of the people. I wouldn't have expected to find people like this within 10 miles of London ...

Fri. 18.—I preached at Hertford. Last year the prospects there seemed fair, but God's servants quarreled among themselves till they destroyed the whole work, so there's no more fellowship; preaching has ceased, and those who had no religion are more hardened than ever. I never saw a more stupid and senseless mob than the one that flocked together in the evening; yet they softened little by little so that at last all were quiet and appeared attentive.

Mon. 21.—I visited the sick in various parts of town, but was surprised that there were so few. I hardly remember so healthy a winter in London. God orders all things so wisely that the poor man may not be destroyed by both hunger and sickness at the same time ...

Thur. 31.—Being greatly embarrassed by the necessities of the poor, we spread all our needs before God in solemn prayer, believing that he would sooner make windows in heaven than suffer his truth to fail ...

1773

Fri. JANUARY 8.—We observed this as a day of fasting and prayer, due to the general lack of trade and the scarcity of provisions. The following week I finished revising my letters, those I'd written and those I'd received. I can only make one remark: that for over 40 years, of all the friends who were once closest to me and later separated from me, they all took the initiative to separate. He left me, not I him [my emphasis]. And from both my letters and their own, the steps they took in doing so are clear and undeniable.

Mon. 18.—In my spare time this week I read *An Account of the European Settlements in America*. But parts of it I can't accept—I mean, regarding the ways of the Native Americans. If it is true that "they all nearly resemble each other," then from my personal knowledge of several American nations, I must judge a great part of this account to be pure, absolute romance. I suspect it to have been copied from some papers that I myself read before I embarked for America ...

Sun. MARCH 7.—In the evening I started out for Bristol and, after spending a few days there, on Monday the 15th went to Stroud and on Tuesday the 16th to Worcester. Here I checked into the "intelligence sent to Mr. Hill from Worcester (as he says in his heated book) of the shocking behavior of some that professed to be perfect." It was supposed that that intelligence came to Mr. Skinner, who loves me and all connected with me. The truth is, a member of the fellowship, after leaving it, behaved extremely badly, but none who professed to love God with all their heart have done anything contrary to that profession ...

Tues. APRIL 13.—As I entered Eyre-court, the street was full of people who yelled loudly as we passed through the market-place. I preached in the open air to a crowd of people, all mannerly and most of them serious. This town has seen a great awakening lately, and many of the most notorious and hopeless sinners have changed entirely and are happy witnesses to the gospel salvation ...

Wed. 21.— ... At Ballihac Ferry, on Tuesday, a band of sailors ran down to the shore to see the stagecoach put into the boat. I was walking a little way from them when I heard them cry out, "Avast! Avast! The coach has turned over into the river!" I thought, "I'm glad my bags are still on shore so my papers aren't ruined." In less than half an hour they fished up the stagecoach and got it safely onto the boat. Since it couldn't hold us all, I got in, leaving the horses to come later. At 3:30 I came to Passage. Finding no post-stage was available, and having no time to spare, I walked the six or seven miles to Waterford and began preaching without delay on "My yoke is easy and my burden is light" [Matt. 11:30] ...

Sun. 25.—As the mayor of Waterford sent word allowing me to preach in the bowling-green, I went there that evening. A huge crowd quickly gathered. My text was, "I saw the dead, small and great, stand before God" [Rev. 20:12]. A few tried to make a disturbance but were unsuccessful; most of the assembly was deeply attentive. But as I was reaching my conclusion, some of the Catholics set to work. They knocked down John Christian and two or three others who tried to quiet them down, and then began to roar like waves crashing on the seashore, but they could go just so far and no further. Some gentlemen standing close to me rushed into their midst, gave heavy blows, seized the ringleader, and turned him over to the constable, and one of them conducted me home. As a result, few received any hurt except the rioters themselves, which I trust will make them more peaceable in the future ...

Fri. 30.—We had a solemn watch-night at Cork. I believe the confidence of many was shaken while I was driving home **"Though I have all faith so as to remove mountains and have not love, I am nothing" [1 Cor. 13:2]. This is a hard saying, but must be insisted on, especially among the people called Methodists. Otherwise, how many of them will build on the sand, on an unloving, unholy faith!** [my emphasis] ...

Thur. MAY 13.—We passed through very dreary country to Galway where, at the recent survey, there were 20,000 Catholics and 500 Protestants. But which of them are Christians, have the mind that was in Christ, and walk as he walked? And without this, what matter does it make whether they are called Catholics or Protestants? At 6 p.m. I preached in the courthouse to a large assembly, who all behaved well ...

Sun. 30 (Whitsunday [Pentecost]).—I dined at Mr. S.'s, a sensible, friendly man. Five clergymen were there besides me, all who attended my preaching every evening. You might have imagined, from the friendliness of the clergy, plus the goodwill of both the bishop and the dean,[308] that the fellowship would increase

---

[308] The head of a cathedral church.

rapidly here. But in fact it doesn't increase at all; it's right where it was two years ago, so little does the favor of man advance the work of God! ...

Wed. JUNE 2.—I said goodbye to the pleasant city of Derry and its congenial people. When we came to the foot of the mountain beyond Dangevan, the horses refused to pull my buggy any farther, so I walked on seven or eight miles, ordering them to follow me to Cookstown ...

Sun. 6 (Trinity Sunday)—At 9 a.m. I explained the great text of St. John[309] to a very large audience. At church the choir anthem was "Praise the Lord, O my soul!" which I don't think I've heard in 50 years, and it was sung in such a way as would have graced any of our English cathedrals. In the evening, the assembly was the largest I've seen in Ulster. And I believe, at least for now, that all were convinced that nothing will prevail without humble, gentle, patient love ...

Sun. 13.—My heart swelled as I preached at 9 a.m. The church service began at 11:30. The rector's assistant read prayers exceptionally well, and the rector himself preached with unusual earnestness. But what I admired most was: 1. the church's cleanliness, equal to any I've seen in England; 2. the serious behavior of the whole congregation; and 3. the excellent singing by 40 or 50 voices, half men and half women. I've heard nothing like this in any church since I came to Ireland.

The rector invited me to dinner, and I spent a pleasant hour with him and his curate. The assembly at 6 p.m. was very large and very serious. We ended the day with the fellowships, coming from all around, and great was our rejoicing. Many were filled with consolation and many weak hands were strengthened ...

Tues. 15.— ... When I came to Belfast, the owner of almost the whole country around came here to give his tenants new leases. But when the tenants came, they found that two merchants of the town had already leased the farms, so that large numbers of them with their wives and children were cast out into the world. No wonder that their lives then were bitter and that they acted as they did. It's rather

---

[309] Likely John 3:16.

a wonder that they didn't go farther than they did. And if they had, who would have been most at fault? Those without home, without money, without food for themselves and their families, or those who drove them to this extremity? ...

Sat. JULY 3.—In Dublin, I sent a message to the commanding officer, asking permission to preach in the barracks, but he replied that "he wouldn't allow innovations," no. Whoredom, drunkenness, cursing and swearing, however, yes, forever!

Mon. 5.—About 11 a.m. we crossed Dublin-bar, and got to Holylake the next afternoon. This was the first night I ever lay awake in my life, though my mind and body were at ease. I believe few can say this: In 70 years I never lost one night's sleep![310] ...

Wed. 21.—We had our quarterly meeting at London, at which I was surprised to find that our income doesn't yet equal our expense. Once again, we were 200 pounds short. My private account is even worse. I've worked as much as many writers, but all my labor has earned me, in 70 years, a debt of 500 or 600 pounds.[311]

Sun. 25.—This was a day of strong consolation, especially at Spitalfields. At 5 p.m. I preached in Moorfields to (we think) the largest congregation that ever assembled there. But my voice was strengthened so that those who were farthest away could hear perfectly well. So the season for field-preaching isn't over yet; and it can't be while so many are in their sins and in their blood.

Tues. AUGUST 3.—Our conference began. I preached mornings as well as evenings, but it was the same as if I'd only preached once a day ...

Sun. 23[22].—I preached at St. Agnes Church (a town), at 8 a.m.; about 1 p.m. at Redruth; and at 5 p.m. in the amphitheater at Gwenap. The people filled both the amphitheater and the ground around it to quite a distance. Supposing the space to be 80 yards square, and to hold five persons in a square yard, there must be over 32,000 people—the largest assembly I ever preached to. Yet I found upon asking that everyone was able to hear, even to the fringes of the

---

[310] Wesley forgets an instance in his youth where he stayed awake all night.
[311] 200 pounds = $47,000; 500 pounds = $118,000; 600 pounds = $141,000 in 2020 USD.

gathering! Perhaps this is the first time that a man of 70 has been heard by 30,000 people at once! ...

Fri. SEPTEMBER 3.—I went over to Kingswood and investigated the basis for the serious charges that had been confidently asserted against the management there. One item was true, and only one, and this fault has now been remedied.

On Saturday September the 4th Ralph Mather talked with three of the students ... These freely confessed their besetting sins and seemed greatly humbled. At 5 p.m., he assembled all the children in the school. During his appeals and admonishments, several were affected. Afterwards, two more were broken and became deeply distressed. One of them, James Whitestone, in less than half an hour, found a clear sense of the love of God. About 7 p.m., the boys in the school came downstairs, and Mr. Mather asked, "Who of you will serve God?" They all seemed thunderstruck, and 10 or 12 fell to their knees. Mr. Mather prayed, then James Whitestone. Immediately one or more cried out, which brought the other boys back in. They were stricken more and more until about 30 were kneeling and praying at the same time. Within a half-hour, 10 of them knew they were accepted in the Beloved. Several more were brought to new birth, and all the children except for three or four were affected to some degree.

Sun. 5.—I questioned 16 of them who asked to partake of the Lord's Supper. Nine or ten had a clear sense of the pardoning love of God. The others were fully determined not to rest till they could witness the same confession.

Eighteen of the children since that time have met in three small groups, besides 12 who met in a trial group. These were remarkable for their love for each other as well as for steady seriousness. They met every day, beside which all the children met in small groups ...

Fri. 10.—I went over to Kingswood and investigated the present status of the children. I found that some of them were walking closely with God; some were not and were in heaviness. In the evening I heard that they were going to pray by themselves in the school, so I went downstairs but, not wanting to disturb them, I stood at the window. Two or three went in first, then more and more till over 30 gathered. Never before or since have I seen such a sight:

Three or four stood and stared as if scared; the rest were all on their knees, pouring out their souls before God in an indescribable way. At times one, sometimes more, prayed aloud, and sometimes a cry went up from them all, till five or six of them who had been in doubt saw the clear light of God's countenance.

Sun. 12.—Four of Miss Owen's children asked permission to partake of the Lord's Supper. I talked with them individually and found that they were still rejoicing in the love of God. And they confirmed the report that "there was only one of their whole number who was not affected on Monday, but all the rest could say with confidence, 'Lord, you know that I love you.'" I suppose that such a divine visitation of children hasn't been known in England in a hundred years! In a marvelous manner, "Out of the mouth of babes and sucklings God has perfected praise!" [Psa. 8:2; Matt. 21:16].

VOLUME 4: 1773-1790

[This book covers the last phase of John Wesley's life and career. He has become immensely popular, so that wherever he goes, people flock to see and hear him—people of all denominations and even of no religious persuasion. He, like Billy Graham of the 20th century, was a phenomenon of his age. Amazingly, he continued to preach until the last weeks of his long life, although having more and more physical ailments, which he details. His brother Charles dies, and John alone is the undisputed head of the Methodist movement. Foreseeing his death, he attempts to establish an organization that will carry on his purposes and ideals after him.]

Mon., SEPTEMBER 13. Still with a cold, I was hardly able to speak. In the evening I was much worse, my palate and throat being very inflamed; still, I preached the best I could. But then I couldn't keep going. I couldn't swallow either liquids or solids, and my windpipe seemed almost stopped up. I lay down at my regular time, but my nose was so runny that I didn't sleep a minute till nearly 3 a.m. I got better over the next nine days.

Fri. 17.—I went to Kingswood and found several of the children still alive to God.

Sat. 18.—I gave them a short, encouraging talk which made me tired but didn't hurt me.

Sun. 19.—I thought I'd be able to speak to the congregation, which I did for half an hour, but afterwards felt pain alternating in my left side and in my shoulder, just as I did at Canterbury 20 years before. In the morning I could hardly lift my hand to my head, but after electricity was applied I was much better, so that I preached fairly easily in the evening, and the next evening read the letters, though my voice was weak. From this point on I slowly recovered both my voice and my strength, and on Sunday the 26th preached without any trouble ...

Wed. OCTOBER 7.—Taking a buggy at 2 a.m., I got to London easily in the evening. The rest of the week I checked my financial accounts the best I could. Some confusion had arisen from the sudden death of my bookkeeper, but it was less than might have been expected ...

Mon. NOVEMBER 1.—I set out for Norfolk and came to Lynn while the assembly was still waiting for me. Once there was a prospect of doing much good here, but it had almost vanished. Calvinism breaking in on them had torn the infant fellowship in pieces. I did all I could to heal the breach, both in public and in private, and having recovered a few persons, I left them in peace and went on to Norwich on Wednesday ...

Mon. 8.—I found that the fellowship at Lakenheath had entirely disappeared. I joined them together once more, and they seriously promised to keep together. If they do, I'll try to see them again; if not, I have better work ...

Sat. DECEMBER 25, and the following days, we had many happy occasions of celebrating the solemn feast-days according to their original purpose. We ended the year with a fast-day, closing with a solemn watch-night.

1774

Tues. JANUARY 12 [11].—I began at the east end of London to visit the fellowship from house to house. I don't know any part of the pastoral office of greater importance than this. But it is so grievous to flesh and blood that I can prevail on few to undertake it, even of our preachers ...

Tues. MARCH 8.—When I arrived in Chippenham, I was told that the floods had made the road by Marshfield impassable. So I went around by Bath and came to Bristol just as brother Charles was leading out with the hymn, and in time to beseech a crowded audience "not to receive the grace of God in vain" [cf. 1 Cor. 15:10] ...

Sat. 19.—At Wednesbury ... I was forced by the crowd of people to preach outdoors in the evening. I strongly urged on them the apostle's words, "How shall we escape if we neglect so great a salvation?" [Heb. 2:3]. If we don't go on to perfection, how shall we escape lukewarmness, antinomianism, hellfire? ...

Tues. 22.—At 5 a.m. I explained that important truth, that God tests us at every moment, weighs all our thoughts, words, and actions, and is pleased or displeased with us according to our works. I see more and more clearly that there's a great gulf between us and all those who, by denying this, sap the very foundation of both inward and outward holiness ...

Sun. APRIL 17.—In Halifax, while at dinner with Dr. Leigh, someone came from Huddersfield to tell me that the vicar was willing for me to preach in the church. Dr. Leigh loaned me his servant and his horse, so I set out immediately and, riding fast, walked into the church while the vicar was reading prayers. It was good that the people had no notice of my preaching till I came into the town. They quickly filled the church. I didn't spare them, but rather fully delivered my own soul.

Mon. 18.—The minister of Heptonstall sent me word that I was welcome to preach in his church. With difficulty we got up the steep mountain, and once at the top, the wind almost blew us away. But the church was filled, not merely with curious, but with serious listeners. Nobody but these would have faced so furious a storm ...

Sun. MAY 1.—At Birstal I preached at 8 a.m. on that clever device of Satan, to destroy the whole religion of the heart by telling people "Not to regard the body, or feelings, but to live by naked faith"—that is, in plain terms, not to regard either love, joy, peace, or any other fruit of the Spirit, not to regard whether they do or don't feel these, whether their souls are in a heavenly or hellish condition! ...

Sun. 15.—[*In Glasgow*] My spirit was moved within me by the sermons I heard, both morning and afternoon. They contained much truth, but were no more likely to awaken one soul than an Italian opera. In the evening a crowd of people assembled on the Green, to whom I earnestly applied these words, "Though I have all knowledge, though I have all faith, though I give all my goods to feed the poor, etc., and have not love, I am nothing" [1 Cor. 13:2] ...

Sat. 21.—I returned to Perth and preached in the evening to a large gathering, but couldn't find the way to their hearts. The people here generally are so wise that they don't need more knowledge and are so good that they don't need more religion! Who can warn those who are brimful of wisdom and goodness to flee from the wrath to come? ...

VOLUME 4: 1773-1790

Sun. JUNE 12.—[*At Weardale.*] The rain drove us into the house, both morning and afternoon. Afterwards I met the poor remnants of the select society. But neither of my two lovely children, Peggy Spence or Sally Blackburn, were there. In fact there had been a whole row like them before, but three-fourths of them were now as careless as ever. In the evening I sent for Peggy and Sally. Peggy came, and I found she had pretty much regained her ground, walking in the light, and having a lively hope of recovering all that she had lost. Sally flatly refused to come and then ran out of doors. At length being found, after a flood of tears, she was brought back almost by force. But I couldn't get a single glance and hardly one word out of her. She seemed to have no hope left. Yet she isn't out of God's reach ...

Mon. 20.—About 9 a.m. I set out for Horsley with Mr. Hopper and Mr. Smith. I took Mrs. Smith and her two little girls in the buggy with me. About two miles out of town, on the brow of the hill, both horses suddenly bolted due to no visible cause and flew down the hill like an arrow. In a minute, John fell off the coach-box. The horses kept going full speed, sometimes to the edge of the ditch on the right, sometimes on the left. A cart passed by them and they just missed it. A narrow bridge was at the foot of the hill, and they ran straight through the middle of it. They ran up the next hill at the same speed, many people coming toward us but getting out of the way. Near the top of the hill was a gate that led into a farmer's yard. It was open. They turned abruptly and ran through it without touching either the gate on one side or the post on the other. I thought, "Surely the gate on the other side of the yard, which is shut, will stop them, but they burst through it as if it were a cobweb and galloped on through the field of grain. The little girls cried, "Grandaddy, save us!" I told them, "Nothing will hurt you; don't be afraid"—feeling no more fear or anxiety (bless God!) than if I had been sitting in my study. The horses ran on till they came to the edge of a steep bank. Just then Mr. Smith, who hadn't caught up with us till then, galloped in between us and the bank. The horses stopped in a moment. If they'd gone on just a little bit, he and we must have gone down together!

I am persuaded that both evil and good angels had a large share in this business—how large, we don't now know, but we'll know in the hereafter ...

Tues. 28.—This is my birthday, the first day of my 72nd year. I was pondering how it is that I'm just as strong as I was 30 years ago. My sight is somewhat better now and my nerves firmer than they were then. How is it that I have none of the infirmities of old age and have lost several I had in my youth? The great cause is the good pleasure of God, who does whatever pleases him. The chief means are: 1. my constantly rising at 4 a.m. for about 50 years; 2. my generally preaching at 5 a.m., one of the most healthy exercises in the world; and 3. my never traveling, by sea or land, less than 4500 miles in a year ...

Mon. JULY 25.—I went on to Sheffield and on Tuesday met the select society, but it had shrunk from 60 to 20, and only half of these kept all they once received. **What a grave error it is to think that those who are saved from sin can't lose what they've gained! It's a miracle if they don't, seeing all earth and hell are so enraged against them, while meantime so very few, even of the children of God, skillfully seek to strengthen their hands** [my emphasis]...

Sat. AUGUST 6.—The conference began and ended in love. It was my full employment Tuesday, Wednesday, and Thursday, and we observed Friday the 12th as a day of fasting and prayer for the success of the gospel ...

Sun. 21.—At 9 a.m. I began the service at St. Daniel's, finishing a little before 12:00. It was a good time. "The power of the Lord was unusually present" [Luke 5:17], both to wound and to heal. Many were compelled to cry out, while others were filled with speechless awe and silent love ...

Thur. 25.—At 11 a.m. I preached within the walls of the old church at the Haye. Here and everywhere I heard the same account of what took place at _____. All who were there told me that the jumpers began in the court and later in the house. Some of them, both men and women, leaped up many times, several feet high, clapping their hands loudly, shaking their heads, distorting their features, and throwing their arms and legs into all kinds of postures. They sang, roared, shouted, and screamed with all their might, terrorizing those around them. One gentlewoman told me she hadn't been herself since and didn't know if she ever would. Meantime, the owner of the house was extremely delighted and said, "Now the power of God has truly come!"[312] ...

Sat. SEPTEMBER 3.—We had the quarterly meeting at Redruth. This is often a dull, heavy meeting, but today it was so lively that we hardly knew how to end it. About 6 p.m. I preached at Treverga, and applied specifically to the Methodists: "What do you do more than others?" [Matt. 5:47]. One cried out, "Damnable doctrine!" True! It condemns all who hear and do not obey it ...

Mon. OCTOBER 3—and on Tuesday and Wednesday, I examined the fellowship.

Thur. 6.—**I met those of our Society who had votes in the upcoming election and advised them 1. to vote, without payment or reward, for the person they believed most worthy; 2. to speak no evil of the person they voted against; and 3. to take care that their spirits weren't embittered against those who voted on the other side** [my emphasis] ...

Sun. 9.—In the evening we had a solemn occasion to renew our covenant with God. This is a means of grace that I'm surprised has been so little used either in Catholic or Protestant churches ...

Wed. 12.—About noon I preached at Langton ... to a large and deeply serious gathering. There is also a small [Methodist] fellowship here, but I didn't find any among them who knew in whom they had believed. In the evening I preached in a meadow near Swanage to a still larger gathering, and here at last I found three or four persons, all of the same family, who seemed to really enjoy the faith of the gospel. Few others of the fellowship (numbering between 30 and 40) appeared to be convicted of sin. I fear the preachers have been more concerned with pleasing than with awakening, or there would have been a deeper work ...

Thur. 13.—I set out early and reached Gosport (72 miles) not long after 6 a.m. Finding a boat ready, I crossed over [to the Isle of Purbeck] and went straight to the preaching-room. It was rather full, so I began without delay and drove home our Lord's words (one of

---

[312] Wesley is skeptical but not quick to outright condemn such phenomena.

my favorite subjects): "My yoke is easy and my burden is light" [Matt. 11:30] ...

Fri. NOVEMBER 5.—In the afternoon, John Downes, who had preached with us many years, was saying, "I feel such a love to the people at West Street that I would be content to die with them. I'm not feeling very well, but I must be with them this evening." He went there and began preaching on "Come to me, you who are weary and heavy laden" [Matt. 11:28]. After speaking 10 or 12 minutes, he sank down and said no more till his spirit returned to God ...

Tues. 8[9].—I baptized two young women, one of whom found a deep sense of the presence of God in his ordinance, and the other received a full assurance of his pardoning love, being filled with joy unspeakable ...

Thur. 16[17].— ... On Friday evening I met the Norwich fellowship and told them plainly that I was determined to have a regulated fellowship or none at all. I then read the rules and asked everyone to consider whether he or she was willing to abide by them or not—in particular, those regarding meeting their class every week, unless prevented by distance or sickness (the only exceptions I could allow), and being constant at church and communion. I asked those who were willing to abide by these rules to meet me the next night, and the rest to stay away. The next night by far the most were there, on whom I enforced the same thing.

Sun. 20.—I spoke to every leader concerning all those under his or her care, and expelled everyone he or she couldn't recommend to me. After this was done, out of 240 members, 174 remained, and these rules shall be enforced if only 50 remain in the fellowship ...

Fri. 25.—I set out between 8 and 9 a.m. in a one-horse buggy, the wind being quite strong and cold. There was a lot of snow on the ground, and much more fell as we crept along over the banks of the marsh. Honest Mr. Tubbs insisted on walking and leading the horse through water and mud above his knees, smiling and saying, "We marsh-men don't mind a little dirt." After we had gone about four miles, the road wouldn't let a buggy go through. So I borrowed a horse and rode forward, but not far, since the ground was all under water. Therefore I then rented a boat, about twice a big as a kneading trough, myself at one end and a boy at the other, who paddled me safely to Erith. There Miss L____ waited for me with another open carriage, which brought me to St. Ives ...

Mon. DECEMBER 12.—I opened the new preaching-house at Sevenoaks [by preaching its first sermon].

Sun. 25.—During the 12 festival days we had the Lord's Supper daily, emblematic of the primitive church. May we follow them in all things, as they were of Christ!

1775

Sun. JANUARY 1.—We had a larger assembly at the renewal of the covenant than we have had for many years, and I don't know that we ever had a greater blessing. Afterwards many wanted to give thanks, either for a sense of pardon, for full salvation, or for a fresh manifestation of his grace, healing all their backslidings ...

Sun. 29.—Finding that many were very downhearted due to the threatening appearance of public affairs, I strongly drove home our Lord's words, "Why are you afraid, O you of little faith?" [Matt. 8:26]. And truly God spoke through his Word. Many were ashamed of their unbelieving fears, and many were enabled to "be anxious about nothing," but simply to make all their "requests known to God with thanksgiving" [Phil. 4:6].

Sun. FEBRUARY 5.—I saw a glorious example of the power of faith. Thomas Vokins, a man of sorrowful spirit, always used to hang his head down like a bulrush, but a few days ago, as he was dying without hope, God broke in on his soul, and since that time he has been victorious over pain and death and rejoicing with joy full of glory ...

Fri. MARCH 17.—In the evening, though it was cold, I had to preach outdoors at Newcastle. One clown tried hard to interrupt me, but as he was bawling, with his mouth wide open, some mischievous boys gave him such a mouthful of dirt that it quite satisfied him ...

On Sunday, APRIL 2, we landed at Dunlary ... On Monday and Tuesday I examined the fellowship. Two years ago there were 376 persons, and I found 376 still, not one more or less, but I found more peace and love among them than I had for many years ...

Sun. 9.—The good old dean of St. Patrick's invited me up within the rails to assist him at the Lord's Supper. This also was a

Serious Joy (John Wesley's *Journal*)

means of removing much prejudice from those who were zealous for the Church ...

Sat. MAY 13.—I preached to a large assembly of Catholics and Protestants in the yard of the customs house, where many could hear inside as well as outside ...

Mon. 22.—I spent two or three hours in one of the loveliest places and with one of the loveliest families in the kingdom ... How willingly I could have accepted the invitation to "spend a few days here"! But no, for now, I "must be about my Father's business" [Luke 2:49]; but I trust to meet them in a still lovelier place ...

Wed. 31.—We rattled on over a miserable road as far as wheels could go, then rode horseback to Listeen. After dinner we hurried to Dargbridge and found a large assembly waiting. They all seemed to be deeply serious. In fact, there is a wonderful reformation spreading throughout this whole country for several miles around. Outward wickedness has disappeared and many, young and old, witness that the kingdom of God is within them ...

Tues. JUNE 6.—The bishop [at New-Buildings] invited me to dinner and told me, "I know you don't like our hours, so I'll order dinner to be on the table between 2 and 3 o'clock." We had a piece of boiled beef and an English pudding. He shows true good breeding. He is entirely easy and unpretentious in his whole behavior, exemplary in all parts of public worship, and plentiful in good works ...

Trinity Sunday. 11.—I preached at 9 a.m. on "God created man in his own image" [Gen. 1:27], and in the evening to a huge assembly, but I couldn't find the way to their hearts ...

Sat. 17.—I was persuaded to send for Dr. Laws, a sensible and skilful physician. He told me that I had a high fever and should stay in bed, but I told him I couldn't do that, since I had appointments to preach at several places and must preach as long as I could speak. He then prescribed a cooling drink with a grain or two of camphor, since my nerves were completely agitated. I took these with me to Tandragee, but when I got there, I was unable to preach, my understanding confused, and my strength gone. Yet I breathed freely and wasn't thirsty, nor did I have any pain from head to foot ...

VOLUME 4: 1773-1790

On the night of Thursday the 22nd, Joseph Bradford came to me with a cup and said, "Sir, you must take this." I thought, "I will if I can swallow, to please him; for it will neither hurt me nor help me." Immediately it set me to vomiting, my heart and pulse began to beat again, and from that hour the extreme symptoms diminished ... On Sunday I came downstairs and sat in the parlor for several hours. On Monday I walked in front of the house. On Tuesday I took some air in the buggy, and on Wednesday, trusting in God, to the astonishment of my friends, I set out for Dublin ...

Tues. JULY 4.—[*At James-Town, near Dublin*] Finding myself a little stronger, I preached for the first time and believe most could hear. I preached on Thursday again, and my voice was clear, though weak. So on Sunday I ventured to preach twice and found no weariness at all.

Mon. 10.—I began my regular routine of preaching morning and evening ...

Wed. 26.—I found one remnant of my illness: My hand shook so that I could hardly write my name, but after electricity was applied, and after driving four or five hours over very rugged, broken pavement, my complaint was gone—my hand was as steady as when I was 10 years old ...

Thur. 27.—I went on to Miss Bosanquet's and prepared for the conference. How willingly I could spend the rest of a busy life in this delightful retreat! But,

> Man was not born in shades to lie!

Up and be doing! Labor on till death

> signs a requiem to the parting soul. ...

Tues. AUGUST 1.—Our conference began. Having received several letters suggesting that many of the preachers were unqualified for the work, without sufficient grace or gifts for it, I decided to examine this serious charge carefully. So I read these letters to the whole conference and begged everyone to freely name and give his reasons about anyone he objected to. The objections

Serious Joy (John Wesley's *Journal*)

were considered at length; committees were appointed for two or three difficult cases; and as a result, we were all fully convinced that the charges made were without foundation, that God has really sent these workers into his vineyard, and that he has qualified them for the work. As a result, we were all more closely united than we have been for many years.

Fri. 4.—I preached at Bradford where the people are all alive. Many here have experienced the great salvation, and their zeal has been a general blessing. Indeed, I always observe this: Whenever a work of sanctification breaks out, the whole work of God prospers. Some are convicted of sin, others justified, and all stirred up to a greater earnestness for salvation …

Sun. 6.— … About this time I received a remarkable letter from one of our preachers at West Bromwick, near Wednesbury, the substance of which follows:

August 16, 1775.

About three weeks ago, someone came and told me that Martha Wood of Darlaston was dying and very much wanted to see me. When I entered the house, which with everything in it was hardly worth five pounds,[313] I found in that poor cottage a jewel such as my eyes had never seen before. Her eyes sparkled with joy and her heart danced like David before the ark. In truth, she seemed to be in the outskirts of heaven, upon the boundaries of glory.

She took hold of my hand and said, "I'm glad to see you; you're my father in Christ. It's been 20 years since I first heard you. You preached on the text, 'Now you have sorrow, but I will see you again, and your heart will rejoice, and no one will take away your joy' [John 16:22]. In that hour God broke into my soul, delivered me from all sorrow, and filled my heart with joy. And blessed be his name, I've never lost it from that hour to this." …

She began to preach with divine power to all who stood near her. She knew everyone, and if anyone entered the room whom she knew to be careless about religion, she called them by name and urged them to seek the Lord while he may be found. At the end she cried out, "I see the heavens opened! I see Abraham, Isaac, and Jacob, with numbers of the heavenly host, coming nearer and nearer. Here they've

---

[313] About $1800 in 2020 USD.

come!" At that word, her soul took its flight to join the heavenly host. We looked for her like Elisha looked for Elijah, and I trust that some of us have caught her mantle ...

Having finished my business in Bristol, on Wednesday the 30th I set out at 3 a.m., and at noon preached in the great Presbyterian meeting-house in Taunton, and indeed with such freedom and openness of spirit as I didn't expect in such a brilliant congregation ...

Sun. SEPTEMBER 3.—I preached at 8 a.m. in St. Agnes' Church on "Believe on the Lord Jesus Christ, and thou shalt be saved" [Acts 16:31]. A young woman followed me into the house, weeping bitterly and crying out, "I've got to have Christ; I will have Christ. Give me Christ, or I'll die!" Two or three of us claimed the promise on her behalf. She was soon filled with joy unspeakable and burst out, "Oh, now let me die! Let me go to him now! How can I bear to stay here any longer?" We left her full of that peace that passes all understanding. About 11 a.m. I preached at Redruth and about 5 p.m. in the amphitheater at Gwenap ...

Tues. 12.— ... On Tuesday the 19th I preached at Frome and on Wednesday at Pensford. From there I went on to the lovely family at Publow, an example for all the boarding schools in England. Everything fit for a Christian to learn is taught here, but nothing unworthy of the Christian character. I gave a short exhortation to the children, which they received eagerly. Many of them have the fear of God and some of them enjoy his love.

Thur. 21.—At the earnest request of the prisoner who was to die the next day and who was willing to do so since, after a deep wrestling of his soul, he had found peace with God, I preached at Newgate to him and a crowded audience, many of whom felt God was there ...

Fri. 29.—We observed this as a fast-day, meeting at 5 and 9 a.m., then again at 1 p.m. and in the evening, and many found a strong hope that God will still be entreated for a guilty land ...

Tues. OCTOBER 17.—In the evening I preached in the large room at the poorhouse in Ramsbury. The people flocked together from all around, and God gave us his blessing ...

Sat. NOVEMBER 11.—I made some additions to my "Calm Address to Our American Colonies." Does anyone need to ask my motive for writing this? Let him just look around. England is in flames!—flames of ill will and rage against the king and almost all in authority under him. I labor to put out this flame. Ought not every true patriot do the same? ...

Mon. 27.—[*Wesley writes a strong letter stating his belief that the Americans are not being abused by the king or British authorities, including in matters of taxation. Only after the Revolution did he accept the break-away as legitimate. He remained a staunch supporter of the king all his life.*]

Wed. DECEMBER 6.—About 1 a.m. I heard a shrill voice in the street, calling and asking me to come to Mr. _____. Going immediately, I found him sick and in a great agony of mind. He fully believed he was at the point of death, nor could any arguments convince him otherwise. We cried to him who has all power in heaven and earth and who keeps the keys of life and death. Mr. _____ suddenly sat up in bed and said with a loud voice, "I won't die, but live!" ....

1776

Mon. JANUARY 1.—About 1800 of us met together in London in order to renew our covenant with God and it was, as usual, a very solemn occasion.

Tues. 2.—I came to Bristol just in time not to see but to bury my brother-in-law, poor Mr. Hall, who died on Wednesday morning, I trust in peace, for God had given him deep repentance. In my 70 years I haven't seen another such manifestation of divine mercy, considering how low he had fallen, and from what a height of holiness! I had planned to see him in the morning, but he didn't stay for my coming. It's enough if, after all his wanderings, we meet again in Abraham's bosom ...

Sun. 14.—In all my free hours during this and the following week, I tried to finish my *Concise History of England.* I'm aware that some will be offended, since in many places I'm unique, especially with regard to those characters greatly wronged, Richard the Third and Mary Queen of Scots. But I must speak my mind, although still waiting for and willing to receive better information.

Sun. 28.—I was asked to preach a charity sermon in Allhallows Church, Lombard Street. In the year 1735, over 40 years ago, I preached in this church at the request of the churchwardens to a large assembly who came, like me, intending to hear Dr. Heylin. That was the first time, having no notes with me, that I preached extemporaneously.

Wed. FEBRUARY 14.—I preached at Shoreham. How the last has become first! No fellowship in the county grows as fast as this, either in grace or number. The main instrument of this glorious work is Miss Perronet, a burning and shining light.

Fri. 23.—I skimmed through Dr. Bolt's *Considerations on the Affairs of India.* Was there ever such a sad picture? How are the mighty fallen! The great Mogul, Emperor of Indostan, one of the mightiest rulers on earth, has become a poor, little, impotent slave to a Company of Merchants! His large, flourishing empire is broken in pieces and covered with fraud, oppression, and misery. And we might even call the myriads who have been murdered happy compared with those who still groan under the iron yoke! Will you not repay for these things, O Lord? …

Sat. MARCH 23.—I had been informed that Mr. Weston, the minister of Campden, was willing for me to preach in his church, but before I arrived he'd changed his mind. However, the vicar of Pebworth was not a weathervane, so I preached in his church on Sunday the 24th, morning and evening, and I believe not in vain …

Wed. APRIL 3.—Having climbed over the mountains, I preached at the New Mills in Derbyshire. The people here are quite earnest and simple, there being no public worship in town except at our chapel, so they go straight forward, knowing nothing of various opinions and caring for nothing but to be Bible Christians …

Fri. 12.—I visited a man, formerly a captain, now a dying sinner. His eyes spoke the agony of his soul; his tongue had nearly forgotten its purpose. With great effort he could barely say, "I … want … Jesus … Christ!" The next day he couldn't say a word, but if he couldn't speak, God could hear …

Tues. 16.—I preached about noon at Chowbent, once the roughest place in the surrounding area. But not the least trace of that remains; such is the fruit of the genuine gospel.

In the afternoon, as we were considering what we would do, since the rain didn't let us meet outdoors, someone asked the vicar for use of the church, and he readily agreed. I began reading at 5:30. The church was crowded—pews, aisles, and galleries—such as I believe it hadn't been for the past 100 years. And God bore witness to his Word ...

Tues. 23.—I preached in the press-yard at Rothwell and have seldom seen an assembly so moved. I then spoke one-by-one to the class of children and found every one of them rejoicing in the love of God. It's remarkable that this work of God among them has broken out all at once. They have all been justified, and one clearly sanctified, within the last six weeks ...

Mon. 29.—I didn't see anyone inattentive at Clough in the evening. What has God wrought since Mr. Grimshaw and I were seized by a furious mob near this place and kept prisoners for some hours! The sons of him who headed that mob now gladly receive what we say ...

Fri. MAY 10.— ... I returned to Glasgow and on Sunday the 12th went in the morning to the High Kirk (to show I was not a bigot) and in the afternoon to the Church of England chapel. The decency of behavior here surprises me more and more. I know nothing like it in these kingdoms except among the Methodists ...

Mon. 20.—About noon I preached at the New Mills, nine miles from Bamff, to a large audience of plain, simple people. As we rode in the afternoon, the heat overcame me, so I was weary and faint before we reached Keith. But I no sooner stood up in the market-place than I forgot my weariness because of the seriousness and attentiveness of the whole gathering, though it was as large as that at Bamff. Mr. Gordon, the parish minister, invited me to supper and told me his kirk was at my disposal. A little fellowship has already formed here and seems likely to increase. But they are in danger of losing their preaching-house, the owner having decided to sell it. So—who would have thought it?—I bought an estate consisting of two houses, a yard, a garden, with three acres of good land. But he told me flatly, "Sir, I'll take no less for it than 16 pounds, 10 shillings,[314] to be paid part now, part at Michaelmas, and the rest next May." ...

Thur. 23.—I read Mr. Pennant's *Journey through Scotland.* He's a lively as well as a judicious writer—judicious, I mean, in most respects. But I can't give up to all the Deists in Great Britain the existence of witchcraft, till I give up the credibility of all history, sacred and profane. At the present I not only have just as strong, but even stronger proofs of this, from eye- and ear-witnesses, than I have of murder, so I can't rationally doubt one anymore than the other ...

Sat. JUNE 8.— ... While at Newcastle, I talked at length with a pious woman whom I had difficulty understanding. I didn't doubt her sincerity or her devotion to God, but she had fallen among some well-meaning enthusiasts who taught her to "listen to the inner voice" to the extent that she had left our fellowship, the preaching, the Lord's Supper, and almost all outward means of grace. I find these people the hardest to deal with; no one knows how to advise them. They mustn't act contrary to their conscience, even if it's in error. And who can convince them that it's in error? None but the Almighty ...

Fri. 28.—Today I'm 73 years old, and far more able to preach than I was at 23. What natural means has God used to produce this wonderful effect? 1. continual exercise and change of air, by traveling 4000 miles a year; 2. always rising at 4 a.m.; 3. being able, whenever I need to, to fall asleep immediately; 4. never losing a night's sleep in my life[315]; 5. two violent fevers and two serious bouts of tuberculosis. True, these were rough medicines, but they've caused my flesh to become like a newborn child again. And, I might add, an even temper. I feel and grieve, but by God's grace I never fret. But still "the help that is done on earth," he does it himself, and this he does in answer to many prayers ...

Wed. JULY 3.— ... In the evening I preached at York on the religion now in fashion commonly called morality, and showed at

---

[314] About $3900 in 2020 USD; an extremely low price.
[315] There was one exception to this that Wesley gave earlier.

length, from the accounts by its most prominent proponents, that it's neither better nor worse than atheism ...

Thur. 4.—In the evening I showed, to an even more crowded audience, the nature and necessity of Christian love, Αγάπη [*agápe*], poorly rendered "charity," to confound English readers. The word was sharper than a two-edged sword, as many of the hearers felt it. God grant the wound may not be healed till he himself binds it up ...

Sun. 14.—I preached in the morning at Gringley, about 1 p.m. at Ouston, and at 4 p.m. in the Epworth market-place, where God "struck with the hammer of his Word and broke the hearts of stone." Afterwards we had a love-feast at which a flame was soon kindled, and it was greatly increased when Mr. Cundy related how God had perfected him in love—a testimony which is always attended with a peculiar blessing ...

Fri. AUGUST 2.—We made pledges toward building a new chapel at the Foundry. At this and the two following meetings, over 1000 pounds[316] were cheerfully pledged ...

Tues. 6.—Our conference began, ending on Friday the 9th, a day we observed with fasting and prayer for our own nation as well as for our brethren in America. In several conferences we have had great love and unity, but in this one, over and above that, there was a general seriousness and solemnity of spirit as we have scarcely had before ...

Tues. 13.—I preached at Taunton and afterwards went with Mr. Brown to Kingston. The big old parsonage is pleasantly situated, close to the churchyard, suitable for a contemplative man. Here I found a clergyman, Dr. Coke, a former gentleman-commoner of Jesus College in Oxford, who came 20 miles on purpose to see me. I had long conversations with him, and a union began which I trust will never end.

Wed. 14.—I preached at Tiverton and on Thursday went on to Launceston. Here I found the clear reason why the work of God had gained no ground in this circuit all this year. The preachers had given up the Methodist testimony: **Either they didn't speak of perfection**

---

[316] About $235,000 in 2020 USD.

at all (the peculiar doctrine committed to our trust), or they spoke of it only in general terms, without urging believers to "go on to perfection," and to expect it every moment [my emphasis]. Wherever this is not earnestly done, the work of God does not prosper ...

Mon. 19.—I once again pulled together the select society which is continually flying apart, though they admit the loss they have suffered by letting this happen. At 11 a.m. I met 50 or 60 children. How much depends on them! All the hope of the rising generation ...

Tues. 27.— ... In the evening I preached in an open place at Mevagissey to most of the inhabitants of the town, where I saw a very rare thing: men quickly growing richer financially but not decreasing in holiness ...

Mon. SEPTEMBER 9. In Bristol, I began doing what I had intended to do for a long time: visiting members of the fellowship from house to house, setting apart two hours a day for this purpose. I was surprised to find the simplicity with which they all spoke of both their temporal and spiritual conditions. Nor could I easily have known any other way how great a work God has done among them. I found very little to correct but rather much for which to praise God. And I noticed one thing that I didn't expect: In visiting all the families outside Lawford-Gate, by far the poorest part of the city, I didn't find one person out of work ...

Fri. 13.—I went on to Midsummer-Norton where the rector, when asked, cheerfully granted me the use of his church and sat in the audience himself. I preached on the words in the Second Lesson, "Oh, you of little faith; why did you doubt?" [Matt. 8:26]. About 2 p.m. I preached in the new preaching-house in Paulton to a plain, simple, loving people, then spent the evening in Kingswood, trying to remove some little offenses that had arisen in the family ...

Sat. 21.—I preached in the paddock[317] at Bedminster. It's clear, despite what some claim, that the time for outdoor preaching isn't over while the people flock to it from all around.

Sun. 22.—After reading prayers, preaching, and administering the sacrament at Bristol, I hurried to Kingswood and preached under

---

[317] An enclosed area for pasturing or exercising animals.

the trees to such a crowd as hadn't been seen there lately. I began in King's Square a little before 5 p.m., where the Word of God was quick and powerful. And I was no more tired at night than when I rose in the morning. Such is the power of God!

After settling matters at Bristol and Kingswood, and visiting the rest of the fellowships in Somersetshire, Wiltshire, and Hants, I returned in OCTOBER to London with Mr. Fletcher ...

Wed. NOVEMBER 13.—When we came to Norwich, finding that many of our friends had been shaken by those who were asserting the Horrible Decree,[318] I took the three following mornings sifting the issue thoroughly. This strengthened many, and I trust they won't be moved from the genuine gospel again.

Thur. 14.—In the evening I laid out what the gospel is and what it is to preach the gospel. The next evening I explained at length the wrong and right meaning of "by faith are you saved" [Eph. 2:8], and many saw how miserably they've been abused by those vulgarly called gospel preachers ...

Mon. 18.—We set out for Yarmouth. Here I didn't know where to preach, since the mayor refused me the use of the town hall. But the chamberlain[319] let me use a larger building, a former church. Here a crowd soon gathered, to whom I described the [Methodist] sect that is bad-mouthed everywhere. I believe all who were attentive will be more honest in the future.

Tues. 19.—I opened the new preaching-house at Lowestoff, a new and well-lit building. It was completely filled with deeply attentive hearers. Surely some of them will bear fruit to perfection ...

Fri. 29.—Back in London, we considered different plans proposed for the new chapel. After we agreed on one, we asked an architect to draw up the details with an estimate of the expense. We then put out proposals to contractors willing to construct any part of the building ...

Tues. DECEMBER 3.—I crossed over to St. Neot's and had an hour's friendly conversation with Mr. V. **Oh that all people would sit as loose to opinions as I do! That they would think and let**

---

[318] The doctrine that, by God's will, most souls are created to be damned, and nothing they do can alter this.
[319] A chief officer.

think! [my emphasis]. I preached in the evening to a large assembly with great enlargement of spirit ...

Fri. 13.—This was the day of the national fast. It was observed not only throughout the city but, as I learned later, throughout the nation, with the greatest solemnity. I won't be surprised if God will now intervene and send us prosperity, since at last we're not too proud to acknowledge that "there's a God who judges the earth." ...

Tues. 31.—We ended the year with solemn praise to God for continuing his great work in our land. It has never ceased one year or one month since the year 1738, in which my brother and I began to preach that strange doctrine of salvation by faith.

1777

Wed. JANUARY 1.—We met as usual to renew our covenant with God. It was a solemn time in which many found his power present to heal and were enabled to push forward with renewed strength ...

Wed. 15.—I began visiting those of our society who lived in Bethnal-Green hamlet. Many of them I found in such poverty as few can imagine without seeing it. Oh, why don't all the rich who fear God constantly visit the poor? Can they spend part of their spare time in any better way? Certainly not. So they will find in that day, when "everyone shall receive their reward according to their own labor." ...

Sun. 26.—I preached again at Allhallows Church, morning and afternoon. I found great liberty of spirit, and the congregation seemed very affected. How is this? Do I still please men? Has the offense of the cross ceased? It seems, after being scandalous nearly 50 years, at last I am becoming an honorable man! ...

Sun. MARCH 2.—It being a warm, sunny day, I preached at Moorfields in the evening. There were many thousands, and all were still as night. Not only is violence and rioting, but even mocking at field-preachers is now past ...

Fri. 21.—I preached at Bath. I often wonder at this: Our chapel stands in the midst of all the sinners, yet coming to or going from it, I never heard an immodest word, only many prayers and blessings ...

Serious Joy (John Wesley's *Journal*)

Mon. APRIL 7.— ... Our new church in Macclesfield is by far the most elegant that I've seen in the kingdom. Mr. Simpson read prayers, and I preached on the first verse of the second lesson (Hebrews 11:1), and I believe many felt their lack of the faith spoken of there. The following evening I preached on Hebrews 12:14: "Without holiness no one will see the Lord." I was enabled to apply this closely, especially to those who expected to be saved by faith. I hope none of them from now on will dream of going to heaven by any faith that doesn't produce holiness ...

Mon. 14.—I preached ... in the evening in Liverpool, where large ships are now dry-docked that had been used for many years in buying or stealing poor Africans and selling them in America for slaves. The men-butchers now have nothing to do at this honorable enterprise; since the American war has broken out, there is no demand for human cattle. So the men of Africa as well as Europe may enjoy their native liberty ...

Sun. MAY 18 (Whitsunday [Pentecost]).—Our service at the Foundry began, as usual, at 4 a.m. I preached in West Street Chapel in the morning and at the Foundry in the evening. In the afternoon, I buried the body of Joseph Guilford, a holy man and a useful preacher. Surely never before did a man of such poor talents do so much good! He died as he lived, in the full triumph of faith, passionately rejoicing and praising God! ...

Sun. JUNE 1.— ... At Peele-Town, Mr. Corbett said he would have asked me to preach but that the bishop had forbidden him to do so. The bishop had also forbidden all his clergy to allow any Methodist preacher to the Lord's Supper. But is any clergyman obligated either by law or conscience to obey such a prohibition? By no means. Even the will of the king doesn't bind any English subject unless it is seconded by express law; how much less the will of a bishop! "But didn't you take an oath to obey him?" No, nor any clergyman in the three kingdoms. This is merely a common error. It's a shame that it should prevail almost universally

Wed. 11.—I had an appointment to preach in the new preaching-house at Colne. Expecting it to be crowded, I went a little early, so the balconies were only half full when I came to the pulpit. Two minutes later, the whole left-hand balcony fell all at once, with 150

VOLUME 4: 1773-1790

to 200 people. Considering the height of the balcony and the weight of the people, one would think many lives would have been lost, but I didn't hear of a single one. Doesn't God give his angels charge over those who fear him? When the disturbance was over, I went to the adjoining meadow and quietly declared the whole counsel of God …

Wed. 18.—I preached at Nottingham to a serious, loving assembly. There is something in the people of this town that I very much approve of. Although most of our society are of the lower class, mainly manufacturing socks, still there is an uncommon gentleness and sweetness in their temperament and something elegant in their behavior which, added to solid, vital religion, make them an ornament to their profession [of faith] …

Sat. 28.—I have now completed my 74th year and, by the favor of God, find my health and strength, and all my faculties of body and mind, just the same as they were at 24 …

Tues. JULY 1.—I preached in the evening at Marton, near Buckingham. The thunder, along with heavy rain, seemed likely to prevent our assembly. We cried to God. The thunder and rain ceased, and we had a fair, sunshiny evening. Many people flocked together, some coming from 12 or 14 miles away. And they didn't labor in vain, for God accompanied his Word with the demonstration of his Spirit …

Sun. 6.— … On Tuesday evening, in Worcester, the rector of the parish attended the preaching—an open-hearted and sensible man. He seemed very surprised, having never dreamed before that there was such a thing as common sense among the Methodists! The fellowship here, by patiently continuing in well-doing, has overcome evil with good. Even the beasts among the people are now tame and don't open their mouths against them …

Sat. 12.— … In the evening I preached to a large assembly in the market-place at Carmarthen. Later I was told that the mayor had sent two constables to forbid my preaching there, but if he did, their hearts failed them, for they didn't say a word …

Sat. 19.—About 11 a.m., I preached at Howton, two miles this side of the ferry. There was a special blessing among the simple-hearted people. At Pembroke, in the evening, we had the most elegant assembly I have seen since we entered Wales. Some of them came in dancing and laughing as if into a theater, but their mood quickly changed, and in a few minutes they were as serious as my subject, Death. I believe, if they don't watch out, they'll remember it—for a week! ...

Sun. 20.—The assembly at St. Daniel's was more than the church could hold. After reading prayers, I preached an hour (unusual with me)[320] on "Not everyone who says to me 'Lord, lord!'" [Matt. 7:21]. Many were cut to the heart, and at the Lord's Supper many were wounded and many healed. Surely now, at least, if they don't harden their hearts, they will all know the day of God's visitation ...

Fri. AUGUST 1.—I asked as many as could to join together in fasting and prayer, that God would restore the spirit of love and of a sound mind to the poor deluded rebels in America. In the evening we had a watch-night at Kingswood, and I was pleasantly surprised that hardly any left till the whole service ended.

Tues. 5.—Our annual conference began. I especially asked every assistant, since the report had been spread far and wide, "Do you have reason to believe, from your own observation, that the Methodists are a fallen people? Is there a decay or an increase in the work of God where you've been? Are the fellowships in general more dead or more alive to God than they were some years ago?" The almost universal answer was this: "If we are to 'know them by their fruits,' there is no decay in the work of God among the people in general. The fellowships aren't dead to God; they're as alive as they've been for many years. And we see this rumor as a mere device of Satan to make our hands hang down." ...

But to sum up the issue: In most places the Methodists are still a poor, despised people, bearing reproach and many inconveniences; therefore wherever the power of God isn't present, they decrease. This is how you can judge clearly: Do the Methodists in general decrease in number? If so, then they decrease in grace; they are fallen or at least are a falling people. But they don't decrease in number; they continually increase; therefore they aren't a fallen people ...

---

[320] Elsewhere it seems that normally Wesley preached about an hour.

VOLUME 4: 1773-1790

Tues. 19.—I went on to Taunton with Dr. Coke, who, being expelled as curate of his parish, has abandoned his honorable title and has decided to cast his lot in with us. In the evening I tried to guard all who love or fear God against that wretched bigotry which many of our mistaken brethren are advancing with all their might ...

Sat. SEPTEMBER 27.—Having received many letters from Dublin telling me that the Society there was in great confusion due to some of the prominent members being excluded from the fellowship by the preachers, and finding my letters insufficient to stop the growing evil, I saw only one way left: to go myself, and that as soon as possible. So the next day I took a buggy with Mr. Goodwin, and headed straight for Mr. Bowen's at Llyngwair in Pembrokeshire, hoping to borrow his sloop and so to cross over to Dublin right away ...

Sat. OCTOBER 4.—When I arrived at Ring's End, Mr. McKenny met me and carried me to his house. Our friends soon flocked from all around, and seemed equally surprised and pleased at seeing me. I didn't enter into any dispute, but asked a few on each side to meet with me at 10 on Monday morning. In the evening, though on short notice, we had a very large gathering to whom, putting all matters of contention aside, I drove home these solemn words: "I must do the work of him who sent me while it is day, for the night is coming when no one can work" [John 9:4] ...

Mon. 6.—At 10 a.m. I met the opposing parties, the preachers on the one hand and the excluded members on the other. I heard them at length, and they pleaded their cases earnestly but also calmly. Four hours weren't enough to hear the whole matter, so we adjourned till the next day. Meanwhile, in order to judge what condition the fellowship was actually in, I examined them myself, meeting part of them Monday and the rest of them Tuesday and Wednesday. I found that 34 persons had been put out of or had left the fellowship ... At the request of the members recently excluded, I now drew up a short statement of the situation. But there was no way I could satisfy them. They were all civil, even affectionate, it seemed, toward me, but they could never forgive the preachers who had expelled them, so I couldn't ask them to return to the fellowship; they could only remain friends at a distance ...

Mon. NOVEMBER 3.—Having been asked many times for nearly 40 years to publish a magazine,[321] I finally complied, and now began collecting materials for it. Once it begins, I am inclined to think it will only end with my life ...

1778

Thur. JANUARY 1.—We had a very solemn occasion of renewing our covenant with God.

Tues. 6.—I spent a pleasant and profitable hour with three German gentlemen, two of them Lutheran ministers and the third a professor of divinity at Leipzig. I admired their good sense, their seriousness, and their good breeding. Few of our clergy exceed or even equal them ...

Mon. MARCH 9.—On this and the following days, I visited the members of our fellowship in Bristol, and found a good increase. This year I personally chose the preachers for Bristol, something I've seldom done, and these were plain men and likely to do more good than has been done in one year for the past 20 years ...

Sun. 22.—I was refreshed by two plain, useful sermons at St. Thomas' Church as well as by the serious and decent behavior of the whole congregation. In the evening, I urged all of our fellowship who had been brought up in the Church to stay in it.

Tues. 31.—We boarded the *Duke of Leinster* and moved quickly down the river with a small side wind, but in the morning, after a dead calm, a contrary wind rose and blew very hard.

Wed. APRIL 1.—The sea was rough, but I went to sleep at my usual time and in the morning found myself in Dublin Bay. About 7 a.m. we landed at the quay ...

Wed. 22.—I went on to Clonmell where, since our preaching-room was small and the weather unsuitable for preaching outdoors, we obtained the largest room in the town, which was in the Quaker workhouse ...

Mon. MAY 4.—In Limerick, in the evening, I felt the spirit of the assembly to be the same as many years ago, but in one regard I noticed a considerable change: I used to have large gatherings at my

---

[321] The *Arminian Magazine*.

first coming to Limerick, but from the first day they gradually decreased. But now it was different: poor and rich, Protestants and Catholics, flocked together from beginning to end. Did they have a premonition that they would never see my face again? ...

Sat. 9.—I wrote "A Compassionate Address to the Inhabitants of Ireland," through which country, as well as through England, the false patriots have tried to spread the alarm as though we were all on the very brink of destruction ...

Tues. 12.—Starting out early, I intended to lodge at Clare-Galway, but we found there was no lodging there. However, they told us there was a good inn at Shreuil not many miles farther on, and there we found a house, but it offered no food for humans or animals. So we were obliged to push on for Ballinrobe, which we reached about 11 p.m. This day we covered 68 English miles, a good day's work for a pair of horses ...

Sun. 17.—At Castlebar, although the weather was rough and turbulent, both Catholics and Protestants flocked at 9 a.m. from all around and God sent down a gracious rain, especially on the backsliders. In the evening, the courthouse was crowded, and the fire of love ran from heart to heart. One prominent backslider, who had drunk in iniquity like water, was utterly broken in pieces and resolved to cut off the right hand at once[322] and to be altogether a Christian ...

Mon. 18.—There were two roads to Sligo, one several miles shorter than the other, but it had some sloughs[323] in it. Since we had a good guide, we chose the shorter route. We got over two sloughs well enough. As we approached the third, seven or eight country fellows ran to help us. One carried me over on his shoulders; others got the horses through, and some carried the buggy. Then we thought we were out of trouble, but half an hour later we came to another slough. After being helped over it, I walked ahead, leaving [my companions] with the buggy, which was stuck fast in the slough. As none of them thought of unharnessing the horses, the traces soon broke, so finally they tied ropes to the buggy and to the stronger

---

[322] Likely an illicit sexual relationship.
[323] (Usually pron. "sloo") Places of deep mud and mire.

horse. With the horse pulling and the men pushing at the same time, they pushed it through the slough onto solid ground. An hour or two later we all met at Ballinacurrah.

While I was walking, a poor man caught up with me who seemed to be in deep distress. He said he owed his landlord 20 shillings' rent, for which he and his family had been evicted, and that he had gone down to his relatives to beg their help but they wouldn't do anything. When I gave him a guinea,[324] he just had to kneel down in the road to pray for me, and then cried out, "Oh, I'll have a house; I'll have a house over my head!" So perhaps God answered that poor man's prayer by my buggy getting stuck in the slough! ...

Sat. 23.—I was asked to preach once more at Coote Hill, which I hadn't seen for many years. Having obtained the use of the Presbyterian meeting-house, I had an extraordinary assembly: To seceders were added many members of the Church of England, Arians, Moravians, and what not. However, I went straight ahead, insisting that "without holiness, no one shall see the Lord" [Heb. 12:14] ...

Tues. JUNE 9.— ... We went on to Belfast, the largest town in Ulster, said to contain 30,000 souls. The streets are well laid out, broad, straight, and well-constructed. The poorhouse stands on a rise, having a beautiful view on every side of the country. The old men and women, the male and female children, are all occupied according to their ability, and all their rooms are airy, sweet, and clean, equal to anything of the sort that I've seen in England ...

Sat. 13.—I stood in the middle of the grove, the people standing in front of me on the gradually rising ground which formed a beautiful theater. The sun glimmered through the trees but not enough to hinder me at all. It was a glorious occasion. The whole assembly seemed to drink of one spirit ...

Sat. 20.—I traveled through a delightful country to Charlemont, where Capt. Tottenham was the commanding officer. We lodged with him in the castle, which stands on a rise and commands the countryside all around. A tent was set up in the castle-yard where the soldiers were mustered at 11 a.m., with crowds of people from many

---

[324] 20 shillings = $240; 1 guinea = $235 in 2020 USD.

miles around who were all attentive [to my preaching]. In the evening their number was considerably greater, but all listened as if their lives depended on it ...

Mon. 22.—I walked to the primate's[325] mansion and went through it, noting all the improvements ... Since he came, the town has a new face. He's repaired the cathedral beautifully, has built a row of neat houses for the choral-vicars, has erected a public library and an infirmary, has caused the free-school to be rebuilt, as large as a little college, and has added a new horse barn, along with a number of comfortable and handsome houses. So Armagh finally is rising out of its ruins into a large and well-populated city. Anyone of large fortune can do just as much good do if they spend it to the best advantage! ...

Wed. 24.— ... I had dinner and supper and lodged with Dr. Lesley, the rector in Tandrogar. He is well-bred, sensible, and, I believe, a pious man. We had family prayers before supper, which he read with admirable appropriateness and devotion, and I don't know that I've spend a more agreeable evening since I entered the kingdom ...

Sun. 28.—Today I am 75 years old and, bless God, I don't find myself any weaker than I was at 25. This too is God's doing.

All this week I visited as many as I could and tried to confirm their love for each other; and haven't known the fellowship to be as united for many years as it is now ...

Tues. JULY 7.—Our small conference began, at which about 20 preachers were present. On Wednesday we heard one of our friends at length on "the duty of leaving the Church [of England]"; but after discussing the matter fully, we all remained firm in our judgment that it's our duty *not* to leave the Church in which God has blessed us and still blesses us ...

Wed. 22.—I went on to Bolton. Our new preaching-house here is the most beautiful in the country. It was quite full in the evening, and I believe many of the audience tasted deeply of the powers of the world to come while I expanded on our Lord's words, "Neither can

---

[325] A primate is the head bishop in a province or nation.

they die anymore, for they are equal to angels and are the children of God, being the children of the resurrection" [Luke 20:36] ...

Sun. AUGUST 2.—At 1 p.m. I preached at the foot of Birstal Hill to the largest gathering ever seen there. Estimates were 12- to 14,000, but later at Leeds there were even thousands more. I think it was the largest gathering I've seen for many years, except at Gwenap in Cornwall ...

Mon. 24.—I went to Redruth, Helston, and Penzance. On Thursday the 27th in the evening, I preached in the market-place at St. Just. Very few of our old fellowship remain; most are now in Abraham's bosom, but the new generation is of the same spirit: serious, earnest, devoted to God, and especially remarkable for simplicity and Christian sincerity ...

Sun. 30.—About 5 p.m. I preached in the natural amphitheater at Gwenap, we estimated, to 24,000 persons. Afterwards I spent a solemn hour with the fellowship, then slept in peace ...

Tue. SEPTEMBER 1.—I went to Tiverton. I was thinking about something I heard a good man say long ago: "Every seven years, I burn all my sermons, because it's a shame if I can't write better sermons now than I could seven years ago." Whoever can do so, I really can't. I can't write a better sermon on "The Good Steward" now than I did seven years ago. I can't write a better one on "The Great Judgment" than I did 20 years ago. I can't write a better one on "The Use of Money" than I did nearly 30 years ago. In fact, I don't know that I can write a better sermon on "The Circumcision of the Heart" now than I did 45 years ago. Certainly I may have read 500 or 600 more books than I had then, and may know a little more history or natural philosophy than I did, but I'm not aware that this has made any essential additional to my knowledge of divinity. Forty years ago I knew and preached every Christian doctrine that I preach now ...

Tues. 8.—In the evening I stood at one side of the market-place of Fromme and declared to a very large audience, "His commandments are not grievous" [1 John 5:3]. They stood as quietly as the people at Bristol, except for a very few so-called (by English courtesy) "gentlemen." How much inferior are they to the barge-men and coalminers! ...

VOLUME 4: 1773-1790

Sun. 13.— ... On Monday, Tuesday, and Wednesday, meeting with the classes, I carefully examined whether there was any truth in the claim that over 100 in our fellowship were involved in bootlegging liquor. The result was, I found two persons doing so and no more.

I got a copy of part of Mr. Fletcher's recent letter to Mr. I., which I think it my duty to publish as full answer to the lying accounts which have been published concerning that bad man. "Mr. Voltaire,[326] finding himself ill, sent for Dr. Tronchin, first physician to the Duke of Orleans, one of his converts to unbelief, and said to him, 'Sir, I ask you to save my life. I'll give you half my fortune if you'll lengthen my days just six months. If not, I'll go to the devil and carry you with me.'" ...

Sat. OCTOBER 3.—Visiting someone at the poorhouse, I was very moved to see such a large group of poor, disfigured, lame, and blind, who seemed to have no one caring for their souls. So I arranged to be there the next day, and at 2 p.m. had all who could, young and old, get out of bed and come into the great hall. My heart was greatly enlarged toward them, and many blessed God for the consolation ...

Fri. 16.—I was asked to preach at Thame when I returned to London. I arrived a little after 10 a.m. The rioters had caused so much trouble there that the preachers wondered whether we should just give up. But I thought I should make one more attempt myself before that was done. The wind was so piercing that it wasn't practical to preach outdoors, so I went into a large building, formerly used by the Presbyterians. It quickly filled, many having to stand outside. But there was no noise, the whole gathering seeming to be "all but their attention dead." We prayed before the service that God would give us a quiet time, and he granted our request.

Right after the service a strange scene occurred. I was asked to visit a woman who had been especially pious, but now had been bedridden for several months and was utterly unable to raise herself up. She asked us to pray that the chain might be broken. A few of us

---

[326] Voltaire, in France, was a contemporary of John Wesley, a writer who was a skeptic and a sharp critic of the Catholic Church. There are conflicting stories about Voltaire's deathbed scenes.

prayed in faith, and soon she got up, dressed herself, came downstairs, and I believe had no further complaint ...

Tues. DECEMBER 1.—I went to Rye. Here as elsewhere, those who begin to flee from the wrath to come are continually caught up in doubtful disputations, puzzled and perplexed with intricate questions concerning absolute and unconditional decrees.[327] Lord, how long will you allow this? How long will these well-meaning zealots destroy the dawning work of grace and strangle the children [of the kingdom] being born? ...

Sun. 20.—I buried the mortal remains of honest Silas Told. For many years he tended to the criminals in Newgate without fee or reward, and I don't think any man of this century has been as successful in this sad office. God had given him special talents for it, and he had amazing success. Most of those he cared for died in peace, and many of them in the triumph of faith ...

1779

Fri. JANUARY 1.—Finally we have a house in London large enough to contain our whole fellowship here. We met there this evening to renew our covenant with God, and we've never met on this solemn occasion without a special blessing ...

Thur. FEBRUARY 18.—I preached at Lowestoff, where there is a great awakening, especially among children and youth, several of whom, between 12 and 16 years old, are an example to all around them ...

Sun. 28.—Immediately after preaching at Spitalfields, I hurried to St. Peter's, Cornhill, and declared to a crowded audience, "God has given us his Holy Spirit" [1 Thes. 4:8]. At 4 p.m. I preached in the New Chapel for the benefit of the Reformation Society. I trust that this too will be a means of uniting the hearts of the children of God of various denominations ...

Mon. APRIL 5.—I preached at Northwich. I used to go from there to Little Leigh. But since Mr. Barker has gone there, that place doesn't know us anymore. I can only wonder at the attachment of people who really love and fear God yet leave most, if not all, of

---

[327] That God has decreed from before Creation who will and who won't be saved.

their inheritance to people who neither love nor fear him! Surely if I did little good with my money while I lived, at least when I died I'd do what good with it that I could.

Tues. 6.— ... When I preached at Nantwich, it was a season of strong consolation. But one young gentlewoman refused to be comforted. She followed me into Mr. S.'s all in tears, and wouldn't touch food or drink. After I'd spent a little time praying, she broke out in prayer herself, and didn't stop till God turned her sorrow into joy unspeakable ...

Mon. 12.—I preached at Bury about 1 p.m. and in the evening at Rochdale. Now was the day of visitation for this town. The people were all on fire. Never was such a flame kindled here before, this mainly by the prayer meetings scattered throughout the town ...

Thur. 22.—I was a little surprised at a passage in Dr. Smollett's *History of England,* Vol. 15, pp. 121-122:

> Imposture and fanaticism still hang on the skirts of religion. Weak minds were seduced by the delusions of a superstition, styled Methodism, raised upon the affectation of superior sanctity, and pretensions to divine illumination. Many thousands were affected with this enthusiasm by the endeavours of a few obscure preachers such as Whitefield and the two Wesleys, who found means to lay the kingdom under contribution.

Poor Dr. Smollett! Thus to transmit to all succeeding generations a heap of notorious falsehoods! ...

Mon. 26.—I preached at Huddersfield, where there is a great revival of the work of God. Many have found peace with God, sometimes 16, 18, even 20 in a day. So the deadly wound they suffered when their predestinarian brethren left them has now been completely healed, and they're not only more alive spiritually, but have increased in number beyond what they were before ...

Wed. 28.—I'd promised to preach at 6 a.m. to the poor prisoners at Whiteley. Though the ground was covered with snow, so many people gathered that I had to preach in the prison courtyard. The snow kept falling and the wind whistled around us, but I trust God warmed many hearts ...

Serious Joy (John Wesley's *Journal*)

Sun. MAY 2.—Dr. Kershaw, the vicar of Leeds, asked me to help him administer the sacrament of communion. We were 10 clergymen and 700 or 800 communicants. Mr. Atkinson asked me to preach in the afternoon. Seldom had such a congregation been seen there. But I preached to a much larger gathering in our own preaching-house at 5 p.m. and felt no lack of strength ...

Sun. 9.—I preached in the market-place in Darlington, and all the assembly behaved well except some of the Queen's dragoons.

Mon. 10.—I preached at Barnard Castle and saw much better behavior in the Durham Militia, the handsomest body of soldiers I ever saw except in Ireland. The next evening they all came, both officers and soldiers, and were an example to the whole assembly ...

Thur. 27.—I went on to Edinburgh. I was pleasantly surprised at the singing in the evening. I haven't heard such female voices, so strong and clear, anywhere in England ...

Sun. 30.—In Glasgow, I went to the English chapel in the afternoon, and how surprised I was! I've seldom seen such decency at West Street [in London] or at the New Room in Bristol: 1. All, both men and women, were dressed plainly; I didn't see one high headdress; 2. No one paid attention to anyone coming in, but after a short prayer sat still; 3. No one spoke to anyone during the service or looked around; 4. All stood—men, women, and children—while the Psalms were sung; 5. Rather than a meaningless organ voluntary, an anthem was sung, one of the simplest and sweetest I've ever heard; 6. The prayers, preceding a sound, useful sermon, were seriously and devoutly read; 7. After the service, no one bowed, curtsied, or spoke, but left quietly and silently ...

Mon. 31.—I returned to Edinburgh, and on June the 1st set out on my northern journey. In the evening, I preached at Dundee. The gathering was, as usual, very large and very attentive, but that was all; I didn't see anyone affected at all. I admire this people! So decent! So serious! And so perfectly unconcerned! ...

Fri. JUNE 4.— ... At 3 p.m. I preached in the kirk at Keith, one of the largest I've seen in the kingdom, but in decay. It was thoroughly filled, and God was there in an uncommon way. He sent forth his voice, even a mighty voice, so that I believe many of the stout-hearted trembled. In the evening I preached once again in the market-place on those awful words, "Where their worm doesn't die and the fire isn't quenched" [Isa. 66:24; Mark 9:44].

Mon. 7.—I came to Grange-Green, near Fores, about noon … Sir Lodowick Grant … received me with warm affection and insisted on my sending for Mrs. Smith and her little girl whom I had left at Fores. Here we were all as if at home in one of the healthiest and most pleasant places in the kingdom, and I had the satisfaction of seeing my daughter clearly recovering her strength almost every hour. In the evening the family was called in to prayers, to whom I first explained a passage of Scripture. So ended this pleasant day! And so God has provided for us in this strange land! …

Wed. 9.—We had another rainy day, so I was driven into the preaching-house again, and again I delivered my own soul to a larger congregation than before. In the morning we had an affectionate farewell, perhaps to meet no more. I'm glad, though, that I've made three trips to Inverness; my labor hasn't been lost …

Sun. 13.—I spoke as directly as I could both morning and evening in Aberdeen, and made a pointed application to the hearts of everyone there. I'm convinced this is the only way we can do any good in Scotland. Even today I heard many excellent truths preached in the kirk, but since there was no application, it was likely to do as much good as the singing of a lark. I'm surprised that the pious ministers of Scotland aren't aware of this. They must be aware that no sinners are convicted of sin and none converted to God by preaching this way. It's strange that neither reason nor experience teaches them to take a better way! …

Thur. 17.—I examined the Edinburgh fellowship. In five years, I find that five members have been added, 99 increasing to 104! What have our preachers been doing all this time? 1. They've preached four evenings during the week and on Sunday morning; they've given up the other mornings. 2. They've been careful not to speak too plainly lest they should give offense. 3. When Mr. Brackenbury preached the old Methodist doctrine, one of them said, "You mustn't preach such doctrine here; the doctrine of perfection isn't suited for the level of Edinburgh." Putting aside all other hindrances, is it any wonder that the work of God hasn't prospered here? …

Sat. JULY 3.—I reached Grimsby, and found a little trial. In this, and many other parts of the kingdom, those young men who call themselves "Lady Huntingdon's preachers" have greatly hindered the work of God. They don't have the sense, courage, or grace to go and attack the devil's strongholds in any place where Christ hasn't been named, but wherever we have entered as by storm and gathered a few souls, often at the risk of our lives, they creep in and, by doubtful disputations, set everyone's sword against his brother. One of these has just crept into Grimbsy and is trying hard to divide the poor little flock, but I hope his labor will be in vain and that they will still hold the unity of the Spirit in the bond of peace ...

Sun. 11.— ... Seldom have we known such a general outpouring of God's Spirit as we had at Epworth this afternoon:

> Like mighty winds or torrents fierce,
> It did opposers all o'errun.

Oh, that they may no more harden their hearts, lest God should swear, "They shall not enter into my rest"! [Psalm 95:11; Heb.3:11] ...

Sat. 17.—I preached at noon in Castle Donnington, but in the open air, for the heat in the preaching-house was unbearable. Still they persuaded me to preach indoors at Nottingham in the evening, where the house was hot as an oven.

Sun. 18.— ... A man who had left us to join the Quakers asked to attend our love-feast, and at the end of which, being unable to contain himself any longer, he burst out saying he must join us again. I went home with him and, after spending some time in prayer, left him full of love and gratitude ...

Sun. 25.—Both our chapels in London were quite full. On Monday, I withdrew to Lewisham to write.

Tues. AUGUST 3.—Our conference began, which continued and ended in peace and love.

Sun. 8.—I was at West Street in the morning and at the New Chapel in the evening, when I said solemn farewell to the affectionate congregation. This was the last night I spent at the Foundry. What has God wrought there in 41 years! ...

VOLUME 4: 1773-1790

Fri. 13.—I was going down steep stairs when my foot slipped and I fell down several steps. Falling on the edge of one of the steps, it broke the case of an almanac in my pocket all to pieces. The edge of another step caught my right shoe buckle and snapped the steel catch in two. But I wasn't hurt. This is how our good Master gives his angels charge over us! In the evening I preached at Brecknock and, leaving my brother Charles there, on Saturday the 14th went on to Carmarthen.

This evening and on the morning of Sunday the 15th, the new preaching-house contained the assembly, but in the afternoon I believe we had the largest gathering I ever saw in Wales. I preached on the Gospel for the day, the story of the Pharisee and the Tax-Collector [Luke 18:10ff.], and believe many were compelled to cry out, at least for the present, "God be merciful to me a sinner!" ...

Fri. 20.—At Haverford, many of us met at noon and spent a solemn hour interceding for our King and country. In the evening the house was completely filled with people of all denominations. I believe they all felt that God was there, and that he's no respecter of persons ...

Mon. 23.—I came once again to Carmarthen. Finding the people here, as everywhere, in deep trouble and confusion due to terrible rumors coming from all around, I cried aloud in the market-place, "Say to the righteous, it will be well with them" [Isa. 3:10]. God made it a seasonable word for them, and many were no longer afraid ...

Thur. 26.—I preached at 5 a.m. and again at 11 a.m. I think this was the happiest time of all. The poor and the rich seemed to be equally affected. Oh, how the times have changed here at Cowbridge, since the people surrounded the house I was in and threw rocks in from every side! But my strength then was equal to my day and, bless God, it still is ...

Tues. 31.— ... SEPTEMBER 1. Here a gentleman who just came from Plymouth gave us a remarkable report: "For two days the combined fleets of France and Spain lay at the mouth of the harbor. They could have entered the harbor with perfect ease ... The island was unable to hinder them, for there was almost no garrison, and the few men there had no wadding at all and only two rounds of powder.

But didn't they have cannon? Yes many, but only two were mounted! 'Why then didn't the enemy go in, destroy the dock, and burn or at least plunder the town?' I believe they themselves could hardly say why. The plain reason was this: The bridle of God was in their teeth, and he had said, 'You can come just so far and no farther.'"

Sun. 12.—I found it quite a job to read prayers, preach, and administer the sacrament to several hundred people. But it was pleasant work, and I was no more tired at the end than at the beginning ...

Thur. 23.— ... In the evening a man sat behind me in the pulpit at Bristol who was one of our first masters at Kingswood. Shortly after he left the school he also left our Society. Riches then flowed upon him, with which, having no relatives, he planned to do much good—after his death. "But God said to him, 'Thou fool!'" Two hours later,[328] he died without a will, and left all his money for others to scramble after.

Reader! If you haven't done it already, make your will before you sleep tonight! [my emphasis]...

Wed. OCTOBER 6.—At 11 a.m. I preached in Winchester, where there are 4,500 French prisoners. I was glad to find that they have plenty of wholesome food and are treated in every way with great humanity.

In the evening I preached at Portsmouth Common.

Thur. 7.—I viewed the army camp adjoining the town, and was surprised to find it as clean and neat as a gentleman's garden. But there was no chaplain! The English soldiers of this generation have nothing to do with God! ...

Sat. NOVEMBER 13.— ... In London, I spent a week examining the rest of our Society, but didn't find the increase I expected. In fact, there was a considerable decrease, clearly due to a senseless jealousy that had crept in between our preachers, grieved the Spirit of God, and greatly hindered his work ...

Sat. DECEMBER 25.—We began the service at the New Chapel, as usual, at 4 a.m. Afterwards, I read prayers, preached, and

---

[328] Does Wesley mean two hours after the service? It's unclear.

administered the Lord's Supper at West Street. In the afternoon, I preached at the New Chapel again, then met the fellowship, and after that the married men and women. But after all this, I wasn't any more tired than when I got up in the morning ...

1780

Sun. JANUARY 28. In the evening I withdrew to Lewisham to prepare articles (who would believe it?) for a monthly magazine[329] ...

Thur. FEBRUARY 24.—I met with the building committee, according to whose accounts, our income finally nearly equals our expenses. If so, our debts will be cleared in a few years ...

Sat. MARCH 25.— ... At Warrington, the evening after Easter, when a few members of our fellowship met together, the power of God came on them mightily. Some fell to the ground; some cried aloud for mercy; some rejoiced with joy unspeakable. Two or three found a clear sense of the love of God. One lively young woman in particular, who until recently was very prejudiced against our way, is now filled with joy unspeakable ...

Fri. APRIL 7.—I went to Delf, a small village in the mountains where a remarkable work of God has just broken out. I had just sat down when the minister sent me word that I was welcome to preach in his church. Hearing this, many people from about a mile around immediately walked there, but 10 minutes later the minister sent word that he had changed his mind. We didn't know what to do until the trustees of the independent meeting offered us the use of their house. It filled up quickly, and God truly bore witness to his Word ...

Sun. MAY 8 [7].— ... At Whitehaven, I had the opportunity of meeting with the select society. I was pleased to find that none of them have lost the pure love of God since they first received it. I was especially pleased with a poor Negro. She seemed more full of love than any of the rest. Not only did her voice have an unusual sweetness, but she chose and uttered her words unusually

---

[329] I.e., *The Arminian Magazine*.

appropriately. Never before have I heard, either in England or America, such a Negro speaker, man or woman ...

Thur. 11.—I reached Newcastle and on Friday the 12th went to Sunderland. Many of our friends prosper in the world. I hope their souls will prosper as well ...

Fri. 19.—I preached at Joppa, a coal-mining town, three miles from Edinburgh. A few months ago, while some of them were cursing and swearing, one of our local preachers, passing through, rebuked them. One of the miners followed the preacher and begged him to give them a sermon, and he did so several times. Afterwards, the travelling preachers went there, and a few of the town quickly agreed to meet together. Some of these now know in whom they've believed and walk worthily of their profession ...

Tues. JUNE 6.—Today was our quarterly meeting, with the largest attendance I've ever seen. At 2 p.m. we held the love-feast, at which several examples of the mighty power of God were shared, by which it appears that his work is still increasing in several parts of this circuit ...

Sun. 25.—Sir William Anderson, the rector, sent a direct order to his curate, who couldn't contradict it, so at 10 a.m. I began reading prayers to such a congregation as I understand hardly ever assembled in this church before. I preached on Luke 8:18, part of the Second Lesson. Not a breath was heard; all was as still "as summer's noontide air." And I believe our Lord then sowed seed in many hearts which will bring forth fruit to perfection ...

Wed. 28.—I can hardly believe that today I've begun my 78th year of life. By God's blessing, I'm just the same as when I entered my 28th year ...

Sun. JULY 9.— ... In the following days, with a few of our preachers, I read over the Large Minutes of our conference, and considered all the articles, one by one, to see whether any should be omitted or altered ...

Mon. 17.— ... On Wednesday my brother Charles and I reached Bath.

A year ago there was such an awakening here as had never been since the beginning, and consequently a rapid and great increase in our fellowship. But just then Mr. McNab, quarreling with Mr.

Smyth, threw wildfire among the people, causing anger, jealousy, judgments, back-stabbing, and tale-bearing without end. And in spite of all the pains we've taken, the wound is not healed to this day.

Both Charles and I now talked to as many as we could, trying to calm and soften their spirits. And on Friday and Saturday I spoke individually to all members of the fellowship who could attend. Friday evening, both in the preaching and at the meeting of the fellowship, the power of God was present once again to heal; also on Saturday, both morning and evening, and a few persons were added to our fellowship …

Mon. 24.— … The people of Bath were still on my mind, so on Thursday the 27th I went there again, and God was truly with us whenever we met. Surely he is healing the breaches of this poor shattered people …

Tues. AUGUST 1.—Our [general] conference began. Always before we've been strained for time. Now we resolved that, for the future, we will allow nine or ten days for each conference, so that everything related to carrying on the work of God may be maturely considered …

Sun. 20.—At 7 a.m. and again at 5 p.m. I preached at the Dock in Plymouth, and in the afternoon in our Plymouth house. It was crowded. After preaching, I made a collection for the house, which amounted to 25 pounds. When I finished, Mr. Jane said, "This isn't enough. We must have a weekly collection both here and at the Dock. Let those who can pledge sixpence a week for one year. I will pledge five shillings[330] a week, and let this be designated for the payment of the debt." This was done, and by this simple method, the most pressing debts were soon paid …

Thur. SEPTEMBER 14.—I read prayers and preached in Clutton Church, but with great difficulty because I was so hoarse, and this got so much worse that in 24 hours I could hardly speak at all. At night I used my never-failing remedy, bruised garlic applied to the soles of my feet. This cured my hoarseness in six hours, and in one hour it cured the pain in the small of my back, which I'd had ever since I came from Cornwall …

---

[330] 25 pounds = about $6000; sixpence = $6; five shillings = $60 in 2020 USD.

Tues. OCTOBER 31.—We had an assembly at noon in Oxford such as I'd never seen there before. What I regarded more than their number was their seriousness. Even the young gentlemen behaved well, nor did I notice one of them smiling, even though I forcibly applied the words, "I am not ashamed of the gospel of Christ" [Rom. 1:16] …

Mon. NOVEMBER 20.—I went on to Chatham and, finding the fellowship there groaning under a large debt, advised them to began a weekly subscription. I gave the same advice to the fellowship at Sheerness. They all cheerfully followed this advice with good results. On Friday the 24th we agreed to follow the same example in London, and in one year we paid off 1400 pounds[331] …

Sun. DECEMBER 10.—Back in London, I began reading and explaining to the fellowship the Large Minutes of the conference. I like to do everything openly and above-board. I would have all the world, and especially all of our Society, see not only all the steps we take but the reasons why we take them …

Sat. 30.—Waking between 1 and 2 a.m. I saw a bright light shining on the chapel. I immediately realized there was a fire nearby, probably in the lumberyard next to our building. If so, I knew it would soon burn us to ashes. First I called all the family to prayer. Then going outside, we found the fire about 100 yards off. It had broken out while the wind was south. But a sailor cried out, "Avast, avast! The wind has suddenly turned!" So it did, to the west, while we were at prayer, and drove the flame away from us. We then thankfully went back home, and I slept well the rest of the night …

1781

Mon. JANUARY 1.—As usual, we began the service at 4 a.m., praising him who, despite all our enemies, has brought us safe to the beginning of another year …

Tues. FEBRUARY 13.—I was asked to preach that evening on "Work out your own salvation with fear and trembling, for it is God working in you both to will and to do his good pleasure" [Phil. 2:13]. Even the Calvinists were satisfied for the present, and they readily

---

[331] About $330,000 in 2020 USD.

acknowledged that we didn't credit our salvation to our own works but to the grace of God ...

Wed. MARCH 28.—I returned to Burslem. How the whole face of this country has changed in about 20 years! Since the potteries were introduced, inhabitants have been flowing in from all around. The wilderness has become a fruitful field. Houses, villages, towns have sprung up, and the people have improved as much as the countryside. The Word of God has had free rein among them. Daily, sinners are awakened and converted to God and believers grow in the knowledge of Christ. In the evening our preaching-house was filled with people and with the presence of God. I felt compelled to extend the service a while longer than I usually do. Likewise, at the meeting of the fellowship, many received strong consolation ...

Mon. APRIL 9.—Wanting to get to Ireland as soon as possible, I hurried to Liverpool ... On Thursday morning, the captain told us the wind was fair. So Mr. Floyd, Snowden, Joseph Bradford, and I, with two of our [Christian] sisters, went on board ... [*The wind turned contrary, the stormed increased, continuing several days, and Wesley became very sick.*] Mrs. S. now crept to me, threw her arms over me, and said, "Oh Sir, we will die together!" By this time we had three feet of water in the hold, though it was a very light vessel ... I called our brothers and sisters to prayer and we found access to the throne of grace. Soon after that, I don't know how, but we got into Holyhead Harbor ...

The more I pondered, the more I was convinced that it wasn't the will of God for me to go to Ireland at this time. So we took the stagecoach right away and the next evening came to Chester ...

Sun. JUNE 4 (Whitsunday [Pentecost]).— ... [*On the Isle of Man.*] Between 6 and 7 p.m. I preached on the seashore at Peel to the largest assembly I've seen on the island. Even the fellowship nearly filled the preaching-house. I soon discerned their spirit. Hardly in England, except perhaps at Bolton, have I found so plain, so earnest, so natural a people ...

Tues. JULY 3.—I preached at Claythorp, three miles from Grimsby. Here, too, there's been an outpouring of the Spirit. I was reminded here of what I saw at Cardiff almost 40 years ago: I couldn't go into any house without it being quickly filled with people, and I was compelled to pray with them in every house, or they wouldn't be satisfied. Several of these are clearly renewed in love and give a plain, scriptural account of their experience, and there's hardly a house in the village where at least one or more aren't earnestly thirsting for salvation ...

Fri. 6.—[*Wesley critiques Dr. Robertson's* History of America, *which never mentions the providence of God.*] The poor American, though not pretending to be a Christian, knew better than this. When the Indian was asked, "Why do you think that the beloved ones[332] take care of you?" he answered, "When I was in the battle, the bullet went on this side and on that side, and this man died and that man died, but I am still alive! So I know the beloved ones take care of me."

It's true, the doctrine of a particular providence (and any but a particular providence is no providence at all) is absolutely out of fashion in England, and a prudent author might write this to gain the favor of his gentle readers. Yet I won't say that this is real prudence, because by it he might lose more than he gains, since the majority even of Britons to this day retain some respect for the Bible ...

Mon. AUGUST 6.— ... On Tuesday our conference began with about 70 preachers in attendance. I invited them to come one by one and help me with their advice in carrying on the great work of God

Wed. 8.—I asked Mr. Fletcher to preach. I'm not surprised that he's so popular, not just because he preaches with all his might but because the power of God is present both in his preaching and his prayer. On Monday and Tuesday we finished the remaining business of the conference, and ended it with solemn prayer and thanksgiving ...

Sun. 26.—Between 1 and 2 p.m. I began my sermon in the new preaching-house at Plymouth. The large assembly paid close attention and gave us reason to hope that even here we'll find some fruit for our labor. In the evening I preached again in the town square on the story of the Pharisee and the tax-collector [cf. Luke 18], to such a gathering as I never saw there before, both for size and seriousness ...

---

[332] I.e., his ancestors.

VOLUME 4: 1773-1790

Tues. 28.—Going through Marazion, I was told that a large crowd was waiting for me, so I stepped down from my buggy and immediately began speaking, and we had a gracious shower. Some were cut to the heart, but more rejoiced with joy unspeakable ...

Sat. SEPTEMBER 1.— ... At 11 a.m. I preached at Cambourn Church-Town, and I believe the hearts of all the people were bowed down before the Lord. After the quarterly meeting in Redruth, I preached in the market-place on the first principle: "By faith are you saved" [cf. Eph. 2:8]. It is also the last point, and it connects the first point of religion with the last.

Sun. 5 [2].—About 5 p.m. I preached at Gwenap. I believe 22- or 23,000 were there, and God so strengthened me in speaking that even those farthest away could hear clearly. I think this is my *ne plus ultra*.[333] I hardly expect to see a larger gathering until we meet in the air.

After preaching at Bodmin, Launceston, Tiverton, and Halberton, on Wednesday the 5th about noon I preached at Taunton. I think that here I ought to tell what some will consider an outstanding example of enthusiasm. Whether that's so or not, I tell the plain facts: An hour after we left Taunton, one of the buggy horses suddenly became so lame that he could hardly set his hoof to the ground. Since it was impossible to obtain any human help, I knew of no remedy but prayer. Immediately his lameness was gone and he went on just as he did before ...

Fri. 8 [7]—I went over to Kingswood and thoroughly investigated the school's management. I found that some of the rules hadn't been followed at all, in particular that of rising early in the morning. Surely Satan has a special hatred of this school! What trouble it has caused me for over 30 years! I can plan, but who will follow through? I don't know. God help me! ...

Sat. 29.—I spent an hour with Mr. Henderson at Hanham and inquired in detail as to his whole approach to working with the mentally ill, and I'm convinced that there's not another house like this for the insane in the three kingdoms. He has a special manner of

---

[333] Farthest limit(?).

governing his patients, not by fear, but by love. The result is that many quickly recover and love him ever after ....

Wed. OCTOBER 10.— At Newport on the Isle of Wight I gave a sermon to open the new preaching-house, just completed. After preaching, I explained the nature of a Methodist fellowship, of which a few didn't have the least idea until then.

Fri. 11[12].—I came to London and was told that my wife had died the previous Monday. This evening she was buried, though I wasn't told about it till a day or two later.[334] ...

Mon. NOVEMBER 5.—[*Back in London*] I began visiting the classes and found quite an increase in the fellowship. I give credit for this mainly to a small group of young people who have kept a prayer meeting going at 5 a.m. every morning. During the following week, I visited most of the rural fellowships and found them increasing rather than decreasing ...

Mon. 26.—I took a little tour through Sussex, and Wednesday the 28th preached at Tunbridge-Wells in the large Presbyterian meeting-house to a well-dressed, yet deeply serious, audience ...

Tues. DECEMBER 11.—Finding many people troubled as though England were on the brink of destruction, I applied those comforting words of Scripture, "I will not destroy the city for the sake of ten" [Gen. 18:32] ...

1782

Mon. JANUARY 14.—Having been told that due to the poor behavior of the preachers, things were in disarray at Colchester, I went down there hoping to "strengthen the things that remained, that were ready to die" [Rev. 3:2]. I found that some of the class leaders had died, and the rest had left the fellowship. The circles were completely dissolved. Morning preaching had been abandoned, and almost no one, except on Sunday, attended the evening preaching. However this evening we had a very large audience to whom I proclaimed "the terrors of the Lord" [cf. Deut. 4:34]. I told them that I would immediately resume the morning preaching, and the next

---

[334] This highlights Wesley's cold relationship with his wife. They had been separated since 1771. Clearly Wesley put his ministry before his marriage.

morning about 100 attended. In the daytime I visited as many as I possibly could in all parts of the town. I then inquired as to who were suitable and willing to meet in circles, and who were most fit to be leaders of either circles or classes. The attendance this evening was larger than last evening, and many again set their hands to the plow. Oh, may the Lord confirm the fresh desires he has put in them, that they may look back no longer! ...

Sun. MARCH 3.— ... Tuesday and Wednesday, after meeting the classes, I visited as many as I could, mainly of the sick and poor ...

Mon. 25.— ... In the evening I preached at Kingswood and afterwards met the circles. The coalminers spoke freely. I was quite surprised. Not only was the substance of what they spoke rational and scriptural, but their words and manner were completely appropriate. "Who teaches like [God]?" ...

Thur. 28.—Coming to Congleton, I found the Calvinists were just breaking in and trying to wreak havoc on our flock. Is this brotherly love? Is this treating us as we would treat them? It's just like highway robbery! But if it's decreed, they can't help it, so we can't blame them.

Good Friday, 29.—I arrived in Macclesfield just in time to assist Mr. Simpson in the heavy work of the day. I preached for him morning and afternoon, and we administered the sacrament to about 1300 persons. While we were doing this, I heard a low, soft, solemn sound, like an Aeolian harp, which continued for five or six minutes and affected so many that they couldn't keep from shedding tears; then it gradually died away. It's strange that no other organist I know should think of this! In the evening I preached in our own preaching room. Here was that harmony which art can't imitate ...

Tues. APRIL 2.—About 10 a.m. I preached at New Mills to a simple people. Realizing they had suffered greatly by not having the doctrine of perfection clearly explained and pressed on them, I preached specifically on that subject, and spoke to the same effect when I met later with the fellowship. The spirits of many greatly revived, and they are now going on to perfection ...

Fri. 5.—About 1 p.m. I preached at Oldham, and was surprised to see the whole street lined with little children—such children as

I've never seen until now. Before preaching, they just ran around and in front of me, but after it, a large group of boys and girls closed me in and weren't content till I shook each one by the hand. I was then asked to visit a dying woman, and as soon as I entered the room, she and her friends were in such an emotional state as I've rarely seen: Some laughed; some cried; all were so moved they could hardly speak. Oh, how much better it is to go to the poor than to the rich, and to the house of mourning than to the house of feasting! ...

Mon. 15.— ... [*Part of a letter from a young man in Amherst, Nova Scotia:*]

> ... On Sunday Mr. Wells, an old Methodist, came to Amherst and gave us an exhortation, in which he said, "Sin and repent, sin and repent, till you repent in the bottomless pit." The words went like a dagger to my heart, and for five weeks and four days I constantly mourned after God until our monthly meeting. I was strongly tempted to commit suicide, but God enabled me to resist the temptation. Two days later an old Methodist, after praying with me, said, "I think you will get the blessing before morning." Two hours after that, while we were singing a hymn, it pleased God to reveal his Son in my heart. Since that time I have had many blessed days and many happy nights ...
>
> WILLIAM BLACK, Junior ...

Sun. MAY 12.—About 8 a.m. I preached at Misterton and about 1 p.m. at Overthorpe. Many of the Epworth children were there, and their spirit spread to all around them. But the huge assembly was in the market-place at Epworth, with the Lord in the midst of them. The love-feast that followed exceeded all I ever knew here before. Several of them were children, but they spoke with the wisdom of the aged although with the fire of youth. So out of the mouth of babes and sucklings God did perfect praise [cf. Matt. 21:16] ...

Tues. 14.—A few years ago, four factories for spinning and weaving were erected at Epworth. In these, many young women and children were employed. Their whole conversation was lewd and profane to the nth degree. But some of them, stumbling in on the prayer meeting, were suddenly cut to the heart, and they never rested till they had won their friends. The whole scene changed. In three of the factories, no more lewdness or profanity was found, for God had put a new song in their mouth, and blasphemies turned into praise. Those three I visited today, and found religion had taken deep root in them. No frivolous word was heard among them, and they watch over each other in love. I found it very good to be there, and we rejoiced together in the God of our salvation …

Sat. JUNE 15.—As I was going downstairs, the carpet slipped under my feet which, I don't know how, turned me around and threw me back headfirst for six or seven steps. There was no way I could recover till I reached the bottom. My head bounced once or twice on the edge of the stone steps, but it felt just as if I had fallen on a cushion or a pillow. Dr. Douglas ran to me anxiously, but he needn't have worried, because I got up as well as ever, having received no injury except losing a little skin from one or two of my fingers. Doesn't God "give his angels charge over us, to keep us in all our ways"? [Psa. 91:22; Luke 4:10] …

Wed. 19.—In Newcastle, on this and the following days, I examined the fellowship. I found they had increased in grace, but not numerically. I think at least four out of five were alive to God. To stir them further, I divided all the classes again according to their places of residence. I noticed another thing: The gatherings were larger, morning and evening, than any I've seen these past 20 years …

Fri. 28.—Today I have entered into my 80th year but, bless God, my time is not labor and sorrow. I find no more pain or bodily infirmities than at 25.

Mon. JULY 1.—Arriving in Sheffield just at the time of the quarterly meeting, I preached on Acts 2:32: "Then the churches had peace and were built up and, walking in the fear of the Lord and in the comfort of the Holy Spirit, were multiplied." This is especially fulfilled in all these parts, in Sheffield in particular …

Sat. 6.—I came to Birmingham and preached one last time in the old, dreary preaching-house.

Sun.7.—I opened our new house at 8 a.m. and it contained the people well enough, but not in the evening, when many were forced to go away …

Wed. 24.—Brother Charles and I paid our last visit to Lewisham and spent a few thoughtful hours with the widow of our good friend,

Mr. Blackwell. We took one more look around the garden and meadow, which he took so much care to improve. For over 40 years this has been my place of retreat when I could spare two or three days from London ...

Tues. AUGUST 13.— ... At 3 p.m. I took the stagecoach. About 1 a.m. on Wednesday we were told that three highwaymen were on the road ahead of us and had robbed all the coaches that passed, some just an hour or two before us. I didn't feel any uneasiness about this, knowing that God would take care of us, and he did so, because before we reached the spot, all the highwaymen were arrested. So we went on unmolested, and early in the afternoon arrived safely in Bristol ...

Sun. 18.—I was very pleased with the decent behavior of the whole congregation at the Exeter Cathedral, as well as with the solemn music following communion—one of the finest compositions I've ever heard. The bishop invited me to stay for dinner. I couldn't help but observe: 1. the lovely situation of the mansion, covered with trees as rural and secluded as if it were in the countryside; 2. the plainness of the furniture, not costly or showy—just fit for a Christian bishop; 3. the dinner sufficient but not extravagant, plain and good, but not delicate; 4. the appropriateness of the company: five clergymen and four of the aldermen; and 5. the genuine, unpretentious courtesy of the bishop who, I hope, will be a blessing to his whole diocese ...

Tues. SEPTEMBER 10. After preaching at Paulton on the 9th, I went on to the simple-hearted coalminers at Colesford, hundreds of whom met me at 6 p.m. in a green meadow, which was delightfully gilded by the rays of the setting sun ...

Fri. DECEMBER 6.—I could find no other transport to St. Albans than in an open buggy. And since the air was freezing cold, I contracted a bad cold ...

Sat. 14.—I found that the cold I'd caught on the way to St. Albans had gotten much worse, having a deep, hacking cough which continued off and on until the spring.

Mon. 16.—I retired to Hoxton for a few days.

Thur. 19.—About 11 p.m. a gun was fired into our bedroom window, and at the same time a big rock was thrown through it—probably someone drunk and having fun. I went right back to sleep.

Sat. 21.—I visited Mr. Maxfield, stricken with a severe stroke. He was unconscious and seemed near death. But we sought God for him, and his spirit revived. I can only believe that this was an answer to prayer.

Sun. 29.—I buried the body of Thomas Forfit, a rich but generous man. He never grew weary in well-doing, and in a good old age, without any pain or struggle, fell asleep.

Tues. 31.—We ended the year with a solemn watch-night.

1783

Wed. JANUARY 1. May I begin to live today!

Sun. 5.—We met to renew our covenant with God. We never meet on this occasion without a blessing. But I don't think we've ever had such a large assembly before …

Sun. 19.—I preached at St. Thomas's Church in the afternoon and at St. Swithin's in the evening. The tide has turned, and now I have more invitations to preach in churches than I can accept …

Tues. FEBRUARY 11.—I buried the body of Sarah Clay, many years a mother in Israel. She was the last of those holy women who, filled with love, 40 years ago devoted themselves wholly to God to spend and be spent in his service. Her death was like her life, calm and easy. She was dressing herself when she dropped down and fell asleep …

Fri. 21. At our yearly meeting to examine financial affairs, we found that the money received just equaled our expenses, which was over 3000 pounds a year. But that's nothing to me. What I receive of it yearly is neither more nor less than 30 pounds.[335]

Today Charles Greenwood went to his rest. He had been a sad man all his life, full of doubts and fears, constantly writing bitter things against himself. When he first got sick, he said he would die, and was miserable through fear of death, but two days before he died, the clouds parted and he was unspeakably happy, telling his

---

[335] 3000 pounds = $705,000; 30 pounds = $7000 in 2020USD.

friends, "God has revealed things to me that it's impossible for man to utter." Just when he died, such glory filled the room that it seemed like a little heaven. No one could grieve or shed a tear, since everyone there seemed to partake of his joy ...

Sun. MARCH 2.—In the evening I took the stagecoach and the next evening preached at Bath.

Thur. 6.—I went on to Bristol and found a family of love, more united than it had been for some years. The following week I met the classes and on Friday had a watch-night at Kingswood. But I was far from being well, the cold I caught coming from Luton getting worse rather than better.

Sat. 15.—I had a deep tearing cough and felt very heavy and weak. Still I forced myself to preach at Weavers' Hall and to meet repentant sinners.

Sun. 16.—I was a good bit worse. However, I preached in the morning, then had such a fever in the afternoon that I had to go to bed.

Now I didn't know what to do, having arranged to begin my journey to Ireland the next morning, and having sent notices to Stroud, Gloucester, and various other places of the days I planned to visit them. But Mr. Collins kindly took it on himself to fill my place at Stroud and the other places as far as Worcester.

Lying down in bed, I swallowed as much as I could of a dose prepared for me. It kept me running to the pot and vomiting, after which I fell asleep ...

Mon. 17.— ... I had a cramp off and on through the night, along with a hacking cough, usually before each cramp. But I had no pain in my back, head, or limbs otherwise. I lay like this till Friday morning, when a terrible cramp took the fever completely away. Seeing this, I took a buggy without delay and reached Worcester in the afternoon. Here I caught up with Mr. Collins, who had filled all my appointments with great blessing to the people. But being exhausted, I found rest was sweet ...

Sun. 23.—Still finding I had a slight fever, with heaviness and tightness in my chest, and a continual tendency to cramp, I got a friend to electrify me thoroughly several times that day, both through the legs and the chest. God blessed this so that I had no more fever or cramp, and no more heaviness and tightness in my chest. In the evening I tried preaching three-quarters of an hour and had no ill effects at all ...

Tues. 29.—Our small conference began [in Dublin] and continued through Friday, May the 2nd. All was peace and love, and I trust the same spirit will spread through the nation ...

Tues. MAY 20.—I met the select society [in Manchester], consisting of 40 to 50 members. Several of these recently became partakers of the great salvation, as were some over 20 years ago. I believe there's no place outside of London where we have as many souls so deeply devoted to God, and so far his hand has not slackened; instead his work rapidly increases all around ...

Fri. 23.—I started out for Derby, but the blacksmith had so lamed one of my horses that many said he'd never be able to work again. I thought: "Even this may be made a matter of prayer," and set out cheerfully. Instead of the horse getting worse and worse, he got better and better, and after I stopped to preach in Leek on the way, he carried me safe to Derby in the afternoon ...

Sun. 25.—I had an easy day's work with Mr. Bailey helping me by reading prayers and serving wine at the Lord's Table ...

Sun. JUNE 15.—[*In Rotterdam, Holland.*] The Episcopal Church here isn't quite as big as our chapel in West Street, [London]. It's very elegant both inside and out. The service began at 9:30 a.m. Such a gathering hadn't often been seen there before. I preached on "God created man in his own image" [Gen. 1:27]. The people "seemed all but their attention dead." In the afternoon the church was filled as it hadn't been for 50 years, so they told me. I preached on "God has given us eternal life, and this life is in his Son" [1 John 5:11]. I believe God applied it to many hearts. If it were just for this hour alone, I'm glad I came to Holland ...

Sun. 22.— ... We spent an hour [in Amsterdam] at Mrs. V.'s, an extraordinary woman. From both her past and present experience, I've no doubt that she is "perfected in love." She said, "I was born in Surinam and brought here from there when I was 10 years old. But when I got here, my guardian wouldn't let me have my inheritance unless I returned to Surinam. However, I got acquainted with some pious people and did whatever I could to live till I was about 16.

Then I sailed for Surinam, but a storm drove us back to the coast of England, where the ship was stranded. I was in great distress, afraid I had sinned by leaving the pious people. But just then God revealed himself to my soul. I was filled with joy unspeakable and boldly assured the people, who thought they were about to die, that God would preserve them all, and so he did. We got on land at Devon but lost everything we had.

"After a time I returned to Amsterdam, and lived four years as a servant. Then I married. Seven years later, it pleased God to do a deeper work in my heart, and since then I've given myself completely to him. I'm always pleased with his will, and was so even when my husband died. I didn't have a single discontented thought; I was still happy in God." ...

Wed. 24 [25].—We took a boat to Harlem ... [and] returned in the afternoon to Amsterdam. In the evening we said goodbye to as many of our friends as we could. How totally mistaken we've been about the Dutch, supposing them to be of a cold, unemotional temperament! I haven't met a more warmly affectionate people in all of Europe—not even in Ireland! ...

Thur. 26.— ... I notice regarding all the pious people in Holland, that with no rule but the Word of God, they dress as plainly as Miss March once did and Miss Johnson does now! And considering the great disadvantage they are under, having no contact with each other, and being under no discipline at all as we are, I wonder at the grace of God that is in them! ...

Sat. 28.— ... Today I have lived 80 years, and by the mercy of God my eyes haven't waxed dim, and what little strength of body or mind I had 30 years ago, I still have just the same. God grant that I may never live to be useless. Rather may I

> My body with my duty lay down,
> And cease at once to work and live ...

Tues. JULY 1.— ... By no means do I regret either the trouble or the expense of this little trip. It opened me to a new world, as it were, where the land, the buildings, the people, the customs, were all such as I'd never seen before. But those with whom I spoke were of

VOLUME 4: 1773-1790

the same spirit as my friends in England. I was as much at home in Utrecht and Amsterdam as in Bristol and London ...

Mon. 14.— ... In the evening I preached in our new preaching-house at Oxford, a well-lit, cheerful place, and quite filled with rich and poor scholars as well as townspeople ...

Wed. 16.— ... In Witney, about 10 p.m. on Friday night, a storm burst over the town with thunder and lightning, or rather sheets of flame, with no letup. Those sleeping woke up, and many thought the Day of Judgment had come. Men, women, and children streamed out of their houses and knelt down together in the streets. The grace of God came down with the flames in the sky, in a way never known before, making a general and lasting impression. After the storm the spirit of seriousness, along with that of grace and supplication, continued. A prayer meeting was set for Saturday night, and the people flocked together, overflowing the preaching-house so that many stood at the doors and windows. On Sunday morning the church was full before the service began; such a sight had never been seen in that church before. The rector himself was deeply moved and delivered a hard-hitting sermon with great zeal. When I came on Wednesday, the same seriousness remained on most of the people. I preached in the evening at Wood Green, where a crowd gathered, on "the Son of Man coming in his glory" [Matt. 25:31]. The Word fell heavily on them, and many of their hearts were as melting wax.

Thur. 17.—At 5 p.m., they were still so eager to hear that the preaching-house couldn't contain the gathering. After preaching, 34 persons asked admission into the fellowship, everyone of whom was, at least for the present, under very serious impressions, and most of them, there's reason to hope, will bring forth fruit with patience [cf. Luke 8:15]. In the evening I preached to a lovely assembly at Stroud, and on Tuesday afternoon came to Bristol ...

Tues. 29.—Our conference began, at which two important points were considered: first, the case of Birstal House, and second, the state of the Kingswood School. With regard to the first, our brethren earnestly requested that I go to Birstal myself, believing this to be the most effective way to bring the trustees to reason. With regard to the second we all agreed that either we should close the school or that its rules should be strictly observed; in particular, that the children should never play,[336] and that a teacher should always be present with them.

Tues. AUGUST 5.—Early in the morning I had violent diarrhea, and added to that, in a few hours, constant cramp, first in my feet, legs, thighs, then in my side and throat. The doctor, considering my condition extreme, gave me a grain and a half of opium in three doses. This soon stopped the cramp, but at the same time took away my speech, hearing, and ability to move, so that I lay still as a log. I then sent for Dr. Drummond, who after that attended me twice a day. For several days I got worse and worse, till on Friday I was moved to Mr. Castleman's. Still my head was not affected and I had no pain, though I had a constant fever. But I continued to recover slowly so as to be able to read or write an hour or two at a time.

On Wednesday the 12th I vomited so much that it nearly shook me to pieces, but I was better after that.

Sun. 17.—and all the following week, my fever gradually decreased, but I was constantly thirsty and had little or no increase of strength. Still, being unwilling to stay idle, on Saturday the 23rd I spent a half-hour with the penitents,[337] and feeling no worse, on Sunday the 24th I preached in the New Room morning and afternoon. Finding my strength in some measure restored, I decided no longer to delay and set out on Monday the 25th, reaching Gloucester in the afternoon. In the evening I preached in the town hall, I think not in vain …

Tues. SEPTEMBER 2.—We went to Leeds, where I was glad to find several preachers.

Wed. 3.—I consulted with the preachers how it was best to proceed with the trustees of Birstal House in order to persuade them to settle it on the Methodist plan. They all advised me to begin by preaching there. So I did that on Thursday evening, then met the fellowship and preached again the next morning.

Fri. 5.—About 9 a.m. I met with the 19 trustees, and after exhorting them to peace and love, said, "All that I ask is that this

---

[336] This is shocking to us of the 21st century, who consider play essential for children. It may hark back to Wesley's strict upbringing. Perhaps unsupervised or unstructured play is meant.

[337] Those confessing and sorrowful for their sins.

house be founded on the Methodist plan, and the same clause be inserted in your deed that is inserted in the deed of the New Chapel in London; namely: 'In case the doctrine or practice of any preacher should, in the opinion of the majority of the trustees, not conform to Mr. Wesley's *Sermons and Notes on the New Testament*, on stating this to the nearest assistants, after a proper hearing, another preacher shall be sent within three months.'"

Five of the trustees were willing to accept our first proposals; the rest were not.

Although I didn't achieve my purpose, and in this respect gained nothing for my labor, I don't at all regret my trip: I've done my part; let others bear their own burden. Going back nearly the same way I came, on Saturday the 13th I reached Bristol. I also had good reward for my labor, recovering my health by a journey of 500 or 600 miles ...

Fri. 26.—Noticing the deep poverty of many of our brothers and sisters, I decided to do what I could for their relief. I spoke individually to some who had the means and received about 40 pounds.[338] Next I asked who were in the direst circumstances and went to their homes. I was surprised to find no complaining spirit among them but many who were truly happy in God. And all of them were very thankful for the small amount of relief they received ...

Wed. OCTOBER 1.— ... I used all my free time this week visiting the rest of the poor and begging for them. Having collected 50 pounds[339] more, I was able to relieve most of those that were in great distress ...

Tues. 14.—I went on to Oxford and found that both the congregation and the fellowship had increased in zeal as well as in number.

Wed. 15.—I came to Witney. The flame kindled here by that providential storm of thunder and lightning has not died out. Indeed, it has continued without intermission ever since. The preaching-house is too small for the congregation ...

---

[338] About $9400 in 2020 USD.
[339] About $12,000 in 2020 USD.

Wed. 22.—I went to Yarmouth. Several times this poor fellowship has been almost broken to pieces, first by Benjamin Worship, then a furious Calvinist, pulling away nearly half of them, next by John Simpson, turning Antinomian and scattering most that were left. Contrary to all human probability, it has pleased God to raise a new fellowship out of the dust—and even more, to give them courage to build a new preaching-house. It is nicely finished and contains about 500 people. I opened it this evening, and those who could get in seemed deeply affected. Who knows but that God is about to repair the waste places and to gather a people who will be scattered no more? ...

Mon. 27.—I talked at length with M.F. I haven't known such a case before. She has been in our Society nearly from the beginning. She found peace with God 25 years ago, and the pure love of God a few years later. For over 30 years she's been a class and a circle leader, and of excellent use. Ten months ago she was accused of drunkenness and of revealing her friend's secret. Being told about this, because I believed the charges, I wrote to Norwich that she must no longer be a leader of class or circle. The preacher told her further that, in his judgment, she was unfit to be a member of the fellowship. At this point she gave up her ticket, together with her circle and class papers. Immediately all her friends (and she had many) forsook her at once. No one claimed to know her or spoke to her. She was treated as if dead and not brought to mind![340]

When I made a closer examination, I found that Mrs. N. (formerly a prostitute) had revealed her own secret to Dr. Hunt and 20 others as well. So the first accusation vanished into the air. And I truly believe the drunkenness she was charged with was in reality her falling down in a fit. So we have thrown away one of the most useful leaders we ever had, for these wonderful reasons! ...

1784

Thur. JANUARY 1.—I took a 2-3 day retreat to Peckham.

---

[340] This is "shunning," practiced by the Amish and certain other sects to punish those who violate their rules.

Sun. 4.—In spite of heavy rain, I believe we had over 1800 people at the renewal of our covenant with God. Many found a special blessing in it; certainly I did, for one ...

Mon. 12.—Wanting to help some that were in dire need, but not having any money of my own left, I thought it proper to ask the help of God. A few hours later, someone from whom I expected nothing less put 10 pounds[341] into my hands.

Wed. 21.—A well-meaning man viciously accused me of many things, especially of covetousness and discourtesy. I referred the matter to three of our brothers. Truly, in these accusations, "I know nothing by myself, but he who judges me is the Lord" [1 Cor. 4:4] ...

Sat. FEBRUARY 14.—I asked all our preachers to meet and to consider thoroughly the idea of sending missionaries to the East Indies. After fully considering the matter, we were unanimous in our judgment that so far we have no calling there, no invitation, and no providential opening of any kind ...

Fri. MARCH 5.—I talked at length with our teachers at Kingswood School, who are now just as I wished for. Finally the rules of the house are promptly obeyed and the children are all in good order ...

Mon. 15.— ... I preached at Stroud where, to my surprise, I found that the morning preaching had been discontinued and also in nearby places. If this is the case when I'm alive, what must it be when I'm gone? Give this up, and Methodism too will degenerate into a mere sect, only distinguished by some opinions and modes of worship ...

Wed. 31.—I reached Burslem, where we had the first fellowship in the country, and it's still the largest and the most earnest. I had to preach outdoors, and the preaching-house would barely contain the fellowships at the love-feast, at which many men and women declared the wonderful works of God ...

Mon. APRIL 5.—About noon I preached at Alpreham to an unusually large assembly. When I came to Chester, I was surprised to find that there, too, morning preaching had been abandoned, for this worthy reason: "Because people won't come, or at least not in

---

[341] About $2,350 in 2020 USD.

the winter." If so, "the Methodists are a fallen people." Here is proof. They've lost their first love, and they never can or won't regain it until they do the first works ...

In the meantime, we're laboring to secure our preaching-houses for the next generation. In the name of God, let us, if possible, secure the present generation from drawing back to perdition! Let all the preachers that are still alive to God join together as one, fast and pray, lift up their voices as a trumpet, be instant in season and out of season, to convince them that they've fallen, and exhort them urgently to "repent, and do the first works." This especially: rising early in the morning, without which neither their souls nor bodies can long remain in health.

Wed. 7.—I crossed over the water to Liverpool. Here I found a people very alive to God. One reason for this is that they've been preaching several mornings in a week, and holding prayer meetings on the other days, all of which they attend regularly ...

Mon. 12.—At Oldham there was a young woman of blameless character (otherwise I wouldn't have given this account any credit) who gave me a remarkable story: She said, "I'd totally lost the sight of my right eye, when I dreamed one night that our Savior appeared to me. I fell at his feet, and he placed his hand over my right eye. Immediately I woke up, and from that moment have seen as well with that eye as with the other."

I applied to a very large assembly the case of the Rechabites (Jer. 35). I asked: 1. Does it seem that these owed more to Jehonadab than the Methodists do to me? 2. Do they regard my advices, although both scriptural and rational (for example, in plain dress and in rising early),[342] as the Rechabites were of his advices (of drinking no wine and of living in tents), which had neither Scripture nor reason to support them? ...

Mon. MAY 3.— ... Our preaching-house at Arbroath was completely filled. I spoke plainly on the difference between building on the rock and building on the sand. Truly these people "approve the things that are excellent" [Phil 1:10], whether they practice them or not.

---

[342] Wesley doesn't give scripture references for these advices, at least not here.

VOLUME 4: 1773-1790

I found this to be a genuine Methodist fellowship: They're all completely united with each other. They love and keep our rules. They long for and expect to be perfected in love. If they keep doing this, they will and must increase in number as well as in grace ...

Wed. 5.— ... In the evening I spoke at length with the preachers and showed them the harm it did both to them and the people for any one preacher to stay six or eight weeks at a time in one place. He can't find enough material to preach on every morning and evening, nor will the people come to hear him. And so he grows cold by lying in bed, as do the people, whereas if he never stays more than two weeks at a time in one place, he may find enough preaching matter, and the people will gladly hear him. They immediately drew up such a plan for this circuit and determined to pursue it[343] ...

Fri. 7.—In Keith I preached about 7 p.m. to the poor of this world (not a silk coat was seen among them), and to most of them again at 5 a.m. And I didn't regret my labor ...

Mon. 10.---I set out for Inverness. I had sent Mr. McAllum ahead on George Whitefield's horse to give notice of my coming. This forced me to take both George and Mrs. McAllum with me in my buggy. To make it easier on the horses, we walked ahead from Nairn, ordering Richard to follow us as soon as they were fed. He did so, but there were two roads. We took one and he the other, and we walked about 12½ miles through heavy rain. We then found Richard waiting for us at a little tavern, and drove on to Inverness. But bless God, I was no more tired than when I set out from Nairn. I preached at 7 p.m. to a far larger assembly than I'd seen here since I preached in the kirk. And surely my labor wasn't in vain, for God sent a message to many hearts ...

Sun. [Thurs.] JUNE 10.—After preaching at 5 a.m., I mounted my horse for the Dales, and about 8 a.m. preached at Cutherston. Here I had the pleasure of seeing some of our brethren cordially reunited who for a long time had differences ...

Sat. 19.—In Whitby, I met such a select society as I haven't seen since I left London. There were about 40 of them, among whom I

---

[343] This is the rationale for the circuit riders. Later we will find appointment of "local" preachers who do serve as pastors for local congregations.

found not one who didn't have a clear witness of being saved from deep-rooted sin. Several of them had lost this witness for a while, but could never rest until they recovered it. And every one of them now seemed to walk in the full light of God's countenance ...

Sun. 20. The new vicar in Scarborough showed plainly why he refused those who asked for me to preach in his church. I've never heard a sharper sermon. So all I've done to persuade the people to attend the Church is overthrown at once! And all who preach like him will drive the Methodists from the Church in spite of all I can do. I preached in the evening on 1 Cor. 13:1-3, and God mightily confirmed his word, applying it to the hearts of many of the hearers ...

Mon. 28.— ... Today I began my 82nd year of life and found myself just as strong for labor and just as fit for bodily or mental exercise as I was 40 years ago. I don't attribute this to secondary causes but to the Sovereign Lord of all. It is he who makes the sun of life stand still as long as it pleases him ...

Sun. JULY 4.—I read prayers and preached in Ouston church, probably filled as it never had been before, and I believe everyone, spiritually awakened or not, felt God was there. The gathering at Epworth market-place in the afternoon was thought to be larger than it had ever been before, and the Holy One of Israel was great in the midst of them ...

Wed. 7.—We estimated that there were 1000 people present in Sheffield at 5 a.m. Afterwards a young gentlewoman was with us at breakfast who was mourning and refused to be comforted. We prayed for her in faith, and in a few hours she was able to rejoice in God her Savior ...

Tues. 13.—I went to Beverley, a place we had tried to reach for many years but without success. Now it seemed the time had come. High and low, rich and poor, flocked together from all around, and all were eager to hear except one man, the town crier. He began yelling loudly till his wife ran to him, grabbed him with one hand, and clapped the other over his mouth, so he couldn't get a word out. God then began a work which I'm persuaded won't soon end ...

Thur. 29.—At Leeds, it being the day for public thanksgiving, there not being enough room for us in the Old Church, I read prayers and preached in our preaching-room. I admired the whole service for the day. The prayers, scriptures, and every part of it pointed to one thing: "Beloved, if God so loved us, we ought also to love one another" [1 John 4:11]. Having five clergymen to assist me, we administered the Lord's Supper, we estimated, to 16- or 1700 persons ...

Fri. AUGUST 20.— ... We went to Haverfordwest, it being the day when the bishop made his visitation. As I was returning in the afternoon from visiting some of the poor people, a carriage in the street forced me to walk very near a clergyman, who made me a low bow. I did the same to him, not knowing at the time that he was the bishop. He has indeed won the hearts of the people in general by his courteous and friendly conduct ...

Thur. 26.—On the road I read through Voltaire's *Memoirs of Himself.* Certainly there never was a more totally proud fool! But even his character is less horrid than that of his royal hero! Surely a more unnatural brute never disgraced a throne before! *Credite Romani; Credite Graii!*[344] A monster who made it a law to let no woman and no priest enter his palace; who not only gloried in the practice of sodomy himself but made it free for all his subjects! What a pity that his father had not beheaded him in his youth and saved him from all this sin and shame ...

Tues. 31.—Dr. Coke, Mr. Whatcoat, and Mr. Vasey came down from London in order to embark for America ...

Wed. SEPTEMBER 8.— ... After preaching to an earnest assembly at Coleford, I met with the fellowship. They contained themselves pretty well during the exhortation, but when I began praying, the flame broke out. Many cried aloud; many sank to the ground; many trembled violently, but all seemed thirsty for God and as if penetrated by the presence of his power ...

Thur. 30.—I had a long conversation with John McGeary, one of our American preachers who just arrived in England. He gave a pleasing account of the work of God there, continually increasing, and he begged me to pay one more visit to America before I die. No,

---

[344] Believe in the Romans; believe in the Greeks!

I won't pay any more visits to new worlds till I go to the world of spirits.

Sat. OCTOBER 2.—It pleased God to pour out his Spirit once more on the family at Kingswood. Many of the children were deeply moved. I talked especially with some who wished to partake of the Lord's Supper. They did so the next morning. Afterwards, I spent a little time with all the children and could easily see an uncommon awe resting on them all ...

Thur. NOVEMBER 18.—I visited two people in Newgate Prison who were sentenced to die. They seemed to have an excellent temperament, being calmly resigned to the will of God. But how much can we make of such impressions, it's hard to say. Often I've known them to disappear as soon as the expectation of death is taken away.

Sat. 20.—At 3 a.m. two or three men broke into our house through the kitchen window, then came up into the parlor and broke into Mr. Moore's bureau, where they found two or three pounds. The night before, I'd stopped him from leaving 70 pounds there that he had just received. They next broke open the cupboard and took some silver spoons. Just at this moment the alarm clock, which Mr. Moore mistakenly had set for 3:30 rather than for 4:00 as usual, went off with a thundering noise. The thieves ran away as quickly as they could, though their work wasn't half done, and the whole damage that we sustained amounted to six pounds[345] ...

Mon. 22.—At Whittlebury, the Presbyterian minister offered me the use of his meeting-house and I willingly accepted. I believe it was able to hold almost as many people as the chapel at West Street, but it still couldn't contain the assembly, and God uttered his voice—yes, and that a mighty voice. Neither the sorrow nor the joy that was felt that night will quickly be forgotten ...

Mon. DECEMBER 13.—and the two following days, I preached at Canterbury, Dover, and Sittingburn.

Thur. 16.—I went to Sheerness, where Mr. Fox read prayers and I preached on those words in the Second Lesson: "If the righteous

---

[345] One pound = $235; 70 pounds = about $16,500; 6 pounds = $1410 in 2020 USD.

scarcely be saved, where will be ungodly and the sinners appear?" [1 Peter 4:18]. I hardly ever spoke stronger words; may God make the application! I never before found this fellowship in the condition they are now, in general all being thirsty for God, and increasing in number as well as in grace ...

Mon. 20.—I went to Hinxworth, where I was glad to meet Mr. Simeon, Fellow of King's College in Cambridge. He has spent some time with Mr. Fletcher at Madeley. They are two kindred souls, resembling each other both in spiritual fervor and their earnest way of expressing themselves. He gave me the pleasing information that there are three parish churches in Cambridge where true scriptural religion is preached and where several young gentlemen gladly drink it in ...

Sun. 26.—I preached the final sermon to condemned criminals in Newgate. Forty-seven had death sentences. While they were entering, there was something awful in the clinking of their chains, but no sound was heard from them or the crowded audience after I gave my text: "There is more joy in heaven over one sinner that repents than over 99 who don't need to repent" [Luke 15:7]. The power of the Lord was strikingly present, and most of the prisoners were in tears. A few days later, 20 of them were executed at the same time, five of whom died in peace. I greatly approved of the spirit and behavior of Mr. Villette, the priest in charge of the prisoners, and rejoiced to hear that it was the same on all similar occasions ...

1785

Sat. JANUARY 1.—Whether this is the last or not, may it be the best year of my life!

Sun. 2.—More people were present this evening at the renewal of our covenant with God than we've ever seen before on this occasion.

Tues. 4.—At this season we usually give out coal and bread to the poor of our fellowship, but now I considered they needed clothes as well as food. So on this and the next four days I walked through the town and begged 200 pounds[346] in order to clothe those who

---

[346] $47,000 in 2020 USD.

needed it most, but it was hard work, as most streets were filled with melting snow, often ankle-deep, so that my feet were steeped in slush nearly from morning till evening. I held out pretty well till Saturday evening, when I was in bed with a severe diarrhea ...

Sun. 23.—Morning and afternoon I preached at West Street, and in the evening in the chapel at Knightsbridge. I think it will be my last time there, since I don't know that I've ever seen a congregation behave worse.

Tues. 25.—I spent two or three hours in the House of Lords. I had often heard that this is the most respectable assembly in England. But was I disappointed! What is a lord but a sinner born to die! ...

Sun. FEBRUARY 6.—[*In London*] We had a love-feast. I couldn't help but notice the way that several of them spoke, one after another. Not just the content, but the language, the accent, the tone of voice, by which illiterate men and women, young and old, spoke such that a scholar needn't be ashamed of. Who teaches like [God]?! ...

Fri. MARCH 4.—I took a walk through the Royal Hospital for sick and wounded sailors. I never saw anything of the kind so complete. Every part is convenient and impressively neat. There is nothing superfluous or purely ornamental, either inside or outside. The only thing that seems to be lacking is a man of faith and zeal to watch over the souls of the poor patients and teach them to take advantage of their affliction ...

Thur. 24.—I had breakfast at Mrs. Price's, a Quaker who keeps a boarding school. I was well pleased with her children, so elegantly plain in their behavior as well as their dress. I was led—I don't know how—to speak to them at length, then to pray, and we were all comforted ...

I pondered how strangely the grain of mustard-seed [*referring to his ministry*], planted about 50 years ago, has grown up. It has spread through all Great Britain and Ireland, the Isle of Wight and the Isle of Man, through the whole Continent, into Canada and Newfoundland. And the fellowships, in all these parts, walk by one rule, knowing that religion is holy dispositions and striving to worship God, not in form only, but also "in spirit and in truth" [John 4:23-24] ...

Sat. 26.—In Quinton, in the evening, my heart was enlarged as I've seldom known, so I held the congregation longer than I usually do. And all the people seemed determined to "glorify God with their body and their spirit" [cf. 1 Cor. 6:20].

Sun. 27 (Easter).—I preached at 7 a.m. on "The Lord is risen indeed" [Luke 24:34], with an unusual degree of freedom. Then I met with the local preachers,[347] several of whom seem to have caught the fashionable disease, desiring to be independent. At first they were quite heated, but at length agreed to act by the rules laid down by the Minutes of the Conference ...

Mon. 28.—I preached a funeral sermon for Sarah Wood, one of the first members of our Society. For over 50 years she adorned the gospel, being an example of all holiness. She was bed-ridden for several months. When asked if she didn't get bored, she replied, "No, the Bible is my delight." "How's that possible," her friend said, "since you can't see?" "Very easily," she replied," because the Lord brings it to my remembrance." So without doubt or fear, she delivered up her soul to her merciful and faithful Creator ...

Wed. APRIL 6.— ... Between 9 and 10 a.m. on Saturday the 9th we went on board the *Clermont* packet boat, but the wind was a dead calm till past 10 a.m. on Sunday the 19th [10th], when those on board asked me to give them a sermon. After doing so, I prayed that God would give us a full and speedy passage. While I was still speaking, the wind sprang up, and in 12 hours brought us to Dublin Bay. Doesn't our Lord still hear prayers? ...

On Tuesday and the next three days, I examined the fellowship. I never found it in such a condition before: Many of them rejoiced in God their Savior, and both men and women wore clothes as plain as those in Bristol and London. I truly believe that many love God with all their heart, and their number increases daily. The total number of the Dublin fellowship is 747. Over 300 of these have been added in a few months—something new and unexpected! ... But such a shower of grace never continues long, and afterwards people may resist the Holy Spirit as before ... What we all must do is to be diligent to encourage as many as possible to press on in spite of the outflowing

---

[347] I.e., preachers staying in a locality; pastors as opposed to evangelists.

tide. And we must especially warn each other not to grow weary or faint in our mind. Perhaps we might see such an amazing work as that recently at Paulton, near Bath, where there was a swift work of God and yet, a year later, out of 100 converted, there wasn't a single backslider! ...

Mon. 27.— ... As I entered Aghrim, the rector, who was waiting at his gate, welcomed me into the country and offered me the use of his church now and whenever I pleased. I preached there at 6 p.m. The church was completely filled with well-behaved hearers. But the Methodist fellowship here, like that at Tyrrell's Pass, has almost shrunk to nothing! Such is the destructive influence of riches! We find this to be true everywhere: The more people increase in worldly goods, with few exceptions, the more they decrease in grace ...

Fri. MAY 6.—In Cork, I examined the condition of the fellowship closely. I found that they numbered about 400, many of whom were very earnest. Many children, especially the girls, were unquestionably justified, and some of them also sanctified and examples of all holiness.

But how will we keep up the flame that is now kindled, not just in Cork, but in many places in Ireland? Not by sitting still, but by stirring up the gift of God that's in them, by constant watchfulness, by warning and exhorting everyone, by besieging the throne [of God] with all the powers of prayer. And after all that, some will and some won't profit from the grace they've received. Consequently, there must be a falling away [at least in part]. We shouldn't let this discourage us but do all we can today, leaving tomorrow to God ...

Sun. 8.—In the afternoon I stood in the empty lot near the preaching-house, capable of holding many thousands. A huge crowd gathered. There was no disturbance. The days of tumult here are gone, and now for a long time God has made our enemies to be at peace with us ...

Wed. 18.—Finding that a little girl had sat up all night and then walked two miles to see me, I took her up in my buggy and was surprised to find her continually rejoicing in God. The person with whom the preachers lodge told me that for two years she has possessed his pure love ...

VOLUME 4: 1773-1790

Thur. 26.—I preached in the assembly room at Swadlingbar, but with difficulty. My cold had gotten so bad that I could only sing or speak in one tone of voice. Still I made the effort to preach in the church at Balliconnell in the evening, though it was packed and very hot.

Fri. 27.—Feeling like I'd felt 11 years ago, and not knowing how much time I might have left to work, I decided to do what little I could while I could. So I began by preaching at 5 a.m., and although I could barely be heard at first, the longer I spoke, the more my voice was strengthened. By the time I was half through my sermon, everyone could hear. To God be all the glory! ...

Tues. 31.— ... At 11 a.m. I preached in the avenue at Armagh again. It rained all the time, yet the assembly was large and attentive. Afterwards a decent woman whom I never saw before or since asked to speak to me and said, "I met you at Caladon. Then I had a violent headache for four weeks, but fully believed that I'd be well if you'd lay your hand on my cheek, which I begged you to do. From that moment I've been completely well." If so, give God the glory ...

Thur. JUNE 2.— ... The fellowship in Londonderry hasn't been as well-established for many years as it is now. What's mainly lacking is zeal for God and entire self-devotion to him ...

Tues. 7.— ... I accepted the offer of the Presbyterian meeting-house at Coleraine, preaching there at noon and at 6 p.m.

Wed. 8.—After preaching in the morning, I left many of the loving people in tears ... In the afternoon I walked over to Gracehill, the Moravian settlement ... Nothing can exceed the neatness of the rooms or the courtesy of the inhabitants, but if they have more courtesy, we have more love. We don't allow a stranger, especially a Christian, to visit us without asking him to "have a bite or take supper" with us. But this is their way, I'm sorry to say. When I called on Bishop Antone in Holland, an old acquaintance whom I hadn't seen for 46 years, till we had both grown gray-headed, he didn't so much as offer to wet my lips! Isn't this way shameful? Isn't it contrary not only to Christianity but to common humanity? Isn't it a way that a Jew, a Muslim, even an honest pagan, would be ashamed of? ...

Serious Joy (John Wesley's *Journal*)

Tues. 28.—By God's good providence, I finished the 82nd year of my life. Is anything too hard for God? It's now 11 years since I've felt anything like weariness. Many times I speak till my voice fails and I can't speak any longer. Often my strength fails, and I can't walk any farther. Yet even then I don't feel any weariness, but am perfectly at ease from head to foot. I dare not credit this to natural causes; it's the will of God …

Wed. JULY 6.—We concluded our conference. I remember few such conferences, either in England or Ireland, where the preachers were completely unanimous and so determined to give themselves up to God …

Mon. 18.—At 5 a.m. in London, not only was the morning chapel well filled, but many stood in the large chapel. I trust they didn't come in vain. The rest of the week I was fully occupied writing for our magazine and preparing for our conference …

Mon. AUGUST 1.—Having weighed the matter thoroughly with a few select friends, I yielded to their judgment and set apart three of our well-tried preachers, John Pawson, Thomas Hanby, and Joseph Taylor, to minister in Scotland, and I trust God will bless their service and show that he has sent them …

Mon. 15.—I preached in Shaftesbury at nine to such a gathering as I'd never seen there before. I was glad to see a gentleman among them who, 30 years ago, sent his officer to prevent me from preaching in his borough …

Sat. 27.—About 9 a.m. I preached at the copper works, near the Hayle in the new preaching-house. I suppose there's none like it in England or in all Europe or even in the whole world. It's round and all the walls are brass—that is, brass slugs. You'd think nothing could destroy it till heaven and earth pass away …

Sun. 28.—At 8:30 a.m. I preached at St Agnes to the largest assembly I ever saw there. Between 1 and 2 p.m. I preached in the streets at Redruth to thousands upon thousands. And my strength was according to my need; still I was afraid that in the evening I couldn't make everyone hear. But although we estimated there were 2- or 3000 more than before, I was later told that they heard to the very outskirts of the gathering while I applied those solemn words: "One thing is needful" [Luke 10:42] …

Thur. SEPTEMBER 1.— ... From Wallington we went on to Ditchet. The people here pay close attention, so all I had to do was to apply the promises. The fellowship is constantly growing, and more and more of the hearers are convicted and justified. The strangest thing is that there are no opposers in the town; rich and poor, all acknowledge the work of God ...

Wed. 7.—In an open place, near the road at Mells, just as I began to speak, a wasp stung me on the lip. I was afraid it would swell up and interfere with my speaking, but it didn't. I spoke distinctly for nearly two hours, and was none the worse for it ...

Sun. OCTOBER 2.—After reading prayers and preaching, I administered the sacrament to many hundreds of communicants. We then solemnly renewed our covenant with God, and while we solemnly acclaimed him to be our God, I believe many felt with holy, humble joy, that he acclaimed us to be his people ...

Tues. NOVEMBER 1.—When I came to Northampton, the use of the new Presbyterian meeting-house was offered to me, twice as large as our own. The large assembly was deeply attentive. Many came again in the morning, I trust not without a blessing ...

Mon. DECEMBER 5.—Throughout this week, I spent every spare hour in the unpleasant but necessary work of going through London begging for the poor men who had worked finishing the New Chapel. It's true that I'm not obligated to do this, but if I don't do it, nobody else will ...

Thur. 22.—I preached at Highgate. Considering how magnificent a place this is, I'm not surprised that so little good has been done here. For what has religion to do with palaces? ...

Mon. 26.—I baptized a young woman brought up an Anabaptist. And God bore witness to his ordinance, filling her heart at the same time with peace and joy unspeakable.

This week I tried to point out all the errors in the eight editions of *The Armenian Magazine.* This I must do myself; otherwise several passages in them will be unintelligible ...

1786

Sun. FEBRUARY 5.—In the morning, in the New Chapel, while I was applying that solemn declaration, "The Lord's hand is not short so that he cannot save, nor is his ear dull so that he cannot hear" [Isa. 59:1], he did indeed speak aloud through his Word so that stout hearts trembled. I broke out into prayer, and the power of God came mightily upon us, and there was a general cry of voices. But the voices of two people were heard over all the rest, one praying and one shrieking as in the agonies of death. God relieved the one praying in a few minutes, but the other not until the evening ...

Sun. 19.—I preached in Horselydown Church where, to my surprise, no one seemed to know me either by face or by name. But before I finished, many of the large congregation knew that God was truly there ...

Wed. MARCH 1.—In the afternoon I went over to Kingswood and found the school in excellent order.

Sun. 5.— ... I read prayers, preached, and served communion to over 500 communicants. At 3 p.m. I preached in Temple Church and at 5 p.m. in the New Room. On Friday I baptized a young Negro, who seemed deeply serious and very emotional, as indeed was the whole congregation ...

Mon. APRIL 3.—About 11 a.m. I preached to a crowded assembly in the new [preaching-] house near Chapel-in-the-Frith. Many of these lively people came from the mountains and strongly reminded me of those fine verses in Latin, paraphrased by Dr. Burton thus: "The hills are a refuge for the wild goats, and so are the stony rocks for the conies." ...

It's primarily among these big mountains that so many have been awakened, justified, and, not long after that, perfected in love. But even while they are full of love, Satan strives to push many of them to extravagance. Here are some examples:

1. Often three or four, or even ten or twelve, pray aloud all together. 2. Some of them, perhaps many, all scream at the same time as loudly as they can. 3. Some of them use improper, even indecent, expressions in prayer. 4. Several drop down as if dead and are as still as a corpse, but after a while they jump up and cry "Glory! Glory!" maybe 20 times in a row.

The French prophets did the same, and so did the Jumpers recently in Wales, bringing the real work of God into contempt. Yet whenever we rebuke them, it should be in the mildest and most gentle manner possible ...

Sun. MAY 7.— ... At St. Margaret's, we had a love-feast in the evening at which many very simply testified to what God had done for their souls. I haven't known this fellowship to be in such a healthy condition spiritually for many years. Surely this is due first, to the exact discipline which they've maintained for some time, and second, to the strong and constant exhortation of the believers to go on to perfection ...

Sun. JUNE 4 (Whitsunday [Pentecost]).—I preached at 8 a.m. to an amazing gathering at Ballast Hill, but at the Fell in the afternoon there was twice that number, and in the evening at the Garth-Heads, the number equaled both gatherings together.

On Monday and Tuesday, the assemblies were larger than I can ever remember ...

Sat. 10.—I went to Darlington. Since I was here last, Mr. _____ died and left many thousand pounds to an idle spendthrift, but not a penny to the poor! Oh, unwise steward of the mammon of unrighteousness! [cf. Luke 26 :9]. How much better for him if he had died a beggar!

Tues. 27.—At 1 p.m. I preached at Belton. During my sermon, three little children, the oldest 6 years old and the youngest two-and-a-half, whom their mother had left eating lunch, left the house and went to the side of a well nearby. The youngest child, leaning over, fell in. While the others were trying to pull him out, the board gave way and they all fell in. The youngest fell under the bucket and didn't move any more. The other two held onto the side of the well for a while and then sank into the water, where it's supposed they lay for half an hour or so. When they had been pulled out and someone told me, I immediately advised to rub them with salt and to breathe strongly into their mouths. They did this, but the youngest one was past help. In two or three hours the others were as well as ever.

Wed. 28.—I began the 83rd year of my life. I'm a wonder to myself ... Surely one natural cause is my constant exercise and change of air ...

Thur. JULY 6.— ... We rode on, in a lovely afternoon and through a lovely country, to Nottingham. I preached to a large and well-behaved audience. I love this people. There is something wonderfully pleasing, both in their spirit and in their behavior ...

Sat. 8.— ... This evening, I believe before I finished my sermon, a remarkable instance of divine justice occurred. One man in the street was cursing another, asking God to "blast my [i.e., his own] eyes." At that moment, he himself was struck blind, and I suppose he remains that way ever since ...

Wed. 12.—At noon I preached in the new chapel at Derrington. Building a chapel here was a great act of mercy, since the church wouldn't hold a fifth, or maybe even a tenth, of the inhabitants. At 6 p.m. I preached in our chapel in Birmingham, and immediately afterwards took the stagecoach for London ...

Fri. 21.—I walked to Kingswood School, now one of the most pleasant places in England. I found everything just as I wished: the rules being followed, and the whole behavior of the children showing that they were now directed with the wisdom that comes from above ...

Tues. 25.—Our conference began, with about 80 preachers attending. We met every day at 6 and 9 a.m. and again at 2 p.m. On Tuesday and Wednesday morning, the characters of the preachers were considered, whether already admitted or not. Thursday afternoon, we allowed anyone in our Society to attend, and we considered what some said about separating from the Church of England. But we all decided to continue in it without dissent. And I don't doubt this decision will stand, at least till I go to a better world ...

Sat. AUGUST 12.—[*In Rotterdam*] Mr. Williams, minister of the Episcopal Church, and Mr. Scot, minister of the Scotch Church, both welcomed me to Holland, but their kindness put me in difficulty: Mr. Scot had arranged for me to preach in his church on Sunday afternoon, but Mr. Williams had given notice that I would preach in his church both morning and afternoon that same day. I wanted to reach a compromise, but neither would give in, so the only way I saw to satisfy both was to prolong my stay by a week ... Perhaps God has more work for me to do in Holland than I'm yet aware of ...

VOLUME 4: 1773-1790

Mon. 14.—Embarking at 8 a.m., we went comfortably through one of the most pleasant summer countries in Europe and reached the Hague between 12 and 1 p.m. Determined not to stay at any more inns, I went with Brother Ferguson to his own lodging and passed a quiet, pleasant night. A few pious people came to us in the evening, whom we quickly found to be kindred spirits. I haven't found anyone else since we crossed the sea who seemed as devoted to God ...

Fri. SEPTEMBER 15.—[*Back in England*] I was very satisfied in the evening at the chapel in Guinea Street, Bristol. It was completely filled, and most of the people seemed very affected while (from Heb. 12:1) I described what I take to be the besetting sin of Bristol: love of money and of ease. Indeed, God has already accomplished a great deliverance for many of them, and we hope an even great deliverance will follow ...

I went to bed at 9:30 p.m., my usual time, feeling in perfect health. But just at midnight I woke up with a terrible diarrhea, which didn't allow me to rest more than a few minutes at a time. Finding that it got worse rather than better, though without the cramp that usually accompanied it, I sent for Dr. Whitehead. He came about 4 a.m., and by God's blessing in three hours I was as well as ever. Nor did I feel at all weak or faint, but preached morning and afternoon, and met with the fellowship in the evening with no weariness. Of such a man [as Dr. Whitehead] I would boldly say, along with Bin Sirach,[348] **"Honor the physician, for God has appointed him"** [my emphasis] ...

Tues. OCTOBER 3.—From Chatham we sailed down, with a pleasant wind, to Sheerness. The preaching-house here is now finished, but by unheard of means: The building was started a few months ago by a handful of men who had no likely means of finishing it, but God so moved on the hearts of people in the Dock that even those who didn't pretend to any religion—carpenters, shipwrights, laborers—ran up, during their off-hours, and worked with all their might, without any pay! By this means a large square house was soon elegantly finished, both inside and out. And it is the

---

[348] Author and title of an apocryphal book, included in the Catholic Bible and some Protestant versions.

neatest building, next to the New Chapel in London, of any in the south of England ...

Tues. 24.—I met the classes at Deptford and was implored to set the Sunday service in our preaching-room at the same time as that of the Church of England. Obviously, this would be a formal separation from the Church. All over England we've timed our morning and evening services so as not to conflict with the Church, in order that those who are members of the Church may attend both services if they so choose. Setting it at the same hour forces them to separate either from the Church or from us, and I judge this not only to be unnecessary but unlawful for me to do ...

Sun. DECEMBER 3.—At Harwich, I administered the Lord's Supper at 8 a.m.,[349] and afterwards attended our parish church. Beside the little group that went with me, and the clergyman and minister, I think we had five men and six women. And this is a Christian country!

There was no way our preaching-house could hold the assembly either in the afternoon or the evening, and at both times the power of God was great in the midst of them. For many years, I haven't seen such a prospect of doing good in this city.

Mon. 4.— ... I heard of a young woman in that country, Sarah Mallett, who had unusual seizures and of another who recently had preached, but I didn't know they were the same person. However, I ran into her in the very house I went to, and talked to her at length ...

A few years ago, she had a deep impression that she should call sinners to repentance. She strongly resisted this, believing herself unqualified both by her sinfulness and her lack of learning till she received the impression, "If you don't do it willingly, you'll do it whether you want to or not." She fell into a fit, and while completely senseless, thought she was in the preaching-house in Lowestoft, where she prayed and preached for an hour to a large audience. Then she opened her eyes and recovered her senses. In a year or two, she had 18 of these fits, in every one of which she imagined herself to be preaching to some assembly or another. She then cried out, "Lord, I

---

[349] I.e., in the Methodist preaching-house. For many years Wesley had resisted administering Holy Communion in his preaching-houses.

will obey you! I will call sinners to repentance!" She's done so occasionally since that time, and she's had no more seizures ...

Sat. 23.—Being begged, I was persuaded, though having little hope of doing good, to visit two of the criminals in Newgate Prison who were sentenced to death. They seemed serious [about their repentance and faith], but I put little stress on appearances of this kind. However, I wrote to a leading citizen, and perhaps for this reason they were given a suspension of their execution ...

1787

Tues. JANUARY 2.—I went to Deptford, but it seemed I had fallen into a den of lions. Most of the leading men of the fellowship were completely unrestrained, arguing for separating from the Church. I tried to reason with them, but in vain; they had neither common sense nor even good manners left. Finally, after meeting the whole fellowship, I told them: "If you're resolved, you may have your services at Church hours, but mark this: From that time on, you'll see my face no more." This struck deep, and from that time on I've heard no more about separating from the Church ...

Mon. 8.—and the four following days, I went around begging for the poor. I hoped to provide food and clothing for those of our fellowship who are in great need but have no weekly income—about 200 people. I was very disappointed. Indeed, six or seven of our brethren gave 10 pounds apiece. If 40 or 50 had done this, I could have reached my goal. However, much good was done with 200 pounds,[350] and many sad hearts were gladdened ...

Mon. FEBRUARY 12.—As there were no seats available on the York coach, Mr. Broadbent and I rode horses cross-country to Hinckley. I asked about that poor wretch who, when I was here last, while he was praying for God to damn his eyes, was at that very moment struck blind. It seems he continued that way for some time, but as soon as he recovered his sight, he was just as irreverent and obscene as before ...

Tues. 27.—We went on to Plymouth-Dock. The large new preaching-house, by far the best in the west of England, was well

---

[350] Ten pounds = $2400; 200 pounds = about $47,000 in 2020 USD.

filled, though on short notice; and they seemed to take my exhortation to heart: "Rejoice in the Lord, O you righteous" [Psalm 33:1].

It satisfied me to find the fellowship here flourishing more than ever. Despite all the pains that have been taken and all the tactics used to tear them apart, they stick together and so increase in number as well as in strength ...

Fri. MARCH 2.—I was asked to go over to Tarpoint, a village on the Cornish side of the water. A large group from the Dock came with us, along with a huge crowd from all around. I suppose many of these had never heard this sort of preaching before. They listened with indescribable attention and I trust not in vain. It's as if God opened the windows of heaven and sent a gracious rain upon his inheritance. I hope for a bountiful harvest springing from the seed that was sown this hour ...

Sun. 4.—At Plymouth-Dock I began the service at 9:30 a.m. and finished before 1 p.m. I suppose such a number of communicants had never been seen there before, but there was no disorder or hurry at all. We had more difficulty in the evening: The throng was so great that it was impossible for me to get through them to the pulpit, so finally they lifted me over the seats. Again God spoke through his Word, I believe to all who could get in; but some were forced to go away ...

Sat. 10.—I had the pleasure of an hour's conversation with Mrs. Fletcher. She seems to be rapidly growing in grace, ripening for a better world. I encouraged her to do all the good she could do during her short stay in Bristol. Accordingly, the following week she met with as many of the classes as her time and strength allowed, and her words were like fire, sending both light and warmth to the hearts of all who heard her ...

Thur. 29.—... The love-feast at Burslem was such as I haven't known for many years. Two or three spoke first, and the power of God fell on all who were present, some praying and others giving thanks, so that their voices could hardly be heard. Two or three were speaking at once till I gently advised them to speak one at a time, and they did so with amazing energy ... Indeed, for some time there's been such an outpouring of the Spirit here as nowhere else in the kingdom, especially in the prayer meetings. Fifteen or twenty have been justified in one day; some of these had been the most notorious, abandoned sinners in all the countryside. And people flock into the fellowship from all around: six, eight, or ten in one evening ...

Sat. 31.—I went on to Macclesfield and found a people still alive to God in spite of rapidly increasing riches. If they keep doing so, it will be the only case of such I've known in over 50 years. I warned them in the strongest terms I could and believe some of them had ears to hear ...

Mon. APRIL 23.— ... At Eyre-Court, I preached on "I am not ashamed of the gospel of Christ" [Rom. 1:16], a subject that seemed suited to the hearers, many whom are held back mainly due to the shame of being completely committed Christians ...

Fri. 27.—We went to Kilkenny, 29 Irish miles from Mountmelick. Religion here was at a low ebb and there was hardly any Methodist fellowship left, when God sent three companies of horse troops, several of them full of faith and love. Since they came, the work of God has revived. I never saw the house so filled since it was built, and the power of God seemed to rest on the gathering as if he would have a people in this place ...

Mon. MAY 7.—The assembly at 5 a.m. was little less than what we used to see on Sunday evening. This time we also had many merry and honorable people, who seem for the moment almost persuaded to be Christians. Oh, what throngs of half-awakened sinners will be wide awake when it's too late! On Tuesday likewise the gatherings were very large, and all paid serious attention ...

Thur. 10.— ... At noon we took a walk to Castle Barnard ... Mr. Barnard closely resembles in features and manner the late Sir George Saville. Though he is by far the richest person in this region, he keeps no racehorses or hounds, but loves his wife and home and spends his time and fortune improving his estate and employing the poor. Gentlemen of this spirit are a blessing to their neighborhood. May God increase their number!

Sat. 12.— ... In Cork, I waited on the mayor, an upright, sensible man, who is busily working from morning to night, doing all the good he can. He has already persuaded the city corporation to make it a law that the 200 pounds[351] a year, which was spent on two entertainments, should be used in the future to relieve suffering freemen, their wives and children. He has carefully set in order the workhouse [for the unemployed], and has instituted a humane society for persons seemingly drowned.[352] And he hasn't grown weary removing abuses of every kind. When will our English mayors imitate the mayor of Cork? ... He was so good as to walk with me all through the city to the workhouse and to go with me through the apartments, which are quite sweet and spacious. One hundred and ninety-two poor are now lodged there, and the master (a pious man, and one of our Society), watches over them, reads with them, and prays with them as if they were his own children ...

Wed. 16.—In Limerick, the assembly at 5 a.m. filled the preaching-house almost as well as it was in the evening. Finding a remarkable spiritual deadness, I asked the reasons for this and found that: 1. For several months there had been a serious misunderstanding between the preachers and the leading members of the fellowship. So on the one hand, the preachers had little life or spirit to preach, and on the other, the congregation dwindled away; 2. Many members had stopped attending their circles, and many others seldom attended their classes; 3. Prayer meetings had been abandoned entirely. No wonder all the people had become dead as stones! ...

After the morning service I met with the stewards and leaders, seeking the cause of the recent misunderstanding. I found that the matter itself was nothing, but impatience on both sides had made a mountain out of a mole-hill. **Oh, how patient, how meek, how gentle toward all ought a preacher, especially a Methodist, to be!** [my emphasis] ...

Sun. 27.—I hastened to Clones, but needn't have hurried, because the church service there didn't begin until noon and ended at 3:30 p.m. The question then was, where would I preach? The strong wind and heavy rain made it impracticable for me to preach at the head of the market-place as I'd intended, but I found a way to stand

---

[351] $47,000 in 2020 USD.
[352] It is unclear to me what this means; perhaps persons lost at sea.

on one side of it in a doorway where I was pretty well sheltered. Although the poor people were exposed to heavy rain all through my sermon, none seemed to pay it any attention. And God did indeed send a gracious rain upon their souls, so that many rejoiced with joy unspeakable ...

Sat. JUNE 9.—We went through lovely country to Antrim. Here likewise the Presbyterian minister offered me the use of a large, spacious house. The Bible in the pulpit was lying open, and I chose for the subject of my message the words that first met my eyes: "When they had nothing to pay, he freely forgave them both" [Luke 7:42] ...

Sun. 17.— ... In the evening the seceders (who would think?) freely gave me the use of their large meeting-house. It was full from one end to another, but a wise young gentleman cracked that I had "quite mistaken my subject, my sermon being calculated for the common people, not for gentlefolks." ...

Thur. 21.— ... In the afternoon it pleased God to bring us safe to Dublin, after an absence of a little over two months.

Fri. 22.—I began visiting the classes, which kept me busy till the following Thursday morning. We found it necessary to exclude 112 members. There remained 1136 ...

Tues. 26.—We were pleasantly surprised with Dr. Coke's arrival. He had come from Philadelphia in 29 days, and gave us a positive account of the work of God in America ...

Sat. 30.—I asked all our preachers to meet me and to consider the condition of our brothers and sisters in America, who have been afraid of their own shadow, as if the English preachers were going to enslave them. I believe that fear is now gone and that they are more aware of Satan's devices ...

Wed. JULY 11.—At 5 a.m. I said a fond farewell to the loving people of Bethesda, having finished all my business there. In the afternoon I went down with my friends, having rented the whole ship, and went on board the *Prince of Wales* ... At 7 p.m. we set sail with a fair, moderate wind. Between 9 and 10 p.m. I lay down as usual and slept till nearly 4 a.m., when I was awakened by an unusual noise, and found the ship beating on a large rock, about a league from Holyhead ... We immediately began praying, and soon the ship—I don't know how—broke free of the rock and sailed on her way with no more damage than to a few of the planks in the hull ...

Fri. 27.— ... We went on to Bolton. Here 800 poor children are taught in our Sunday schools by about 80 teachers, whose only pay is what their Great Teacher will pay them [in the end]. About 100 of them, boys and girls, are taught to sing, and they sang so correctly that, all together, they seemed to be but one voice. The house was completely filled while 1 explained and applied the first commandment. Without this, what is all morality or religion? Just a castle in the air. In the evening, since many of the children were still hovering about, I asked 40 or 50 to come in and sing ... Though some remained silent, not being able to sing because of their tears, the harmony was such as I believe wouldn't be equaled in the king's chapel ...

Tues. AUGUST 14.— ... [*Sailing to Guernsey*] It "so happened" (to use a common phrase) that three or four who sailed with us from England, a gentleman with his wife and sister, were close relatives of the governor. He came to us this morning and, when I went into the room, behaved with the utmost courtesy. This little incident may remove prejudice and make a more open way for the gospel ...

Thur. 16.— ... In the evening I preached at the other end of Guernsey town in our own preaching-house. So many people squeezed in (though not nearly all who tried) that it was as hot as an oven. But no one seemed to pay this any attention, for the Word of God was sharper than a two-edged sword [cf. Heb. 4:12] ...

Sun. 19.—Joseph Bradford preached at 6 a.m. at Mont-Plaiser les Terres to a large gathering. I preached at 8:30, and the preaching-house contained the assembly. At 10 a.m. I went to the French church, where there was large and well-behaved congregation. At 5 p.m. we had the largest assembly of all, of whom I took a solemn and affectionate farewell, as it is likely I may never see them again till we meet in Abraham's bosom ...

Wed. 22.—[*On St. Helier's Island*] In the evening the preaching-room couldn't contain the people, so I had to stand in the lot beside it. I preached on Romans 3:22-23, and spoke very plainly.

VOLUME 4: 1773-1790

Even the gentry listened with close attention. God turns even little things to his own glory; probably many of these gather because I've lived so many years! Even this may be the means of their living forever!

Sat. 25.— ... This morning I had a detailed conversation like I had had once or twice before with Jeannie Bisson here of Jersey, such a young woman as I've hardly seen anywhere else. She seems to be completely devoted to God and to have constant communion with him. Her understanding is clear and strong, and I don't sense the least trace of enthusiasm. I'm afraid she won't live long. I'm amazed at the grace of God manifested in her. I think she is far beyond Madame Guyon [in France], in deep communion with God, and I don't think I've found her equal in England. Precious as my time is, it would have been worth my while to have come to Jersey if only to see this marvel of grace ...

Wed. 29.— ... I looked over Archbishop's Usher's *Letters,* and was surprised to find that great man was fully convinced, 1. that the Septuagint[353] translation continually adds to, takes from, and changes the Hebrew text at pleasure; 2. that this could not possibly be by mistake but on purpose; 3. that the original translation of it was lost long ago, and whatever since has gone under that name is a false copy, with many omissions, additions, and alterations of the Hebrew text, yet not in such a way that destroys the foundation.[354] ...

Tues. SEPTEMBER 4.— ... In the afternoon we drank tea at a friend's house, who mentioned a captain who had just arrived from France and planned to sail in the morning for Penzance. The wind would be suitable to go there but not to Southampton. We saw the clear hand of God in this and agreed with him immediately, so in the morning of Thursday the 6th we went on board with a fair, moderate wind. But no sooner did we embark than the wind died away. We cried to God for help, and the wind soon sprang up, just right, and didn't die until it brought us into Penzance Bay ...

---

[353] The translation into Greek of the Hebrew Bible or Old Testament, around 200 B.C. It was very influential in the early church.
[354] From my own comparison of the LXX (Septuagint) and the Masoretic (Hebrew) text, I can verify that items 1 and 2 are true; also the conclusion to 3.

Mon. OCTOBER 1.—On this and the following three days, I spoke to members of our fellowship one by one and was very refreshed, as the love of many had not grown cold and their number had considerably increased ...

Wed. 10.—I withdrew and spent the rest of the week answering letters and writing articles for *The Armenian Magazine* ...

Mon. 29.—I reviewed all the manuscripts I'd collected for the magazine, trashed what I didn't think worth publishing, and corrected the rest ...

Sat. NOVEMBER 3.—I had a long conversation with Mr. Clulow on that detestable law called the Conventicle Act.[355] ...

Mon. 5.—The congregation in Dorking was, as usual, large and serious, but our fellowship hasn't increased at all, so we haven't gained anything by having our service at the same time as the Church, which some imagined would have done wonders. I don't know that it's done any good anywhere in England, although in Scotland, I believe it has ...

Mon. 19.—I began the unpleasant work of visiting the classes in Spitalfields. I continue to do this in London and Bristol, Cork and Dublin, but my assistants supply my lack in other fellowships.

Sun. 25.—I preached two charity sermons at West Street on behalf of our poor children. In these I tried to warn them, and those who brought them, against that English sin, ungodliness, the reproach of our nation, in which we exceed all other people on earth ...

Tues. DECEMBER 4.—I withdrew to Rainham to prepare another edition of the New Testament for the press ...

Fri. 7.—I returned to London and again considered what we should do in our current financial situation. After lengthy consultation with my brethren, they asked me: 1. to appoint a few of them to divide the town among them, and to ask our brethren who were able to help in this necessary business; and 2. that a collection should be made in all our preaching-houses for the same purpose.

---

[355] The Conventicle Act 1664 was an Act of the Parliament of England (16 Charles II) that forbade conventicles, defined as religious assemblies of more than five people other than an immediate family, outside the auspices of the Church of England. (Wikipedia)

Over 300 pounds[356] were raised by these means and the whole debt cleared.

Sun. 9.—I went downstairs at 5:30 a.m. but found no preacher in the chapel, even though there were three or four preachers in the house; so I preached myself. Afterwards, asking why none of my family attended the morning preaching, they said it was because they sat up too late. I was determined to put an end to this, and so ordered: 1. that everyone under my roof should go to bed at 9 p.m., and 2. that everyone should attend the morning preaching. And they have done so ever since …

Sat. 22.—An artist persuaded me to sit for an hour and a half total for my portrait. I think it was the best ever done of me. But what is the portrait of a man over 80 years old!?

Mon. 24.—We had another meeting of the committee which, after a calm and loving discussion, deemed it best: 1. that the men and women should continue sitting separately; and 2. that no one should claim any pew as his own, either in the New Chapel or in West Street.

1788

Mon. FEBRUARY 25.—I took a solemn leave of the congregation at West Street by applying once again what I had proclaimed 50 years before: "By grace are you saved, through faith" [Eph. 2:8]. At the meeting after the preaching, the presence of God filled the place in a marvelous way. The next evening we had a large gathering at the New Chapel to whom I declared the whole counsel of God. I seemed to have finished my work in London now. If I see it again—good; if not, I pray God to raise up others who will be more faithful and more successful in his work! …

Mon. MARCH 3.—[*In Bristol*] On Tuesday I announced that on Thursday evening I would preach on the subject now one everyone's mind—slavery. As a result, that evening the preaching-house was filled from one end to the other with noblemen and commoners, rich and poor. I preached on that ancient prophecy, "God shall enlarge Japhet, and he shall dwell in the tents of Shem; and Canaan shall be

---

[356] About $71,000 in 2020 USD.

his servant" [Gen. 9:26]. Halfway through my message, while all were paying deep attention, a tremendous noise occurred—no one could tell how—and shot like lightning through the whole assembly. The terror and confusion were indescribable ... The people rushed at each other violently; the benches were broken into pieces; and $9/10^{th}$s of the congregation seemed to be struck with the same panic. In about six minutes the storm ceased, almost as suddenly as it arose. And all being calm, I went on without further interruption.

It was the strangest incident of the kind that I can remember, and I don't believe anyone can explain it without supposing some influence outside of nature. Satan fought lest his kingdom be delivered up. We set Friday apart as a day of fasting and prayer, that God would remember those poor human outcasts, and (what seems impossible with men, considering the wealth and power of their oppressors) make a way for them to escape and break off their chains ...

Thur. 20.—I went to Stourport ... Here a few years ago Mr. Cowell paid most of the expenses to build a preaching-house where both Calvinists and Arminians could preach, but when it was completed, the Arminian preachers were totally excluded. Rather than contest the matter legally, Mr. Cowell built another preaching-house, even larger and more spacious. I preached there at noon to a large gathering and to an even larger one in the evening. Several Anglican clergymen were present and were as attentive as any of the people. I believe it probable that there will be a deep work of God at this place ...

Sun. APRIL 6.—The new church[357] was half filled in the morning but completely filled in the afternoon, and great was our rejoicing in the Lord, both then and at 6 p.m. ...

Sat. 19.—We went on to Bolton, where I preached in the evening in one of the most elegant preaching-houses in the kingdom, and to one of the conregations most alive [to God]. And I must declare that there isn't such a choir in any [other] of the Methodist congregations in the three kingdoms. There can't be, because [here] we have nearly 100 such sopranos, selected out of our Sunday

---

[357] Note, again, the language, moving from "preaching-house" to "church."

schools and rightly trained, as aren't found together in any chapel, cathedral, or music room within the four seas. Besides, the spirit with which they all sing and the beauty of many of them fits the melody so well, that I defy any to exceed it, except the singing of angels in our Father's house ...

Sun. 20.—[Our children in Bolton] are an example to the whole town. Their usual pastime is to visit the poor that are sick (sometimes six, eight, or 10 going together), to encourage, comfort, and pray with them. Often 10 or more of them gather to sing and pray by themselves; sometimes 30 or 40. They are so seriously involved in singing, praying, and crying alternately, that they don't know how to part. You children that read or hear this, why shouldn't you go and do likewise? Isn't God here as well as at Bolton? Let God arise and maintain his own cause! Even "out of the mouth of babes and sucklings" [Psalm 8:2; Matt. 21:16].

Mon. 21.—I went on over miserable roads to Blackburn where, despite the constant rain, the new preaching-house was completely filled with serious, well-behaved people.

Tues. 22.—Over equally "good" roads we got to Paddiham. I preached to an assembly as quiet, but not as alive, as that at Bolton. From there we went in the afternoon through still more "wonderful" roads to Haslingden—roads sufficient to lame any horse or shake any carriage to pieces. N.B.-I'll never try to travel on these roads again till they are completely repaired! ...

Thur. MAY 1.—[*In Huddersfield*] The gathering at 5 a.m. was very large, people coming from many miles around, but that at Shelly, a solitary place, six or seven miles away, where I was forced to preach outdoors at 9 a.m., was six or seven times larger—in fact, the largest I've seen since I left Manchester. And the power of God was especially present, both to wound and to heal. I believe the assembly at Wakefield in the evening was still larger, and the greenness of the trees, the smoothness of the meadow, the calmness of the evening, and the stillness of the whole assembly, made it a delightful sight ...

Sat. JUNE 7.—Our brethren in Stanhope thought the preaching-house would contain the assembly at 5 a.m. It was a large upper room. But before I began to speak, it was very crowded, the main beam that supported it gave way, and the floor began to sink. Some yelled, "The room is falling!" One man jumped out of the window; the rest left slowly and quietly without the least bit of hurry or confusion. The only thing hurt was a poor dog that was under the window. I then preached outdoors to two or three times as many as the room would have contained, and all paid close attention. Oh, how white these fields are unto harvest! [cf. John 4:35] …

Sun. 8.— … I preached at Gateshead Fell, I suppose, to twice as many as were at Ballast-hills, on the joy in heaven "over one sinner that repents" [Luke 15:7]. Although the sun was very hot and the wind very cold, the people paid no attention to either one; they seemed only to attend to the voice of God and the breathing of his Spirit …

Sun. 15.— … [*At Whitby*] After preaching at 5 a.m. on the education of children, I made a collection for Kingswood School, especially using the opportunity to refute the threadbare slander of my "getting so much money." We ended our service with a comforting love-feast …

Sun. 22.—Mr. Clark, the vicar, invited me to preach in the high church. I explained what it is to build our house on the rock and applied it as strongly as I could. I dined with Mr. Clark at the vicarage, finding him to be a friendly, sensible man whom I truly believe fears God. By the providence of God, all three of the resident ministers seem to be the same. Mr. Clark said he never saw the church so full before, but it was even more packed in the afternoon when, at Mr. Clark's request, I preached on St. James' beautiful teaching about "the wisdom that is from above" [James 3:17] …

Sat. 28.—Today I enter into my 85th year of life … It's true that I'm not as agile as I once was; I don't run or walk as fast. My eyesight has been affected; my left eye has dimmed and hardly serves me to read. Every day I have some pain in the ball of my right eye as well as in my right temple (due to a blow I received some months ago), and pain in my right shoulder and arm which I blame partly on a sprain and partly on arthritis. I also find some decay in my memory with respect to names and recent events, though not at all with regard to what I've read or heard 20, 40, or 60 years ago. Nor do I find any decay in my hearing, smell, taste, or appetite, though I eat just a third of what I once did. I still feel nothing like weariness, either in traveling or preaching, and I'm unaware of any decline in writing sermons, which I do as readily—and I believe as correctly—as ever.

To what cause can I credit this, that I am as I am? First, doubtless, to the power of God, fitting me for the work to which I am called, as long as he pleases to continue me in it, and secondarily, to the prayers of his children ...

Fri. JULY 4.—I set out early from Raithby and at 8 a.m. preached in Horncastle. My plan was to have preached a serious message, for which I chose the text, "The harvest is past, the summer is gone, and still we are not saved" [Jer. 8:20]. But somehow—I can't tell how—I was turned another way, and could hardly preach anything but consolation. I believe this is exactly what the people needed, although I didn't know it ...

Sun. 6.—[*At Epworth*] I very much want to keep our members here from leaving the Church of England, but can't do it. Mr. G. [the rector] isn't a pious man, but rather an enemy to piety, who often preaches against the truth and those who hold and love it. With all my influence, I can't persuade them to listen to him or to attend Holy Communion administered by him. If I can't carry this point even while I'm alive, who'll be able to do it when I die? And the situation at Epworth is the same at every church where the minister neither loves nor preaches the gospel. The Methodists won't attend his services. What then is to be done?

Sun. 13.—[*At Nottingham*] I began the service at 10 a.m., but didn't know if I would make it to the end, being almost exhausted when I finished my sermon. But Mr. Dodwell, though very weak with the fever, came and helped me administer the Lord's Supper. After preaching in the evening, I made a collection for Kingswood School. Today I had just as much work as I was able to do ...

Wed. 16.—[In Newark] I consulted with a few friends about the state of affairs, which was better than I expected. The fellowship has increased, and those who usually attend, in all parts of the town, haven't decreased. Meantime there is reason to hope that the work of God progresses, though little by little. On the following days I looked over my books and papers and set them in order as far as I could.

Sat. 19.—I spent an hour in Chesterfield Street with my [brother Charles'] widowed sister and her children. They all seemed inclined to make the right use of the late providential inheritance ...

Sun. 27.— ... I preached at the New Chapel every evening during the conference, which continued nine days, beginning on Tuesday July the 29th and ending on Wednesday, August the 6th. We scarcely had enough time, having to pass over many things very briefly that deserved fuller consideration ...

Mon. AUGUST 4.— ... One of the most important points considered at this conference was that of leaving the Church of England. The sum of a long conversation was this: That in the course of 50 years, we hadn't varied from it in one article, either of doctrine or of discipline either by forethought or willingly ... [but] that we have, through the years, out of necessity and not by choice, slowly and cautiously varied in some points of discipline, by preaching outdoors, by extemporary prayer, by using lay preachers, by forming and regulating fellowships, and by holding annual conferences. But we did none of these things till we were convinced we could no longer neglect them except at the peril of our souls ...

The next three days I withdrew, revised my papers, and finished all the work I had to do in London.

Sun. 10.— ... I preached in the morning at West Street to a large audience, but to a far larger one at the New Chapel in the evening. It seems that people generally don't expect that I will stay among them much longer after my brother [Charles], and that therefore they want to hear me while they can ...

Wed. SEPTEMBER 3.—I made just the beginning of an account of my brother Charles' life. If I don't live to finish it, may it fall into better hands! ...

Fri. 5.—We had a solemn watch-night at Kingswood. The school is now just as I want it to be. Mr. McGreary has three devout and able assistants, chosen from those who were brought up in the school, and I'm confident it will supply enough teachers for the time to come ...

VOLUME 4: 1773-1790

Sat. 20.—[*In Bristol*] I met with the trustees for the new room, who were all willing to add a codicil to the deed of trust, assigning to the conference, after me, the sole right of appointing preachers in it ...

Fri. OCTOBER 10.—[*In London*] I appointed a committee to audit my accounts and to supervise the business of the bookroom, which I don't doubt will be managed very differently from what it has been until now ...

Sat. NOVEMBER 1 (All Saints' Day).—I preached at Snowsfields on Rev. 14:1, a comforting subject, and I always find this a comforting day ...

Wed. 19.—I crossed over to Bedford, but didn't know where to find lodging. Someone met me in the street and said Mr. _____ asked me to go straight to his house. Doing so, I found myself in a true palace, by far the best house in town. There I was entertained not only with great courtesy but also, I believe, with sincere affection. Our preaching-room was quite crowded in the evening and pretty well filled in the morning. And since there is an end to all disputes, there's reason to hope that the work of God will increase here also ...

Wed. DECEMBER 10.—and the following days, I corrected my deceased brother's unpublished poems, being short psalms (except for a few) on the four Gospels and the Acts of the Apostles. They make five volumes in quarto, containing 18- or 1900 pages. They were finished April 25, 1765 ...

Many of these are little, if at all, inferior to his earlier poems, having the same justness and strength of thought with the same beauty of expression; indeed, the same keen wit, on proper occasions as bright and piercing as ever ...

1789

Thur. JANUARY 1.—If this is to be the last year of my life, according to some prophecies, I hope it will be the best ...

Mon. 5.—At the earnest request of Mrs. T., I once again sat for my portrait. Mr. Romney is indeed an artist. He struck off an exact likeness at once, and did more in one hour than Sir Joshua did in ten!

Fri. 9.—I left no money to anyone in my will because I had none. But considering that after I'm gone money will come from the sale of my books, I added a few legacies, by a codicil, to be paid as soon as feasible. But I would still like to do a little good while I live, for who can tell what will come after him? ...

Thur. 15.—I withdrew to Camberwell and worked on my *Journal*, probably as far as I will live to write it. I preached once more at Peckham, and didn't withhold from those who had ears to hear the whole counsel of God ...

Fri. FEBRUARY 6.—This being the quarterly day for meeting the local preachers, between 20 and 30 of them met at West Street and opened their hearts to each other. Using the occasion of having them all together at the watch-night, I strongly insisted on St. Paul's advice to Timothy: "Hold fast to that which has been committed to you" [1 Tim. 6:20], especially **the doctrine of Christian perfection, which God has peculiarly entrusted to the Methodists** [my emphasis] ...

Sat. MARCH 21.—I had a day of rest, only preaching morning and evening ...

Fri. 27.—We went on to Holyhead and at 8 p.m. boarded the *Claremont* packet. The wind was fair for three or four hours, then it turned and blew hard against us. I don't remember ever being this sick at sea before, but it was almost nothing compared to my cramp, which continued through the night with little letup. All Saturday we were beating to and fro, and I was so sick throughout the day that I was good for nothing, but I slept well that night, and about 8 a.m. on Sunday the 29th we arrived safe in Dublin quay. I went straight to the new preaching-room. We had an assembly as large and serious as if we had been at West Street in London ...

Sun. APRIL 5.—I preached in the new preaching-room [in Dublin] at 7 a.m., then at 11 a.m. went to the cathedral. I asked those of our Society who didn't go to their parish churches to go with me to St. Patrick's. Many of them did so. We were told that the number of communicants was about 500—more than went there the whole year before Methodists were known in Ireland ...

VOLUME 4: 1773-1790

Wed. 8.—I visited and administered the sacrament to our poor widows, of whom 24 are provided for reasonably well in our widows' house ...

Sun. 12.—Being Easter, we had a solemn assembly indeed, with many hundreds of communicants in the morning and, in the afternoon, far more attending than our room would contain, even though it has been considerably enlarged. Afterwards I met the fellowship and explained to them at length **the original plan of the Methodists; namely, not to be a distinct denomination, but to stir up all denominations** [my emphasis], Christians or heathens, to worship God in spirit and in truth, but the Church of England in particular, to which they belonged from the beginning ...

Mon. 20.—I preached about 11 a.m. at B_____ and at 6 p.m. in the church at Aghrim. It was more filled than when I preached here before, and many Catholics were there who, as the minister told me, had attended the church ever since I was there last ...

Wed. MAY 13.—I wasn't quite up to preaching in the morning, so Joseph Bradford took my place, but about 11 a.m. I did preach at Pallas, about 12 miles from Limerick ... Many of the Palatine families around here have been deeply convicted, many converted to God, and some perfected in love. Some fellowships have doubled in number, and some have increased six- or even tenfold. All the gentry of the area likewise gathered, so that no house could contain them, and I was forced to stand outside. It seemed the people swallowed every word, and great was our rejoicing in the Lord ...

Tues. 26.— ... [*At Brooksborough, Ireland*] I haven't found a more affectionate family in the kingdom than Mr. McCarty's. This was most apparent on Wednesday morning. When we were talking together one, then another, fell on their knees all around me, and most of them burst into tears and intense cries, the like of which I've seldom heard, so that we found it difficult to separate ...

Mon. JUNE 8.—We went on to Belfast. At first I thought of using the Linen Hall, but since the weather was very uncertain, I went to the heads of the large meeting-house requesting its use, which they granted in the most courteous way. It's the most complete place of public worship I've ever seen: It's oval-shaped and, judging by eye, is 100 feet long and 70 or 80 feet across. It's very high, with two rows of large windows, so it's as well-lit as our New Chapel in London; and the rows of pillars, along with everything else, are so finely proportioned that it's of the utmost beauty.

The house was so crowded inside and out, and in fact with some of the most respectable people in town, that I had great difficulty getting in, but I found that I didn't go in without the Lord. I had great liberty speaking to them, and great was our glorying in the Lord ...

Thur. 11.— ... Before 2 p.m. I set out for Tandragee, but in about half an hour the iron part of my front axle-tree broke. So I walked ahead with two of our brothers ... but before we came to Loch Brickland, I was so exhausted that I was glad to stop at a little inn and send ... for a post carriage. It came soon after 6 p.m., and I set out immediately. I had gone about a mile when Mrs. Lesley met me with her buggy ... and took me with her to Tandragree. A crowd was waiting when, finding no lack of strength, I earnestly proclaimed, "God was in Christ reconciling the world to himself" [2 Cor. 5:19]. I haven't seen such a gathering since I entered the kingdom, nor such a pleasant place, shaded with tall, spreading trees, near which ran a clear river; and all the people listened with quiet and deep attention to "Drink of the water of life freely" [Rev. 21:6] ...

Sun. 14.—In the evening I preached in the castle-yard at Dungannon on "There is one God" [1 Tim. 2:5], with the demonstration of the Spirit. It is a lovely place and contained a huge audience ...

Sun. 28.—Today I enter my 86th year of life. I'm growing old: 1. My sight is decayed, so that I can't read small print except in strong light; 2. My strength has decayed, so that I walk much slower than I did some years ago; 3. My memory of names both of persons and places has decayed till I stop a little to recall them. What I would be afraid of, if I took thought for tomorrow, is that my body would weigh down my mind and create stubbornness, by the decrease of my understanding, or fretfulness, by the increase of bodily infirmities. But you will answer for me, O Lord my God.

Fri. JULY 3.—Our little conference began in Dublin and ended on Tuesday the 7th. I remark about this that: 1. I never had between

40 and 50 such preachers together in Ireland before, all of them, we had reason to hope, alive to God and earnestly devoted to his service; 2. I never saw such a number of preachers before unanimous in all points, particularly about not leaving the Church (which none of them had the least thought of doing). No wonder that this year there has been such a large increase in our society ...

Sat. 18.—I asked the opinion of Dr. Easton, as my thirst and fever had greatly increased. His medicine took effect immediately, and I was much better on Sunday morning. I preached and, with Dr. Coke's assistance, administered the sacrament to 11- or 1200 communicants. I preached again in the evening, but it was too much for me, and brought back my fever ...

Thur. AUGUST 6.—We started out early, and between 4 and 5 a.m. reached Hinxworth. I now felt inclined to rest, but as a crowd soon gathered, I didn't want to disappoint them, and preached on "We love him because he first loved us" [1 John 4:19]; and after preaching and travelling 80 miles, I wasn't more tired than when I started out in the morning.

Fri. 7.—We reached London between 1 and 2 p.m. and found great reason to praise the gracious Power that had preserved us by land and sea, from all known and unknown dangers, to the present hour.

Sat. 8.—I settled all my worldly affairs, and in particular chose a new editor for *The Armenian Magazine,* being obliged, though unwillingly, to discharge Mr. O., for two reasons: 1. The errors are unbearable. I've borne them for the past 12 years but can tolerate them no longer; 2. Several pieces, both in prose and in verse, have been inserted without my knowledge. I must try whether these things can't be corrected for the brief remainder of my life ...

Wed. 12.— ... [*At Plymouth*] I preached to a large audience in the afternoon, and although the day was extremely hot, I found myself better yesterday and today than I've been for several months ...

Tues. 18.—We went on to Truro where I had arranged to preach at noon. But here we met with an unforeseen obstacle. I couldn't get through the main street to our preaching-house; it was totally blocked with soldiers to the east and with innumerable tin-miners to the west.

The crowd of tin-miners, many of whom were nearly starved, came either to beg or to demand an increase in their wages, without which they couldn't live. So we were forced to withdraw to the other end of town, where I preached under the Coinage Hall to twice as many people, rich and poor, as the preaching-house would have contained. And many of them, except for these circumstances, wouldn't have come at all. How wise are all the ways of God!

In the afternoon, since we couldn't go by the main road, we got permission to drive around by some fields and reached Falmouth in good time. The last time I was here, over 40 years ago, I was taken prisoner by a huge mob, gazing stupidly and roaring like lions. But now the tide has turned: High and low now lined the street from one end of the town to the other out of pure love and kindness, gazing and staring as if the king were passing by ...

Wed. 26.—I returned to Redruth and applied to the assembly, "God was in Christ, reconciling the world to himself" [2 Cor. 5:19]. I then met the fellowship and explained at length the origin and the nature of Methodism, and I still declare **that I've never read or heard of, in either ancient or modern history, any other church that builds on so broad a foundation as the Methodists do, requiring of its members no conformity either in opinions or modes of worship, but this one thing only: to "fear God and work righteousness"** [my emphasis] ...

Sun. SEPTEMBER 27.—I preached at the New Room morning and evening, and in the afternoon at Temple Church. But it was all that I could do. I believe that from here on I must not try to preach more than twice a day ...

Thur. OCTOBER 29.—I returned to Oxford, and since notice had been given (though without my knowledge) of my preaching at noon, I did so, on "There is one God" [1 Tim. 2:5], to a very serious audience. But in the evening such a crowd pressed in that they kept each other from hearing by their noise; by their very eagerness to hear, they defeated their own purpose ...

Mon. NOVEMBER 16.—After suspending morning preaching for many weeks because of a dry mouth, I determined to try if I could do it at 5 a.m. I was able to do so without much difficulty, and now hope to hold on a little longer ...

Wed. DECEMBER 16.—Being quite hoarse, I couldn't sing or speak, but was determined at least to show up where I had arranged to preach. Coming to Sandwich about noon, and finding the audience was waiting, I trusted in God and started to speak. The more I spoke, the more my voice was strengthened, so that after a few minutes I believe everyone could hear. And many, I believe, were aware that what they heard was not the word of man but of God ...

Sun. 27.—I preached in St. Luke's, our parish church, in the afternoon to a large audience, on "The Spirit and the Bride say, 'Come'" [Rev. 22:17]. So the tables are turned, and I now have more invitations to preach in churches than I can accept ...

1790

Fri. JANUARY 1.—I'm now an old man, decaying from head to foot. My eyes are dim; my right hand shakes a lot; my mouth is hot and dry every morning. I have a lingering fever almost every day. I move about weakly and slowly. But bless God, I don't slack my labor. I can still preach and write.

Sat. 2.—I preached at Snowsfields to the largest congregation I've seen there this year, on "I'm not ashamed of the gospel of Christ" [Rom. 1:16].

Sun. 3.—I suppose nearly 2000 met at the New Chapel to renew their covenant with God!—a scriptural means of grace, now almost everywhere forgotten except among the Methodists ...

Fri. 29.—We had our general quarterly meeting, in which it appeared that our Society received and spent about 3000 pounds[358] during the year. But our expense still exceeded our income ...

Sun. FEBRUARY 14.—I preached a sermon to the children at West Street Chapel. They flocked together from all around, and truly God was in their midst, applying those words, "Come, little children, listen to me, and I will teach you the fear of the Lord" [Psalm 34:11].

Fri. MARCH 5.—Hearing that Mr. W. of Bolton was dying, I went over and spent an hour with him. His spirit was comforted, and in a few days he was nearly as well as ever ...

---

[358] About $705,000 in 2020 USD.

Sun. 14.—This was a pleasant day. In the morning I met with the Strangers' Society, founded solely for the relief, not of our own Society, but for poor, sick, friendless strangers. I don't know that I ever heard or read of such an institution till within a few years ago. So this also is one of the fruits of Methodism ...

Thur. 25.—I finished my sermon on the Wedding Garment, perhaps the last I'll write. My eyes have become dim, my natural force is diminished. However, while I can, I'd like to do a little for God before I drop into the dust ...

Mon. JUNE 7.—I recorded the stations of the preachers ...

Tues. 8.—I wrote a form for settling the preaching-houses, without any unnecessary words, which will be used for the time to come, verbatim, for all the houses to which I contribute anything. I'll no longer encourage that compiling of words lawyers use, which is the scandal of our nation ...

Thur. 24.—The dissenting minister offering me the use of his chapel in Bridlington, twice as large as our own (the wind being too strong for me to stand outdoors), I willingly accepted his offer ...

Mon. 28.—Today I enter my 88th year of life. For over 86 years, I had none of the infirmities of old age ... But last August, I found an almost sudden change: My eyes became so dim that no glasses could help me. My strength is now just about gone and probably won't return in this world. But I feel no pain from head to toe. It just seems that nature is exhausted and, humanly speaking, will sink more and more ...

Tues. AUGUST 31.—William Kingston, the man born without arms, came to see me of his own accord. Some time ago he received a clear sense of the favor of God, but after some months was persuaded by some of his old buddies to join in a favorite diversion, which caused him to lose sight of God and to lose all that he'd gained. But God has now touched his heart again, and he's once more earnestly seeking to save his soul. He's of medium height and proportion, of pleasing appearance and voice, and has an agreeable manner. At breakfast he shook off his custom-made shoes, took the tea-cup between his toes, and the toast with his other foot. He also writes fairly well and does most things with his feet that the rest of us do with our hands ...

VOLUME 4: 1773-1790

Sun. SEPTEMBER 5.—At 10 a.m. we had a large assembly in Bath, and more communicants than I ever saw here before. Today I stopped that despicable custom—I don't know when or how it began—of the same preacher preaching three times a day to the same assembly. This is enough to wear out the bodies and minds of both the speaker and his hearers. Surely God is returning to this Society! ...

Sat. 25.—Mr. Hay, the Presbyterian minister of Lewensmead meeting, came to ask me if he could use our preaching-house on Sundays during the times when we weren't using it ourselves, which were around 10 a.m. and 2 p.m. I willingly consented, and he preached an excellent sermon there the next day at 2 p.m. I preached at 5 a.m. to more than the house could well hold ...

Thur. OCTOBER 7.— ... [*At Winchelsea*] Here I stopped at the house of a very devout woman, Mrs. Jones, who told me a strange story. Many years ago she suffered a great deal preparing for childbirth. She had several doctors but got worse and worse till, seeing she wasn't getting any better, she stopped seeing them. She had constant pain in her groin, along with a prolapsed uterus, which confined her to bed, where she lay for two months. She was helpless and hopeless until a thought came to her mind one day: "Lord, if you will, you can make me whole. Let it be according to your will!" Immediately the pain and disorder ceased. Feeling well, she got up and dressed herself. Her husband coming in and seeing her in tears asked, "Are those tears of serious joy?" She said, "Of joy!" At which they wept together. From that hour she has felt no pain and rather has enjoyed perfect health. I don't think our Lord ever worked a more obvious miracle, even in the days of his flesh ...

Wed. 13.— ... I went to Yarmouth and finally found a fellowship at peace and all united. In the evening, the assembly was too large for the meeting-house to hold, yet the people were much less noisy than usual. After supper a little group went to prayer, and the power of God fell upon us, especially when a young woman broke out in prayer, to the surprise and comfort of us all ...

Wed. 20.—I had arranged to preach at Disa, a town near Scoleton, but there was a difficulty: Where could I preach? The Anglican minister was willing for me to preach in the church but feared offending the bishop, who had left for London and was a few miles out of town. But a gentleman [caught up with him and] asked the bishop if he had any objections to my preaching, who replied, "None at all." I think this church is one of the largest in the county, and suppose it hasn't been filled so full in the past 100 years ...

Fri. 22.—We returned to London.

Sun. 24.—I explained to a large congregation in Spitalfields church, "the whole armor of God" [Eph. 6:11ff.]. St. Paul's, Shadwell, was even more crowded in the afternoon, while I drove home that important truth, "One thing is needful" [Luke 10:42], and I hope many even then resolved to choose the better part.

END OF JOURNAL

Details Of John Wesley's Final Days
(as recorded by friends)

During the remaining part of the autumn and winter, till the middle of February 1791, he carried on, constantly praying, "Lord, let me not live to be useless." He preached at his usual places in London and its vicinity, generally meeting the fellowship after preaching in each place, and exhorting them to "love as brothers and sisters, fear God, and honor the king," which he wanted them to consider as his final advice. He then most often concluded with that verse,

> Oh that, without a ling'ring groan,
> I may the welcome word receive;
> My body with my duty lay down,
> And cease at once to work and live …

Thursday, February 17, 1791, he preached at Lambeth, but returning home said he felt out of order and had taken cold. The next day, however … he preached at Chelsea … although with some difficulty, having a high fever. In fact, he had to stop once or twice, telling the people that his cold was affecting his voice …

On Monday the 21st he seemed much better and kept an appointment to dine at Twickenham. On his way there he dropped in on Lady Mary Fitzgerald, with whom he had a profitable conversation and which proved to be his last visit. On Tuesday … he preached in the evening at the Chapel in the City Road and seemed better than he had been for some days. On Wednesday he went to Leatherhead and preached to a small group on "seek the Lord while he is near" [Isa. 55:6]. This proved to be his last sermon and the end of his public labor …

[*Several days of ups and downs and a doctor's visit followed.*] After this the fever was very high and at times affected his mind, but even then, though his mind was temporarily deranged, his heart was wholly engaged in his Master's work. In the evening he got up again and, while sitting in his chair said, "How essential it is for everyone to be on the right foundation!

Serious Joy (John Wesley's *Journal*)

<pre>
I the chief of sinners am
But Jesus died for me."
</pre>

Monday 28.—His weakness increases; he sleeps most of the time, but when he does speak, it is about care of the fellowships, the glory of God, and the furtherance of his kingdom. Once he said, in a low but clear voice, "There's no way into the holiest but by the blood of Jesus." ... He suffered very little pain except once in the left side of his chest. Tuesday morning he sang two verses of a hymn and wanted to write, but when someone brought him pen and ink, he couldn't do it. Before noon he said he'd get up, and while they were getting his clothes, he astonished everyone by singing,

<pre>
"I'll praise my Maker while I've breath,
And when my voice is lost in death,
Praise shall employ my nobler powers:
My days of praise shall ne'er be past,
While life, and thought, and being, last,
Or immortality endures!" ...
</pre>

[*They got him into his chair and noticed that he was dying. But with a weak voice he sang two lines of another hymn.*] Here his voice failed, but after gasping for breath he said, "Now we have done all." He was then laid in the bed, never to rise again. After resting a little, he called those who were with him "to pray and praise." They knelt down, and the room seemed to be filled with the divine presence. He said a loud "Amen" to one prayer in particular, and when the group rose from their knees, he took their hands and, with great serenity, spoke to them saying, "Farewell, farewell." ...

A little later, with his remaining strength, he cried out, "The best of all is, God is with us!" which he repeated. [*He affectionately greeted his brother Charles' widow when she came in.*] On wetting his lips he said, "We thank you, O Lord, for these and all your mercies. Bless the Church and king, and grant us truth and peace through Jesus Christ our Lord forever and ever!" [*He uttered a few more phrases Tuesday.*]

[*On Wednesday morning he died*]

Details Of John Wesley's Final Days

At the request of many of his friends, his body was place in the New Chapel and remained there the day before his interment. His face during that time had a heavenly smile on it, and a beauty that was admired by all who saw it.

About The Editor

Robert Hunt Morris II grew up in small-town West Tennessee, the son of a well-known and -loved physician. His parents were devout Christians of different denominations, his home full of books, and he was a voracious reader. He attended Rhodes College in Memphis and spent his junior year abroad in France. There he underwent a crisis of faith and for several years, though he loved Jesus, he didn't believe in the biblical God and didn't pray. He became an earnest spiritual seeker as a New Ager, a Quaker, a Pentecostal, and a charismatic, obtaining his master's degree in Biblical Literature at Oral Roberts University in 1992, attaining proficiency in NT Greek, then completing all the coursework for a Ph.D. in Midrash (rabbinic interpretation) during three years at Jewish Theological Seminary of America, where he won an award for excellence in the Hebrew language. When he joined a Wesleyan church some 20 years ago, he became fascinated by the person and life of John Wesley.

The editor has been married for 53 years to Jeanne Sokol Morris from New York State. They have had three children (one died), and have four grandchildren. After living in four different states, he and Jeanne returned in 1996 to his home state of Tennessee.

www.ingramcontent.com/pod-product-compliance
Lightning Source LLC
Chambersburg PA
CBHW021752230426
43669CB00006B/59